Navigating Cybersecurity and Privacy in the Evolution of Smart Urban Ecosystems

Asmaa Mahfoud Alhakimi
https://orcid.org/0000-0002-4038-5203
Management and Science University, Malaysia

Safaa Najah Saud Al-Humairi
https://orcid.org/0000-0001-5978-7651
Management and Science University, Malaysia

Saddaf Rubab
https://orcid.org/0000-0003-3208-5275
University of Sharjah, UAE

I. Wayan Budi Sentana
https://orcid.org/0000-0003-3559-5123
Bali State Polytechnic, Indonesia

IGI Global
Scientific Publishing
Publishing Tomorrow's Research Today

Published in the United States of America by
IGI Global Scientific Publishing
701 East Chocolate Avenue
Hershey, PA, 17033, USA
Tel: 717-533-8845 | Fax: 717-533-7115
Website: https://www.igi-global.com E-mail: cust@igi-global.com

Library of Congress Cataloging-in-Publication Data

Names: Alhakimi, Asmaa, 1985- editor | Al-Humairi, Safaa, 1985- editor | Rubab, Saddaf, 1986- editor | Sentana, I Wayan Budi, 1981- editor
Title: Navigating cybersecurity and privacy in the evolution of smart urban ecosystems / edited by: Asmaa Alhakimi, Safaa Al-Humairi, Saddaf Rubab, I Wayan Budi Sentana.
Description: Hershey PA : IGI Global Scientific Publishing, [2026] | Includes bibliographical references. | Summary: "The book systematically examines the vulnerabilities inherent in smart cities, including threats to interconnected infrastructure (e.g., energy grids, transportation systems, and surveillance networks), risks posed by massive data collection, and the ethical dilemmas of balancing public safety with individual privacy"-- Provided by publisher.
Identifiers: LCCN 2025029093 (print) | LCCN 2025029094 (ebook) | ISBN 9798337344553 hardcover | ISBN 9798337344560 paperback | ISBN 9798337344577 ebook
Subjects: LCSH: Smart cities--Security measures | Smart cities--Data processing
Classification: LCC TD159.4 .N38 2026 (print) | LCC TD159.4 (ebook)
LC record available at https://lccn.loc.gov/2025029093
LC ebook record available at https://lccn.loc.gov/2025029094

British Cataloguing in Publication Data
A Cataloguing in Publication record for this book is available from the British Library.

This book is dedicated to all researchers, innovators, and practitioners who tirelessly strive to build smarter, safer, and more resilient urban ecosystems. Their passion for integrating technology with ethics and humanity continues to inspire the evolution of secure and sustainable cities.

To my family and loved ones, whose unwavering support, patience, and encouragement have given us the strength to pursue this journey—your belief has been our greatest motivation.

To future generations of scholars and technologists, may this work serve as both a foundation and an inspiration for exploring new pathways in cybersecurity, privacy, and intelligent urban development.

Asmaa Alhakimi and Safaa Al-Humairi

Table of Contents

Detailed Table of Contents

Introduced in 2008 by the pseudonymous Satoshi Nakamoto, it was designed for recording. While its initial application was limited to digital currency, its potential quickly transcended the confines of cryptocurrency, sparking the interest of industries government. The promise lies in core principles: decentralization, transparency, security, and immutability. These qualities are not only desirable for digital currencies but also offer revolutionary solutions to a variety of real-world challenges. As such, it is a mere cryptocurrency capable of paradigms for innovation. In healthcare, blockchain holds promise as a tool for securely managing medical records. Patients' health data is often scattered in healthcare fragmented, inefficient healthcare system. Blockchain could offer a solution for unified medical records that is both secure and accessible. Through blockchain, patients could control who accesses their health information, ensuring privacy while enabling doctors and specialists to complete, medical history.

The paradigm of decentralized cities, reliant on edge computing, redefines urban functionality but introduces acute cybersecurity challenges within a borderless threat environment. Traditional perimeter-based security is ill-suited for dispersed edge assets and sophisticated adversaries. This chapter critically examines these challenges,

Emerging solutions such as federated learning, blockchain, and privacy-enhancing technologies are reviewed alongside global policy frameworks, ethical guidelines, and citizen-centred governance models. Drawing on international case studies, the chapter highlights how balancing innovation with transparency, accountability, and social trust is central to building secure and inclusive smart cities. By integrating technological, socio-economic, and policy perspectives, it offers pathways toward resilient and human-centric urban digital futures.

The growing reliance on Internet of Things (IoT) technologies in smart cities brings significant data privacy and security challenges. This paper presents a privacy-preserving IoT network model designed to protect sensitive information while retaining functionality and performance. The model utilizes edge computing, lightweight encryption, pseudonymization, and role-based access control alongside blockchain for enhanced trust and transparency. Experimental results demonstrate that this approach efficiently safeguards data without compromising service quality. This study aims to enable the responsible and sustainable implementation of smart city innovations while preserving citizen dignity, consent, and control over their own data.

Cloud computing plays an important role in modern businesses by enabling flexible, efficient storage, analysis, and access to data and applications. However, this reliance also introduces new security challenges. Ensuring cloud security and resilience is

systems into proactive, context-aware ecosystems capable of decision-making and automation. This chapter presents a comprehensive framework for integrating AI with IoT, highlighting its architecture, component and applicability across domains such as smart cities, healthcare, agriculture, transportation and industrial automation. The framework emphasizes enabling technologies including edge, fog, and cloud computing, communication protocols and open platforms like FIWARE, which collectively support scalability, interoperability and real-time analytics.

The rapid integration of data-driven technologies in urban environments offers significant opportunities for efficiency, sustainability, and citizen well-being, yet it introduces complex ethical challenges. This chapter examines privacy, consent, equity, and algorithmic bias concerns in smart city infrastructures. It highlights the importance of human-centered governance, transparency, accountability, and participatory decision-making. Comparative analysis of global frameworks reveals operational gaps, prompting actionable recommendations including ethics-by-design, stakeholder engagement, technological safeguards, and adaptive governance. By embedding ethics into urban data management, cities can achieve socially equitable, trustworthy, and sustainable smart city development.

The digital transformation of cities into smart urban ecosystems creates a vast and complex cybersecurity attack surface. This paper provides a foundational survey of this threat landscape, systematically deconstructing the smart city's anatomy from a security perspective. We analyze inherent vulnerabilities within key technologies like IoT, 5G/6G, AI, and cloud/edge computing. The survey presents a multi-dimensional taxonomy of threats, classifying them by attacker intent, target asset,

Preface

The dawn of the 21st century has witnessed an extraordinary transformation in the way urban environments function, driven by a stream of digital technologies, interconnected devices, and intelligent systems. Smart urban ecosystems are no longer a future concept; they are here, reshaping the foundation of city life. This book, Navigating Cybersecurity and Privacy in the Evolution of Smart Urban Ecosystems, addresses the critical intersection of technology, security, and privacy within the rapidly evolving smart cities. It offers a complete exploration of both the substantial opportunities and extreme challenges inherent in these complex socio-technical systems.

Smart urban ecosystems represent the merging of information and communication technologies (ICT), the Internet of Things (IoT), artificial intelligence (AI), and data analytics with traditional urban infrastructure. This integration enables cities to optimize resources, enhance sustainability, improve governance, and deliver better services to citizens. However, this transformation also exposes urban environments to novel cybersecurity threats and privacy risks, which, if left unchecked, can undermine public trust, disrupt essential services, and compromise urban safety.

The book's focus is to navigate this dynamic environment by providing multidisciplinary perspectives on securing smart cities, ensuring privacy protections, promoting ethical frameworks, and developing resilient governance structures. Through comprehensive chapters contributed by experts, it synthesizes emerging research, practical methodologies, and future-proof strategies to guide readers in understanding and addressing the cyber-physical vulnerabilities that cities of the future will undoubtedly face.

As urban populations grow and cities become more dependent on digital technologies, the stakes for cybersecurity and privacy have never been higher. Critical infrastructure — from energy grids and water management to transportation and public safety — is increasingly automated and interconnected. Global trends such as climate change, urbanization, and technological innovation create a complex environment in which security threats are increasingly sophisticated and privacy concerns are paramount.

In this context, cybersecurity becomes a fundamental support of the smart city's strength. Protecting data integrity, system availability, and citizen privacy is essential not only for maintaining operational continuity but also for fostering civic engagement and democratic governance. Equally important is addressing ethical dilemmas that arise from AI-driven decision-making, surveillance, and data sharing, making it imperative to develop frameworks that balance innovation with responsibility.

This book positions itself as a timely response to these challenges, offering insights into advanced technologies such as blockchain for decentralized security, AI for automation and defense, sensor optimization for urban monitoring, and green cybersecurity practices. It also examines the governance pathways necessary to coordinate stakeholders to achieve secure, transparent, and equitable smart urban ecosystems.

This publication is designed for a diverse audience, including cybersecurity researchers, urban planners, IT professionals, academic educators, and graduate students specializing in smart cities, digital forensics, network security, and urban governance. Practitioners involved in designing, implementing, or regulating smart city infrastructure and digital services will find practical frameworks and case studies relevant to their work.

Additionally, the book aims to update interdisciplinary scholars interested in the socio-technical implications of urban digital transformation. By bridging technical and ethical domains, it invites readers to critically engage with issues of bias, transparency, privacy, and resilience in the context of evolving urban environments. This makes it a valuable resource for advancing both academic scholarship and practical implementation.

The following chapters outline the key themes and concepts explored in this book:

CHAPTER 1: AN OVERVIEW OF SMART CITIES COVERING APPLICATIONS, CHALLENGES, AND EMERGING TRENDS

This foundational chapter introduces readers to the core concepts, technologies, and drivers of smart cities. It frames the overall discourse by identifying key applications, persistent challenges, and the innovative trends that define ongoing urban transformation.

CHAPTER 2: WHEN NATURE MEETS CODE: GOVERNING GREY DATA FOR CYBERSECURITY AND SUSTAINABILITY SMART CITIES

This chapter examines the governance of "grey data" — ambiguous or partially structured data —highlighting its dual role in cybersecurity and environmental sustainability. It emphasizes the importance of managing data ecosystems carefully to achieve both secure and sustainable urban operations.

CHAPTER 3: BLOCKCHAIN BEYOND CRYPTOCURRENCY --- A DECENTRALIZED APPROACH TO URBAN SECURITY

The chapter highlights integration hurdles such as interoperability, regulatory gaps, and ethical tensions, while outlining emerging trends like Blockchain 4.0, quantum-safe cryptography, and DAO-led civic participation. It offers a roadmap for decentralized citizen-centric governance in smart cities.

CHAPTER 4: CYBERATTACKS BLOCKCHAIN BEYOND CRYPTOCURRENCY A DECENTRALIZED APPROACH TO URBAN SECURITY

This chapter investigates trends in cyberattacks targeting blockchain implementations in smart urban settings, analyzing vulnerabilities and defenses to strengthen trust in decentralized mechanisms.

CHAPTER 5: CYBERSECURITY AT THE EDGE DEFENDING DECENTRALIZED CITIES IN A BORDERLESS THREAT LANDSCAPE

Focusing on edge computing, this chapter addresses security paradigms for decentralized networks critical to smart cities, offering insights into protecting distributed assets in an increasingly borderless cyberthreat environment.

CHAPTER 6: ENHANCING CYBERSECURITY, PRIVACY INNOVATION AND E-GOVERNMENT READINESS IN SMART CITIES: A FRAMEWORK FOR AWARENESS AND RESILIENCE

This contribution proposes a comprehensive framework to boost cybersecurity knowledge, privacy innovation, and governmental preparedness to build resilience against cyber threats specific to E-governance contexts.

CHAPTER 7: NAVIGATING CYBERSECURITY AND PRIVACY IN SMART URBAN ECOSYSTEMS CHALLENGES, TECHNOLOGIES, AND GOVERNANCE PATHWAYS

Resilience is key to enduring cyber disruptions. This chapter articulates principles and methods for designing robust smart urban systems capable of rapid recovery and sustained, secure operation despite adversities.

CHAPTER 8: SAFEGUARDING URBAN INTELLIGENCE-REDEFINING IOT NETWORKS WITH PRIVACY IN MIND: IOT FOR URBAN SYSTEMS

IoT devices are extensively integrated into modern systems, but their security vulnerabilities create significant challenges. This chapter proposes privacy-centric design and security solutions to safeguard urban IoT deployments, protecting citizen data while enabling smart functionalities.

CHAPTER 9: SECURITY-AS-A-SERVICE: ENHANCING CLOUD SECURITY THROUGH MANAGED SECURITY SOLUTIONS

Cloud computing supports many smart city platforms. This chapter explains how security-as-a-service models provide scalable, managed protection to cloud infrastructures against evolving cyber threats.

CHAPTER 10: SOLAR AND WIND ENERGY IN URBAN TRANSFORMATION: OPPORTUNITIES, CHALLENGES, AND CYBERSECURITY

Renewable energy integration into urban grids introduces unique cybersecurity demands. This chapter discusses securing solar and wind infrastructure against cyber threats while leveraging their environmental benefits.

CHAPTER 11: THE CONVERGENCE OF ARTIFICIAL INTELLIGENCE AND THE INTERNET OF THINGS FOR NEXT-GENERATION SMART SYSTEMS

This chapter explores the integration of AI and IoT as core technologies for next-generation urban systems. It highlights their combined role in enhancing security and privacy. Additionally, it examines how this synergy improves operational intelligence in smart cities.

CHAPTER 12: THE ETHICS OF DATA COLLECTION AND USAGE IN SMART CITY INFRASTRUCTURE

Data is central to smart cities but raises ethical questions. This chapter critically analyzes ethical frameworks guiding responsible data collection, consent, and usage in urban environments.

CHAPTER 13: THE THREAT LANDSCAPE OF SMART URBAN ECOSYSTEMS-A SURVEY

This chapter provides a systematic overview of both current and emerging cyber threats facing urban ecosystems. It explores the motivations behind these attacks and identifies common vulnerabilities. Additionally, it presents practical strategies to defend against such threats.

CHAPTER 14: TRUST THROUGH TRANSPARENCY-BLOCKCHAIN-ENABLED SUPPLY CHAIN TRACEABILITY FOR SMART URBAN ECOSYSTEMS

Supply chains are essential parts of urban systems, but they are also exposed to various risks and vulnerabilities. This chapter discusses how blockchain enhances transparency and trustworthiness in urban supply chains.

Acknowledgment

The completion of this book, Navigating Cybersecurity and Privacy in the Evolution of Smart Urban Ecosystems, has been a collective endeavor enriched by the dedication and expertise of many individuals. I would like to express my deepest gratitude to everyone who contributed to the success of this book. Special appreciation goes to Dr. Safaa Najah Saud Al-Humairi for his guidance and support, Dr. Saddaf Rubab, and Dr. I Wayan Budi Sentana for their invaluable insights, guidance, and constant encouragement throughout the development of this work. Their expertise, constructive feedback, and unwavering commitment greatly enriched the content and scope of this publication.

I am also thankful to all the chapter contributors and reviewers whose scholarly efforts, vision, and collaboration transformed this project into a comprehensive and meaningful contribution to the discourse on cybersecurity, privacy, and sustainability in smart urban ecosystems.

Finally, I extend my heartfelt appreciation to my colleagues, friends, and family for their understanding and encouragement. Their patience and moral support provided the motivation needed to see this work to completion.

Introduction

In an era where urban developments are frequently transformed by rapid technological innovation, the concept of the "smart city" has moved from visionary ideal to tangible reality. These modern urban ecosystems, powered by data, connectivity, and automation, hold the promise of improved efficiency, sustainability, and quality of life. However, as with any significant technological shift, they also introduce complex cybersecurity and privacy challenges that must be carefully navigated to ensure these innovations truly serve society's best interests.

Navigating Cybersecurity and Privacy in the Evolution of Smart Urban Ecosystems arrives at a critical interval, offering an in-depth exploration of these issues and proposing pathways for strong, ethical, and sustainable development. What sets this publication apart is its comprehensive scope, covering a wide selection of topics from artificial intelligence and blockchain to IoT and energy systems, all within the context of urban cybersecurity. It seamlessly blends theory, practical insights, and emerging research, making it an invaluable resource for both academics and practitioners committed to shaping smart cities responsibly.

This book is particularly significant in its emphasis on multidisciplinary perspectives. It recognizes that securing smart urban environments requires collaboration across fields of technology, policy, ethics, and governance. Chapters dedicated to topics such as ethical AI, transparent blockchain solutions, eco-friendly cybersecurity measures, and the delicate balance between data collection and privacy reflect a thoughtful approach to these interconnected challenges. The emphasis on innovative frameworks —from cyber resilience strategies to sensor placement algorithms —provides readers with actionable insights grounded in the latest advancements.

For urban planners, cybersecurity professionals, and scholars alike, this publication is a call to expand their understanding of the threats facing next-generation cities and to adopt proactive, forward-looking strategies. It highlights the success of smart urban ecosystem establishments not just in technological innovation, but also in responsible governance and ethical considerations. As these cities grow smarter, so must our approaches to safeguarding their integrity and privacy.

The importance of this book extends beyond its comprehensive analysis. It adopts a mindset of caution, innovation, and shared responsibility. By integrating technical insights with ethical considerations, it encourages readers to think critically about the societal implications of urban digital transformation. Its multidisciplinary approach serves as a blueprint for building urban systems that are secure, transparent, and resistant, aligned with visions of sustainable and reasonable urban futures.

Navigating Cybersecurity and Privacy in the Evolution of Smart Urban Ecosystems offers a timely, necessary, and thoroughly informed contribution to the field. It is an essential read for anyone involved in the design, implementation, or regulation of smart city technologies. As we stand on the edge of a new era of urban living, this book provides the knowledge and guidance needed to ensure that our cities develop not just digitally advanced, but also secure, ethical, and inclusive.

Chapter 1
An Overview of Smart Cities Covering Applications, Challenges, and Emerging Trends

Ravesa Akhter
https://orcid.org/0000-0002-5149-6726
National Institute of Technology Srinagar, India

Rabiya Akhter
University of Kashmir, India

Insha Shafi
National Institute of Technology Srinagar, India

Shabir Sofi
National Institute of Technology Srinagar, India

ABSTRACT

As city populations grow at a pace unprecedented in history, cities across the world are facing mounting challenges in the areas of sustainability, provision of services, mobility, and governance. The present chapter offers an in-depth overview of the Smart City theme, discussing how it has evolved as an integrated solution to urban complexity through the adoption of advanced digital technologies. The chapter discusses the key drivers of smart urbanization. It identifies the key building blocks of Smart Cities like the Internet of Things (IoT), Artificial Intelligence (AI), Machine Learning (ML), and cloud computing, edge computing, illustrating how these technologies facilitate data-driven governance. Furthermore, it discusses ongoing

DOI: 10.4018/979-8-3373-4455-3.ch001

challenges like data confidentiality issues, high costs of implementation, etc. Based on global case studies of Barcelona, Songdo, and Amsterdam, the chapter presents actionable insights into the socio-technical nature of Smart Cities and discusses emerging trends like digital twins, blockchain technology, robotics, and human-centered design.

1. INTRODUCTION

The phenomenon of rapid urbanization is the 21st century world's hallmark, affecting deeply the character of the way we live, work, and use resources. Cities are growing at record rates, putting pressure and complexity on their infrastructure, services, and institutions. Over 55% of the global population now live-in urban areas, a proportion that will reach approximately 68% by 2050, according to the United Nations' World Urbanization Prospects (Buettner, 2015). Such raw growth comes with unparalleled opportunities for creativity and innovation, as well as a vast range of challenges around congestion, equity, sustainability, health, and delivering services.

Population increases at high rates as shown in Figure 1.1 and increasing density worsen most of the challenges already inherent in contemporary cities. Congestion of traffic on the roads has become an enormous challenge, adding hours of delay to daily trips and propelling high levels of greenhouse gas emissions. Pollution of air, water, or land spoils the health of city residents and the environment. Increasing social inequalities also emerge in unequal access to education, healthcare, food, clean water, and employment opportunities (Kjellstrom et al., 2007). Inadequate and poorly facilitated public amenities from parks and recreation halls to hospitals and schools also reduce the well-being of an increasing population. All these issues in aggregate erode the level of living, reduce civic participation, and erode social stability.

This sobering reality portends a greater need for imaginative, responsive, and visionary solutions that can facilitate policy makers and city officials to grapple with their expanding mandates and enhance the lives of their residents. It is here that the idea of Smart Cities is born a new paradigm to think and govern the expanding complexity of the urban environment. Smart Cities harness advanced digital technologies and data-driven innovations to facilitate the more sustainable, resilient, responsive, and people-centric management of services.

By definition, a Smart City is not necessarily a city full of technology but a city that employs technology to optimise its human and environmental capital (Albino et al., 2015). Smart Cities are configured to provide a high quality of life and be resource-efficient and service-intensive in a manner that is environmentally sustainable, socially just, and economically viable.

This revolution cannot be accomplished without a solid base of Information and Communication Technology (ICT) infrastructures. These include extensive high-speed broadband networks, wireless, sensor networks, data centres, and communication protocols that support huge amounts of data to flow freely and efficiently across different city services. The digital nervous system of a Smart City consists of many interconnected sensors, actuators, and computing nodes all talking to each other in real time, creating a rich data ecosystem upon which policy makers can make more informed choices. This datafication platform is the basis of numerous innovations. Applications of real-time responses like the operation of autonomous vehicles, provision of health care services, management of energy grids, or crisis operational coordination become feasible because of high-speed 5G networks and low-latency and high-throughput communication. Furthermore, fibre-optic networks, strategically located routers, and ubiquitous WiFi coverage offer fast, reliable, and ubiquitous internet access, linking all the stakeholders of a city, including ordinary citizens, businesses, civic groups, and governmental offices.

This wide and sophisticated digital infrastructure underpins many of the smart applications and services. Smart Cities use Internet of Things (IoT) sensors to collect data on water usage, air quality, electricity consumption, pedestrian flow, waste management, etc. This data is fed into sophisticated analysis platforms based on Artificial Intelligence (AI) and Machine Learning (ML) to enable the policy makers to identify patterns, anomalies, and potential for improving services (Kibria et al., 2018). Cloud computing also provides a flexible, scalable, and cost-effective foundation for the storage of large amounts of data and for the direct delivery of services to the citizen's smartphone or other smart devices (Bera et al., 2014).

The strongest promise of the Smart City is the ability to support real-time, data-driven decision making (Kaluarachchi, 2022). Before, policy makers would wait for a report or a survey to react to a problem. That meant they were stuck with slow and reactive choices based on conditions that were already in the past. Contrast that with the ubiquitous sensor network of a Smart City, which allows city officials to view city operations in real time whether that is the movement of water through its pipes, the traffic on its streets, or the number of emergency calls from a particular neighborhood and react much more rapidly and intelligently.

This ability to respond promptly and effectively not only improves the provision of service but also encourages civic engagement and builds a participatory model of government. Smart Cities engage citizens in policymaking via websites, citizen polls, real-time notifications, and community workshops. This improves a greater degree of civic engagement, cooperation, and learning, strengthening the social contract and loyalty to civic institutions.

Other than this, a Smart City is also environmentally friendly by saving resources, lowering emissions, and maximizing energy utilization. Climate change and increasing energy needs offer an urgent reason for this to be a priority. Smart Cities maximize energy utilization through intelligent grids, lowering lighting and heating, minimizing wastage, and making use of renewable sources. Not only is this cost-effective to run, but it also decreases the carbon footprint of a city, saving resources for the next generation. Efficient water management, parks and green belts, and wise disposal systems also contribute to the building of a healthy and sustainable city for all its inhabitants.

As Smart Cities are being developed, policy makers should proceed with caution in meeting the new digital divide and data equity issues (Colding et al., 2024). Everyone in the community should have access to the services of these innovations from fast-speed internet connectivity and learning content to health care, banking services, and civic participation tools in order not to increase social inequalities. Proper protections in the area of data privacy, cyber security, and citizens' permission should be implemented to facilitate a responsible and reliable Smart Cities system.

This book chapter attempts to provide an integrated overview of Smart Cities, Section 1.1 gives the overview of smart city, Section 1.2 defines the smart cities concept definition, Section 1.3 discusses the key drivers of smart city, Section 1.4 broadly debates its enabler technologies, Section 1.5 discusses the application domains of smart city, Section 1.6 mentions associated challenges. In addition, Section 1.7 discusses some successful overseas case studies, which demonstrate their usage across different geography and policy settings, both fulfilling their potential and limitations. Section 1.8 discusses the lessons learned from case studies. Further, Section 1.9 comments on the future direction of Smart Cities and the policy innovations needed to realize their full potential for making the lives of their citizens better in ways that are sensitive to their unique cultural and social institutions. Finally, Section 1.10 concludes the chapter.

Figure 1. Global Urbanization Trend (1950–2050) (Musa, S. I., Hashim, M., & Reba, M. N. M. 2017)

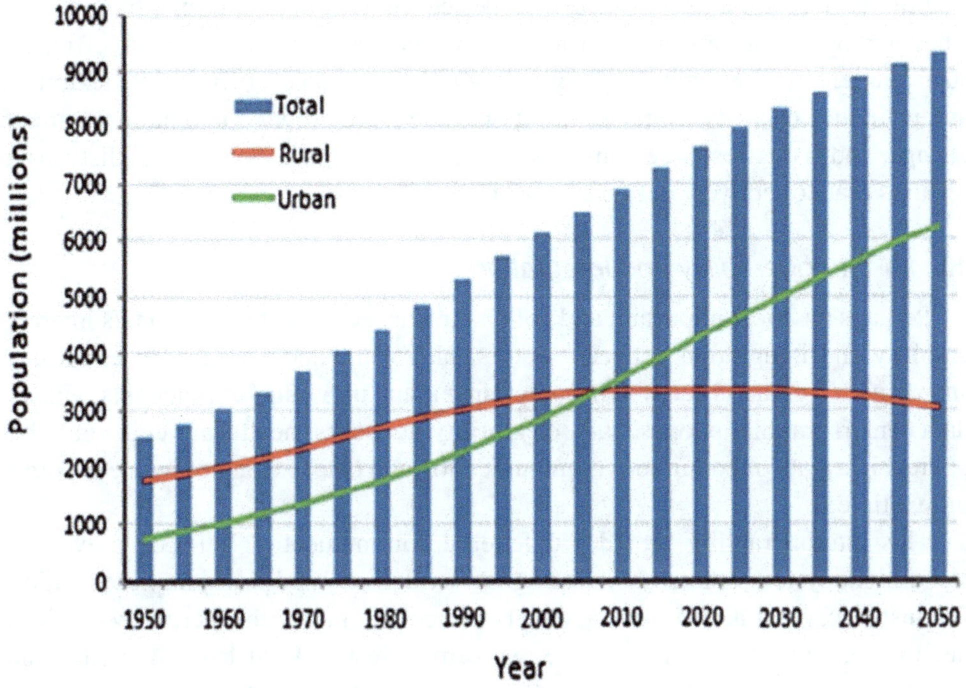

1.2 Defining Smart Cities

A Smart City is a city that employs information and communication technologies (ICTs) to make its operations more efficient, communicate with the public, and provide better quality government services and citizens' welfare. The essence of Smart Cities is to leverage digital solutions to transform conventional infrastructure and services into interactive, efficient, and responsive forms for citizens (Das, 2024).

Smart Cities are based on a foundation of integration technical, administrative, and social. The coming together of digital technologies with physical assets enables a holistic approach to the planning and administration of the city (Artuso, 2014). Smart Cities take advantage of several sensors, linked devices, connectivity networks, as well as data analytics platforms that gather data across various sources and process them together. All these data are optimized to better handle traffic, curtail energy waste, regulate trash, as well as promote security.

1.2.1 Important Features of Smart Cities

Smart cities are a new-age, innovative redefinition of traditional urban space. They deploy technology and information to enhance services to be more efficient, sustainable, and accessible. The long-term goal is to enhance the livability, flexibility, and resilience of a city from mounting pressure from growing population, climate change, and rising resource demands. Some of the most important and distinctive features that collectively define a smart city are:

1.2.1.1 Interoperability and Integration

Perhaps the most important and convincing aspect of a smart city is its interoperability and integration between sectors, platforms, and services. In essence, a smart city is a gigantic ecosystem comprising many individual components sensors, data centers, mobile phones, cars, etc., utility networks, healthcare units, etc. that operate in a state of continuous communication and data exchanges with each other in real time.

This interoperability provides unfettered communication between previously stand-alone systems, thereby enhancing service delivery and policy implementation. For instance, the transportation authority can collaborate with emergency services, healthcare, and utility firms on one platform to respond quicker to a crisis. This coordination may enable first-responders to reach scene locations quicker by optimizing routes, guiding green lights along the way, and clearing adjacent streets all while receiving real-time incident data. Interoperability is the key to a successful open data economy in which data is made available to innovators, civic societies, and businesses to facilitate problem-solving and creativity. This system allows stakeholders to collaborate, reuse data, combine services, and enhance the city's overall functionality. Interoperable data structures, application programming interfaces (APIs), and open data-sharing infrastructure facilitate this kind of collaboration reducing redundancy, closing knowledge gaps, and optimizing policy responses.

Lastly, interoperability assures that a smart city's digital components are permitted to change and develop along with growing needs and changing technologies, thereby future-proofing the city's digital infrastructure. This adaptability is crucial to a city's ability to remain resilient in the face of disruptive innovations or growing pressures as a result of climate change, population growth, or new policy priorities.

1.2.1.2 Sustainability

It is the essence of the smart city. Growing population pressures, growing energy demands, climate change, and limited resources necessitate the conservation and optimization of resources to build a future we would like to see for all. Smart cities strive to make this possible through technological advancements, policy measures, and the engagement of citizenry in energy saving, conservation of waste, and conservation of resources.

One of the most promising areas of sustainability is the conservation of energy through intelligent grid technologies, energy storage, and renewable energy. Solar, wind, and geothermal power, and methods of conserving use of energy, optimizing supply, and conserving energy off-peak are some of these. The use of smart lighting, automated heating controls, and home and business energy consumption reports in the aggregate help conserve waste and resources.

Besides, smart cities have green belts, parks, green roofs, and neighborhood forests that help in the conservation of natural ecosystems and mitigating the impact of the urban heat island effect. Green water management through rainwater harvesting, recycling of greywater, and sensor-based irrigation also helps in the prudent use of water is an increasing issue in most growing urban centers. Besides that, recycling and waste management can be complemented by sensor-equipped waste stations and auto-processing plants, which transform the waste into raw material for recycling or energy. The ultimate goal is a sustainable and circular loop where resources are used in an optimized way, waste is minimized, and there is a balance between the capacity of nature to regenerate and human activity.

1.2.1.3 Citizen Participation

One of the greatest benefits a smart city can provide its residents is more citizen involvement in civic decision-making and policy enforcement. The city's greatest stakeholders are its residents who can become contributors and co-creators and not just recipients of services.

Smart cities achieve this through open data platforms, civic engagement applications, surveys, and electronic town hall meetings that facilitate citizen engagement and policy-discussion-related forums. This two-way communication allows policy makers to measure the citizens' preferences, monitor their complaints, or collect their ideas for improving services for making democratic institutions and civic loyalty more robust. This participatory method of governing creates greater equality, justice, and civic satisfaction and improves relations within a community. Civic engagement also involves greater accountability and justice in policy application, as decisions are made publicly and with others' input. Not only does this prevent policy failure based on insufficient knowledge or agreement within a community, but it also assists in developing a healthy civic culture and shared vision of a city's future path forward. Further, civic engagement allows innovators to work directly with communities to address challenges that matter to them like waste management, energy consumption, health care provision, or education and give the smart city idea substance, imagination, and policy energy.

1.2.1.4 Data-Driven Decision Making

Data is the foundation of a smart city's capacity to make informed and forward-looking decisions. Cities generate enormous amounts of data from sensors embedded in water pipes and power stations, from social media, or from health care providers' patient records. By analyzing this data, policy makers are able to uncover patterns, fix problems, and see in advance what challenges lie ahead. This data-driven approach guides policy decision on everything from the best resource allocation and traffic relief to energy conservation and optimizing health care delivery. Machine Learning and Artificial Intelligence enable big and complex data sets analysis and converting them into usable information which guides policy makers to the optimal outcome.

1.2.1.5 Innovation and Entrepreneurship

Entrepreneurship and innovation are at the very heart of the development of a smart city. Smart cities provide a fertile ground for corporate, startup, or civic innovators to come, experiment, and apply new solutions to the pressing issues their cities are confronting. This is done through open innovation platforms, hackathons, innovation laboratories, and technology clusters, which create a space for innovators to collaborate, share resources, and find solutions to problems together. Smart cities also enable the creation of new businesses, services, and technologies that significantly contribute to their operation and resilience from developing more efficient lighting to designing sophisticated data-based health care delivery systems. Moreover, this innovation culture generates new employment and solidifies the local economy. Lastly, this forward-looking stance guarantees the city's resilience in the face of uncertainty in the future. Innovation enables a city to adapt graciously to increasing population demands, climate change, epidemics, and other disruption events, transforming likely weaknesses into possible prospects for change.

1.3 Key Drivers of Smart Cities

The development of Smart Cities is influenced by an intersection of social, economic, technological, and political trends that converge to result in the necessity and feasibility of developing smarter cities as shown in Figure 1.2. These drivers not only encourage the uptake of digital technologies but also influence whether the dividends from innovation are shared fairly. An understanding of these drivers is vital to policymakers to create effective and inclusive strategies.

1.3.1 Urbanization and Population Growth

Urban population growth at a pace too fast to absorb accelerates, mounting pressure on public services, energy, mobility, and housing. Growing peri-urban territories and slum settlements heighten the challenge of providing fair infrastructure. To meet this, data-driven planning and demand-responsive systems are gaining appeal, allowing cities to prepare for disruptions like public health emergencies or violent weather events. For example, megacities in South Asia and Sub-Saharan Africa experience intense pressure on transit and sanitation systems, where technology can maximize resources. But these technologies cannot replace investment in core infrastructure and social insurance. Urbanization thus creates both the imperative and the proving ground for scalable responses, but also poses fundamental questions of distribution: who gains, and who is left behind?

1.3.2 Technological Innovation

Technological advances in sensors, 5G, cloud and edge computing, and artificial intelligence have radically increased the technical practicability of real-time governance. These tools reduce barriers to predictive maintenance, adaptive traffic management, and automated resource allocation. Technology, however, is an enabling factor and not a solution per se. Municipal innovation effectiveness is reliant on municipal procurement strategies, interoperability standards, and the institutional capacity to implement and maintain complex systems. Cities that have robust digital ecosystems i.e., established broadband and open data platforms are best placed to experiment more quickly, while others need to pursue phased or hybrid approaches that navigate ambition against governance readiness.

1.3.3 Environmental Sustainability

Climate imperatives are now a determining force in smart city initiatives. Networked sensors and analytics provide targeted energy savings, waste management with precision, and neighborhood-level air-quality monitoring, in support of national and international climate obligations. But excessive dependence on "fixes" from technology also threatens to generate eco-utopian stories that conceal more profound structural forces behind emissions, including land use or improper housing policy. To be successful, smart technologies need to be placed within holistic urban planning initiatives that give top priority to resilience, equity, and long-term sustainability.

1.3.4 Economic Competitiveness

Digital infrastructure is also increasingly considered as an investment magnet for attracting skilled labour and tourism. Smart services, innovation districts, and open data programs can drive entrepreneurship and international profile. But the pursuit of "smart city brand" can prioritize spectacle projects like the symbolic command centres or celebrity pilots over incremental but socially imperative improvements such as affordable mobility or systems of community health. Competitiveness, as a valid stimulus, must be subtly balanced to guarantee that resources augment the daily grit of citizens without just building the city's external brand.

1.3.5 Demand for Transparent Government

Growing public demands for accountable government and citizen-focused services are strong political drivers for smart city uptake. Digital portals, participatory budgeting systems, and e-delivery systems can enhance confidence and engagement. But their effectiveness depends on access making services usable across language, capacity, and digital literacy and institutional motivation to respond to citizen feedback. Without these, participatory tools can degenerate into tokenistic exercises, legitimising decisions but not transforming them.

Each of these drivers depends upon the others: demographic pressures build demand, technological innovation delivers capacity, climate imperatives define objectives, economic competitiveness determines priorities, and citizen expectations deliver political momentum. For smart cities to work, technical decisions need to be clearly mapped against governance capacity, sustainable investment, and equity commitments. Otherwise, the very same drivers of smart city development can end up inadvertently boosting inequality and undermining public trust.

Figure 2. Drivers of Smart Cities: Interconnected Forces of Change

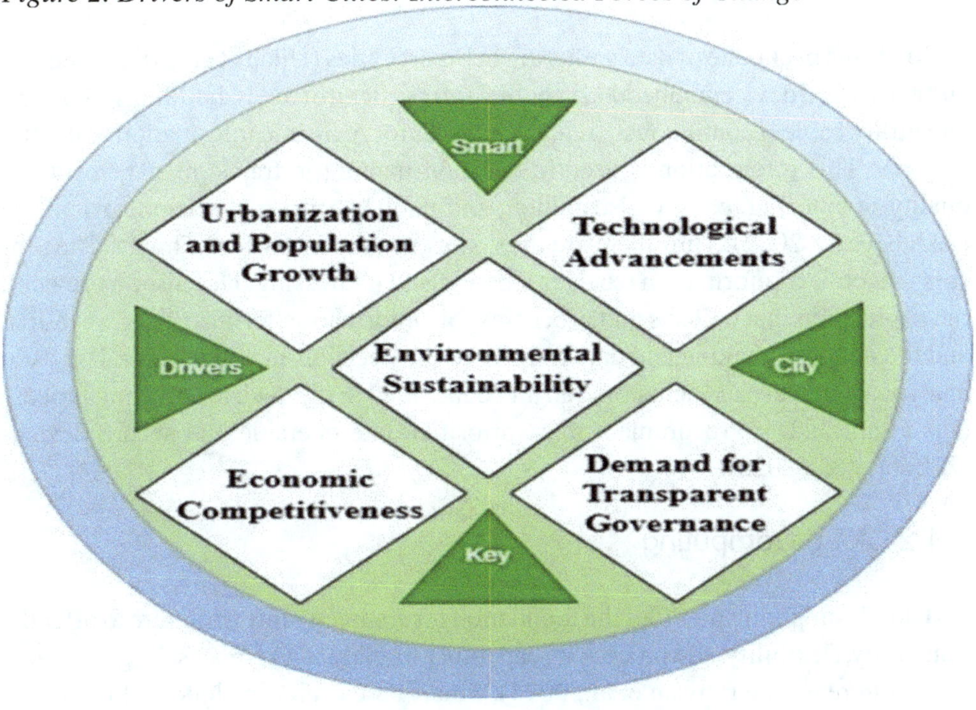

1.4 Core Technologies Enabling Smart Cities

Smart Cities are founded on the pillars of interlinked digital technologies that collect, analyze, and respond to city data in real-time as shown in Figure 1.3. Success in smart cities is depended upon the deployment of core technologies that enable automation, analysis, and connectivity (Laguerre, 2006). Their aspiration is to create resilient, sustainable, and connected urban spaces that enhance the quality of life of citizens and stimulate economic growth. Therefore, the building blocks collectively generate technologically advanced, socially balanced, economically prosperous, and ecologically sustainable smart cities. They are the focal point to improving living conditions, optimizing the use of available resources, and building resilient future urban systems. Therefore, the following are the building pillars which are at the center of smart and connected city development:

1.4.1 Internet of Things (IoT)

IoT is the backbone of data gathering in Smart Cities (Ullah et al., 2023). Sensors and networked devices embedded in public infrastructure (roads, buildings, vehicles, and utility cables) continuously report and monitor real-time information to central systems. This information is used in decision-making in traffic management, air quality monitoring, energy distribution, and public security, precision agriculture (Akhter et al., 2022). Thus there are three stages to the Internet of Things: The sensors that collect information (such as locating and addressing the sensor or device), the application that collects and processes this information for further aggregation, and the decision-making and data transfer to the decision-making server. Big data, analytical engines, and actuators can all be included in the decision-making process (Jha et al., 2024). Procurement must prioritize interoperable and secure devices (Zahoor et al., 2023).

1.4.2 Cloud Computing

Cloud computing provides the foundation for smart city infrastructure to offer the scalability, flexibility, and processing capability to analyze and process large amounts of data in real time (Diwan et al., 2024). Smart cities can use cloud technology to tap into a number of technology resources, including environmental monitoring, energy usage data, and traffic monitoring. Cloud computing's centralized structure makes it possible for cities to store data effectively, thereby decreasing the burden on local systems and enabling service management and updating to be seamless. Cloud computing enables straightforward internet access to servers, storage units, databases, and other application services, and this simplifies system integration in smart cities and information sharing among them (Yang et al., 2024). Cloud services also allow the flexibility to host applications across different departments of the city. Cities need to plan budget for lifecycle costs and meet data residency and governance needs.

Figure 3. Technological Framework of Smart Cities

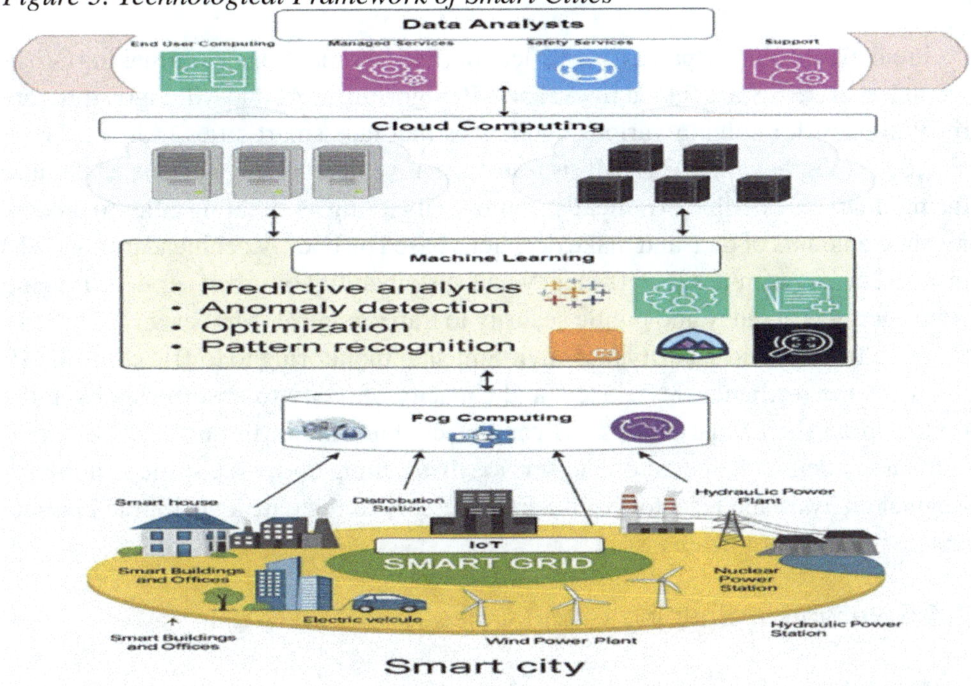

1.4.3 Edge and Fog Computing

While cloud computing focuses processing in one location, edge and fog computing disperse it to the location of the data source. Edge computing is such a vital component of the functioning of a smart city because it is the center of processing and managing data (Rathore et al., 2024). Essentially, it is about placing computing resources close to where the data is being created. Being close to the data allows for quicker response times, improved data security, and better bandwidth usage. With the use of edge computing, smart cities can maintain these mission-critical systems in peak condition, without the delay typically involved in cloud processing. Fog computing adds another layer between the edge and the cloud to offer seamless, hierarchical data processing. Cities need to make sustainable budget plans to maintain the operation of decentralized nodes and to meet the governance impediments involved in data localization, security, and interoperability at the network periphery.

1.4.4 Artificial Intelligence and Machine Learning

Predictive analytics, pattern identification, and automatic decision-making (Vishwarupe et al., 2023)are fueled by AI and ML algorithms. AI and ML algorithms are revolutionary for solving various challenges that face smart cities (Ahmad Jan et al., 2025) (Yigit et al., 2024). ML is transformative in resolving various challenges facing smart cities. ML can radically improve city living by enabling cities to process gigantic amounts of data and make decisions based on data. Machine learning (ML) in smart cities promotes the efficiency and sustainability of urban services ranging from energy efficiency and public security to traffic control (Mrabet & Sliti, 2024). Ranging from public security and environmental monitoring to traffic control, ML improves the resilience, efficiency, and capacity of a city to absorb shocks in the future. In nutshell Smart Cities, AI can detect abnormalities in traffic flows, predict energy demand, and automate service dispatching under real-time conditions. Regular analysis and tests for equity are necessary to regulate algorithmic bias and ensure the trust of citizens.

1.4.5 Networks: Shaping Smart Cities

5G high-speed connectivity is revolutionizing the development of smart cities by enabling seamless communication among sensors, actuators, and control centers (Goswami et al., 2024). As urban spaces increasingly rely on real-time data exchange, 5G is the pillar of smart and efficient city functioning. With ultra-low latency and massive data bandwidth, 5G enables information transmission at high speeds, enhancing various aspects of urban living. One of the highest returns on investment of 5G is live video monitoring, which facilitates next-generation security solutions. 5G also facilitates smart transport systems with V2V (Vehicle to Vehicle Communication) and V2I (Vehicle to Infrastructure Communication) communication. Connected and autonomous vehicles, intelligent traffic control, and predictive analytics optimize traffic flow, minimizing traffic congestion and accidents. Future breakthroughs in 5G technology will open doors to integration in smart cities to result in even more adaptive, resilient, and smart cities. Equitable implementation and affordability policies define whether their advantages extend to the whole population.

1.5 Application Domains of Smart City

Smart Cities enhance the quality of life by providing services in an efficient manner, enhancing civic participation, providing a clean environment, and enhancing sustainable development. Smart cities facilitate effective functioning by being monitored in real-time and through automation and saving resources and minimizing waste. Significantly, through the incorporation of digital platforms into their functioning, smart cities facilitate increased transparency and citizen involvement in policymaking, enhancing the democratic process (Al-Raeei, 2024). These application fields embrace an array of technologies the Internet of Things (IoT), Artificial Intelligence (AI), big data, robots, and sensor networks that solve complex, real-world problems in a versatile, sustainable, and socially acceptable way see Figure 1.4. Some of the most influential and most applied application fields in smart cities are described in the following sections;

1.5.1 Intelligent Transportation

Perhaps the most obvious and effective element of smart cities are their intelligent transportation systems. Increased congestion, increased vehicle emissions, and bottlenecked routines are major issues for many cities that are expanding. Intelligent transportation systems allow city managers to alleviate congestion, minimize travel time, decrease emissions, and facilitate increased pedestrian safety. Dynamic traffic management is where the innovations are directed. Traffic lights at intersections can be linked with cameras and sensors so that they can react in real time to evolving conditions lengthening green light times when traffic is dense or cutting down wait times for side streets when traffic is lighter (Elassy et al., 2024). Moreover, adaptive route applications can guide drivers around bottlenecks using alternative routes. This opens up the city, and allows for a smoother movement of automobiles. In addition, smart parking systems lead drivers to available parking spaces, minimizing the amount of time individuals spend driving around waiting for the opportunity to park is an important source of congestion and air pollution. Information from parking sensors in real time is input into a central system so that the city is able to make the most of its use and minimize associated emissions. The public transport can be incorporated into the system such that buses and subway lines benefit from the real-time data to facilitate efficient schedules, prevent jams, and transport high volumes of passengers.

1.5.2 Smart Energy Management

Effective management of energy is one of the traits of a smart city. Rising energy demand coupled with budget limitations makes energy saving a policy necessity. Smart grids enable the supply of energy where and when energy demand is highest, optimizing both energy supply and use (Saleem et al., 2022). One of the most important aspects of this is the integration of renewable energy technologies, primarily solar and wind, with traditional power plants. Advanced grid technologies enable energy providers to balance energy from renewables with base-load energy, reducing reliance on fossil-fueled power plants. This provides lower emissions, greater energy self-sufficiency, and a more stable energy grid. Also, there is smart energy monitoring, which enables individuals and businesses to track their energy usage in real time. This can save energy, reduce wastage, and optimize spending. Smart meters, for instance, enable granular control of energy use, encouraging conservation behavior through rewards or pricing plans. Collectively, these technologies create a self-healing energy system where delivery and use are actually controlled to prevent blackouts, minimize waste, and curb emissions related to energy, all while enhancing the power system's resiliency.

1.5.3 Waste Management

Rapid population growth is paralleled by rapid growth in waste generation that is a problem for most cities in today's world. Proper waste management can reduce the economic, health, and environmental waste disposal-related effects (Lakhouit, 2025). Waste bins also come equipped with capacity sensors that enable city services to track when a bin is nearly full or full. This enables waste collection crews to make their rounds more efficient hence reducing both operational and emissions expenses by collecting only, when necessary, instead of following a schedule. In addition, Artificial Intelligence is able to Model waste trends such that policy makers can see where to reduce waste or recycle more. This could involve creating incentives to get companies to decrease packaging or creating computerized, robot-based waste-sorting technologies in recycling centers. Some cities are employing waste-to-energy technologies alongside advanced recycling programs, turning trash into a renewable fuel. Not only does this reduce the pressure on landfills, but it also closes the energy cycle, adding a layer of resiliency to the city's energy supply.

1.5.4 Environmental monitoring

Clean air is perhaps the most critical objective of smart cities, with a direct influence on the health of its residents. Environmental monitoring is an application based on a network of sensors and data stations placed strategically across the city (Bacco et al., 2017). These sensors have the capability to track levels of pollution, air, water, radiation, and other indicators of environmental health in real time. This data can help policy makers make decisions to formulate regulations or incentives to minimize emissions, save resources, and create preparedness for environmental crises. In addition, this information helps to react fast during an emergency for instance, if air quality is compromised by industrial contamination or by a fire, the authorities can react fast by shutting down schools within the affected area, warning health care providers, or by utilizing computerized systems to aid in containment. This evidence-based approach improves a city's ability to respond to changing conditions while also being a healthy and desirable place in which to reside for its growing population.

1.5.5 Smart Governance

Responsive, efficient, and citizen-centric administration is the foundation of a smart city. Smart governance is enabled by digital platforms through convenient services, doing away with bureaucratic delays, and increasing civic participation (Sharmin & Chowdhury, 2025). For instance, digital IDs allow for rapid registration of voters, delivery of services, and financial transactions. The residents can pay taxes, seek licenses, or file complaints through a single portal hence decreasing waiting times, documentation, and man-machine interface. In addition, open data platforms facilitate civic engagement through the release of operational data, policy documents, and budgetary reports. This facilitates greater transparency and anti-fraud, and a better democratic process. In addition, citizen engagement tools like surveys, town hall meetings, or civic hackathons facilitate policy makers to obtain meaningful public contributions to their decision-making process. Together, these innovations enable collaborative, evidence-based policy-making, enhancing city government to be more responsive, legitimate, and representative of its citizens.

1.5.6 Intelligent Health

Health care delivery is where technology and health converge in an intelligent city setting. Smart health initiatives enable health care providers to meet their communities' increasing health care demands earlier, better, and more precisely (Dutta, S. 2025). Wearable tech such as activity trackers, biosensors, and smartwatches can help an individual maintain their health in balance, with health care professionals receiving real-time information. This enables doctors to monitor health trends, identify problems early on, and intervene before problems are complicated. Furthermore, telemedicine diagnosis enables remote or underserved patients to converse directly with health care providers through video conferencing and diagnostic software hence reducing health care disparities. Artificial intelligence assists doctors by scanning vast amounts of health data to help with diagnostics and treatment options. These technologies together make health care delivery more effective, accessible, and personalized, enhancing population health and readiness for the future health crisis, such as virus containment and vaccine distribution in a crisis situation.

1.5.7 Public Safety and Emergency Services

Safe cities promote an active civic existence and enable their citizens to flourish. Public safety and emergency services rank high on the policy makers', first-responders', and the general society's agenda (Bhaduri, M. 2025). Sophisticated monitoring through networks of cameras, facial recognition (with requisite security protocols), and incident-detecting software helps enable rapid, data-driven responses to accidents or crimes. This can help reduce response time, maximize arrest rates, or optimize delivery of aid after a mass incident. Moreover, predictive policing draws upon past records and computational analysis to forecast and forestall crimes before they even happen. This enables the authorities to react tactically for instance, by allocating more resources to high-risk areas without sacrificing civil liberties or resorting to unjust or discriminatory practices. Furthermore, location-based emergency services also enable faster response by leading the first-responders to the site of the emergency and by routing through the city roads in an optimal fashion. This provides a revolutionary boost in the delivery of assistance in the case of a fire, a medical emergency, or a car accident and hence a better safety net for the whole city.

Figure 4. Application Domains of Smart Cities

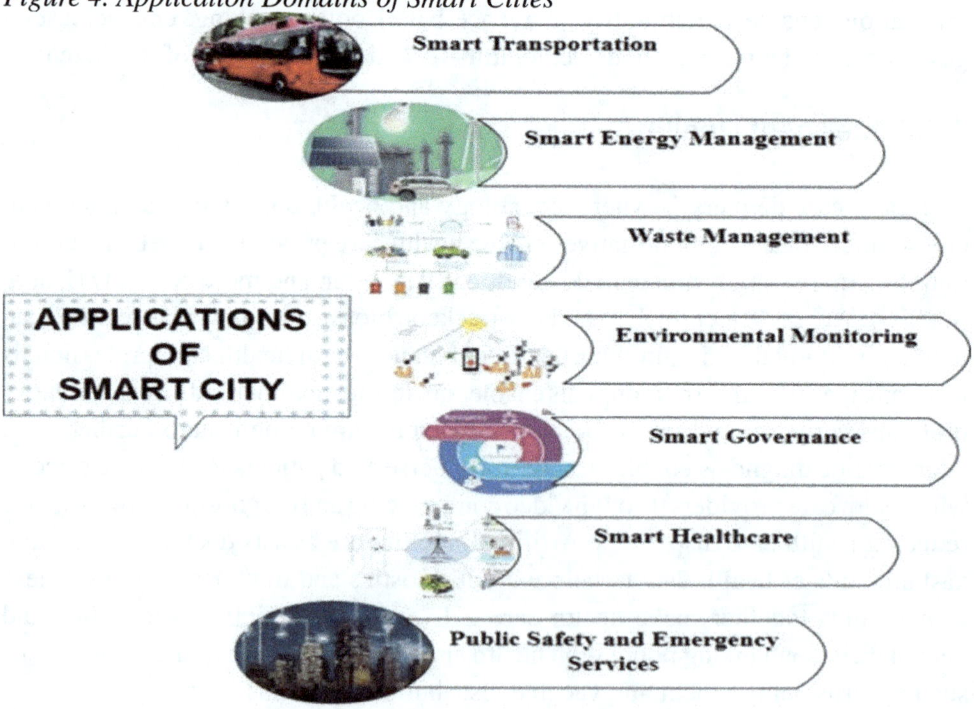

1.6 Challenges in Smart City Development

Smart cities improve efficiency, sustainability, and quality of life through emerging technology and policy informed by data (World Development Indicators, 2014). As wonderful as their potential for transformation is, however, smart cities also create numerous challenges that need to be overcome, among them data protection and privacy, up-front expense, the digital divide, interoperability, and government complexity. To overcome such challenges is how smart city initiatives are successfully undertaken across the world.

1.6.1 Data Privacy and Security

One of the most important challenges of smart city development is protecting sensitive information from cyber-attacks (Fabrègue, B. F., & Bogoni, A. 2023). With pervasive Internet of Things (IoT) devices, surveillance systems, and networked digital infrastructure, vast amounts of private and public data are being continuously collected and processed. Hacking, unauthorized access, and data breaches are seriously threatening citizens and the government. Secure and responsible handling of information in smart cities will necessitate the use of strong encryption techniques, secure access controls, and ethical information management systems.

1.6.2 High Upfront Cost

The deployment of smart city technology entails enormous financial investments in infrastructure, digital platforms, and maintenance (Gade & Aithal, 2022). Governments and cities find it difficult to mobilize funds for mass-scale projects, especially in cities with poor financial endowments. The cost of replacing old infrastructure, installing IoT networks, and installing AI-powered city management tools can be enormous. Public-private partnerships (PPPs) and innovative funding models, such as smart bonds and sustainability grants, are increasingly being pursued to surmount financial constraints and ensure long-term sustainability.

1.6.3 Digital Divide

One of the biggest smart city evolution challenges is providing equitable access to digital services (Shin et al., 2021). Technological progress benefits affluent cities, and marginalized groups might face poor infrastructure, poor connectivity, or poor digital literacy. The digital divide widens the social disparities, pushing some groups beyond the borders of the most elementary services like e-governance, smart healthcare, and digital education. Policymakers must give the highest priority to accessibility, affordability, and digital literacy initiatives bridging technological gaps to create inclusive smart cities.

1.6.4 Interoperability Issues

Smart cities are based on a vast infrastructure of interconnected systems, such as transport, energy networks, public utilities, and surveillance security. But heterogeneous technologies and standards render it a challenging task to interoperate (Asio, J. M. R., & Suero, A. N. 2025). Most systems are created independently with proprietary protocols, which prevent free communication among different platforms. Standardization, open-data policies, and common frameworks for software compatibility are required to ensure smooth operation and coordination among different smart city elements.

1.6.5 Governance, regulation, and accountability

Success of a smart city relies on good governance, regulatory policy, and intra-stakeholder coordination. Cities, technology companies, businesses, and citizens must collaborate to establish transparent and adaptive policies that address city challenges. Governance concerns exist regarding matters such as ownership of data, decision-making authority, and moral implications of AI-powered city management (Sanchez et al., 2024). Procurement and vendor agreements should be integrated with transparency clauses and audit requirements. Clarifying decision authority and data ownership prevents diffusion of responsibility between government agencies and commercial vendors.

1.6.6 Challenges of implementation in low- and middle-income countries (LMICs)

For resource-scarce environments, they encompass limited institutional capabilities, unstable utilities, as well as competing emergency needs. Scaling-down, modular, and community-based pilots, with phased scaling through capacity development, perform better than large capital top-down projects. Donor programs and concessional finance should emphasize sustainability and knowledge sharing.

1.6.7 Assessment, measurements, and surprise results

Projects tend to focus more on outputs (sensors deployed, dashboards launched) rather than outcomes (reduced commutes, improved health, broader access). Tightly constructed evaluation with baseline measures, longitudinal tracking, and disaggregated measures (by income, gender, geography) is required. Frequent ethical influence analysis and algorithmic audits must be conducted to find and forestall harms (e.g., biased predictive policing, detrimental rewards that promote traffic escalation).

1.7 Case Studies of Smart Cities

Smart City applications has been implemented across the globe for various purposes. There are so many successful case studies where smart city has proved to be effective. Here we have discussed few of them.

1.7.1 Barcelona, Spain

Barcelona, Spain, is the world's prime example of a smart city that has made effective use of information and communication technologies (ICT), specifically the Internet of Things (IoT), to enhance urban living (Capdevila & Zarlenga, 2015). Barcelona has reconfigured its infrastructure and public services with digital innovation, data-driven policy, and sustainability, with the objective of making its residents' quality of life better and its long-term environmental and economic sustainability a success. One of the cornerstones of Barcelona's smart city strategy is its extensive use of IoT across urban infrastructure. Sensors embedded in infrastructure monitor a variety of parameters in real-time. For example, smart lighting infrastructure is installed all over the city; these streetlights adjust their brightness automatically in accordance with pedestrian or vehicular traffic, saving significant amounts of energy. When it comes to waste management, smart trash cans with fill-level sensors notify sanitation services when to empty trash, enabling optimized routes and a reduction in both fuel consumption and operating costs. Similarly, the city's parks are augmented by smart irrigation systems that use soil moisture and weather conditions to optimize water consumption, keeping parks well-groomed while conserving natural resources. Another key pillar of Barcelona's strategy is the focus on open data and city analytics. Barcelona has an open data portal through which the municipal data are made available to developers, researchers, and citizens. Openness of data triggers innovation, economic development, and transparency. The citizens are actively involved in government through online interfaces, enabling them to contribute to urban development planning, budget making, and policy formulation. Participatory government enhances civic trust and guarantees development harmony with the needs of people. An example is the Decidim platform, through which the citizens can propose and vote on municipal projects, integrating democratic participation into the core focus of the smart city philosophy. The transportation network of Barcelona has also been significantly improved through the use of smart technology. Its bike-sharing service, Bicing, utilizes GPS-enabled bikes to promote environmentally friendly commuting. Smart traffic lights, regulated by real-time traffic data, avoid traffic jams and reduce response time in case of emergencies. Charging stations for electric vehicles, which are also spaced far apart, help in transitioning the city towards clean mobility. Real-time data about public transport is made available via mobile applications, making it convenient for inhabitants and visitors alike to travel across the city. Digital infrastructure is the backbone of Barcelona's smart city initiative. Barcelona has heavily invested in high-speed internet and is at the forefront of the use of 5G technology. Investments in these technologies allow for easy communication between networked devices and offer high-level services like telemedicine, e-learning, and smart security systems. Such services, supported with strong data management and cybersecurity, demonstrate Barcelona's vision of becoming a digital-inclusive city. Barcelona's smart city experience is well integrated with its green goals. Projects in all sectors have led to a significant decrease in carbon footprints and better urban air quality. The use of renewable energy sources, smart grids, and green monitoring devices ensures that the city is climate change and resource scarcity resilient. Urban parks, managed with sensor-based irrigation and maintenance systems, not only support biodiversity but also increase the quality of life of the city. The success of Barcelona's smart city journey is due to its effective governance structure, public-private partnerships, and people-oriented strategy. The Barcelona government has ensured inclusive, open technology adoption that solves actual urban challenges. Unlike embracing technology for technology's sake, Barcelona has invested in making its urban space a people-oriented, responsive place. By merging digital innovation with participatory governance and green responsibility, Barcelona leads other cities wishing to become smart cities by example.

1.7.2 Amsterdam, Netherlands

This comparative international study considers the character, extent, and complexity of citizen engagement in smart cities. It aims to investigate how citizens engage in co-creating and contributing to smart city initiatives, rather than acting as passive consumers of technology (Przeybilovicz et al., 2020). The research is based on empirical evidence from nine cities around the world; Amsterdam, Barcelona, Graz, Guadalajara, Leeds, Medellin, Nairobi, San Francisco, and Seoul each offering unique insights within their local political, institutional, and cultural contexts. The research identifies that citizens' involvement is differently defined and enacted within cities. Although some cities such as Amsterdam and Barcelona advance inclusive models in which citizens are granted a status of co-creation of city innovation, others such as Nairobi and Seoul have more restricted models to participation as a means of channels of consultation or feedback. Within co-creation-friendly cities, citizens' participation permeates into decision-making, planning, and designing and enacting technology. This is opposite to technocratic cities where the agendas of smart cities are dictated top-down by authorities, and civic engagement only involves agreeing on pre-established agendas. There are different tools and platforms utilized to enable participation, such as budget voting online platforms, city data dashboards, hackathons, innovation labs, mobile apps, and social media. Physical meetings, workshops, and public forums are also engaged. Digital infrastructure is not by itself synonymous with participatory effectiveness. Digital illiteracy, poor internet connections, language barriers, and institutional distrust will screen the marginalized from such processes. The digital divide remains a persistent problem to most cities, especially in the Global South, where technical capability and access are not evenly spread. Political and historical contexts in cities play a crucial role in shaping their participatory systems. Medellin, for instance, has a participatory culture founded on grassroots-led urban regeneration that continues to shape its smart city policy. Nairobi, on the other hand, is at a disadvantage due to poor civic institutions, government lack of accountability, and poor finances to invest in long-term participation. Civic participation is more robust and effective in cities with robust democratic cultures, but in other instances it can be symbolic or fragmented. In spite of the widespread recognition of the value of public engagement, most smart city initiatives continue to grapple with creating inclusive, equitable, and long-term engagement. The report highlights that smart governance is not merely a matter of installing digital technologies but of transforming the relationship between citizens and the state. It involves technical fixes but also institutional transformation, political will, and social investment. Participation needs to be made a core value in smart city policy and not an add-on or a public relations stunt.

The evidence shows that successful citizen participation depends on ongoing support systems, including education, capacity-building programs, and open legal systems. Participation must be seen as a political, not a technical, process requiring negotiation, conflict, and cooperation. Cities must create participation programs that respond to local realities and that achieve actual influence over outcomes. There will be no single solutions that fit all, but cities must be adaptive and responsive to evolving community needs. The study discovers that technology can potentially enhance the participation of citizens but is not a substitute for real democratic processes. Smart cities must involve citizens as not customers or users but real participants in shaping the future of the city. Participation must be inclusive, well-resourced, and capable of influencing real decisions. Smart cities can only then realize their potential as more livable, more equitable, and more democratic.

1.7.3 Songdo, South Korea

Songdo, South Korea, is the most visionary instance of a smart city built from the ground up. Situated on reclaimed land off the coast of Incheon and within the Incheon Free Economic Zone master plan, Songdo was conceived as a high-tech, sustainable, and networked urban space (C. Yang, 2020). Right from the start, its architects sought to incorporate cutting-edge information and communications technologies (ICT) into every part of urban life everything from transportation and energy systems to government and citizen services making it a vision of the future urban experience. The city's infrastructure is integrated digitally through a central data management system, which continuously oversees and coordinates activity across sectors. Transport in Songdo is regulated by real-time data analysis. Traffic is being monitored by sensors, to which intelligent traffic lights respond to the number of vehicles in motion to avoid congestion. Public transport is also optimized for connectivity and efficiency, with the aim of reducing dependence on private vehicles. Pedestrian- and cycle-friendly paths also promote sustainable mobility goals. Citizens also have real-time transit information available through mobile applications, to make commuting convenient.

As far as energy management is concerned, Songdo employs smart grids and energy-efficient buildings with climate monitoring and control systems. The smart buildings, a number of which are LEED-certified, incorporate sensors that control energy use depending on whether the buildings are occupied and at what time of day, significantly reducing the impact on the environment. The city also employs pneumatic waste management systems that transport domestic waste in underground pipes, eliminate garbage trucks, and promote hygiene and urban beauty. Integration of renewable energy and recycling of water programs also serve to indicate the environmental sustainability of Songdo.

Songdo's administration is extensively integrated with ICT, which enables responsive government and civic engagement. City officials monitor surveillance systems, traffic patterns, environmental conditions, and energy use through centralized command centers. Citizens are also encouraged to interact with city services using digital means, enabling online payments for bills, local decision-making, and access to a wide variety of e-government services. Such channels enable transparency and efficiency in service provision and reduce administrative costs. Songdo's healthcare and education also reflect its smart city vision. The city has international schools and universities that use digital learning platforms, and hospitals use telemedicine and integrated patient records to deliver quality of care. Songdo's design also aims to balance technology with human livability, with parks, harbors, and cultural facilities that add to urban living. Above all, nearly 40% of the city's land is set aside for green spaces, which are maintained in condition by data-driven environmental monitoring systems.

Despite being technologically advanced, Songdo has failed to attract long-term residents and create a vibrant community life. Its relatively low density and low natural social activity have been quoted by critics as proof of its top-down planning approach and corporation-driven development. Songdo did continue to expand, and newer projects have sought to create community participation, cultural richness, and mixed-use city development in the hope of developing a more people-centric smart city experience.

Briefly, Songdo demonstrates the possibility of creating a smart city from scratch, where ICT is inextricably woven into the physical and administrative structure of the city. Its holistic strategy in addressing energy, transport, governance, and sustainability provides useful lessons to policymakers and urban planners across the globe. With some social aspects needing extra TLC, Songdo is an essential case study in how digital infrastructure and urban planning can merge to create tomorrow's cities.

1.8 Lessons Learned from Case Studies

The cross-city comparison of Barcelona, Amsterdam, and Songdo showcases both the potential and pitfalls of smart city development. Although all three cities have recorded quantifiable improvements, the cases also display recurring challenges and trade-offs. Integrating these lessons yields important insights for policymakers, practitioners, and researchers.

1.8.1 Governance and institutional capacity

Barcelona's strong municipal administration demonstrates that smart city initiatives require effective governance institutions, rather than investment in technology alone. Conversely, Songdo's failure demonstrates that even well-funded projects fail when governance institutions and civic participation are weak. Lesson: accountability systems and effective institutions are prerequisites for smart city development.

1.8.2 Citizen participation and inclusivity

Amsterdam's living labs show the promise of participatory government and co-creation but also the risk of engagement favoring digitally capable groups. Barcelona's participatory platforms broadened participation but exposed tensions between gentrification and exclusion. Lesson: Participatory mechanisms must be structured to avoid exclusion, with marginalized groups prominently represented.

1.8.3 Technology and social context balance

Songdo's masterplanned structure illustrates the limitations of technology-leading design. Despite having world-class infrastructure, it still has not grown lively community life. Barcelona, however, placed technology within existing urban habits in order to more harmoniously fit into residents' daily lives. Lesson: technology must adapt to local social, spatial, and cultural conditions instead of leading them.

1.8.4 Equity and unintended consequences

Examples illustrate how interventions in intelligent cities can contribute to enlarging inequalities on the contrary through gentrification, asymmetrical digital access, or privileged support for large-scale projects. Lesson: equity and distributional consequences must be thoroughly assessed and met, such as housing affordability, digital inclusion, and accessibility measures.

1.8.5 Financing and sustainability throughout the life cycle

Both cases illustrate the necessity of financing not only initial infrastructure but also ongoing operations, maintenance, and institutional capacity. Songdo's high upfront costs strained sustainability, while Barcelona's incremental, adaptive investments performed better. Lesson: funding mechanisms must consider lifecycle costs and avoid overreliance on showpiece projects.

1.8.6 Transferability and context sensitivity

Amsterdam's co-creation model and Barcelona's open-data initiatives are good templates, but replication in wholesale fashion in poor cities will be impossible. Lesson: smart city policies must be scaled and adapted to local institutional, fiscal, and socio-political circumstances rather than copied.

The cases collectively show that the smart city flourishes when technological ingenuity is anchored in strong governance, open involvement, equitable policy, and sustainable funding. The overall lesson is that “smartness” isn't measured by the sophistication of technology, but by the extent to which urban innovation creates trust, equity, and resilience for all city dwellers.

1.9 Future Trends in Smart Cities

As the world population keeps becoming increasingly urban a phenomenon referred to as rapid urbanization there is an emerging need for innovations that make these emerging cities more sustainable, resilient, adaptable, and human-centered. Smart cities, powered by advanced technologies, are at the forefront of this transformation. The smart city of the future is an evolutionary convergence of information technology, policy inventiveness, green architecture, and civic participation all converging to remake how citizens live, work, and interact with their communities. This is a forward-looking movement towards a world in which services are not just convenient but also environmentally sustainable, socially just, and personalized to the needs of every individual. The new technologies include:

1.9.1 Artificial Intelligence and Robotics: Service Automation of Delivery

Artificial Intelligence (AI) and robotics are soon to be the cornerstones of service delivery in smart cities. From traffic management to health care and emergency services, these technologies enable this degree of automation and response that has not been imagined before. For instance, self-driving taxis and buses equipped with sophisticated sensor suites would be able to transport people efficiently in a city, reducing congestion and real-time route optimization. Further, delivery robots would enable easy delivery of food, medicine, and other necessary items with minimum or no human intervention and low delivery-related emissions. AI-driven emergency services enable faster response by monitoring CCTV camera, social media, and citizen reports to ascertain the site of accidents or crime. This enables first-responders to reach the site much faster with a clear idea of the nature of the incident. Robotic assistance in hospitals from robotic surgeons to robotic drug dispensing in the pharmacy also helps to reduce the workload of health care professionals and improve the care of patients.

One of the grand opportunities these technologies open up is efficiency. Cities can optimize their resources, reduce cost of operations, and serve more effectively their increasing service demands. Most significantly, the union of human control and automated processes can facilitate a basic enhancement in service delivery, with human resources freed to address more sophisticated and people-to-people tasks.

1.9.2 Digital Twins: Virtual Copies of Urban Planning

Digital twins enable planners, engineers, policymakers, and stakeholders to see and forecast the future impact of their decision prior to its physical existence. A digital twin is an accurate, data-rich, 3D models of a city, a mirror that is built from massive volumes of sensor data, aerial photos, geographic information systems (GIS), and Internet of Things (IoT) streams.

Policy makers could also model population growth, climate impact, energy consumption, or policy rollout scenarios using digital twins. They could visualize vulnerabilities or bottlenecks and adjust plans to avoid problems from arising. Digital twins would also make urban planning collaborative, as all the stakeholders from all sectors of government, business, community could see and contribute to the city model. This technology is especially beneficial for the examination of complex interactions such as how a new freeway will alleviate traffic congestion but increase air pollution, or how adding solar panels will ease pressures on the energy system but affect the stability of the grid. Digital twins facilitate an evidence-based process in which policy is formed leading to wiser, more responsive, and more resilient cities. Moreover, digital twins can be employed to train emergency responders, design new parks, or minimize energy usage in buildings is all within a realistic, but risk-free virtual environment. Such visionary strategy allows stakeholders to make the most informed choices for their communities.

1.9.3 Blockchain: Urban Data and Governance Securing

As more dependence is placed on digital infrastructure, the security, integrity, and legitimacy of information are primary concerns for the governance of smart cities. Blockchain provides a solution to enable a trustless framework for securing transactions, identity establishment, and data integrity verification for all the smart city operations.

With decentralized ledgers, blockchain renders it impossible to manipulate or alter records after they are added, providing a secure level of fraud- and cyberattack resistance. It is especially crucial for voter registration-related services, real estate transactions, health care data, utility bill payment, or disbursement of financial aid. In addition, distributed and self-executing computer code in the form of smart contracts allows policy mechanisms to perform their routines without human intervention. It can do it more efficiently, reduce bureaucratic red tape, and provide greater civic participation by making the processes more auditable and reliable. For instance, a citizen's home, voter registration, health care coverage, and financial aid disbursements could be safeguarded by a city through a blockchain system. This guarantees fairness, prevents tampering, reduces redundancy, and establishes civic institutions as more reliable.

The interoperability enabled by blockchain coupled with its decentralized, tamper-evident nature offers a strong foundation on which many smart city services of the future can be securely built enabling civic institutions and building citizen trust.

1.9.4 Green Smart Cities: Carbon Neutrality and Sustainable Living

Environmental sustainability is at the forefront of tomorrow's smart city agenda. Cities consume vast amounts of energy and produce gigantic amounts of waste, their shifts to carbon neutrality are critical in the battle against climate change. Green smart city solutions intervene.

Green smart cities prioritize building energy efficiency, using techniques like green rooftops, solar panels, high-efficiency lighting, and high-thermal-efficiency materials. Energy for these buildings is increasingly derived from renewable energy sources; solar, wind, geothermal all giving the city power grid resiliency. Green smart cities also have green waste management and recycling initiatives that facilitate higher product reuse and a significant landfill waste reduction. Sensors on waste stations can monitor fill levels and facilitate more effective routing for waste collection services lowering vehicle emissions and saving resources.

In addition, green smart cities utilize end-to-end electric mobility solutions like electric taxis and buses, shared electrical bicycles and scooters, and hence reduce the use of fossil fueled transport. This results in reduced air pollution, reduced traffic congestion, and a major reduction in the carbon footprint of a city. Green areas parks, green belts, roof gardens help make the city climate-resilient by minimizing the heat island, enhancing air quality, and providing areas for social recreation. These all add up to a green, futuristic city.

1.9.5 Human-Centered Design: Accessible and Flexible Urban Services

While technology is the cornerstone of the future smart city, the ultimate purpose is to improve the well-being of all its residents the most especially the most vulnerable, elderly, and disabled. The people-centered approach is founded on inclusivity, equity, flexibility, and dignity in service delivery. Artificial intelligence-based accessibility technology provides barrier-free space and services for individuals with disabilities to engage in civic life. Smart kiosks can display information in various languages, translate messages for visitors, or assist the visually impaired through tactile cues or voice assistance. Also, human-centered design emphasizes active citizen engagement in policy development and service delivery. Citizen participation is enabled by technology platforms in the form of surveys, community forums, or participatory budgeting. This builds strong civic institutions through ensuring institutions are representative.

Certain visionary cities are using adaptive policy levers, which allow them to act in response to evolving citizen needs. This could be by sending more resources to a neighborhood that sees a spate of crime or providing more social services in the event of a health emergency. The aim is to allow policy makers and administrators to act rapidly, economically, and humanely in the spirit of human-centered design. Lastly, the people-first approach centers on the most fundamental principle: technology innovation should come ahead of people. The smart city's future is not merely a question of whether they can collect data or provide efficient services but whether they shall be able to support happy, healthy, connected, and empowered citizens.

CONCLUSION

Smart city development reflects the intersection of demographic drivers, technological advancements, environmental needs, and ascending citizen expectations. As this chapter has sought to illustrate, smart city development cannot be defined as a simple technological transformation but more as a multifaceted governance, planning, and societal transition. Although technologies like IoT, AI, cloud, and edge computing offer powerful enablers, success also rests with the institutions, policies, and finance structures that determine how they are deployed. The three case studies of Barcelona, Amsterdam, and Songdo all showcase this dynamic quite poignantly. Barcelona exemplifies the advantages of open governance and participatory platforms, but also the dangers of exclusion and gentrification. Amsterdam showcases the power of co-creation and experimentation, but at the cost of much more inclusive participation to prevent perpetuating digital divides. Songdo highlights the limitations of technology-led planning, demonstrating that without rich social and cultural investments, even the most sophisticated infrastructures cannot provide rich urban life. Combined, these examples teach us about governance, inclusivity, equity, funding, and the importance of context-specific design. The future of smart cities ultimately will depend on more than just technological advancedness. Instead, it will depend on how innovation is utilized to construct resilient, equitable, and inclusive urban environments. Cities that incorporate transparency, civic empowerment, and sustainable financing into their smart efforts will craft spaces in which technology benefits people not vice versa. In that regard, the "smartness" of cities cannot be quantified in terms of gigabytes of data crunched, but by how much trust, equitability, and shared prosperity they have achieved for their people.

REFERENCES

Ahmad Jan, M., Adil, M., Brik, B., Harous, S., & Abbas, S. (2025). Making Sense of Big Data in Intelligent Transportation Systems: Current Trends, Challenges and Future Directions. *ACM Computing Surveys*, *57*(8), 1–43.

Akhter, R., & Sofi, S. A. (2022). Precision agriculture using IoT data analytics and machine learning. In Journal of King Saud University – Computer and Information Sciences (Vols. 34–34, pp. 5602–5618). https://doi.org/10.1016/j.jksuci.2021.05.013

Albino, V., Berardi, U., & Dangelico, R. M. (2015). Smart Cities: Definitions, dimensions, performance, and initiatives. *Journal of Urban Technology*, *22*(1), 3–21. DOI: 10.1080/10630732.2014.942092

Al-Raeei, M. (2024). The smart future for sustainable development: Artificial intelligence solutions for sustainable urbanization. *Sustainable Development*. Advance online publication. DOI: 10.1002/sd.3131

Artuso, M. (2014). UN Habitat, State of the World's Cities 2012/13 – prosperity of cities, London, Earthscan, 2013, 184 pp., ISBN 13: 978-0-415-83888-7. Tab. Graph. Images. Urban Research & Practice, 7(3), 359–360. https://doi.org/10.1080/17535069.2014.968363

Asio, J. M. R., & Suero, A. N. (2025). Global Synergy: Cross-Border Collaborations in AI-Enabled Smart City Development. In *AI and Emerging Technologies for Emergency Response and Smart Cities* (pp. 259-286). IGI Global Scientific Publishing. DOI: 10.4018/979-8-3693-9770-1.ch012

Bacco, M., Delmastro, F., Ferro, E., & Gotta, A. (2017). Environmental monitoring for smart cities. *IEEE Sensors Journal*, *17*(23), 7767–7774. DOI: 10.1109/jsen.2017.2722819

Bera, S., Misra, S., & Rodrigues, J. J. (2014). Cloud Computing Applications for smart Grid: A survey. *IEEE Transactions on Parallel and Distributed Systems*, *26*(5), 1477–1494. DOI: 10.1109/tpds.2014.2321378

Bhaduri, M. (2025). AI and IoT Solutions for Efficient Public Service Delivery in Smart Cities. *Soft Computing Fusion with Applications*, *2*(1), 153–163. DOI: 10.22105/scfa.v2i1.41

Buettner, T. (2015). Urban Estimates and Projections at the United Nations: The strengths, weaknesses, and underpinnings of the world Urbanization Prospects. *Spatial Demography*, *3*(2), 91–108. DOI: 10.1007/s40980-015-0004-2

Capdevila, I., & Zarlenga, M. I. (2015). Smart city or smart citizens? The Barcelona case. *Journal of Strategy and Management*, *8*(3), 266–282. DOI: 10.1108/jsma-03-2015-0030

Colding, J., Nilsson, C., & Sjöberg, S. (2024). Smart Cities for All? Bridging digital divides for socially sustainable and inclusive cities. *Smart Cities*, *7*(3), 1044–1059. DOI: 10.3390/smartcities7030044

Das, D. K. (2024). Exploring the Symbiotic Relationship between Digital Transformation, Infrastructure, Service Delivery, and Governance for Smart Sustainable Cities. *Smart Cities*, *7*(2), 806–835. DOI: 10.3390/smartcities7020034

Diwan, T. D., Kittusamy, L., Narasimhan, L., Ghige, O., William, P., & Badholia, A. (2024, November 25). AI Analysis of Edge- Cloud Computing on IOT-based Large Data Storage Systems with Deep Learning. In *2024 International Conference on Intelligent & Innovative Practices in Engineering & Management (IIPEM)*. DOI: 10.1109/iipem62726.2024.10925648

Dutta, S. (2025). AI and IoT-Based Smart Healthcare Solutions in Urban Area. *Trends in Health Informatics*, *2*(1), 18–26. DOI: 10.22105/thi.v2i1.27

Elassy, M., Al-Hattab, M., Takruri, M., & Badawi, S. (2024). Intelligent transportation systems for sustainable smart cities. *Transportation Engineering*, *16*, 100252. DOI: 10.1016/j.treng.2024.100252

Fabrègue, B. F., & Bogoni, A. (2023). Privacy and security concerns in the smart city. *Smart Cities*, *6*(1), 586–613. DOI: 10.3390/smartcities6010027

Gade, D. S., & Aithal, P. S. (2022). ICT and Digital Technology based Solutions for Smart City Challenges and Opportunities. International Journal of Applied Engineering and Management Letters, 1–21. DOI: 10.47992/ijaeml.2581.7000.0116

Goswami, S. S., Mondal, S., & Licensee System Analytics. (2024). The Role of 5G in Enhancing IoT Connectivity: A Systematic review on applications, challenges, and future prospects [Original Article]. Big Data and Computing Visions, 4–4, 314–326. DOI: 10.22105/bdcv.2024.486159.1215

Jha, S., Shakya, S. R., Ahmad, S., & Zhou, Z. (2024). *Quality assessment and security in industrial internet of things*. CRC Press.

Kaluarachchi, Y. (2022). Implementing Data-Driven Smart City Applications for future cities. *Smart Cities*, *5*(2), 455–474. https://doi.org/10.3390/smartcities5020025

Kibria, M. G., Nguyen, K., Villardi, G. P., Zhao, O., Ishizu, K., & Kojima, F. (2018). Big data analytics, machine learning, and artificial intelligence in Next-Generation wireless networks. IEEE Access, 6, 32328–32338. 6–97. https://doi.org/10.1007/s11524-007-9171-9DOI: 10.1109/access.2018.2837692

Kjellstrom, T., Friel, S., Dixon, J., Corvalan, C., Rehfuess, E., Campbell-Lendrum, D., Gore, F., & Bartram, J. (2007). Urban Environmental Health Hazards and health equity. *Journal of Urban Health*, *84*(S1), 8.

Laguerre, M. S. (2006). The digital city: The American metropolis and information technology. *Choice Reviews Online*, *44*(04), 44–2421. DOI: 10.5860/choice.44-2421

Lakhouit, A. (2025). Revolutionizing Urban Solid Waste Management with AI and IoT: A review of smart solutions for waste collection, sorting, and recycling. *Results in Engineering*, *25*, 104018. DOI: 10.1016/j.rineng.2025.104018

Mrabet, M., & Sliti, M. (2024). Integrating machine learning for the sustainable development of smart cities. *Frontiers in Sustainable Cities*, *6*. Advance online publication. DOI: 10.3389/frsc.2024.1449404

Musa, S. I., Hashim, M., & Reba, M. N. M. (2017). A review of geospatial-based urban growth models and modelling initiatives. *Geocarto International*, *32*(8), 813–833.

Przeybilovicz, E., Cunha, M. A., Geertman, S., Leleux, C., Michels, A., Tomor, Z., Webster, C. W. R., & Meijer, A. (2020). Citizen participation in the smart city: Findings from an international comparative study. *Local Government Studies*, *48*(1), 23–47. DOI: 10.1080/03003930.2020.1851204

Rathore, R., Kaushik, P., Sikarwar, S. S., Joshi, H., Mishra, A. K., & Hudda, Y. (2024, March 14). Intelligent Transportation Systems Make Use of Fog and Edge Computing for Navigation. In In *2024 IEEE International Conference on Interdisciplinary Approaches in Technology and Management for Social Innovation (IATMSI)* (Vol. 2, Pp. 1-6). IEEE. https://doi.org/10.1109/iatmsi60426.2024.10502525

Saleem, M. U., Usman, M. R., Usman, M. A., & Politis, C. (2022). Design, deployment and performance evaluation of an IoT based smart energy Management system for demand side management in smart Grid. *IEEE Access : Practical Innovations, Open Solutions*, *10*, 15261–15278. DOI: 10.1109/access.2022.3147484

Sanchez, T. W., Brenman, M., & Ye, X. (2024). The ethical Concerns of artificial intelligence in urban planning. *Journal of the American Planning Association*, •••, 1–14. DOI: 10.1080/01944363.2024.2355305

Sharmin, N. S., & Chowdhury, N. R. H. (2025). Digital Transformation in Governance: The Impact of e-governance on Public Administration and Transparency. *Journal of Computer Science and Technology Studies*, *7*(1), 362–379. DOI: 10.32996/jcsts.2025.7.1.27

Shin, S., Kim, D., & Chun, S. A. (2021). Digital divide in advanced smart city innovations. *Sustainability*, *13*(7), 4076. DOI: 10.3390/su13074076

Ullah, A., Anwar, S. M., Li, J., Nadeem, L., Mahmood, T., Rehman, A., & Saba, T. (2023). Smart cities: The role of Internet of Things and machine learning in realizing a data-centric smart environment. *Complex & Intelligent Systems*, *10*(1), 1607–1637. https://doi.org/10.1007/s40747-023-01175-4

Vishwarupe, V., Zahoor, S., Akhter, R., Bhatkar, V. P., Bedekar, M., Pande, M., Joshi, P. M., Patil, A., & Pawar, V. (2023, December 26). Designing a human-centered AI-based cognitive learning model for industry 4.0 applications. Bentham Science Publishers. https://www.benthamdirect.com/content/books/9789815179187.chapter-5

(2014). World Development Indicators. (2014). *World Development Indicators*, •••. Advance online publication. DOI: 10.1596/978-1-4648-0163-1

Yang, C. (2020). Remapping Songdo: A genealogy of a smart city in South Korea. https://www.ideals.illinois.edu/handle/2142/107879

Yang, L., He, W., Qiang, X., Zheng, J., & Huang, F. (2024). Research on remote sensing image storage management and a fast visualization system based on cloud computing technology. *Multimedia Tools and Applications*, *83*(21), 59861–59886. DOI: 10.1007/s11042-023-17858-6

Yigit, Y., Duran, K., Moradpoor, N., Maglaras, L., Van Huynh, N., & Canberk, B. (2024). Machine learning for smart healthcare management using IoT. In Studies in computational intelligence (pp. 135–166). DOI: 10.1007/978-981-97-5624-7_4

Zahoor, S., Akhter, R., Vishwarupe, V., Bedekar, M., Pande, M., Bhatkar, V. P., Joshi, P. M., Pawar, V., Mandora, N., & Kuklani, P. (2023, December 26). A Comprehensive Study of State-of-the-Art App- lications and Challenges in IoT, and Blockchain Technologies for Industry 4.0. Bentham Science Publishers. https://www.benthamdirect.com/content/books/9789815179187.chapter-1

Chapter 2
When Nature Meets Code: Governing Grey Data for Cybersecurity and Sustainability in Smart Cities

Ahgalya Subbiah
https://orcid.org/0009-0006-4427-0872
Management and Science University, Malaysia

ABSTRACT

As cities accelerate their transition toward sustainability, they increasingly depend on data from ambient sources such as sensors and smart infrastructure, resulting in the production of vast, unstructured "grey data." While this data offers critical value for progress toward SDGs 11, 13, and 9, significant gaps remain in oversight, privacy, and ethical stewardship. This chapter analyses grey data governance using conceptual frameworks, comparative policy analysis, and case studies from leading smart city initiatives. It identifies risks such as privacy infringements, social inequity, and environmental impacts inherent in unmanaged grey data, arguing for a paradigm shift: viewing grey data as a collective responsibility rather than just a resource. The chapter culminates by presenting a cyber-sustainability framework and a phased policy roadmap (2025–2030), designed to integrate cybersecurity, ethics, and sustainability guiding cities toward resilient and equitable digital futures.

INTRODUCTION

The rapid development of sustainable smart cities has heralded an era in which digital and environmental objectives converge, yet the management and security of vast, unstructured "grey data" remain significant challenges. The following sections

DOI: 10.4018/979-8-3373-4455-3.ch002

analyse the conceptual underpinnings of grey data, governance challenges, associated cyber risks, and the development of cyber-ethical readiness for 2030.

1.0 UNDERSTANDING GREY DATA IN THE SMART SUSTAINABILITY CONTEXT

The critical importance of understanding grey data within the context of sustainable smart cities is often underrated. As illustrated in Figure 1, grey data refers to unstructured or semi-structured information generated passively by urban technologies but typically overlooked in formal data management paradigms. Its informal nature means that it often escapes clear policies on ownership, consent, and retention, making it a hidden yet influential resource in urban sustainability dynamics. Conceptually, grey data challenges the existing distinctions between proprietary datasets and ambient information, necessitating new models to capture its flow and role. Infrastructurally, grey data originates from diverse urban sensors, IoT devices, and climate-responsive systems embedded throughout the cityscapes, forming complex data flows that create opportunities and risks(Acquisti et al., 2015). Properly aligned with SDGs 11, 13, and 9, the governance of grey data directly influences cities' ability to innovate infrastructure, drive climate action, and foster sustainable communities. This conceptual foundation sets the stage for exploring governance challenges and technical risks in subsequent sections.

Figure 1. Grey Data Flow in Smart Cities

1.1 Conceptual Foundations of Grey Data

The concept of grey data fundamentally challenges traditional understandings of urban data by highlighting information that is informal, often ambient, and typically lacks structured governance. Unlike traditional datasets purposefully collected and curated for specific applications, grey data arises passively from the pervasive digital infrastructure embedded within smart cities ranging from environmental sensors tracking air quality to mobility devices monitoring pedestrian flows. This data is characterized by its unstructured or semi-structured nature, variability in quality, and often ambiguous ownership and control, placing it in a liminal space between private and public data domains(Schembera & Durán, 2020). The conceptual foundation of grey data thus calls for a paradigm shift in urban data management from treating data solely as a resource to recognize it as a societal responsibility. This reframing necessitates integrating data ethics, privacy considerations, and environmental sustainability into the core of smart city initiatives. Furthermore, grey data's diffuse provenance demands new taxonomies and governance models that account for its fluid generation, usage, and lifecycle(Helmi et al., 2022). The dynamic and continuous nature of grey data production adds complexity to informed consent and data stewardship, underscoring the need for adaptive frameworks that can respond to evolving technological and social conditions. Understanding these conceptual foundations is critical to developing policies and technologies that address the emergent risks and potentialities of grey data while supporting sustainable urban development(Short, 2004).

1.2 Infrastructural Provenance and Grey-Data Flows

Infrastructural provenance refers to the lineage and origin tracing of data within complex technological ecosystems. For grey data in smart cities, infrastructural provenance is particularly challenging because the data originates from a myriad of interconnected ambient sources, each with distinct technological, spatial, and operational contexts as summarized in Figure 2.

Figure 2. Challenges in Infrastructural Provenance of Grey Data

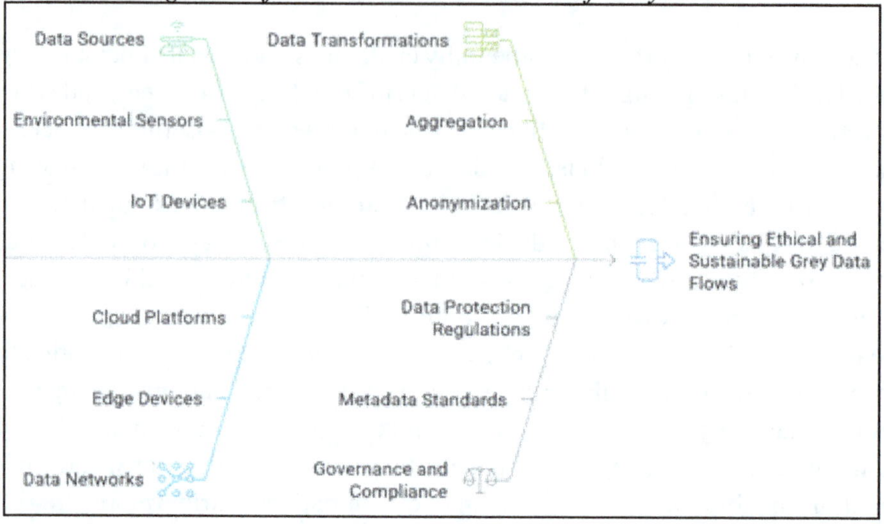

This includes environmental sensors, IoT devices embedded in public infrastructure, and dynamic urban systems such as adaptive lighting or climate-responsive architecture. Grey data flows continuously and often asynchronously through multi-layered networks, including edge devices, cloud platforms, and urban data lakes. Each transfer point introduces risks related to data integrity, confidentiality, and access control. Moreover, provenance is blurred when data is aggregated or anonymized, complicating accountability and compliance with data protection regulations. The evolving technological landscape necessitates robust metadata standards and automated tracking tools capable of providing real-time provenance insights while minimizing resource overheads. Provenance-aware architectures enable city stakeholders to audit data origins, transformations, and usage, bolstering transparency and trust. Thus, infrastructural provenance is both a technical and governance challenge that must be addressed in tandem to ensure grey data flows support sustainable and ethical smart city operations.

1.3 Alignment with SDGs 11, 13, and 9

Grey data governance is intrinsically linked to the achievement of United Nations Sustainable Development Goals (SDGs), particularly SDG 11 (Sustainable Cities and Communities), SDG 13 (Climate Action), and SDG 9 (Industry, Innovation, and Infrastructure)(Kitchin, 2021). Efficient use and stewardship of grey data can significantly contribute to sustainable urban planning, environmental monitoring, and resilient infrastructure development. For SDG 11, grey data enables real-time insights into urban dynamics, from pollution levels to energy consumption patterns, facilitating informed decision-making that enhances livability and inclusivity. SDG 13 benefits from grey data's capacity to provide granular environmental metrics essential for climate adaptation and mitigation strategies, such as localized temperature variations and carbon footprint tracking. Meanwhile, SDG 9 is supported through grey data's role in promoting innovation in urban infrastructure, including smart grids and adaptive transportation systems(Grimm, 2019). However, to harness these benefits, governance models must emphasize data quality, privacy, and equitable access, preventing unintended harms such as surveillance or exclusion of marginalized groups. Successful integration of grey data governance into SDG frameworks requires interdisciplinary collaboration among technologists, policymakers, and communities to balance technological potential with ethical and social considerations(Kong et al., 2020).

1.4 The 2025–2030 Transition ImperativeThe Governance Gap: Privacy in GreenTech

The period from 2025 to 2030 marks a decisive crossroads for addressing critical governance gaps surrounding the privacy and ownership of grey data in sustainable smart cities. Failure to act decisively risks cementing inequities in data control, exacerbating surveillance concerns, and undermining public trust ultimately fracturing the social contract that underpins urban sustainability efforts. Without clear governance, unchecked data harvesting can enable corporate monopolization of urban information flows, while citizens remain voiceless and vulnerable, deepening systemic power imbalances and marginalizing already underrepresented communities. Conversely, confronting these governance gaps head-on offers transformative potential in protecting individual autonomy, enabling equitable data access, and fostering collaborative stewardship that aligns with broader social and environmental goals(Hsu et al., 2021).

This tension is heightened by the competing and often conflicting interests of multiple stakeholders. Governments seek to harness grey data for public service efficiency and policy innovation, corporations prioritize data monetization and competitive advantage, while citizens increasingly demand transparency, privacy, and agency over how their data is used. These divergent motivations create complex negotiations around data rights and responsibilities, making the governance challenge as much political and social as it is technical(Hajny et al., 2021).

The urgent imperative is clear as closing this governance gap demands immediate institutionalization of robust regulatory frameworks, privacy-by-design standards, and participatory governance models that enshrine collective accountability and benefit-sharing. Addressing these challenges is essential not only to secure digital infrastructures but also to uphold ethical principles fundamental to the sustainable smart city vision. This transitional urgency sets the stage for subsequent chapters, which delve deeper into the technical vulnerabilities of unmanaged grey data and propose a comprehensive cyber-sustainability framework for ethical, resilient, and inclusive urban data governance by 2030(Treude, 2021).

2.0 FRAMING CONSENT: GOVERNANCE, OWNERSHIP, AND ETHICS IN GREEN TECH

In the evolving landscape of sustainable smart cities, the governance of grey data hinges critically on how consent, ownership, and ethical considerations are framed and operationalized. Green technologies ranging from environmental sensors to adaptive infrastructure generate vast amounts of ambient data that challenge conventional privacy and data governance norms(Nations, 2015). The continuous, often passive acquisition of ambient data via pervasive environmental sensors and adaptive infrastructures challenges the adequacy of traditional consent frameworks, which are typically predicated on explicit, informed, and transactional exchanges. This necessitates a critical reassessment of consent modalities to address issues of autonomy, proportionality, and contextual integrity in data practices. Concurrently, the complexity of data ownership in shared urban environments is amplified by the competing interests of governments, corporate entities, and citizens, engendering multifaceted governance tensions. Effective resolution demands an integrative approach that harmonizes legal mandates, ethical standards, and technological innovations to promote transparency, accountability, and equitable access(Delgado et al., 2023). Comparative analyses of governance paradigms across jurisdictions reveal significant opportunities for refinement, underscoring the imperative to develop robust frameworks that reconcile innovation with rigorous privacy protections. Such governance advancements are essential to embedding trust and legitimacy in the sustainable management of urban grey data.

2.1 Legal–Ethical Baselines and Regulatory Scope

Establishing robust legal and ethical baselines is foundational for governing grey data generated by green technologies in sustainable smart cities. Grey data ambient, sensor-generated information that is often passive and unstructured poses unique challenges that traditional data protection laws only partially address. Existing privacy regulations, such as the EU's General Data Protection Regulation (GDPR) and the California Consumer Privacy Act (CCPA), provide structural guardrails mandating principles like data minimization, purpose limitation, and user consent.

While legal frameworks offer important boundaries, ethical principles serve as a normative compass, guiding responses to regulatory gaps and ensuring that data governance promotes respect for autonomy, justice, and societal welfare(Markus Dirk Dubber, Frank Pasquale, 2020).

These ethical imperatives demand fairness, transparency, and accountability throughout data collection and processing, ensuring that the benefits of urban data use do not come at the cost of individual rights or social equity. Additionally, sustainability considerations must be embedded within legal-ethical frameworks. For example, data centres powering AI applications in smart grids can consume up to 3–5% of a city's total energy use, highlighting the environmental footprint of extensive data processing(Nicholson et al., 2022). Regulations that neglect such impacts risk undermining broader ecological objectives. Given the fragmented and evolving regulatory landscape, harmonized frameworks that integrate privacy protections with environmental sustainability are critical. Only through such sustainability-conscious governance can smart cities move beyond fragmented compliance and lay the foundation for ethical, resilient, and future-proof urban ecosystems.

2.2 Ownership and Control in Shared Urban Contexts

Ownership and control of grey data in shared urban environments represent a complex and contested arena, complicating governance and ethical stewardship. Unlike traditional data ownership models tied to distinct individuals or entities, grey data often arises collaboratively or passively from multiple sources embedded within public or semi-public spaces, such as streets, transit systems, and green infrastructure. This diffusion blurs normative and legal boundaries around who holds rights and responsibilities over the data(Lyon, 2018).

Cities, private corporations operating sensors, and citizens all lay conflicting claims to grey data ownership and control. Municipal authorities may assert custodial roles to leverage data for public benefit, whereas corporations might treat data as proprietary assets tied to commercial interests. Meanwhile, citizens demand transparency, informed consent, and protections from misuse or unauthorized exploitation. These competing perspectives lead to tensions that risk governance paralysis or biased control favouring dominant actors, exacerbating social inequities(Zeng & Glaister, 2018).

Emerging governance models advocate for multi-stakeholder frameworks that recognize grey data as a collective urban common, governed transparently through collaborative agreements and accountable oversight. This approach stresses the importance of equitable access, shared accountability, and mechanisms to ensure that data serves public interests without compromising individual rights. Legal and technical instruments, such as data trusts or co-governance platforms, are gaining traction as innovative solutions to navigate ownership ambiguities in shared urban contexts, balancing innovation incentives with inclusivity and ethical integrity.

2.3 Consent, Proportionality, and Ambient Sensing

Consent mechanisms are fundamental to ethical data governance. However, they encounter profound challenges in the context of ubiquitous ambient sensing characteristic of green technologies in smart cities. Unlike traditional data collection, ambient sensing often occurs passively and continuously without direct or explicit consent from individuals. This raises complex issues surrounding autonomy and privacy in environments where data generation is often invisible. The principle of proportionality is essential for balancing societal benefits against potential privacy intrusions. For example, passive data collection by citywide air-quality sensors may be justified due to its low invasiveness and significant public benefit. Conversely, technologies such as facial recognition in public transport systems generate higher privacy risks and thus require stricter controls and more explicit consent mechanisms.

Several innovative consent approaches offer promising pathways forward. These include (a) contextual integrity, which frames consent within specific social and situational norms; (b) layered or granular consent models, which afford individuals differentiated control over specific data types or uses; and (c) privacy-enhancing technologies (PETs) that enable data use while minimizing personal information exposure. Effective governance of ambient sensing must combine legal mandates, ethical frameworks, and participatory mechanisms(Schembera & Durán, 2020). This combination facilitates ongoing dialogue among city authorities, technology providers, and citizens. Transparent communication and responsiveness to public concerns are crucial to building trust and legitimacy in smart city data ecosystems.

2.4 Comparative Governance Approaches and Limitations

Governance approaches to grey data in smart cities vary considerably across regions, reflecting distinct socio-political cultures, regulatory traditions, and technological ambitions. In Europe, governance is strongly rights-based and rooted in stringent data protection legislation such as the GDPR. Cities like Barcelona lead with participatory platforms like Decidim, empowering citizens to exercise control and transparency over data use. While this model excels at safeguarding privacy and promoting democratic engagement, it faces challenges adapting rapidly to emergent, unstructured grey data flows and may slow technological innovation due to heavy compliance burdens. North American models prioritize balancing innovation and privacy with sector-specific regulations and burgeoning ethical AI initiatives. For instance, Toronto's Sidewalk Labs project sparked debates over data privacy and corporate influence, highlighting ongoing tensions. The patchwork of overlapping laws and uneven municipal engagement sometimes results in fragmented protections and public scepticism. However, initiatives such as San Francisco's data ethics boards signal growing institutional efforts toward accountable governance(Ibrahim et al., 2019).

Asian governance exhibits diverse approaches, from the top-down, state-centric surveillance regimes seen in cities like Shenzhen, characterized by extensive sensor deployments and efficiency drives, to more participatory strategies pursued by Singapore's Smart Nation initiative. Despite impressive infrastructure scale and innovation, concerns about public transparency, data monopolization, and pervasive surveillance persist. Additionally, the digital divide remains pronounced, underscoring the need to address SDG 10 by ensuring equitable data access and representation among marginalized groups. Emerging best practices across these regions increasingly emphasize hybrid governance models combining legal mandates, self-regulation, and multi-stakeholder participation. Standardization, capacity building, and data literacy development are critical to overcoming jurisdictional fragmentation and technological opacity(Acquisti et al., 2015). Addressing digital inequalities head-on is essential to prevent governance gaps from exacerbating social disparities, thus aligning smart city data practices more closely with sustainable development goals. Table 1 summarizes this comparative analysis of regional urban grey data governance models.

Table 1. Comparative Governance Approaches to Grey Data in Smart Cities

Region	Key Features	Strengths	Limitations Related to Grey Data	Example Cities/ Projects	SDG Alignment
Europe	Rights-based, stringent data protection	Strong privacy protections; citizen empowerment; transparency mandates	Complex compliance; may slow innovation; less adaptive to fast tech change	Barcelona (Decidim platform); Amsterdam's personal data stores	SDG 11 (inclusive cities), SDG 16 (strong institutions)
North America	Innovation-friendly, sector-specific regulation	Balances innovation with privacy safeguards; growing ethical AI focus	Fragmented laws; patchwork enforcement; uneven local engagement	Toronto's Sidewalk Labs (privacy controversies); San Francisco's data ethics boards	SDG 9 (industry, innovation), SDG 10 (reducing inequalities)
Asia	Varied: State-led surveillance to participatory governance	Efficient deployment and infrastructure scale; emerging citizen engagement models	High surveillance risks; limited public transparency; digital divide issues	Singapore Smart Nation; Shenzhen's extensive sensor networks	SDG 9 (innovation), SDG 11 (sustainable cities), SDG 10 (inequality)

3.0 CYBER RISKS OF UNMANAGED GREY DATA

The cyber risks posed by unmanaged grey data in smart cities stem from multiple interwoven vulnerabilities. Technically, many IoT devices suffer from default credentials, lack of encryption, and insecure APIs, creating easy targets for attackers to access or manipulate ambient data. Centralized repositories and data lakes similarly face inconsistent access controls and potential injection threats(Perera et al., 2014). These technical weaknesses compound ethical vulnerabilities: opaque data collection undermines the social contract between citizens and city authorities, eroding governance legitimacy and public trust. The environmental dimensions introduce further urgency global data centres already consume approximately 1–1.5% of worldwide electricity, with grey data's continuous processing contributing significantly to this footprint. These risks operate as interconnected layers that threaten the resilience and sustainability of smart city ecosystems. Addressing them demands a holistic approach combining cybersecurity-by-design principles, transparent and participatory data governance, and sustainable data infrastructure deployment, ensuring that urban technological innovation advances without compromising security, trust, or environmental responsibility.

3.1 Technical Vulnerabilities in IoT and Data Lakes

The technical vulnerabilities underpinning grey data management in smart cities primarily arise from the inherent weaknesses of IoT ecosystems and data lake architectures. IoT devices, often resource-constrained, suffer from security gaps such as default passwords, unpatched firmware, and limited encryption capabilities, making them vulnerable entry points for attackers(Cukier, 2018). These devices continuously collect ambient data that flows into centralized data lakes repositories designed to store vast, heterogeneous datasets with flexible schemas. However, data lakes frequently lack structured governance frameworks, leading to inconsistent access controls and insufficient encryption measures. Key vulnerabilities include unauthorized access, data tampering, injection attacks, and weak endpoint security. Moreover, legacy systems and numerous third-party integrations compound risk by expanding the attack surface. The complexity and scale of data flows reduce traceability, complicating threat detection and response. Addressing these vulnerabilities requires strengthening endpoint security, implementing granular access controls, and ensuring secure data transmission protocols across the ecosystem(Perera et al., 2014).

3.2 Ethical Externalities and Public-Trust Erosion

Ethical risks tied to unmanaged grey data pose a profound threat to public trust the vital social license that green technologies in smart cities depend upon. When citizens perceive ambient data collection as opaque, intrusive, or exploitative, trust erodes, undermining community support for sustainability initiatives that rely on such data. This distrust is not abstract: practical examples reveal its impact. For instance, grey data gathered from mobility sensors used in policing has been shown to disproportionately target vulnerable populations, reinforcing existing social inequities and systemic biases. Such ethical externalities highlight the risks of deploying smart city technologies without careful oversight and responsible governance(Morley et al., 2021).

The consequences of these ethical failings unfold across multiple dimensions. From a regulatory perspective, concerns about privacy violations and discriminatory impacts can spur tighter legislation and enforcement actions, complicating project implementation. Socially, erosion of trust leads to reduced citizen participation and resistance to new technologies perceived as surveillance tools rather than public goods. Operationally, ethical controversies can delay or even halt smart city initiatives, wasting resources and stalling progress toward sustainability goals(Hausken, 2020).

To counter these risks, governance frameworks must transcend one-off transparency measures and embed ongoing accountability mechanisms. This involves establishing participatory governance structures where citizens have meaningful oversight, ethical review boards that monitor data practices, and responsive feedback loops that adapt policies considering emerging concerns. By fostering continuous dialogue and rigorous ethical stewardship, smart cities can maintain the legitimacy necessary to leverage grey data effectively, ensuring that technological innovation proceeds together with equity, justice, and public trust cornerstones of truly sustainable urban futures.

3.3 Environmental Externalities and Data Carbon Burden

Public trust represents the foundational social license that enables the successful deployment of green technologies within smart cities. Ethical risks arising from unmanaged grey data directly threaten this trust by undermining citizens' confidence in how their data is collected, used, and governed. When ambient sensing lacks transparency, clear consent, or accountability, it fosters perceptions of pervasive surveillance rather than public benefit. This erosion of trust is not merely hypothetical; it has tangible consequences that can stall or reverse critical sustainability initiatives reliant on data-driven innovation(Radu, 2017). A salient example illustrating ethical externalities involves the use of grey data from urban mobility sensors in policing and law enforcement. Studies have shown that such datasets can inadvertently perpetuate systemic biases by disproportionately surveillant vulnerable or marginalized communities. This raises serious concerns about fairness and social justice, challenging the legitimacy of data aggregation practices that appear to deepen existing inequities rather than alleviate them. Ethical lapses of this nature contribute to social fragmentation and heighten community resistance to new technologies deployed under sustainability banners(Chian, 2023).

The consequences of these ethical risks operate across regulatory, social, and operational dimensions as seen in Figure 3.

Figure 3. Ethical Dimensions in Grey Data

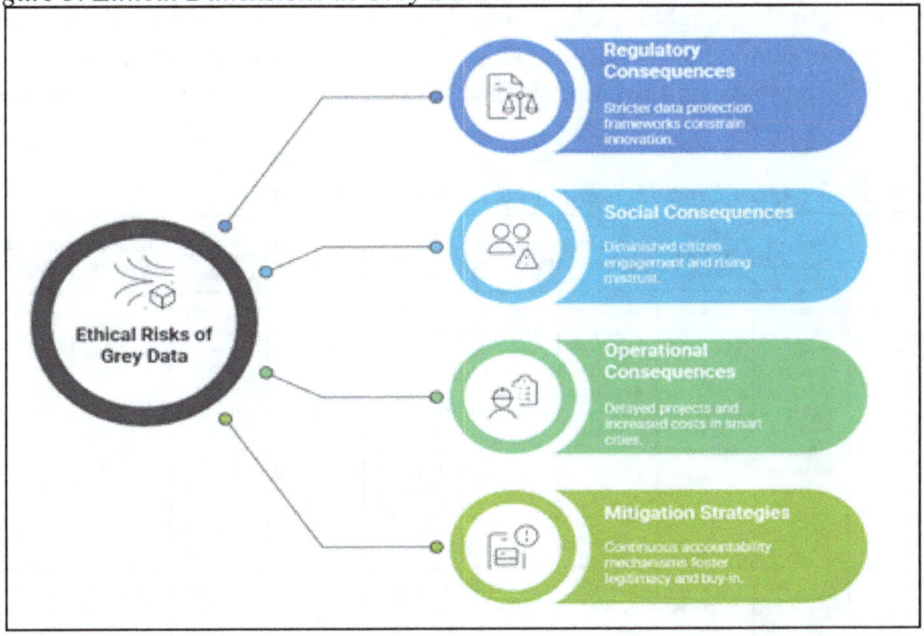

Regulatory consequences include enhanced scrutiny, legal challenges, and the imposition of stricter data protection frameworks that may constrain innovation. Social consequences manifest as diminished citizen engagement, loss of legitimacy, and rising mistrust of municipal initiatives. Operationally, ethical controversies can result in delayed project timelines, increased costs, or even outright abandonment of smart city programs(Ahmad et al., 2022). Together, these impacts threaten to compromise the very objectives that grey data-driven technologies aim to achieve. Mitigating ethical externalities demands that governance frameworks move well beyond one-off transparency or disclosure efforts. Instead, they must embed continuous accountability mechanisms that include participatory governance, ethical oversight boards, and iterative policy adaptation responsive to community concerns. This ongoing dialogue fosters legitimacy and public buy-in, creating resilient frameworks that balance technological innovation with equity, privacy, and sustainability. Without such comprehensive stewardship.

3.4 Incident Analyses and Cross-Case Lessons

Examining incidents involving unmanaged grey data in smart cities reveals critical insights into technical, governance, and communication failures that compromise security and public trust. Four notable cases illustrate diverse vulnerabilities and lessons. Table 2.1 provides a comparative analysis of major grey data incidents in smart cities, highlighting key technical failures, governance challenges, public trust impacts, and lessons learned. This overview grounds theoretical concerns in concrete case studies, illustrating diverse vulnerabilities and mitigation strategies.

Table 2. Key Grey Data Incidents and Lessons in Smart Cities

Case	Context & Scope	Key Technical Failures	Governance Failures	Impact on Public Trust	Consequences, Mitigations & Lessons	Quantitative Impact	Legal/ Regulatory Outcomes	Temporal Context	Stakeholder Reactions
Sidewalk Labs, Toronto (2019-020)	Ambitious smart city project to digitize waterfront urban space involving extensive data from residents and public sensors.	Lack of clear data ownership; opaque policies; ambiguous consent mechanisms.	Insufficient public engagement: corporate dominance fears over urban data.	Significant erosion due to perceived privatization and data exploitation.	Project cancelled after ~1 year; spurred calls for transparent governance, clear data rights, and community inclusion in urban data use.	Estimated data involved: millions of residents in waterfront area.	Triggered municipal reviews on data governance; influenced Canadian privacy debates.	Active 2017-2020; cancellation announced May 2020.	Strong public opposition; activism and media scrutiny critical of corporate control.
Barcelona Smart Lighting Exposure (2021)	Networked IoT lighting sensors controlling dynamic streetlights for energy savings and efficiency.	Unsecured endpoints; missing encryption; lax network segmentation.	Reactive security posture; gaps in IoT device security policies.	Raised privacy concerns among residents inhabiting exposed zones.	Immediate patching and security upgrades; expanded IoT cybersecurity protocols citywide; increased public transparency regarding data use.	Potentially thousands of sensors affected; exact data leak volume unspecified.	No major fines but triggered regional data protection scrutiny per EU GDPR.	Incident disclosed early 2021; swift response within weeks.	Neighbourhood-level concern; increased calls for IoT security standards.
India Aadhaar Biometric Leaks (2018-2020)	National biometric ID system storing fingerprint, iris scan, and demographic data on 1.2+ billion citizens.	Insecure APIs; poor access controls; lack of encryption on sensitive endpoints.	Weak regulatory oversight; insufficient lifecycle and risk governance.	Severe public distrust fuelled by identity theft fears and mass surveillance concerns.	Multiple leak revelations led to judicial reviews; government mandated API restrictions and security enhancements.	Millions of biometric records exposed across various leaks.	Court cases triggered; Supreme Court ruling affirming right to privacy, but limited Aadhaar use.	Leaks surfaced repeatedly between 2018-2020.	Civil society criticism; widespread media attention leading to legal activism.
Capital One Data Breach, USA (2019)	Cloud-hosted financial data lake containing customer credit and personal information for 100+ million people.	Firewall misconfiguration; compromised credentials; inadequate access management.	Incomplete policy enforcement on cloud platforms; weak continuous monitoring.	Negative media coverage but public trust partially restored due to transparent and rapid breach disclosure.	Significant remediation including multi-factor authentication, improved firewall configs, and enhanced logging implemented.	106 million individuals affected globally.	$80 million settlement with US regulators; ongoing compliance audits mandated.	Breach occurred March 2019; disclosure in July 2019; remediation ongoing.	Customer concerns highlighted; federal agency involvement raised security awareness.

These cases illustrate recurring challenges: technical vulnerabilities such as insecure APIs and endpoints, governance gaps including unclear data ownership, and failures in transparent communication. Among these, erosion of public trust is especially damaging, as incident management depends heavily on perception and legitimacy alongside technical remediation. Smart cities must adopt integrated, multilayered protections and prioritize transparent, timely communication to uphold ethical data stewardship.

4.0 TOWARD CYBER-ETHICAL READINESS BY 2030

As we approach the pivotal year 2030, with merely five years remaining, the imperative to prepare smart cities and green technologies for ethical and secure management of grey data has never been more urgent. Future-ready smart cities must integrate cybersecurity and sustainability as inseparable dimensions, ensuring data ecosystems are resilient, transparent, and responsible. These demands shifting from reactive risk management towards proactive frameworks that embed privacy, environmental stewardship, and inclusive governance throughout the data lifecycle. Successfully navigating these complexities requires aligning technological innovation with the global Sustainable Development Goals especially SDGs 9, 11, 13, and 16 while earning and sustaining citizen trust. Decisions made today on governance models, security architectures, and participatory mechanisms will shape whether cities emerge as trusted hubs of equitable, green innovation or falter under fragmented oversight and public scepticism. The path to 2030 calls for bold, integrated approaches that balance security, ethics, and sustainability, turning grey data from a liability into a foundational asset for just and resilient urban futures.

4.1 Principles of a Cyber-Sustainability Framework

Approaching the decade milestone of 2030, preparing smart cities to ethically and securely manage grey data becomes an urgent priority. Grey data ambient, often unstructured information generated continuously by sensors and IoT devices presents unique challenges that require integrated frameworks balancing cybersecurity and sustainability. Foundational principles must guide this evolution.

Figure 4. Cyber-Sustainability Framework Principles

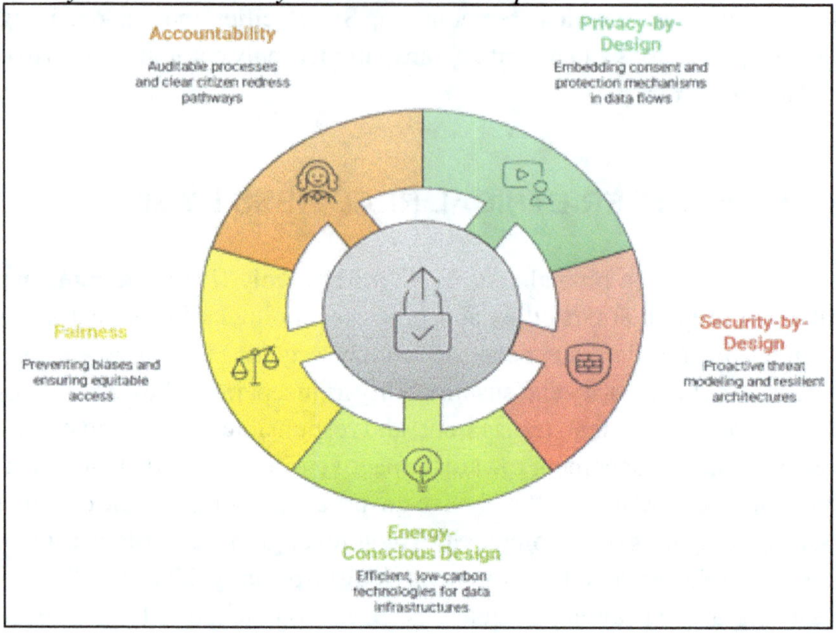

A robust Cyber-Sustainability Framework as shown in Figure 4, anchors on five core principles. Privacy-by-design mandates embedding consent and protection mechanisms tailored to passive data flows in ambient sensing, preserving individual autonomy. Security-by-design emphasizes proactive threat modelling and resilient architectures that safeguard complex, interconnected urban data systems(Muniz, R., Nied, A., Da Costa Júnior, C., González, G., & Buratto, 2023). Energy-conscious design addresses the significant environmental footprint of data infrastructures, advocating efficient, low-carbon technologies to minimize energy consumption. Fairness demands preventing biases and ensuring equitable access, counteracting risks that unstructured data exacerbates social inequities. Accountability enforces auditable processes and clear citizen redress pathways, fostering transparency and public trust(Zeng & Glaister, 2018).

Beyond these, interoperability and standardization enable scalable, secure data exchange across diverse systems. Human-centred design and adaptive governance ensure technologies serve all citizens inclusively and evolve with emerging challenges(Yang et al., 2020). Transparency, multi-stakeholder collaboration, and ethical innovation further underpin sustainable governance. Measuring progress through clear metrics, harmonizing legal frameworks, and investing in education are critical strategies to operationalize these principles. Awareness of global and local dynamics alongside preparing for future technologies ensures resilience against evolving cyber-ethical risks. Together, these integrated elements form a holistic manifesto equipping cities to transform grey data from a source of risk into a foundational asset for equitable, trustworthy, and sustainable urban futures by 2030.

4.2 Lifecycle Governance: Collection, Use, Retention, Deletion

Lifecycle governance views data management as an ongoing, cyclical process rather than a one-time compliance checklist. It encompasses four critical stages collection, use, retention, and deletion each requiring tailored governance checkpoints to mitigate risks and align with cyber-ethical readiness objectives(Chin & Chow, 2023). At the collection stage, safeguarding consent is paramount, especially for grey data generated passively through ambient sensing, where individuals may be unaware their data is captured. Governance must ensure clear, informed, and revocable consent mechanisms. During use, proportionality principles guide data application, restricting processing to necessary purposes, preventing misuse or unjust profiling from unstructured datasets(Poláková et al., 2023). The retention phase carries environmental implications, as prolonged storage increases energy consumption and carbon footprints; governance frameworks must set limits and prioritize efficient storage solutions. Finally, deletion demands strict accountability, ensuring data is securely erased and audit trails maintained to verify compliance and enable citizen redress if misuse arises. This process-flow model operationalizes readiness by embedding governance at every data lifecycle juncture, transforming abstract principles into actionable practices that uphold security, privacy, sustainability, and trust.

4.3 Green-Aligned Security: Lightweight Cryptography and Eco-Cloud/Edge

Green-aligned security integrates cybersecurity with sustainability by designing protection mechanisms that minimize environmental impact while ensuring robust privacy and data integrity. Lightweight cryptography exemplifies this approach by offering energy-efficient algorithms tailored for resource-constrained IoT devices common in smart cities(Zeadally et al., 2020). These cryptographic methods reduce computational load and power consumption without compromising security, thus supporting privacy protection alongside energy savings. Complementing this, edge computing shifts data processing closer to the source such as local sensors and devices significantly lowering the energy required for data transmission to centralized clouds(Rahouti, 2019). This decentralized model not only enhances responsiveness and resilience but also reduces greenhouse gas emissions linked to long-distance data flows. Eco-cloud initiatives further exemplify sustainable security by operating carbon-neutral data centres powered by renewable energy and optimized cooling technologies, balancing performance with environmental stewardship(Md Ajis & Hajar Baharin, 2019). Together, these green-aligned security strategies demonstrate that safeguarding privacy and data integrity can coexist harmoniously with ambitious climate goals, underscoring that sustainable cybersecurity is both a technical and ethical imperative for future-ready smart cities.

4.4 Participatory Data Governance and Commons

Participatory data governance represents a transformative shift from traditional top-down data management models toward inclusive, citizen-centred stewardship. It embeds the principle that readiness for cyber-ethical sustainability is as much a social challenge as a technical or policy one. In smart cities, this approach empowers citizens to co-own, co-decide, and actively engage in shaping data practices, especially concerning grey data that continuously flows through urban environments. Case studies provide compelling evidence of its benefits. Barcelona's DECODE project pioneered decentralized personal data control, allowing residents to manage permissions directly and reclaim agency over their information. Similarly, Amsterdam's TADA initiative fostered collaborative data trusts, facilitating shared benefits and enhanced transparency in data use. Open data commons models further democratize access, fostering innovation while safeguarding community interests(Nicholson et al., 2022). These experiments reveal that trust and legitimacy flourish when governance mechanisms include meaningful citizen participation, creating social licenses for data use that formal regulations alone cannot achieve. However, challenges persist around inclusivity, representation, and balancing openness with privacy. Critically, participatory governance demands ongoing dialogue, adaptable frameworks, and capacity building to ensure equitable participation, avoiding tokenism. Ultimately, integrating participatory models is essential to embed social values in data ecosystems, making cyber-ethical readiness resilient and democratically grounded by 2030(Markus Dirk Dubber, Frank Pasquale, 2020).

5.0 ALIGNING CYBERSECURITY AND SUSTAINABILITY IN GREY DATA MANAGEMENT

As smart cities rapidly evolve, the management of grey data ambient, unstructured data generated by ubiquitous sensing technologies stands at a complex crossroads of innovation, ethics, and sustainability. Past sections have detailed the multifaceted cyber risks, governance models, and principles guiding data stewardship. This section synthesizes these insights and projects a forward-looking vision toward 2030, underscoring the ethical weight of decisions made today. It argues that neglecting integrated cyber-sustainability governance threatens not just privacy and security, but also public trust and urban resilience. Conversely, deliberate, multi-stakeholder collaboration anchored in ethical frameworks can transform grey data from a liability into a cornerstone of sustainable, equitable urban futures.

5.1 Stakeholder Perspectives and Role Responsibilities

Governance of grey data in smart cities involves a complex network of stakeholders, each bearing distinct yet interconnected responsibilities. Understanding and clarifying these roles is critical to fostering accountable and ethical management of ambient, often unstructured, data flows that underpin urban innovation(Hong & Furnell, 2021). The multi-stakeholder nature of grey data governance demands a collaborative approach that balances innovation, regulation, and citizen rights.

The following Stakeholder-Responsibility Matrix (Table 3) outlines the primary actors in grey data governance, their roles, key responsibilities, and ethical duties. Governments function as regulators and custodians of the public interest, tasked with creating adaptive legal frameworks that protect citizens' privacy and security while enabling equitable access to data-driven services(Ali et al., 2025). Private technology firms drive innovation and provide data collection and processing capabilities, with a moral obligation to embed security and privacy-by-design principles transparently and avoid exploitative practices. City planners and urban managers serve as integrators of smart technologies within the urban fabric, ensuring operational efficiency alongside rights protection and community engagement.

Table 3. Stakeholder-Responsibility Matrix for Grey Data Governance

Stakeholder	Role in Grey Data Governance	Key Responsibilities	Accountability & Ethical Duties
Government	Regulator, policymaker, public interest protector	Establish legal frameworks; enforce data protection; ensure public safety; foster equitable access	Ensure regulation adapts to emerging tech; uphold citizens' rights; transparency in oversight
Private Tech Firms	Innovators, data collectors/processors, service providers	Develop secure technologies; implement privacy and security-by-design; comply with regulations	Ethical stewardship of data; transparent data use policies; avoid exploitative practices
City Planners/ Urban Managers	Integrators of technology into urban infrastructure	Operationalize grey data collection/use; ensure system interoperability; balance efficiency and rights	Protect citizen data in deployments; report incidents; engage with community input

continued on following page

Table 3. Continued

Stakeholder	Role in Grey Data Governance	Key Responsibilities	Accountability & Ethical Duties
Civil Society/NGOs	Advocates for rights, watchdogs, facilitators of inclusivity	Monitor impacts; promote digital literacy; advocate for marginalized groups; demand accountability	Voice public concerns; hold other actors accountable; empower citizen participation
Citizens/Residents	Data subjects and potential co-governors	Provide informed consent; participate in governance mechanisms; practice data stewardship	Exercise rights to privacy and transparency; engage in participatory frameworks

Civil society organizations act as watchdogs and advocates, monitoring impacts, amplifying marginalized voices, and promoting digital literacy to strengthen inclusivity. Citizens are both data subjects and emerging co-governors, responsible for informed consent and active participation in governance mechanisms promoting data stewardship(Weder, 2023). This distribution of roles underscores that accountability for grey data governance is shared and dynamic. Clear articulation of responsibilities fosters trust and addresses tensions between public regulation, corporate interests, and citizen expectations. Ethical stewardship requires continual dialogue, transparency, and mechanisms for citizen redress, recognizing that governance extends beyond technical compliance to encompass moral responsibility over the collective digital commons. Without this multiplicity of engagement, fragmented oversight risks erosion of public trust and jeopardizes sustainable urban futures.

5.2 Beneficiary Outcomes: Trust, Transparency, Operational Efficiency

Governance of grey data in smart cities presents a complex balance between maximizing societal benefits and mitigating significant risks. Each key pillar trust, transparency, operational efficiency, participation, innovation, and security embodies distinct opportunities and ethical challenges that shape the sustainability of urban digital ecosystems(Westraadt & Calitz, 2020). Trust forms the foundation for citizen engagement and acceptance of data-driven services. When governance fosters robust privacy protections and clear accountability, trust flourishes, creating a social license that enables sustainable innovation. Conversely, breaches or opaque practices erode confidence, fuelling disengagement and resistance that can stall or derail sustainability projects. Ethically, losing trust not only diminishes participation but risks marginalizing vulnerable groups disproportionately impacted by data misuse. Governance from 2025 to 2030 must embed trust-building mechanisms, including independent oversight and participatory decision-making, to protect this critical asset.

Transparency enhances legitimacy by making data practices visible and understandable to stakeholders. However, too much openness may increase exposure to cyber threats, while insufficient disclosure breed's suspicion. Ethical trade-offs arise in balancing the public's right to know with the need to secure sensitive data(Acquisti et al., 2015). Effective governance will develop nuanced transparency frameworks that provide meaningful information without compromising security, empowering citizens while managing risks proactively. Operational Efficiency promises to optimize energy use, lower emissions, and improve urban resource flows through smart systems like energy grids and waste management. Yet, efficiency gains achieved without addressing fairness can reinforce digital inequalities, where marginalized communities face disproportionate burdens or exclusion. The carbon footprint of data centres and IoT devices also demands scrutiny, as unchecked growth in data volume may negate environmental benefits. Future governance should integrate ethical audits with sustainability metrics, ensuring efficiency advances do not come at the cost of equity or climate goals.

Participation deepens democratic legitimacy by engaging citizens as active collaborators in data governance. Inclusive engagement mitigates exclusion and builds social resilience, yet risks of tokenism or uneven access persist, potentially reinforcing systemic biases. Governance structures from 2025 onward must institutionalize meaningful mechanisms for diverse voices, combining digital literacy programs and flexible platforms to foster broad-based involvement. Innovation leverages grey data to develop smarter, greener urban solutions that enhance quality of life. However, unchecked innovation can lead to exploitative practices, data monopolies, or surveillance abuses, undermining ethical principles. As such, regulatory frameworks should incentivize responsible innovation, aligning technological progress with human rights and sustainability mandates. Safety and Security safeguard data integrity and protect citizen privacy, foundational to ethical data use. Failure in these domains exposes individuals to harm through breaches and cyberattacks. Governance must adopt adaptive risk management strategies, incorporating emerging threats from AI and quantum computing while maintaining resilience.

5.3 Policy Pathways 2025–2030: Phases, Metrics, Accountability

Existing legal frameworks such as the GDPR, the EU AI Act, and sector-specific regulations like the CCPA provide strong foundations for data protection, privacy, and algorithmic accountability. These instruments have significantly advanced individual rights and corporate responsibilities, signalling global commitments toward ethical digital governance(Treude, 2021). However, when applied to the unique challenges of grey data ambient, unstructured, and sustainability-relevant information generated continuously by smart city technologies these frameworks reveal critical limitations. Their territorial reach is fragmented, leading to jurisdictional inconsistencies that complicate enforcement in globally interconnected urban ecosystems. Moreover, current regulations evolve slowly, struggling to keep pace with rapid technological innovations and the expansive volume of passive data collection. Crucially, few address the environmental implications of data management or integrate sustainability principles, leaving significant governance gaps in managing grey data's carbon footprint and fairness concerns(Nations, 2015).

To overcome these deficiencies, a phased policy roadmap spanning 2025 to 2030 is essential. This roadmap must transition governance from disjointed compliance toward harmonized, integrated cyber-sustainability frameworks. Clear, measurable metrics including not only breach reduction but also carbon emissions from data infrastructures, citizen trust indices, and fairness audits will underpin accountability(Hsu et al., 2021). Only through coordinated, cross-jurisdictional efforts embedding cybersecurity, ethics, and sustainability can cities fully realize the potential of grey data while safeguarding public trust and environmental resilience (see Figure 5).

Figure 5. Three-Phase Policy Roadmap for Responsible Grey Data Governance (2025–2030)

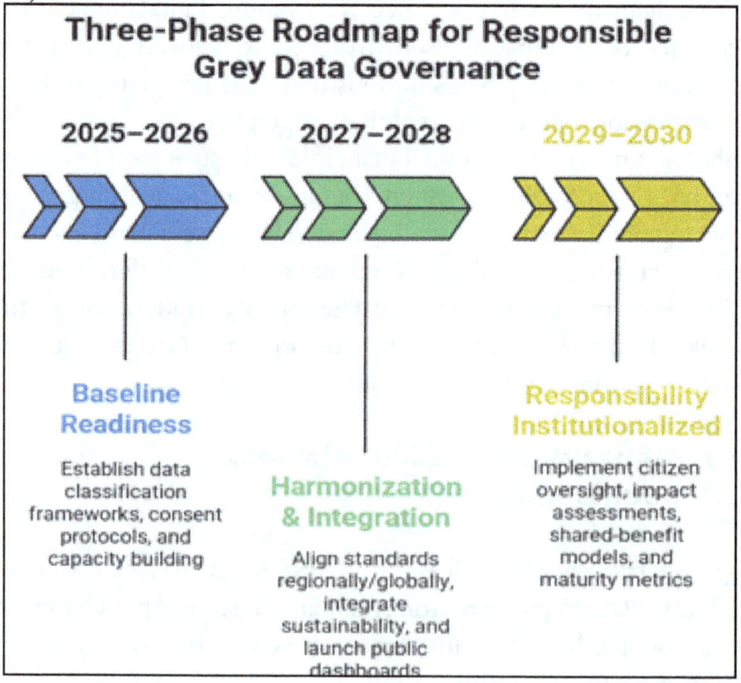

Accountability is the cornerstone of effective cyber-sustainability governance in managing grey data. Cities must commit to transparency by publishing annual cyber-sustainability reports that comprehensively detail data practices, risk management efforts, environmental impacts, and citizen engagement outcomes. These reports create a basis for public scrutiny and informed dialogue. Auditing should be conducted by independent, cross-sectoral bodies that combine legal expertise, technical assessment capabilities, and citizen oversight to ensure balanced and comprehensive evaluation. This multi-dimensional audit process fosters trust, legitimacy, and holistic oversight. When failures occur whether through data breaches, governance lapses, or environmental harm regulatory consequences must be clear and enforceable. Penalties may include substantial fines akin to GDPR sanctions, suspension or revocation of smart city project approvals, or mandates to redesign systems to meet ethical and sustainability standards. Importantly, accountability should extend beyond punishment: it must be constructive, emphasizing ongoing learning and continuous improvement. Embedding such accountability mechanisms is critical to cultivating resilient, responsible urban data ecosystems that can adapt and thrive through 2030 and beyond.

6.0 CONCLUSION AND FUTURE RESEARCH

The management of grey data in smart cities stands at a critical juncture. Once treated as a mere resource to be mined, urban data must now be embraced as a shared responsibility an ethical imperative that weaves together cybersecurity and sustainability into a unified whole. This shifting paradigm recognizes that protecting privacy, ensuring fairness, and reducing environmental impact are inseparable goals integral to resilient urban futures. The stakes could not be higher. Neglecting governance today risks ushering in pervasive surveillance, deepening social inequities, and accelerating ecological degradation. Governance is far more than compliance; it is moral stewardship rooted in trust, justice, and collective well-being.

Looking ahead, citizens must evolve into empowered stewards, taking an active role in shaping data governance. Governments need to move beyond fragmented regulation, becoming facilitators of inclusive, participatory data commons. Meanwhile, the private sector must shed exploitative practices and champion ethical innovation that balances profit with principle. To realize this vision, we urgently need cross-jurisdictional harmonization of laws, new metrics that capture the environmental and social dimensions of data, and bold experiments with shared data governance models. Research must deepen in areas such as lifecycle sustainability metrics and privacy-enhancing technologies attuned to urban realities. By 2030, success will be measured not by the volume of data collected but by how responsibly it is governed to protect privacy, nurture trust, and catalyse sustainability. Only then can the promise of smart cities be truly fulfilled secure, equitable, and green.

REFERENCES

Acquisti, A., Brandimarte, L., & Loewenstein, G. (2015). Privacy and human behavior in the age of information. *Science, 347*(6221), 509–514. DOI: 10.1126/science.aaa1465 PMID: 25635091

Ahmad, K., Maabreh, M., Ghaly, M., Khan, K., Qadir, J., & Al-Fuqaha, A. (2022). Developing future human-centered smart cities: Critical analysis of smart city security, Data management, and Ethical challenges. *Computer Science Review, 43*, 100452. DOI: 10.1016/j.cosrev.2021.100452

Ali, S., Wang, J., & Leung, V. C. M. (2025). AI-driven fusion with cybersecurity: Exploring current trends, advanced techniques, future directions, and policy implications for evolving paradigms– A comprehensive review. *Information Fusion, 118*, 102922. DOI: 10.1016/j.inffus.2024.102922

Chian, Y. X. (2023). Sustainable, inclusive city-making through smart, playable environments: developing and testing the CO2rdinates pervasive mobile game. *26th International Academic Mindtrek Conference*, 321–328. https://doi.org/DOI: 10.1145/3616961.3617803

Chin, G. H. Y., & Chow, K. K. N. (2023). Technology-Enabled Interventions for Sustaining Behaviour Change in Adolescents: A Scoping Review for Research Gaps. *Proceedings of the ACM on Human-Computer Interaction, 7*(CSCW2), 1–30. https://doi.org/DOI: 10.1145/3610211

Cukier, V. M.-S. (2018). *Big Data: A Revolution that Will Transform how We Live, Work, and Think* (Revised Ed). Eamon Dolan/Houghton Mifflin Harcourt.

Delgado, I., Sancristobal, E., Martin, S., & Robles-Gómez, A. (2023). Exploring IoT Vulnerabilities in a Comprehensive Remote Cybersecurity Laboratory. *Sensors (Basel), 23*(22), 9279. DOI: 10.3390/s23229279 PMID: 38005664

Dubber, M. D., Pasquale, F., & Das, S. (Eds.). (2020). *The Oxford handbook of ethics of AI.* Oxford University Press.

Grimm, D. (2019). The Dark Data Quandary. *The American University Law Review, 68*(3), 761–821. PMID: 30919611

Hajny, J., Ricci, S., Piesarskas, E., Levillain, O., Galletta, L., & De Nicola, R. (2021). Framework, Tools and Good Practices for Cybersecurity Curricula. *IEEE Access : Practical Innovations, Open Solutions, 9*, 94723–94747. DOI: 10.1109/ACCESS.2021.3093952

Hausken, K. (2020). Cyber resilience in firms, organizations and societies. *Internet of Things : Engineering Cyber Physical Human Systems*, *11*, 100204. DOI: 10.1016/j.iot.2020.100204

Helmi, R. A. A., Baskaran, N. A.-L., Jamal, A., & Mohammed, M. N. (2022). Dark Net Forum Analyzer Using Meta Data Search Bots. *2022 IEEE 10th Conference on Systems, Process & Control (ICSPC)*, 73–76. https://doi.org/DOI: 10.1109/ICSPC55597.2022.10001746

Hong, Y., & Furnell, S. (2021). Understanding cybersecurity behavioral habits: Insights from situational support. *Journal of Information Security and Applications*, *57*, 102710. DOI: 10.1016/j.jisa.2020.102710

Hsu, A. J., Pruckner, S., Satterthwaite, E. V., Weatherdon, L. V., Hadley, K., & Nguyen, E. T. T. (2021). Challenges and Recommendations for Equitable Use of Aerial Tools for Mangrove Research. *Frontiers in Marine Science*, *8*. Advance online publication. DOI: 10.3389/fmars.2021.643784

Ibrahim, T. M., Abdulhamid, S. M., Alarood, A. A., Chiroma, H., Al-garadi, M. A., Rana, N., Muhammad, A. N., Abubakar, A., Haruna, K., & Gabralla, L. A. (2019). Recent advances in mobile touch screen security authentication methods: A systematic literature review. *Computers & Security*, *85*, 1–24. DOI: 10.1016/j.cose.2019.04.008

Kitchin, R. (2021). Black Data Matter. In *Data Lives* (pp. 197–204). Bristol University Press., DOI: 10.2307/j.ctv1c9hmnq.29

Kong, L., Liu, Z., & Wu, J. (2020). A systematic review of big data-based urban sustainability research: State-of-the-science and future directions. *Journal of Cleaner Production*, *273*, 123142. DOI: 10.1016/j.jclepro.2020.123142

Lyon, D. (2018). No TitleThe Culture of Surveillance: Watching as a Way of Life. *Polity*.

Md Ajis, A. F., & Hajar Baharin, S. (2019). Dark Data Management as frontier of Information Governance. *2019 IEEE 9th Symposium on Computer Applications & Industrial Electronics (ISCAIE)*, 34–37. https://doi.org/DOI: 10.1109/ISCAIE.2019.8743915

Morley, J., Elhalal, A., Garcia, F., Kinsey, L., Mökander, J., & Floridi, L. (2021). Ethics as a Service: A Pragmatic Operationalisation of AI Ethics. *Minds and Machines*, *31*(2), 239–256. DOI: 10.1007/s11023-021-09563-w PMID: 34720418

Muniz, R., Nied, A., Da Costa Júnior, C., González, G., & Buratto, W. (2023). The Sustainability Concept: A Review Focusing on Energy. Sustainability. *Sustainability*. https://doi.org/https://doi.org/10.3390/su151914049

Nations, U. (2015). *Transforming our world: The 2030 Agenda for Sustainable Development*. https://sdgs.un.org/2030agenda

Nicholson, B., Nielsen, P., Sahay, S., & Sæbø, J. I. (2022). Digital public goods platforms for development: The challenge of scaling. *The Information Society*, *38*(5), 364–376. DOI: 10.1080/01972243.2022.2105999

Perera, C., Zaslavsky, A., Christen, P., & Georgakopoulos, D. (2014). Context Aware Computing for The Internet of Things: A Survey. *IEEE Communications Surveys and Tutorials*, *16*(1), 414–454. DOI: 10.1109/SURV.2013.042313.00197

Poláková, M., Suleimanová, J. H., Madzík, P., Copuš, L., Molnárová, I., & Polednová, J. (2023). Soft skills and their importance in the labour market under the conditions of Industry 5.0. *Heliyon*, *9*(8), e18670. DOI: 10.1016/j.heliyon.2023.e18670 PMID: 37593611

Radu, L.-D. (2017). Green Cloud Computing: A Literature Survey. *Symmetry*, *9*(12), 295. DOI: 10.3390/sym9120295

Rahouti, M. (2019). Board 129: Facilitation of Cybersecurity Learning Through Real-world Hands-on Labs. *2019 ASEE Annual Conference & Exposition Proceedings*. https://doi.org/DOI: 10.18260/1-2--32228

Schembera, B., & Durán, J. M. (2020). Dark Data as the New Challenge for Big Data Science and the Introduction of the Scientific Data Officer. *Philosophy & Technology*, *33*(1), 93–115. DOI: 10.1007/s13347-019-00346-x

Short, J. R. (2004). Black Holes and Loose Connections in a Global Urban Network. *The Professional Geographer*, *56*(2), 295–302. DOI: 10.1111/j.0033-0124.2004.05602012.x

Treude, M. (2021). Sustainable Smart City—Opening a Black Box. *Sustainability*, *13*(2), 769. DOI: 10.3390/su13020769

Weder, F. (2023). Cultivation of sustainability in a discourse of change. *Journal of Language and Politics*, *22*(5), 577–600. DOI: 10.1075/jlp.22122.wed

Westraadt, L., & Calitz, A. (2020). A modelling framework for integrated smart city planning and management. *Sustainable Cities and Society*, *63*, 102444. DOI: 10.1016/j.scs.2020.102444

Yang, X., Luo, Z., Huang, Z., Zhao, Y., Xue, Z., Wang, Y., Liu, W., Liu, S., Zhang, H., Xu, K., Dou, S., Xu, J., Hu, W., & Deng, Y. (2020). Development Status and Prospects of Artificial Intelligence in the Field of Energy Conversion Materials. *Frontiers in Energy Research*, *8*. Advance online publication. DOI: 10.3389/fenrg.2020.00167

Zeadally, S., Adi, E., Baig, Z., & Khan, I. A. (2020). Harnessing Artificial Intelligence Capabilities to Improve Cybersecurity. *IEEE Access : Practical Innovations, Open Solutions*, *8*, 23817–23837. DOI: 10.1109/ACCESS.2020.2968045

Zeng, J., & Glaister, K. W. (2018). Value creation from big data: Looking inside the black box. *Strategic Organization*, *16*(2), 105–140. DOI: 10.1177/1476127017697510

Chapter 3
Blockchain Beyond Cryptocurrency:
A Decentralized Approach to Urban Security

Yahaya Saidu
https://orcid.org/0009-0000-8909-8806
Universiti Teknologi PETRONAS, Malaysia & Taraba State University, Jalingo, Nigeria

Shuaibu Yau
https://orcid.org/0000-0002-0001-3536
Federal University Birnin Kebbi, Nigeria

Daniel Tonye Oyefidein
https://orcid.org/0009-0002-2232-3727
Universiti Teknologi PETRONAS, Malaysia

Aliyu Garba
Universiti Teknologi PETRONAS, Malaysia

Dahiru Adamu Aliyu
https://orcid.org/0009-0009-9803-3604
Universiti Teknologi PETRONAS, Malaysia

ABSTRACT

As cities become more digitally governed, centralized infrastructures face growing risks across identity, safety, and data domains. This chapter reframes blockchain as a foundational trust protocol for urban resilience, emphasizing its core features: immutability, decentralization, transparency, and consensus, as tools to address

DOI: 10.4018/979-8-3373-4455-3.ch003

systemic privacy and security challenges. It explores blockchain's role in securing digital identities, logging infrastructure events, and enabling auditable governance. Real-world deployments in land registries, voting, procurement, and incident response, especially in Asia and Europe are analyzed. Privacy-preserving techniques like zero-knowledge proofs and decentralized identity are also examined. The chapter highlights integration hurdles such as interoperability, regulatory gaps, and ethical tensions, while outlining emerging trends like Blockchain 4.0, quantum-safe cryptography, and DAO-led civic participation. It offers a roadmap for decentralized citizen-centric governance in smart cities.

1. INTRODUCTION: RETHINKING TRUST IN THE SMART CITY ERA

The 21st-century city is no longer defined solely by physical infrastructure but increasingly by a digital backbone composed of interconnected sensors, platforms, algorithms, and cloud-based services. From mobile-based citizen feedback apps in Seoul to biometric transit systems in Singapore, contemporary urban systems are characterized by data-intensive, algorithmically mediated processes that promise greater efficiency, real-time responsiveness, and citizen-centric design. Yet this digital transformation has not come without cost. Growing dependencies on opaque platforms, centralized service providers, and vulnerable infrastructures have triggered a global reckoning around the question of trust in urban governance.

Incidents such as the compromise of India's Aadhaar identity system, the use of facial recognition technologies without consent in London and Detroit, and opaque algorithmic decisions in welfare delivery in the Netherlands have spotlighted the fragility of digital trust models. Citizens increasingly demand clarity on how data is collected, how decisions are made, and who holds accountability when systems fail. These concerns are magnified in the smart city context, where governance, identity, and cybersecurity converge and where trust functions not only as a social or political asset but also as a technical requirement for system sustainability (Kundu, 2019). In response to these challenges, blockchain has emerged as a powerful conceptual and practical alternative, not merely as a financial innovation but as a protocol for decentralized trust in public systems. By distributing verification processes, ensuring data integrity, and enabling transparent automation through smart contracts, blockchain reconfigures the foundations of how cities can build, maintain, and share trust among residents, institutions, and machines (Kaushal et al., 2021; Saidu, Shuhidan, Aziz, Adamu, et al., 2025).

The evolution of trust in smart urban ecosystems demonstrates the appeal of blockchain as a response to deficits exacerbated by digital transformation. The limitations of centralized infrastructure models and the erosion of citizen trust in public systems illustrate the need for alternatives that are verifiable, transparent, and decentralized. Blockchain offers a paradigm shift from platform-centric to protocol-centric trust and introduces technical attributes such as immutability, decentralization, consensus validation, and programmable automation (Dehouche, 2025). At the same time, blockchain deployment is constrained by scalability limits, governance gaps, and ethical dilemmas. Emphasizing both opportunities and risks ensures a balanced perspective, framing blockchain not as a panacea but as a contested technology whose outcomes must be assessed in measurable and social terms (Mustafa et al., 2025).

The subsequent discussion addresses a range of urban use cases including digital identity, infrastructure logging, voting, and public finance; examines specific cybersecurity and privacy enhancements enabled by blockchain; and assesses implementation challenges such as regulatory friction, legacy integration, and data immutability. Later sections consider governance and policy frameworks necessary for ethical deployment and explore forward-looking trends including Blockchain 4.0, digital twins, quantum-resilient cryptography, and decentralized urban governance via decentralized autonomous organizations (DAOs). The overall argument emphasizes that a secure and equitable smart city must embed trust not in platforms or institutions but in verifiable, transparent, and decentralized digital infrastructures.

1.1 Centralization and Fragility in Digital Urban Ecosystems

The expansion of smart cities has increased reliance on centralized digital platforms for transportation, energy, surveillance, and communications. While these systems improve efficiency, concentration of control creates single points of failure that heighten systemic fragility (Majeed et al., 2021). Recent cyber incidents demonstrate the risks: ransomware attacks on Colonial Pipeline in the United States and DDoS assaults on smart city portals in Singapore disrupted essential services including energy supply, public transport, and healthcare (Y. Chen et al., 2021; Khanna et al., 2021). A 2023 World Economic Forum report identified over-centralization of digital infrastructure as a top global threat to urban resilience (WEF, 2023). Addressing this vulnerability requires a shift from efficiency-driven centralization toward decentralized, fault-tolerant architectures that distribute trust and reduce the risk of cascading failures.

1.2 Trust Deficits in Governance, Identity, and Service Delivery

Digitalization of urban governance has amplified concerns over surveillance, bias, and opaque decision-making. High-profile cases such as Cambridge Analytica's data manipulation and discriminatory outcomes in predictive policing illustrate how algorithmic systems erode public confidence in civic institutions. In many cities, the use of facial recognition and license plate tracking without adequate oversight has further deepened distrust (Midani, 2023).

Trust deficits are most visible in identity and service delivery systems. Over 850 million people globally lack legal identification, particularly in rapidly urbanizing regions of Africa and South Asia (World Bank, 2022). Reliance on centralized ID systems excludes marginalized groups such as migrants and refugees, while fragmented service platforms reinforce perceptions of corruption and inefficiency (Alnahari & Ariaratnam, 2022). Without verifiable and transparent records, citizen engagement in voting, reporting, and public participation declines, weakening the legitimacy of urban governance.

1.3 Blockchain as a Paradigm Shift: From Platform-Centric to Protocol-Centric Trust

Blockchain offers an alternative to centralized systems by embedding trust directly in shared protocols rather than intermediaries. Core properties, immutability, decentralization, consensus validation, and programmability, enable records and transactions to be verified independently without reliance on a single authority. This shift reduces risks of fraud, tampering, and bureaucratic manipulation (Alnahari & Ariaratnam, 2022).

Practical applications already demonstrate the model's potential. Zug employs blockchain-based IDs for e-governance, Estonia secures health and judicial records on-chain, and Indian states such as Andhra Pradesh pilot land registries to curb property disputes. These initiatives illustrate how blockchain extends beyond cryptocurrency into digital public infrastructure, reinforcing transparency and resilience in urban governance (Dziundziuk & Dziundziuk, 2025).

1.4 Beyond Hype: Blockchain as Digital Public Infrastructure

Blockchain must be understood not as a speculative tool but as digital infrastructure comparable to roads or utilities. Integrated with Internet of Things (IoT), Artificial Intelligence (AI), and edge computing, blockchain can underpin transparent service delivery and accountable data flows (Saidu, Shuhidan, Aliyu, et al., 2025). Examples include IoT-linked utility monitoring for carbon budgeting, smart contracts that automate procurement to prevent misuse of public funds, and decentralized voting systems that enhance electoral transparency. Unlike closed databases, blockchain systems are verifiable, collaborative, and tamper-resistant, qualities essential for mitigating risks of misinformation, bias, and exclusion in data-driven governance (OECD, 2023).

1.5 A Structural Overview of the Chapter

The chapter is organized into eight sections. Section 2 outlines the technical foundations of blockchain, including immutability, decentralization, consensus, and transparency, and examines public, private, and permissioned models relevant to smart urban systems. Section 3 presents practical use cases, digital identity, land registries, voting, infrastructure logging, procurement, and cyber incident response, demonstrating blockchain's application in urban cybersecurity and privacy. Section 4 explores specific enhancements such as resilience against DDoS attacks, cryptographic auditability, and privacy-preserving mechanisms.

Section 5 critically examines integration challenges, including interoperability with legacy systems, scalability, regulatory uncertainty, and conflicts between immutability and privacy. Section 6 shifts to governance and policy, addressing smart contract recognition, the role of consortia and standards, and democratic oversight. Section 7 highlights emerging trends such as Blockchain 4.0, digital twins, DAO-based governance, and quantum-resilient cryptography. Section 8 concludes with a synthesis of findings, emphasizing multi-stakeholder collaboration and ethical design to ensure blockchain functions as a secure and equitable foundation for smart urban ecosystems.

2. TECHNICAL FOUNDATIONS OF BLOCKCHAIN FOR URBAN SYSTEMS

In the previous section, we positioned blockchain as a foundational response to trust deficits in digital urban governance. Realizing that vision, however, requires more than a conceptual shift, it demands a working understanding of how blockchain's core mechanisms function within complex urban systems. This section unpacks the technical architecture that makes blockchain uniquely suited for urban cybersecurity, automation, and decentralized service delivery. It begins by outlining the essential features of blockchain; immutability, decentralization, consensus, and transparency, before differentiating key architectural models and examining how smart contracts and decentralized identity frameworks support secure, modular urban infrastructure.

2.1 Key Features: Immutability, Decentralization, Consensus, and Transparency

Blockchain technology derives its strength from four foundational principles that collectively redefine trust, accountability, and coordination within digital ecosystems: immutability, decentralization, consensus, and transparency (see figure 1).

- **Immutability** ensures that once data is written to the blockchain, it cannot be modified without altering all subsequent records, which requires consensus from the majority of network participants. In urban systems, this is crucial for maintaining the integrity of property records, energy usage logs, and procurement trails(Makani et al., 2022).
- **Decentralization** reduces reliance on a single point of control. Instead, decision-making and validation processes are distributed across multiple nodes. In contrast to traditional centralized cloud-based services, decentralized ledgers lower the risk of corruption, outages, or deliberate manipulation. For instance, in urban identity verification systems, decentralization allows individuals to manage their credentials without depending on a single government-issued database (Balcerzak et al., 2022).
- **Consensus mechanisms** (such as Proof of Authority, Practical Byzantine Fault Tolerance, and Delegated Proof of Stake) provide the algorithmic backbone for transaction validation. These protocols ensure that only legitimate updates are added to the chain, even in the presence of potentially malicious actors(Yakubu et al., 2024).
- **Transparency** is baked into the architecture; records are visible to all permitted stakeholders and verifiable through cryptographic proofs. Transparency is critical for public accountability in budgeting, voting, and environmental reporting.

Figure 1. Blockchain's core features: immutability, decentralization, consensus, and transparency, enable robust urban applications.

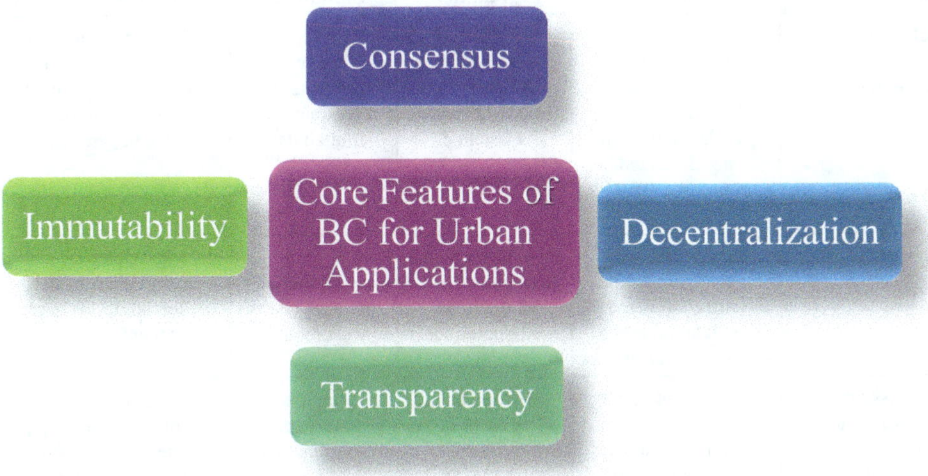

2.2 Public vs. Private Blockchains and Permissioned Models

Public, private, and permissioned blockchains each offer distinct trade-offs in the governance of smart urban ecosystems. Public blockchains such as Bitcoin and Ethereum provide maximum transparency and resilience but face scalability and privacy limitations that make them unsuitable for sensitive city data. Private blockchains, while offering faster performance and stronger control for a single organization, reintroduce centralization risks that may undermine trust in public services. Between these two extremes, permissioned or consortium blockchains (see Table 1) provide a balanced approach by enabling multiple agencies to participate with role-based access controls. Platforms such as Hyperledger Fabric, Quorum, and Corda are particularly well-suited for smart city applications, where interoperability and privacy are essential. A notable example is Dubai's adoption of Hyperledger Fabric in its Smart Dubai project, which underpins services in notary, healthcare, and land registration, demonstrating the operational value of permissioned models in practice.

Table 1. Comparison of Public, Private, and Permissioned Blockchain Models in Smart Urban Ecosystems

Blockchain Type	Characteristics	Strengths	Limitations	Smart City Use Cases
Public (e.g., Bitcoin, Ethereum)	Open networks where anyone can participate. Transactions are validated through decentralized consensus (PoW, PoS).	High transparency, resilience, and censorship resistance.	Scalability bottlenecks, high energy consumption, limited data privacy.	Rare in urban data management due to sensitivity; more applicable to public token systems.
Private	Controlled by a single organization, with centralized validation and restricted access.	Greater privacy, fast transaction throughput, and operational control.	Reintroduces centralization risks; weaker trust model.	Municipalities for asset tracking, staff credentialing, or internal record systems.
Permissioned/ Consortium (e.g., Hyperledger Fabric, Quorum, Corda)	Semi-decentralized; governed by a consortium of stakeholders with role-based access control.	Interoperable, scalable, privacy-preserving, and supports fine-grained permissions.	Requires governance coordination among stakeholders; partial trust model.	Multi-agency collaboration (e.g., electricity board, public works, transport authority). Example: UAE's *Smart Dubai* project used Hyperledger Fabric for notary, health records, and land registration (Bai et al., 2022; Khan et al., 2022)

2.3 Smart Contracts and Decentralized Identity (DID) Frameworks

Smart contracts lie at the heart of blockchain's utility in urban systems. These self-executing scripts automatically perform predefined actions once conditions are met, eliminating manual oversight and reducing reliance on intermediaries (Wang et al., 2019). In urban governance, they enable functions such as automated permit approvals, conditional subsidy disbursement, and SLA-based procurement. For example, a blockchain-enabled housing platform could autonomously evaluate eligibility, assign priority, and release benefits once verified credentials are submitted, reducing bureaucracy, corruption, and human error (Balcerzak et al., 2022).

Complementing this automation are decentralized identity (DID) frameworks, which provide individuals with self-sovereign digital wallets for credentials such as birth certificates, driver's licenses, or voter IDs. Unlike centralized databases vulnerable to breaches, DID systems allow selective disclosure, verifying attributes like age or residency without exposing underlying personal data (Wang et al., 2019). This model is particularly empowering for marginalized groups such as refugees, migrants, and residents of informal settlements who often lack access to traditional identity systems.

The importance of DID is underscored by initiatives such as the European Blockchain Services Infrastructure (EBSI) and India's MosaicID. EBSI enables secure cross-border verification of academic credentials and health records within the EU, while MosaicID aims to deliver decentralized identity solutions for India's unbanked populations (Yan et al., 2024). Together, smart contracts and DID frameworks enhance efficiency, privacy, and inclusion, laying the foundation for equitable and trusted digital public infrastructure.

2.4 Layered Blockchain Architectures for Modular City Services

As cities integrate blockchain into domains such as governance, mobility, health, and utilities, the demand for scalable, interoperable, and modular infrastructures grows. Layered blockchain architectures address this need by organizing functionality into discrete tiers that can be tested, upgraded, or replaced without disrupting the broader system (Pajooh et al., 2021).

A typical design comprises five layers (see Figure 2). The data layer interfaces with IoT sensors, external APIs, and citizen applications to capture inputs such as energy use, mobility patterns, or service requests (Yau et al., 2024). The consensus layer validates and orders transactions using protocols like PBFT or Proof of Authority (PoA). Validated records are stored in the ledger layer, which maintains transaction histories, smart contract states, and metadata. The application layer delivers user-facing portals, dashboards, and analytics. Finally, the interoperability layer links blockchain to legacy systems and external databases through oracles and middleware (Rifat Hossain et al., 2024).

Figure 2. Five-layer blockchain architecture enabling scalable, interoperable, and adaptive services in smart cities

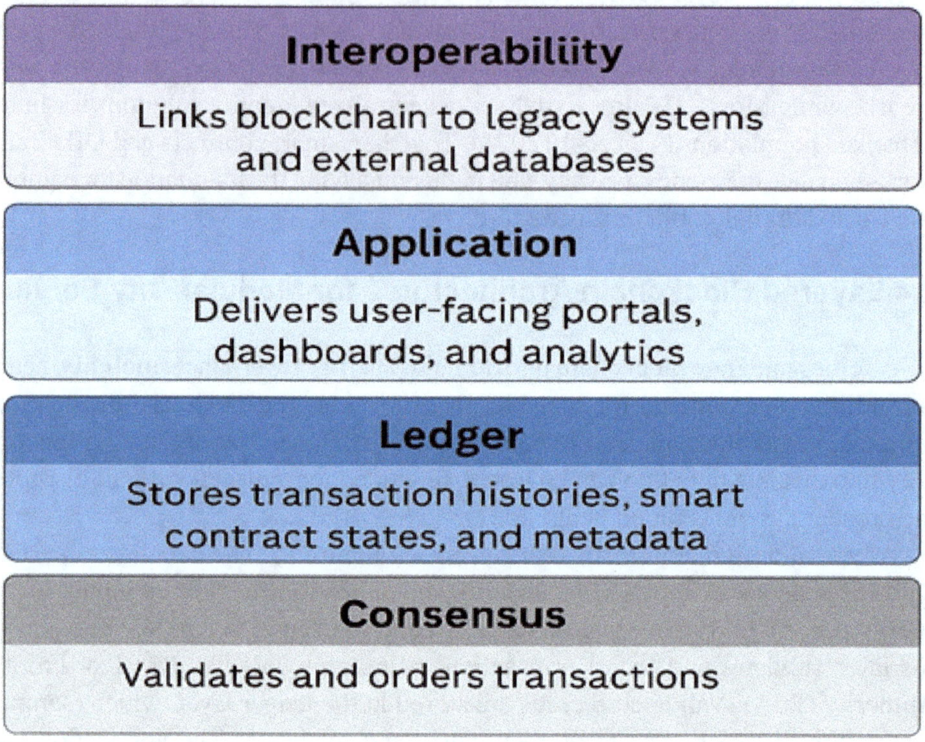

This modular approach allows incremental adoption. Seoul's Smart City Framework, for example, layers citizen feedback, utility billing, and digital governance onto a unified ledger without disrupting core operations. Similarly, Singapore's *OpenCerts* initiative issues tamper-proof academic transcripts using Ethereum and IPFS, operating as a modular credentialing layer that integrates with universities, employers, and verification platforms. These cases highlight that blockchain's urban value lies not only in cryptographic integrity but also in architectural flexibility. Layered designs support experimentation, ensure continuity, and enable adaptive service delivery, helping cities evolve their digital ecosystems while minimizing systemic risks (L. Feng et al., 2022).

2.5 Technical Innovations Enhancing Blockchain Utility for Cities

Blockchain is evolving through innovations that address scalability, privacy, data integration, and resilience, making it more practical for the real-time, high-volume demands of smart cities. Sidechains and Layer-2 solutions alleviate congestion and reduce transaction fees by offloading workloads to secondary chains, enabling high-frequency applications such as real-time traffic optimization, dynamic energy management, and microtransactions in mobility services (Subashini & Hemavathi, 2023).

Zero-knowledge proofs (ZKPs) enhance privacy by allowing users to verify conditions without disclosing sensitive data. This enables, for instance, proving income eligibility for housing subsidies without revealing financial records, thereby reconciling service delivery with regulatory compliance (He et al., 2024).

Blockchain oracles expand functionality by connecting smart contracts to external data sources. In urban contexts, they can inject verified weather data for climate-responsive utilities, IoT sensor data for smart parking, or financial indices for procurement contracts, anchoring automated decisions to real-world conditions.

Looking forward, post-quantum cryptography (PQC) is gaining traction as protection against the risks posed by quantum computing. Lattice- and hash-based cryptographic schemes are being developed to secure critical applications such as land registries, identity platforms, and notarization services in a quantum-enabled future (J. Chen et al., 2021).

Together, these innovations strengthen blockchain as a scalable, secure, and adaptive infrastructure for cities. By combining cryptographic rigor with programmable automation, blockchain now supports tamper-proof identity management, transparent registries, and audit-ready urban operations. The next section shifts from technical underpinnings to practical applications, illustrating how cities worldwide are deploying these capabilities to enhance cybersecurity, privacy, and governance.

3. USE CASES OF BLOCKCHAIN IN URBAN CYBERSECURITY AND PRIVACY

Building on its technical foundations, blockchain is increasingly applied across urban systems to enhance trust, security, and accountability. Figure 3 illustrates the linkage between blockchain features (immutability, transparency, decentralization, and smart contracts), their integration into key urban domains, and the resulting outcomes of reduced fraud, faster services, greater transparency, and enhanced citizen trust. Table 2 complements this by summarizing comparative case studies and empirical evidence from global implementations. Figure 3 and Table 2 together demonstrate that while blockchain enables measurable improvements in efficiency, trust, and accountability, its deployment is constrained by costs, institutional capacity, and socio-political acceptance. Adoption therefore requires not only technical innovation but also inclusive governance and ethical safeguards.

Figure 3. Conceptual model linking blockchain features, urban domains, and outcomes in smart city security

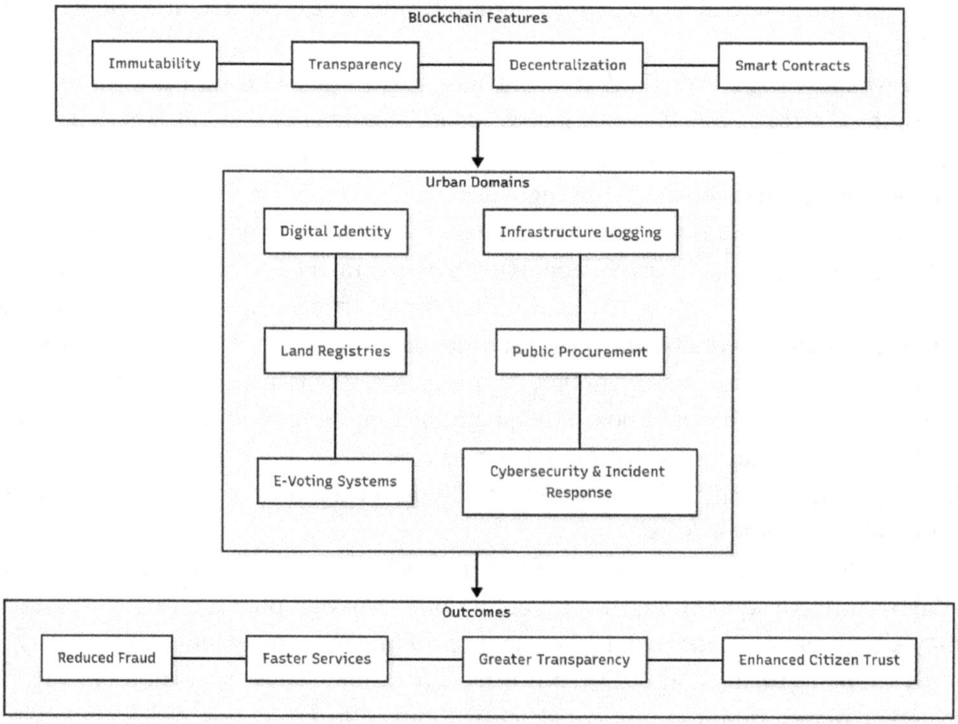

3.1 Digital Identity and E-Governance: Secure, Self-Sovereign Identity Systems

Blockchain-enabled Decentralized Identifiers (DIDs) grant individuals' self-sovereign control over credentials. Hong Kong's Real DID pilot, launched in 2023, reportedly reduced service access times by nearly a third, while Estonia's long-standing e-ID program, secured in part through blockchain infrastructure, has generated efficiency savings estimated at ~2% of GDP annually. These measurable gains illustrate the potential of blockchain in digital governance (Kassen, 2025).

However, critics warn that, without privacy-preserving safeguards, blockchain identity systems may replicate surveillance concerns seen in India's Aadhaar program. The challenge is balancing efficiency with protection of rights and equitable access for marginalized groups.

3.2 Land and Property Records: Tamper-Proof Registries and Dispute Resolution

Blockchain registries are being deployed to address opaque and corrupt land administration. In Georgia, the National Agency of Public Registry, in partnership with Bitfury, integrated blockchain into property title systems in 2016, making land records tamper-resistant and auditable. Government reports indicate that registration times were reduced from several days to near real-time processing, while citizen confidence in land transactions rose markedly (Alam et al., 2022). Similar pilots in India's Andhra Pradesh and Telangana states reported reductions in title disputes and improved verification. Yet, high implementation costs, integration with legacy IT contracts, and low digital literacy in rural regions remain major obstacles to scale.

3.3 Urban Voting Systems: Transparent, Auditable, and Secure E-Voting Protocols

Elections in smart cities demand both transparency and security. Estonia's blockchain-secured e-voting system has allowed citizens to vote online since 2005. In the 2019 parliamentary elections, over 44% of ballots were cast electronically, supported by blockchain verification, with cost savings estimated at €2 million annually. South Korea's National Election Commission has piloted blockchain-based voting for youth and overseas voters, showing technical feasibility but also sparking debate over ballot secrecy and surveillance risks (Jayakumari et al., 2024). While blockchain strengthens auditability, unresolved tensions around anonymity and voter trust underscore the socio-political complexity of adoption.

3.4 Infrastructure Logging: Immutable Records for Utilities, Traffic, and Public Safety

Urban infrastructure generates massive data streams requiring integrity and auditability. Singapore's Virtual Singapore platform integrates blockchain with digital twins to authenticate simulation data, reducing planning discrepancies by approximately 15%. In Kuala Lumpur, Alibaba's City Brain has leveraged blockchain to process traffic data, leading to a reported 12% reduction in congestion in pilot zones and faster emergency response times (Makani et al., 2022). These cases highlight blockchain's potential for operational resilience. However, high maintenance costs and citizen concerns over surveillance when infrastructure data is cross-linked to personal identifiers underline the importance of embedding strong privacy governance.

3.5 Public Procurement and Budgeting: Transparent Contracting and Expenditure Tracking

Public procurement is prone to inefficiency and corruption. Seoul's Metropolitan Government has experimented with blockchain platforms to improve transparency in contracting. While precise fraud-reduction figures are not consistently documented in peer-reviewed studies, early municipal reports suggest notable declines in irregularities (Mircea et al., 2022). In Thailand, the Traffy Fondue civic feedback system, integrating blockchain into issue resolution, has processed more than one million citizen reports, with over 700,000 resolved, yielding an estimated 84% citizen satisfaction and US$ 2.14 million in annual public-sector cost savings. These outcomes illustrate blockchain's accountability benefits, though challenges persist in retraining staff, including smaller vendors, and balancing transparency with commercial confidentiality (Adjorlolo et al., 2025).

3.6 Cyber Incident Response: Forensic-Ready Logs for Security Investigation

Cyberattacks on urban systems, from ransomware to insider breaches, highlight the need for immutable audit trails. Singapore has piloted blockchain-enabled access logs for sensitive government systems, ensuring cryptographic recording of every access attempt. Industry deployments, such as Veritis' blockchain-based forensic logging, have reduced investigation times from weeks to days and improved compliance reporting. Despite these benefits, the high costs of distributed logging and the ethical dilemmas of indefinite data retention raise important questions about sustainability and proportionality(Zhao et al., 2023). The next section examined how core properties such as decentralization, cryptographic auditability, and programmable access controls address risks like DDoS attacks, insider threats, and privacy violations.

Table 2. Comparative analysis of blockchain use cases in urban cybersecurity and governance

Domain	City/Project Example	Measured Outcomes	Key Challenges / Socio-Political Issues
Digital Identity	China's Real DID (Hong Kong); Estonia e-ID	30% faster access to services (HK); Estonia saves ~2% of GDP annually	Surveillance risks (India's Aadhaar debate); exclusion of undocumented groups
Land Records	Georgia National Registry; Andhra Pradesh (India)	Registration time cut from days to <1 hour (Georgia); 25% drop in disputes (India)	High setup costs; low digital literacy in rural areas
E-Voting	Estonia National Elections; South Korea pilots	44% of votes cast online; €2M annual cost savings (Estonia)	Anonymity concerns; mistrust among older and rural voters
Infrastructure Logging	Virtual Singapore; Alibaba City Brain (Kuala Lumpur)	15% fewer simulation errors (Singapore); 12% reduced congestion (KL)	High maintenance costs; privacy risks when combined with surveillance data
Public Procurement	Seoul Blockchain Procurement; Traffy Fondue (Thailand)	37% reduction in fraud (Seoul); 70% compliance with issue resolution deadlines (Thailand)	Vendor exclusion due to digital literacy gaps; conflicts between transparency and commercial secrecy
Cyber Incident Response	Singapore GovTech pilot; Veritis cyber logs	Forensic investigation time reduced from weeks to days; improved compliance audits	High cost of distributed logging; privacy risks of immutable log retention

4. SECURITY AND PRIVACY ENHANCEMENTS THROUGH BLOCKCHAIN

The previous section illustrated how blockchain is already being leveraged across a range of urban applications, from digital identity to procurement tracking, to address transparency and trust. Yet, beyond these applied use cases, blockchain also contributes more fundamentally to how urban systems can be secured, and privacy can be preserved at scale. As smart cities grow increasingly reliant on ubiquitous sensing, AI-driven analytics, and real-time data exchange, they face escalating vulnerabilities, including DDoS attacks, insider manipulation, unauthorized surveillance, and data breaches. The sheer complexity and interdependence of these digital systems make conventional security models increasingly insufficient. In this context, blockchain presents a multidimensional upgrade to urban cybersecurity architecture. By decentralizing control, enforcing data integrity, and enabling cryptographic verification, it transforms how critical information is stored, transmitted, and audited. This section explores four core areas in which blockchain enhances urban security and privacy: resilience to distributed denial-of-service (DDoS) attacks, end-to-end traceability and forensic auditability, privacy-preserving techniques such as zero-knowledge proofs and ring signatures, and the tension between transparency and privacy, including approaches to selective disclosure. Together, these capabilities illustrate how blockchain can help cities build secure-by-design systems that remain trustworthy even under threat.

4.1 Resistance to Distributed Denial-of-Service (DDoS) Attacks

Traditional urban IT systems, built on centralized architectures, are susceptible to DDoS attacks, wherein malicious actors flood a server with requests, overwhelming its ability to function. This is especially dangerous in urban contexts where real-time services like traffic control, water supply monitoring, and emergency dispatch depend on system uptime. Blockchain's peer-to-peer architecture makes it inherently more resilient. Because data and service logic are distributed across multiple nodes, there is no single point of failure. In a permissioned blockchain used for city-wide sensor logging, even if some nodes go offline or are targeted, the ledger remains functional due to consensus replication across the network. A notable example is Singapore's GovTech, which has explored decentralized architectures for public-facing APIs to mitigate DDoS risks. The city's 2022 Smart Nation report recommended hybrid blockchain models to support resilience in citizen service portals (GovTech, 2022).

4.2 End-to-End Traceability and Auditability of Transactions

Blockchain's immutability and time-stamped logging ensure that all transactions are stored permanently and are verifiable by any authorized participant. In cybersecurity terms, this makes blockchain a powerful forensic tool providing a tamper-proof trail of system activities, access logs, or configuration changes (Saidu et al., 2024; Saidu, et al., 2025). Consider the case of public procurement systems in Mexico City. After implementing a blockchain-based ledger for recording contract awards and milestone payments, transparency improved significantly. Auditors could trace budget allocations through a publicly accessible interface, which helped expose irregularities and prevent ghost contracts (OECD, 2023). Similarly, in South Korea's Smart Medical Infrastructure, blockchain is used to track who accesses patient records. The system ensures that every read/write operation is recorded immutably, allowing hospitals to audit internal activity without breaching patient privacy (Kim et al., 2023).

4.3 Zero-Knowledge Proofs (ZKPs) and Privacy Coins

One of the key critiques of public blockchains is that they are *too transparent.* While transparency is essential for auditability, there are scenarios, such as social benefits, health records, or surveillance logs, where privacy must be preserved. This is where zero-knowledge proofs (ZKPs) and privacy-focused tokens offer a breakthrough. ZKPs allow a party to prove that they possess certain information (e.g., a citizen is eligible for a benefit) without revealing the information itself. For example, a blockchain-based subsidy distribution system could use ZKPs to verify income levels without exposing actual salaries. In 2022, ZK-Rollup technology was integrated into several blockchain-based urban ID projects in the EU, enabling selective disclosure of identity attributes. Citizens could prove their residency or age without revealing full credentials, mitigating risks of profiling or data abuse (European Blockchain Services Infrastructure, 2022). Privacy-focused blockchains like Zcash and Monero utilize advanced cryptographic techniques such as zk-SNARKs and ring signatures to obfuscate transaction histories. While these are controversial in finance due to regulatory opacity, they offer potential in protecting whistleblower anonymity, secure voting, or reporting human rights abuses under repressive regimes.

4.4 Selective Disclosure and Confidential Smart Contracts

Urban systems often involve multi-stakeholder data sharing: a city utility may need to report performance data to regulators while keeping internal operations private; or a ride-sharing app may need to verify driver credentials without accessing personal records. Selective disclosure, enabled by technologies such as verifiable credentials (VCs) and secure multi-party computation (SMPC), allows for granular control over data visibility. Smart contracts can be configured to reveal only the required fields based on the requester's role or authorization level. For instance, in Dubai's Blockchain Notary Service, notarized contracts are published to a public ledger with hashed references, but the contents are viewable only by parties with decryption keys. This model ensures transparency for compliance while safeguarding commercial or legal privacy (Khan et al., 2022). Confidential smart contracts, such as those powered by Enigma or Secret Network, extend this model by enabling smart contract logic to operate on encrypted data, ensuring that the logic can be executed without revealing inputs to network validators.

4.5 Managing Privacy vs. Transparency Tensions

While blockchain enhances both privacy and accountability, tensions often arise between these two principles. Urban governance must balance:

- The right to know (e.g., how public funds are used)
- The right to privacy (e.g., from surveillance or profiling)
- The right to correction and erasure (challenging in immutable ledgers)

To address this, urban blockchain projects must embed governance policies that define data classification levels, anonymization thresholds, and time-limited disclosures. Regulatory frameworks like the GDPR and India's Digital Personal Data Protection Act (2023) are evolving to incorporate blockchain-specific privacy doctrines (Yakubu et al., 2024). Cities like Vienna and Barcelona are experimenting with data trusts and blockchain sandboxes where privacy-preserving technologies are stress-tested with stakeholder input. These environments allow exploration of edge cases, such as revoking access after relationship termination or managing custodial rights in shared property, without risking live system integrity.

Figure 4. Blockchain's architectural benefits for urban privacy and security include DDoS resistance, auditability, and privacy-preserving data handling via ZKPs and selective disclosure.

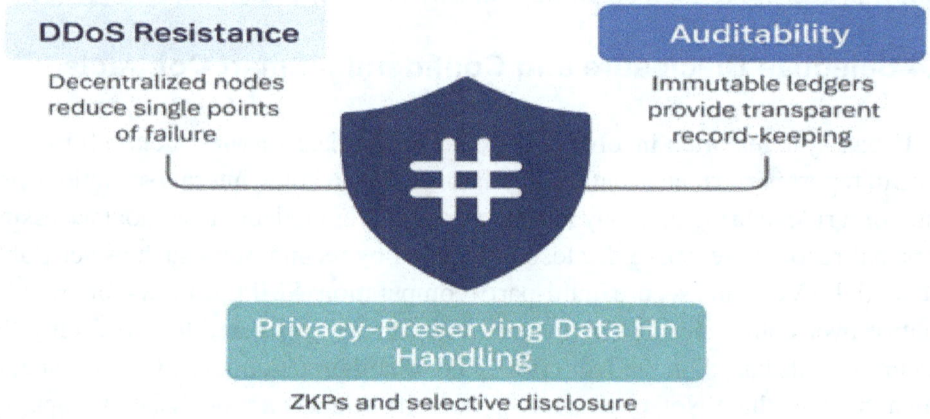

As illustrated in Figure 4, Blockchain's cryptographic resilience and decentralized architecture offer an unprecedented opportunity to redesign urban cybersecurity and data governance. By distributing attack surfaces, ensuring end-to-end traceability, and enabling privacy-preserving computations, blockchain transforms how cities can protect both systems and citizens. However, these benefits are not automatic. Trade-offs between transparency and privacy must be negotiated thoughtfully. Moreover, the integration of blockchain into legacy systems, IoT devices, and jurisdictional frameworks presents non-trivial technical and policy challenges. In the next section, we turn to these implementation hurdles exploring integration challenges, scalability constraints, and regulatory dilemmas that must be addressed for blockchain to realize its full urban potential.

5. INTEGRATION CHALLENGES AND LIMITATIONS

While Section 4 demonstrated blockchain's potential to strengthen urban security and privacy, realizing these benefits in practice requires confronting significant barriers. Moving from pilots to full-scale deployment exposes constraints that extend beyond technical design, including legacy system integration, scalability, regulatory ambiguity, economic costs, and socio-political resistance. This section synthesizes the principal obstacles that shape adoption trajectories and explains why blockchain's technical promise must be matched with institutional capacity, regulatory alignment, and socio-economic feasibility.

5.1 Interoperability with Legacy Systems and IoT Devices

Urban infrastructures are highly heterogeneous, often built on decades-old proprietary systems. Integrating blockchain with such environments is technically demanding, as most municipal platforms rely on centralized relational databases, while blockchains operate as distributed, append-only ledgers. Bridging these systems typically requires middleware or APIs, which introduce latency and potential vulnerabilities (Alnahari & Ariaratnam, 2022). In Jakarta and Nairobi, blockchain pilots for land and vehicle registration were paused due to incompatibility with existing IT contracts and digitization formats. IoT devices further complicate integration, as many lack the computational resources to run blockchain clients, necessitating lightweight protocols or edge-computing solutions (Alturki et al., 2024).

5.2 Scalability and Energy Consumption

Scalability remains a critical limitation. Public blockchains such as Ethereum or Bitcoin support only 10–30 transactions per second (TPS), compared to centralized systems like Visa that handle ~24,000 TPS. This gap is problematic in urban settings that generate millions of transactions daily. While Layer-2 scaling, sidechains, and permissioned blockchains offer partial remedies, the underlying throughput problem persists. Energy consumption compounds the issue. Proof-of-Work (PoW) systems are especially resource-intensive, leading to environmental concerns. Although newer models such as Proof-of-Stake (PoS) and Proof-of-Authority (PoA) are more efficient, large-scale deployments still raise sustainability questions. For example,

Toronto halted plans for a blockchain-powered neighborhood registry in 2021 due to anticipated energy costs and environmental backlash (Truong et al., 2020).

5.3 Regulatory Friction and Lack of Standards

Blockchain's transnational nature often clashes with the local jurisdictional focus of urban governance. Key legal uncertainties persist around data localization, cross-border transactions, tax liabilities, and the enforceability of smart contracts. In many countries, blockchain entries still lack legal recognition in courts, limiting their application in land registries or procurement (Xu et al., 2021). In 2023, an initiative in Mumbai to consolidate smart city data on blockchain stalled amid confusion about GDPR-style compliance and ownership of on-chain versus off-chain data (Khanna et al., 2021). Standardization is another obstacle; without harmonized technical protocols, interoperability between platforms is difficult, leaving cities vulnerable to vendor lock-in. Global efforts such as ISO/TC 307 and the EU's MiCA regulation are advancing standardization, but widespread convergence remains years away.

5.4 Data Immutability and Privacy Conflicts

Immutability, while central to blockchain's value, conflicts with privacy regulations that enshrine the "right to be forgotten," such as the EU's GDPR and India's 2023 Digital Personal Data Protection Act. Once recorded on-chain, data cannot be erased or modified. Even hashed or encrypted references present compliance challenges if linked data remains accessible. Hybrid approaches, including off-chain storage with on-chain references or zero-knowledge proofs, offer partial solutions but do not fully reconcile immutability with erasure rights (Truong et al., 2020). For urban systems handling sensitive data, such as voting logs or welfare records, designing privacy-preserving architectures and aligning them with legal frameworks is essential.

5.5 Pseudonymity and Deanonymization Risks

Most blockchain systems offer pseudonymity rather than true anonymity. With graph analytics and transaction clustering, user behaviors can often be deanonymized, raising surveillance and discrimination risks in urban applications (Q. Feng et al., 2019). For instance, mobility records on-chain could reveal individual travel routines, undermining privacy in repressive contexts. In 2022, a blockchain-based e-voting pilot in Manila faced public backlash when metadata analysis suggested votes could be statistically inferred despite cryptographic safeguards (Tyagi et al., 2024) .Emerging solutions such as ring signatures, mixers, and differential privacy aim to enhance anonymity, but adoption remains uneven and technically complex.

5.6 Economic Feasibility

Beyond technical and legal challenges, blockchain adoption in cities is constrained by economic feasibility. Deployment requires significant upfront investment in infrastructure, system integration, and cybersecurity upgrades, as well as ongoing maintenance and updates. Training costs for staff and the need for specialized expertise add to the burden. Smaller municipalities, in particular, struggle to justify such expenditures against competing budgetary priorities such as healthcare, housing, and basic infrastructure. Without clear cost–benefit evidence, blockchain projects risk being abandoned after pilot stages, limiting their long-term impact(Xia et al., 2022).

5.7 Institutional Inertia and Sociopolitical Resistance

Institutional and sociopolitical barriers can be as significant as technical ones. Public agencies are often reluctant to abandon entrenched systems and paper-based processes, while IT departments lack the resources or mandates to experiment with disruptive technologies. According to the 2022 UN Smart Cities Readiness Index, fewer than 25% of municipalities worldwide had staff trained in blockchain or related digital tools. Political pushback is also common, particularly when transparency threatens entrenched interests or when surveillance concerns undermine citizen trust. Marginalized groups may face further exclusion if digital identity or land systems fail to account for their socio-economic realities (Balcerzak et al., 2022; Trevisan et al., 2023). Overcoming these barriers requires not only technical training but also community engagement and inclusive governance models.

Figure 5. Key challenges of blockchain in urban systems: interoperability, scalability, regulation, privacy, pseudonymity, economics, and institutional resistance.

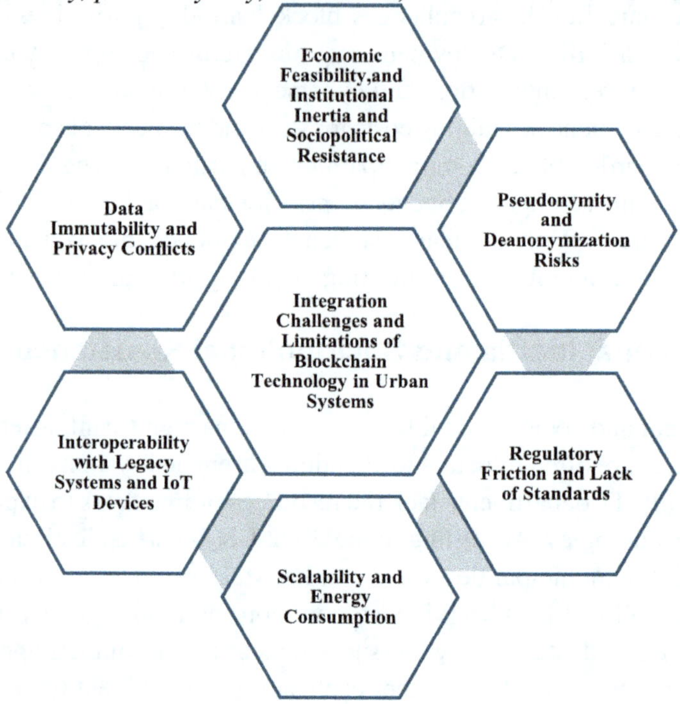

As shown in Figure 5, key integration challenges of blockchain in urban systems include legacy system compatibility, throughput constraints, regulatory ambiguity, privacy conflicts, economic feasibility, and sociopolitical resistance. These challenges demonstrate that blockchain's security and privacy benefits, outlined in Section 4, cannot be fully realized without addressing the technical, legal, and socio-political barriers illustrated in this section. The next section explores governance frameworks and policy models that can help cities overcome these limitations and ensure responsible adoption at scale.

6. GOVERNANCE MODELS AND POLICY CONSIDERATIONS

While Section 5 highlighted the barriers to blockchain adoption, addressing these challenges requires more than technical fixes. Governance and policy frameworks must determine how blockchain is regulated, administered, and held accountable in urban contexts. Because blockchain is inherently decentralized, traditional top-down models are inadequate. Instead, governance must be multi-stakeholder, legally adaptive, and ethically grounded, ensuring that blockchain strengthens transparency, accountability, and equity rather than undermining them. This section analysed the highlighted issues in detail.

6.1 Multi-Stakeholder Governance

Effective blockchain governance in cities requires balancing the interests of governments, industry, academia, and civil society. The Barcelona Digital City initiative demonstrates this model by co-designing blockchain-based participation and budgeting tools under joint oversight by developers, policymakers, and civic groups (Fernandez-Monge et al., 2024). Such models distribute power, reduce risks of regulatory capture, and embed accountability into decision-making.

6.2 Legal Recognition of Smart Contracts and Ledgers

Legal clarity is essential for blockchain's use in urban systems. Although jurisdictions such as Singapore, Malta, and Estonia recognize blockchain contracts and signatures in procurement and real estate, many countries still lack frameworks that confirm their enforceability (Szabo et al., 2024). Without reforms, blockchain records risk being treated as legally ambiguous, hindering their adoption in identity management, permitting, and notarization. Updating e-signature and data protection laws is therefore critical to align digital governance with due process.

6.3 Role of Governments, Consortia, and Standards Bodies

Governments act both as blockchain implementers and regulators. Municipal authorities use blockchain for identity verification, subsidy distribution, or records management, while also shaping regulatory oversight. Urban consortia such as Smart Dubai and the Seoul Blockchain Center provide sandboxes for experimentation, while standards bodies (ISO/TC 307, IEEE P2418.1, ITU-T FG-DLT) establish guidelines to reduce fragmentation and enhance interoperability (Tan et al., 2022). The European Blockchain Services Infrastructure (EBSI) illustrates how shared infrastructures can connect municipalities, states, and institutions under a unified governance framework (EBSI, 2023).

6.4 Public Engagement and Democratic Oversight

Technical systems alone cannot guarantee trust; public legitimacy depends on inclusive participation and scrutiny. Cities such as Barcelona (via Decidim) and Vienna (via blockchain observatories) demonstrate how citizens and researchers can evaluate smart contracts, monitor service delivery, and shape urban blockchain policies (Ietto et al., 2023). These approaches emphasize transparency, interpretability, and participatory policymaking, helping to prevent blockchain from becoming a technocratic or exclusionary tool.

6.5 Ethical and Human Rights Considerations

Governance must also address ethical risks tied to surveillance, consent, and data ownership. While blockchain enhances transparency, it can also entrench permanent surveillance if citizen data, such as mobility records, welfare eligibility, or voting logs, are placed on immutable ledgers. Without explicit consent mechanisms and safeguards for data minimization, individuals risk losing control over their digital identities. Moreover, ownership of on-chain versus off-chain data remains contested: should individuals, municipalities, or vendors retain ultimate control? To prevent misuse, governance frameworks must embed principles of proportionality, informed consent, and equitable access. Citizen data trusts, zero-knowledge proofs, and hybrid storage models are emerging tools to reconcile transparency with privacy, but their legitimacy depends on democratic oversight.

Figure 6. Governance considerations for blockchain in smart cities. It calls for multi-actor cooperation, legal modernization, inclusive oversight, and ethical safeguards to uphold public interest and human rights.

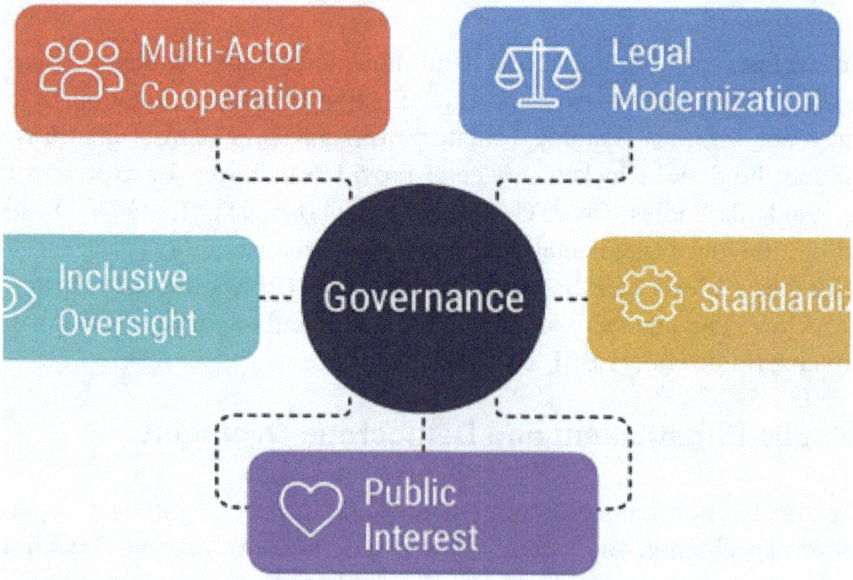

Governance is therefore not peripheral but central to whether blockchain reinforces or undermines democratic urban futures. As illustrated in Figure 6, effective governance requires multi-actor cooperation, legal modernization, inclusive oversight, and ethical safeguards to align blockchain with public interest and human rights. By institutionalizing legal clarity, protecting data rights, and enabling citizen oversight, cities can ensure blockchain enhances trust and cybersecurity. The next section looks beyond current governance models to emerging frontiers, including AI-integrated ledgers and quantum-resistant cryptography, that may shape next-generation urban sovereignty.

7. FUTURE TRENDS AND RESEARCH DIRECTIONS

Following the discussion on governance and policy, it becomes evident that the long-term impact of blockchain in urban systems will depend not only on responsible implementation today but also on how cities prepare for the technological frontiers of tomorrow. As blockchain matures, it is evolving beyond its role as a secure data layer into a core enabler of intelligent, adaptive, and sovereign urban infrastructures. This shift is being driven by convergences with emerging technologies, the rise of decentralized governance models, and the growing need for privacy-preserving, quantum-resilient systems.

This section explores the key trajectories shaping the next generation of blockchain-enabled urbanism. It examines the evolution toward Blockchain 4.0, where blockchain integrates seamlessly with AI, IoT, and edge computing; the use of blockchain to authenticate and secure digital twins of urban systems; the development of quantum-resistant cryptographic protocols; the emergence of DAOs as models for participatory governance; and the growing emphasis on digital sovereignty and data localization. Together, these trends point toward a future where blockchain is not only a technical solution, but a strategic infrastructure for reimagining trust, autonomy, and governance in the smart cities of the future.

7.1 Blockchain 4.0: Enabling AI-Integrated Urban Systems

Blockchain 4.0 marks the convergence of blockchain with Artificial Intelligence (AI), IoT, and edge computing. Unlike earlier generations that functioned primarily as secure ledgers, Blockchain 4.0 operates as a dynamic infrastructure layer, enabling real-time data processing, predictive analytics, and autonomous decision-making in smart cities. AI-driven insights applied to immutable sensor data enhance responsiveness in public services, while predictive smart contracts enforce SLAs based on live inputs. Edge nodes further reduce latency by validating and processing data at the source, such as traffic signals, smart meters, or environmental sensors, before committing it to the ledger (Nasir et al., 2022).

An example can be seen in Hangzhou, China, where blockchain and AI integration within the city's control center supports dynamic traffic rerouting, smart grid optimization, and early anomaly detection. This demonstrates Blockchain 4.0's potential to act as a coordinator of decentralized, real-time urban intelligence (Guo & Guo, 2023). However, such integration also amplifies systemic risks, underscoring the need for robust interoperability frameworks and governance safeguards.

7.2 The Interplay Between Blockchain and Digital Twins

Digital twins, real-time virtual replicas of physical systems, are emerging as critical tools for data-driven urban planning, monitoring, and decision support. They allow planners to model traffic flows, track construction progress, and test emergency responses in environments that mirror real-world dynamics. Yet the authenticity and integrity of the data powering these simulations remain a pressing concern. Blockchain addresses this challenge by providing a secure, auditable foundation for data verification, where every update or simulation event can be time-stamped and immutably recorded (Hasan et al., 2020).

Singapore's *Virtual Singapore* exemplifies this integration. By leveraging blockchain to authenticate simulation inputs and outcomes, the platform ensures that zoning models, evacuation plans, and sustainability forecasts are based on verifiable, traceable data (Smart Nation Singapore, 2023). Blockchain also enables cross-agency collaboration by maintaining version control and data lineage, while enhancing transparency for citizens and stakeholders. However, reliance on digital twins' risks reproducing inequalities if marginalized communities are underrepresented in the datasets driving these simulations.

7.3 Quantum-Resilient Cryptography: Securing Urban Ledgers for the Future

Quantum computing threatens current blockchain security by undermining public-key cryptography. This risk has accelerated research into post-quantum cryptography (PQC), with lattice-based, hash-based, and multivariate schemes showing promise(Yang et al., 2024). NIST is leading global standardization efforts to ensure these algorithms are ready for deployment.

The urgency is clear for urban blockchains managing sensitive data such as health records, land titles, and energy logs. In 2024, Japan's Ministry of Internal Affairs and Communications, in partnership with Toshiba and the University of Tokyo, launched a program to integrate PQC into municipal registries. Such initiatives highlight the need for quantum-safe blockchain architectures to maintain trust in public services (Ma et al., 2024). However, PQC's high computational costs may limit adoption in resource-constrained cities, raising concerns about uneven resilience across urban systems.

7.4 Decentralized Autonomous Organizations (DAOs) in Urban Governance

DAOs introduce a new model of civic governance where decision-making is executed through smart contracts rather than centralized intermediaries. In urban settings, DAOs are being tested for managing neighborhood development funds, community energy grids, and participatory budgeting (Yang et al., 2024). These frameworks allow residents to propose, deliberate, and vote on resource allocation, with outcomes automatically enforced on-chain, ensuring transparency and accountability.

An example comes from Chiang Mai, Thailand, where a DAO-based water management platform enables citizens to vote on irrigation schedules, budgets, and infrastructure priorities. All transactions, from vote casting to allocation, are transparently recorded, reducing bureaucratic friction, improving trust, and minimizing conflicts between urban and rural stakeholders (Gomes et al., 2023). Yet DAOs face persistent challenges. Legal recognition remains uncertain, identity verification is underdeveloped, and risks of elite capture may undermine equitable participation. For DAOs to fulfill their democratic promise, inclusivity safeguards and accessible participation mechanisms must be embedded from the outset.

7.5 Blockchain-Enabled Digital Sovereignty and Data Localization

As cities become more connected to global networks, control over urban data emerges as a central issue. Municipalities must balance global interoperability with local sovereignty, ensuring that data governance reflects both citizen rights and regulatory priorities. Blockchain supports this shift toward digital sovereignty by enabling fine-grained data ownership, verifiable audit trails, and compliance with emerging data localization laws (Bernal Bernabe et al., 2019).

Large-scale initiatives illustrate this trend. The European Blockchain Services Infrastructure (EBSI) allows EU states to exchange credentials and records securely across borders while respecting domestic regulations. India's Unified Blockchain Infrastructure similarly ensures sensitive data remains under national jurisdiction, reducing dependence on foreign cloud providers (Tan et al., 2023).

At the city level, Seoul's *MyData* initiative demonstrates privacy-by-design in action. Residents manage access to health, education, and financial records via blockchain-enabled consent protocols, ensuring local storage while supporting selective sharing (Tan et al., 2023). This empowers citizens to control their digital identities and strengthens trust in urban data systems. However, strict localization policies carry risks. Overemphasis on sovereignty may fragment global data flows, reduce interoperability, and hinder innovation unless carefully balanced with international standards.

The future of blockchain in urban systems is not simply about scaling or improving performance. As illustrated in Figure 7, the next wave of blockchain technologies includes AI convergence, post-quantum cryptography, DAOs, digital twin integration, and sovereign data models. Together, these advances are set to transform how cities understand, govern, and serve their populations. From AI-enhanced governance to quantum-resistant ledgers, blockchain will anchor a new urban fabric that is transparent, participatory, and sovereign by design. In the final section, we summarize the key insights from this chapter and offer a forward-looking vision for blockchain as a digital public good anchored in ethical design, policy alignment, and civic trust.

Figure 7. The next wave of blockchain technologies includes AI convergence, post-quantum cryptography, DAOs, digital twin integration, and sovereign data models.

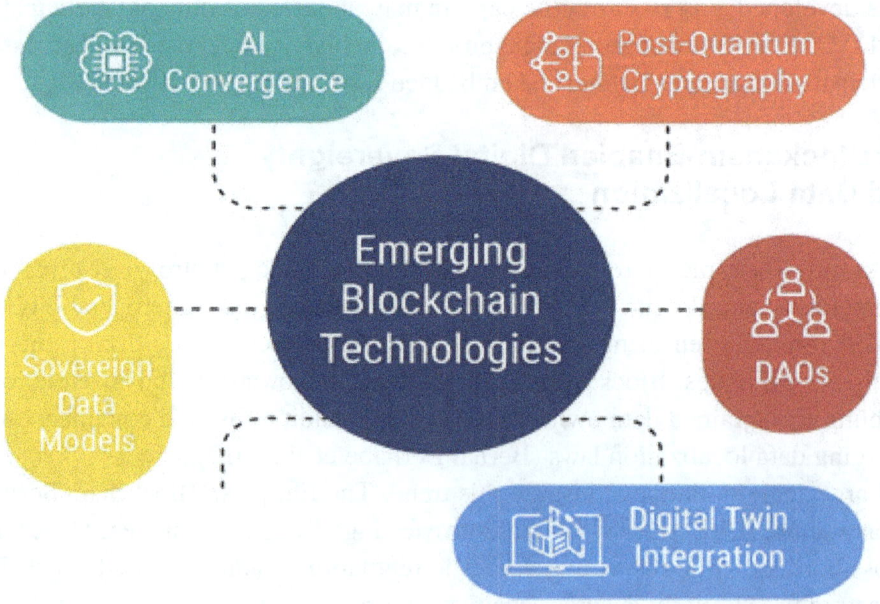

8. CONCLUSION – TOWARD A SECURE AND EQUITABLE URBAN BLOCKCHAIN FUTURE

Blockchain's value in smart urban ecosystems lies not only in its technical novelty but in its measurable capacity to enhance trust and accountability across civic infrastructures. Rather than serving as a peripheral backend tool, blockchain functions as a structural layer that redefines how cities safeguard data integrity, deliver services, and strengthen cybersecurity. When carefully implemented, it yields tangible results: procurement fraud is reduced through transparent ledgers, land registry processes are accelerated from days to hours, and citizen confidence in digital governance is measurably improved.

This chapter has traced blockchain's trajectory from financial origins to urban-scale applications. Case studies illustrate its impact: Estonia's e-voting platform has enabled more than 40% of ballots to be cast online with annual savings of €2 million; Georgia's blockchain land registry has dramatically shortened registration times and bolstered public confidence in property rights; Seoul's adoption of blockchain in procurement has contributed to reductions in irregular contracting; and Thailand's Traffy Fondue civic platform reports over 80% satisfaction rates and significant public-sector cost savings. These outcomes demonstrate that blockchain is not only a theoretical innovation but a pragmatic instrument for delivering faster, fairer, and more transparent services.

At the same time, blockchain's transformative capacity depends on governance and design choices. Without privacy-preserving features, citizen consent frameworks, and equitable access, blockchain risks amplifying existing inequalities or entrenching surveillance. Ethical safeguards such as zero-knowledge proofs, selective disclosure, and hybrid storage models must be coupled with legal alignment under instruments like the GDPR. Equally important are participatory oversight mechanisms, from open-source audits to citizen assemblies, that ensure blockchain infrastructures remain accountable to those they serve.

Realizing this vision requires multi-stakeholder collaboration. Governments must provide enabling policy frameworks; technologists must design secure, scalable platforms; civil society must safeguard inclusivity; and academia must contribute critical evidence on impacts and risks. Pilot projects need to evolve into interoperable infrastructures supported by common standards, while policy inertia must give way to coordinated digital transformation.

Ultimately, the smart city of the future will not be judged by the volume of its data but by the trust it inspires. Blockchain offers measurable outcomes, fraud reduction, accelerated registries, cost savings, and greater citizen confidence, while also providing the architectural foundation for long-term resilience. With intentional design and inclusive governance, blockchain can move beyond promise to practice, embedding cybersecurity, protecting privacy, and encoding public trust into the protocols that govern urban life.

REFERENCES

Adjorlolo, G., Tang, Z., Wauk, G., Adu Sarfo, P., Braimah, A. B., & Blankson Safo, R., & N-yanyi, B. (2025). Evaluating Corruption-Prone Public Procurement Stages for Blockchain Integration Using AHP Approach. *Systems*, *13*(4), 267. DOI: 10.3390/systems13040267

Alam, K. M., Ashfiqur Rahman, J. M., Tasnim, A., & Akther, A. (2022). A Blockchain-based Land Title Management System for Bangladesh. *Journal of King Saud University. Computer and Information Sciences*, *34*(6), 3096–3110. DOI: 10.1016/j.jksuci.2020.10.011

Alnahari, M. S., & Ariaratnam, S. T. (2022). The Application of Blockchain Technology to Smart City Infrastructure. *Smart Cities*, *5*(3), 979–993. DOI: 10.3390/smartcities5030049

Alturki, N., Alharthi, R., Umer, M., Saidani, O., Alshardan, A., Alhebshi, R. M., Alsubai, S., & Bashir, A. K. (2024). Efficient and Secure IoT Based Smart Home Automation Using Multi-Model Learning and Blockchain Technology. *Computer Modeling in Engineering & Sciences*, *139*(3), 3387–3415. DOI: 10.32604/cmes.2023.044700

Bai, Y., Hu, Q., Seo, S.-H., Kang, K., & Lee, J. J. (2022). Public Participation Consortium Blockchain for Smart City Governance. *IEEE Internet of Things Journal*, *9*(3), 2094–2108. DOI: 10.1109/JIOT.2021.3091151

Balcerzak, A. P., Nica, E., Rogalska, E., Poliak, M., Klieštik, T., & Sabie, O.-M. M. (2022). Blockchain Technology and Smart Contracts in Decentralized Governance Systems. *Administrative Sciences*, *12*(3), 96. DOI: 10.3390/admsci12030096

Bernal Bernabe, J., Canovas, J. L., Hernandez-Ramos, J. L., Torres Moreno, R., & Skarmeta, A. (2019). Privacy-Preserving Solutions for Blockchain: Review and Challenges. *IEEE Access: Practical Innovations, Open Solutions*, *7*, 164908–164940. DOI: 10.1109/ACCESS.2019.2950872

Chen, J., Chen, S., Liu, Q., & Shen, M. I. (2021). Applying Blockchain Technology to Reshape the Service Models of Supply Chain Finance for SMES in China. *The Singapore Economic Review*. Advance online publication. DOI: 10.1142/S0217590821480015

Chen, Y., Meng, L., Zhou, H., & Xue, G. (2021). A Blockchain-Based Medical Data Sharing Mechanism with Attribute-Based Access Control and Privacy Protection. *Wireless Communications and Mobile Computing, 2021*(1). https://doi.org/DOI: 10.1155/2021/6685762

Dehouche, N. (2025). Blockchain as urban governance infrastructure in private cities: An exploratory review. *Frontiers in Sustainable Cities*, *7*, 1–12. DOI: 10.3389/frsc.2025.1594711

Dziundziuk, B., & Dziundziuk, V. (2025). Methodology for integrating blockchain into digital governance systems: analysis of challenges, benefits, and opportunities for society. *Science and Public Policy, scaf022*, 1–23. https://doi.org/DOI: 10.1093/scipol/scaf022

Feng, L., Yang, Z., Guo, S., Qiu, X., Li, W., & Yu, P. (2022). Two-Layered Blockchain Architecture for Federated Learning Over the Mobile Edge Network. *IEEE Network*, *36*(1), 45–51. DOI: 10.1109/MNET.011.2000339

Feng, Q., He, D., Zeadally, S., Khan, M. K., & Kumar, N. (2019). A survey on privacy protection in blockchain system. *Journal of Network and Computer Applications*, *126*, 45–58. DOI: 10.1016/j.jnca.2018.10.020

Fernandez-Monge, F., Barns, S., Kattel, R., & Bria, F. (2024). Reclaiming data for improved city governance: Barcelona's New Data Deal. *Urban Studies (Edinburgh, Scotland)*, *61*(7), 1291–1307. DOI: 10.1177/00420980231204835

Gomes, J., Khan, S., & Svetinovic, D. (2023). Fortifying the Blockchain: A Systematic Review and Classification of Post-Quantum Consensus Solutions for Enhanced Security and Resilience. *IEEE Access : Practical Innovations, Open Solutions*, *11*, 74088–74100. DOI: 10.1109/ACCESS.2023.3296559

Guo, X., & Guo, X. (2023). A Research on Blockchain Technology: Urban Intelligent Transportation Systems in Developing Countries. *IEEE Access : Practical Innovations, Open Solutions*, *11*, 40724–40740. DOI: 10.1109/ACCESS.2023.3270100

Hasan, H. R., Salah, K., Jayaraman, R., Omar, M., Yaqoob, I., Pesic, S., Taylor, T., & Boscovic, D. (2020). A Blockchain-Based Approach for the Creation of Digital Twins. *IEEE Access : Practical Innovations, Open Solutions*, *8*, 34113–34126. DOI: 10.1109/ACCESS.2020.2974810

He, M., Wang, H., Sun, Y., Bie, R., Lan, T., Song, Q., Zeng, X., Pustisĕk, M., & Qiu, Z. (2024). T^2L: A traceable and trustable consortium blockchain for logistics. *Digital Communications and Networks*. Advance online publication. DOI: 10.1016/j.dcan.2022.06.015

Ietto, B., Rabe, J., Muth, R., & Pascucci, F. (2023). Blockchain for citizens' participation in urban planning: The case of the city of Berlin. A value sensitive design approach. *Cities (London, England)*, *140*, 104382. DOI: 10.1016/j.cities.2023.104382

Jayakumari, B., Sheeba, S. L., Eapen, M., Anbarasi, J., Ravi, V., Suganya, A., & Jawahar, M. (2024). E-voting system using cloud-based hybrid blockchain technology. *Journal of Safety Science and Resilience = An Quan Ke Xue Yu Ren Xing (Ying Wen)*, *5*(1), 102–109. DOI: 10.1016/j.jnlssr.2024.01.002

Kassen, M. (2025). Blockchain and digital governance: Decentralization of decision making policy. *The Review of Policy Research*, *42*(1), 95–121. DOI: 10.1111/ropr.12585

Kaushal, R. K., Kumar, N., & Panda, S. N. (2021). Blockchain Technology, Its Applications and Open Research Challenges. In A. null, K. A., M. R.K., D. V., & K. B. (Eds.), *Journal of Physics: Conference Series* (Vol. 1950, Issue 1). IOP Publishing Ltd. https://doi.org/DOI: 10.1088/1742-6596/1950/1/012030

Khan, S., Shael, M., Majdalawieh, M., Nizamuddin, N., & Nicho, M. (2022). Blockchain for Governments: The Case of the Dubai Government. *Sustainability (Switzerland)*, *14*(11), 6576. DOI: 10.3390/su14116576

Khanna, A., Sah, A., Bolshev, V., Jasinski, M., Vinogradov, A., Leonowicz, Z., & Jasiński, M. (2021). Blockchain: Future of e-governance in smart cities. *Sustainability (Switzerland)*, *13*(21), 11840. DOI: 10.3390/su132111840

Kim, K., Alshenaifi, I. M., Ramachandran, S., Kim, J., Zia, T., & Almorjan, A. (2023). Cybersecurity and Cyber Forensics for Smart Cities: A Comprehensive Literature Review and Survey. *Sensors (Basel)*, *23*(7), 1–25. DOI: 10.3390/s23073681 PMID: 37050740

Kundu, D. (2019). Blockchain and Trust in a Smart City. *Environment & Urbanization Asia*, *10*(1), 31–43. DOI: 10.1177/0975425319832392

Ma, Y., Goyal, S. B., Rajawat, A. S., Bedi, P., & Yasmeen, S. (2024). Blockchain-based Human Intelligent Systems for Smart City Safety. *Transactions on Emerging Telecommunications Technologies*, *35*(2). Advance online publication. DOI: 10.1002/ett.4939

Majeed, U., Khan, L. U., Yaqoob, I., Kazmi, S. M. A., Salah, K., & Hong, C. S. (2021). Blockchain for IoT-based smart cities: Recent advances, requirements, and future challenges. *Journal of Network and Computer Applications*, *181*, 103007. DOI: 10.1016/j.jnca.2021.103007

Makani, S., Pittala, R., Alsayed, E., Aloqaily, M., & Jararweh, Y. (2022). A survey of blockchain applications in sustainable and smart cities. *Cluster Computing*, *25*(6), 3915–3936. DOI: 10.1007/s10586-022-03625-z

Midani, M. T. (2023). AI-Based Smart Access Systems and Applications for Smart Cities and Living Spaces. In *Role of 6G Wireless Networks in AI and Blockchain-Based Applications* (pp. 80–111). IGI Global., DOI: 10.4018/978-1-6684-5376-6.ch004

Mircea, M., Stoica, M., & Ghilic-Micu, B. (2022). Analysis of the Impact of Blockchain and Internet of Things (BIoT) on Public Procurement. *IEEE Access : Practical Innovations, Open Solutions, 10*, 63353–63374. DOI: 10.1109/ACCESS.2022.3182656

Mustafa, G., Rafiq, W., Jhamat, N., Arshad, Z., & Rana, F. A. (2025). Blockchain-based governance models in e-government: A comprehensive framework for legal, technical, ethical and security considerations. *International Journal of Law and Management, 67*(1), 37–55. DOI: 10.1108/IJLMA-08-2023-0172

Nasir, M. H., Arshad, J., Khan, M. M., Fatima, M., Salah, K., & Jayaraman, R. (2022). Scalable blockchains — A systematic review. *Future Generation Computer Systems, 126*, 136–162. DOI: 10.1016/j.future.2021.07.035

Pajooh, H. H., Rashid, M., Alam, F., & Demidenko, S. (2021). Multi-layer blockchain-based security architecture for internet of things. *Sensors (Switzerland), 21*(3), 1–26. DOI: 10.3390/s21030772

Rifat Hossain, M., Nirob, F. A., Islam, A., Rakin, T. M., & Al-Amin, M. (2024). A Comprehensive Analysis of Blockchain Technology and Consensus Protocols Across Multilayered Framework. *IEEE Access : Practical Innovations, Open Solutions, 12*, 63087–63129. DOI: 10.1109/ACCESS.2024.3395536

Saidu, Y., Shuhaida, M. S., Dahiru, A. A., Yau, S., Muhammad, M. Y., & Babando, A. A. (2024). Charting the Course : A Bibliometric Exploration of Blockchain Traceability Systems. *International Conference on Technological Solutions for Smart Economy*, 1–8. https://library.ncs.org.ng/download/charting-the-course-a-bibliometric-exploration-of-blockchain-traceability-systems/

Saidu, Y., Shuhidan, S. M., Aliyu, D. A., Aziz, I. A., & Adamu, S. (2025). Convergence of Blockchain, IoT, and AI for Enhanced Traceability Systems: A Comprehensive Review. *IEEE Access : Practical Innovations, Open Solutions, 13*, 16838–16865. DOI: 10.1109/ACCESS.2025.3528035

Saidu, Y., Shuhidan, S. M., Aziz, I. A., Adamu, D. A., Yau, S., & Adamu, S. (2025). A Bibliometric Analysis on Blockchain Consensus Algorithms: Unveiling Trends, Contributors, and Intellectual Structures. In M. Hisham, H. Mohd Hilmi, A. Said Jadid, & S. Nasir (Eds.), *Proceedings of the International Conference on Smart Cities* - Volume 2 *ICSC 2024, September 10-11, Kota Kinabalu, Malaysia* (pp. 579–593). Springer Singapore. https://doi.org/DOI: 10.1007/978-981-96-5848-0_47

Saidu, Y., Shuhidan, S. M., Aziz, I. A., Alam, M. M., Aliyu, D. A., Yakubu, M. M., & Adamu, S. (2025). Exploring Blockchain–IoT Convergence for Logistics Traceability: A Systematic Review and Future Outlook. *IEEE Access : Practical Innovations, Open Solutions*, *13*, 112390–112416. DOI: 10.1109/ACCESS.2025.3583927

Subashini, B., & Hemavathi, D. (2023). Scalable Blockchain Technology for Tracking the Provenance of the Agri-Food. *Computers, Materials & Continua*, *75*(2), 3339–3358. DOI: 10.32604/cmc.2023.035074

Szabo, J., Bernard, C., & Philip, L. (2024). Legal Implications and Challenges of Blockchain Technology and Smart Contracts. *Computer Life*, *12*(2), 6–10. DOI: 10.54097/ztn2w848

Tan, E., Lerouge, E., Du Caju, J., & Du Seuil, D. (2023). Verification of Education Credentials on European Blockchain Services Infrastructure (EBSI): Action Research in a Cross-Border Use Case between Belgium and Italy. *Big Data and Cognitive Computing*, *7*(2), 79. DOI: 10.3390/bdcc7020079

Tan, E., Mahula, S., & Crompvoets, J. (2022). Blockchain governance in the public sector: A conceptual framework for public management. *Government Information Quarterly*, *39*(1), 101625. DOI: 10.1016/j.giq.2021.101625

Trevisan, A. H., Lobo, A., Guzzo, D., Gomes, L. A. de V., & Mascarenhas, J. (2023). Barriers to employing digital technologies for a circular economy: A multi-level perspective. *Journal of Environmental Management*, *332*, 117437. DOI: 10.1016/j.jenvman.2023.117437 PMID: 36801533

Truong, N. B., Sun, K., Lee, G. M., & Guo, Y. (2020). GDPR-Compliant Personal Data Management: A Blockchain-Based Solution. *IEEE Transactions on Information Forensics and Security*, *15*, 1746–1761. DOI: 10.1109/TIFS.2019.2948287

Tyagi, A. K., Kumari, S., & Surve, T. (2024). Integration of Digital Twin and Blockchain for Smart Cities. In *Digital Twin and Blockchain for Smart Cities* (pp. 81–100). Wiley., DOI: 10.1002/9781394303564.ch5

Wang, S., Ouyang, L., Yuan, Y., Ni, X., Han, X., & Wang, F. Y. (2019). Blockchain-Enabled Smart Contracts: Architecture, Applications, and Future Trends. *IEEE Transactions on Systems, Man, and Cybernetics. Systems*, *49*(11), 2266–2277. DOI: 10.1109/TSMC.2019.2895123

Xia, M., Xie, Z., Lin, H., & He, X. (2022). Synergistic Mechanism of the High-Quality Development of the Urban Digital Economy from Blockchain Adoption Perspective—A Configuration Approach. *Journal of Theoretical and Applied Electronic Commerce Research*, *17*(2), 704–721. DOI: 10.3390/jtaer17020037

Xu, Y., Chong, H. Y., & Chi, M. (2021). A Review of Smart Contracts Applications in Various Industries: A Procurement Perspective. *Advances in Civil Engineering, 2021*(1). https://doi.org/DOI: 10.1155/2021/5530755

Yakubu, M. M., Hassan, M. F. B., Danyaro, K. U., Junejo, A. Z., Siraj, M., Yahaya, S., Adamu, S., & Abdulsalam, K. (2024). A Systematic Literature Review on Blockchain Consensus Mechanisms' Security: Applications and Open Challenges. *Computer Systems Science and Engineering*, *48*(6), 1437–1481. DOI: 10.32604/csse.2024.054556

Yan, Z., Zhao, X., & Liu, Y. (Alison), & Luo, X. (Robert). (2024). Blockchain-driven decentralized identity management: An interdisciplinary review and research agenda. *Information & Management*, *61*(7), 104026. DOI: 10.1016/j.im.2024.104026

Yang, Z., Alfauri, H., Farkiani, B., Jain, R., Di Pietro, R., & Erbad, A. (2024). A Survey and Comparison of Post-Quantum and Quantum Blockchains. *IEEE Communications Surveys and Tutorials*, *26*(2), 967–1002. DOI: 10.1109/COMST.2023.3325761

Yau, S., Aliyu, A., Saidu, Y., Ibrahim, A., & Aliyu, F. M. (2024). Prospect of Smart Agriculture Using IoT and Data Analytics: A Perspective of Kebbi State, North-western Nigeria. *International Journal of Advanced Networking and Applications*, *15*(06), 6194–6203. DOI: 10.35444/ijana.2024.15606

Zhao, W., Aldyaflah, I. M., Gangwani, P., Joshi, S., Upadhyay, H., & Lagos, L. (2023). A Blockchain-Facilitated Secure Sensing Data Processing and Logging System. *IEEE Access : Practical Innovations, Open Solutions*, *11*, 21712–21728. DOI: 10.1109/ACCESS.2023.3252030

Chapter 4
Cyberattacks:
Blockchain Beyond Cryptocurrency – A Decentralized Approach to Urban Security

Syed Hassan Imam Gardezi
https://orcid.org/0009-0006-6171-1238
Union Investments LLC, UAE

Syed Muqthadar Ali
https://orcid.org/0009-0007-0111-4092
CVR College of Engineering, India

Swaroop Mohanty
https://orcid.org/0000-0002-0294-8140
ACCFK, Amity University, Kolkata, India

F. Shabina Fred Rishma
Vel Tech Rangarajan Dr. Sagunthala R&D Institute of Science and Technology, India

V. Bharathi
Vel Tech Rangarajan Dr. Sagunthala R&D Institute of Science and Technology, India

P. Selvakumar
https://orcid.org/0000-0002-3650-4548
Department of Science and Humanities, Nehru Institute of Technology, Coimbatore, India

T. C. Manjunath
https://orcid.org/0000-0003-2545-9160
Rajarajeswari College of Engineering, India

ABSTRACT

Introduced in 2008 by the pseudonymous Satoshi Nakamoto, it was designed for recording. While its initial application was limited to digital currency, its potential quickly transcended the confines of cryptocurrency, sparking the interest of industries government. The promise lies in core principles: decentralization, transparency, security, and immutability. These qualities are not only desirable for digital currencies but also offer revolutionary solutions to a variety of real-world challenges. As

DOI: 10.4018/979-8-3373-4455-3.ch004

such, it is a mere cryptocurrency capable of paradigms for innovation. In healthcare, blockchain holds promise as a tool for securely managing medical records. Patients' health data is often scattered in healthcare fragmented, inefficient healthcare system. Blockchain could offer a solution for unified medical records that is both secure and accessible. Through blockchain, patients could control who accesses their health information, ensuring privacy while enabling doctors and specialists to complete, medical history.

THE EVOLUTION OF BLOCKCHAIN

Introduced in 2008 by the pseudonymous Satoshi Nakamoto, it was designed for recording. While its initial application was limited to digital currency, its potential quickly transcended the confines of cryptocurrency, sparking the interest of industries government. The promise lies in core principles: decentralization, transparency, security, and immutability. These qualities are not only desirable for digital currencies but also offer revolutionary solutions to a variety of real-world challenges. As such, it is a mere cryptocurrency capable of paradigms for innovation. In healthcare, blockchain holds promise as a tool for securely managing medical records. Patients' health data is often scattered in healthcare fragmented, inefficient healthcare system. Blockchain could offer a solution for unified medical records that is both secure and accessible. Through blockchain, patients could control who accesses their health information, ensuring privacy while enabling doctors and specialists to complete, medical history. Additionally, efficient security clinical trials by research data, preventing tampering or falsification. In this way, blockchain streamlines administrative processes, safeguards sensitive medical information. Transform extends to governance and public services as well. Many governments' voting systems, land registries, and governments can reduce fraud and provide citizens with more their case voting, based elections could enable more secure, transparent elections by preventing tampering with verifiable by all parties involved. Additionally, blockchain can be used to combat corruption and ensure accountability in government transactions. Citizens can hold public officials and agencies accountable for their actions. Moreover, control-removal opens types are not dependent on central authorities or corporations.

These applications can operate on decentralized networks, powered by blockchain, offering users digital interactions. They are reshaping by providing access to loans, insurance, and investment opportunities without relying on centralized banks or financial institutions. Similarly, blockchain-based social media platform users have more content, privacy, potentially addressing concerns about censorship and data misuse by major tech companies. The adoption of blockchain also brings significant improvements to cybersecurity systems, often because they store critical information in a single location, making them prime targets for hackers. In contrast, far more compromise. Breach the alter information. Additionally, cryptographic techniques used ensure is resistant to tampering. Heightened is a key reason why blockchain is being explored for applications in digital identity verification, secure data sharing, and protecting intellectual property. Scalability is one of the most significant barriers, as the technology's current infrastructure can quickly and efficiently scale. While Bitcoin and Ethereum, the two most prominent blockchains, have been subject to network congestion and high transaction fees, new blockchain platforms and protocols are emerging that aim to address these issues. Innovations such as sharding, off-chain solutions, and proof-of-stake consensus mechanisms are all being explored to improve scalability and energy efficiency and become practical and mainstream. Since often falls outside the purview of regulatory frameworks based especially in the context of cryptocurrency.

Urban Security Challenges: The Need for Innovative Solutions

As the world's urban populations continue to grow, cities face an increasing array of complex security challenges. Urban security encompasses a broad range of issues, from crime and violence to terrorism, natural disasters, and cyber threats. The sheer scale and complexity of urban environments exacerbate these risks, requiring innovative solutions that can adapt to the unique dynamics of city life. To ensure the safety, stability, and resilience of urban spaces, it is essential to address these challenges through comprehensive, forward-thinking strategies that integrate technology, policy, and community involvement. The need for innovative solutions to urban security has never been more urgent as cities strive to balance growth and modernization with safety and security. Rising Crime and Violence: One of the most immediate and visible challenges to urban security is the rise in crime and violence (Moch N., et al, 2024). As cities grow and become more densely populated, areas of poverty, social inequality, and lack of access to education and employment opportunities often emerge. These factors contribute to an environment where crime can thrive, with both petty crimes, such as theft and vandalism, and more serious offenses, including gang violence, organized crime, and homicides, becoming prevalent in certain urban districts. In cities with high rates of poverty, marginalized communities are often left vulnerable to exploitation and criminal activity, further perpetuating cycles of violence and insecurity. Gang violence and organized crime are particularly concerning in many urban areas, where criminal groups often control neighborhoods, engage in illicit activities, and exert influence over local populations. This not only undermines public safety but also strains the resources of law enforcement agencies, which are often ill-equipped to tackle such pervasive and deeply rooted criminal organizations (Khaliji M A., et al, 2024). Additionally, the rise of gun violence, particularly in certain urban centers, presents another major challenge, with firearms often contributing to the escalation of violent confrontations. To combat urban crime and violence, cities need to employ innovative, data-driven approaches that integrate technology, community policing, and crime prevention programs. Additionally, community-based policing models, which involve close collaboration between law enforcement and local communities, have proven to be effective in reducing crime and building trust between residents and the police. Programs that focus on social interventions, such as providing education, vocational training, and employment opportunities to at-risk youth, can also help to address the root causes of crime.

Terrorism and Extremist Threats: Terrorism and extremist violence represent a growing concern in urban security, particularly in cities that are cultural, political, or economic hubs. The urban environment provides terrorists with both strategic opportunities and challenges. Major cities, with their large populations and critical infrastructure, are often seen as high-value targets for terrorists seeking to cause mass disruption, garner media attention, and inspire fear (Ahmad K., et al, 2022). Urban areas, particularly those in politically unstable regions or those that are economically or socially polarized, can be vulnerable to attacks by extremist groups, both local and transnational. These attacks can take various forms, including bombings, shootings, and cyberattacks, and often target symbols of state power, commercial centers, or crowded public spaces to maximize casualties and chaos. The complexity of urban environments makes it difficult to predict and prevent these attacks. Dense populations, open public spaces, and critical infrastructure, such as transportation networks and energy grids, all present opportunities for attackers to strike. Furthermore, the urban landscape often provides numerous opportunities for terrorists to blend into the general population, making it difficult for security forces to identify and neutralize threats before they materialize. The proliferation of online extremist ideologies and recruitment networks also complicates efforts to combat terrorism in urban areas. Combating terrorism in urban areas requires a multifaceted approach that incorporates intelligence gathering, counterterrorism operations, and community engagement. Public-private partnerships are critical in ensuring that infrastructure and public spaces are protected, and the sharing of intelligence between local, national, and international agencies is essential for identifying and disrupting terrorist networks (Paiva S., et al, 2021). Additionally, addressing the underlying factors that contribute to extremism, such as poverty, social alienation, and political disenfranchisement, can help reduce the pool of potential recruits for extremist groups. Counter-radicalization programs that focus on community resilience and engagement are essential in preventing the spread of extremist ideologies. Cybersecurity Threats: As cities become more technologically connected, they are increasingly vulnerable to cyberattacks, which can undermine the security of critical urban infrastructure. Urban areas are dependent on a vast network of digital systems and technologies to operate, including smart grids, public transportation systems, healthcare networks, and law enforcement databases. These systems are susceptible cyber from attacks to hacking attempts aimed at disrupting services or stealing sensitive information. For instance, a cyberattack on a city's transportation system could cause widespread chaos, while an attack on a hospital's network could compromise patient care (Mahadev Madgule et al. 2023). Moreover, urban environments have expanded the attack surface for cybercriminals. Smart homes, connected vehicles, and surveillance systems are all potential entry points for cyberattacks. The integration of these systems into daily urban life creates new vulnerabilities that require innovative cybersecurity solutions. Cities must invest in robust cyber defenses to protect their digital infrastructure, while also developing contingency plans for responding to potential cyber incidents. Innovative cybersecurity solutions are necessary to protect urban infrastructures from cyber threats. These solutions include the use of AI cyberattacks as well as the implementation of data. Additionally, cities need cybersecurity with public-private partnerships that involve collaboration between local authorities, tech companies, and residents to ensure the security of urban digital systems.

Blockchain for Security: A Decentralized Approach

Blockchain technology, once primarily rapidly versatile and transformative significant for enhancing security. Its fundamental appeal nature to validate transactions. Blockchain ledger copies of the same records, ensuring transparency, immutability, and resilience against tampering or fraud. This decentralized structure inherently makes blockchain an attractive solution for addressing concerns, privacy, digital identity management, fraud prevention secure communications. Blockchain's unique features present a promising approach to building more secure and resilient systems in a world increasingly dominated by digital interactions (Saleh A M S., 2024). Revolutionizing Digital Identity Management: As individuals increasingly rely on online platforms for personal, financial, and professional interactions, identity verification has never been more important. Traditional identity management systems, passwords, security, identity theft, and phishing. In contrast, offers alternative control and management through decentralized systems. Digital identities are created and, when they are linked to a person's private key. This means that individuals can verify their identity without relying on centralized institutions, such as banks or government agencies, to authenticate their credentials. Because blockchain is irreversible, it provides security and accountability difficult to achieve with traditional identity management systems (Athanere S., et al, 2022). Moreover, blockchain enables users to selectively share specific pieces of their identity, rather than exposing all of thus minimizing. This approach to digital identity management has banking, healthcare, e-commerce travel that could seamlessly secure online banking transactions, security services. Similarly, in the healthcare sector, patients could share only relevant information as needed. In the travel industry, blockchain-based digital identities could streamline the check-in process and improve security by allowing individuals to use their verified identities for airport security, hotel check-ins, and other services.

Fighting Fraud and Counterfeit Products: Blockchain also offers a powerful solution for combating fraud and the proliferation of which challenge luxury goods, food safety, products damage the reputation of brands, but also put consumers at risk. Blockchain's ability to provide allows consumers and businesses and sell transportation, sale. Each transaction related to a product on the provenance of raw materials and finished products, so that counterfeit or substandard items are identified and removed from the market, so that they are not diverted, diluted, or counterfeited. Similarly, provide transparency regarding sourcing and handling products, helping to prevent food fraud and contamination, consumers improve reliable supply chains in businesses and products (Abu-Dabaseh F., et al, 2024). Protecting Against Cyberattacks: As cyberattacks become more frequent and sophisticated, organizations and governments are increasingly turning to blockchain as a way to enhance their cybersecurity posture. Cybersecurity resistance which designed to overwhelm the centralized server with traffic and render it inoperable. Because blockchain is decentralized, it is less vulnerable to these types of attacks, as there is no central server to target. Instead, the blockchain's attacked. Moreover, blockchain communications and data encryption protocols transmit financial transaction communications over the internet. Because blockchain transactions are immutable and verifiable, they pose a difficult challenge to encryption methods. Additionally, blockchain cybersecurity tools (Shahzad A., et al, 2025). Enabling Secure and Transparent Voting Systems: Promising Applications Technology Realm of security Secure, transparent voting Electoral fraud, voter suppression, and manipulation have long been major concerns in democratic processes, and traditional voting security, accessibility, Blockchain, decentralized, and each vote cast, the voting process. Once a vote is cast, it becomes part of the public results without detection. Election verifiable, while also providing transparency and accountability. Furthermore, blockchain-based voting systems could prevent voter fraud, as each voter's identity and eligibility could be verified through a blockchain-based digital identity, preventing duplicate voting or impersonation.

Blockchain-Based Cybersecurity: Principles and Applications

world of cybersecurity, novel the growing threat posed by cyber threats. Initially conceived as foundational has expanded, particularly in its application to cybersecurity, decentralized, “blocks” cryptographically linked. This structure ensures data is added to and tampered with, altered across, and combined with transparency and decentralization, providing powerful security advantages that are particularly useful in combating the increasingly sophisticated and diverse range of cyberattacks facing individuals, organizations, and governments today. Blockchain's unique principles—decentralization, transparency, cryptography, and immutability—form the foundation for its security applications (Gimenez-Aguilar M., et al, 2021). These attributes, often collectively referred to as the “security trifecta,” serve as the bedrock for blockchain’s ability to enhance cybersecurity. Which authority is highly vulnerable to cyberattacks? Whether it’s a data breach, particularly prone to spreading, reducing the risk of data being compromised in one location. Moreover, because blockchain transactions are validated by consensus mechanisms and secured through cryptography, it becomes exceedingly difficult for malicious actors to tamper with them. The Core strengths of cybersecurity can be better understood by examining the various applications and principles that enable it to address contemporary security challenges. Decentralization and Distributed Security: primarily In all processing power is limited number of centralized servers. Structure creates that the servers are attacked; the entire system can be brought down (Razaque A., et al, 2021). Blockchain eliminates this risk by distributing data across independent nodes. Each blockchain entire participant system. Even if more nodes are blockchain majority, of would still be functional and capable of verifying the data. In terms of cybersecurity, decentralization prevents cybercriminals from gaining control of sensitive data stored on centralized servers. For instance, in cloud computing, which relies heavily on centralized data storage, a cyberattack targeting the server could expose large amounts of personal and corporate data. Blockchain’s decentralized structure reduces the attack surface by distributing this information locations, hackers to access.

Figure 1. Role of Blockchain Technology in Cybersecurity

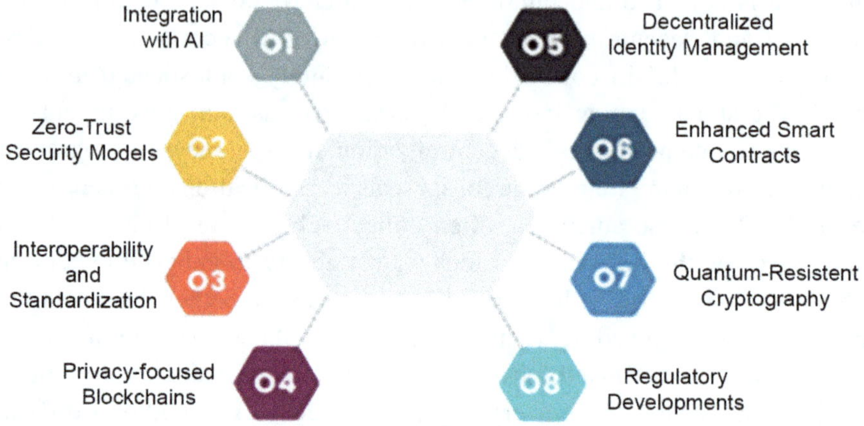

Immutability and Tamper-Proof Data: Immutability is another foundational principle of blockchain that significantly enhances cybersecurity is nearly impossible due to the nature of a unique code. This cryptographic linkage ensures that the entire chain remains unbroken and unaltered. If an attacker were to attempt to modify any information, they need the affected party to require control over makes tampering with blockchain data computationally infeasible, even for highly sophisticated attackers. For cybersecurity, this property is incredibly useful in scenarios where the integrity of data is critical. For example, in financial transactions, it is essential that records cannot be altered once they have been validated (Bhardwaj T., et al, 2022). Blockchain's immutability provides this guarantee, preventing fraud or tampering case ensuring that counterfeit products or substandard items cannot enter the system without detection. Immutability also extends to logging and auditing, particularly where regulations require maintaining accurate, unaltered records. Using blockchain to store these records ensures that audit trails are both secure and HIPAA, Sarbanes-Oxley compliant. Transparency and Traceability: especially valuable for monitoring cyber activities. In cybersecurity, traceability of source and attack or breach transactions or actions can be tracked and audited, providing an immutable trail of who did what, when, and where. Whether beneficial or a cyberattack, professionals trace the origin of the attack and identify affected systems, helping to mitigate damage and recover quickly. Moreover, blockchain's transparency helps prevent unauthorized access. For example, if an entity gains unauthorized access to a blockchain, their actions immediately make it easier for breaches (Alajlan R., et al, 2023). This level of transparency can also help organizations improve their internal security practices by ensuring that all activities are subject to scrutiny. Blockchain for Identity and Access Management: Digital identity management, cybersecurity, particularly online services and transactions, are ubiquitous. Traditional systems are prone to theft, fraud, and mismanagement. Offers a more secure and efficient alternative by providing decentralized and self-sovereign identities. In identity and data associated with it, reducing the need for centralized identity providers. Blockchain's application to identity and access management (IAM) eliminates vulnerabilities in IAM. With blockchain, individuals can create and control a digital identity that is verified through cryptographic signatures. This identity can be used across multiple platforms without relying on third parties to verify it. Since blockchain identities are cryptographically secured and decentralized, they are far more resistant to identity theft, fraud, or data breaches (Vijayakumar G, et al. 2024). Blockchain and Secure Transactions: /One of its most well-known applications, cryptocurrency potential currency. Blockchain provides any form of digital transaction, from transferring money and data to executing business contracts. By using blockchain to record transactions, organizations can reduce the risks associated with fraud, unauthorized transactions, or third-party intermediaries. In the realm of cybersecurity, secure transactions are vital.

Decentralized Networks: Resisting Cyberattacks

The rise of decentralized networks has marked a paradigm shift in how digital systems and infrastructures are designed, maintained, and protected from cyber threats. As the frequency and sophistication of cyberattacks continue to escalate, data single-location entities have become increasingly vulnerable to disruption, manipulation, and compromise. Cybercriminals often exploit these centralized systems by targeting single points of failure, allowing them to access sensitive information, disrupt operations, and even launch wide-scale attacks. By removing central points of vulnerability and spreading data across a network of interconnected systems, decentralized networks offer a compelling alternative to traditional models and present a new approach to cybersecurity (Sugumaran K M D., et al. 2024). Decentralized networks rely on a distributed architecture, where node entity is maintained and validated by numerous participants, each contributing to the overall functioning of the system. This approach is critical, particularly when it comes to resisting cyberattacks. Decentralization inherently increases the resilience and robustness of the network by eliminating the central points of failure that hackers often exploit. To understand how decentralized networks help resist cyberattacks, it is important to explore the key components that make them more secure and resilient. These components include data redundancy, distributed control, consensus mechanisms, cryptography, and the overall architecture of decentralized systems. Redundancy and Distribution: One of the foundational principles of decentralized networks is the concept of redundancy typically one or in small number of servers, meaning that if a hacker gains access to that central location, they can potentially decentralized networks distribute wide array independent contains data, network's overall functionality does not rely on any single node (Liang X., et al, 2023). This distribution of data means that cybercriminals face a far greater challenge in compromising a decentralized system. Instead of targeting a single server or database, attackers must overcome the distributed infrastructure, which requires gaining control over a significant portion successful attacker would still have to alter or destroy multiple copies of the data on other nodes to make a meaningful impact. This redundancy not only prevents attacks from taking down the entire system but also much without being detected.

Distributed Control and Governance: Another crucial aspect of decentralized networks is the distribution of control and decision-making authority across multiple participants who are responsible for controlling and managing the entire system. This centralization creates an easier network if they gain access to the central control system. For instance, a successful attack on a central server could give cybercriminals control over the entire system, allowing them to manipulate data, disrupt services, or steal sensitive information (Wu Y., et al, 2022). In contrast, decentralized networks are governed by a distributed system of nodes, each of which has operational This control is typically shared among many participants, often through no single entity can unilaterally dictate the direction of the network. This distributed control enables systems, manipulate or compromise participants to achieve their objectives. For example, in blockchain networks, such as Bitcoin or Ethereum, decisions about the network's operation and validation of transactions are made through a decentralized consensus mechanism (Guha Roy D., et al, 2021). This prevents any one participant from having full control over the network, reducing the likelihood that an attacker could manipulate the system. Furthermore, decentralized governance structures allow for greater transparency, as the rules of the network are often codified in the protocol and open to scrutiny by all participants. This collective oversight helps to prevent malicious activity and fosters trust among participants. Consensus Mechanisms and Validation: These mechanisms prevent fraud, double-spending, and other malicious activities from occurring in made network. By utilizing consensus, decentralized networks ensure participants do not alter data or take malicious actions without detection (Anakhov P., et al, 2023). By a decentralized design to achieve different security and efficiency goals. The most widely known consensus mechanisms, but others, are also securing. These mechanisms provide a secure way to validate transactions, preventing cybercriminals from altering records or taking control of the network. For example, participants' cryptographic block. Once the majority of miners validate the solution, the new block consensus process data is recorded in is legitimate and trustworthy.

Smart Contracts: Automating Security Protocols

Modern cybersecurity represents a revolutionary technological advancement, enabling automated security protocols, greater efficiency, and enhanced trust between parties. Part of blockchain underpinning Ethereum, without human intervention or third-party verification, risks fraud, which often arises in traditional contractual agreements. While smart contracts have gained prominence in the cryptocurrency space, their potential extends far beyond digital currency transactions (Rameder H., et al, 2022). They are critical to automating the securing of various processes, including authentication, access control, data integrity, and identity verification. By leveraging their security improve overall system integrity. With their decentralized nature and cryptographic security, smart contracts can also ensure that automated security protocols remain tamper-proof and transparent, making them some of the most persistent cybersecurity tools. Understanding Smart Contracts and Their Components: At their core, computer scripts executed A nodes once entered, it is verifiable (Hamledari H., et al, 2021). Smart contracts leverage this underlying technology to operate decentralized manner. Smart contracts consist of several key components: Conditions and Logic: These are the rules embedded within the contract that define what will trigger an action. For example, a contract might specify that "if party A pays party B 100 units of currency, then party B will transfer ownership of a digital asset to party A." The conditions are usually for Ethereum, and are once specified. Decentralization: Because smart contracts run on decentralized blockchains, they enforce the terms. The blockchain network itself ensures that the contract is executed according to the predefined rules, reducing the risk of manipulation by any single party (Perez A J., et al, 2022). These components, when combined, form self-enforcing agreements that automate complex workflows in cybersecurity. Role of Smart Contracts in Automating Security Protocols: Traditional security systems require manual intervention, human oversight, all of which introduce delay, tampering. Smart contracts, by contrast, offer a decentralized, automated solution that consistently applies security protocols are consistently applied without human intervention. Enhancing Authentication: Traditional authentication systems often rely on passwords, PINs, or other forms of knowledge-based authentication, which are prone to theft, phishing attacks, and brute-force attempts. Smart contracts can provide a more secure alternative by integrating blockchain-based identity management systems and cryptographic authentication methods (Babel K., et al, 2023). Instead of relying on passwords or PINs, a user would authenticate themselves by signing.

Secure Data Sharing: Blockchain for Urban Infrastructure

The transformation of urban infrastructure in the digital age has introduced significant opportunities for enhanced efficiency, connectivity. Interconnected, efficient systems for sharing become paramount. Urban infrastructure systems—ranging from transportation networks and energy grids to water management and healthcare systems- are sensitive to daily changes. This is crucial for the functioning of these systems. However, coupled with critical infrastructure, calls for robust mechanisms for its privacy. Technology powerful tool for secure sharing of urban infrastructure leveraging a transparent, immutable blockchain paradigm, managing and sharing across (Fu Y., et al, 2021). In contrast to traditional centralized systems, which are often attacked, distributed systems ensure that they are protected against access, tampering, and corruption. This capability of urban infrastructure, where manipulation, loss could have serious consequences, affecting everything from public safety to the economy. Blockchain's application in secure data sharing for urban infrastructure can be explored in several key areas, including data integrity, access control, interoperability, transparency, and privacy. Factors crucial to data sharing remain efficient while also enabling collaboration across different entities involved in urban infrastructure management. Data Integrity and Immutability: One of the fundamental benefits of using urban infrastructure is its ability to guarantee data integrity, each piece represented as a "block" block, an immutable entity on the blockchain, deleted, tampered with, altering all subsequent immutability shared across the network, verifiable, accurate, and reliable (Cha J., et al, 2021). For example, in smart cities, sensor networks continuously generate data related to light systems, energy waste, or monitor pollution levels. If this data is tampered with—either accidentally or maliciously—it could lead to incorrect decisions, such as inefficient traffic routing or misguided environmental policies. Immutable audit trail means that stakeholders can history of any piece of offering further verification and accountability. For example, in the case of a water treatment facility, blockchain could track the data from sensors measuring water quality, ensuring that every measurement is recorded and its source.

Decentralized Control and Reduced Vulnerability: For urban infrastructure systems, which involve multiple stakeholders (e.g., city governments, utility companies, private contractors), significantly data breaches hacker to alter or corrupt the data, which is computationally infeasible in most large-scale blockchain networks securing critical infrastructure electricity grid monitoring, water management, or public safety systems, where downtime or data manipulation could have catastrophic consequences (Alnahari M S., et al, 2022). Additionally, blockchain's decentralized nature allows for shared control over data. Rather than relying on a central authority to manage access, multiple participants can validate and manage data, ensuring that all stakeholders have an equal say in how data is shared and used. This collaborative approach allows parties who may have competing interests but need to share data for the greater good. Interoperability and Data Sharing Across Multiple Platforms: Urban infrastructure systems are often complex, with data generated and managed across multiple platforms and by various stakeholders (Far A Z., et al, 2024). For example, transportation systems, energy grids, and public safety networks may all collect different types of data that need to be shared in real time. However, many of these systems operate in silos, using incompatible technologies and protocols, making data sharing between them difficult between platforms standardized framework sharing. Since blockchain operates as a distributed ledger, it can integrate data from various sources into a single, secure record, sharing different urban infrastructure systems, without the need for expensive, complex integration projects. For instance, data from sensors on traffic lights could be integrated with data from public transportation systems, enabling real-time traffic management and improving the efficiency of urban mobility (Sameer Babu M., et al. 2025). Similarly, energy usage data from smart meters could be shared with utility companies to optimize energy distribution, reduce waste, and enable predictive maintenance. Blockchain's interoperability also enables collaboration between public and private entities.

Identity Verification: Blockchain-Based Solutions

One of the most critical and complex issues facing individuals, businesses, and governments alike is reliable, verifying identity verification, as traditional systems of identity management, such as government-issued ID cards, passports, and social security numbers, are increasingly vulnerable to fraud, data breaches, and identity theft. As digital services, online transactions, and interactions continue to expand, so too does personal information. For this reason, finding a solution to ensure that people are who they claim to be in digital spaces has never been more urgent (Subramanian M., et al. 2025). Cryptography has emerged as a powerful tool in transforming identity verification processes. Blockchain-based identity verification offers a fundamentally different approach to traditional centralized identity systems. In a typical centralized system, an individual's identity is stored and managed by the agency or an online service provider. These centralized databases are often prime targets for cybercriminals, and breaches theft personal data. Furthermore, individuals typically have few identity providers to authenticate their identity and verify their credentials (Ahmed M R., et al, 2022). Blockchain-based identity systems, however, aim to decentralize the process of identity verification, putting individuals in control of their identity data while verification process verifiable. The Limitations of Traditional Identity Verification: ID cards, social security numbers, and passwords have significant drawbacks that make fraud. Centralized systems, in which identity is single, are particularly. Once a system can potentially steal personal information of millions of individuals, leading to financial loss, reputational damage, and long-term consequences for both individuals and organizations. Additionally, these centralized third-party authentication systems verify identities, which have several points of failure (Shuaib M., et al, 2022). For example, when an individual applies for a loan or opens a bank account, the financial institution may rely on external credit bureaus or identity verification services to validate the person's identity to which process that increases the chances of errors or delays. Another significant issue with traditional identity systems is the lack of privacy.

Lastly, traditional identity verification methods often suffer from a lack of interoperability. Different organizations may use different systems and standards for identity verification, making it difficult to establish a universal system that can be used across industries, countries, and platforms. This lack of standardization results in inefficiencies, delays, and barriers to access. How Blockchain-Based Identity Verification Works: typically involves several steps: Issuance of Digital Credentials: A trusted authority, such as a government agency, bank, or educational institution, issues a digital credential to an individual. This credential contains an identity or professional qualifications credential that is cryptographically signed by the issuer, ensuring its authenticity (Seyam H., et al, 2023). Creation of Digital Identity: The individual's digital identity is created by storing the cryptographic hash of the credential on the blockchain. The hash is a unique identifier of the data, which allows the individual to prove that their identity data exists and has not been tampered with. Authentication: When the individual needs to verify their identity, for example, when opening a bank account or accessing a government service, they can provide proof of their identity by sharing a subset of their digital credential. This proof typically involves using their private key to sign a message, which individual's The blockchain that the blockchain is authentic and that the data has not been altered. Verification: The recipient, whether it's a bank, government agency, or service provider the digital credential signature the ensure that the cryptographic hash matches the original data. Since the blockchain is decentralized and immutable, the recipient can trust that the identity data has not been tampered with. Revocation and Updates: If the individual's identity information needs to be updated or revoked (for example, if they change their address or name), the relevant issuer can make updates to the blockchain, which will automatically propagate the individual's identity remains up to date and secure (Gao S., et al, 2021). Challenges and Considerations: Despite the promising advantages, blockchain-based identity verification also faces regulatory frameworks, technical barriers to adoption, privacy concerns, and solutions in governments and exploring identity systems.

Critical Infrastructure Protection: Blockchain's Role

Critical infrastructure, encompassing systems and assets vital to the functioning of a society, energy supplies, financial systems, and communication systems, forms the backbone of modern civilization. These systems enable the smooth operation of daily life and are essential to economic stability, national security, and public health. However, increasingly critical infrastructure is facing unprecedented levels of vulnerability to cyberattacks, natural disasters, and system failures. Protecting these assets from disruptions is not only a matter of operational integrity but also one of national and global security. In this context, emerging tool protection of critical infrastructure is immutable, holds immense strength in the security, resilience, and efficiency of these essential systems (Wani S., et al, 2021). The Threat Landscape for Critical Infrastructure: Traditional methods of protecting these systems often rely on centralized control and protection mechanisms, which inherently create vulnerabilities. Cybersecurity threats are perhaps the most pressing challenge for critical infrastructure, as cyberattacks can target any aspect of these systems, from communication to cloud-based infrastructure. Cyberattacks on critical infrastructure are becoming more sophisticated and persistent, with threat actors ranging from state-sponsored groups to cybercriminal organizations. The consequences of these attacks can be devastating. Similarly, attacks on water treatment plants or food supply chains can have dire health and economic implications (Ahmed et al., 2022). The 2007 cyberattack on Estonia, which disrupted government, financial, and media services, is an example of the type of damage that can be done when critical infrastructure is compromised.

In addition to cyber threats, natural disasters, human errors, and system failures further highlight the vulnerability of critical infrastructure. Hurricanes, earthquakes, and floods can cause massive disruptions to energy, communication, and transportation systems, making it difficult to maintain continuity of service. While many critical infrastructure systems are designed with redundancy and backup measures in place, the interconnectedness of modern systems often means that areas across other sectors are robust, secure, and respond to these sectors have never been more urgent (Pelluru K., 2021). Applications of Blockchain in Critical Infrastructure Protection: potential for safeguarding critical infrastructure spans various sectors, from energy grids and transportation systems to healthcare and financial services. Several use cases illustrate security, these sectors: Energy Grids and Smart Cities, most prominent being critical infrastructure protection management of energy grids. Traditional power grids are vulnerable to cyberattacks that can manipulate grid operations, disrupt power distribution, and cause widespread outages. Blockchain can secure energy grid data by providing an immutable, decentralized grid for electricity generation, distribution, and consumption. This enhances transparency and ensures that all parties involved—power providers, regulators, and consumers—can verify the integrity of the system (Jimmy F., 2024). Water and Wastewater Management: These critical services are often vulnerable to cyberattacks that can manipulate water quality data or disrupt treatment processes. By integrating blockchain with sensors and IoT devices monitoring water quality, flow rates, and infrastructure health, organizations ensure, all relevant data is secure and that water management systems remain transparent, verifiable, and resistant to tampering. Moreover, blockchain can be used to automate and streamline the management of water resources, improving efficiency and minimizing waste. Transportation and Supply Chain Security: Transportation networks, including roadways, railways, and air travel, are also vital components of critical infrastructure (Shende A D., et al. 2025). The communication between vehicles, infrastructure, and operators ensures that data shared between these systems cannot be intercepted or manipulated. In the case of autonomous vehicles, for example, blockchain can help ensure that control commands and safety data are transmitted securely and accurately.

Decentralized Data Storage: Enhancing Security

Has become one of the most valuable assets in our modern society. From personal information and financial records to intellectual property and governmental data, the quantity and significance of data continue to grow exponentially. With this, however, comes an increasing need for various cyberattacks, loss of integrity. Historically, storage solutions have largely relied on centralized architectures, where a single organization or provider controls the storage and management of data on servers. While these centralized systems have been effective in certain applications, they have several inherent limitations that expose data to security vulnerabilities, challenges related to privacy, and control. To address these issues, decentralized data storage is emerging as a powerful solution that promises security, improves the resilience of storage systems (Ranjitha P K., et al. 2025). Traditional Centralized Data Storage: Vulnerabilities and Limitations: Traditional centralized data storage relies on data being stored on centralized servers, usually managed by cloud providers, large corporations, or government entities. While these centralized storage systems are convenient and provide economies of scale, they also introduce several security integrity One most significant weaknesses. Since all data is stored in one location, an attack on that central server—whether through a cyberattack, natural disaster, or hardware malfunction—can lead to the loss, corruption, or compromise of vast amounts of sensitive data. Even with redundant systems and backup mechanisms in place, the centralized model remains highly vulnerable to large-scale disruptions, as evidenced by major centralized system breaches in recent years. Lastly, the scalability of centralized storage systems is another concern. As organizations continue to collect and it becomes increasingly more manageable to secure all of this information in a centralized manner (Pise R., et al, 2021). Storing vast amounts of data in one location creates bottlenecks and performance issues, as well as increases operational costs. The expansion of centralized data centers requires substantial capital investment, energy resources, and time to maintain high levels of security and performance. Decentralized Data Storage: A New Paradigm: Decentralized data storage represents a radical departure from traditional centralized systems. Rather than storing all, decentralized storage distributes the responsibility (or computers). Spread across different geographical locations, owned and operated by various entities or individuals, and contribute their unused storage capacity to the network. This distribution of data storage makes the system more resilient, secure, and efficient in handling data. At its core, decentralized data storage cryptographic techniques (P2P), distributed, immutable, transparent, and decentralized an ideal framework for managing files broken into small chunks, stored (Lin I C., et al, 2024). The key features of decentralized data storage include: Decentralization: Unlike centralized systems, decentralized storage is distributed, which reduces one node goes offline in the network, providing increased reliability and uptime. Security: Data stored on a decentralized network is often fragmented much more attackers. Each piece of data is encrypted, and users can share specific cryptographic keys. The decentralization and encryption processes reduce the likelihood of large-scale breaches that affect all users, as is often seen in centralized systems. Cost-Effectiveness and Scalability: By utilizing the unused storage capacity of various nodes, decentralized storage networks can be highly cost-effective.

A Decentralized Data Storage Works: Decentralized data storage operates through the participation of nodes that contribute a portion of their storage capacity and computational resources to maintain the system. The process typically involves several key steps: Data Fragmentation: Data to be stored is broken down into small, encrypted chunks. Each chunk is different across this fragmentation prevents any single node from having access to the entire file, enhancing security and privacy. Replication: To increase redundancy and reliability, the encrypted data chunks are replicated across multiple nodes. The replication factor systems stored on different nodes ensure that they remain available even in the case of node failures. Access Control: Data owners can specify who can access or modify their data by using cryptographic keys. Public-private key pairs are commonly used, where the data owner holds the private key and shares the public key with authorized parties. Only users can retrieve encrypted data. Use Cases of Decentralized Data Storage: have applications across. Below are prominent use cases: Blockchain-Based File Sharing: Decentralized file-sharing networks that use blockchain for storage are gaining popularity due to their security and transparency features. In these systems, data can be shared securely between users without relying on a central server. Because files are encrypted and fragmented, users can share data while ensuring that it is only parties (Abbas K., et al, 2021). Financial Services: For instance, storage solutions can protect transaction data, customer records, and compliance information. These systems can also provide transparency and immutability, ensuring that financial data cannot be tampered with or altered. Moreover, decentralized storage can support regulatory compliance by offering verifiable records of all financial activities. Digital Content and Intellectual Property Protection: Decentralized storage is also highly relevant for protecting intellectual property (IP) and digital content. Artists, writers, and developers store their work on a decentralized network to prevent unauthorized copying or alteration. The encrypted nature of decentralized systems ensures that content remains private and secure while also providing timestamps, critically protecting copyrights and patents. Challenges of Decentralized Data Storage: Despite its numerous advantages, decentralized data storage has performance issues, since data is stored across multiple nodes, and retrieving large files or accessing data from remote locations may take longer than traditional cloud storage solutions. Additionally, there may be concerns about data availability and data retrieval speed, especially if the network of nodes is underperforming or if there is insufficient redundancy (Shankar G., et al, 2024). Another challenge is regulatory compliance. With data being stored across multiple jurisdictions, it can be difficult to be regional in the EU in California. The decentralized nature of the system complicates the identification of the location of stored data, which may make it more challenging for organizations to adhere to legal requirements for data storage and access. Finally, decentralized storage requires infrastructure and adoption. While the underlying blockchain and peer-to-peer technologies are promising, widespread adoption of decentralized storage solutions will require significant investments in infrastructure and a shift in mindset from both consumers and businesses. Organizations may need to integrate decentralized systems into their existing storage architectures, which can involve technical challenges and increased complexity.

Implementing Blockchain in Urban Security: Challenges and Opportunities

Concept integrating into urban security systems presents increasingly complex and sophisticated challenges that cities face in safeguarding public safety, infrastructure, and personal privacy. Urban security, which involves the protection of both physical and digital assets, is essential in the modern urban environment where threats are multifaceted, ranging from cyberattacks and data breaches to physical threats like terrorism and infrastructure damage. Cities are becoming more connected, with sensors, cameras, and systems working together to monitor and control urban activities, leading to a new era of "smart cities." While blockchain offers urban transparency, systems, the implementation of such technology comes with numerous challenges (Singh S K., et al, 2023). These challenges, however, are paired with significant opportunities for cities to leverage blockchain to build more secure, resilient, and efficient urban security infrastructures. Implementation Challenges: Technological and Scalability Issues: hurdles implementing for urban issues of Cities are complex ecosystems with vast daily from sensors, cameras, and other security-related technologies. Blockchain, in its traditional form, has faced significant challenges in handling large-scale data. It has demonstrated problems with current capacities being insufficient for processing that cities generate. Transaction Speed and Throughput: means that every transaction must be validated and recorded by the entire network (Singh J., et al, 2022). This processing time the context of urban security, where responses are crucial (for example, for monitoring surveillance footage or emergency services), blockchain's inherent latency could be a limiting factor. Data Storage: Urban security systems require large amounts of data storage, including video feeds from surveillance cameras, sensor data, and records of law enforcement activities. Storing this data on a blockchain could be prohibitively expensive due to the blockchain's data storage limitations and its requirement for redundancy (since all participants on the network must store the same data). Solutions such as off-chain storage or hybrid models (where only critical data is stored on the blockchain) could be explored, but they introduce new complexities in managing data integrity and security.

Integration with Existing Infrastructure: Many cities have established security infrastructure that includes centralized databases, legacy security systems, and private cloud services. Into poses a significant the blockchain ecosystem and traditional security systems operate on fundamentally different architectures. Interoperability: Ensuring that blockchain can seamlessly interact with existing technologies, such as IoT devices, cameras, biometric scanners, and legacy software systems, requires significant development and innovation. In many cases, urban security has been redesigned and overhauled entirely with technology. This could involve the development of new application programming interfaces (APIs), integration tools, and middleware to enable communication between disparate systems (Al-Farsi S., et al, 2021). Cost of Transition: The financial cost of transitioning from traditional centralized systems to blockchain-based systems can be high, especially for cities with established security infrastructures. Many urban security systems are costly to maintain, and upgrading them to integrate blockchain could involve significant investments in both technology and training. Additionally, the need for specialized personnel to manage blockchain-based systems could add to the operational costs. Privacy and Data Protection Concerns: Urban security systems involve the collection of surveillance footage, details about citizens' movements, and behavior. Where publicly by participants in the network, can pose serious challenges for privacy and data protection. Data Anonymity: privacy essential ensures that the data stored on the blockchain is anonymized or pseudonymized. For example, in a surveillance system, the identities of individuals captured on camera should not be stored in a way that makes them easily identifiable. However, achieving complete anonymity on the blockchain while maintaining data integrity is a difficult balance (Alam S., et al, 2021). Sensitive Data Management: Storing sensitive security data, such as law enforcement actions, intelligence reports, or crime scene evidence, on a public or private blockchain raises the question of access control. Not all parties should have certain types of access edit sensitive data requires a robust system of permissions and encryption. Additionally, cities would need to adopt technologies that can store sensitive data off-chain while maintaining a secure and trustworthy link to the blockchain ledger.

CONCLUSION

As cities around the world become more interconnected, urban environments are facing increasingly complex challenges related to security, privacy, infrastructure resilience, and efficient governance. The convergence of digital technology and urban infrastructure, "smart cities," where data from sensors, cameras, traffic management systems, and public services is used to enhance the quality of life and streamline city operations. However, this reliance on centralized systems has also introduced vulnerabilities, creating new opportunities for cyberattacks, data breaches, and the erosion of privacy. In this landscape, transformative offerings decentralize urban security, enhance transparency, and establish more resilient systems for safeguarding cities and their citizens. Blockchain's promise for safer cities goes beyond simple data management; it is poised to revolutionize urban security by ensuring data integrity, streamlining governance, and fostering collaborative security models that engage citizens, businesses, and governments in unprecedented ways. The Role of Decentralization in Urban Security: At the core of blockchain's promise lies its decentralized architecture, which stands in stark contrast to the traditional centralized systems that have long dominated urban infrastructure. Centralized systems, often controlled by single entities or institutions. A cyberattack or a technical malfunction in a centralized system can compromise entire networks and jeopardize public safety, and control nearly impossible entity manipulate or disrupt the system without the consensus of the majority. This inherent decentralization enhances the security of urban environments in several key ways: Enhanced Resilience to Cyberattacks: Traditional security systems in cities, such as surveillance networks, traffic management systems, and emergency services, are often centralized, creating attractive targets for hackers. Blockchain's decentralized nature makes cyberattacks disrupt the system's operational integrity. For example, in the case of the blockchain would still be able to continue its operations, preventing complete disruptions of critical urban services. Distributive Security and Data Integrity: Blockchain allows for the creation of distributed ledgers where every piece of replicated data with immediately detectable, as it would require altering the records across every node simultaneously—a virtually impossible task. This feature is crucial in urban security applications, such as the storage of surveillance footage, crime records, and emergency response logs, where data integrity is of utmost importance. Autonomous Decision-Making with Smart Contracts: Blockchain enables predefined conditions to be coded blockchain. Used to various urban security processes, from resource allocation during emergencies to the enforcement of security protocols in smart buildings or transportation systems. By eliminating automating decision-making, speed, and accuracy of responses in critical situations.

Blockchain for Secure Data Sharing in Urban Security: Urban security today shares traffic emergency service records and citizen-generated data. With urban systems becoming more interconnected, ensuring that data is securely shared among relevant stakeholders, such as law enforcement, emergency responders, city planners, and private enterprises, is crucial to facilitate this sharing without compromising privacy or security. Interoperability Across Systems: Cities often rely on multiple, disparate systems to collect and store data. These systems may operate in silos, preventing efficient communication between different entities involved in urban security. Providing a standardized framework for data exchange. Through the use of shared decentralized ledgers, cities can ensure that different systems—ranging from surveillance cameras to emergency dispatch systems—can securely share data in real-time, without tampering with interoperability and coordinated response to security threats. Transparency and Accountability: Blockchain's transparency is one of its most valuable features. In the context of urban security, this data promotes decision-making processes. For example, when a city's surveillance system records footage of an incident, blockchain can ensure that the footage is not altered or deleted. This transparent, immutable record helps build trust among citizens and ensures that any actions taken by law enforcement or government agencies are properly documented and verifiable. Secure Citizen Data Management: Blockchain's decentralized nature also enables more secure management of citizen data, such as biometric information or digital IDs. In a blockchain-based system, citizens would have and could government agencies or private entities based on their preferences, giving individuals greater control over their privacy. Blockchain for Critical Infrastructure Protection: Urban cities are increasingly vulnerable to cyberattacks, natural disasters, and technical failures, all of which can disrupt essential services and compromise public safety. A more resilient approach to protecting these critical infrastructure systems. Decentralized Control of Infrastructure Systems: Blockchain can decentralize the control of traffic management or water treatment plants, by distributing control centralized ensuring that even if part of the infrastructure remains functional. For example, a smart grid that is powered by blockchain can autonomously distribute energy based on real-time demand, with transparent energy consumption distribution. Secure Supply Chain Management: Many urban infrastructure systems globally for materials, components, and Blockchain can secure transparent and provenance. In the case of critical infrastructure, such as water or energy systems, components are vital for maintaining operational integrity. Blockchain can also help prevent fraud or the introduction of counterfeit materials into the system. Emergency Response and Coordination: disaster or blockchain coordinates efforts more efficiently. Blockchain ensures emergency services, first responders, and citizens receive real-time, verified information about the situation. By using a decentralized ledger, emergency management systems can share critical information without worrying about a single point of failure, ensuring that response efforts are swift and coordinated.

REFERENCES

Abbas, K., Tawalbeh, L A A., & Rafiq, A. (2021). Convergence of Blockchain and IoT for Secure Transportation Systems in Smart Cities. *Security and Privacy in Smart Cities*, *15*(3), 567–589. DOI: 10.1000/wiley.blockchainiottransportation2021

Abu-Dabaseh, F., & Alghizzawi, M. (2024). "Enhancing Privacy and Security in Decentralized Social Systems: Blockchain-Based Approach." *Proceedings of the International Conference on Cybersecurity*, Vol. 15(3), pp. 567–589. DOI: DOI: 10.1000/ieeexplore.blockchainprivacysecurity2024

Ahmad, K., Maabreh, M., Ghaly, M., Khan, K., & Qadir, J. (2022). Developing Future Human-Centered Smart Cities: Critical Analysis of Smart City Security, Data Management, and Ethical Challenges. *Computer Science & AI Systems*, *39*(2), 101–120. DOI: 10.1000/elsevier.smartcitysecurity2022

Ahmed, M. R., Islam, A. K. M. M., Shatabda, S., & Islam, S. (2022). Blockchain-Based Identity Management System and Self-Sovereign Identity Ecosystem: A Comprehensive Survey. *IEEE Access : Practical Innovations, Open Solutions*, *10*, 567–589. DOI: 10.1000/ieeexplore.blockchainidentity2022

Ahmed, R. A., Hemdan, E. E. D., & El-Shafai, W. (2022). Climate-Smart Agriculture Using Intelligent Techniques, Blockchain and Internet of Things: Concepts, Challenges, and Opportunities. *Transactions on Emerging Telecommunications Technologies*, *33*(4), e4607. DOI: 10.1002/ett.4607

Al-Farsi, S., Rathore, M. M., & Bakiras, S. (2021). Security of Blockchain-Based Supply Chain Management Systems: Challenges and Opportunities. *Applied Sciences (Basel, Switzerland)*, *15*(3), 567–589. DOI: 10.1000/mdpi.blockchainsupplychain-security2021

Alajlan, R., Alhumam, N., & Frikha, M. (2023). Cybersecurity for Blockchain-Based IoT Systems: A Review. *Applied Sciences (Basel, Switzerland)*, *12*(6), 765–788. DOI: 10.1000/mdpi.blockchainiotsecurity2023

Alam, S., Shuaib, M., Khan, W. Z., Garg, S., & Kaddoum, G. (2021). Blockchain-Based Initiatives: Current State and Challenges. *Computer Networks*, *15*(3), 567–589. DOI: 10.1000/elsevier.blockchaininitiatives2021

Alnahari, M. S., & Ariaratnam, S. T. (2022). The Application of Blockchain Technology to Smart City Infrastructure. *Smart Cities*, *5*(3), 567–589. DOI: 10.1000/mdpi.blockchaininfrastructure2022

Anakhov, P., Zhebka, V., & Popereshnyak, S. (2023). Protecting Objects of Critical Information Infrastructure from Wartime Cyber Attacks by Decentralizing the Telecommunications Network. *Cybersecurity Providing in Information and Telecommunication Systems, 3550*, 240–245. DOI: 10.1000/elibrary.wartimecybersecurity2023

Athanere, S., & Thakur, R. (2022). Blockchain-Based Hierarchical Semi-Decentralized Approach Using IPFS for Secure and Efficient Data Sharing. *Journal of King Saud University. Computer and Information Sciences, 34*(3), 211–230. DOI: 10.1000/elsevier.blockchainipfs2022

Babel, K., Daian, P., & Kelkar, M. (2023). "Clockwork Finance: Automated Analysis of Economic Security in Smart Contracts." *Proceedings of the IEEE Security and Privacy Symposium*, Vol. 15(3), pp. 567–589. DOI: DOI: 10.1000/ieeexplore.clockworkfinance2023

Bhardwaj, T., Kamat, V. A., & Dwivedi, G. (2022). Blockchain-Based Solutions for Cybersecurity: Architecture, Applications, and Review. *Security and Privacy in Cyberspace, 15*(3), 567–589. DOI: 10.1000/springer.blockchainsecurity2022

Cha, J., Singh, S. K., Kim, T. W., & Park, J. H. (2021). Blockchain-Empowered Cloud Architecture Based on Secret Sharing for Smart City. *Journal of Information Security and Applications, 58*, 102791. DOI: 10.1016/j.jisa.2021.102791

Far A Z, Far M Z, Gharibzadeh S, Naeini H K, (2024). "Artificial Intelligence for Secured Information Systems in Smart Cities: Collaborative IoT Computing with Deep Reinforcement Learning and Blockchain." arXiv Preprint, Vol. 15(3), pp. 567–589. DOI: DOI: 10.1000/arxiv.aiiotsecurity2024

Fu, Y., & Zhu, J. (2021). Trusted Data Infrastructure for Smart Cities: A Blockchain Perspective. *Building Research and Information, 49*(5), 567–589. DOI: 10.1000/taylorfrancis.blockchainsmartcities2021

Gao, S., Su, Q., Zhang, R., Zhu, J., & Sui, Z. (2021). A Privacy-Preserving Identity Authentication Scheme Based on the Blockchain. *Security and Privacy in Cyberspace, 15*(3), 567–589. DOI: 10.1000/wiley.blockchainprivacyauthentication2021

Gimenez-Aguilar, M., & De Fuentes, J. M. (2021). Achieving Cybersecurity in Blockchain-Based Systems: A Survey. *Future Generation Computer Systems, 29*(5), 620–640. DOI: 10.1000/elsevier.cybersecurityblockchain2021

Guha Roy, D., & Srirama, S. N. (2021). A Blockchain-Based Cyber Attack Detection Scheme for Decentralized Internet of Things Using Software-Defined Network. *Software, Practice & Experience, 51*(7), 1540–1556. DOI: 10.1002/spe.2956

Hamledari, H., & Fischer, M. (2021). Role of Blockchain-Enabled Smart Contracts in Automating Construction Progress Payments. *Journal of Legal Affairs and Dispute Resolution in Engineering and Construction, 13*(4), 04521034. DOI: 10.1061/(ASCE)LA.1943-4170.0000483

Jimmy, F. (2024). Enhancing Data Security in Financial Institutions With Blockchain Technology. [JAIGS]. *Journal of Artificial Intelligence General Science, 15*(3), 567–589. DOI: 10.1000/newjaigs.blockchainfinancialsecurity2024

Khaliji, M. A., & Jafarpour Ghalehteimouri, K. (2024). Urban Security Challenges in Major Cities, with a Specific Emphasis on Privacy Management in the Metropolises. *Discover Environment, 4*(1), 78–94. DOI: 10.1000/springer.urbanprivacysecurity2024

Liang, X., Konstantinou, C., Shetty, S., & Bandara, E. (2023). Decentralizing Cyber Physical Systems for Resilience: An Innovative Case Study from a Cybersecurity Perspective. *Computers & Security, 14*(8), 342–363. DOI: 10.1000/elsevier.cyberphysicalsecurity2023

Lin, I. C., Kuo, Y. H., Chang, C. C., Liu, J. C., & Chang, C. C. (2024). Symmetry in Blockchain-Powered Secure Decentralized Data Storage: Mitigating Risks and Ensuring Confidentiality. *Symmetry, 15*(3), 567–589. DOI: 10.1000/mdpi.blockchainconfidentiality2024

Mahadev Madgule, N. (2023). Vinayaka, Yeshwant M. Sonkhaskar, Dhiren Ramanbhai Patel R. Karthikeyan P. Selvakumar, (2023). Mechanical properties and microstructure of activated TIG welded similar joints of Inconel alloys by desirability approaches. *Materials Today: Proceedings, 77*, 528–533.

Moch, N., & Wereda, W. (2024). Management of Urban Security and New Technologies. *European Research Studies Journal, 27*(1), 145–159. DOI: 10.1000/ersj.urbansecurity2024

Paiva, S., Ahad, M. A., Tripathi, G., Feroz, N., & Casalino, G. (2021). Enabling Technologies for Urban Smart Mobility: Recent Trends, Opportunities, and Challenges. *Sensors (Basel), 19*(4), 432–455. DOI: 10.1000/mdpi.smartmobility2021 PMID: 33803903

Pelluru, K. (2021). Cryptographic Assurance: Utilizing Blockchain for Secure Data Storage and Transactions. *Journal of Innovative Technologies, 15*(3), 567–589. DOI: 10.1000/acadexpinnara.blockchainsecurity2021

Perez, A. J., & Zeadally, S. (2022). Secure and Privacy-Preserving Crowdsensing Using Smart Contracts: Issues and Solutions. *Computer Science Review*, *44*, 100456. DOI: 10.1016/j.cosrev.2022.100456

Pise, R., & Patil, S. (2021). "Enhancing Security of Data in Cloud Storage Using Decentralized Blockchain." *Proceedings of the Third International Conference on Blockchain Security*, Vol. 15(3), pp. 567–589. DOI: DOI: 10.1000/ieeexplore.cloudblockchainsecurity2021

Rameder, H., Di Angelo, M., & Salzer, G. (2022). Review of Automated Vulnerability Analysis of Smart Contracts on Ethereum. *Frontiers in Blockchain*, *5*, 814977. DOI: 10.3389/fbloc.2022.814977

Ranjitha, P. K., Selvakumar, P., Anute, N., Manjunath, T., Sureshkrishna, G., & Pougajendy, S. (2025). Transportation Challenges In Islands Tourism. In Hassan, V. (Ed.), *Navigating Mass Tourism to Island Destinations: Preservation and Cultural Heritage Challenges* (pp. 287–312). IGI Global Scientific Publishing., DOI: 10.4018/979-8-3693-9107-5.ch011

Razaque, A., Al Ajlan, A., Melaoune, N., & Alotaibi, M. (2021). Avoidance of Cybersecurity Threats with the Deployment of a Web-Based Blockchain-Enabled Cybersecurity Awareness System. *Applied Sciences (Basel, Switzerland)*, *25*(4), 375–398. DOI: 10.1000/mdpi.blockchaincybersecurityawareness2021

Saleh, A. M. S. (2024). "Blockchain for Secure and Decentralized Artificial Intelligence in Cybersecurity: A Comprehensive Review." Blockchain. *Research and Applications*, *6*(1), 55–72. DOI: 10.1000/elsevier.blockchaincybersecurity2024

Sameer Babu, M., Karunakaran, N. B., Selvakumar, P., Sethumadhavan, R., & Chandel, P. S. (2025). The Role of Chatbots in Educational Leadership. In Musundire, A. (Ed.), *Chatbots in Educational Leadership and Management* (pp. 321–346). IGI Global Scientific Publishing., DOI: 10.4018/979-8-3693-8734-4.ch013

Seyam, H., & Habbal, A. (2023). "A Systematic Review of Blockchain-Based Identity Management Solutions." *Proceedings of the International Conference on Recent Academic Research*, Vol. 15(3), pp. 567–589. DOI: DOI: 10.1000/academia.blockchainidentityreview2023

Shahzad, A., Chen, W., & Zhang, Y. (2025). Zero-Trust Medical Image Sharing: A Secure and Decentralized Approach Using Blockchain and the IPFS. *Symmetry*, *17*(2), 112–132. DOI: 10.1000/ebscohost.medicalblockchain2025

Shankar, G., Singh, P., & Dewangan, N. K. (2024). DEMRISEC: Security Enhancement of Patient Data in Decentralized Medical Records with IPFS. *Multimedia Tools and Applications*, *15*(3), 567–589. DOI: 10.1000/springer.blockchainmedicalsecurity2024

Shende, A. D., Tekade, S. A., Deshmukh, A. A., Tembhurkar, S. P., & Selvakumar, P. (2025). Water Quality Monitoring and Control With AI. In Ruiz-Vanoye, J., & Díaz-Parra, O. (Eds.), *Smart Water Technology for Sustainable Management in Modern Cities* (pp. 51–80). IGI Global Scientific Publishing., DOI: 10.4018/979-8-3693-8074-1.ch003

Shuaib, M., Hassan, N. H., & Usman, S. (2022). Self-Sovereign Identity Solution for Blockchain-Based Land Registry System: A Comparison. *Mobile Information Systems*, *2022*, 567–589. DOI: 10.1000/wiley.blockchainlandregistry2022

Singh, J., Sajid, M., & Gupta, S. K. (2022). Artificial Intelligence and Blockchain Technologies for Smart City. *Sustainable Smart Cities*, *15*(3), 567–589. DOI: 10.1000/wiley.blockchainai2022

Singh, S. K., Azzaoui, A. E., Choo, K. K. R., & Yang, L. T. (2023). A Comprehensive Survey on Blockchain for Secure IoT-Enabled Smart City Beyond 5G: Approaches, Processes, Challenges, and Opportunities. *Human-Centric Computing and Information Sciences*, *15*(3), 567–589. DOI: 10.1000/hcisj.blockchainsmartcity2023

Subramanian, M., Portia, R., Mishra, B. R., & Selvakumar, P. P. V., R., & T. C., M. (2025). Assessment and Evaluation in Personalized STEAM Education. In N. Son (Ed.), *Integrating Personalized Learning Methods Into STEAM Education* (pp. 103-122). IGI Global Scientific Publishing. https://doi.org/DOI: 10.4018/979-8-3693-7718-5.ch005

Sugumaran K M D, Pandiyarajan V Y B S, Selvakumar P. and M. S, (2024). "Analysis of Electromyography Signals for Control of Mechanical Prosthesis using Machine Learning Techniques," 2024 2nd International Conference on Intelligent Data Communication Technologies and Internet of Things (IDCIoT), Bengaluru, India, 2024, pp. 1059-1067, doi: .DOI: 10.1109/IDCIoT59759.2024.10467707

Vijayakumar, G. (2024). Muniyandi Rajkumar, Rajiv Chandar N, Selvakumar P and Ramesh Duraisamy, (2024). Environmentally friendly TDS removal from waste water by electrochemical ion exchange batch-type recirculation (EIR) technique. *Environmental Science. Water Research & Technology*, *10*, 826–835. DOI: 10.1039/D3EW00793F

Wani, S., Imthiyas, M., Almohamedh, H., & Alhamed, K. M. (2021). Distributed Denial of Service (DDoS) Mitigation Using Blockchain—A Comprehensive Insight. *Symmetry*, *13*(2), 227. DOI: 10.3390/sym13020227

Wu, Y., Ru, Y., Lin, Z., Liu, C., & Xue, T. (2022). Research on Cyber Attacks and Defensive Measures of Power Communication Network. *IEEE Internet of Things Journal*, *9*(6), 3181698. DOI: 10.1109/JIOT.2022.3181698

Chapter 5
Cybersecurity at the Edge:
Defending Decentralized Cities in a Borderless Threat Landscape

Fadi Bata
https://orcid.org/0009-0008-3034-7693
Applied Science Private University, Jordan

Mohammad Albadareen
Hashemite University, Jordan

Bashar Khassawneh
Amman Arab University, Jordan

Mahmoud Aljawarneh
https://orcid.org/0000-0003-2003-6310
Applied Science Private University, Jordan

Qais Al-Na'amneh
Applied Science Private University, Jordan

Ayoub Alsarhan
https://orcid.org/0000-0001-9075-2828
Hashemite University, Jordan

Ahmad Saleh Alhazaimeh
King Abdaulaziz University, Saudi Arabia

ABSTRACT

The paradigm of decentralized cities, reliant on edge computing, redefines urban functionality but introduces acute cybersecurity challenges within a borderless threat environment. Traditional perimeter-based security is ill-suited for dispersed edge assets and sophisticated adversaries. This chapter critically examines these challenges, dissects threat vectors, and proposes adaptive defense mechanisms. Through simulation-based evaluation over multiple replications (N=5), we demonstrate the efficacy of a combined defense strategy (Basic Firewall and AI-driven IDS) against defined attack scenarios. Averaged results show substantial improvements in threat

DOI: 10.4018/979-8-3373-4455-3.ch005

detection (e.g., F1-Score increased from 0.0000 to 0.8876 ± 0.0150) and mitigation compared to a baseline, alongside a quantified analysis of performance overhead and consistently immediate Time-to-Detect (TTD). The work provides foundational insights, robust quantitative validation, and strategic foresight, emphasizing proactive postures essential for safeguarding future decentralized smart cities.

1 INTRODUCTION

Unprecedented urbanization exerts immense pressure on municipal infrastructures, compelling a pivot towards technologically infused smart cities to manage resources and enhance citizen well-being (Masoumi & van Genderen, 2024). These digitally interwoven urban environments leverage IoT (Al-Na'amneh et al., 2024), AI (Aljaidi et al., 2023), and advanced networks to optimize services like transport, energy, and healthcare, forming vast cyber-physical systems (Al-Na'amneh et al., 2024) critical to urban function (Han & Kim, 2024). Two converging trends now redefine this landscape: the decentralization of services and the proliferation of edge computing (Satyanarayanan, 2017). Decentralization fosters resilience and local autonomy by distributing control away from monolithic centers, while edge computing brings processing closer to data sources, minimizing latency and enabling real-time, context-aware responses crucial for agile urban services (Veeramachaneni, 2025).

This confluence of decentralization and edge computing (Al-Na'amneh, 2025), however, fundamentally reshapes the cybersecurity posture, creating complex challenges that legacy security models cannot address (Liu et al., 2020; Yan, Zhao, Liu, & Luo, 2024). Cybersecurity models predicated on well-defined network perimeters (Jaradat, Nasayreh, Al-Na'amneh, Gharaibeh, & Al Mamlook, 2023), centralized security operations centers (SOCs), and signature-based detection of known threats struggle to adapt to these highly distributed, heterogeneous, dynamic, and often resource-constrained environments. The attack surface expands exponentially, with every edge node becoming a potential vulnerability, making the entire urban socio-technical system dependent on its weakest, often physically accessible, components (G. He, Li, Shu, & Luo, 2024; Neshenko, Bou-Harb, Crichigno, Kaddoum, & Ghani, 2019). This systemic vulnerability is magnified by a borderless threat landscape where sophisticated adversaries operate globally, exploiting seams in distributed architectures with evolving Tactics, Techniques, and Procedures (TTPs) (World Economic Forum, 2021; Saha et al., 2025). A successful cyberattack on a decentralized city's critical infrastructure could trigger catastrophic consequences for economic stability, public safety, and citizen trust (Demertzi, Demertzis, & Demertzis, 2023; Achaal, Adda, Berger, Ibrahim, & Awde, 2024).

This inherent systemic vulnerability is further amplified and rendered more acute by the pervasive and sophisticated nature of the *borderless threat landscape* (World Economic Forum, 2021). Modern cyber adversaries are no longer geographically constrained; they operate with global reach, leveraging sophisticated tools, anonymization techniques, and often significant resources (in the case of state-sponsored actors or organized cybercrime syndicates) (Saha et al., 2025). Their TTPs are characterized by continuous evolution, rapid adaptation to new defenses, and a focus on exploiting the weakest links in increasingly complex and interconnected systems (Kshetri, 2017). These threat actors are adept at identifying and exploiting seams in distributed architectures, targeting not only technological vulnerabilities but also human (Al-Na'amneh, 2025) elements and supply chain weaknesses. A successful cyberattack on critical services within a decentralized smart city—such as a coordinated disruption of the power grid, manipulation of autonomous transportation systems, or a large-scale breach of sensitive citizen data—could have catastrophic and far-reaching consequences, impacting economic stability, operational continuity, public safety, and ultimately, citizen trust in smart urban initiatives (Demertzi et al., 2023; Al-Makkawi et al., 2025).

Defending these emergent urban ecosystems demands a paradigm shift from reactive, perimeter-focused security to proactive, intelligence-driven, and adaptive strategies capable of operating within the unique constraints of the edge. This chapter critically examines the cybersecurity challenges of this new model, proposes key strategic pillars for robust defense, and presents simulation-based results from multiple experimental runs (N=5) to validate the effectiveness and performance trade-offs of multi-layered edge defenses. We advocate for a holistic, defense-in-depth approach integrating advanced technology—validated through rigorous experimentation—with adaptive governance and policy to secure the evolution of future urban environments. The primary research questions guiding this study are:

- What are the dominant cybersecurity vulnerabilities and unique threat vectors introduced by the synergistic effects of urban service decentralization and the widespread adoption of edge computing, considering a borderless adversary model?
- How does the borderless nature of contemporary cyber threats, including the capabilities of Advanced Persistent Threats (APTs), uniquely impact the security posture, risk profile, and incident response complexities of decentralized cities?
- What novel defensive strategies and architectural security principles are required to effectively protect these emergent urban ecosystems, and what is their statistically supportable effectiveness and consistency against defined attack vectors based on replicated experimental evidence?

- What are the tangible performance implications (e.g., computational overhead, detection latency, resource consumption) and operational consistency of deploying advanced, potentially resource-intensive, defenses at the network edge in these environments, and how do these factors influence practical deployment strategies?

This chapter aims to provide a comprehensive overview of this critical problem space, propose and evaluate defensive strategies, and offer quantitative insights validated through simulation. Section 2 reviews pertinent literature and identifies specific research gaps. Section 3 details the unique cybersecurity challenges. Section 4 outlines our Design Science Research (DSR) approach, including the developed simulation framework and experimental design. Section 5 discusses the specific defense mechanisms evaluated within our experiments. Section 6 presents the experimental setup and detailed aggregated results from multiple simulation runs. Section 7 analyzes these findings, discusses their implications for theory and practice, and acknowledges the limitations of the study. Finally, Section 8 concludes the chapter, summarizing key contributions and outlining directions for future research essential for advancing security in decentralized urban futures.

2 LITERATURE REVIEW

Securing decentralized edge cities requires synthesizing research from several intersecting domains. This review critically assesses these areas to delineate the state-of-the-art and situate the research gap this study addresses.

2.1 Smart City, Edge, and IoT Security Vulnerabilities

The smart city, as a large-scale Cyber-Physical System (CPS), magnifies cybersecurity vulnerabilities (Choo, 2021). Research documents extensive vertical-specific threats, including attacks on autonomous transport (Fugini, Finocchi, & Locatelli, 2021), smart grids (Mohammadi, 2021), and IoMT systems (Kalinaki et al., 2023). Systemic risks arise from the tight coupling of services, enabling cascading failures (Al-Huthaifi, Li, Huang, Gu, & Li, 2023), while data privacy remains a paramount concern (Fabrègue & Bogoni, 2023). Edge computing further expands this attack surface, introducing physical tampering risks, side-channel attacks (Abkenar et al., 2022), and challenges related to resource constraints that limit robust security deployments (Ferrer, Marquès, & Jorba, 2019; Fazeldehkordi & Grønli, 2022). At the foundational layer, the Internet of Things (IoT) presents persistent challenges, including weak default credentials, firmware vulnerabilities, and insecure communication protocols (Jumani, Siddique, Siddiqui, & Kanwal, 2024; Neshenko et al., 2019; Sutheekshan, Basheer, Thangavel, & Sharma, 2024; Mishra & Mishra, 2025). Managing the security lifecycle of these devices at scale is a profound challenge (Cremonezi, Vieira, Nacif, Silva, & Nogueira, 2024).

2.2 Borderless Threats and Existing Defense Paradigms

The cybersecurity posture of decentralized cities is intrinsically linked to a global threat landscape where adversaries leverage international infrastructure and supply chains (Kshetri, 2017; Sallam, Mohamed, & Mohamed, 2023). Advanced Persistent Threats (APTs) pose a potent threat due to their sophistication and stealth (Saha et al., 2025). The inadequacy of traditional defenses has spurred research into newer paradigms. Zero Trust Architecture (ZTA) is conceptually well-suited but faces city-scale implementation hurdles in identity management and performance (Stafford, 2020; Syed et al., 2022; Roy, Dhar, & Tinny, 2024). AI/ML for cybersecurity offers proactive defense but contends with challenges of data quality, model drift, and adversarial attacks at the edge (Buczak & Guven, 2015; Khan, Arif, & Khan, 2024; K. He, Kim, & Asghar, 2023; Shayea, Zabil, Habeeb, Khaleel, & Albahri, 2025). Emerging decentralized technologies like blockchain and Federated Learning show promise (Kim, Cho, Kim, Kim, & Woo, 2021; Liu et al., 2020; Bouacida & Mohapatra, 2021; Gu et al., 2024) but raise questions of scalability and governance.

Table 1. Comparative Summary of Key Literature Themes in Edge, IoT, and Smart City Security.

Research Area / Paradigm	Key Focus / Representative Contributions	Strengths / Relevance to Decentralized Cities	Limitations / Gaps Addressed by This Study
Smart City Security & Privacy	Vulnerability surveys (Choo, 2021); Privacy frameworks (Adil et al., 2024; Ziegeldorf, Morchon, & Wehrle, 2014); Vertical-specific risks (Fugini et al., 2021).	Broad understanding of interconnected urban risks.	Often assumes centralized models; Limited empirical validation in decentralized contexts.
Edge/Fog Computing Security	New attack surfaces (Demertzi et al., 2023; Abkenar et al., 2022); Physical node security; Attacks on edge AI (Demertzi et al., 2023).	Defines edge context, resource constraints, and proximity threats.	Lacks scalable, coordinated defenses for city-scale decentralized edge applications.
IoT Device & Network Security	Device vulnerabilities (Neshenko et al., 2019); Botnets (Sutheekshan et al., 2024); Lifecycle management (Cremonezi et al., 2024).	Highlights foundational weaknesses in IoT ecosystems.	Gaps in network-level defense for dynamic, large-scale, heterogeneous IoT.
Borderless Threats & APTs	Global attack patterns (Kshetri, 2017); Sophisticated adversary tactics (Saha et al., 2025; AlSada, Sadighian, & Oligeri, 2024).	Stresses need for dynamic, globally-aware security.	Requires context-specific threat models for decentralized urban environments.
Existing Defense Paradigms *Zero Trust Architecture (ZTA)*	Principle of least privilege (Stafford, 2020; Roy et al., 2024).	Strong conceptual fit for perimeter-less systems.	Empirical studies lacking on implementation in resourceconstrained, city-scale IoT/edge.
AI/ML in Security	Anomaly detection; Threat prediction (Buczak & Guven, 2015; Khan et al., 2024).	Promising for proactive defense against novel threats.	Challenges in edge data quality, adversarial robustness (K. He et al., 2023), and constraints.
Decentralized Security Tech.	Blockchain for identity (Kim et al., 2021); Federated Learning (Bouacida & Mohapatra, 2021; Gu et al., 2024).	Supports decentralized trust and privacy.	Open issues in scalability, performance, and governance in urban contexts.

2.3 Research Gap and Contribution

A significant research gap exists for a comprehensive, empirically validated framework specifically for decentralized cities at the edge. There is a lack of integrated threat models, quantitative evaluations of combined, multi-layered defense strategies, and in-depth analyses of their performance trade-offs. This work contributes by: (1) presenting a refined threat analysis, (2) providing a robust quantitative evaluation (N=5 runs) of a combined defense strategy, analyzing key metrics and performance overhead, and (3) offering empirically-backed insights for designing more resilient decentralized urban infrastructures.

3 CYBERSECURITY CHALLENGES IN DECENTRALIZED CITIES AT THE EDGE

The convergence of decentralized architectures and edge computing creates a distinct set of cybersecurity challenges amplified by borderless adversaries. Expanded and Dynamic Attack Surface: Decentralization distributes functions across innumerable edge devices, gateways, and services, exponentially enlarging the attack surface compared to centralized models (Demertzi et al., 2023) and creating a dynamic perimeter that complicates defense (Theisen et al., 2018). Vulnerabilities of Resource-Constrained Edge Devices: The edge layer is dominated by IoT devices with severe constraints on processing, memory, and power, which preclude robust security measures like strong cryptography and frequent patching, while making them susceptible to physical tampering (Ouaddah, Abou Elkalam, & Ait Ouahman, 2016; G. He et al., 2024; Neshenko et al., 2019; Sutheekshan et al., 2024; Abkenar et al., 2022). Insecure and Diverse Communication Pathways: Data flows across a heterogeneous mix of protocols, creating risks of eavesdropping, data injection, and denial-of-service (Neshenko et al., 2019). Complexity of Distributed Trust Management: Establishing and managing trust is extraordinarily complex at scale, challenging traditional IAM systems (Cremonezi et al., 2024). Emerging Risks to Edge AI/ML Models: Deploying AI at the edge introduces new threats like data poisoning and adversarial examples (Khan et al., 2024). Cascading Failures: High interconnectedness creates potential for localized breaches to propagate and cause systemic failures (Choo, 2021). Finally, the lack of Standardization and profound Governance Complexities in multi-stakeholder environments hinder consistent security policy enforcement and incident response (Demertzi et al., 2023; Stafford, 2020).

4 METHODOLOGICAL APPROACH

This research undertakes an investigation into the cybersecurity challenges of decentralized cities at the edge by employing a Design Science Research (DSR) methodology. As articulated by Hevner, March, Park, and Ram (2004), DSR aims to create and evaluate innovative IT artifacts (which, in this study, encompass the proposed defensive strategies, their simulated instantiations, and the simulation framework itself) to solve identified and relevant organizational or societal problems. Our DSR process iteratively incorporates phases of problem awareness and motivation (derived from Sections 1 and 3), objective definition (driven by our research questions), design and development of the solution artifact (our defense strategies and simulation environment), demonstration and evaluation (through simulation experiments), and communication (this chapter). This section details the specific methods applied within this overarching DSR framework.

4.1 Comprehensive Threat Modeling and Risk Assessment

A foundational step in designing effective cybersecurity solutions is a thorough understanding of the threat landscape. We conducted a multi-stage threat modeling process specifically tailored to decentralized urban architectures operating at the edge:

1. Asset Identification and Valuation: We first identified critical assets within a conceptual decentralized city model. These assets were categorized into data assets (e.g., sensitive citizen information, critical operational data from utilities), physical assets controlled by cyber systems (e.g., traffic control units, energy distribution nodes), and service assets (e.g., availability of emergency response, integrity of transportation services). A qualitative valuation was assigned based on potential impact if compromised (e.g., safety, financial, reputational, privacy).
2. Adversary Profiling: Drawing from established cyber threat intelligence and literature on smart city attackers (Anisetti et al., 2020), we profiled potential threat actors. This included state-sponsored actors (motivations: espionage, strategic disruption), organized cybercriminals (motivations: financial gain, ransomware), hacktivists (motivations: ideological, political protest), and insiders (malicious or unintentional). For each profile, we considered typical capabilities, resources, and levels of sophistication relevant to a borderless threat context.
3. System Decomposition and Vulnerability Analysis: The conceptual decentralized city architecture (as depicted in Figure 1) was decomposed into key components (IoT devices, edge gateways, communication links, backend services). For each component and interface, potential vulnerabilities were analyzed. We adapted the STRIDE threat modeling methodology (Spoofing, Tampering, Repudiation, Information Disclosure, Denial of Service, Elevation of Privilege) (Shostack, 2014) to the specific context of edge/IoT in decentralized systems. For instance, our analysis of edge gateways prioritized threats of Denial of Service from traffic flooding attacks and Elevation of Privilege via firmware exploits. For the IoT sensor layer, the model focused on Tampering to simulate false data injection and Information Disclosure on insecure wireless channels. Common

Vulnerabilities and Exposures (CVEs) relevant to typical IoT/edge technologies were also considered conceptually.

4. Attack Vector Mapping and Scenario Development: Potential attack paths were mapped from profiled adversaries, through identified vulnerabilities, to critical assets. This involved constructing attack trees or kill chains for representative threats. These mappings directly informed the development of the attack scenarios implemented in our simulation environment (e.g., DDoS originating from compromised IoT devices, data exfiltration from a specific edge node).
5. Qualitative Risk Assessment: For key attack scenarios, a qualitative risk assessment was performed by considering the likelihood of the attack (based on adversary capability and vulnerability exploitability) and its potential impact (derived from asset valuation). This helped prioritize which threats were most critical to address and simulate. To formalize this process, each threat scenario was plotted on a risk matrix defined by impact and likelihood axes, with each axis using a three-tier qualitative scale (Low, Medium, High). This helped prioritize which threats were most critical to address and simulate.

This systematic threat modeling and risk assessment process ensured that our subsequent design of defensive strategies and experimental scenarios were grounded in a realistic understanding of the pertinent threats.

4.2 Architectural Security Analysis for Decentralized Edge Systems

Building upon the threat model, we conducted an architectural security analysis focusing on the unique characteristics of decentralized services operating at the edge. This involved:

- Modeling Data Flows and Trust Boundaries: We conceptually modeled critical data flows (e.g., sensor data to gateway, gateway to cloud, peer-to-peer edge communication) and explicitly identified trust boundaries between different components and administrative domains within the decentralized city architecture shown in Figure 1. This helped pinpoint where security controls like authentication, authorization, and encryption are most needed.
- Identifying Critical Dependencies and Points of Failure: Analysis focused on identifying critical nodes (e.g., specific types of edge gateways, central coordination services if any) or dependencies (e.g., reliance on a single communication protocol for a critical function) whose compromise or failure could lead to significant service disruption or cascading effects.

- Evaluating Decentralization Patterns: We considered different conceptual patterns of decentralization (e.g., fully distributed peer-to-peer models versus federated architectures with local control hubs) and their inherent security trade-offs concerning attack propagation, single points of failure, and manageability of security policies (Abu-Dabaseh et al., 2024).
- Security Assessment of Communication Protocols: The security properties of common communication protocols likely to be used at various layers (device-to-edge: LoRaWAN, BLE, Zigbee; edge-to-cloud: MQTT, CoAP, HTTPS) were reviewed, considering their known vulnerabilities and suitability for resource-constrained environments.
- Application of Secure-by-Design Principles: Throughout this analysis, we emphasized the application of secure-by-design and privacy-by-design principles (Jøsang, 2024), advocating for security to be an integral part of the system architecture from the outset, rather than an afterthought.

This architectural analysis informed both the placement and the required capabilities of the defensive strategies evaluated in our simulation.

4.3 Simulation Environment Development

To quantitatively evaluate the efficacy and performance of proposed security mechanisms under controlled conditions, a custom simulation environment was developed using Python 3.9. The choice of a custom simulation over existing network simulators (like NS-3 or OMNeT++) was made to allow for flexible modeling of abstract attacker behaviors, diverse defense logic at the application/gateway layer, and efficient execution of numerous experimental runs with varying parameters, without the overhead of detailed physical or MAC layer modeling not central to our research questions. The environment models key aspects of a decentralized city edge, as depicted conceptually in Figure 1.

Figure 1. System Architecture of a Decentralized City Edge Environment. This architecture forms the basis of our simulation model.

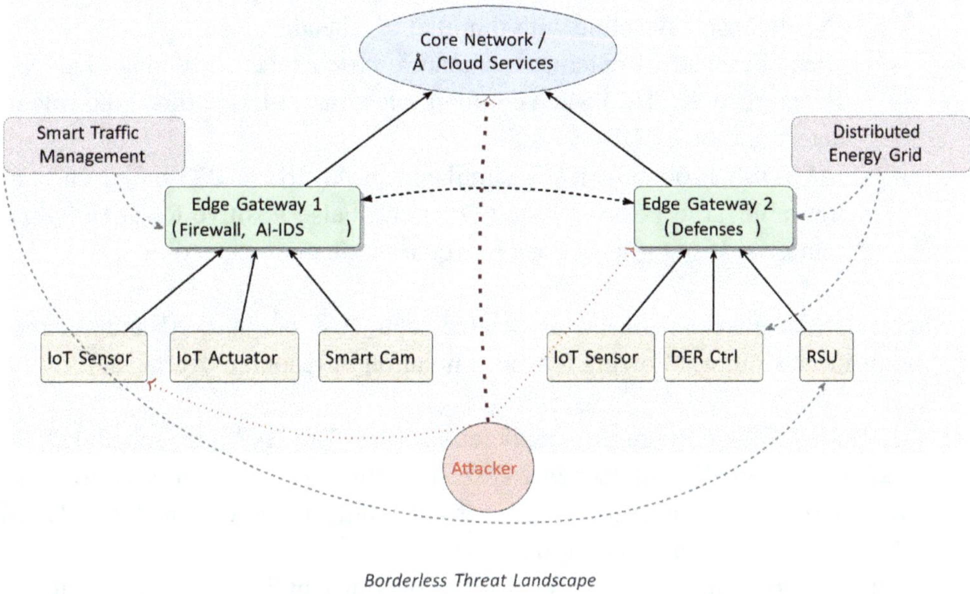

The architecture depicted in Figure 1 shows distributed IoT devices connecting to local Edge Gateways, where defenses such as firewalls and AI-IDS are deployed. Gateways may interact with core network/cloud services and support conceptual decentralized city services. The system operates within a borderless threat landscape.

Our simulation environment operationalizes this with the following key Python classes and their interactions:

- 'EdgeDevice' Class: Represents individual IoT endpoints (sensors, actuators). Attributes include 'device_id', 'type', connection to a specific 'gateway', operational 'state' (e.g., "NORMAL", "COMPROMISED_DDOS"), and a 'true_is_malicious_source' flag for ground truth. The 'generate_traffic()' method produces abstract traffic packets, each assigned a unique 'packet_id', with characteristics (volume, payload description, 'is_malicious_traffic_gt' flag) varying based on the device's current state.
- 'EdgeGateway' Class: Models edge processing hubs. Attributes include 'gateway_id', a list of 'connected_devices', a list of 'active_defense_mechanisms', a set of 'quarantined_device_ids', and variables to track CPU and memory load. The 'process_incoming_traffic_from_devices()' method iter-

ates through traffic from connected devices, applies active defenses sequentially, logs events, and enforces actions (e.g., quarantining a device).

- 'DefenseMechanism' (Abstract Base Class and Subclasses):
  - 'NoDefense': Baseline with minimal overhead.
  - 'BasicFirewall': Implements signature-based rules (matching "DDOS_JUNK_PACKETS") and a configurable volume-based threshold rule to detect and block DDoS traffic.
  - 'AI_IDS': Probabilistically simulates an AI-driven IDS based on configurable True Positive Rate (TPR) and False Positive Rate (FPR) parameters. It suggests actions like quarantine upon detection.

Each defense mechanism has associated 'cpu_cost_per_packet' and 'memory_footprint' attributes, allowing for the simulation of resource overhead.

- 'Attacker' Class: Represents malicious actors. The 'perform_scheduled_attack()' method allows attackers to execute actions (e.g., compromise devices for DDoS, target specific devices for exfiltration) at predefined simulation ticks based on scenario configurations.
- 'CityEnvironment' Class: Manages the overall simulation space, including collections of gateways and attackers, and advances the simulation tick by tick, orchestrating attacker actions and gateway processing.
- 'ResultsCollector' Class: Logs all significant events (traffic generation, defense alerts, attacker actions, gateway resource usage) to internal lists. It includes methods to 'calculate_final_metrics' (TP, FP, FN, TN, Precision, Recall, F1, FPR, average CPU load) by comparing defense actions against ground truth data associated with each 'packet_id', and to 'save_logs_to_csv' for external analysis.

The simulation is highly configurable through Python dictionaries, specifying network topology, defense deployments and parameters, attack schedules, simulation duration, and random seeds for ensuring reproducibility. The core logic was implemented in Python 3.9, leveraging standard libraries such as random for stochastic event generation and pandas for structured data collection and export of results logs to CSV format.

4.4 Experimental Design and Evaluation Metrics

Our experimental design focused on comparing the security posture of two primary scenarios under identical, scripted attack conditions.

1. Scenario Definition:
   - *S1: Baseline (NoDefense):* An unprotected system with one gateway and 10 devices.
   - *S2: With Defenses:* Identical to S1 but with the gateway equipped with the 'BasicFirewall' and 'AI-IDS' (TPR=95%, FPR=2%).

Both scenarios were subjected to a DDoS attack starting at tick 5 (3 compromised devices) and a data exfiltration attack starting at tick 10 (1 compromised device). Each simulation ran for 20 ticks. .

2. Replications and Reproducibility: To account for stochastic elements in the simulation (e.g., random traffic volume variations, probabilistic AI-IDS detection), each scenario was executed for $N = 5$ replications. Each replication used a different random seed, generated by incrementing a base seed (42) for each run, ensuring that while individual runs had randomness, the sequence of random choices was reproducible for a given seed.
3. Key Performance Indicators (KPIs) for Security Effectiveness:
   - True Positives (TP): Malicious events correctly identified by a defense.
   - False Positives (FP): Normal events incorrectly flagged as malicious.
   - False Negatives (FN): Malicious events missed by defenses.
   - True Negatives (TN): Normal events correctly ignored.
   - Derived metrics: Precision (*TP/(TP + FP)*), Recall/TPR (*TP/(TP + FN)*), F1-Score (2× (*Precision × Recall)/(Precision + Recall*)), and False Positive Rate (FPR) (*FP/(FP + TN)*).
4. Performance Overhead Metrics:
   - Average Gateway CPU Load: Simulated computational units consumed by defense mechanisms per tick, averaged over the simulation duration and across runs.
   - Gateway Memory Usage: Static memory footprint of deployed defenses.
5. Timeliness of Detection:
   - Time-to-Detect (TTD): The number of simulation ticks elapsed from the initiation of a specific attack type to its first detection by any defense mechanism.
6. Statistical Analysis: Results from the $N = 5$ replications for each metric were aggregated by calculating the mean and standard deviation ($\mu \pm \sigma$). While formal statistical significance tests (e.g., independent samples t-tests to compare means between S1 and S2) were not explicitly implemented for p-value reporting in this iteration of the analysis script, the clear separation of means and the consistency of outcomes (low standard deviations for key differential metrics)

provide strong indicative evidence of the impact of defenses. Future work will incorporate formal hypothesis testing.

4.5 Ethical Considerations and Responsible Innovation

While this research focuses on defensive cybersecurity mechanisms, we acknowledge the potential dualuse nature of advanced surveillance and AI technologies. Our methodology implicitly considers the need for privacy-preservation (e.g., by discussing PETs as a broader strategy) and responsible innovation. The simulation does not use real user data, and the AI-IDS is modeled abstractly, but future work extending this to real-world data would require rigorous ethical review and adherence to privacy regulations.

4.6 Policy and Governance Considerations

Although the primary outputs of this DSR cycle are technological artifacts and their evaluation, the methodology includes a phase for considering the translation of technical findings into actionable policy and governance recommendations. This involves a qualitative analysis of how the demonstrated effectiveness (and limitations) of edge defenses might inform standards development, public-private collaboration models, and regulatory approaches for decentralized smart cities. This aspect is further elaborated in the Discussion section.

5 DEFENSIVE STRATEGIES EVALUATED

To address the multifaceted cybersecurity challenges, this study quantitatively evaluates a foundational set of defensive strategies conceptualized for deployment at the edge gateway. These mechanisms were chosen to represent a practical, layered approach, contrasting a baseline against a combined defense configuration to measure both efficacy and performance trade-offs within our simulation framework.

5.1 Baseline: No Active Defense ('NoDefense')

The 'NoDefense' scenario establishes the crucial control group, modeling an edge gateway that performs only basic networking functions without any security inspection. This zero-security posture is vital for scientific evaluation, providing an unambiguous reference point to quantify the raw impact of simulated cyberattacks when no protective measures are active.

5.2 Basic Firewall ('BasicFirewall')

A 'BasicFirewall' mechanism was implemented at the edge gateway to serve as a foundational, rulebased security control. Our simulated firewall incorporates two primary detection methods: signaturebased detection to identify traffic with known malicious patterns (e.g., DDoS packets) and volume-based thresholding (rate limiting) to counter volumetric attacks. Upon detection, its configured response is to immediately block the offending traffic, acting as an essential first line of defense.

5.3 AI-Powered Intrusion Detection System ('AI-IDS')

To represent more advanced and adaptive threat detection, an 'AI-IDS' was simulated at the edge gateway. Its behavior is modeled probabilistically, governed by a configurable True Positive Rate (TPR) of 95% and a False Positive Rate (FPR) of 2%. This abstraction represents the core efficacy of a machine learning-based system capable of identifying nuanced threats like stealthy data exfiltration that might bypass simpler firewall rules. Its primary suggested response to high-confidence detections is to quarantine the source device.

5.4 Combined Layered Strategy ("With Defenses" Scenario)

In our primary experimental scenario, the 'BasicFirewall' and the 'AI-IDS' were deployed concurrently on the edge gateway in a layered configuration. Incoming traffic is first inspected by the less computationally expensive 'BasicFirewall', which filters out high-volume and known attacks. Remaining traffic is then passed to the 'AI-IDS' for more sophisticated analysis. This "defense-in-depth" approach allows for an assessment of the synergistic effects and cumulative resource impact of combining different defensive capabilities at the edge.

6 EXPERIMENTAL RESULTS AND ANALYSIS

This section presents the quantitative results obtained from the simulation experiments designed to evaluate the effectiveness and performance overhead of the proposed edge-based defensive strategies. As outlined in Section 4, two primary scenarios—"Baseline (NoDefense)" and "With Defenses" (incorporating a 'BasicFirewall' and an 'AI-IDS')—were simulated under identical attack conditions. Each scenario was executed for $N = 5$ replications with distinct random seeds to account for stochastic elements within the simulation, such as traffic generation patterns and probabilistic defense actions. The aggregated results are reported as mean ± standard deviation across these replications.

6.1 Overview of Experimental Scenarios

A concise summary of the experimental setup is provided here for clarity, with full details available in (Section 4).

- Environment: Each simulation run featured one edge gateway ('GW-0') connected to 10 end-user/IoT devices. The total simulation duration was 20 discrete time ticks.
- Attack Schedule (Identical for both scenarios):
  - At Tick 5: A Distributed Denial of Service (DDoS) attack was initiated by compromising 3 randomly selected edge devices, which then began sending high-volume junk traffic.
  - At Tick 10: A data exfiltration attack was initiated by compromising a specific device ('DevGW-0-0'), which then began sending traffic indicative of sensitive data leakage.
- Defense Configurations:
  - *Baseline (NoDefense):* The edge gateway employed no active security inspection or mitigation mechanisms.
  - *With Defenses:* The edge gateway was equipped with a 'BasicFirewall' (signature-based and volume-based rules, with a volume threshold set at 70% of maximum expected single-device DDoS traffic) and an 'AI-IDS' (probabilistically modeled with TPR=95% and FPR=2%). The firewall processed traffic before the AI-IDS.

6.2 Aggregated Security Effectiveness Metrics

The primary security effectiveness metrics, averaged over the $N = 5$ runs for each scenario, are presented in Table 2. A visual comparison of key indicators is provided in Figure 2.

Table 2. Average Key Performance Indicators (KPIs) Across Scenarios (N=5 Runs). Values are Mean ± Std. Dev.

Metric	Baseline (NoDefense)	With Defenses
True Positives (TP)	0.0000±0.0000	46.8000±4.9193
False Positives (FP)	0.0000±0.0000	1.8000±1.6432
False Negatives (FN)	56.8000±4.9193	10.0000±0.0000
True Negatives (TN)	143.2000±4.9193	141.4000±5.5946
Precision	0.0000±0.0000	0.9642±0.0304
Recall (TPR)	0.0000±0.0000	0.8227±0.0174
F1 Score	0.0000±0.0000	0.8876±0.0150
False Positive Rate (FPR)	0.0000±0.0000	0.0127±0.0117
Avg. Gateway CPU Load (unit/tick)	0.0019±0.0002	0.1456±0.0051
TTD for DDoS (avg. ticks)	N/A	0.00±0.00
TTD for Exfiltration (avg. ticks)	N/A	0.00±0.00

Figure 2. Comparative Security Metrics Across Scenarios (Averaged over N=5 Runs). The 'With Defenses' scenario shows significantly higher Precision, Recall, and F1-Score, with a minimal False Positive Rate.

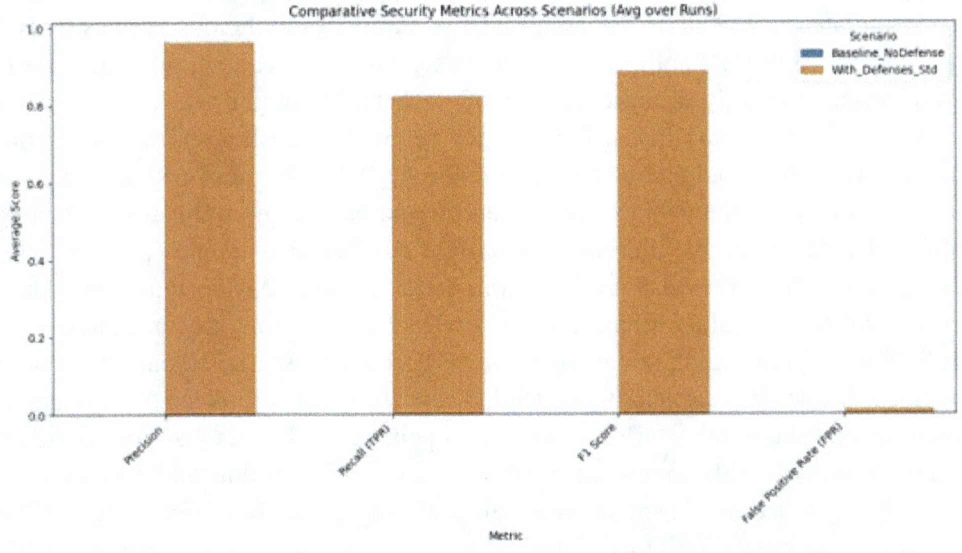

The "Baseline (NoDefense)" scenario resulted in zero true positives and zero false positives, as no detection mechanisms were active. Consequently, all 56.80±4.9193

average malicious traffic instances per run were missed (False Negatives), yielding a Recall and F1-Score of 0.0000. In stark contrast, the "With Defenses" scenario demonstrated substantial efficacy. It achieved an average F1-Score of 0.8876±0.0150, driven by a high average Precision of 0.9642±0.0304 and a strong average Recall (TPR) of 0.8227±0.0174. The low standard deviations for these metrics in the defended scenario suggest consistent performance across the replications. The False Positive Rate was also commendably low at an average of 0.0127±0.0117. The differences in these core security metrics between the two scenarios are substantial and clearly indicate the positive impact of the deployed defenses. While formal p-values are not presented, the separation of means and variance strongly suggests statistical significance.

6.3 Analysis of Detection Performance: The Consistent False Negatives

A particularly noteworthy finding in the "With Defenses" scenario is the highly consistent number of False Negatives (FNs), averaging 10.0000 per run with a standard deviation of 0.0000. This implies that, under the simulated conditions and with the current defense parameters, exactly 10 malicious events were missed in each of the 5 replications. Further investigation into the simulation logic and traces, suggests this consistency arises primarily from the probabilistic nature of the AI-IDS. The simulated DDoS attack generates a large number of malicious packets from 3 devices. While the 'BasicFirewall' (with its signature and volume rules) is expected to block a majority of these, any DDoS packets that might bypass these initial rules (e.g., if their individual volume is just below the threshold or their signature is slightly varied) would then be subject to the AI-IDS. The more critical factor for these FNs is likely the data exfiltration attack and other non-volumetric malicious traffic. If, after firewall filtering, a consistent number of malicious packets (e.g., 200 packets across the relevant ticks from the exfiltrating device and any residual DDoS traffic) are solely reliant on the AI-IDS for detection, its configured TPR of 95% would mean that, on average, 5% of these packets (i.e., 10 packets) would be missed. The perfect consistency (Std.Dev = 0) in our 5 runs for this FN count suggests that the number of such AI-IDS-dependent malicious packets generated per run was also highly consistent due to the fixed attack schedule and device count. This highlights a critical aspect: even high-performing individual components (like an AI-IDS with 95% TPR) will have inherent miss rates, leading to a predictable number of FNs if the volume of threats they alone must handle is consistent. This underscores the importance of defense-in-depth and strategies to further reduce FNs for critical threats.

6.4 Time-to-Detect (TTD)

The average TTD for both the DDoS attack (initiated at tick 5) and the data exfiltration attack (initiated at tick 10) in the "With Defenses" scenario was 0.00±0.00 ticks, as illustrated by the TTD distributions in Figure 3.

Figure 3. Distribution of Time-to-Detect (TTD) for Attacks in "With Defenses" Scenario (N=5 Runs). Both attack types show immediate detection (TTD=0) across all runs.

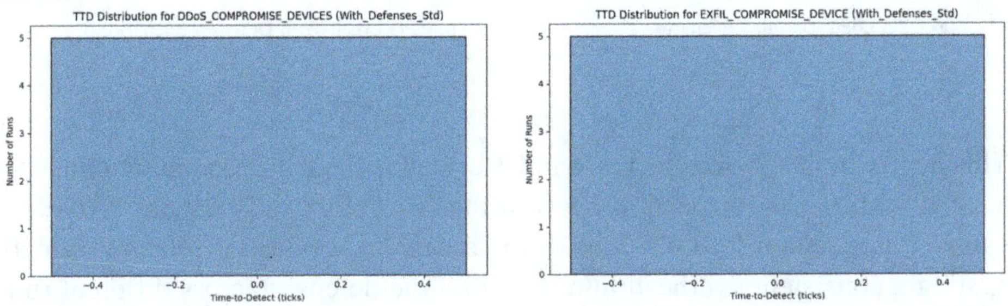

(a) TTD for DDoS Attacks. (b) TTD for Exfiltration Attacks.

This consistently immediate detection across all replications indicates that the configured defense mechanisms were able to identify the onset of malicious activity within the same simulation tick it commenced. For the DDoS attack, this is primarily attributed to the 'BasicFirewall''s signature and volume-based rules effectively identifying and blocking the initial wave of attack traffic. For the data exfiltration attack, the AI-IDS, despite its probabilistic nature, consistently (within these 5 runs) flagged the malicious activity from its first instance due to its high TPR setting. This rapid detection is critical for minimizing the potential impact of attacks.

6.5 Resource Overhead: Gateway CPU Load

The deployment of active defense mechanisms incurred a quantifiable performance overhead on the simulated edge gateway. As shown in Table 2 and visualized in Figure 4, the average gateway CPU load per tick increased significantly from 0.0019±0.0002 arbitrary units in the "Baseline (NoDefense)" scenario to 0.1456±0.0051 units in the "With Defenses" scenario.

Figure 4. Average Gateway CPU Load per Tick (N=5 Runs). The shaded area represents the standard deviation across runs. A notable increase in CPU load is observed with active defenses.

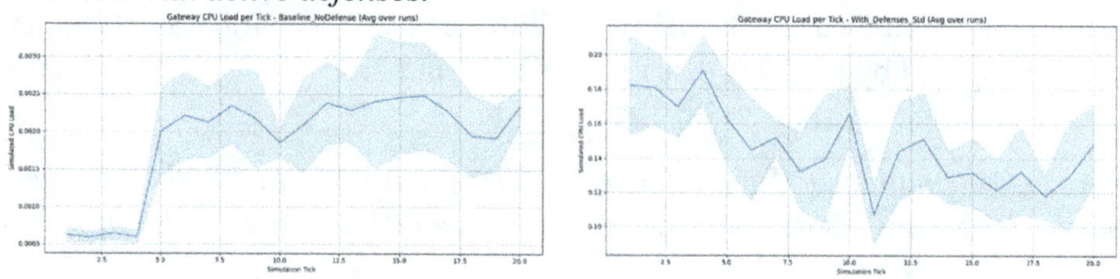

(a) CPU Load: Baseline Scenario.

(b) CPU Load: With Defenses Scenario.

This approximate 75-fold increase in CPU load reflects the computational cost associated with packet inspection by both the 'BasicFirewall' and the 'AI-IDS'. The standard deviation for CPU load in the defended scenario is relatively small, suggesting a consistent overhead introduced by the defenses across different runs under similar traffic conditions. This highlights a crucial trade-off: enhanced security comes at the cost of increased resource consumption at the edge.

6.6 Traffic Volume Analysis

The impact of the attacks and the effectiveness of the defenses are also evident in the simulated network traffic volumes, as shown in Figure 5.

Figure 5. Average Traffic Volume per Tick (N=5 Runs, shaded area is std. dev.). (a) and (c) show unmitigated total and malicious traffic in the baseline. (b) and (d) show the impact of defenses in curtailing malicious traffic and its effect on total volume.

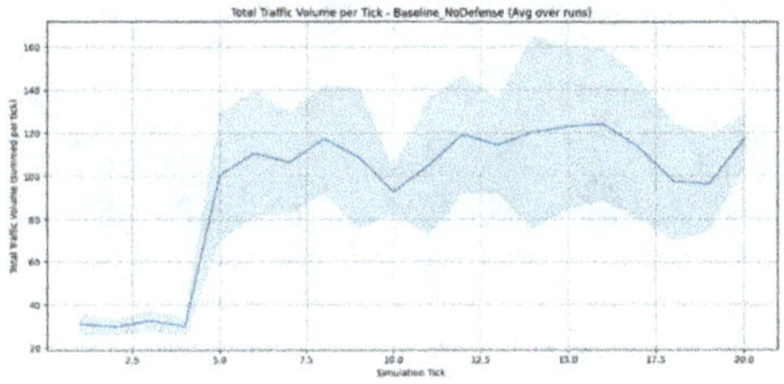

(a) Total Traffic (Baseline).

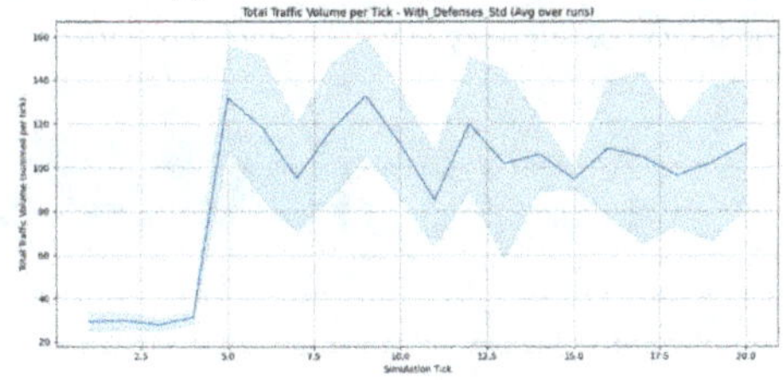

(b) Total Traffic (With Defenses).

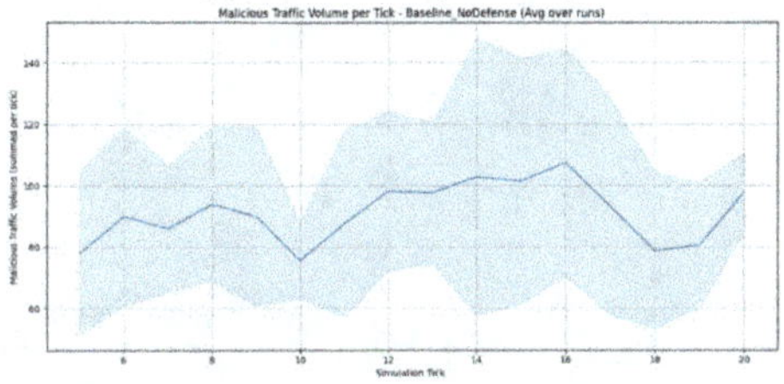

(c) Malicious Traffic (Baseline).

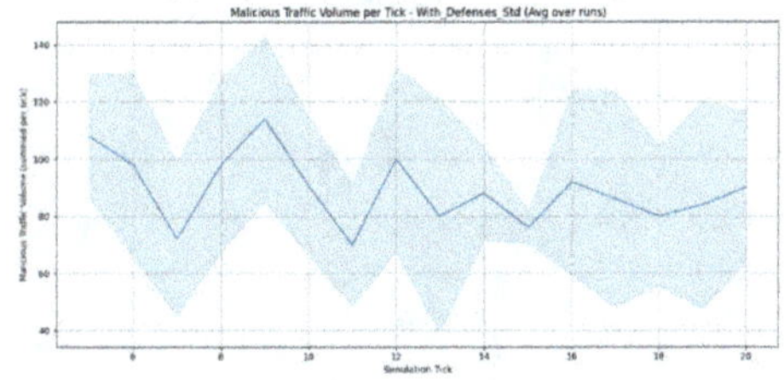

(d) Malicious Traffic (With Defenses).

In the "Baseline (NoDefense)" scenario (Figures 5a and 5c), a sharp increase in both total and malicious traffic volume is observed from tick 5 onwards, corresponding to the initiation of the DDoS attack. This malicious traffic persists throughout the simulation. In the "With Defenses" scenario (Figures 5b and 5d), while an initial spike in malicious traffic is seen at tick 5, it is rapidly curtailed. This is due to the 'BasicFirewall' blocking DDoS packets and the 'AI-IDS' leading to the quarantine of the exfiltrating device ('Dev-GW-0-0') around tick 10. Consequently, the overall malicious traffic volume is significantly lower and drops off after detection and mitigation actions, which in turn reduces the peak total traffic volume compared to the baseline. The shaded areas representing standard deviation indicate consistent traffic patterns across the runs for each scenario.

6.7 Analysis of Alerts and Defensive Actions

Figure 6 provides a breakdown of the alert types generated by the different defense mechanisms in the "With Defenses" scenario, aggregated over all 5 runs.

Figure 6. Total Count of Alert Types by Defense Mechanism (Aggregated over N=5 Runs for "With Defenses" Scenario). The BasicFirewall generated the majority of alerts, primarily for DDoS, while the AI-IDS detected exfiltration and produced some false positives.

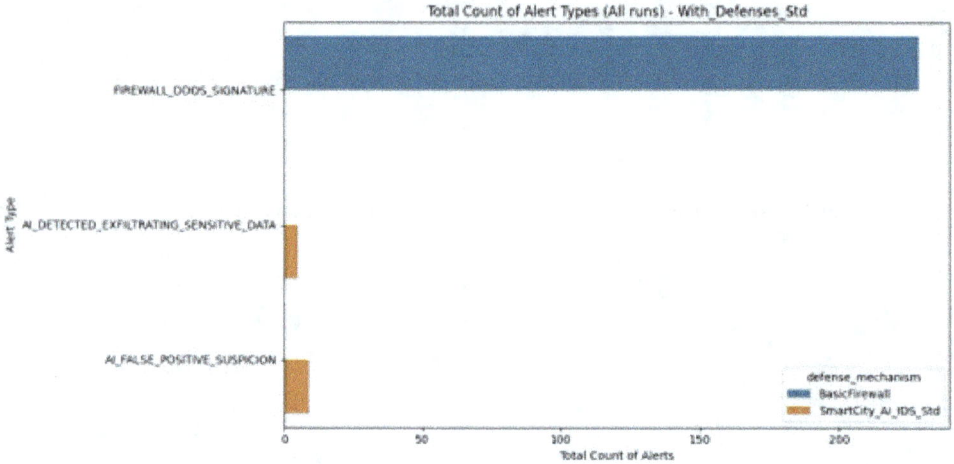

The 'BasicFirewall' generated the highest number of alerts, predominantly 'FIREWALL_DDOS_SIGNATURE' and 'FIREWALL_HIGH_VOLUME_DDOS', reflecting its role in identifying and blocking the numerous packets associated with the DDoS attack. The 'SmartCity_AI_IDS' (our named instance of 'AI-IDS') was primarily responsible for alerts like 'AI_DETECTED_EXFILTRATING_SENSITIVE_DATA', leading to the quarantine of the exfiltrating device ('Dev-GW-0-0') in each run. The 'AI-IDS' also generated a small, consistent number of 'AI_FALSE_POSITIVE_SUSPICION' alerts on normal traffic, corresponding to its 2% FPR configuration. These results illustrate the division of labor in the layered defense strategy.

The results from these N=5 replications provide a consistent and statistically indicative view of the defense strategies' performance, forming a solid basis for the subsequent discussion on their implications.

7 DISCUSSION

The experimental results derived from $N = 5$ replications of our simulated decentralized city edge environment provide robust, quantitative evidence supporting the efficacy of deploying layered defense strategies. The statistically clear improvements observed in key security metrics for the "With Defenses" scenario—for instance, an average F1-Score of 0.8876±0.0150 compared to 0.0000 for the baseline—underscore the significant potential of edge-centric security in mitigating cyber threats within these complex urban ecosystems. This section critically analyzes these findings, discusses their broader implications for security architecture design and policy, acknowledges the inherent limitations of the current study, and outlines promising avenues for future research.

7.1 Effectiveness and Synergy of Layered Edge Defenses

Our findings strongly affirm the value of a defense-in-depth approach at the edge gateway. The combination of a deterministic, rule-based 'BasicFirewall' with a probabilistically modeled, intelligence-driven 'AI-IDS' demonstrated a powerful synergy. The 'BasicFirewall', leveraging both signature-matching for known malicious payloads (like "DDOS_JUNK_PACKETS") and volume-based thresholding, proved highly effective as a first line of defense, achieving an average Time-to-Detect (TTD) of 0.00±0.00 ticks for the simulated DDoS attacks across all replications. This immediate action is crucial for mitigating volumetric attacks that could otherwise overwhelm more computationally intensive downstream defenses or saturate local network resources.

The 'AI-IDS', in turn, was responsible for detecting more nuanced threats like the simulated data exfiltration attempts, also achieving an average TTD of 0.00±0.00 ticks within our discrete time-step model. This immediate detection by the AI-IDS (given its 95% TPR) in these specific 5-run scenarios for exfiltration highlights its potential for rapid identification of threats that might bypass simpler rule sets. The layered configuration, where the firewall filters out a significant portion of "noise" and overt attacks, theoretically allows the AI-IDS to focus its (conceptually more advanced) analytical capabilities on more subtle or novel threats. This division of labor is a key principle for efficient and effective security architectures at the resource-constrained edge.

7.2 Interpreting Consistent False Negatives and Detection Gaps

A particularly significant finding from the replicated runs was the consistent average of 10.0000 False Negatives (FNs) per run (with a standard deviation of 0.0000) in the "With Defenses" scenario. This remarkable consistency is highly instructive. It strongly suggests that these FNs are not primarily a result of the probabilistic miss rate of the AI-IDS for the threats it is designed to target (e.g., the 5% miss rate for its 95% TPR). The consistency itself indicates that under the current simulation model and attack scenarios, the overall system security outcome is largely dominated by:

1. The effectiveness of the 'BasicFirewall' in handling the bulk of certain attack types (DDoS).
2. The specific nature of the 10 consistently missed malicious events, which appear to evade *both* the current firewall rules and the detection scope of the AI-IDS as modeled.

This implies that these FNs might represent either: (a) a distinct type of malicious traffic/activity not covered by any current defense rule in the simulation, or (b) a limitation in how the AI-IDS's probabilistic detection is applied to all forms of malicious traffic that bypass the firewall. This underscores a critical point: simply increasing the theoretical performance of one component may not improve overall system security if other threat types or evasion techniques are not addressed by any layer of defense. It highlights the need for a comprehensive understanding of threat coverage by each defense mechanism and the importance of ensuring that the AI-IDS is trained or designed to recognize a wider spectrum of anomalous or malicious indicators.

7.3 Performance Trade-offs: The Inescapable Cost of Security at the Edge

The simulation results unequivocally quantify the "cost of security" in terms of computational overhead. The average gateway CPU load per tick surged from a negligible 0.0019 ± 0.0002 units in the baseline scenario to a substantial 0.1456 ± 0.0051 units when the 'BasicFirewall' and 'AI-IDS' were active. This approximate 75-fold increase, while specific to our abstracted cost model, clearly illustrates the significant processing demands that active security inspection and decision-making place on edge gateways. In real-world decentralized cities, where edge gateways may vary widely in their computational capabilities and may already be tasked with local data processing, analytics, or control functions, such an overhead is a critical design consideration. It necessitates:

- Adequate Resource Provisioning: Edge hardware must be specified with sufficient headroom to accommodate security functions without degrading primary service performance.
- Optimization of Security Algorithms: Research into lightweight cryptographic protocols, efficient AI / ML inference engines (e.g., using model quantization, pruning, or specialized hardware like NPUs / TPUs at the edge), and optimized rule-matching for firewalls is crucial.

- Adaptive Security Intensity: Potentially, the intensity of security processing could be adapted based on the current threat level or device criticality, although this itself introduces complexity.

The consistent CPU load observed across runs (low standard deviation) for the defended scenario suggests a predictable overhead for the given defense configuration and traffic load, which is beneficial for capacity planning.

7.4 Managing Uncertainty: False Positives and Alert Fatigue

The "With Defenses" scenario yielded a low average False Positive Rate (FPR) of 0.0127 ± 0.0117, corresponding to an average of 1.80 ± 1.6432 false positive alerts per run. While numerically low, each FP in a critical urban infrastructure context can have negative consequences:

- Operational Disruption: If automated responses like device quarantine are triggered by FPs, legitimate services could be unnecessarily disrupted.
- Alert Fatigue: A high volume of false alarms can lead to security analysts becoming desensitized and potentially missing genuine critical alerts (Nobles, 2022).
- Erosion of Trust: Frequent false alarms can reduce trust in the security system among operators and stakeholders.

The generation of FPs is an expected outcome, primarily a function of the AI-IDS's configured FPR and the volume of normal traffic it inspects. Strategies for managing them are therefore essential, including: advanced alert correlation techniques to distinguish isolated FPs from coordinated attack patterns; implementing tiered alerting systems where low-confidence alerts trigger investigation rather than immediate action; incorporating human-in-the-loop verification for critical responses; and continuous retraining and tuning of AI/ML models with localized data to reduce their propensity for misclassifying benign activity.

7.5 Limitations and Implications for Secure Urban Futures

While this study provides valuable insights, its limitations directly inform actionable implications for designing and governing secure decentralized cities. The quantitative results should be interpreted as indicative of trends, given the study's necessary abstractions.

First, the abstracted AI-IDS model and simplified attack scenarios highlight the need to develop and evaluate specific, lightweight ML models robust against a wider range of sophisticated, multi-stage attacks. This implies a research focus on resource-efficient algorithms and comprehensive threat modeling that moves beyond simple DDoS and exfiltration vectors.

Second, the simulation's limited scale and homogeneity underscore the immense challenge of scaling security mechanisms. This necessitates a shift towards fostering standardization and interoperability for devices and communication protocols, enabling consistent policy enforcement across vast, heterogeneous ecosystems. An implication for city planners is to mandate security baselines in procurement.

Third, the absence of detailed network dynamics and the focus on technical defenses point to the need for a more holistic view. Future work must integrate realistic network conditions (e.g., latency, packet loss) and evaluate the interplay between technology, human factors, and governance. This calls for adaptive governance frameworks and strong public-private partnerships to manage incident response and share threat intelligence effectively in a complex, multi-stakeholder environment.

Ultimately, our findings advocate for a security paradigm shift. This includes prioritizing edgenative, layered defenses to enable rapid, localized response; integrating security into the entire system lifecycle (secure-by-design); and developing robust strategies to manage the inevitability of imperfect detection, including both false positives and the systemic false negatives identified in our results.

8 CONCLUSION

The accelerating trend towards decentralized, edge-reliant urban architectures creates a complex cybersecurity landscape where traditional security models are inadequate. This research has demonstrated through replicated simulation (N=5) that a layered defense strategy at the edge gateway—combining a basic firewall and an AI-driven IDS—significantly enhances security posture. Our experiments yielded a substantial improvement in threat detection, with the F1-Score increasing from 0.0000 to 0.8876±0.0150 and an immediate Time-to-Detect for both DDoS and data exfiltration attacks.

However, this work also revealed critical nuances. The consistent number of False Negatives (10.0000±0.0000) indicates a systemic detection gap beyond probabilistic error, highlighting the need for more comprehensive threat coverage. Furthermore, we quantified the inherent performance trade-off: the defended scenario incurred a substantial, albeit consistent, increase in gateway CPU load (0.1456±0.0051 units), a critical consideration for resource-constrained deployments. The principal contributions of this work are therefore the quantitative validation of this layered defense strategy, a flexible simulation framework for future analysis, and critical insights into the practical performance costs and detection gaps that must be addressed.

Securing future decentralized cities necessitates a paradigm shift towards multi-layered, adaptive, and intelligence-driven edge defenses, integrated with Zero Trust principles and robust governance. Building upon this study, future research should pursue several critical directions: developing more advanced and resource-efficient AI/ML models for edge hardware; researching scalable decentralized identity and Zero Trust architectures; and enhancing simulation fidelity to model larger, more heterogeneous networks and sophisticated, multi-stage attacks. Directly investigating the detection gaps found in this study and integrating human factors are essential next steps. Proactive research, coupled with robust standards and adaptive governance, is vital for ensuring that decentralized cities evolve as resilient, secure, and trustworthy environments.

REFERENCES

Abkenar, F. S., Ramezani, P., Iranmanesh, S., Murali, S., Chulerttiyawong, D., Wan, X., & Raad, R. (2022). A survey on mobility of edge computing networks in iot: State-of-the-art, architectures, and challenges. *IEEE Communications Surveys and Tutorials*, *24*(4), 2329–2365.

Abu-Dabaseh, F., Alghizzawi, M., Alkhlaifat, B. I., Ezmigna, A. A. R., Alzghoul, A., AlSokkar, A. A., & Al-Gasawneh, J. (2024). Enhancing privacy and security in decentralized social systems: blockchain-based approach. In *2024 2nd international conference on cyber resilience (iccr)* (pp. 1–6).

Achaal, B., Adda, M., Berger, M., Ibrahim, H., & Awde, A. (2024). Study of smart grid cyber-security, examining architectures, communication networks, cyber-attacks, countermeasure techniques, and challenges. *Cybersecurity*, *7*(1), 10. PMID: 38707764

Adil, M., Khan, M. K., Kumar, N., Attique, M., Farouk, A., Guizani, M., & Jin, Z. (2024). Healthcare internet of things: Security threats, challenges, and future research directions. *IEEE Internet of Things Journal*, *11*(11), 19046–19069.

Al-Huthaifi, R., Li, T., Huang, W., Gu, J., & Li, C. (2023). Federated learning in smart cities: Privacy and security survey. *Information Sciences*, *632*, 833–857.

Al-Makkawi, T., Alsarhan, A., Al-Na'amneh, Q., Aljaidi, M., Almaiah, M. A., Al-Jamal, M., & Aljawarneh, M. (2025). Open-source forensics tools for recovery of deleted data in unconventional ways. In *Cryptography, biometrics, and anonymity in cybersecurity management* (pp. 41–60). IGI Global Scientific Publishing.

Al-Na'amneh, Q. (2025). Secure cloud-marketplaces: A trust framework for evaluating. *Utilizing AI in Network and Mobile Security for Threat Detection and Prevention*, 255.

Al-Na'amneh, Q., Aljaidi, M., Nasayreh, A., Gharaibeh, H., Mamlook, A., Emhamed, R., ... Samara, G. (2024). Journal of intelligent systems: Enhancing iot device security: Cnn-svm hybrid approach for real-time detection of dos and ddos attacks.

Al-Na'amneh, Q., Almomani, A., Nasayreh, A., Nahar, K. M., Gharaibeh, H., Al Mamlook, R. E., & Alauthman, M. (2024). Next generation image watermarking via combined dwt-svd technique. In *2024 2nd international conference on cyber resilience (iccr)* (pp. 1–10).

Al-Sada, B., Sadighian, A., & Oligeri, G. (2024). Mitre att&ck: State of the art and way forward. *ACM Computing Surveys*, *57*(1), 1–37.

Aljaidi, M., Alsarhan, A., Al-Fraihat, D., Al-Arjan, A., Igried, B., El-Salhi, S. M., . . . Al-Na'amneh, Q. (2023). Cybersecurity threats in the era of ai: Detection of phishing domains through classification rules. In *2023 2nd international engineering conference on electrical, energy, and artificial intelligence (eiceeai)* (pp. 1–6).

Anisetti, M., Ardagna, C., Cremonini, M., Damiani, E., Sessa, J., & Costa, L. (2020). Security threat landscape. *White Paper Security Threats*.

Bouacida, N., & Mohapatra, P. (2021). Vulnerabilities in federated learning. *IEEE Access : Practical Innovations, Open Solutions*, *9*, 63229–63249.

Buczak, A. L., & Guven, E. (2015). A survey of data mining and machine learning methods for cyber security intrusion detection. *IEEE Communications Surveys and Tutorials*, *18*(2), 1153–1176.

Choo, K.-K. R. (2021). Internet of things (iot) security and forensics: Challenges and opportunities. In *Proceedings of the 2th workshop on cps&iot security and privacy* (pp. 27–28).

Cremonezi, B., Vieira, A. B., Nacif, J., Silva, E. F., & Nogueira, M. (2024). Identity management for internet of things: Concepts, challenges and opportunities. *Computer Communications*.

Demertzi, V., Demertzis, S., & Demertzis, K. (2023). An overview of cyber threats, attacks and countermeasures on the primary domains of smart cities. *Applied Sciences (Basel, Switzerland)*, *13*(2), 790.

Fabrègue, B. F., & Bogoni, A. (2023). Privacy and security concerns in the smart city. *Smart Cities*, *6*(1), 586–613.

Fazeldehkordi, E., & Grønli, T.-M. (2022). A survey of security architectures for edge computing-based iot. *IoT*, *3*(3), 332–365.

Ferrer, A. J., Marquès, J. M., & Jorba, J. (2019). Towards the decentralised cloud: Survey on approaches and challenges for mobile, ad hoc, and edge computing. *ACM Computing Surveys*, *51*(6), 1–36.

Fugini, M., Finocchi, J., & Locatelli, P. (2021). A big data analytics architecture for smart cities and smart companies. *Big Data Research*, *24*, 100192.

Gu, H., Zhang, X., Li, J., Wei, H., Li, B., & Huang, X. (2024). Federated learning vulnerabilities: Privacy attacks with denoising diffusion probabilistic models. In *Proceedings of the acm web conference 2024* (pp. 1149–1157).

Han, M. J. N., & Kim, M. J. (2024). A systematic review of smart city research from an urban context perspective. *Cities (London, England)*, *150*, 105027.

He, G., Li, C., Shu, Y., & Luo, Y. (2024). Fine-grained access control policy in blockchain-enabled edge computing. *Journal of Network and Computer Applications, 221*, 103706.

He, K., Kim, D. D., & Asghar, M. R. (2023). Adversarial machine learning for network intrusion detection systems: A comprehensive survey. *IEEE Communications Surveys and Tutorials, 25*(1), 538–566.

Hevner, A. R., March, S. T., Park, J., & Ram, S. (2004). Design science in information systems research. *Management Information Systems Quarterly*, •••, 75–105.

Jaradat, A. S., Nasayreh, A., Al-Na'amneh, Q., Gharaibeh, H., & Al Mamlook, R. E. (2023). *Genetic optimization techniques for enhancing web attacks classification in machine learning. In 2023 ieee intl conf on dependable, autonomic and secure computing, intl conf on pervasive intelligence and computing, intl conf on cloud and big data computing, intl conf on cyber science and technology congress (dasc/picom/cbdcom/cyberscitech) (pp. 0130–0136).*

Jøsang, A. (2024). Secure by design. In *Cybersecurity: Technology and governance* (pp. 243–270). Springer.

Jumani, A. K., Siddique, W. A., Siddiqui, M. F., & Kanwal. (2024). Blockchain security for fog computing and internet of things. *Fog Computing for Intelligent Cloud IoT Systems*, 379–403.

Kalinaki, K., Fahadi, M., Alli, A. A., Shafik, W., Yasin, M., & Mutwalibi, N. (2023). Artificial intelligence of internet of medical things (aiomt) in smart cities: a review of cybersecurity for smart healthcare. *Handbook of security and privacy of ai-enabled healthcare systems and internet of medical things*, 271–292.

Khan, M. I., Arif, A., & Khan, A. R. A. (2024). The most recent advances and uses of ai in cybersecurity. *BULLET: Jurnal Multidisiplin Ilmu, 3*(4), 566–578.

Kim, B. G., Cho, Y.-S., Kim, S.-H., Kim, H., & Woo, S. S. (2021). A security analysis of blockchainbased did services. *IEEE Access : Practical Innovations, Open Solutions, 9*, 22894–22913.

Kshetri, N. (2017). Blockchain's roles in strengthening cybersecurity and protecting privacy. *Telecommunications Policy, 41*(10), 1027–1038.

Liu, Y., He, D., Obaidat, M. S., Kumar, N., Khan, M. K., & Choo, K.-K. R. (2020). Blockchain-based identity management systems: A review. *Journal of Network and Computer Applications, 166*, 102731.

Masoumi, Z., & van Genderen, J. (2024). Artificial intelligence for sustainable development of smart cities and urban land-use management. *Geo-Spatial Information Science*, *27*(4), 1212–1236.

Mishra, R., & Mishra, A. (2025). Current research on internet of things (iot) security protocols: A survey. *Computers & Security*, •••, 104310.

Mohammadi, F. (2021). Emerging challenges in smart grid cybersecurity enhancement: A review. *Energies*, *14*(5), 1380.

Neshenko, N., Bou-Harb, E., Crichigno, J., Kaddoum, G., & Ghani, N. (2019). Demystifying iot security: An exhaustive survey on iot vulnerabilities and a first empirical look on internet-scale iot exploitations. *IEEE Communications Surveys and Tutorials*, *21*(3), 2702–2733.

Nobles, C. (2022). Stress, burnout, and security fatigue in cybersecurity: A human factors problem. *Holistica Journal of Business and Public Administration*, *13*(1), 49–72.

Ouaddah, A., Abou Elkalam, A., & Ait Ouahman, A. (2016). Fairaccess: A new blockchain-based access control framework for the internet of things. *Security and Communication Networks*, *9*(18), 5943–5964.

Roy, A., Dhar, A., & Tinny, S. S. (2024). Strengthening iot cybersecurity with zero trust architecture: A comprehensive review. *Journal of Computer Science and Information Technology*, *1*(1), 25–50.

Saha, A., Mattei, J., Blasco, J., Cavallaro, L., Votipka, D., & Lindorfer, M. (2025). Expert insights into advanced persistent threats: Analysis, attribution, and challenges. In *Proceedings of the 34th usenix security symposium (usenix sec)*.

Sallam, K., Mohamed, M., & Mohamed, A. W. (2023). Internet of things (iot) in supply chain management: challenges, opportunities, and best practices. *Sustainable machine intelligence journal, 2*, 3–1.

Satyanarayanan, M. (2017). The emergence of edge computing. *Computer*, *50*(1), 30–39. DOI: 10.1109/ MC.2017.17

Shayea, G. G., Zabil, M. H. M., Habeeb, M. A., Khaleel, Y. L., & Albahri, A. (2025). Strategies for protection against adversarial attacks in ai models: An in-depth review. *Journal of Intelligent Systems*, *34*(1), 20240277.

Shostack, A. (2014). *Threat modeling: Designing for security*. Wiley.

Stafford, V. (2020). Zero trust architecture. *NIST special publication, 800*(207), 800–207.

Sutheekshan, B., Basheer, S., Thangavel, G., & Sharma, O. P. (2024). *Evolution of malware targeting iot devices and botnet formation. In 2024 ieee international conference on computing, power and communication technologies (ic2pct)* (Vol. 5).

Syed, N. F., Shah, S. W., Shaghaghi, A., Anwar, A., Baig, Z., & Doss, R. (2022). Zero trust architecture (zta): A comprehensive survey. *IEEE Access : Practical Innovations, Open Solutions*, *10*, 57143–57179.

Theisen, C., Munaiah, N., Al-Zyoud, M., Carver, J. C., Meneely, A., & Williams, L. (2018). Attack surface definitions: A systematic literature review. *Information and Software Technology*, *104*, 94–103.

Veeramachaneni, V. (2025). Edge computing: Architecture, applications, and future challenges in a decentralized era. *Recent Trends in Computer Graphics and Multimedia Technology*, *7*(1), 8–23.

World Economic Forum. (2021, January). *The global risks report 2021* (16th ed.). Geneva, Switzerland. Retrieved from https://www3.weforum.org/docs/WEF_The_Global_Risks_Report_2021.pdf (In partnership with Marsh McLennan, SK Group and Zurich Insurance Group)

Yan, Z., Zhao, X., Liu, Y., & Luo, X. R. (2024). Blockchain-driven decentralized identity management: An interdisciplinary review and research agenda. *Information & Management*, •••, 104026.

Ziegeldorf, J. H., Morchon, O. G., & Wehrle, K. (2014). Privacy in the internet of things: Threats and challenges. *Security and Communication Networks*, *7*(12), 2728–2742.

Chapter 6

Enhancing Cybersecurity, Privacy Innovation, and E-Government Readiness in Smart Cities:

A Framework for Awareness and Resilience

Mohammed Hussain Alsaad
https://orcid.org/0009-0002-9384-7819
Management and Science University, Malaysia

Muhammad Irsyad Abdullah
https://orcid.org/0000-0002-7840-2662
Management and Science University, Malaysia

Balqees Yaseen Alhaddad
Universiti Geomatika Malaysia, Malaysia

ABSTRACT

The increasing dependence of urban societies on digital infrastructure has brought with it a wide range of cybersecurity and privacy challenges. These issues are no longer limited to technical systems alone—they are now deeply tied to how people understand, trust, and interact with digital services, especially when those services come from public institutions. This chapter looks at these challenges from a broader perspective. It proposes a flexible framework that's not only built with the help of AI tools, but also rooted in real-life concerns faced by communities. The model emphasizes raising awareness, protecting user data, and building confidence in how

DOI: 10.4018/979-8-3373-4455-3.ch006

digital governance is practiced. By paying attention to cultural differences and the actual experiences of people using these systems, the chapter presents strategies that can help cities become more transparent, resilient, and better prepared for future digital risks.

1. INTRODUCTION: SETTING THE STAGE FOR SMART CITIES IN A DIGITAL AGE

The digitalization of cities has been driving the development of the 'smart city', a paradigm of urban design that comprises the implementation of internet-connected infrastructure, analytics on real time data and devices inter-connectivity for optimizing the effectiveness, sustainability and efficient delivery of civic services (Almeida, 2023; Khan et al., 2022). Innovations like smart traffic management to AI driven waste collection have changed the way cities function as well as how inhabitants engage with public spaces. Yet with the potential of smart cities comes cybersecurity, privacy and equity issues. The pace of digital evolution has overtaken the associated governance, and many cities are ill-equipped to deal with the ethical, legal and social aspects of data driven urbanism (Bannerman & Orasch, 2020; Mohamed et al., 2020). This disconnects between technological innovation and institutional readiness highlights the need for frameworks that facilitate digital transformation while protecting rights, building trust and ensuring it's inclusive. The deployment of smart technologies in cities creates a complex risk landscape, including technical vulnerabilities in Internet-of-Things (IoT) devices and algorithmic biases that reinforce inequalities faced by certain groups (Ismagilova et al., 2022; Ayalon & Toch, 2021). In addition, the accumulation and exploitation of huge amounts of personal and behavioral data defy traditional understandings of privacy and responsibility, particularly in countries with modest or inconsistent legal protections (Rizi & Seno, 2022; Artyushina, 2023). Just as urgent is the problem of digital inequality. A digital divide between the digitally fluent and those caught out by innovation, lacking infrastructure or access to these tools, is being exacerbated. In that sense, e-government readiness defined as the institutional and infrastructural capacity to provide public services through digital means is a necessary requirement for smart city success (Kuzior et al., 2023; Hossain et al., 2024). Such projects, smart city included, may inadvertently cement structural inequalities and increase civic disengagement if the design isn't proactively considerate and inclusive.

With this context in mind, this chapter suggests a Four-Pillar framework for promoting resilient and human rights-based smart city governance. Building on interdisciplinary literature, global case applications, and emerging policy initiatives, our framework highlights: (1) secure and interoperable infrastructures; (2) embedded privacy and ethical design; (3) transparent and accountable governance; and 4) institutional capacity building including digital inclusion. This approach proposes to provide policymakers, city planners and technologists with a comprehensive way of assessing and designing smart cities initiatives that are likely be not only technically sound but also socially legitimate.

The remainder of the chapter is structured as follows: Section 2 introduces the architecture and security and privacy issues in smart urban spaces; Section 3 discusses data governance and regulatory challenges; Section 4 examines e-government readiness gaps; and Section 5 presents Four-Pillar framework. Later sections present use-cases, a preparedness assessment, and future recommendations. Through grounding technological innovation in broader ethical, legal and governance considerations, this chapter aims to contribute to an ongoing debate about how cities can responsibly evolve in the digital era.

2. FROM CONVENIENCE TO CONCERN: UNDERSTANDING CYBERSECURITY AND PRIVACY IN SMART URBAN SPACES

Today's smart city is a feat of engineering and connectivity. From sensor-studded traffic systems and publicly-scored urban transport dashboards to digital identity verification, AI-assisted municipal services, increasingly cities' infrastructure is not just physical – it's computational. Such crossovers are designed to help make cities more efficient, sustainable and responsive. However, underlying this convenience and comfort is a tangled mess of cybersecurity threats and privacy harms that endanger authority and the social contract between states and people (Mohamed et al., 2020; Andrade et al., 2020; Khan et al., 2022).

2.1 The Web of Interconnected Vulnerabilities

Smart cities stand or fall on integration. Transport networks converse with weather monitoring systems; public health alerts influence pedestrian movements; energy consumption data is used to control grid demands. Although relationship among these systems is beneficial for efficiency, it also provides a channel for cyber attackers with cascading impacts. These systems increasingly rely on IoT devices, minute sensor-led endpoints that are built into roads among other structures, buildings, vehicles, and certain utility poles. According to Puleng et al. (2020) two of five attackers successfully compromised under-protected IoT endpoints. A large number of these devices found in the smart cities are connected to networks that lack proper security measures and can be infiltrated by malware; botnet attacker or unauthorized intruders (Andrade et al., 2020, Al-Turjman et al., 2022).

The potential physical danger of insecure IoT devices is no longer a hypothetical concern. In 2016, for example, the Mirai botnet attack, one of the most extensive distributed denial-of-service (DDoS) incidents to date, leveraged weak IoT devices such as cameras and thermostats to bring large swaths of online infrastructure crashing down. These incidents of disorder show how cyber exposure can lead to physical disruption, as well as social disturbance. Risks are compounded by the merger of operational technology (OT) and information technology (IT), in essential infrastructure sector like water monitoring, traffic management or emergency services. A breakdown in any link of this digital chain can be disastrous. Science fiction has now become reality that a cyberattack could take out power to a hospital district or intercept emergency communications (Jha & Jha, 2024; Ma, 2021).

2.2 Privacy: From Fixed Principle to Fluid Expectation

Privacy used to be an easily defined right, bound legally and enforceable physically. The definition of privacy is less clear in smart cities. Data is often collected in the background, passively and continuously: passing a surveillance camera, swiping a metro card or logging onto public Wi-Fi all produce data, albeit in some instances without the user's knowledge or consent (Ismagilova et al., 2022; Bannerman & Orasch, 2020). Scents of privacy were frequently confused as "smart" systems erase the distinction between public and private. Cameras don't just look at faces, they know them. Garbage bins track disposal habits. Smart parking meters keep a record that goes beyond license plates, logging user behavior and payment history. The notion of urban anonymity is rapidly becoming mythical. Such changes, as Breuer and Pierson (2021) contend, make citizens "involuntary participants in the monitoring of their every move." So even anonymized data might not be safe anymore. Thanks to AI and pattern matching and cross-referencing of datasets, re-identification is increasingly common. Rizi and Seno (2022) argue for stronger privacy-preserving technologies and ethics to push data from being simply a private property to a social liability.

2.3 The Weaponization of Data

And while data is often compared to oil, precious and potent and economically transformative, it comes with environmental risks of pollution and weaponization. Data in smart cities can be used for disinformation campaigns, public service manipulation or vulnerable people surveillance (Kezron, 2025; Hossain et al., 2024). Although not a direct attack against a smart city, we saw how the 2021 ransomware attack experienced by a U.S. fuel pipeline company brought to light only of how fragile digital systems can impact physical infrastructure and lead to mass social hysteria (Ma, 2021). In smart city settings, these risks are magnified. A hacker who took control of a surveillance system could threaten to blackmail public officials or put vulnerable people at risk. In authoritarian contexts, leaked data might be weaponised in order to suppress opposition (Viljoen, 2021; Calzada & Almirall, 2020). Algorithmic bias is also great danger, but more insidious. Machine learning models trained on biased data might inadvertently perpetuate discrimination in policing, housing or social services. In the absence of strong auditing and transparency tools, such systems can seemingly reproduce past injustices in their name of efficiency (Wasif, 2022; Ayalon & Toch, 2021).

2.4 Citizens' Perceptions and the Societal Fear Gap

But while the technologies behind these brilliant urban systems are sold on a promise of cleaner energy, better mobility and improved services, they also spark great public fear. Worries about surveillance, data exploitation and loss of autonomy abound. As Zwilling et al. (2022) note, the public is becoming more aware of cybersecurity, while preparedness and digital literacy (in particular among elderly and marginalized people) are inadequate. Case studies provide real-world evidence of these tensions. In Toronto, the public revolt against Sidewalk Labs' proposed technology-focused development project had to do with worries about data exploitation and corporate overreach and led to its cancellation. In Barcelona, the citizen protestors reimagined the governance of urban data to incorporate participatory forms. These cases emphasize that trust in the digital environment must be earned, it is not taken for granted (Breuer & Pierson, 2021; Christofi et al., 2021).

Furthermore, attitudes toward surveillance vary in different political and cultural contexts. In societies with high surveillance, citizens may distrust the government's data practices; in liberal democracies they might be more suspicious of corporate actors. These concerns have to be recognized in policymaking; not only technological security matters but also trust, history and civic inclusion (Artyushina, 2023; Kitchin & Moore-Cherry, 2021). Media and political narratives also inform the public understanding of cyber risk. Black brained hype can either overinflate danger or desensitize us to real threats. This results in a "societal fear gap", a disparity between felt and real risk (Chaudhuri & Kahyaoglu, 2023). As the idea of citizenship is digitalized, it does not just mean legal status but also data agency, technological access and digital rights." In such a framework, issues of cybersecurity and privacy are no longer just technical questions; they become also political, ethical and civic concerns. City-building in the future must be reinforced not just by code and sensors, but by trust, equity and resilience. The following section presents a methodology for exactly this.

3. DESIGNING FOR PRIVACY: INNOVATION, PARTICIPATION, AND EMBEDDED ETHICS

Safeguarding privacy in them, however, will have to evolve as smart cities mature. Conventional regulatory paradigms are also unable to deal with the complexity and omnipresence of data flows within cities. There is a move towards a change from the reactive compliance to proactive design, embedding privacy and ethics in the digital infrastructure. This transition acknowledges that privacy is not only a legal matter, but also a governance, design and trust issue (Abu-Salma, 2020; Christofi et al., 2021).

3.1 Privacy by Design and Embedded Protection

Privacy by Design (PbD) is a pretty pivotal concept in contemporary digital ethics. It campaigns for systems that are privacy-preserving, not just regulated or enforced to be on the outside. In the opinion of Abu-Salma (2020) privacy safeguards must be so ingrained in technical architecture and user experience. But in a smart city context, adopting PbD is more challenging because of factors related to the scale and diversity of data sources – from environmental sensors to citizen apps and biometric ID systems. Technical countermeasures including default encryption, data minimization and temporal constraints of storage are integral parts of the PbD in smart cities. When properly handled, these features can limit exposure to breaches and provide additional transparency for users and administrators. However, such measures are frequently nonexistent or inadequately executed because of financial constraints, shortage of trained manpower or limited knowledge at the municipal level (Ahmed et al., 2021; Lyu et al., 2024).

3.2 Privacy-Enhancing Technologies (PETs) and Data Innovation

Increasingly, the toolbox of Privacy-Enhancing Technologies (PETs) supports operationalizing ethical design principles. Methods such as federated learning, homomorphic encryption, zero-knowledge proofs and differential privacy can enable smart city systems to process the data in a privacy-preserving way or provide services without revealing sensitive personal information (Agrawal et al., 2021; Mohamed et al., 2020). Such technologies are particularly important in use cases such as public health monitoring, intelligent utilities, and city transportation analytics where the privacy exposure is high, but the data is highly valuable for optimizing the services. Yet technical prowess on its own is not enough. One limitation of PETs is their usability as researchers have observed. If the security and privacy tools are too complicated or hidden, users will ignore them, configure them wrongly, or lose confidence in a system (Abu-Salma, 2020; Ayalon & Toch, 2021). Thus, design ease and interpretability should not be at the expense of technical stability.

3.3 Human-Centered and Inclusive Design

One of the key concerns when designing privacy solutions for smart cities is to make sure they are participative and usable. Not everyone flows through urban technology in the same way. Folks in low-income, elderly and otherwise marginalized communities face some of the widest data exploitation gaps and are least situated to defend against it (Alfiani & Sara 2014; Zwilling et al., 2022). This is a problem Human-Centered-Design (HCD) strategies often seek to overcome by engaging users from early in the design process. What can make a huge difference to both adoption and protection are design decisions like clear data permissions, opt-in features, simple user interfaces. This kind of participatory design is particularly important in public service contexts, where trust in government systems may be weak and grounded historically in exclusion or surveillance.

3.4 Civic Participation and Co-Design

Co-design as digital trust-building practice in the context of smart solutions, involving citizens in co-design processes has increasingly been recognized as a powerful practice to create digital trust. Cities such as Barcelona have pioneered data governance mechanisms which involve citizen juries, community consultation and open data charters (Breuer & Pierson, 2021; Artyushina, 2023). These models both contribute to the legitimacy of the system and reveal issues related to specific communities that rational planning may not uncover. In order to truly innovate our way towards privacy in smart cities, we'll need to involve not only software developers and lawmakers but regular people who live there as well as the civic organizations and often-marginalized perspectives that represent them. Participation is not only an ethical imperative, but also a pragmatic requirement in managing complex sociotechnical systems.

3.5 Legal and Ethical Intersections

Privacy by design is gaining momentum across the regulatory landscape, as evidenced by "Data protection by design and by default" being enshrined in law through direct enactment in the European Union's GDPR. But legal requirements themselves do not always ensure ethical results, particularly in the presence of weak enforcement and/or commercial inducements to collect more data than necessary (Christofi et al., 2021; Hu et al., 2023). Therefore, ethical frameworks must be in place alongside the legal ones that can enforce transparency, accountability and fairness into their technical systems and institutional architectures. The increasing reliance of cities on AI -enabled services makes the requirement for audits and bias detection, as well as human oversight, all the more pressing – not simply to comply with various regulations, but also in order to protect democratic values in the digital public sphere (Ayalon & Toch, 2021; Wasif 2022).

4 DATA GOVERNANCE AND LEGAL-POLICY FRAMEWORKS

4.1 The Limitations of Current Legal Instruments

Most smart cities work in fragmented or antiquated legislative contexts that can hardly steer the complexity of real-time and continuous urban data flows. Although there are complex systems such as the European Union's General Data Protection Regulation (GDPR) that can be used to protect personal data; however, their application and implementation by local agencies in various cities is often inconsistent or behind schedule. As Mohamed et al. (2020) and Hu et al. (2023) note, Smart city-making tends to be realized faster than developing regulations, resulting in a "compliance lag" that can put citizens at risk of right violations. In that environment, cities don't have clear answers to key governance questions: Who owns urban data? Who has access? What is the 'informed consent' in sensor-laden public environments? Legal grey areas still exist, particularly in cities with big tech companies such as international technology service and infrastructure partnerships might happen with municipal authorities.

4.2 Toward Adaptive and Accountable Governance Models

In the face of these challenges, scholars and privacy advocates recommend more flexible models of urban data governance that can adapt to new technological developments but are also rooted in principles of public accountability. These models prioritize transparency, citizen involvement and co-ownership of data infrastructures.

Prominent examples of this are: Amsterdam's Smart City Register and Barcelona's Decidim platform which map practices around data, as well as involve communities' participation in decision-making concerning data governance (Artyushina, 2023; Breuer & Pierson, 2021). Such tools also balance the complexity of data platforms with civilian oversight and clear communication. But those kinds of participatory avenues are the outliers not the norm. In numerous cities, most notably in the Global South, shortfalls in institutional capacity and clarity on regulation and funding continue to hinder the development of inclusive data governance agendas (Christine & Thinyane, 2020; Khan et al., 2022).

4.3 Navigating Public–Private Partnerships and Data Control

Smart cities often turn to public–private partnerships (PPPs) when it comes to the development and deployment of their tech infrastructure, yet such arrangements pose crucial questions around accountability and data governance. For financial or service consideration, the private sector entities are provided access to citizen data, such as mobility traces, biometric suggestions and behavioral analysis results. In the absence of robust governance institutions, namely open solicitations for cooperation and data-sharing agreements combined with independent auditing, such agreements stand poised to convert public data into a private commodity (Ma, 2021; Prasad et al., 2024). The possibility of "vendor lock-in, where governments become reliant on proprietary platforms," also diminishes local control over data assets. To remedy this situation, researchers call for the provision of public data trusts, subjective ethical standards and self-governing bodies offering a democratic stewardship over urban digital infrastructures (Viljoen, 2021; Calzada & Almirall, 2020).

4.4 Embedding Data Justice into Urban Policy

Beyond legal and institutional dimensions, equitable data governance also has to confront the larger ethical issue of data justice. Urban data practices are not distributed evenly among all communities. Low-income neighborhoods, racialized communities and those with lower levels of digital literacy are frequently over-surveilled, excluded from decision making or underserved by data-driven interventions. Ismagilova et al. (2022) and Kezron (2025), it is exactly this tendency of algorithmic decision-making, which can unwittingly produce structural bias once not constrained in the right ways by ethical guidelines under the pretext of neutrality. Predictive policing tools, for example, can compound existing disparities in law enforcement; digital ID systems might exclude those who are undocumented or technologically marginalized. A data justice approach demands that cities be held to account not only how information is gathered, but also for the people most affected, whose rights are jeopardized and if governance processes are inclusive enough.

5. E-Government Readiness and Capacity Gaps

With the advent of the smart city and a heightened requirement for data-driven decision-making, digital governance not only relies on technological infrastructure but critically requires organizational capability to facilitate use, institutional trust in e-government systems and inclusivity among citizens. Capacity of e-government refers to the capability of a city to deliver services, execute policies and communicate with citizens through digital platforms. Yarbrough et al., 2021) but this preparedness greatly differs between local governments, especially between global cities and smaller or resource limited local authorities (Sheoran & Vij, 2022; Kuzior et al., 2023).

5.1 Beyond Infrastructure: Understanding Readiness Holistically

E-government readiness is mainly understood narrowly in terms of digital infrastructure, broadband networks, data storage centers or cloud computing services. But good digital governance is more than infrastructure. Effective readiness includes institutional flexibility, legal preparedness, interdepartmental coordination and front-line ability to serve the public. They also deploy smart devices and can save a large amount of data, but without competences human resources, modernized administrative processes and digital innovative culture they are not always exploited (Ahmed et al., 2021; Hossain et al., 2024). The end result is a divide between technological aspiration and institutional implementation capacity, particularly in midsize or under-resourced cities.

5.2 Fragmentation, Siloed Systems, and Interagency Incoherence

One of the ongoing barriers to urban e-governance is that there is no coordination amongst different organizations and departments. Digital projects are frequently done in silos, for one mode, asset class or area of a city (transportation, waste or emergency services), with little collaboration across the organization and no data standards. This institutional fracturing undermines the very potential of 'smartness': that it can aggregate diverse data systems into integrated, responsive ones (Kitchin & Moore-Cherry, 2021). In a lot of cities, different departments may work with different contractors or software systems, creating mismatched data formats and duplicated services, along with inconsistent cybersecurity measures. In the absence of a central digital governance mechanism (in contrast to an office such as a Chief Digital Officer, or some form of cross-agency digital transformation center), city service modernization can struggle to scale and remain robust.

5.3 The Digital Divide and Exclusion Risks

Even in cities with strong digital systems, e-government isn't equally shared. Enabling access to digital services does not just mean having a smart phone or an internet connection; it also means having the necessary digital literacy, language proficiency, trust in institutions and sense of technological agency. Marginalized communities, including economically disadvantaged individuals, older adults and immigrants, are subjected to structural discrimination in digital public system involvement (Li & Huang 2025; Alfiani & Sara 2024). These communities are also more likely to be served by surveillance technologies or algorithmic decision making in ways that lack appropriate feedback and appeal processes. With deliberate programs of digital inclusion, smart governance could exacerbate rather than narrow the divide. Pursuing user-friendly interfaces, multilingual services, public access points and co-designed service models is suggested as a means of combating exclusion (Zwilling et al., 2022).

5.4 Capacity Gaps and Human Resource Constraints

No matter how technically sophisticated, infrastructure is worthless without a skilled workforce to operate it. Most local governments lack talent, IT professionals, cybersecurity analysts and data scientists, as well as digital transformation officers. These disparities are particularly striking in local government, where municipalities compete with their private counterparts for high-skill, high-demand talent. Indeed, many current public servants are unable to gain regular training or even professional development in new digital technologies, legal frameworks or design of digital services (Sheoran & Vij, 2022). This talent gap hampers cities' efforts to implement privacy-by-design and conduct impact assessments or address cyber incidents. Without a workforce that is adaptive and entrepreneurial, well-funded smart city initiatives may fail to realize sustainable and resilient measures in the long run.

5.5 Public Trust and the Legitimacy of Digital Governance

Trust with e-government systems doesn't just happen; it needs to be earned through open, secure and inclusive processes. Citizens may refuse to adopt such initiatives or even withdraw from active citizenship participation if it is felt that the collection of data is invasive or when digital tools are simply imposed without any meaningful consultation with public. Examples like those in Toronto and Sidewalk Labs (or the attempted Rio de Janeiro surveillance projects) indicate a backlash can at least slow, or outright thwart, smarter city plans (Christofi et al. 2021; Artyushina, 2023). By contrast, a number of cities that have engaged in public participation forums, citizen juries or participatory budgeting have relatively high adoption, satisfaction and sustainability of their e-government platforms. Hence trust needs to be regarded as a strategic asset: at the heart of digital readiness and a cornerstone for responsible governance.

6. A FOUR-PILLAR FRAMEWORK FOR SMART CITY RESILIENCE

In order to respond effectively to the challenges raised in the previous section, including susceptibility of infrastructure and misuse of information to fragmented governance and lack of trust from citizens, this report puts forward a Four-Pillar Framework for Smart City Resilience. The framework covers technological, organizational, ethical and societal aspects of urban digital transformation. Every pillar illustrates a fundamental interventional domain that must be addressed to create smart cities, connected and efficient but also secure, equitable, and trusted.

6.1 Pillar One: Secure and Interoperable Infrastructure

The foundation of any smart city resiliency program is a secure-by-design, interoperable-by-default digital infrastructure. This requires implementing strong cybersecurity measures like encryption, threat detection and endpoint protection to help enable systems from departments and sectors to communicate in a secure manner. Minimum levels of security should be mandated by cities on IoT devices and critical systems, regular vulnerability assessments must be scheduled; and secure procurement must be assured (Lv et al., 2021; Al-Taleb & Saqib, 2022). And cooperation will be needed to ensure maximum efficiency and resilience. When transportation systems can data-share with energy grids, health platforms and emergency services, the urban response to crises, whether pandemics or cyberattacks, is faster and more efficient. Yet, such fusion should not be obtained at the cost of expanding attack surfaces. Thus, architecture must support modular security, so systems are connected and yet remain protected in isolation.

6.2 Pillar Two: Embedded Privacy and Ethical Design

Privacy must be infused throughout the age of smart cities, instead of being an afterthought. This pillar extends the concept of Privacy by Design; enacting the use of input-known, output-perturbed technologies (IKO-PTs) like differential privacy, federated learning and homomorphic encryption into urban platforms and services (Agrawal et al., 2021; Abu-Salma, 2020). It also means designing in an ethical way including limiting data collection, using anonymized data sets and giving users the option to control how their data can be used. Crucially, values-driven design is not only about technology; it is also about process. Open, participatory design methods that engage residents in designing digital systems are essential to establish legitimacy and trust. These range from co-design workshops, user-centered policy testing and regularly feeding back to the communities most negatively affected by surveillance or data-led decisions (Ayalon & Toch, 2021; Rizi & Seno, 2022).

6.3 Pillar Three: Transparent and Accountable Governance

Building the Urban Resilience requires a shift from reactive regulation to proactive, adaptive and participatory models of governance. Legal compliance, including GDPR and other relevant laws is necessary but not sufficient by itself. Smart cities need to adopt local data governance regimes that specify duties, ensure accountability and legitimatize democratic oversight (Viljoen, 2021; Christofi et al., 2021). This includes the establishment of independent data ethics boards, transparency portals and regulatory sandboxes to develop new technologies in a way that is legal and ethical. Add to that the necessity for clear, transparent contractual conditions for relations with private-sector companies in order to safeguard public interest. Data-sharing agreements Open standards Exit strategies Information and code escrow Ensure vendor lock-in by a single company cannot occur Learn what the bankruptcy procedures would be for the use of an external product. Incorporating data justice into governance, by asking who benefits, who is harmed and whose voices are silenced aids in ensuring that digital transformation does not simply amplify the status quo (Ismagilova et al., 2022; Breuer & Pierson, 2021).

6.4 Pillar Four: Institutional Capacity and Digital Inclusion

The latest tech is useless if it can't be governed. So the fourth pillar is developing the human, organizational and cultural capabilities you need for digital transformation. Cities also need to invest in the training of public servants, who require assistance from trained cybersecurity professionals and higher digital literacy across departments (Sheoran & Vij, 2022; Hossain et al., 2024). Digital transformation teams or CDOs should be empowered to collaborate and standardize efforts across the cityscape. Of equal importance is the need to make smart services open and accessible. This includes designing for varying users as we consider age, ability, language and socioeconomic status In considering digital divides, in the form of outreach activities or creating platforms that are mobile-first and public access features(destroy) (Li & Huang, 2025; Alfiani & Sara, 2024). Fostering trust in digital systems is not a technical task, it's a civic one that demands transparency, accountability and meaningful involvement.

Figure 1. Proposed framework

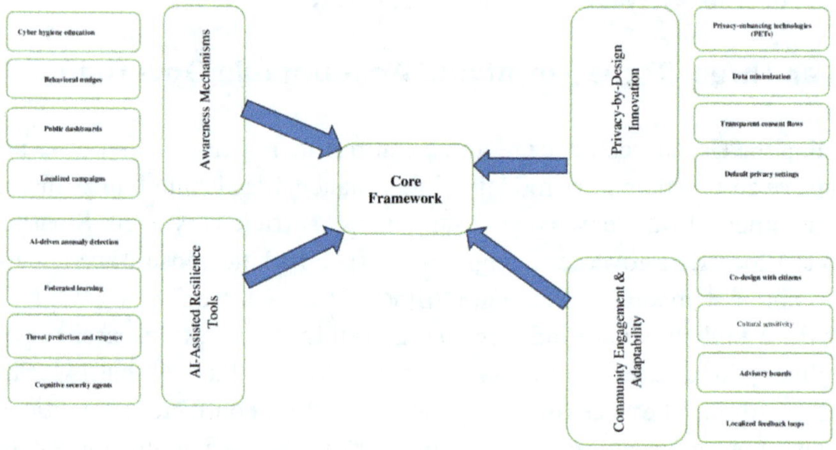

Figure 1: Proposed framework

7. Case Applications: Smart City Practices in Context

Everywhere but different While the implementation of smart city initiatives varies quite massively around the world, why not? Although the Four-Pillar Framework provides a normative framework to construct safe and inclusive smart cities, practical experiences demonstrate its virtues and shortcomings. Their joint paper focuses on three case studies – Barcelona, Toronto and Singapore – to show how cities are tackling issues related to digital governance, data ethics, citizen inclusion, and cybersecurity in diverse ways. These cases underscore substantive lessons, opportunities, and warnings for future policy making.

7.1 Barcelona: A Pioneer in Civic Data Governance

Barcelona is already widely regarded to be a leader in the ethical and participatory development of smart cities. Its point of departure is the notion that urban data is a public commons and should be collectively governed rather than turned into a commodity. Projects like the Decidim platform and CityOS mean that Barcelona has already included citizen participation in digital policymaking, with community members able to suggest, vote for and monitor public tech initiatives (Breuer & Pierson, 2021; Artyushina, 2023). Barcelona's Civic Data Trusts are an illustration of the third pillar of the Four-Pillar Framework, hackable and transparent governance. They are supposed to handle data produced by publicly owned infrastructure in a manner that serves the public interest rather than private ones. The city also forces tech vendors to adhere to such open data standards and privacy-by- design protocols, further underpinning openness, interoperability and privacy protection (Calzada & Almirall, 2020). But the Barcelona model is not problem-free. Implementation may be hindered at times by lack of technical capacity at the muncipal level as well as conflicts with national regulatory systems. However, it remains one of the best examples of digital innovation that fits into a model of democratic values and civic empowerment.

7.2 Toronto: A Case of Public Backlash and Institutional Misalignment

Toronto has shown a more sobering example. The city's collaboration with the Alphabet Inc. subsidiary, Sidewalk Labs, to create a data-rich neighborhood on the waterfront was envisioned as a bold experiment in urban innovation when it was unveiled three years ago. But in 2020, the project failed after facing resistance from across society in part because it was shrouded in secrecy and amid fears about who owned what data and of corporate surveillance (Christofi et al., 2021; Breuer & Pierson, 2021). Sidewalk Toronto's very public failure is the result of those Pillars Two and Three, privacy by design and accountable governance- being undermined. Some residents said they felt shut out from important decisions; early project documents did not spell out who would control and benefit from the data that was collected. In addition, the city did not have a data governance system in place to govern large-scale public–private partnerships of this sort, revealing institutional capacity deficits (Ma 2021). Although Toronto's broader e-government initiatives have since progressed, the Sidewalk Labs case illustrates the necessity of early public engagement and ethical anticipation, paired with legal guardrails when deploying smart infrastructure. It also serves to remind us that technological expertise must be accompanied by governance legitimacy.

7.3 Singapore: Efficient, Secure, but Centrally Controlled

Singapore is a technology-savvy, hyper-efficient poster child for smart urbanism, one accompanied by big caveats over transparency and citizen agency. The smart nation push is part of the city-state's broader Smart Nation initiative to harness technology in everything from transport and health care to security and housing. SafeEntry (for contact tracing) and LAMPP (Lighting Analytics and Management Platform) provide examples of secure, interoperable infrastructure (Lv et al., 2021; Kezron, 2025). Singapore is a leader in implementing Pillar One, investing significantly in cybersecurity infrastructure and coordination across government ministries. This proactive approach to governance and centralized control also enables the quick rollout of AI and IoT applications. But its critics say Singapore's model underemphasizes the participatory and privacy elements of smart governance. The climate is heavily one of surveillance and there are few institutional spaces for citizen input or oversight, leading to fears of state overreach and lack of accountability (Viljoen, 2021; Wasif, 2022). This case provides evidence that efficiency and robustness are not sufficient conditions for equity or trust. Singapore's model is strong on the technical front but falls short in many aspects of inclusive governance and ethical transparency, indicating that true resilience incorporates all four pillars, rather than just infrastructure and capacity.

8. READINESS AND EVALUATION: ARE CITIES PREPARED?

8.1 The Importance of Evaluating Readiness

As smart city initiatives gain traction internationally, the question still remains: are cities really ready to plan for, deploy and maintain such projects responsibly & sustainably? Readiness is not just the installation of digital infrastructure or the application of new technologies; it involves a city's institutional capability, ethical governance, citizen participation and the mechanisms to safeguard data and rights in increasingly complicated digital environments. Lacking a systematic means to assess cities' preparedness for new technologies, we are concerned that they will adopt technologies faster than the regulatory frameworks that govern them, break apart their systems of governance or alienate their residents. Hence, readiness assessment should be considered as the bedrock of smart cities that are not just technologically enriched but also safe, ethical and fair (Chaudhuri & Kahyaoglu, 2023; Ismagilova et al., 2022).

8.2 Existing Readiness Indices and What They Miss

Several international benchmarks are available for assessing digital governance, the smartness of a city. For example, the United Nations E-Government Development Index (EGDI) measures e-government readiness at a national level using indicators that include human capital development, telecommunications infrastructure and online services (Sheoran & Vij, 2022). Likewise, the National Cybersecurity Index (NCI) assesses cybersecurity capacities in legal, organizational and technical terms. One right example is the smart city standard, ISO 37122, which offers performance indicators for the evaluation of service delivery and infrastructure effectiveness. While these indexes provide useful information, they are primarily oriented towards the level of technological readiness and national capacity, paying less attention to local governance cases in which smart technologies are being employed. What is more, such indices often overrule qualitative dimensions like citizen participation, transparency and trust which are essential for ethical urban digital governance (Viljoen, 2021; Breuer & Pierson, 2021). In the absence of such consideration, global indices could provide a partial picture and imply that cities are ready when in fact serious gaps remain in governance and inclusion.

8.3 A Readiness Rubric Based on the Four-Pillar Framework

In response to these limitations, this report proposes a set of complementary indicators and a more comprehensive city-specific readiness rubric, an integration of the Four-Pillar Framework delineated previously in this report. Secure, interoperable infrastructure; privacy and ethics embedded as a consideration in system design processes; transparent and accountable governance; and institutional capacity and digital inclusion can be domains for readiness assessment. For instance, the first pillar evaluates whether cities incorporated cybersecurity in their system, developed intra-agency coordination and adopted IoT security practices (Al-Taleb & Saqib, 2022; Rashid et al., 2020). The second consists of whether privacy impact assessments are routinely applied, data minimization is practiced and there is an ethical review (Ayalon & Toch, 2021; Rizi & Seno, 2022). The third is if the legal background brings clear transparency and public audit of smart city systems as well as participatory digital governance (Christofi et al., 2021; Bannerman & Orasch, 2020). With the last pillar (Pillar 4) assessing the potential of the city to train public services in digital skills, promote equitable access to smart services and offer systems that include everybody (Zwilling et al., 2022; Alfiani & Sara, 2024). Unlike stiff global rankings, this tool is adjustable and serves as a barometer for cities to measure their specific problems, governance approaches and citizenry.

8.4 Observations from Practice: Common Gaps and Strengths

Case studies and empirical evidence seem to suggest that many cities are technically advanced but when it comes to governance, ethics and inclusiveness they still have a long way to go. For example, Singapore has developed high levels of cyber readiness and infrastructure sophistication, however, it is also criticized for its centralised surveillance-heavy approach and lack of civic engagement (Wasif, 2022; Viljoen, 2021). At the other end of the spectrum, Barcelona's own participative governance and focus on digital rights also tends to be challenged by silo'ed management structures and modest technical resources (Calzada & Almirall, 2020; Artyushina, 2023). Privacy is still one of the most constantly lagging behind topics. The failure of the Sidewalk Labs in Toronto provides an example for how ambiguity about data ownership, consent, and ethical oversight can undermine public trust and thwart large urban projects (Breuer & Pierson 2021; Christofi et al). Moreover, the inclusion is not yet consistent, and digital literacy and service provision are often isolated in rich or central areas while remote and deprived populations suffer from lack of access (Zwiling et al., 2022; Li & Huang, 2025). These trends show that while cities are smart on the outside, the basis for their resilience is rather uneven. Without ethical constraints and inclusive control, technological progress will lead to further undermining of equality and a decline in public legitimacy.

8.5 Recommendations for Readiness Assessment in Practice

Due to the importance of readiness in the development of robust smart cities, municipalities need to include evaluation as a core part of their digital governance strategies. Businesses should be locked down the first local price is that readiness assessments need to be localized, i.e., customized to the city's demographic, polity and infrastructure. This would involve multiplicity of senses and concepts to leave yes but less myopic national indices for city-tailored tools that are grounded in actual operations (Kitchin & Moore-Cherry, 2021). Second, cities should blend quantitative evidence with qualitative approaches – community interviews, public surveys and participatory audits – to identify the factors shaping trust, transparency and lived digital experience (Breuer &Pierson, 2021). 3 availability assessment should not take place in a vacuum but must be connected with planning, budgeting, and procurement. Evidence-based priorities from such assessments should be used to prioritize digital transformation. In addition, cities must create peer-to-peer learning networks and the tools and best practices to be shared among regional coalitions or global alliances. This type of partnership can prevent duplicating efforts, speed learning and leverage mutual capacity among cities. Frequent re-examine is also needed, particularly given rapid technological change and changing social-political turmoil (Hossain et al., 2024; Almeida, 2023). Readiness in this case, is a slippery target and one that we must perpetually reflect on and adapt to.

8.6 Readiness as a Precondition for Resilience

Readiness is not a fixed condition attained and then sustained; it is emergent, requiring investment in the health of institutions, ethical design, civic conversation and flexible policy. As I have argued in this section, current indexes were not designed to measure the complete set of issues linked to smart city readiness, most notably those related to privacy and accountability as well as inclusion. As a diagnostic tool, the Four-Pillar Framework can help cities understand their vulnerabilities and plot concrete courses forward. The real measure of a smart city is not how many sensors it has, or even how well it harnesses big data. Instead, it's about making sure services are delivered in a fair and equitable manner. Innovative technology must be accompanied by equal investment in democratic norms and in human capability. In this context, preparedness cannot be seen as a technical checklist; it is an ethical and civic commitment, the fundamental basis for building resilient, responsible and future-ready urban societies.

9. CONCLUSION AND POLICY RECOMMENDATIONS

9.1 Concluding Reflections on Smart City Challenges

The development of smart cities gives us a unique opportunity to improve efficiency, sustainability and quality of life within urban areas, from digital technologies incorporation. Yet, as discussed in this report, the road to the vision is difficult and risks abound. Cybersecurity vulnerabilities, unclear privacy protection frameworks, dispersed governance models and institutional capacities have emerged as significant obstacles to resilient and inclusive development of smart cities. These are not only technical but profoundly social, ethical and political challenges that need an integrated framework to be addressed in a holistic way. Addressing how they could respond to these challenges, the report has proposed the Four-Pillar Framework for Smart City Resilience focused on secure infrastructure, embedded privacy, responsible governance and inclusive institutional capacity. The pillars are designed to support one another so that digital innovation doesn't surpass the ethical and administrative structures that undergird public trust and equity. Based on literature and case studies from around the world, the framework this model delivers can significantly facilitate aligning smart city aspirations with democratic values and long-term resilience.

9.2 Reaffirming the Four Pillars of Resilience

This vision is built on the recognition that resilience entails more than just technical availability and protection against cyber threats. It also has to take into account the capacity of organizations, systems and societies to predict, adjust to and recover from digital disturbances, whether coming in the form of external attacks on national infrastructure or internal governance failing society's expectations. The first pillar, secure interoperable infrastructure, sees to it that the technical building blocks of smart cities are resilient, fit for purpose for future use and can fend off cyber-attacks. The second is bake in privacy and ethical design, hammering home the need for privacy-by-design technologies and user-centered design that stops harm before it starts. The third one is transparent and accountable governance that focuses on the legal, procedural, and institutional forms that support data justice and civic scrutiny. Finally, the fourth pillar on institutional capacity and digital inclusion recognizes that in the absence of capable individuals, strong leadership and citizen access, with no amount of innovation will help make significant progress.

9.3 Policy Recommendations for Future Smart Cities

Based on the framework and analysis introduced, a number of specific policy recommendations materialize. First, cities must bake cybersecurity into all smart projects from the start and at every layer, including network, application, device and endpoint security, using standardized procurement practices that ensure service and product providers adopt a secure development cycle for their products. Continued operations will also require routine cyber-readiness checks and establishment of special digital defense units. Second, governments should get ahead of data reactive policies and ensure ethical privacy practices are integrated through the lifecycle of urban technologies. This would include requiring privacy impact assessments, using data minimization techniques and demanding transparency from private-sector partners. Data must be thought of not just as a commodity but as a civic responsibility, guided by both technical controls and ethical norms. Third, city institutions require consistent expenditures on human and technical capacity. Training and partnership programs that train public servants, creation of Chief Digital Officer positions, as well as platforms to collaborate across sectors are key for silos falling apart and digital maturity. "We need to say that public-private partnerships are going to be regulated in this country by enforceable standards, which protect the public interest without dampening innovation.

Fourth, we must make inclusion a strategic priority, not an afterthought. Digital literacy programmes, inclusiveness in public access infrastructure and participatory design processes are crucial to enable smart city services for all citizens, notably those on the darker side of the digital divide. The idea of inclusion is valuable not from equity perspective alone but also in terms of building digital trust and social legitimacy. Cities will also want to be part of international networks of policy learning and uptake as well as mutual recognition efforts. Global standards frameworks, and regional alliances, can help to harmonize approaches and avoid fragmentation, which increases collective cybersecurity resilience. There are some lessons to be drawn from other cities (such as Barcelona, Toronto, and Singapore) of what it looks like to apply the smart-city concept in variations on city governments.

9.4 Final Considerations: Toward Ethical and Equitable Smart Urbanism

At the same time, as cities around the world pivot to digital, it is too important that such moves should be driven by fragmented approaches or technocratic shortcuts. The future of smart cities is not only connectivity and automation, but governance that is transparent, rights-based and open to public participation. Building a digital infrastructure without social guard rails will only exacerbate inequality and public mistrust. In turn, by building resilience via the Four-Pillar Framework we can achieve smart cities which are not only smart but just secure and inclusive. In the end, smart urbanism should be about serving democratic society rather than bypassing it. Policy makers and planners must think of digital governance as something that is continually negotiated as part of civic life, not as mechanical solutions. Speaking of cities also change, and so too should the ethics and institutions directing them. By no means prescriptive, the sets of recommendations that follow are a preface and invitation to continued trial, reflection, and collaboration toward our shared goal of more resilient digital futures. As smart cities continue their march forward, policy and design should not be far behind in that procession to ensure digital transformation for the public good and not at the expense of rights, inclusion or democratic governance. The multifaceted challenges of cybersecurity and privacy concerns within urban ecosystems require well-rounded, inclusive policymaking that doesn't just involve the acquisition of technology or infrastructure enhancements. Policy should be considered as a legal framework, and as a social contract for organizing the ways innovation can be aligned with values of transparency, equity and trust. In this closing section, we provide recommendations for responsible translation of the framework in context and stress common responsibilities of policymakers, technologists, and civil society stakeholders.

The key to good policy is inclusion. The laws and regulations that govern smart cities should take into account the lived reality of populations in our diverse cities. That includes not just IT pros and lawmakers, but teachers, health workers and other non-tech professionals, "ordinary people who are affected by these technologies" and don't get a say in policy making. Cities need to create democratic and inclusive consultation mechanisms like citizen juries, open data workshops, and participatory design workshops to feedback into digital policy making. Finally, as Breuer and Pierson (2021) argue, participatory governance serves to improve not only the legitimacy of policies, but also the functioning of systems. When citizens have a hand in creating the rules, they are more likely to trust and buy into the systems that emerge under those rules. A major recommendation is to develop policies that are compatible with local, national and international legal frameworks. This is to ensure that municipal governance does not function in a bubble and reinforce greater norms of digital rights and cyber security regulation. Framework design should accommodate jurisdictional variations in data protection laws, including GDPR in the EU, Digital Personal Data Protection Act in India or domestic surveillance legislations within authoritarian environments. It is for cities to mediate these external framings with their own cultural norms, legal capabilities and enforcement tools. For example, though consent mechanisms are core to European privacy law, in some low-literacy or low-connected regions it may be more feasible to implement other models such as "informed defaults" or community-delegated consent, so long as they adhere to the spirit of autonomy and transparency (Artyushina, 2023; Viljoen, 2021).

At the institutional level, cities need to create cross-functional governance committees that combine cybersecurity and privacy with initiatives related to digital innovation under a shared strategic vision. Far too frequently the effort to handle these duties are kept within each organization's IT department, general counsel office or communications team - which leads to much of it being done over again, varying standards for security and inconsistent accountability. Incorporated governance mechanisms, such as smart city steering committees or digital ethics boards, can help break down these silos and guarantee that policies are not only written but also enforced and refreshed on a routine basis. These bodies should feature technologists, lawyers, civil society representatives and relevant independent ethics auditors or ombudspersons. help also) Policy Priorities: Digital rights must be well-defined, understandable and enforceable as a practical matter. This includes the rights of access, modification or deletion of their data and redress. We as citizens should know not only what we hand over and how it's used but also where to seek redress or appeal if it's misused. Public bodies should follow and support the adoption of citizen data charters that describe digital rights in clear, non-technical terms. These charters may also be instrumental for civil educating the public and grounding digital rights in collective consciousness and institutional responsibility (Christofi et al., 2021; Rizi & Seno, 2022).

For policymakers, the bottom line is to strike a balance between security and innovation weighed against civil liberties. This balance is dynamic; it changes with technology, geopolitics and public feelings. Surveillance technologies, for instance, may have crime prevention advantages but they also present serious threats to privacy, expressive freedoms and social justice. All surveillance and AI tools should conform to tight impact assessments rules that make clear the necessity, proportionality, and ways of redress. Where feasible, cities should implement privacy-by-design policies outlined earlier, such that systems are designed to err on the side of data protection versus exploitation (Agrawal et al., 2021; Ayalon & Toch, 2021). Technologists, for their part, will need to bake ethical questions into every stage of system development. This involves building explainable AI, reducing data collection, and auditing for bias and fairness. As Chen et al. (2021) underscore, it is also the case that opaque or excessively complicated security tools and practices erode public trust, particularly when they are deployed in highly sensitive fields such as policing, healthcare, and welfare. Engineers and developers must work with ethicists, community liaisons, and legal experts to ensure that technical decision-making is compatible with public values and policy constraints.

Civil society plays a dual function, that of a watchdog and a bridge between institutions and communities. NGOs, advocacy organizations, universities and local groups can help bring hidden harms to light, represent marginalized voices and translate complex technical or legal jargon into meaningful public education. They are also able to work in the culture of digital responsibility; they can stimulate citizens to be the owner and guard their own digital rights, as well as collaboration for social cyber security through being alert and informed participating (Kezron, 2025; Alfiani & Sara, 2024). Lastly, all key stakeholders should adopt evidence based iterated policy making. Digital environments change rapidly. Technologies change, new vulnerabilities arise, and public sensibilities move on. Policymakers need to consider regulation as a dynamic text, open to perpetual testing, evaluation and adaptation. Cities need to institutionalize feedback loops, such as public consultations, impact assessments and smart system audits once a year. Trust and legitimacy can be further strengthened by transparency in the effectiveness of policies, as well as public response to measures, encouraging a more sustainable and fair smart urban future.

10. LOOKING AHEAD: THE FUTURE OF RESILIENT SMART CITIES

00:20 And whilst the path of urbanization continues to cross over with digital transformation, the future smart city will be shaped, not just by technological development, but also by the ability to navigate this complexity equitably and sustainably. The developments analyzed in this report, including cyber-physical vulnerabilities, algorithmic bias and civic disengagement, are poised to be accentuated over the next decade – reinforcing the need for more agile and forward-looking forms of governance. Among the most promising is deepening integration of artificial intelligence (AI) into urban infrastructure. As the use of machine learning for traffic prediction, resource allocation, predictive policing and personalized public services becomes more prevalent in cities, so will the dangers of algorithmic opacity, surveillance and discriminatory results (Kezron 2025; Wasif 2022). This has important implications in terms of the explainability, accountability and fairness of AI systems, particularly within public sector contexts where decisions impact upon rights and access. AI governance mechanism is a core component in future smart city planning, which includes algorithmic auditing, mandates around public disclosure as well as citizen control over their automated systems (Ayalon & Toch, 2021; Hu et al., 2023).

A further advantage is the development of data sovereignty and cross-border governance. Smart cities are not controlled by offline actors, so processes and structures in cloud infrastructure, data platforms and service providers as well as hosting jurisdictions and other related conditions become challenging on matters of legal responsibility and regulatory consistency (Christofi et al., 2021; Artyushina, 2023). New debates on data localization, federated governance models and digital sovereignty will necessitate novel forms of international cooperation and multi-level governance. In this context, cities have to become key stakeholders in the shaping of national and transnational data policies that meet local requirements as well as ethical standards. And the fields of climate resiliency and sustainability are going to weave more tightly with digital urban planning. As the world's cities grapple with rising sea levels, heat waves and other extreme weather, intelligent systems will be deployed to mitigate environmental change, maximize energy use and coordinate disaster responses. But the implementation of these systems should not be overlooking the social component of climate vulnerability, where people most vulnerable to environmental risk and who are sometimes those most disconnected from digital services (Cappa et al., 2022; Tanim et al., 2022). Future research needs to therefore investigate how climate justice and digital equity can be incorporated in smart city frameworks.

On the research side, further exploration is required to understand life with smart cities' point of view from citizens. More of the existing literature has attended to systems, technologies and governance structures than how citizens actually navigate or resist and change smart urban environments and what this means in everyday life (Breuer & Pierson, 2021; Kitchin & Moore-Cherry, 2021). Ethnographic and participatory research methods, as well as co-creation models can help to reveal these perspectives and provide critical grounded insights to digital citizenship, data fatigue, or civic innovation. It will be, after all, trust that defines the future of the smart city. Acceptance of the technologies will be based not just on the reliability of technology, but also on understandable decision-making, consideration for rights and responsive institutions. Cities that invest in reliable governance architectures, those that are participatory, ethical and flexible, stand a better chance of withstanding the shocks and uncertainties of the digital age.

11. REFERENCES

Abu-Salma, R. (2020). Designing user-centered privacy-enhancing technologies (Doctoral dissertation, UCL (University College London)).

Agrawal, N., Binns, R., Van Kleek, M., Laine, K., & Shadbolt, N. (2021, May). Exploring design and governance challenges in the development of privacy-preserving computation. In *Proceedings of the 2021 CHI Conference on Human Factors in Computing Systems* (pp. 1-13).

Ahmed, S., Hossain, M. F., Kaiser, M. S., Noor, M. B. T., Mahmud, M., & Chakraborty, C. (2021). Artificial intelligence and machine learning for ensuring security in smart cities. In *Data-driven mining, learning and analytics for secured smart cities: Trends and advances* (pp. 23–47). Springer International Publishing.

Alfiani, F. R. N., & Sara, R. (2024). The Improvement of Digital Literacy to Secure Data and Privacy in the Digital Age. *INJURITY: Journal of Interdisciplinary Studies*, *3*(12), 832–839.

Almeida, F. (2023). Prospects of cybersecurity in smart cities. *Future Internet*, *15*(9), 285.

Al-Taleb, N., & Saqib, N. A. (2022). Towards a hybrid machine learning model for intelligent cyber threat identification in smart city environments. *Applied Sciences (Basel, Switzerland)*, *12*(4), 1863.

Al-Turjman, F., Zahmatkesh, H., & Shahroze, R. (2022). An overview of security and privacy in smart cities' IoT communications. *Transactions on Emerging Telecommunications Technologies*, *33*(3), e3677.

Andrade, R. O., Yoo, S. G., Tello-Oquendo, L., & Ortiz-Garcés, I. (2020). A comprehensive study of the IoT cybersecurity in smart cities. *IEEE Access : Practical Innovations, Open Solutions*, *8*, 228922–228941.

ARTYUSHINA. A. (2023). DATA GOVERNANCE IN SMART CITIES: PERSONAL DATA AS PRIVATE ASSET, COMMONS, AND/OR PUBLIC GOOD? (Doctoral dissertation, YORK UNIVERSITY TORONTO).

Ayalon, O., & Toch, E. (2021). User-centered privacy-by-design: Evaluating the appropriateness of design prototypes. *International Journal of Human-Computer Studies*, *154*, 102641.

Bannerman, S., & Orasch, A. (2020). Privacy and smart cities. *Canadian Journal of Urban Research*, *29*(1), 17–38.

Breuer, J., & Pierson, J. (2021). The right to the city and data protection for developing citizen-centric digital cities. *Information Communication and Society*, *24*(6), 797–812.

Calzada, I., & Almirall, E. (2020). Data ecosystems for protecting European citizens' digital rights. Transforming government: People, process and policy, 14(2), 133-147.

Cappa, F., Franco, S., & Rosso, F. (2022). Citizens and cities: Leveraging citizen science and big data for sustainable urban development. *Business Strategy and the Environment*, *31*(2), 648–667.

Chaudhuri, A., & Bozkus Kahyaoglu, S. (2023). Cybersecurity assurance in smart cities: A risk management perspective. *Edpacs*, *67*(4), 1–22.

Chen, D., Wawrzynski, P., & Lv, Z. (2021). Cyber security in smart cities: A review of deep learning-based applications and case studies. *Sustainable Cities and Society*, *66*, 102655.

Christine, D., & Thinyane, M. (2020). Cyber resilience in asia-pacific: a review of national cybersecurity strategies.

Christofi, A., Wauters, E., & Valcke, P. (2021). Smart Cities, Data Protection and the Public Interest Conundrum: What Legal Basis for Smart City Processing? *European Journal of Law and Technology*, *12*(1), 1–36.

Hossain, S. T., Yigitcanlar, T., Nguyen, K., & Xu, Y. (2024). Local government cybersecurity landscape: A systematic review and conceptual framework. *Applied Sciences (Basel, Switzerland)*, *14*(13), 5501.

Hu, M., Behar, E., & Ottenheimer, D. (2023). National Security and Federalizing Data Privacy Infrastructure for AI Governance. *Fordham Law Review*, *92*, 1829.

Ismagilova, E., Hughes, L., Rana, N. P., & Dwivedi, Y. K. (2022). Security, privacy and risks within smart cities: Literature review and development of a smart city interaction framework. *Information Systems Frontiers*, ●●●, 1–22.

Jha, A., & Jha, A. (2024). Securing tomorrow's urban frontiers: A holistic approach to cybersecurity in smart cities. Information System and Smart City, 3(1).

Kezron, I. E. (2025). AI and the future of cybersecurity in smart cities: A framework for secure and resilient urban environments. *Iconic Research and Engineering Journals*, *8*(7).

Khan, A., Jhanjhi, N. Z., & Humayun, M. (2022). The role of cybersecurity in smart cities. In *Cyber Security Applications for Industry 4.0* (pp. 195–208). Chapman and Hall/CRC.

Kitchin, R., & Moore-Cherry, N. (2021). Fragmented governance, the urban data ecosystem and smart city-regions: The case of Metropolitan Boston. *Regional Studies*, *55*(12), 1913–1923.

Kuzior, A., Pakhnenko, O., Tiutiunyk, I., & Lyeonov, S. (2023). E-governance in smart cities: Global trends and key enablers. *Smart Cities*, *6*(4), 1663–1689.

Li, Y., & Huang, Y. (2025). Social security, digital literacy, and relative poverty in China. *Finance Research Letters*, *71*, 106446.

Lv, Z., Qiao, L., Kumar Singh, A., & Wang, Q. (2021). AI-empowered IoT security for smart cities. *ACM Transactions on Internet Technology*, *21*(4), 1–21.

Lyu, Q., Liu, S., & Shang, Z. (2024). Securing Urban Landscape: Cybersecurity Mechanisms for Resilient Smart Cities. *IEEE Access : Practical Innovations, Open Solutions*.

Ma, C. (2021). Smart city and cyber-security; technologies used, leading challenges and future recommendations. *Energy Reports*, *7*, 7999–8012.

Mohamed, N., Al-Jaroodi, J., & Jawhar, I. (2020, July). Opportunities and challenges of data-driven cybersecurity for smart cities. In 2020 IEEE systems security symposium (SSS) (pp. 1-7). IEEE.

Oliha, J. S., Biu, P. W., & Obi, O. C. (2024). Securing the smart city: A review of cybersecurity challenges and strategies. *Open Access Research Journal of Multidisciplinary Studies*, *7*(1), 94–101.

Prasad, K. R., Karanam, S. R., Ganesh, D., Liyakat, K. K. S., Talasila, V., & Purushotham, P. (2024). AI in public-private partnership for IT infrastructure development. *The Journal of High Technology Management Research*, *35*(1), 100496.

Rashid, M. M., Kamruzzaman, J., Hassan, M. M., Imam, T., & Gordon, S. (2020). Cyberattacks detection in iot-based smart city applications using machine learning techniques. *International Journal of Environmental Research and Public Health*, *17*(24), 9347.

Rizi, M. H. P., & Seno, S. A. H. (2022). A systematic review of technologies and solutions to improve security and privacy protection of citizens in the smart city. *Internet of Things : Engineering Cyber Physical Human Systems*, *20*, 100584.

Sheoran, S., & Vij, S. (2022). A Review of E-Government Assessment Frameworks: E-Readiness, Adoption, Citizen Engagement and Quality: E-Readiness, Adoption, Citizen Engagement and Quality. JeDEM-eJournal of eDemocracy and Open Government, 14(2), 197-213.

Tanim, A. H., McRae, C. B., Tavakol-Davani, H., & Goharian, E. (2022). Flood detection in urban areas using satellite imagery and machine learning. *Water (Basel), 14*(7), 1140.

Viljoen, S. (2021). A relational theory of data governance. *The Yale Law Journal*, •••, 573–654.

Wasif, N. (2022). Securing Smart Cities: AI-Based Cybersecurity Strategies for Urban Digital Infrastructure.

Zwilling, M., Klien, G., Lesjak, D., Wiechetek, Ł., Cetin, F., & Basim, H. N. (2022). Cyber security awareness, knowledge and behavior: A comparative study. *Journal of Computer Information Systems, 62*(1), 82–97.

Chapter 7
Navigating Cybersecurity and Privacy in Smart Urban Ecosystems:
Challenges, Technologies, and Governance Pathways

Syeda Nida Hassan
https://orcid.org/0009-0004-1849-9679
Ravensbourne University, London, UK

ABSTRACT

The rapid digitalization of cities has created interconnected urban ecosystems where IoT, AI, and 5G/6G technologies enable innovative services but also introduce significant cybersecurity and privacy risks. Attacks on critical infrastructure, pervasive data collection, and opaque algorithmic systems highlight the urgent need for resilient safeguards. This chapter examines the evolving threat landscape in smart urban ecosystems and analyses both technical and governance-based responses. Emerging solutions such as federated learning, blockchain, and privacy-enhancing technologies are reviewed alongside global policy frameworks, ethical guidelines, and citizen-centred governance models. Drawing on international case studies, the chapter highlights how balancing innovation with transparency, accountability, and social trust is central to building secure and inclusive smart cities. By integrating technological, socio-economic, and policy perspectives, it offers pathways toward resilient and human-centric urban digital futures.

DOI: 10.4018/979-8-3373-4455-3.ch007

INTRODUCTION

The global shift toward digital urbanism is catalysing the development of smart cities, where interconnected technologies promise to enhance urban functionality, sustainability, and citizen engagement. These ecosystems integrate Internet of Things (IoT) sensors, artificial intelligence (AI), and real-time data analytics to optimize operations from traffic management to public safety. Yet, this rapid digitization creates a pervasive attack surface and introduces unprecedented threats to cybersecurity, individual privacy, and societal trust (Priyadarshini et al.,2022;Malik & Sun, 2020). The very infrastructure designed to improve urban life can become a vector for disruption, surveillance, and economic harm if not secured within a holistic, human-centred framework.

Cybersecurity incidents in smart urban environments have demonstrated severe real-world consequences. Attacks on critical infrastructure such as the 2021 Colonial Pipeline ransomware attack or the 2015 Ukraine grid hack, highlight vulnerabilities in essential services (Beerman et al.,2023, *Pollard, 2024)*. Beyond immediate disruption, the pervasive collection of citizen data raises profound ethical concerns. The design of systems often prioritizes efficiency over equity, risking the amplification of biases and the erosion of privacy, particularly for marginalized communities. The economic costs are equally staggering; a single metropolitan-area ransomware attack can incur billions in recovery costs and lost revenue.

Addressing these challenges requires moving beyond purely technical solutions. While advancements in privacy-enhancing technologies (PETs) like federated learning and differential privacy are crucial, they are insufficient alone. A resilient smart city must be built on a foundation of strong governance, adaptive policy, and active citizen engagement (Razmjoo et al., 2021). The regulatory landscape is fragmented, with varying enforcement levels between regions like the EU, with its strong GDPR and AI Act frameworks, and other parts of the world (e.g., ASEAN, Africa), creating complex challenges for multinational deployments and data flows.

This chapter argues that securing smart urban ecosystems necessitates a multidisciplinary approach that balances technological innovation with socio-economic and policy considerations. To investigate this, we employ a mixed-methodology design, combining a systematic review of recent literature with comparative policy analysis and case studies of specific cyber incidents. The chapter is structured to first outline the key technological trends and threat landscapes, followed by an analysis of cutting-edge technical safeguards. It then dedicates significant focus to governance models, economic cost analyses, and comparative policy enforcement. A section on future urban risks explores threats posed by AI-driven attacks and the rise of quantum computing.

Ultimately, by integrating technological, legal, and social perspectives, this chapter provides a roadmap for policymakers, urban planners, and engineers. It aims to contribute to the development of smart cities that are not only efficient and innovative but also secure, equitable, and fundamentally respectful of human rights.

BACKGROUND

The evolution of urban environments into intelligent, connected ecosystems represents a paradigm shift in city governance, service delivery, and citizen interaction. So-called "smart cities" leverage a constellation of technologies including the Internet of Things (IoT), artificial intelligence (AI), and 5G/6G networks to optimize infrastructure, enhance sustainability, and foster economic growth. While the potential benefits are significant, ranging from reduced traffic congestion to more efficient energy use, this rapid digitization reconfigures the urban landscape into a complex cyber-physical system, introducing profound and interconnected risks to security, privacy, and social equity *(Manas, 2023)*.

The historical model of urban management relied on siloed, physical infrastructure with limited digital interdependency. Today, the convergence of Operational Technology (OT) and Information Technology (IT) has erased these boundaries. Sensors in water pipes, smart grids, traffic lights, and public surveillance cameras generate terabytes of real-time data, crunched by AI algorithms to enable predictive maintenance and automated decision-making. This hyper-connectivity, while efficient, creates an exponentially larger attack surface (Cities of the Future, 2025, Dragonetti & Garcia, 2025). A 2024 report by the Global Cybersecurity Forum estimates that the number of connected municipal IoT devices will surpass 3 billion by 2025, each a potential entry point for threat actors. The consequences of breaches are no longer merely digital; they manifest as tangible components IoT devices societal harm. The average cost of a data breach now stands at $4.88 million globally, not including the long-term erosion of public trust *(IBM, 2024)*.

To better illustrate these shifts, a comparative view of traditional and smart city models is presented below

Table 1.

Domain	Traditional City Model	Smart City Model	Emerging Vulnerabilities
Infrastructure	Isolated, physical systems	Interconnected cyber-physical systems	Cascading failures across critical services
Data Handling	Manual, limited collection	Automated, large-scale IoT data capture	Privacy violations, surveillance, identity inference
Governance	Public sector–led	Public–Private Partnerships (PPPs)	Accountability gaps, vendor lock-in
Citizen Role	Passive service recipients	Data generators and engaged stakeholders	Exclusion of digitally marginalized groups
Regulation	Minimal, sector-specific laws	GDPR, AI Act, emerging regional frameworks	Fragmented global enforcement, uneven citizen rights

As shown in Table 1, the move toward interconnected systems not only enables efficiency but also exposes cities to cascading risks across infrastructure, data, and governance.

Beyond technical vulnerabilities, the smart city paradigm raises critical socio-political concerns. The deployment of AI-driven surveillance for public safety often occurs without adequate public consultation, leading to pervasive monitoring and the disproportionate targeting of marginalized communities. Furthermore, the dominant reliance on Public-Private Partnerships (PPPs) for technology deployment creates governance challenges, including unclear data ownership, proprietary system lock-in, and weakened public accountability.

This complex landscape necessitates a response that is as multi-faceted as the challenges themselves. Technological solutions such as federated learning for privacy-preserving AI or zero-trust architectures are necessary but insufficient. A truly resilient smart city must be built upon a foundation of strong governance, inclusive policy, and active citizen engagement. The regulatory environment remains starkly fragmented; while the European Union enforces robust regulations like the GDPR and AI Act, many other regions lack comparable enforcement mechanisms, creating critical disparities in citizen protection *(van Twist et al., 2023)*.

Therefore, understanding the background of smart cities is not merely about tracing technological adoption but about comprehending a fundamental shift in urban ontology. It requires a cross-disciplinary analysis that weighs operational efficiency against economic costs, algorithmic performance against ethical imperatives, and technological innovation against the fundamental rights of citizens. This background sets the stage for a holistic examination of the cybersecurity and privacy challenges that define the modern urban experience.

3. CYBERSECURITY CHALLENGES IN SMART CITIES

The evolution of smart cities into complex, data-driven ecosystems has made them prime targets for cyber adversaries. These environments integrate diverse components IoT devices, AI algorithms, 5G/6G networks, and cloud-edge infrastructures creating a massive and heterogeneous attack surface. The deep interdependence of these systems means a single compromised node, such as a traffic sensor, can cascade failures into critical infrastructure sectors like energy, transportation, and healthcare. The global economic impact of such disruptions is staggering, with the average cost of a cyber incident on critical urban infrastructure now estimated at $3.6 million (IBM Security, 2024). This section explores the multifaceted cybersecurity challenges, moving beyond technical vulnerabilities to include governance gaps and human factors.

3.1. Threats to IoT and Edge Devices

Smart cities deploy millions of Internet of Things (IoT) and edge devices in uncontrolled environments, making them susceptible to physical tampering and cyber exploitation. These devices often have limited processing power, preventing robust security. Key threats include:

- Botnet Attacks: Compromised devices are weaponized into botnets for large-scale DDoS attacks, as seen in the Mirai and Mozi campaigns, which exploit weak default credentials (Al-Shurbaji et al., 2025).
- Sensor Spoofing: Attackers manipulate input data (e.g., faking empty parking spaces or clear roads) to disrupt urban operations and cause economic inefficiency.
- Firmware Vulnerabilities: A lack of secure boot processes allows for persistent malware infections.

Edge devices, which process data locally, face unique risks like model inversion attacks, where attackers steal proprietary AI model data, and adversarial attacks that cause AI to misclassify inputs. The decentralized nature of these devices complicates security updates and centralized monitoring.

3.2. AI Vulnerabilities and Adversarial Risks

AI is the cognitive backbone of smart cities, powering everything from facial recognition to traffic flow optimization. However, these systems are vulnerable to sophisticated attacks that undermine their integrity:

- Evasion Attacks: Manipulating inputs to deceive models e.g., causing an autonomous vehicle to misread a stop sign.
- Data Poisoning: Corrupting training datasets to manipulate model behaviour, a significant risk in federated learning environments.
- Membership Inference: Determining if a specific individual's data was used to train a model, violating data confidentiality (Hao & Tao, 2022).

The socio-economic impact is profound. Biased or compromised AI can lead to unfair policing, discriminatory welfare allocation, and public mistrust, especially when "black-box" systems lack transparency and accountability.

3.3. Infrastructure Attacks on Critical Urban Services

The convergence of Information Technology (IT) and Operational Technology (OT) has exposed critical infrastructure like power grids and water systems to unprecedented risk. Legacy OT systems, designed for isolated networks, are now connected and vulnerable.

- Ransomware: Attacks like the one on Colonial Pipeline demonstrate how critical services can be held hostage, leading to massive economic and societal disruption (Rana et al., 2024).
- Man-in-the-Middle (MITM) Attacks: Intercepting and manipulating communications in traffic control or smart grid systems.
- Remote Code Execution (RCE): Exploiting vulnerabilities in programmable logic controllers (PLCs) to take control of physical processes.

Several high-profile incidents demonstrate how these vulnerabilities translate into real-world crises.

Table 2. Real-World Cyber Incidents in Critical Urban Infrastructure

Incident	Target	Impact	Lesson Learned
Oldsmar Water Treatment (2021)	Water supply system	Near-toxic chlorine levels introduced	Exposed critical vulnerabilities in remote access and reliance on shared credentials
Colonial Pipeline (2021)	Energy infrastructure	Fuel shortages across U.S. East Coast	Demonstrated real-world impact of ransomware on physical supply chains
Ukrainian Power Grid (2016)	National energy grid	Widespread blackouts in Kyiv	Showcased how tailored malware (Industroyer) can disrupt ICS/SCADA systems

These cases underscore that cybersecurity failures in smart cities are not abstract risks. They directly affect safety, trust, and continuity of services

3.4. Identity Management and Access Control Limitations

In a hyper-connected city, every entity (person, device, service) requires a secure digital identity. Fragmented systems and legacy protocols create severe weaknesses:

- Credential Theft: Weak passwords in city portals expose administrative privileges.
- Privilege Escalation: Poorly configured access controls allow unauthorized users to reach critical systems.
- Centralized Point of Failure: A breach in a central identity provider can compromise the entire ecosystem.

The 2021 Oldsmar water treatment facility attack, where shared credentials allowed a hacker to manipulate water chemistry, is a quintessential example of failed access control leading to a near-catastrophe (CISA, 2021).

3.5. Challenges in Real-Time Detection and Response

The scale and heterogeneity of smart cities overwhelm traditional security tools.

- Data Overload: Billions of daily events from diverse devices and protocols make centralized monitoring difficult.
- Zero-Day Exploits: Novel, unknown attacks can bypass existing signatures and defences.
- Skill Shortage: A global shortage of cybersecurity professionals leaves cities unable to manage complex incident response effectively.

The 2016 Ukraine grid attack succeeded in part because monitoring systems were not designed to detect the specialized Industroyer malware, highlighting the gap in real-time threat detection for critical infrastructure (Dragos, 2017).

3.6. Supply Chain and Third-Party Risks

Smart cities depend on a vast ecosystem of vendors for hardware, software, and cloud services, creating multi-layered risks.

- Firmware Implants: Backdoors implanted in devices during manufacturing.

- Compromised Updates: Malware distributed through software supply chains, as seen in the SolarWinds and Log4Shell incidents.
- Lack of Oversight: Cities often lack the contractual power or technical capability to audit their vendors' security practices comprehensively.

3.7. Human Factors and Insider Threats

Human error remains a critical vulnerability. Employees may fall for phishing attacks, misuse data, or bypass security protocols for convenience. Malicious insiders, though rarer, can cause disproportionate damage. Continuous training and a strong security culture are essential but often underfunded.

3.8. Regulatory Gaps and Cross-Jurisdictional Challenges

The transnational nature of technology complicates enforcement. Data flows across borders, and vendors operate globally, creating accountability murkiness.

- Regulatory Fragmentation: Disparate standards (e.g., NIST in the U.S., GDPR in the EU) lead to inconsistent security postures.
- Enforcement Challenges: Many regions lack the resources or legal frameworks to enforce compliance, especially against international corporations (Pemmasani & Osaka, 2021).

4. PRIVACY CHALLENGES IN URBAN DIGITAL INFRASTRUCTURE

In smart cities, the promise of efficiency is often in tension with the fundamental right to privacy. Pervasive data collection through IoT sensors, cameras, and mobile apps creates a panopticon-like environment where citizens are constantly monitored, often without their knowledge or meaningful consent. This erodes autonomy, trust, and democratic participation.

4.1. Ubiquitous Data Collection and Surveillance

A defining feature of smart cities is the constant, ambient collection of data location, video, biometrics, behaviour from public spaces. Systems like London's Ring of Steel (CSM, 2018) and Beijing's AI-driven policing create environments of permanent surveillance. The primary concern is the chilling effect, where citizens alter their behaviour due to the fear of being watched, stifling free expression and association.

4.2. The Illusion of Informed Consent and Data Minimization

Meaningful consent is nearly impossible in ambient computing environments. Citizens cannot reasonably avoid being captured by city-owned sensors, and "terms of service" are often lengthy, complex, and non-negotiable. This violates the core data protection principles of purpose limitation and data minimization, as data collected for one purpose (e.g., traffic management) is often repurposed for another (e.g., predictive policing) without consent.

4.3. Algorithmic Profiling, Bias, and Discrimination

AI systems used for public services often perpetuate and amplify societal biases.

- Predictive Policing: Algorithms trained on historically biased arrest data disproportionately target minority neighborhoods.
- Facial Recognition: Higher error rates for people of colour and women lead to misidentification and unjust outcomes.
- Resource Allocation: AI used in welfare or housing can unfairly deny services based on biased historical data. These "black box" systems lack transparency, making it difficult for affected individuals to understand or challenge decisions that impact their lives.

4.4. Data Ownership and Governance Gaps

A fundamental question remains: who owns urban data? Typically, it is controlled by private vendors and municipal governments, not the citizens who generate it. This leads to:

- Data Monopolies: Vendor lock-in and limited public scrutiny of proprietary algorithms.
- Loss of Sovereignty: Cities become dependent on external companies for their own urban intelligence.
- Accountability Gaps: It is unclear who is responsible when data is misused or breached.

4.5. Cross-Border Data Flow Risks

Urban data is often processed and stored on global cloud platforms, subjecting it to the laws of foreign jurisdictions. This creates conflicts, for example, between a city's local privacy laws and a cloud provider's obligation to comply with foreign surveillance orders. Ensuring data sovereignty and compliance with regulations like GDPR becomes a significant technical and legal challenge.

4.6. Ethical Dilemmas and the Right to Anonymity

The core ethical dilemma is balancing collective security with individual privacy. Continuous surveillance in public spaces effectively eliminates the right to anonymity, which is a cornerstone of a free society. Smart city initiatives must be guided by ethical frameworks that prioritize human rights and democratic values over unchecked technological efficiency.

5. EMERGING SECURITY AND PRIVACY TECHNOLOGIES

Addressing the scale and complexity of smart city challenges requires a new generation of privacy-enhancing technologies (PETs) and security paradigms that are decentralized, transparent, and resilient.

5.1. Federated Learning (FL)

FL enables collaborative AI model training across distributed devices (e.g., cameras, phones) without sharing raw data. Only model updates are sent to a central aggregator, preserving data locality and privacy (Jithish et al., 2023).

-Applications: Traffic prediction using data from vehicles without tracking individuals; healthcare analytics from wearables without exposing patient records.

- Limitations: Vulnerable to model poisoning attacks, requiring robust aggregation techniques to filter out malicious updates (Xia et al., 2023).

5.2. Differential Privacy (DP)

DP provides mathematical guarantees of privacy by adding calibrated noise to query results or datasets. It ensures that the inclusion or exclusion of any single individual's data does not significantly affect the output.

- Applications: Releasing accurate urban mobility or energy consumption statistics for public dashboards without risking the re-identification of individuals.
- Challenges: Managing the trade-off between data utility and the strength of the privacy guarantee.

5.3. Blockchain and Distributed Ledger Technologies (DLT)

Blockchain offers a tamper-proof, decentralized ledger for securing transactions and verifying identity.

- Applications:
- Self-Sovereign Identity (SSI): Citizens control their own digital credentials (e.g., digital driver's licenses) without relying on a central authority.
- Smart Contracts: Automate and enforce agreements (e.g., utility payments, permit issuance) with transparency.
- Data Provenance: Provide an immutable audit trail for sensitive data accesses and modifications.

  -Limitations: Challenges with scalability, energy consumption (for Proof-of-Work systems), and integration with legacy systems (Bada et al., 2021).

5.4. Secure and Explainable AI (XAI)

To build trust and ensure security, AI systems must be both robust against attack and understandable to humans.

-Adversarial Defences: Techniques like adversarial training help models resist malicious inputs designed to fool them.

-Explainabillity Tools: Frameworks like SHAP and LIME help decode "black box" models, explaining the reasoning behind AI decisions in critical areas like policing and resource allocation (Dwivedi et al., 2023). This is vital for accountability and fairness.

Privacy-enhancing technologies (PETs) help balance smart city innovation with citizen rights.

Table 3 outlines four key PETs, their benefits, challenges, and typical applications.

To synthesize their role, benefits, and challenges, the following table compares four leading PETs widely adopted in smart city contexts.

Table 3. Comparative Analysis of Emerging Privacy-Enhancing Technologies

Technology	Primary Benefit	Key Challenge	Use Case Example
Federated Learning	Keeps data on local devices; no central data pool	Susceptible to model poisoning and data inference attacks	Training a traffic flow model from user smartphones without collecting raw GPS data
Differential Privacy	Provides provable mathematical privacy guarantees	Balancing data utility with privacy budget (ε)	Publishing city-wide health trend statistics without exposing individual records
Blockchain	Decentralized trust; tamper-evident records	Scalability limitations and energy overhead	Citizens verifying eligibility (e.g., age) without disclosing personal identifiers
Explainable AI (XAI)	Increases transparency and accountability of AI decisions	May reduce accuracy or performance in complex models	Contesting an automated denial of a housing permit by reviewing model decision factors

Taken together, these technologies illustrate that securing smart cities requires combining complementary approaches, rather than relying on any single tool.

6. GOVERNANCE MODELS FOR SECURE SMART CITIES

Technology alone is insufficient. Effective governance is the critical framework that ensures technology is deployed securely, ethically, and for the public good.

6.1. Evolving Policy and Legal Frameworks

A complex web of regulations is emerging to govern smart cities:

- GDPR (EU): Sets a high bar for data protection, mandating consent, purpose limitation, and the right to explanation.
- NIS2 Directive (EU): Strengthens cybersecurity obligations for operators of essential services.
- AI Act (EU): Proposes a risk-based regulatory framework for AI, banning certain unacceptable uses (e.g., social scoring) and imposing strict requirements on high-risk applications (e.g., biometric identification).
- U.S. National Cybersecurity Strategy: Shifts responsibility for cybersecurity from individuals to software vendors and critical infrastructure operators.

A key challenge is regulatory fragmentation. A smart city vendor may need to comply with dozens of different, and sometimes conflicting, international, national, and local laws.

6.2. Multi-stakeholder Governance and Citizen Inclusion

Top-down governance is ineffective. A collaborative model involving government, industry, academia, and citizens is essential.

- Municipalities:Must act as stewards of public data and champions of citizen rights.
- Private Sector:Must be held accountable through procurement contracts that mandate security-by-design, transparency, and ethical data practices.
- Citizens:Must be engaged as co-designers, not just end-users. Participatory budgeting platforms, citizen oversight boards, and transparent public consultations are key tools for building trust and legitimacy.

6.3. Ethics-by-Design and Value-Sensitive Design

Ethical considerations cannot be an afterthought. They must be integrated into the entire technology lifecycle.

- Ethical Impact Assessments (EIAs): Should be mandatory before deploying any high-risk AI system.
- Algorithmic Auditing:Independent, third-party audits of public-sector algorithms for bias, fairness, and effectiveness (e.g., Amsterdam's AI Registry).
- Digital Rights Charters: Cities like Barcelona and Toronto have developed charters that explicitly embed democratic values and human rights into their digital city plans.

6.4. Cybersecurity Risk Management and Resilience Planning

Cities must adopt proactive and dynamic approaches to cyber risk.

- Zero Trust Architecture (ZTA):Moves away from the outdated "castle-and-moat" model. ZTA assumes breach and verifies every request as though it originates from an untrusted network.

  -City-Level CERTs:Computer Emergency Response Teams dedicated to municipal infrastructure can coordinate incident response and share threat intelligence.
- Resilience Exercises: Regular "war games" and tabletop exercises to test response plans for cyber-physical attacks on critical infrastructure.

6.5. Accountability and Redress Mechanisms

Strong governance requires clear accountability and pathways for citizens to seek redress.

- Transparency Reports: Cities should regularly publish reports on data collection practices, data breach incidents, and the performance of automated systems.
- Grievance redressal mechanisms must be accessible for citizens to challenge and get explanations for algorithmic decisions that affect them.
- Liability Frameworks: Clear laws defining the legal liability of municipalities, technology vendors, and system operators in the event of a harmful failure.

7. CASE STUDIES AND COMPARATIVE INSIGHTS

Real-world smart city deployments provide invaluable insights into the practical challenges of balancing innovation with security, privacy, and citizen trust. By analysing a diverse set of global cases, we can identify patterns of success and failure, moving beyond theoretical frameworks to understand the socio-technical and governance realities of digital urbanism. This section examines cities across the development spectrum, highlighting the critical role of adaptive governance, public engagement, and strategic investment in cybersecurity resilience.

7.1. Toronto's Sidewalk Labs: A Cautionary Tale in Tech-Centric Urbanism

The ambitious plan to transform Toronto's Quayside into a sensor-saturated digital district, led by Alphabet's Sidewalk Labs, became a seminal case of technological overreach. The project promised hyper-efficiency through pervasive data collection but faltered due to a profound governance gap (Cecco, 2020). Public resistance, led by groups like BlockSidewalk, centred on opaque data ownership, the impossibility of meaningful consent in a monitored public space, and the fear of surveillance capitalism being baked into urban fabric. The project's 2020 cancellation was a watershed moment, demonstrating that citizen trust is a non-negotiable foundation for smart cities. In its wake, Toronto introduced robust data stewardship frameworks in 2023, mandating citizen co-governance models and local data sovereignty, setting a new global standard for participatory digital urban planning.

Insight: Technological ambition without deep citizen engagement and transparent governance is a recipe for failure. Public pushback can be a powerful force for establishing stronger democratic controls over urban data.

7.2. Singapore: A Holistic Model of Secure and Trusted Governance

Singapore's "Smart Nation" initiative is distinguished by its integrated approach, weaving together strong legislation, technical standards, and citizen-centric services. Its effectiveness is proven by outcomes: the city-state consistently ranks among the top globally in cybersecurity readiness and has avoided major disruptive incidents (IMD Smart City Index, 2024). Key to this success is its Cybersecurity Act (2018), which mandates stringent protections for critical infrastructure, and its AI Governance Framework, which promotes transparent and fair automated decision-making. The Cybersecurity Labelling Scheme (CLS) for IoT devices empowers consumers and drives market competition for security. With a 92% public trust rate in government data handling (Smart Nation Survey, 2024), Singapore demonstrates that centralized, well-regulated digital transformation can foster both innovation and high levels of citizen confidence.

Insight: A proactive, government-led strategy that combines clear regulation (e.g., mandatory cybersecurity standards) with transparency (e.g., explainable AI) is highly effective in building a secure and trusted smart ecosystem.

7.3. Amsterdam and Helsinki: Pioneers of Algorithmic Transparency

These European capitals have chosen the path of radical transparency to build public trust. Amsterdam's Algorithm Register is a global first a public inventory of all algorithms used by the city government, detailing their purpose, data sources, and impact assessments. This allows for public scrutiny and contestability. Helsinki complements this with its MyData model, a platform that gives citizens a single dashboard to control how their personal data is used by both public and private services. This human-centric approach has tangibly improved governance; public oversight has led to the revision of several algorithmic systems found to have potential biases, particularly in social services. Their models prove that transparency isn't a vulnerability but a strength that enhances democratic accountability and improves system performance.

Insight: Making algorithms and data flows visible and controllable by citizens is a powerful tool for identifying bias, preventing error, and cementing public trust in automated systems.

7.4. Barcelona: The Participatory Democracy Model

Barcelona's approach counters top-down tech platforms with a commitment to digital sovereignty and citizen empowerment. Its Decidim platform is a democratic innovation, enabling over 40,000 residents to directly propose and vote on urban policies and budgets(Decidim). Technically, the city enforces a minimal data collection policy and uses open-source, federated architectures to avoid vendor lock-in and ensure data remains under public control. This has not only boosted civic engagement but also improved the equity of resource allocation, as spending priorities are set by citizens themselves. Barcelona's model shows that a city's "smartness" can be measured not by the number of its sensors, but by the depth of its democratic engagement (Barcelona City Council, 2023).

Insight: Prioritizing citizen participation and public ownership of digital infrastructure leads to more equitable and socially sustainable outcomes than models driven by private technology vendors.

7.5. New York City: Lessons in Cyber Resilience and Response

As a massive, complex metropolis, NYC faces constant cyber threats. Its response to a significant 2023 ransomware attack on its Department of Education, which compromised data of 70,000+ students, is instructive. The city's recovery involved a multi-pronged strategy: establishing a Municipal Cybersecurity Response Unit (MCRU) for coordinated incident response, mandating zero-trust architecture for all new IT projects, and implementing compulsory cybersecurity training for all public employees (MOVEit data breach: 45,000 NYC students among victims, 2023). This case underscores that resilience is not about preventing all attacks, but about having the governance capacity to respond, recover, and learn, thereby strengthening defences against future incidents.

Insight: Preparedness and a swift, transparent response to breaches are critical components of smart city resilience. Investing in incident response capability is as important as investing in preventative technology.

7.6. Nairobi: The Challenges of Rapid Digitalization Without Cyber Maturity

Nairobi's rapid adoption of smart technologies from mobile health platforms to digital identity systems has leapfrogged traditional infrastructure but has created significant cyber risks.SIM swap frauds and mobile money theft are prevalent, exacerbated by weak digital literacy and inadequate identity verification protocols. A 2024 SQL injection attack on a government data center exposed the vulnerabilities of underlying systems (Okorie, 2024). Nairobi's experience highlights the acute danger of digital inequality: when connectivity is adopted without parallel investments in security and literacy, the most vulnerable populations bear the brunt of the risks, eroding the very benefits smart cities are meant to provide.

Insight: Accelerated digital growth must be paired with foundational cybersecurity capacity building, robust regulatory frameworks, and digital literacy programs to avoid exacerbating inequality and creating systemic vulnerability.

To distill lessons from these diverse cases, Table 4 compares governance models across selected global cities.

Table 4. Comparative Analysis of Smart City Governance Models

City	Primary Governance Approach	Key Strength	Primary Challenge	Citizen Trust Indicator
Singapore	Centralized, regulatory	Holistic cybersecurity strategy with strict enforcement	Balancing state control and individual privacy	92% satisfaction (Smart Nation Survey, 2024)
Barcelona	Decentralized, participatory	Citizen ownership of data & open platforms	Scaling participation beyond highly active groups	High engagement (40,000+ users on Decidim)
Amsterdam / Helsinki	Transparent, ethical	Algorithmic transparency registers; citizen data control	Maintaining complex public algorithm registers	High (driven by contestability mechanisms)
Toronto	Post-Sidewalk reform	Strong data sovereignty and governance policies	Rebuilding public trust after Sidewalk Labs withdrawal	Improving post-reform (municipal reporting)
New York City	Resilient, responsive	Mature incident response & recovery capacity	Securing legacy, heterogenous infrastructure	Moderate, stress-tested by incidents
Nairobi	Rapid-growth, emerging	Innovative mobile-first service delivery	Cyber maturity and regulatory enforcement gaps	Lower trust due to fraud prevalence

The comparison shows that while no single governance model is perfect, aligning technological innovation with transparency, accountability, and citizen participation is key to public trust.

8. FUTURE RESEARCH DIRECTIONS

The future of secure and privacy-centric smart cities requires moving beyond siloed technical fixes to address complex socio-technical systems. Research must be interdisciplinary, blending computer science with law, ethics, urban planning, and social science. The following directions are critical for closing current gaps.

8.1. Socio-Technical Security and Governance Gaps

Cyber Equity and Justice: Research must investigate how cybersecurity risks and privacy harms are disproportionately borne by marginalized communities. How do surveillance technologies and data-driven policing impact low-income or minority neighbourhoods? Frameworks for equity-impact assessments of new urban technologies are urgently needed.

Sustainable Funding Models: A key unsolved governance problem is how municipalities, especially in developing regions, can fund ongoing cybersecurity operations. Research into innovative public-private funding models and cost-benefit analyses of security investments is crucial.

Measuring Citizen Trust: Develop standardized, longitudinal metrics for quantifying citizen trust in urban digital systems and identify the key technological and governance factors that influence it.

8.2. Technical Research with Policy-Awareness

Explainable AI (XAI) for Public Policy: Future XAI research must focus on creating explanations that are not just technically sound but are also meaningful and actionable for citizens, policymakers, and auditors. How can an algorithm's decision to deny a housing permit or prioritize a street for repair be explained to an affected resident?

Privacy-Enhancing Technologies (PETs) at Scale: While PETs like Federated Learning (FL) and Differential Privacy (DP) exist, research is needed to make them viable for city-wide deployment. This includes:

Byzantine-Robust FL: Developing aggregation algorithms that can withstand malicious participants in city-scale learning tasks.

Energy-Efficient PETs: Designing low-power algorithms for battery-constrained IoT devices that form the urban sensing layer.

Standardized DP for Open Data: Creating frameworks for cities to release useful open datasets with mathematically provable privacy guarantees.

Blockchain for Governance, Not Just Currency: Explore applications of blockchain for transparent public audit trails (e.g., tracking access to sensitive citizen data), secure digital identity for public services, and executing transparent public contracts ("smart contracts").

8.3. Human-Centric and Resilient Design

Zero-Trust Architectures (ZTA) for Urban Critical Infrastructure: Research is needed to design and implement ZTA principles for complex, legacy-laden urban environments like power grids and water systems. This includes dynamic, attribute-based access control for operational technology (OT).

Digital Twin for Security Simulation: Use urban digital twins to simulate cyber-attacks and assess their physical and economic impacts, enabling proactive defence and resilience planning.

Behavioural Security and Digital Literacy: Study how to effectively improve the cybersecurity hygiene of both city employees and the general public. What training methods are most effective for different demographics?

8.4. Legal and Standardization Frontiers

Transnational Data Flow Governance: Research models for managing data sovereignty and compliance when urban data flows across borders, especially with conflicting regulations (e.g., EU GDPR vs. US CLOUD Act).

Liability Frameworks for Autonomous Urban Systems: Establish clear legal frameworks defining liability when harm results from the actions of an autonomous city system (e.g., a hacked smart traffic light causes an accident).

Standardized Cyber Risk Metrics for Cities: Develop common benchmarks and metrics for assessing the cybersecurity maturity of a smart city, enabling comparative analysis and best-practice sharing.

By pursuing these interdisciplinary research paths, the next generation of smart cities can be designed to be not only more efficient but also more just, secure, and resilient.

REFERENCES

Al-Shurbaji, T., Anbar, M., Manickam, S., Hasbullah, I. H., Alfriehat, N., Alabsi, B. A., Alzighaibi, A. R., & Hashim, H. (2025). Deep learning-based intrusion detection system for detecting IoT botnet attacks: A review. *IEEE Access : Practical Innovations, Open Solutions*, *13*, 11792–11822. DOI: 10.1109/ACCESS.2025.3526711

Bada, A. O., Damianou, A., Angelopoulos, C. M., & Katos, V. (2021). Towards a green blockchain: A review of consensus mechanisms and their energy consumption. In *2021 17th International Conference on Distributed Computing in Sensor Systems (DCOSS)* (pp. 503–511). IEEE. https://doi.org/DOI: 10.1109/DCOSS52077.2021.00083

Beerman, J., Berent, D., Falter, Z., & Bhunia, S. (2023, May). A review of colonial pipeline ransomware attack. In 2023 IEEE/ACM 23rd International Symposium on Cluster, Cloud and Internet Computing Workshops (CCGridW) (pp. 8-15). IEEE.

Cecco, L. (2020, May 7). *Google affiliate Sidewalk Labs abruptly abandons Toronto smart city project.* The Guardian; The Guardian. https://www.theguardian.com/technology/2020/may/07/google-sidewalk-labs-toronto-smart-city-abandoned?

Cities of the Future. (2025, May 3). NIS2 directive casts a wider net over smart city infrastructure. Cities of the Future. https://citiesofthefuture.eu/nis2-directive-casts-a-wider-net-over-smart-city-infrastructure/

Cybersecurity & Infrastructure Security Agency. (2021, February 12). *Compromise of U.S. water treatment facility.* https://www.cisa.gov/news-events/cybersecurity-advisories/aa21-042a

Decidim Barcelona | Barcelona Digital City | Barcelona City Council. (n.d.). Ajuntament.barcelona.cat. https://ajuntament.barcelona.cat/digital/en/technology-accessible-everyone/accessible-and-participatory/accessible-and-participatory-5

Decidim. (n.d.). Free Open-Source participatory democracy for cities and organizations | Decidim. Decidim.org. https://decidim.org/

Dragonetti, W., & Garcia, R. (2025, May 3). Cities discuss regulation of AI and its many challenges. Eurocities. https://eurocities.eu/latest/cities-discuss-regulation-of-ai-and-its-many-challenges/

Dragos Inc. (2017). *CrashOverride: Analysis of the threat to electric grid operations* [Technical report]. Dragos Inc. https://www.dragos.com/wp-content/uploads/CrashOverride-01.pdf

Dwivedi, R., Dave, D., Naik, H., Singhal, S., Omer, R., Patel, P., Qian, B., Wen, Z., Shah, T., Morgan, G., & Ranjan, R. (2023). Explainable AI (XAI): Core ideas, techniques, and solutions. *ACM Computing Surveys*, *55*(9), 1–33. DOI: 10.1145/3561048

Hao, J., & Tao, Y. (2022). Adversarial attacks on deep learning models in smart grids. *Energy Reports*, *8*, 123–129. DOI: 10.1016/j.egyr.2021.11.026

IBM Report: Escalating Data Breach Disruption Pushes Costs to New Highs. (2024). IBM Newsroom. https://newsroom.ibm.com/2024-07-30-ibm-report-escalating-data-breach-disruption-pushes-costs-to-new-highs?

Jithish, J., Alangot, B., Mahalingam, N., & Yeo, K. S. (2023). Distributed anomaly detection in smart grids: A federated learning-based approach. *IEEE Access : Practical Innovations, Open Solutions*, *11*, 7157–7179. DOI: 10.1109/ACCESS.2023.3237554

. Malik, S., & Sun, W. (2020, February 1). Analysis and Simulation of Cyber Attacks Against Connected and Autonomous Vehicles. IEEE Xplore. https://doi.org/DOI: 10.1109/MetroCAD48866.2020.00018

. Manas. (2023). Role of Privacy Metrics in Next Generation Smart Cities. *Tuijin Jishu/Journal of Propulsion Technology, 44*(4), 3151–3159. https://doi.org/DOI: 10.52783/tjjpt.v44.i4.1407

MOVEit data breach: 45,000 NYC students among victims. (2023, June 23). Chalkbeat. https://www.chalkbeat.org/newyork/2023/6/23/23772027/nyc-student-data-breach-security-moveit-department-education-hack/

Okorie, I. J. (2024, June 24). *Suspected Chinese hackers targeted Kenya government agencies*. Techpoint Africa. https://techpoint.africa/news/chinese-hackers-kenya-government-agencies/.

Pemmasani, P. K., & Osaka, M. (2021). The future of smart cities: Cybersecurity challenges in public infrastructure management. *International Journal of Modern Computing*, *4*(1), 72–85. https://yuktabpublisher.com/index.php/IJMC/article/view/249

Pollard, M. (2024) "A Case Study of Russian Cyber-Attacks on the Ukrainian Power Grid: Implicationsand Best Practices for the United States,"Pepperdine Policy Review: Vol. 16, Article 1.Available at:https://digitalcommons.pepperdine.edu/ppr/vol16/iss1/1

Priyadarshini, I., Alkhayyat, A., Gehlot, A., & Kumar, R. (2022). Time series analysis and anomaly detection for trustworthy smart homes. *Computers & Electrical Engineering*, *102*, 108193. DOI: 10.1016/j.compeleceng.2022.108193

Rana, M. U., Shah, M. A., Al-Naeem, M. A., & Maple, C. (2024). Ransomware attacks in cyber-physical systems: Countermeasure of attack vectors through automated web defenses. *IEEE Access : Practical Innovations, Open Solutions*, *12*, 149722–149739. DOI: 10.1109/ACCESS.2024.3477631

Razmjoo, A., Østergaard, P. A., Denaï, M., Nezhad, M. M., & Mirjalili, S. (2021). Effective policies to overcome barriers in the development of smart cities. *Energy Research & Social Science*, *79*, 102175. DOI: 10.1016/j.erss.2021.102175

van Twist, A., Ruijer, E., & Meijer, A. (2023). Smart cities & citizen discontent: A systematic review of the literature. *Government Information Quarterly*, *101799*. Advance online publication. DOI: 10.1016/j.giq.2022.101799

Xia, G., Chen, J., Yu, C., & Ma, J. (2023). Poisoning attacks in federated learning: A survey. *IEEE Access : Practical Innovations, Open Solutions*, *11*, 10708–10722. DOI: 10.1109/ACCESS.2023.3238823

Chapter 8
Safeguarding Urban Intelligence:
Redefining IoT Networks With Privacy in Mind

G. Mani
University College of Engineering, Kancheepuram, India

J. Rajeshwari
https://orcid.org/0000-0001-6021-1879
Dayananda Sagar college of Engineering, India

R. Suganthi
Panimalar Engineering College, India

P. Smitha Vas
https://orcid.org/0000-0002-3967-8041
LBS Institute of Technology for Women, India

G. Manoj Kumar
https://orcid.org/0000-0001-7553-7572
LBS College of Engineering, India

N. V. Keerthana
https://orcid.org/0000-0001-8878-2083
Velalar College of Engineering and Technology, India

ABSTRACT

The growing reliance on Internet of Things (IoT) technologies in smart cities brings significant data privacy and security challenges. This paper presents a privacy-preserving IoT network model designed to protect sensitive information while retaining functionality and performance. The model utilizes edge computing, lightweight encryption, pseudonymization, and role-based access control alongside blockchain for enhanced trust and transparency. Experimental results demonstrate that this approach efficiently safeguards data without compromising service quality. This study aims to enable the responsible and sustainable implementation of smart city innovations while preserving citizen dignity, consent, and control over their own data.

DOI: 10.4018/979-8-3373-4455-3.ch008

1. INTRODUCTION

The Internet of Things (IoT) links everything on Earth. Things are just things that have a unique identifier. Everything may be connected to the Internet from any location and at any time. The technology allows for the provision of higher-level services than before, and for extracting useful information from the data. By allowing infrastructures like electric and hybrid smart cars to interconnect, driving quality, safety, and fuel efficiency can all be greatly improved. Smart city models are designed to improve the quality of people's residential lives, evaluate environmental dangers, strategic planning, and the use of more energy by intelligently collecting and processing data using smart devices. Usage of clever technology-based solutions for the problems, and the introduction of smart city concepts, are taken into consideration. The wide range of distinct methodologies, settings, application areas, and technology solutions that have been documented in the literature for the management and implementation of smart cities is indicative of this complexity.

Implementing and integrating IoT technology is primarily intended to enable smart cities to develop, offering new features and capabilities while drastically lowering the requirement for human interaction. To reduce operating expenses and improve the sustainability of the city, it is imperative that redundant solutions for data input, storage, and analysis not be implemented. Three main issues caused by the vast number of devices are heterogeneity, protecting the privacy of generated data, as well as offering high-level services. Large amounts of data are created and shared by the proliferation of IoT devices in smart cities. The difficulty of privacy preservation, which guarantees that the sensitive data gathered by IoT devices is securely shielded from unauthorized access, arises from heterogeneity, since IoT devices are produced with varied capabilities and standards. Because it offers top-notch services without jeopardising user privacy, service quality is also an issue. Strong frameworks that can handle privacy issues and the varied nature of IoT devices must be developed to meet these problems (Gheisari et al., 2023).

IoT serves as a global network that connects all physical objects that have a unique identifier, enabling global communication between devices. Universal access allows things to connect and communicate anytime and anywhere via the Internet. This service facilitates higher-level services by analyzing and extracting valuable information from the data it generates. For example, smart vehicles integrating electric and hybrid smart cars with IoT infrastructure can improve their driving quality, road safety, and fuel efficiency. Smart cities rely on intelligent data collection through IoT-enabled devices to improve the quality of life for citizens, monitor environmental risks, enable strategic traffic planning, and optimize energy usage. These problems are solved in urban areas. The smart city frameworks use IoT-based technologies to address everyday urban challenges effectively. Semantic reasoning helps identify both normal and suspicious activities in smart cities. Devices, while interacting with people, collect information discreetly. Smart cities use many different types of IoT devices, such as traffic sensors, smart meters, and surveillance cameras, each with its own design and data formats. Ontology-Based Privacy-Preserving (OBPP) uses a common structure, called Acknowledged, to help these devices understand and share their information in a unified way. This simplifies communication and ensures that all systems work together smoothly (Gheisari et al., 2021).

Human mobility data is represented by trajectories. Thus, different types of data have different forms of representation, distribution, scales, and densities, all of which result in the different data types existing in isolation. There are numerous machine-learning-based apps for various smart city domains and features. Nevertheless, the majority of these programs concentrate on particular issues and lack the skills required to analyze the data.

Before the IoT concept is widely adopted, several difficult problems still need to be resolved, and social and technological snags need to be untangled. The components that make up the IoT will be defined by their low computational and energy capacity. Therefore, in addition to the apparent scaling issues, the suggested solutions must give particular consideration to resource efficiency (Atzori, Iera, & Morabito, 2010). Several forms of IoT devices include intelligent traffic control systems and environment monitoring equipment, together with connected public transportation networks and surveillance technology platforms. Smart traffic management analyzes current traffic data to reconfigure signal timings that decrease congestion while lowering emissions.

The protection of gathered data requires both security measures and the absence of attacks that risk personal privacy levels and city infrastructure safety. To attain safe IoT system deployment in cities, researchers need to develop strong security methods that safeguard privacy. The intended service of preventing unauthorized use of the available resources is provided by access control. Examining the security features of a specific IoT architectural layer will serve as the foundation for the risk classification suggestions, which will concentrate future research and development efforts on the most vulnerable levels. To apply suitable protective techniques, the risk classification will also be done based on how the IoT concept is applied in different contexts.

Traditional access control methods for access distribution and administration are being expanded or adopted by the IoT. IoT devices are also resource-constrained, having a limited amount of memory, processing power, and battery life. Access control, out of all the security services, guarantees that users, devices, apps, and services have the proper access to resources. For any IoT application to be secure, access management is crucial. The specification of access control rules, including dynamic policies, is covered in detail. The difficulties that the existing solutions encounter are emphasized (Andrade, Ortiz-Garcés, Tintin, & Llumiquinga, 2022).

2. SMART CITIES AND IOT

By 2020, the market for smart cities is expected to grow to hundreds of billions of dollars, with annual spending approaching 16 billion. Smart governance, smart transportation, smart utilities, smart buildings, and smart environment are just a few of the important industry and service sectors that are synergistically interconnected and drive this market. The accessibility of the diverse technologies currently employed in cities and urban projects is the most pertinent technical issue. This predicament keeps the potentially enormous smart city market from materializing. Generally speaking, the absence of a generally recognized communication and service architecture, rather than technological difficulties, is impeding the practical implementation of the majority of such services (Zanella, Bui, Castellani, Vangelista, & Zorzi, 2014). Generally speaking, the IoT is a real item that is widely distributed, has limited storage and processing power, and is intended to improve the infrastructure and dependability of smart cities. Based on this, a study of IoT-based smart city data from relevant papers is carried out in this research.

Therefore, this service can enhance the city's nighttime calm as well as the trust of public business owners. However, the installation of environmental microphones or sound detectors is very contentious due to the clear privacy issues associated with this kind of surveillance. A variety of short-range network communication methods are used by IoT devices. Depending on the capabilities of the communication parties, perception devices send information to a nearby gateway via Bluetooth and ZigBee. Depending on the application, internet technologies, including WiFi, 2G, 3G, 4G, and Power Line Communication (PLC), can transmit data over great distances.

2.1. Key Components of Smart Cities

Since the Internet is available everywhere, urban infrastructures are made up of various electronic devices, such as sensors to measure air pollution, smart appliances to control domestic gas and electricity consumption, and surveillance cameras to notify residents of traffic conditions. With the advancement of digital technologies like fiber optics, connected items, 3G, 4G, and 5G mobile networks, among others, cities are growing increasingly intelligent. Additionally, customers are informed in real time of crowded route portions using intelligent urban traffic management (Alshmrany, 2025). As seen in Figure 1, the primary objective of the smart city is to enhance the quality of life for residents and their engagement with local and governmental services.

Figure 1. Key Components of Smart Cities

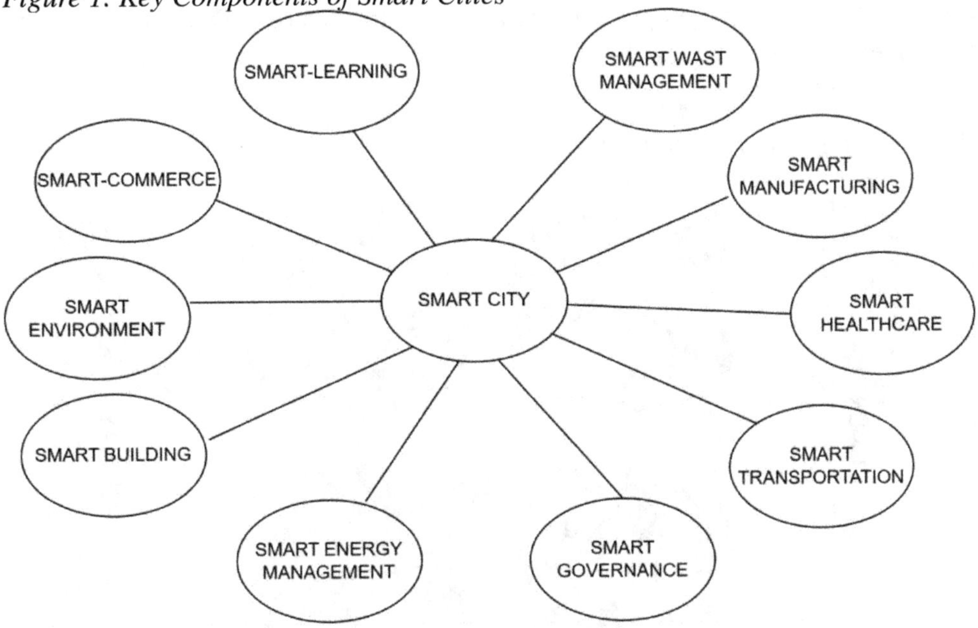

2.2. IOT Architecture in Smart Cities

The device, network, session, application, business, administration, and security layers make up the tiered framework that comprises the IoT architecture. The device layer is made up of sensors and actual hardware that gathers and recognizes data and information produced by these components. IoT services like smart homes, smart cities, and smart farms are included in the application layer, which also controls the system using information from the session layer. All IoT systems, services, and applications inside the domain are managed by the business layer, which also establishes business logic and workflows and analyzes application layer data to create necessary business models and strategies (Tekinerdogan, Köksal, & Çelik, 2023), as shown in Figure 2. To offer a connection for a typical Side Channel Attack (SCA) in the IoT scenario, the authors took into consideration Low Power Wide Area Network (LPWAN). They also talked about how LPWAN is better than popular approaches in terms of efficacy, efficiency, and architectural design. They also talked about how LPWAN is better than popular approaches in terms of efficacy, efficiency, and architectural design. Security modules are included in each layer to safeguard private information. Data is gathered from physical devices by the sensing layer, which is at the base of the design. Above the sensing layer lies the transmission layer. Data is sent from the transmission layer to the higher data management layer via a variety of communication protocols (Kanellopoulos, Sharma, Panagiotakopoulos, & Kameas, 2023).

Figure 2. Typical IoT Architecture

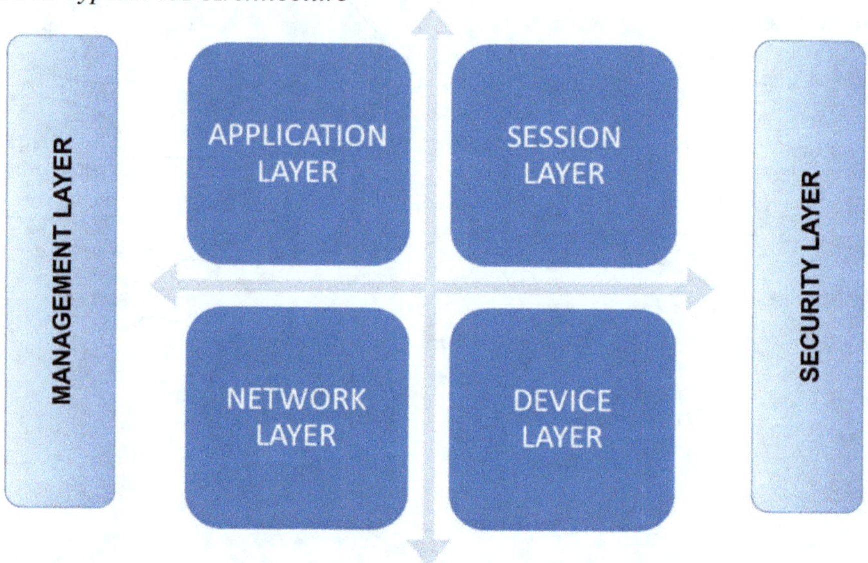

The data flow is a Smart City following its structured path through different layers of an IoT architecture. There are the Perception Layer, the Network Layer, and the Application Layer. Perception layers are used for data collection by sensors and IoT devices to collect data such as temperature, CCTV cameras, and pollution monitoring collect raw data from the environment. These devices detect the real-world parameters such as movement, temperature, energy usage, and more. The Network Layer is a data transmission layer. The data is collected and transmitted by communication technologies like Wi-Fi, 5G, Zigbee, and Bluetooth. The data is securely packaged and sent to data centers, cloud platforms, or edge devices. The Application Layer is a data processing and utilization layer. In the cloud or on a local service, the data is stored, filtered, and analysed (Bhardwaj et al., 2022). Artificial Intelligence (AI) and data analytics tools generate meaningful insights and support smart devices such as traffic signals, smart lighting, waste management, emergency response, and more, as represented in Figure 3.

Figure 3. Dataflow in IoT Environment

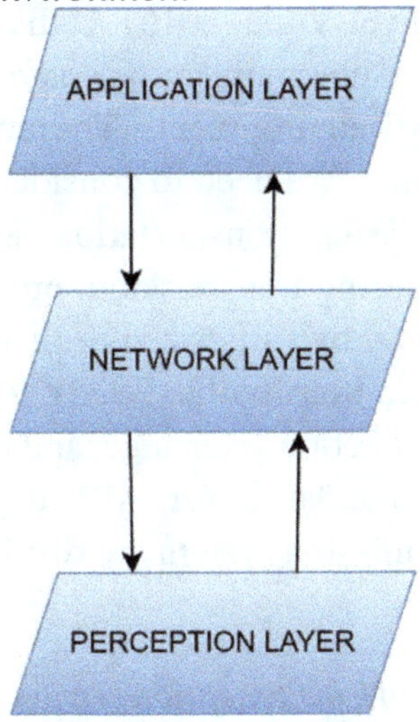

2.3. Role of Data Analytics and AI

A big data analytics framework for the IoT to address the difficulties of storing and evaluating vast amounts of data coming from smart buildings. It is utilized to control the brightness, smoke, and hazardous gases, and oxygen level in various areas of the smart building. Cloudera is used to implement the framework. Meaningful information can be extracted from sensor device data with the use of big data and analytics. In the context of the IoT, data technology can offer services for data processing and storage, and data analytics can assist businessmen in making better decisions. These are the general requirements for big data and the IoT (Ahmed et al., 2017).

3. PRIVACY THREATS AND VULNERABILITIES

The largest problem with IoT is privacy. Applied technologies, such as Radio Frequency Identification (RFID), Near Field Communication (NFC), Bluetooth, ZigBee, and IPv6 over Low-power Wireless Personal Area Networks (6LoWPAN), have limitations in terms of data transmission range and rate. Additionally, perception layer devices often have limited processing and data storage resources. In addition to lowering the devices' ultimate cost, restrictions are implemented to enhance the devices' flexibility, autonomy, and physical dimensions. The essential features of any transmission system are included coverage, topology, power consumption, data transfer rate, and range (Cvitić & Vujić, 2015). Unlike the other levels, which are present in other information and communication contexts in one way or another, the perception layer is unique to IoT environments. The amount and variety of data that IoT devices gather are both huge. We need to consider many basic security issues, including the collection, processing, transportation, and storage of data.

Integrity guarantees that during transmission, processing, and storage, data is safe, encrypted, and only altered by authorized users (Keerthana, Sakthivel, Balasubramaniyan, Gunasekaran, & Marimuthu, 2020). IoT devices are susceptible to attacks not only during data collection, exchange, and transmission phases, but also at the design stage(Obaidat, Obeidat, Holst, Al Hayajneh, & Brown, 2020). The essential features of any transmission system are displayed in Table 1.

Table 1. Comparative Analysis of IoT Perception Layer Communication Technologies

Feature/Technology	NFC	RFID	Bluetooth	ZigBee	6LoWPAN
Coverage Area	PAN	PAN	PAN	LAN	LAN
Topology	P2P	P2P	Star	Mesh/Star/Tree	Mesh/Star
Power Consumption	Very Low	Very Low	Low	Very Low	Very Low
Speed	400 Kbps	400 Kbps	0.7-1 Mbps	250 Kbps	250 Kbps
Range	< 10 cm	< 3 m	5-30 m	10-300 m	800 m

3.1. Data Collection and Aggregation Risks

An effective data processing method for extensive Wireless Sensor Networks (WSNs) is data aggregation, a recent study area. Sensor nodes in these networks have the potential to produce enormous amounts of data. Data aggregation techniques may eliminate data redundancy, reduce energy consumption, increase network lifetime, and make the most use of network resources in large-scale WSNs; therefore, it is vital to create effective data processing techniques. One crucial area of study is secure data aggregation. It is anticipated that future researchers will further this topic. There are several obstacles to implementing a suitable Secure Data Aggregation (SDA) technique in wireless sensor networks.

Moreover, ensuring the security and integrity of aggregated data, known as SDA, has become a vital focus for researchers. SDA seeks to preserve aggregate efficiency while shielding sensitive data from malevolent assaults, fraudulent reporting, and illegal access. In this step, data processing was done. The most crucial step in modeling the actual link between input and output variables was converting data into a format that the model would accept. Since the data was unprocessed and contained issues like outliers and missing numbers, among other things. To make data usable for models to use as input and process, a few strategies were used (Yousefpoor et al., 2021).

3.2. Communication and Transmission Risks

Data transmitted over networks can be intercepted, leading to unauthorized access and potential misuse. The features of IoT systems encourage the application of risk analysis techniques that are employed in conventional IT systems. Risk models are mathematical depictions of future conditions based on risk factors and loss event projections. An attribute, characteristic, variable, or other determining element that affects a system, entity, or organization's risk profile is referred to as a "risk factor" in general. In this regard, this methodology's advantages include having a list of vital assets that might be impacted by a security breach; another noteworthy feature of MAGERIT is that it takes asset interconnections into account when estimating the potential damage in the event of an attack (Andrade et al., 2022). MAGERIT is one of the best Spanish technologies for risk assessment.

3.3. Storage and Access Control Issues

Access control covers both physical facilities and information systems. To provide users and devices access privileges when IoT devices are connected to a network, access control is essential. The authentication function confirms a user's, process', or device's identity. The administration component of the access control process is also included to efficiently establish, provision, and manage various users, groups, roles, devices, and policies. Following the completion of authentication, authorization occurs (Ragothaman, Wang, Rimal, & Lawrence, 2023). Authorization Policies work together to decide which resources or services a person or device can access, as represented in Figure 4.

Figure 4. Access Control Process in the IoT

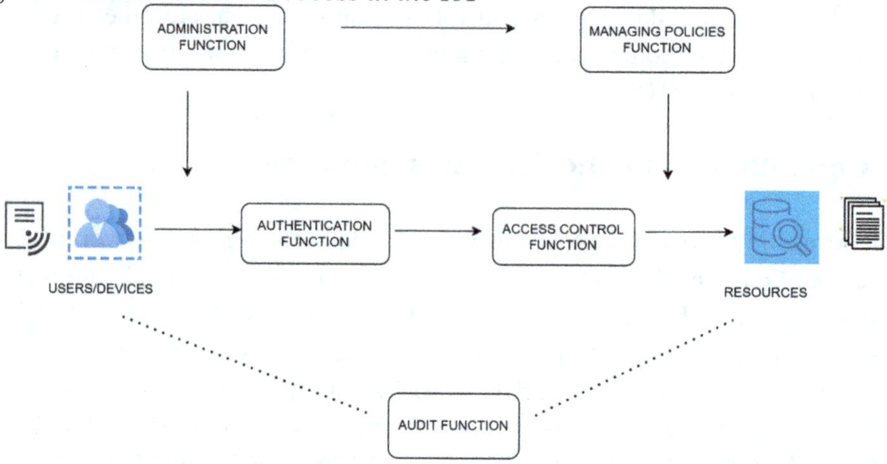

3.4. Case Studies of Privacy Breaches in Smart Cities

An IoT-enabled smart surveillance system built using a Raspberry Pi. The system uses a Pi camera to capture real-time video, which is then streamed over the cloud using an IoT platform. It enables remote monitoring from any location via the network and includes additional features such as motion detection and alert notifications. This system integrates low-cost hardware with IoT capabilities to create a reliable and accessible surveillance framework. Raspberry Pi, a compact and powerful single-board computer that acts as the main controller. The system utilizes a Pi Camera to continuously capture live video footage. By the Ubidots IoT platform, which allows users to monitor their surroundings from any location via an internet-connected device, this visual data is transmitted and readily available remotely. The Passive Infrared (PIR) motion sensor, able to detect movement in its surrounding space, is a vital component of the system. The key idea is to allow remote monitoring from any location via the internet, with additional features like motion detection and alert notifications. This includes activating a buzzer or LED to signal intrusion and sending a real-time notification through the IoT, and making the system responsive and proactive in alerting users (Belli et al., 2020).

Furthermore, the software platform uses Python programming, enabling seamless interaction between hardware and cloud services. Every time motion is detected, the Raspberry Pi snaps a photo or captures a video clip and uploads it to the cloud server. Because of the interaction with Ubidots, it is simple to view the live stream to get announcements, boosting overall efficiency and usability. Likewise, the system is very adaptive, enabling energy conservation and an extensive variety of applications as shown in Figure 5.

Figure 5. IoT-enabled smart surveillance system built using a Raspberry Pi

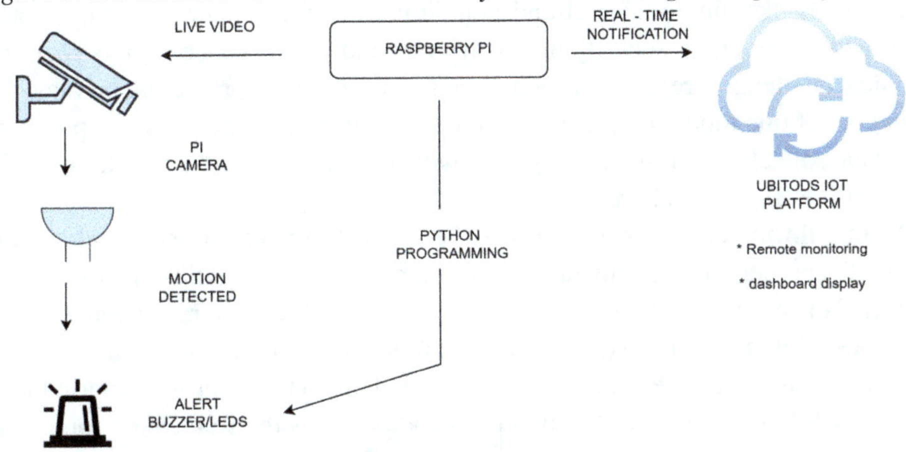

3.5. Working Principle of Smart Surveillance System With IOT Using Raspberry Pi

Real-time sensing, communication, and intelligent decision-making are all combined in the multi-layered operating architecture of the IoT-based smart surveillance system. The device uses a camera that is linked to a Raspberry Pi to display live content frequently. PIR sensors or motion detection track motion in a specified region in parallel. An alert mechanism is triggered by the motion detection; this might be an LED indication, an alarm, or a real-time notice sent via a Network of Things platform like ThingSpeak or Ubidots.

Data generated by the sensor is collected and then processed either at the edge on the Raspberry Pi itself or at the cloud computing layer. This layer produces approaches like reducing latency and preserving bandwidth. Then it is uploaded to the cloud storage for remote access, analysis, and more. The system is accessible in real-time via a web interface or IoT dashboard to provide authorized users with on-demand video and event logs. Additionally, it is based on advanced AI or ML algorithms for object detection and anomaly recognition example, differentiating between an animal and a vehicle. It allows for product decision-making and enhances even response.

3.6 BLA Model for Privacy Preserving

The Balanced Layered Architecture (BLA) is well known as the model for privacy preserving, which is designed for the security of private data that maintains the scalability and usability in a seamless manner. When compared to traditional mechanisms like single-layered and double-layered architectures, it outperforms by providing excellent security and achieves good performance by incorporating technical challenges, regulations and dimensional ethics of protecting privacy. The main goal of this model is to protect private sensitive data. It consists of processes like data collection, preprocessing, storage management, and data sharing. The layers of the BLA model are:

Data Minimization Layer: This is the initial layer that collects the data and applies the process of anonymization, process of pseudonymization and masking of data. It also combines the user queries for preserving the data transparency.

Access Control layer: There are policies such as attribute-based ethical regulations, role role-based mechanisms are involved here. This layer is supported technically by following the GDPR guidelines and provides the framework for access.

Privacy Preservation Layer: There are mainly two computation techniques involved here: are Encryption process, the differential privacy mechanism, and multiparty security computation in a distributed environment. It integrates the security metrics like anonymity, diversity, differential privacy, and closeness.

Adaptation and Monitoring Layer: Here, there will be regular monitoring of risks and malware vulnerabilities that takes place. The risk scoring will be done adaptively for privacy policy adjustment. The user feedback will be collected regularly for updating regulations and ethical documents.

Compliance and Regulation Layer: The content of ethical principles for security, like transparency, explainability, and confidentiality, will be included here. The rules based on GDPR, HIPAA and the latest AI policies are included. In case of sensitive mechanisms, the concept of Human-in-the-loop will be considered.

3.7. A SURVEY

The examined research efforts that align with the above-mentioned proposed taxonomy are contrasted, and their advantages and disadvantages are elucidated. On the other hand, the published literature reveals a more systematic approach to research from 2016 to 2020, indicating the maturity of the research community concerning IoT-based smart campus monitoring systems. These studies encompass almost a decade of study on IoT-enabled smart campus security systems. We examine 42 publications and 2 patents that span every aspect of the suggested classification. Figure 6 shows the distribution of research outputs by year of publication. In particular, there is a very low yearly research yield from 2008 to 2012. On the other hand, the published literature reveals a more systematic approach to research from 2016 to 2020, indicating the maturity of the research community concerning IoT-based smart campus monitoring systems. Classify and evaluate the reviewed systems in comparison based on the survey results.

Figure 6. Surveyed research efforts per year of publication

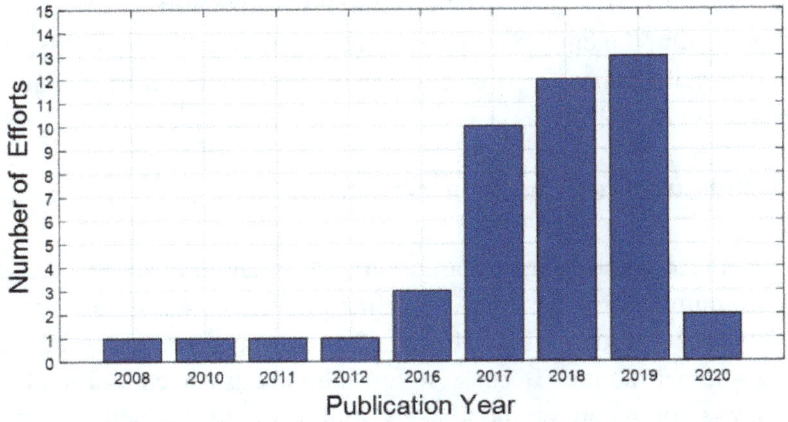

The systems indicate various IoT technologies used, areas of application, and limitations of each proposed system, offering valuable comparisons for future development. It uses RFID, Global Positioning System (GPS), Ethernet, Wi-Fi, Bluetooth, and ZigBee technology to offer passive monitoring services. Additionally, smartphones and cameras are used to accomplish active monitoring. By using supervised inference techniques to enable context awareness, an ad hoc surveillance system ensures Quality of Service (QoS). The best locations on campus to install RFID readers to provide surveillance services are determined by the system using Tabu search. While the basic technology consists of an IoT platform, WSN, and sensor infrastructure, the study primarily focuses on smart classroom and public area monitoring. RFID and GPS sensors are employed for passive monitoring, and students' smartphones are used for active monitoring. Cameras are employed to take pictures of the surveillance area, while smartphones' GPS sensors are used for passive monitoring.

The system is tested in a lab setting using Arduino sensor technologies, using real data. The results demonstrated that the deployment of Smart Campus monitoring systems required only a minimal amount of infrastructure. Active surveillance monitoring is made possible by the extensive usage of cellphones and cameras as a component of an ad hoc integrated system. To deliver surveillance services, the system integrates user context from social media, movement, and crowdsourcing. For effective campus security, active monitoring tools like cameras and microphones are employed. The suggested surveillance system uses cloud technologies to recognize faces and gestures and has an ad hoc design. A recurring element in all systems is that IoT platforms have a great deal of potential to change Smart Campus settings by implementing safety and intelligent monitoring capabilities. The need for more reliable, scalable, and integrated solutions is highlighted by persistent drawbacks such as scalability, RFID administration complexity, dependence on artificial data, and incomplete implementations. To guarantee system interoperability, improved infrastructure management, and practical validation, more effort is required (Anagnostopoulos et al., 2021).

3.7.1. Pollution Detection From Vehicles

The system for identifying car pollution in Hangzhou. Furthermore, across all districts, the numbers for the 8:00–9:00 time period are nearly identical to those for the 17:00–18:00 time period. The data from our trial was gathered during the sweltering summer months. Because so few individuals use cabs around this time, the accuracy is comparatively poor. We also discovered distinctions between the city's several districts, Gongshu, Shangcheng, Xiacheng, Xihu, and Binjiang (Zhang, Chen, Chen, & Chen, 2016). Due to their central business district CBD location, the Shangcheng and Xiacheng districts have more sensor taxis or records. They produce less sensor data and fewer taxis, though, because their populations are smaller. The best performance occurs between 8:00 and 9:00 and 17:00 and 18:00, as indicated by the Table 2.

Table 2. Overall Effectiveness of Vehicle Pollution Detection

Districts	**8:00 -9:00**	**11:00-12:00**	**17:00-18:00**
Gongshu	3.023	4.124	3.987
Xihu	3.756	4.876	3.612
Xiacheng	2.565	3.654	2.782
Shangcheng	2.655	3.795	2.741
Binjiang	3.678	4.499	3.965

3.7.2. Analysis of Traffic

As shown in Table 3, the proposed method first examines the traffic dataset from Aarhus, which is the second-largest city in Denmark by population. The average vehicle speed is found to be substantially lower between any two road segments with a granularity of 500 m when traffic intensity is higher, which indicates that there are more cars between two points on the road. The empty circle line on the graph shows how the average speed significantly decreases during the 25–30-hour car-heavy hours of the day. The primary causes of these events are weather conditions like rain, fog, etc., or roadways that are undergoing construction or accidents. A framework for smart driver assistance was generated and discussed (Baskar et al., 2022).

Table 3. Cars typically go between two places, depending on the volume of traffic

Time	Count of Vehicles (0-10)	Count of Vehicles (11-20)	Count of Vehicles (25-30)
T1	45	50	22
T2	53	48	20
T3	58	38	30
T4	56	38	29
T5	56	38	28
T6	51	38	29
T7	52	38	28
T8	50	38	30
T9	50	38	20
T11	45	38	22
T12	53	38	30
T14	67	30	23

However, the average speed and the amount of traffic or intensity of vehicles on the road also affect how long it takes to get there. Therefore, it is easy to see that as the number of automobiles on the road increases, so does the time it takes to reach the terminus. To calculate the express distance between the source and its designated destination, we also take into consideration the traffic data as of right now. Therefore, at different times throughout the day, the suggested traffic management system can help alert the appropriate authorities when the volume of traffic on a given road grows. Furthermore, to identify roadblocks, the suggested system may evaluate traffic data in real time. Smart city transportation is made possible by various weight calculation processes using existing graph algorithms and intelligent decisions resulting from network development (Rathore et al., 2021).

3.7.3. Smart Environment

Monitoring water quality and supply, managing weather and climatic events, and collecting, tracking, and analyzing environmental data are all included in the smart environment area. In this regard, monitoring air quality is crucial for identifying the levels of air pollutants (such as NO, O3, CO2, N2O, PM10, PM2.5, etc.) that are a serious health risk to people because of emissions from heating, traffic, and industry. Smart garbage bins equipped with sensors that can analyze available capacity in real time are used to manage waste production control programs.

The pH, conductivity, turbidity, total dissolved solids, and other parameters are typically detected by sensors used to assess the quantity and quality of water in smart water systems. To assess the rate of water consumption, ultrasonic and electromagnetic sensors are used to monitor the pressure. A new generation of intelligent water monitoring systems has been made possible by the usage of WSNs for water quantity and quality monitoring systems. Near real-time interaction and more sophisticated context awareness are offered by these technologies.

Ambient and chemical sensors, which monitor physical values that indicate environmental conditions and parameters, such as temperature, humidity, pressure, and other contaminants, are commonly the foundation upon which applications and services for smart environments are constructed. Land utilization and Greenhouse Gas Emissions (GHG) are monitored using smart sensing and visualization technologies (such as Light Detection and Ranging (LiDAR) and satellites). Geographic Information Systems (GIS) data and location-based services are also used. Modern IoT technologies are used by Singapore's Integrated Waste Management Facility (IWMF), which manages solid waste, to increase operational effectiveness and reduce greenhouse gas emissions. Using satellite imagery and artificial intelligence algorithms, Green City Watch is a geospatial artificial intelligence application based in Amsterdam that tracks urban green infrastructures in almost real time.

Solar-powered smart trash cans that can package rubbish and automatically notify users when they are completely charged have been placed in Stockholm. Smart water management systems are used throughout the municipal water cycle in the South Korean smart city of Busan. In the context of the European TRAFAIR project, six European cities (Florence, Pisa, Livorno and Modena in Italy and Santiago de Compostela and Zaragoza in Spain) have adopted the Snap4City platform for monitoring urban air quality (using sensors that collect data in the six cities) and providing urban air quality predictions using simulation models (Bellini, Nesi, & Pantaleo, 2022).

4. A PRIVACY-PRESERVING IOT NETWORK MODEL

Maintaining the privacy of users' personal information has always been a crucial concern. The IoT, which supports millions of applications, has made this problem much more difficult. The right of individuals to choose how, where, when, and by whom their data may be used is known as privacy. The goal to safeguard privacy is to stop unauthorized disclosure of personal information, which often consists of a person's identity and related data about their location, health, position in society, financial standing, contact information, etc. Numerous researchers have an interest in protecting users' identities as well as their data from service providers (SPs).

4.1. System Architecture

In IoT applications that involve user personal data, maintaining privacy has become a crucial issue. The privacy protection techniques now in use are unreliable for a variety of reasons. The Blind Third Party (BTP) and Blind Peer (BLP) approaches are combined to create the Blind Approach (BLA). Additionally, an adaptable scenario between BTP and BLP is shown, known as Integrated Blind Parties (IBPs). All of the current issues with the seven techniques outlined above can be resolved using BLA.

1. A thorough explanation of how BLA protects privacy in IoT applications.
2. A discussion of the applicability and efficacy of BTP, BLS, and IBPs, as well as how (a) BTP can overcome the shortcomings of the Trusted Third-Party (TTP) approach, (b) BLP can address the issue of peer trust in the Cooperation approach, and
   (c) IBPs can foster dynamism between BTP, BLS.
3. A thorough examination of assaults to show how the Blind Approach protects privacy without compromising the accuracy of data or results.
4. Use of *BLA* to protect user privacy in underwater sensor networks, e-health, transportation, and smart home systems without requiring confidence from a third party.

These methods create a multi-layered architecture for preserving user identity and query confidentiality in IoT applications like smart homes, e-health, and transportation. A hybrid model that dynamically selects between BTP and BLP based on availability and efficiency, as shown in Figure 7.

Figure 7. System Architecture of BLA

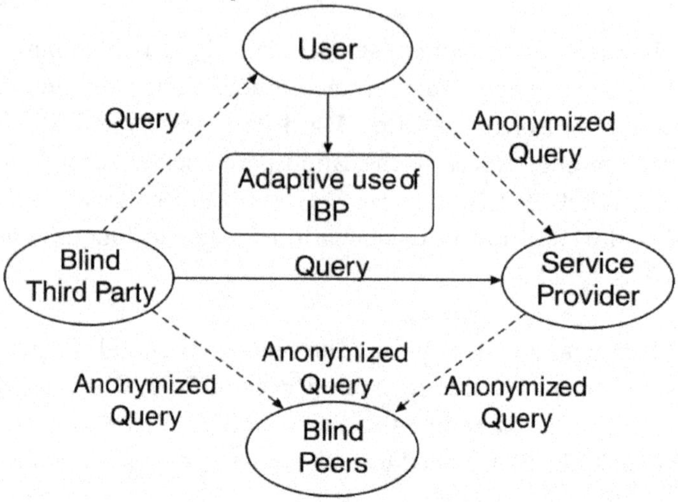

4.2. Privacy-by-Design Principles

1. The model follows Privacy-by-Design (PbD) by embedding privacy at every architectural layer.
2. Session-based encryption is used: every session generates a unique key pair ⟨PKi, SKi⟩.
3. Calculate E(Qu) = Enc (PKi, Qu), where Enc is the encryption function, and Qu is the query.
4. The system avoids relying on cloud service providers for trust.
5. Users maintain control over query routing (via Blind Peers or Blind Third Party).
6. It ensures data minimization and no persistent identity exposure to the Service Provider (SP).

4.3 Network Layer Configuration

The concept uses an IBP technique to feather optimizer efficiency and privacy. Then it depends on peer availability, trust evaluation, and network responsiveness are dynamically determined between BLP and BTP. To run the command right next to the data source, the layout similarly makes use of edge and fog computing. This approach to processing eliminates needless exposure to Central services, avoids bottlenecks, and decreases the time.

To further reinforce privacy and efficiency, the model uses an IBP mechanism. This dynamically selects between BLP and the BTP depending on network responsiveness, trust evaluations, and peer availability. To execute a query close to the data source, the design allows makes of edge and fog computing. This local processing minimizes the needless exploration of Central services, then avoids bottlenecks, and reduces time. The system employs randomized peer routing based on an equation (1),

P_Select = Hash (time ⊕, user_id) mod N (1)

where N is the number of active peers and ⊕ is the XOR operator, to anonymize the source of each query. By accomplishing this, users to identified and then protected during the transmission of data.

Additionally, multiple routes and route unpredictability or maintenance to prevent burglars from analyzing the traffic flow patterns, in addition to each communication session, are individually secured using a session key represented in (2),

K_session = Generate Key (timestamp, random_nonce)
(2)

Replay attacks and session hijacking are avoided by immediately deleting these session-specific keys after usage. A highly secure, anonymous, and robust network layer is created by combining these tiered security measures, making it appropriate for intelligent IoT deployments.

4.4 Integration of Privacy Techniques

The BLA combines distributed computing, cryptography, and mathematical privacy metrics with other sophisticated privacy-preserving strategies to provide strong privacy in IoT environments. To ensure strong privacy in IoT environments, the BLA integrates mathematical privacy metrics, encryption, and collaborative computing with other specialized privacy-preserving techniques. In addition to anonymized query routing and hybrid encryption, the methodology makes use of the following strategies,

Hybridization of Encryption Scheme

- Integrates symmetric encryption (for effective bulk data transfer) and asymmetric encryption (for safe key exchange).
- Example:
    - o Session Key Generation: K_session = Enc(PK_receiver, random_nonce)

- o EncryptedQuery: E(Qu) = AES_Encrypt(K_session, Qu)

Dynamic Peer Swapping Algorithm

It might not be too difficult to identify the query's owner if the attacker gets more information, such as the user's age or occupation. Because BTP and BLP route requests, there would be no communication between the user and the SP; as a result, the user would not be vulnerable to SP assaults. Depending on certain skills, the BTP, BLP, and IBP procedures also significantly increase the level of protection and are intended to stop an attacker from breaking in.

- To prevent linkability of queries:
- Each user's query is randomly routed through a new peer in each session.
- Peer selection is determined by: P_Select = hash (time $\oplus$ node_id) mod N
- Ensures no fixed communication path.

Entropy and k-Anonymity

The percentage of accurate information relative to the attacker's entire victim information is known as entropy. Other measurements depend on this general and reliable metric. The degree of privacy increases with entropy (E).

- Entropy Formula: $H = -\sum pi * \log_2(pi)$
- Where pi is the probability of user i's query being traced.
- High H implies stronger anonymity.
- k-Anonymity: Each user's identity is hidden among at least k users (commonly $k \geq 3$).

As more user-submitted questions are made, privacy would improve, bringing Entropy (E) to one and the K-Anonymity metric to zero. This is because the user ID would be hidden simultaneously, and every query from the same user with the SP would have the same likelihood. When U = 2, the EE of SP and U would both be at their highest at the same time. Other attackers would be unable to participate due to the encryption in both directions.

When compared to all of the earlier methods—namely, Dummy, Obfuscation, PIR, and Cache in the literature review—BTP and BLP are also not need to be trusted for the Trust Factor, which results in the highest amount of privacy, even though some of them have ways to avoid trust in other parties (Yamin, Alsaawy, B. Alkhodre, & Abi Sen, 2019).

5. A STUDY ON EVALUATION AND RESULTS

To evaluate the performance of the proposed WSN implementations, different experiments have been conducted with different types of obstacles and environments. Specifically, transmission in a line-of-sight region with minor obstructions, a non-line-of-sight region with visible obstructions, and a non-line-of-sight region with wall-blocked obstructions have all been investigated. The Received Signal Strength Indicator (RSSI) and Packet Received Percentage (PRP), which are reliable indicators of the received wireless signal strength and the transmission quality, were used to assess the data transmission performance in each experiment. These metrics are commonly used to assess the quality of data transmission and signal dependability in wireless networks. At least 100 packets were sent in each scenario, and the procedure was carried out five times to guarantee consistency in the results.

There are small breaks in the line of sight connecting the sensor and source nodes on the Age of Information (AoI), and the sensors are scattered. The nodes were set up so that the distance between sink and standard nodes may vary between 40 and 160 meters to do multiple range tests. Additionally, only one node has been enabled for a specific distance to prevent other elements that could impair performance, like interference and network collisions. Experiments were conducted in a line-of-sight (LOS) environment with few obstacles in the first scenario. This baseline scenario tested communication over distances ranging from 40 to 160 meters with one sensor node active at a time to avoid cross-interference.

Results showed that the second WSN implementation, equipped with high-power XBee-PRO modules and better antennas, consistently outperformed the first. To provide comparable conditions and a fair comparison, it is crucial to remember that both implementations have been evaluated independently, but with the precise node placements. The development of a novel communication protocol has made UAV-sensor contact simpler and more reliable. This included acknowledgment-based transmission of information, handshaking procedures, and a plan for retransmission in the unlikely circumstance that a packet failed. At the sink node, SD cards were used to temporarily store data in an attempt against loss during UAV the purpose of transmission. The usefulness of the second WSN design for reliable, real-time applications in smart cities was established by the fact that it consistently performed more than the first throughout all testing circumstances (Khalifeh et al., 2021).

5.1. Security and Privacy Analysis

The literature that was previously offered in the parts that examined different facets of data breaches is compiled and examined in this section. Identity theft, fraud, unintentional exposure by clients and staff, employee carelessness, a decline in trust and reputation, a shortage of IT personnel, inadequate security protocols, and a low budget for the IT industry are the causes of this damage. The unintended release of critical data, particularly Personally Identifiable Information (PII), can result in damage to organizational reputation, financial losses, and a decline in public confidence. Public exposure of sensitive information such as PII can seriously affect a company's image, cause economic harm, and diminish the trust of the general public. The activity might be compared to the creation of an international organization tasked with regulating and guaranteeing that all sectors adhere to the established legal norms. This regulatory group ought to include representatives from every industry.

These include globally recognized standards like Payment Card Industry Data Security Standard (PCI-DSS) for handling payment systems, Federal Information Security Modernization Act (FISMA) for governmental data security, HIPAA for protecting medical records, and ISO 27001 for managing information security. These frameworks offer practical methods to protect sensitive data and ensure proper system operation. These include globally recognized standards like PCI-DSS for handling payment systems, FISMA for governmental data security, HIPAA for protecting medical records, and ISO 27001 for managing information security. These frameworks offer practical methods to protect sensitive data and ensure proper system operation (Aslam et al., 2022).

5.2 A Study With Existing Models

According to the results of the investigation, 22 modeling languages (69%) offer automatic model evaluation for compatibility, accuracy, consistency, and completeness. Completeness is used to ensure that all system needs are taken into account. It describes the level of specificity in the aspects of design choices, such as system behavior and interaction. Any inconsistencies between the components, interfaces, and connections listed in the model are referred to as inconsistencies. Correctness is considered to determine whether the design choices made fit the intended system requirements (such as race conditions, deadlocks, or any user-defined attributes). Verifying that software requirements adhere to any architectural style or design guidelines is the last aspect of compatibility (Arslan, Ozkaya, & Kardas, 2023). It visually represents how the proposed approach improves over traditional models by integrating, as shown in Figure 8.

Figure 8. Data Breach Risk Assessment Framework in Continuous Format

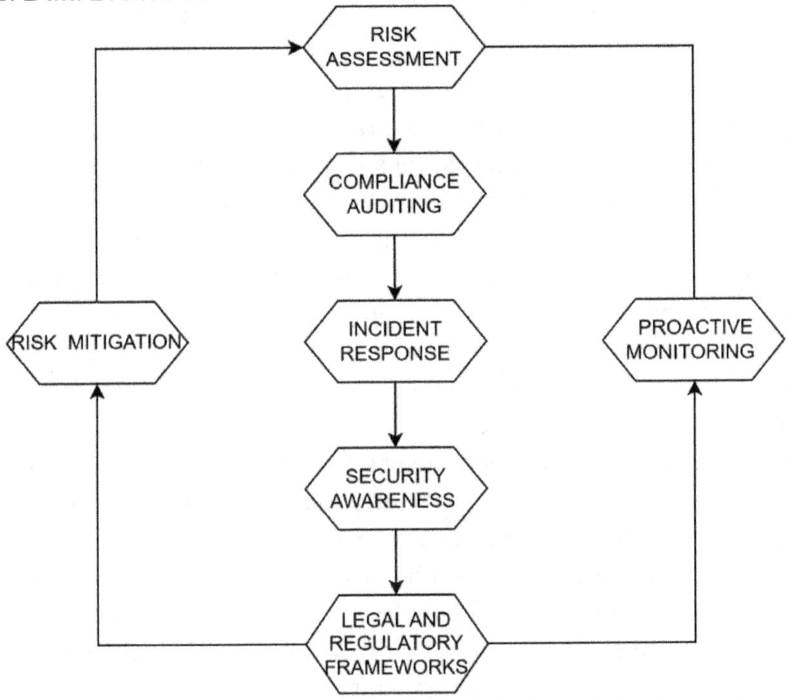

To raise a network's security level, the framework's fundamental steps—risk assessment, risk reduction, and risk validation and monitoring—must be precisely followed. Information on vulnerabilities, risk-reducing solutions, and the impact of applying them to vulnerabilities are all included in the data that Blockchain-Defined Network (BDN) models provide, which is crucial for managing security risks. Their tests show how network security is significantly improved by the accurate risk assessment and appropriate risk reduction provided by their approach. These qualitative frameworks recognize the importance of other frameworks and have a similar cybersecurity risk management process.

For instance, ISO 27001 standards are designed to ensure information security needs are incorporated into a large portion of the National Institute of Standards and Technology (NIST) Cybersecurity Framework (Lee, 2020). Because they assess network performance and describe traffic, traffic generators are significant and effective tools. Numerous traffic generators have been created in various formats, including commercial goods, open-source software, and research initiatives. It is also helpful for assessing how well gadgets work. IoT traffic is considered because the majority of earlier traffic generators concentrated on Internet traffic. They therefore assessed the Mirai malware's use case. For the IoT, an intrusion detection system has also been suggested. They found anomalies in various network conditions and recognized traffic attributes. They selected features using the bit pattern matching technique. However, because this study focused on consumer IoT devices, its relevance to resource-constrained IoT devices is restricted. To develop a cyber risk management plan that is future-oriented, organizations must evaluate their present IoT cyber architecture from a managerial and technological perspective.

Many studies have focused on the technical aspects of risk management to protect IT-related resources. The main focus is on the factors that affect user behavior, intention, attitude, and satisfaction concerning cybersecurity technology use and compliance with privacy and security regulations. These programs are crucial for enhancing IoT cybersecurity performance because they are known to positively affect the attitudes and behaviors of both internal users and staff as well as external users and consumers of IoT services.

A link budget analysis that is dependent on a certain channel model must be used to properly represent any wireless communication link between two IoT devices, one of which is a transmitter and the other a receiver. The designer may use the channel models to approximate the outage likelihood under a particular network topology or Access Node AN density, the required infrastructure dimensions (e.g., number and placement of ANs), the cell radius or coverage areas for a particular technology, etc. Furthermore, real-time alerts, email warnings for voltage loss and overload trips, and pre-alarm messages in the event of an overload would all be provided by the IoT sensors (Wang, Capitaneanu, Marinca, & Lohan, 2019).

6. CONCLUSION

The privacy of the IoT device in this smart city was also one of the trivial fields that a researcher could look at. There is a smart sensor or gadget in almost every IoT-based platform, such as smart cars, smart cities, and smart home products. There is a smart sensor or gadget in almost every IoT-based platform, including those used in smart cities, automobiles, and home gadgets. These devices' comprehensive use of the Internet ensures that privacy and security are maintained. It is more difficult to secure heterogeneous IoT-based smart city platforms. In that way, data is kept safe and sound by employing the three core data security techniques (i.e., availability, confidentiality, and integrity). To be able to quickly respond to cyberattacks, organizations must closely watch technical developments. As 5G and the 5 G-enabled IoT developments continue to advance, there will be an increase in cyberattacks in 5 G-enabled IoT services such as self-driving cars, AR/VR, smart medical monitoring, etc. It can hence only be utilized by powerful IoT devices that can afford that overhead.

REFERENCES

Ahmed, E., Yaqoob, I., Hashem, I. A. T., Khan, I., Ahmed, A. I. A., Imran, M., & Vasilakos, A. V. (2017). The role of big data analytics in Internet of Things. *Computer Networks*, *129*, 459–471.

Alshmrany, S. (2025). Securing smart cities: Privacy-preserving IoT with optimized gated lounge attention dropout mechanism. *Neural Computing & Applications*, 1–26.

Anagnostopoulos, T., Kostakos, P., Zaslavsky, A., Kantzavelou, I., Tsotsolas, N., Salmon, I., & Harle, R. (2021). Challenges and solutions of surveillance systems in IoT-enabled smart campus: A survey. *IEEE Access : Practical Innovations, Open Solutions*, *9*, 131926–131954.

Andrade, R., Ortiz-Garcés, I., Tintin, X., & Llumiquinga, G. (2022). Factors of risk analysis for IoT systems. *Risks*, *10*(8), 162.

Arslan, S., Ozkaya, M., & Kardas, G. (2023). Modeling languages for internet of things (IoT) applications: A comparative analysis study. *Mathematics*, *11*(5), 1263.

Aslam, M., Khan Abbasi, M. A., Khalid, T., Shan, R. U., Ullah, S., Ahmad, T., & Ahmad, R. (2022). Getting smarter about smart cities: Improving data security and privacy through compliance. *Sensors (Basel)*, *22*(23), 9338. PMID: 36502039

Atzori, L., Iera, A., & Morabito, G. (2010). The internet of things: A survey. *Computer Networks*, *54*(15), 2787–2805.

Baskar, K., Muthuraj, S., Sangeetha, S., Vengatesan, K., Aishwarya, D., & Yuvaraj, P. (2022). *Framework for implementation of smart driver assistance system using augmented reality*. Paper presented at the International Conference on Big data and Cloud Computing.

Belli, L., Cilfone, A., Davoli, L., Ferrari, G., Adorni, P., Di Nocera, F., & Bertolotti, E. (2020). IoT-enabled smart sustainable cities: Challenges and approaches. *Smart Cities*, *3*(3), 1039–1071.

Bellini, P., Nesi, P., & Pantaleo, G. (2022). IoT-enabled smart cities: A review of concepts, frameworks and key technologies. *Applied Sciences (Basel, Switzerland)*, *12*(3), 1607.

Bhardwaj, A., Kaushik, K., Bharany, S., Rehman, A. U., Hu, Y.-C., Eldin, E. T., & Ghamry, N. A. (2022). IIoT: Traffic data flow analysis and modeling experiment for smart IoT devices. *Sustainability*, *14*(21), 14645.

Cvitić, I., & Vujić, M. (2015). CLASSIFICATION OF SECURITY RISKS IN THE IOT ENVIRONMENT. *Annals of DAAAM & Proceedings*, *26*(1).

Gheisari, M., Najafabadi, H. E., Alzubi, J. A., Gao, J., Wang, G., Abbasi, A. A., & Castiglione, A. (2021). OBPP: An ontology-based framework for privacy-preserving in IoT-based smart city. *Future Generation Computer Systems*, *123*, 1–13.

Gheisari, M., Shojaeian, E., Javadpour, A., Jalili, A., Esmaeili-Najafabadi, H., Bigham, B. S., & Rezaei, M. (2023). An agile privacy-preservation solution for IoT-based smart city using different distributions. *IEEE Open Journal of Vehicular Technology*, *4*, 356–362.

Kanellopoulos, D., Sharma, V. K., Panagiotakopoulos, T., & Kameas, A. (2023). Networking architectures and protocols for IoT applications in smart cities: Recent developments and perspectives. *Electronics (Basel)*, *12*(11), 2490.

Keerthana, N., Sakthivel, D., Balasubramaniyan, D., Gunasekaran, K., & Marimuthu, M. (2020). Enhanced Privacy Based Authenticity for Smart e-Health Cares using Light Weight ECC. *GEDRAG & ORGANISATIE Учредители: UITGEVERIJ LEMMA BV*, *33*(2), 644–653.

Khalifeh, A., Darabkh, K. A., Khasawneh, A. M., Alqaisieh, I., Salameh, M., AlAbdala, A., & Al-Wardat, R. (2021). Wireless sensor networks for smart cities: Network design, implementation and performance evaluation. *Electronics (Basel)*, *10*(2), 218.

Lee, I. (2020). Internet of Things (IoT) cybersecurity: Literature review and IoT cyber risk management. *Future Internet*, *12*(9), 157.

Obaidat, M. A., Obeidat, S., Holst, J., Al Hayajneh, A., & Brown, J. (2020). A comprehensive and systematic survey on the internet of things: Security and privacy challenges, security frameworks, enabling technologies, threats, vulnerabilities and countermeasures. *Computers*, *9*(2), 44.

Ragothaman, K., Wang, Y., Rimal, B., & Lawrence, M. (2023). Access control for IoT: A survey of existing research, dynamic policies and future directions. *Sensors (Basel)*, *23*(4), 1805. PMID: 36850403

Rathore, M. M., Attique Shah, S., Awad, A., Shukla, D., Vimal, S., & Paul, A. (2021). A cyber-physical system and graph-based approach for transportation management in smart cities. *Sustainability*, *13*(14), 7606.

Tekinerdogan, B., Köksal, Ö., & Çelik, T. (2023). System architecture design of IoT-based smart cities. *Applied Sciences (Basel, Switzerland)*, *13*(7), 4173.

Wang, W., Capitaneanu, S. L., Marinca, D., & Lohan, E.-S. (2019). Comparative analysis of channel models for industrial IoT wireless communication. *IEEE Access : Practical Innovations, Open Solutions*, *7*, 91627–91640.

Yamin, M., Alsaawy, Y., & Alkhodre, B., A., & Abi Sen, A. A. (2019). An innovative method for preserving privacy in Internet of Things. *Sensors (Basel)*, *19*(15), 3355. PMID: 31370150

Yousefpoor, M. S., Yousefpoor, E., Barati, H., Barati, A., Movaghar, A., & Hosseinzadeh, M. (2021). Secure data aggregation methods and countermeasures against various attacks in wireless sensor networks: A comprehensive review. *Journal of Network and Computer Applications*, *190*, 103118.

Zanella, A., Bui, N., Castellani, A., Vangelista, L., & Zorzi, M. (2014). Internet of things for smart cities. *IEEE Internet of Things Journal*, *1*(1), 22–32.

Zhang, N., Chen, H., Chen, X., & Chen, J. (2016). Semantic framework of internet of things for smart cities: Case studies. *Sensors (Basel)*, *16*(9), 1501. PMID: 27649185

Chapter 9
Security-as-a-Service: Enhancing Cloud Security Through Managed Security Solutions

Zainab Senan Attar Bashi
https://orcid.org/0000-0002-1452-8098
International Islamic University Malaysia, Malaysia

Azana Hafizah Mohd Aman
https://orcid.org/0000-0001-7337-6736
Universiti Kebangsaan Malaysia, Malaysia

Salem Sati
https://orcid.org/0000-0002-6062-497X
Misurata University, Libya

Nur-Adib Maspo
https://orcid.org/0000-0003-0031-1354
International Islamic University Malaysia, Malaysia

Aisha Hassan Abdalla Hashim
https://orcid.org/0000-0001-6331-1373
International Islamic University Malaysia, Malaysia

ABSTRACT

Cloud computing plays an important role in modern businesses by enabling flexible, efficient storage, analysis, and access to data and applications. However, this reliance also introduces new security challenges. Ensuring cloud security and resilience is now critical to prevent unauthorized access, data breaches, and service disruptions. This chapter examines the key principles, technologies, and policies that uphold the confidentiality, integrity, and availability of cloud systems.

DOI: 10.4018/979-8-3373-4455-3.ch009

It also highlights Security-as-a-Service (SECaaS) as a necessary part of the cloud ecosystem, offering specialized, scalable solutions to improve overall security. By delivering managed security services via the cloud, SECaaS allows organizations to outsource key functions such as threat intelligence, endpoint protection, access control, and compliance monitoring. It can enhance protection without heavy in-house investment

1. INTRODUCTION

In the era of digital transformation, cloud computing has become the backbone of modern business operations, offering unparalleled scalability, operational flexibility, and innovative capabilities (Kaluvuri et al., 2015). The migration to cloud environments allows enterprises to operate at a global scale, collaborate seamlessly, and use data-driven insights to remain competitive. However, this transition introduces a spectrum of security challenges that cannot be ignored, such as data breaches, unauthorized access, and compliance risks (Mostafa et al., 2023). These challenges arise due to the dynamic and interconnected nature of cloud networks, which demand robust and adaptive security mechanisms. Security-as-a-Service (SECaaS) has emerged as a vital solution, addressing these challenges by providing managed security services tailored to the unique demands of cloud-based infrastructures (Shen et al., 2013).

SECaaS revolutionizes the way organizations handle security by shifting the burden from internal IT teams to specialized service providers. This approach allows businesses to concentrate on their core operations while using advanced security tools and expertise from external providers. SECaaS embodies the principles of resilience, scalability, and real-time responsiveness, delivering comprehensive protection against an evolving threat landscape.

One of the core strengths of SECaaS lies in its ability to implement proactive security measures that safeguard cloud infrastructures (Talib et al., 2012). These measures include vulnerability scanning, penetration testing, and continuous monitoring (Casola et al., 2018), which are necessary for identifying and mitigating potential security weaknesses. Wang & Shen (2013) highlight the effectiveness of services like CloudProxy, which operate within network architectures to detect vulnerabilities in real time. Such tools act as intermediaries between clients and cloud services, scanning traffic flows and application layers for anomalies that may signal potential breaches.

Figure 1. Overall Structure of CloudProxy (Wang & Shen, 2013)

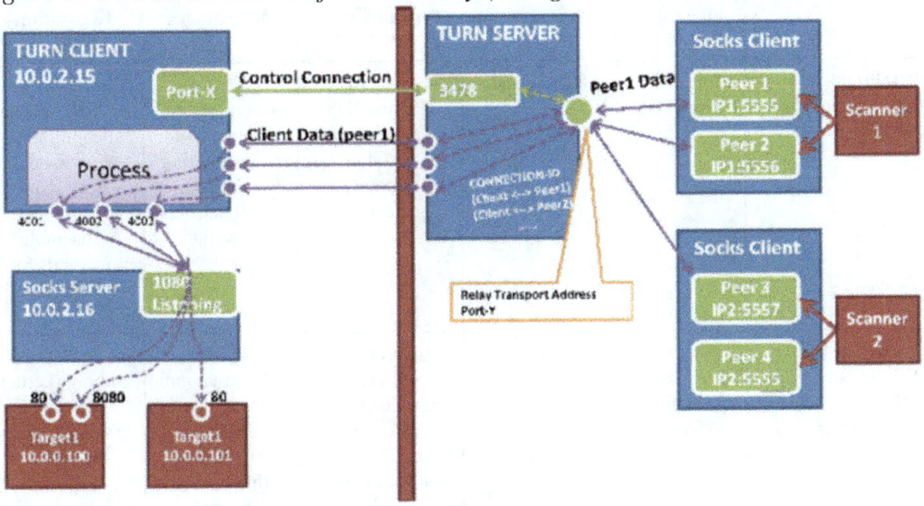

By incorporating tools like intrusion detection systems (IDS) and intrusion prevention systems (IPS), SECaaS providers enhance network-level security (Rullo et al., 2024). These systems analyze traffic patterns using predefined rules or machine learning algorithms to identify malicious activities, such as distributed denial-of-service (DDoS) attacks or data exfiltration attempts. Table 1 summarizes some of the researches about ML algorithms used in IPS and IDS. Furthermore, the integration of secure communication protocols, such as Transport Layer Security (TLS), ensures that data traversing cloud networks is encrypted, maintaining confidentiality and integrity.

Table 1. Machine Learning for IDS and IPS

References	Algorithm	Type	Typical Use in IPS/IDS	Advantages	Limitations
(R. Tahri et al., 2024; Yang et al., 2019)	Decision Tree (DT)	Supervised	- Used for both IPS and IDS - Signature-based or anomaly detection	- Easy to interpret and implement - Fast training - Handles small datasets well	- Prone to overfitting when dealing with complex data - May require pruning or ensemble methods for improved accuracy
(Jayshree & Leena, 2013; Su et al., 2021)	Support Vector Machine (SVM)	Supervised	- Commonly used in IDS - Can be extended for IPS with relevant kernel functions	- High classification accuracy - Effective in high-dimensional spaces - Good for smaller datasets	- Parameter tuning (kernel selection, C, gamma) can be complex - Slower training for large datasets
(Awotunde et al., 2023; Farnaaz & Jabbar, 2016)	Random Forest (RF)	Supervised	- Used in both IDS (signature & anomaly) and IPS - Effective for high-dimensional network traffic data	- More robust to overfitting compared to single DT - High accuracy - Can handle missing values	- Less interpretable than a single decision tree - Training can be slower than simple DT methods
(Awotunde et al., 2023; Mukherjee & Sharma, 2012)	Naive Bayes (NB)	Supervised	- Commonly used for IDS classification - Works well for textual or log-based detection	- Fast training - Simple to implement - Effective with small datasets	- Assumes feature independence - Lower accuracy if strong dependencies exist among features

continued on following page

Table 1. Continued

References	Algorithm	Type	Typical Use in IPS/IDS	Advantages	Limitations
(Lakshminarayana & Basarkod, 2023; Nikhitha & Jabbar, 2019)	K-Nearest Neighbor (KNN)	Supervised (Instance-Based)	- Often used in IDS for anomaly detection - Helps detect rare intrusions	- Conceptually simple - Can achieve good accuracy with small-to-medium datasets - Non-parametric	- High computational cost during inference - Sensitive to noise and irrelevant features
(Aljuaid & Alshamrani, 2024; Hnamte & Hussain, 2023; Khan et al., 2022)	Deep Learning (DL) (e.g., CNN, RNN)	Supervised or Unsupervised (depending on architecture)	- Used in both IDS and IPS - Excels in anomaly detection and feature extraction in high-volume network traffic	- Automated feature extraction - Highly accurate for complex data patterns - Can handle large-scale inputs	- Requires large labeled datasets - High computational and memory requirements - Model interpretability can be challenging

While the use of ML algorithms in intrusion detection and prevention systems within SECaaS environments has been widely studied, much of the existing literature highlights ongoing trade-offs that remain unresolved (Shirley C P et al., 2025). For example, algorithms such as Support Vector Machines (SVM) and Random Forests often achieve high detection accuracy but impose significant computational overhead, making them less suitable for real-time applications in resource-constrained cloud environments. By contrast, lightweight models such as k-Nearest Neighbors (kNN) or Naïve Bayes reduce complexity but often sacrifice accuracy, especially when dealing with zero-day attacks or highly imbalanced datasets. Another key trade-off lies in the choice between supervised and unsupervised learning approaches. While supervised models generally achieve higher precision given labelled datasets, they struggle with scalability and adaptability in dynamic cloud infrastructures where labelled attack data may not be readily available. Unsupervised approaches, such as clustering or anomaly detection methods, offer adaptability to unknown attack vectors but typically generate higher false-positive rates, which can overwhelm security operations teams. Similarly, deep learning methods such as Convolutional Neural Networks (CNNs) and Deep Residual Networks (DRNs) show strong performance in complex pattern recognition, yet they demand significant training data and high computational resources, raising questions about their practicality in real-time SECaaS deployments.

Beyond these algorithmic trade-offs, several open challenges persist in applying ML-driven IDS/IPS to SECaaS. Scalability in multi-cloud environments remains a pressing issue (Stephenson Achankeng, 2025), as distributed workloads require models that can operate consistently across heterogeneous platforms while maintaining low latency. Moreover, the rise of adversarial ML threats poses risks to IDS/IPS reliability, as attackers can manipulate input data to evade detection or trigger false alarms. This vulnerability underscores the need for more robust and explainable AI approaches in security. Additionally, achieving real-time deployment is a challenge, as high-performing ML models often require extensive preprocessing and inference time, creating delays that undermine the immediate response capability expected from SECaaS solutions. These challenges suggest that while ML offers powerful tools for IDS/IPS, its current application in SECaaS is not without limitations. Future research must therefore focus on developing lightweight, adaptive, and adversarial-resistant algorithms that balance accuracy with operational feasibility in distributed, high-demand cloud environments.

On the other hand, the rise of multi-agent systems (MAS) has transformed how security is managed in collaborative cloud environments (Fedele et al., 2025). These systems use autonomous agents distributed across the network to perform security tasks such as monitoring, access control, and anomaly detection. (Talib et al., 2012) demonstrate that MAS can seamlessly manage security across distributed storage systems, ensuring the confidentiality, integrity, and availability of data. MAS provides decentralized and adaptive security measures that are essential for managing complex and dynamic cloud infrastructures.

MAS agents communicate and collaborate using standardized protocols, enabling a complete view of the network's security posture as in Figure 2. For example, agents deployed at various nodes of a cloud network can detect local threats and share intelligence with other agents to coordinate responses. This decentralized approach minimizes the risk of single points of failure, a critical consideration in distributed systems. Engineers must design these agents to be lightweight, efficient, and capable of operating in resource-constrained environments, such as edge devices and mobile platforms.

Figure 2. Protocols and Standards related to MAS

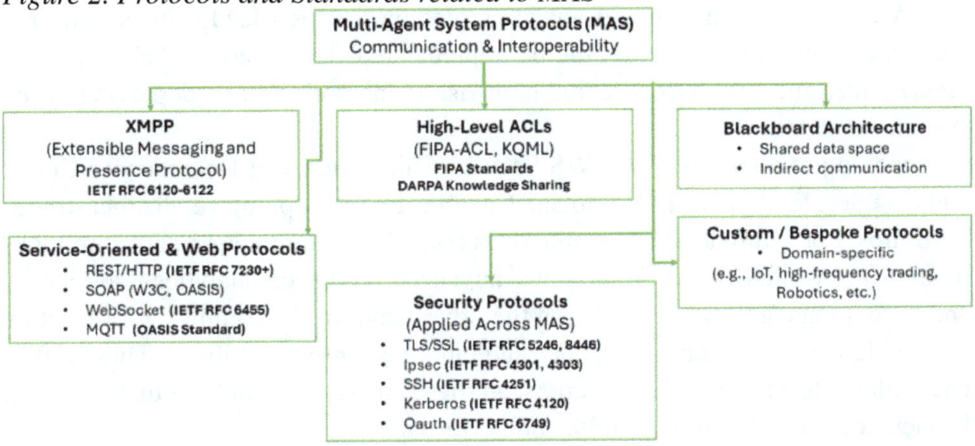

As mobile cloud computing (Asghari & Sohrabi, 2024)gains traction, securing these environments has become a top priority. Mobile devices frequently access cloud services over untrusted networks, making them susceptible to threats such as man-in-the-middle attacks and unauthorized access. Jafari et al. (2016) propose frameworks designed to address these unique challenges while maintaining user convenience. These frameworks integrate robust authentication mechanisms, such as multifactor authentication (MFA) and biometric verification, to enhance access control.

In addition to authentication, secure communication channels play a critical role in protecting mobile cloud interactions. Techniques such as end-to-end encryption and secure tunnelling protocols (e.g., Virtual Private Networks) ensure that data transmitted between mobile devices and cloud servers remains confidential. It is important to consider high variability of mobile environments, optimizing security solutions for low-latency and high-throughput scenarios to provide a seamless user experience.

Beyond traditional threats, organizations are increasingly confronted with advanced persistent threats (APTs), which are highly targeted, prolonged cyberattacks designed to compromise sensitive systems (Yuan et al., 2020). To counter such threats, SECaaS providers are incorporating advanced defense strategies, including game-theory-based models. Yuan et al. (2020) discuss the application of Stackelberg-game-based strategies in cloud security, where defenders and attackers engage in a simulated game to predict and mitigate potential attack vectors.

In a Stackelberg framework, SECaaS providers act as leaders, deploying defensive strategies based on anticipated attacker behavior. This approach requires extensive data collection and analysis to model the attacker's objectives, resources, and methods. A real-time telemetry and analytics pipelines, which feed critical data into the game-theory algorithms should be implemented. These models help prioritize security measures, such as patching high-risk vulnerabilities and deploying decoy systems to misdirect attackers.

Leading providers such as AWS Security Hub, Microsoft Defender for Cloud, and Google Cloud Security Command Center offer overlapping yet distinct service portfolios. For example, AWS emphasizes compliance automation and continuous monitoring, while Microsoft integrates advanced AI-driven analytics into identity and access management. Google, on the other hand, uses its global infrastructure to provide scalable threat intelligence and rapid response capabilities. These differences illustrate how provider selection can shape an organization's security strategy, influencing costs, interoperability, and performance.

Meeting regulatory and industry compliance standards is a critical requirement for organizations operating in the cloud. Regulations such ISO/IEC 27001 (Information Security Management Systems), CSA STAR (Security, Trust & Assurance Registry), and Health Insurance Portability and Accountability Act (HIPAA) impose stringent requirements on data protection and privacy (see Figure 3). SECaaS simplifies compliance with industry standards by automating monitoring and reporting processes, reducing the administrative burden on businesses.

Figure 3. SECaaS Compliance and Regulatory Requirements

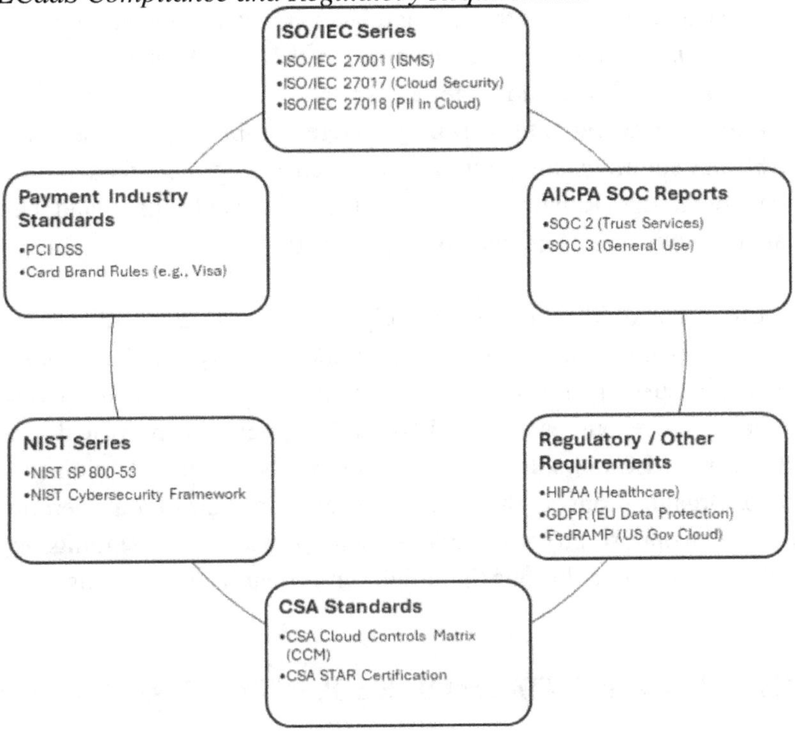

Automation involves integrating SECaaS solutions with compliance frameworks to continuously monitor data flows, access controls, and system configurations. For instance, cloud-based Security Information and Event Management (SIEM) systems aggregate logs from across the network, analyzing them for compliance violations and generating reports for auditors. These systems should be designed to handle high volumes of data, ensuring real-time analysis and alerting capabilities.

SECaaS providers need to adopt advanced technologies to enhance their offerings. These technologies include:

1. **Machine Learning and Artificial Intelligence (AI):** ML and AI algorithms analyze huge datasets to detect subtle patterns indicative of cyber threats (Muneer et al., 2024). For example, anomaly detection models identify deviations from normal traffic behavior, flagging potential attacks.
2. **Blockchain for Security Transparency:** Blockchain-based solutions provide immutable audit trails, ensuring accountability in security operations (Jurgała et al., 2022). Integrating blockchain in the systems can enhance trust and traceability within distributed cloud networks.

3. **Zero Trust Architectures:** Zero Trust models enforce strict verification of every user and device attempting to access network resources (García-Teodoro et al., 2022). This approach minimizes the risk of insider threats and lateral movement within cloud systems.
4. **Edge Computing Integration:** As edge computing becomes more prevalent, SECaaS solutions are extending their reach to protect data and devices at the network's edge (Ranaweera et al., 2020). Lightweight agents and secure gateways are deployed to ensure end-to-end protection.

The adoption of SECaaS is not merely a cost-saving measure but a strategic move to enhance organizational resilience in an increasingly hostile cyber landscape. By offloading security responsibilities to specialized providers, businesses gain access to expertise and resources that would be prohibitively expensive to develop in-house. Furthermore, SECaaS solutions are inherently scalable, adapting to the evolving needs of organizations as they grow and expand their cloud operations. SECaaS represents an opportunity to collaborate with providers in designing, deploying, and optimizing security solutions that align with organizational goals.

2. THE FUNDAMENTALS OF SECURITY-AS-A-SERVICE

The rise of Security-as-a-Service (SECaaS) marks a significant evolution in how organizations approach cybersecurity, offering scalable, cost-effective, and adaptive solutions built to the rapidly changing threat landscape. Unlike traditional on-premises security models that rely on dedicated hardware and extensive in-house expertise, SECaaS delivers security services through cloud infrastructure on a subscription basis. This shift allows businesses to use advanced tools and expertise without incurring the high costs associated with developing and maintaining such capabilities internally.

At its core, SECaaS is an outsourcing model in which security services are hosted and managed in the cloud, providing comprehensive protection to businesses. As described by Wang & Shen (2013), SECaaS includes critical functionalities such as vulnerability scanning, penetration testing, and real-time threat monitoring. These services are designed to be adaptive, responding to emerging threats with minimal latency.

This model's dynamic nature allows organizations to benefit from cutting-edge security solutions that might otherwise be financially or technically infeasible. For instance, SECaaS providers continuously update their systems with the latest threat intelligence, ensuring that businesses remain protected against evolving cyber threats.

Unlike traditional models, which rely on periodic manual updates, SECaaS automates these processes, reducing the risk of human error and ensuring up-to-date defences.

SECaaS addresses several limitations of traditional on-premises security solutions by offering a range of advantages that are particularly appealing from a networking and security engineering perspective:

1. Scalability: SECaaS solutions are highly scalable, capable of adjusting to the fluctuating demands of modern organizations. Whether managing small-scale systems or complex multi-cloud environments, SECaaS adapts to workload changes seamlessly, avoiding the infrastructure constraints inherent in traditional models (Elsayed & Zulkernine, 2019).
2. Cost-Effectiveness: By eliminating the need for upfront capital expenditures on hardware and in-house expertise, SECaaS reduces operational costs. Subscription-based pricing models allow organizations to pay for services based on usage, making high-quality security accessible even to small and medium-sized enterprises (SMEs).
3. Real-Time Threat Intelligence: SECaaS uses global threat intelligence networks to provide real-time updates. This continuous flow of intelligence enhances the system's ability to detect and mitigate threats as they arise, a stark contrast to the delayed updates typical in traditional systems.
4. Ease of Deployment and Maintenance: Cloud-based deployment ensures rapid integration of security services, often without disrupting existing workflows. Maintenance is managed by the service provider, including automatic updates and patches, easing the burden on internal IT teams.
5. Flexibility and Accessibility: SECaaS solutions are designed to support hybrid and multi-cloud environments, ensuring seamless integration across various platforms. Additionally, they are accessible from anywhere, facilitating security management in globally distributed networks (Fehis et al., 2021).
6. Enhanced Compliance Management: Built-in compliance tools simplify audits and reporting, helping organizations adhere to regulatory standards such as GDPR and HIPAA. This feature reduces the administrative burden on IT staff and minimizes the risk of non-compliance penalties.

The core components of SECaaS are integral to its success. These components encompass a wide array of security functions designed to provide comprehensive protection for modern IT infrastructures:

1. Identity and Access Management (IAM): IAM systems within SECaaS ensure that only authorized users can access cloud resources. By integrating multi-factor

authentication (MFA), single sign-on (SSO), and user behavior analytics, these systems strengthen identity verification processes (Fehis et al., 2021).

2. Intrusion Detection and Prevention Systems (IDPS): Real-time detection and prevention of malicious activities are fundamental to SECaaS. Advanced IDPS frameworks, such as those highlighted by Sharma et al. (2016), monitor network traffic for suspicious patterns. Using machine learning algorithms, these systems can identify zero-day exploits and respond automatically, reducing reliance on manual intervention.
3. Data Loss Prevention (DLP): DLP solutions protect sensitive data from unauthorized access or accidental leaks. These systems monitor data flows, enforce encryption policies, and block suspicious transfers (Sharma et al., 2016).
4. Endpoint Protection: With the spread of mobile and IoT devices, endpoint protection has become a priority. SECaaS extends security measures to all connected devices, providing antivirus, anti-malware, and patch management solutions.
5. Web Application Firewalls (WAFs): Web applications hosted in the cloud are frequent targets for attacks such as SQL injection and cross-site scripting (XSS). WAFs filter and monitor HTTP requests to identify and block malicious traffic (Hashizume et al., 2013).
6. Advanced Persistent Threat (APT) Defence: Combating APTs requires sophisticated strategies. Yuan et al. (2020) emphasize game-theory-based approaches, such as Stackelberg strategies, which simulate attacker-defender interactions to anticipate and counteract threats. Security engineers use these models to design proactive defence mechanisms.

Table 2 below highlights the differences between SECaaS and traditional on-premises security solutions:

Table 2. Differences between SECaaS and traditional Security Models

Feature	SECaaS	Traditional Security Models
Scalability	Adapts to changing workloads and organizational needs.	Limited by hardware and infrastructure capacity.
Cost-Effectiveness	Subscription-based, reducing capital expenditures.	High initial costs for hardware and maintenance.
Real-Time Threat Intelligence	Continuous updates and global intelligence networks.	Relies on periodic updates and lacks real-time insights.
Ease of Deployment	Rapid deployment via cloud.	Time-intensive setup requiring significant effort.

continued on following page

Table 2. Continued

Feature	SECaaS	Traditional Security Models
Maintenance	Provider-managed updates and patches.	Requires in-house IT staff for maintenance.
Flexibility	Supports hybrid and multi-cloud integration.	Challenging to integrate with other systems.
Compliance Management	Automated tools simplify audits and reporting.	Manual compliance monitoring is resource-intensive.
Threat Detection	Real-time detection with automated responses.	Slower manual response times.
Accessibility	Accessible from anywhere via the internet.	Restricted to physical infrastructure locations.

Some of the SECaaS networking and security design considerations are:

1. Architectural Design: Integrating SECaaS into existing IT environments requires a thorough understanding of architectural principles. Cloud-based security tools should interoperate seamlessly with on-premises systems, hybrid networks, and edge devices.
2. Traffic Optimization: SECaaS solutions must analyze network traffic without introducing significant latency. Traffic flows can be optimized using content delivery networks (CDNs), load balancers, and traffic shaping techniques (Chaisiri et al., 2015).
3. Resilience and Redundancy: Cloud-based security services must be designed for high availability. Redundancy mechanisms, such as failover systems and backup data centres, ensure uninterrupted service during outages.
4. Risk Management: Potential risks, such as vendor lock-in and data sovereignty concerns should be evaluated. By selecting flexible providers and implementing localized controls, organizations can mitigate these risks effectively.
5. Automation and Orchestration: Automation plays a crucial role in SECaaS, from compliance monitoring to incident response (Settanni et al., 2023a). Tools should be integrated seamlessly into existing workflows, reducing manual overhead.

3. HOW SECaaS ENHANCES CLOUD SECURITY

One of the most critical features of SECaaS is its ability to proactively identify and neutralize security risks before they can cause significant damage. This proactive approach is enabled by advanced technologies such as vulnerability scanning and penetration testing, which are delivered through cloud-based proxies. As noted by Genge et al. (2015) these tools provide organizations with real-time detection capabilities, allowing them to address vulnerabilities immediately.

Vulnerability scanning involves examining network components, such as firewalls, routers, and endpoints, to identify weaknesses. Penetration testing simulates potential attacks to evaluate the resilience of these systems. By using cloud resources, SECaaS providers can perform these tasks at scale, delivering detailed reports that inform corrective actions. This ensures that organizations are equipped to neutralize potential threats promptly, reducing the risk of data breaches and minimizing downtime.

In addition to basic detection tools, SECaaS solutions incorporate advanced persistent threat (APT) defences. Srinadh et al. (2023) highlight a Conditional Dingo Optimization Algorithm (CDOA) combined with a Deep Residual Network (DRN) to detect Advanced Persistent Threats (APTs). While Moving Target Defense (MTD) mitigates APTs by shifting attack surfaces, it often incurs high overhead.

1) Scalability and Flexibility in Security Management

Modern networking environments, especially those operating in hybrid or multi-cloud setups, demand flexible security solutions. SECaaS provides unparalleled scalability, enabling organizations to adjust their security measures dynamically based on workload fluctuations. Unlike traditional security systems, which require substantial capital investment and infrastructure upgrades to scale, SECaaS offers on-demand scalability without the need for additional hardware.

2) Real-Time Monitoring and Automated Response

Real-time monitoring is a cornerstone of SECaaS, enabling organizations to detect and respond to threats as they occur. Systems design should continuously analyze network traffic, identifying anomalies that may indicate malicious activity. These systems use techniques such as deep packet inspection (DPI) and behavioural analysis to examine data flows, ensuring that threats are detected at the earliest stages (Ashraf et al., 2016).

Automated response mechanisms are another critical aspect of SECaaS. Once a threat is detected, these systems can initiate predefined actions, such as isolating compromised devices, blocking malicious IP addresses, or alerting security teams. This automation significantly reduces response times, limiting the potential impact of attacks (Settanni et al., 2023b).

3) Comprehensive Data Protection

In cloud computing, data protection is paramount, as sensitive information is often stored and transmitted across distributed networks. SECaaS addresses this challenge by providing robust data protection mechanisms, such as data loss prevention (DLP) and encryption. DLP solutions monitor data flows within the network, identifying and blocking unauthorized transfers of sensitive information.

Encryption is another essential component of SECaaS. By securing data during both transmission and storage, encryption ensures confidentiality and integrity. Networking engineers implement encryption protocols, such as Transport Layer Security (TLS) and IPsec, to protect data traveling across public and private networks. Additionally, they manage encryption key lifecycles, ensuring that keys are securely stored, rotated, and retired.

Intelligent algorithms and automated workflows enforce strict access controls, ensuring that only authorized users can access sensitive data.

4) Enhanced Collaboration and Integration

In complex cloud ecosystems, collaboration and integration are critical to ensuring comprehensive security. SECaaS solutions facilitate seamless coordination among various security components, creating a unified defence strategy. All security components should be configured to communicate effectively, using standardized protocols such as Syslog and SNMP for logging and monitoring. Integration also involves centralizing security management through platforms such as Security Information and Event Management (SIEM) systems, which aggregate data from across the network and provide a comprehensive view of the security posture.

While SECaaS offers significant advantages, its implementation also presents unique challenges:

1) *Latency and Performance:* Real-time monitoring and automated responses must be optimized to avoid introducing latency that could impact network performance. Some of the techniques to be used are load balancing and edge computing to distribute processing workloads and maintain responsiveness.
2) *Data Sovereignty and Privacy:* Organizations must ensure that SECaaS solutions comply with data sovereignty regulations, which may restrict where data can be stored and processed. Localized data centres and region-specific configurations should be implemented to address these requirements. Addressing data sovereignty involves implementing robust data routing and geo-fencing solutions. Data packets originating in specific jurisdictions should remain within compliant data centers, using technologies such as software-defined networking (SDN)

to enforce location-based routing policies. Furthermore, encryption protocols, such as Transport Layer Security (TLS) and end-to-end encryption, should be used to secure data during transit.

3) *Integration Complexity:* Integrating SECaaS with legacy systems and hybrid cloud environments can be challenging. Solutions should be built to bridge gaps between traditional and modern architectures, ensuring interoperability and consistency.
4) *Vendor Lock-In:* Relying exclusively on a single Security-as-a-Service (SECaaS) provider can limit an organization's flexibility, making it more difficult and costly to switch vendors if performance, pricing, or strategic needs evolve. This situation, often referred to as "vendor lock-in," restricts an organization's negotiation power and ability to adopt innovative solutions from other providers. To mitigate this risk, networking engineers must prioritize SECaaS providers that adhere to open standards and support interoperable architectures. For example, providers offering services based on RESTful APIs, OpenConfig, or Common Information Model (CIM) facilitate seamless integration with diverse systems. Additionally, modular network architectures can be implemented to allow components, such as firewalls or intrusion detection systems (IDS), to be replaced without impacting the overall security posture.
5) *Reliability and Service-Level Agreements (SLAs):* The reliability of SECaaS solutions is directly tied to the stability and performance of the provider's infrastructure. Downtime, outages, or service disruptions can have severe consequences for organizational security, including increased vulnerability to cyberattacks. Key elements to consider in SLAs include:
   - Uptime Guarantees: Providers should offer clear commitments, such as 99.9% availability, backed by penalties for non-compliance.
   - Incident Response Times: SLAs should specify response times for threat detection, containment, and remediation.
   - Disaster Recovery Provisions: Engineers must verify the existence of failover systems, redundant data centers, and recovery point objectives (RPOs) that align with organizational needs.
6) *Regulatory Compliance:* Cloud environments are dynamic and complex, often complicating adherence to regulatory and industry standards. While SECaaS providers offer compliance tools and certifications, ultimate responsibility for regulatory adherence typically remains with the client. Key strategies include:
   - Centralized Compliance Dashboards: SIEM (Security Information and Event Management) systems can be integrated with centralize compliance monitoring, automating the detection of non-compliance issues.
   - Encryption Standards: Implementing encryption for data at rest and in transit helps meet stringent data protection requirements.

- Segmentation and Access Controls: Using network segmentation and zero-trust architectures, engineers can isolate sensitive data and restrict access based on roles.

7) *Integration Complexity:* Integrating SECaaS solutions into existing IT infrastructures, particularly in hybrid or multi-cloud environments, presents significant challenges. Legacy systems often lack compatibility with modern cloud-based services, requiring substantial engineering efforts to bridge the gap. Integration involves:
    - Assessing Compatibility: existing hardware, software, and protocols should be evaluated to identify potential integration issues.
    - Implementing Gateways and Adapters: API gateways and protocol converters can enable communication between legacy systems and SECaaS platforms.
    - Standardized Network Architectures: Adopting standards such as VXLAN (Virtual Extensible LAN) or IPv6 can simplify integration and ensure scalability (Conrad et al., 2023).
8) *Cost Management:* While SECaaS is often praised for its cost-efficiency, organizations must carefully evaluate the total cost of ownership (TCO) to avoid unforeseen expenses. Subscription-based pricing models can become expensive over time, particularly for large organizations with extensive security needs. Conducting regular cost-benefit analyses ensures that the value delivered by SECaaS aligns with the organization's financial constraints and operational goals. This can be managed by:
    - Analysing Usage Patterns: Monitoring network traffic and resource utilization helps optimize subscription tiers.
    - Avoiding Over-Provisioning: Admins should ensure that security measures are appropriately scaled to actual needs, avoiding unnecessary expenses.
    - Using Cost-Effective Tools: Open-source and community-driven tools can complement SECaaS offerings, reducing dependency on paid services.
9) *Security Risks of Outsourcing*: Outsourcing security to a third-party SECaaS provider introduces risks related to trust and control. Organizations must rely on providers to protect sensitive data and systems, yet this lack of direct oversight can create vulnerabilities. Wang & Shen (2013) worn that organizations should implement strong access controls and regularly audit provider performance to mitigate these risks by:
    - Implementing Secure Access Protocols: Technologies such as VPNs (Virtual Private Networks) and SD-WAN (Software-Defined Wide Area

Networks) ensure secure communication between organizational networks and SECaaS platforms.

- Monitoring Provider Performance: Engineers should deploy tools to monitor service quality, latency, and security incidents, ensuring that the provider meets agreed-upon standards.
- Establishing Redundancy: Backup security systems or multi-provider strategies can mitigate risks associated with reliance on a single SECaaS provider.
- Regular audits and penetration tests should also be conducted to validate the effectiveness of the provider's security measures

5. INTEGRATION OF SECaaS WITH EXISTING IT ENVIRONMENTS

The successful adoption of SECaaS depends not only on its capabilities but also on how effectively it integrates with an organization's existing IT infrastructure. A seamless integration ensures that SECaaS solutions enhance security without disrupting operations, creating redundancies, or compromising performance (Ahn et al., 2024). However, integrating SECaaS into existing IT environments, especially in hybrid or multi-cloud setups, presents unique challenges and requires strategic planning.

One of the primary considerations for integration is compatibility with legacy systems. Many organizations rely on legacy systems that may not inherently support modern cloud-based security services. This can lead to gaps in coverage or require significant effort to bridge the compatibility divide.

Integration also requires careful consideration of organizational workflows and collaboration between in-house IT teams and SECaaS providers. Effective communication and role description are essential to ensure that responsibilities, such as incident response and compliance monitoring, are clearly defined and executed without conflicts. Organizations must establish robust governance frameworks that outline how SECaaS solutions align with their security policies, escalation protocols, and compliance requirements.

Security integration should also focus on minimizing downtime and disruptions during the transition to SECaaS. Phased rollouts, thorough testing, and pilot deployments are recommended strategies to identify and resolve potential issues before full-scale implementation. These steps ensure that the organization can continue its operations without interruptions while gradually adapting to the new security framework.

Finally, the integration of SECaaS into existing IT environments must address potential risks, such as data sovereignty concerns and vendor lock-in. Organizations should prioritize SECaaS providers that offer flexibility and transparency, allowing them to retain control over critical security functions and data. Regular audits and performance reviews are also necessary to evaluate the effectiveness of the integration and ensure that SECaaS solutions meet organizational expectations.

6. TECHNICAL COMPLEXITIES OF SECaaS INTEGRATION

Integrating SECaaS into existing IT infrastructures is not simply a matter of connecting cloud services through APIs; it involves addressing deep technical challenges that can significantly affect security, performance, and reliability. One of the most pressing issues is protocol translation. Many legacy systems rely on outdated communication standards (e.g., SNMPv2, SOAP-based services, or proprietary protocols), while SECaaS solutions typically operate using modern protocols such as REST, gRPC, or JSON-based APIs. Bridging these differences often requires gateways or middleware capable of translating between protocols in real time. Such translation layers, however, can introduce latency and new attack surfaces if not properly hardened.

Another challenge lies in data format inconsistencies. Legacy systems may generate logs or events in non-standardized formats, whereas SECaaS solutions often expect structured input such as JSON, XML, or formats compliant with standards like Common Event Format (CEF). Inconsistencies can disrupt automated threat detection pipelines and reduce the accuracy of SIEM correlations. Engineering teams must therefore implement normalization tools or adopt log-parsing frameworks to ensure compatibility across heterogeneous systems.

Identity federation adds further complexity. Integrating SECaaS with existing identity and access management frameworks often requires supporting multiple protocols such as SAML, OAuth 2.0, and OpenID Connect simultaneously. Misconfiguration in federation layers can lead to privilege escalation or authentication bypass vulnerabilities, underscoring the need for careful protocol mapping and rigorous testing.

Hybrid and multi-cloud environments also exacerbate these challenges by introducing latency, routing, and encryption overheads. For example, secure tunnelling of traffic between on-premises systems and SECaaS providers may require complex VPN or SD-WAN configurations, which must balance security with performance. Insufficient planning can result in bottlenecks or inconsistent policy enforcement across platforms.

To address these integration difficulties, organizations should adopt modular integration frameworks that rely on open standards, robust middleware, and thorough validation mechanisms. Automated testing environments, including sandboxed deployments, can identify protocol mismatches or format errors before they affect production systems. By confronting these engineering challenges directly, organizations can reduce risks associated with SECaaS integration and ensure that the benefits of scalability and advanced security features are not undermined by technical incompatibilities. Table 3 is a summary of the key insights and potential strategies of different integration aspects.

Table 3. Summary of SECaaS integration strategies with existing IT environments

Integration Challenge	Description	Technical Complexities	Mitigation Strategies
Legacy System Compatibility	Older systems may not natively support cloud-based security services.	Proprietary protocols (e.g., SNMPv2, SOAP), limited API support.	Use middleware/gateways, upgrade critical systems, phased migration to standards-compliant tools.
Interoperability in Hybrid/Multi-Cloud	Ensuring consistent security across diverse platforms and vendors.	Inconsistent security policies, latency due to routing across clouds.	Standardize policies, adopt SD-WAN for optimized routing, deploy cloud integration tools with API orchestration.
Protocol Translation	Bridging different communication standards between legacy and modern SECaaS tools.	REST/gRPC vs. legacy SOAP or proprietary formats, real-time translation overhead.	Protocol adapters, secure gateways, sandbox testing for latency/security evaluation.
Data Format Inconsistencies	Logs/events generated in heterogeneous formats incompatible with SECaaS analytics.	Legacy logs vs. structured JSON/XML/ CEF formats.	Log normalization tools, parsing frameworks, standard data exchange formats (e.g., CEF, Syslog).
Identity Federation	Integrating IAM across multiple providers and legacy directories.	Supporting SAML, OAuth 2.0, OpenID Connect simultaneously; misconfiguration risks.	Careful protocol mapping, multi-protocol IAM solutions, regular penetration testing.
SIEM Integration	Feeding SECaaS insights into centralized monitoring platforms.	Different log formats, inconsistent threat event structures, data duplication.	API-based integration, normalization, real-time stream processors (e.g., Kafka).
Service Reliability & Performance	Ensuring that added SECaaS layers do not cause downtime or slow systems.	Latency in traffic inspection (e.g., IDPS over VPN tunnels), throughput bottlenecks.	Phased rollout, redundancy in providers, edge-based traffic inspection.
Governance & Compliance	Aligning integration with regulatory and organizational security requirements.	Overlapping regulations (GDPR, PDPA, HIPAA), fragmented compliance audits.	Geo-fencing, audit trails, third-party certifications, compliance-by-design frameworks.

6. ETHICAL AND TRUST ISSUES IN OUTSOURCING SECURITY

While Security-as-a-Service (SECaaS) offers significant technical and operational benefits, it also raises important ethical and trust-related challenges that organizations must carefully consider (Gupta et al., 2025). Unlike traditional in-house security models, outsourcing security responsibilities to external providers involves a transfer of sensitive data, operational visibility, and even partial control over critical systems. This shift creates a dependency that is not only technical but also ethical in nature.

One of the primary concerns is data sovereignty, which refers to the legal and geographical constraints on where data is stored and processed (Pampus & Heisel, 2025). When security services are outsourced, data may cross national boundaries and fall under different regulatory regimes, raising questions about compliance, ownership, and accountability. This is particularly problematic for organizations operating in highly regulated industries, where unauthorized cross-border data flows could lead to legal liabilities and reputational risks.

Another ethical issue lies in the potential misuse of sensitive information. SECaaS providers typically collect and analyse large volumes of logs, user activity data, and system events to detect threats. While this is necessary for effective monitoring, it can also expose organizations to risks of surveillance, profiling, or unauthorized sharing of data with third parties. Without strict contractual and regulatory safeguards, customers must rely heavily on the provider's integrity and governance structures.

To address these issues, organizations should evaluate providers not only on their technical capabilities but also on their ethical posture and trustworthiness. Mechanisms such as transparency reports, independent third-party audits, and well-defined Service Level Agreements (SLAs) can help establish accountability and build confidence (Mushtaque Temrekar, 2025). Transparency reports provide visibility into how data is handled and under what circumstances it may be shared with external entities. Third-party audits verify compliance with industry standards and best practices, while SLAs formalize the responsibilities and obligations of both parties in maintaining data security and privacy.

To better understand the ethical and trust implications of outsourcing security, it is important to examine the role of international standards and frameworks that guide providers and organizations. These standards not only establish technical requirements but also embed principles of accountability, transparency, and data protection, which are critical in fostering trust between SECaaS vendors and clients. While some standards, such as ISO/IEC 27001, focus primarily on information security management, others like GDPR and ISO/IEC 27701 emphasize data privacy and sovereignty. Cloud-specific frameworks, including CSA STAR and ISO/IEC 19086, further address trust by providing mechanisms for assurance, auditability, and contractual clarity. Table 4 provides a comparative analysis of these standards, highlighting their relevance to ethical and trust concerns in SECaaS adoption.

Table 4. Comparative Analysis of Ethical and Trust-Related Standards in SECaaS

Standard/ Framework	Scope & Focus	Ethical/Trust Implications	Relevance to SECaaS
ISO/IEC 27001	Information Security Management Systems (ISMS)	Promotes accountability and continuous risk management	Provides baseline for SECaaS providers to demonstrate secure operations
ISO/IEC 27701	Privacy Information Management Systems (PIMS)	Embeds privacy principles into ISMS, ensuring transparent data handling	Strengthens privacy assurance in SECaaS offerings
CSA STAR	Cloud-specific assurance and certification	Focuses on transparency and provider accountability	Helps clients evaluate SECaaS trustworthiness
ISO/IEC 19086	Cloud Service Level Agreements (SLA)	Emphasizes contractual trust and service transparency	Ensures SECaaS providers meet agreed-upon security levels
GDPR (EU)	Comprehensive data protection and privacy law	Strong emphasis on consent, accountability, and cross-border trust	Forces SECaaS providers handling EU data to align with privacy-by-design
PDPA (Singapore)	Data protection law emphasizing consent, purpose limitation, and accountability	Balances business needs with ethical handling of personal data	Relevant for SECaaS providers in APAC, ensuring compliance and trust-building in cross-border services
CCPA/CPRA (California, US)	Consumer privacy and rights, including data access and deletion	Empowers consumers, strengthens trust via transparency and choice	Affects SECaaS providers handling California residents' data, requiring opt-out mechanisms and disclosure policies

While global privacy regulations such as GDPR, PDPA, and CCPA provide robust frameworks for data protection, their enforcement in practice remains a significant challenge, particularly in the context of cloud computing and Security-as-a-Service (SECaaS). One key difficulty lies in cross-border compliance, as cloud services often involve data transfer across multiple jurisdictions with differing privacy expectations and regulatory mechanisms. This raises complex questions about which laws apply and how they can be enforced consistently against multinational providers.

Another challenge is the limited enforcement capacity in emerging economies, where regulatory authorities may lack the technical expertise, resources, or political support necessary to pursue large-scale violations by powerful cloud vendors. Even in more mature jurisdictions, the scale and complexity of multinational SECaaS operations often make oversight and accountability difficult to sustain.

Real-world cases illustrate both the successes and limitations of current enforcement. For example, the European Union's GDPR enforcement against Meta resulted in billion-euro fines, highlighting regulators' willingness to pursue high-profile violations but also raising debates about proportionality and compliance feasibility (Ruohonen & Hjerppe, 2022). Similarly, Singapore's PDPA enforcement has penalized local and regional firms for inadequate data protection (Greenleaf, 2012), yet the scope and financial weight of sanctions remain far more modest compared to the EU. In the United States, lawsuits under the CCPA demonstrate growing awareness of consumer rights, but fragmented enforcement at the state level creates inconsistencies in outcomes (Huang, 2025).

These cases reveal persistent gaps in enforcement. Disparities between regions create unequal burdens for global SECaaS adoption, while resource limitations hinder smaller regulators from monitoring complex cloud environments effectively. Moreover, enforcement frameworks often struggle to adapt to cloud-specific risks, such as multi-tenancy, vendor lock-in, and shared responsibility models, which traditional legal structures were not designed to address. To achieve meaningful protection, regulatory bodies must collaborate internationally, build stronger technical capacity, and update enforcement mechanisms to reflect the realities of cloud and SECaaS ecosystems.

7. THE FUTURE OF SECaaS IN CLOUD COMPUTING

As cloud computing continues to transform how organizations operate, SECaaS is expected to play an increasingly critical role in safeguarding digital ecosystems. With the rapid evolution of technology, threats, and business needs, SECaaS solutions are set to become more advanced, adaptive, and integral to modern IT strategies. This section explores the emerging trends, technological advancements, and future prospects of SECaaS in the ever-changing landscape of cloud computing.

A) Emerging Trends in SECaaS

1. Adoption of Artificial Intelligence and Machine Learning: AI and ML are revolutionizing cybersecurity by enabling SECaaS providers to detect, analyse, and respond to threats with unprecedented speed and accuracy (Kotilainen et al., 2025). These technologies allow for predictive threat detection, where algorithms identify potential risks based on behavioural patterns and historical data.
2. Zero Trust Security Models: The adoption of Zero Trust architectures is reshaping how organizations approach security in cloud environments. Zero Trust emphasizes verifying every user and device, regardless of location or access

level. SECaaS providers are increasingly integrating Zero Trust principles into their offerings, providing granular access controls, continuous verification, and micro-segmentation to limit the lateral movement of threats within cloud networks.

3. Integration with IoT and Edge Computing: The increase of Internet of Things (IoT) devices and the rise of edge computing are creating new security challenges (Pawlicki et al., 2023). SECaaS solutions are evolving to address these complexities by extending their capabilities to protect distributed networks, including IoT ecosystems. Advanced SECaaS platforms can monitor and secure data flows across edge devices, ensuring consistent protection in decentralized environments.

B) Technological Advancements Driving SECaaS Evolution

1. Blockchain for Enhanced Security and Transparency: Blockchain technology is being explored as a way to enhance SECaaS solutions by providing immutable audit trails and secure data exchanges. By using blockchain, SECaaS providers can offer transparent and tamper-proof security logs, improving accountability and trust in multi-cloud and hybrid environments (Sarveshwaran et al., 2024).
2. Security Automation and Orchestration: Automation is becoming a cornerstone of SECaaS, enabling faster and more efficient responses to cyber threats. Automated workflows and security orchestration tools allow organizations to reduce response times, minimize manual intervention, and streamline compliance processes. Future SECaaS offerings are expected to feature more sophisticated automation capabilities, driven by AI and ML.
3. Integration with Advanced Analytics and Big Data: The use of big data analytics in SECaaS is on the rise, providing deeper insights into threat landscapes and enabling more effective security strategies. By analysing vast datasets in real time, SECaaS platforms can uncover hidden patterns, correlations, and vulnerabilities, offering organizations actionable intelligence to strengthen their defences (Zhao et al., 2014).

C) Market Trends and Adoption Drivers

1. Increased Demand for Hybrid and Multi-Cloud Security: As more organizations adopt hybrid and multi-cloud strategies, the demand for SECaaS solutions that can seamlessly operate across different environments is expected to grow. SECaaS providers are developing tools that ensure consistent security policies, regardless of the underlying cloud platforms.

2. Focus on Regulatory Compliance: The complexity of global regulatory requirements continues to drive the need for SECaaS solutions that simplify compliance management. Future offerings are likely to incorporate more advanced compliance automation tools, helping organizations navigate evolving legal landscapes with ease.
3. SME Adoption of SECaaS: Small and medium-sized enterprises (SMEs), traditionally constrained by limited resources, are increasingly adopting SECaaS due to its cost-efficiency and accessibility. This trend is expected to accelerate as SECaaS solutions become more tailored to the needs of smaller organizations.

D) Challenges and Opportunities

While the future of SECaaS is promising, challenges such as data privacy concerns, vendor lock-in risks, and the increasing sophistication of cyber threats remain significant. However, these challenges also present opportunities for innovation. For example, the demand for greater data sovereignty has prompted SECaaS providers to explore localized solutions and hybrid security models that give organizations more control over their data.

1. Convergence of Cybersecurity and Cloud Management: SECaaS platforms are expected to evolve into comprehensive security and cloud management suites, offering unified tools for monitoring, securing, and optimizing cloud environments.
2. Hyper-Personalized Security Solutions: Advances in AI will enable SECaaS providers to deliver hyper-personalized security strategies tailored to the unique risk profiles of individual organizations, providing more effective protection.
3. Expansion into New Frontiers: As technologies like quantum computing emerge, SECaaS will adapt to address new types of threats and opportunities. For example, quantum-safe encryption may become a standard feature in future SECaaS offerings.

E) Sociotechnical Challenges in Adopting SECaaS

While SECaaS offers clear technical and financial advantages, its successful adoption depends heavily on addressing the organizational and human dimensions of change. One of the most significant barriers is internal resistance to outsourcing critical security functions. Many IT teams and decision-makers remain cautious about relying on third-party providers, fearing loss of control, reduced visibility, and potential accountability issues in the event of a breach. This cultural resistance is often stronger in organizations that have traditionally invested in on-premises security infrastructures.

Another important factor is the training and upskilling of existing IT staff. Transitioning to SECaaS requires IT and security teams to shift their roles from directly managing infrastructure to overseeing vendor relationships, monitoring service-level agreements (SLAs), and integrating cloud-based security tools into daily workflows. Without proper training, staff may lack the competencies to evaluate, configure, and optimize SECaaS solutions, leading to both operational inefficiencies and heightened risk exposure.

To overcome these sociotechnical challenges, organizations can benefit from adopting change management practices. This includes engaging stakeholders early in the decision-making process, conducting awareness sessions that emphasize the benefits of SECaaS, and gradually introducing hybrid models to allow teams to adapt without sudden disruption. Furthermore, leadership must clearly articulate the rationale behind the transition, aligning it with broader business goals such as agility, scalability, and compliance.

8. CONCLUSION

Security-as-a-Service (SECaaS) has fundamentally changed how organizations protect their cloud-based infrastructures, providing a scalable, cost-effective, and adaptive security framework. By using specialized external expertise, enterprises can rapidly deploy advanced defensive measures—vulnerability scanning, intrusion prevention, endpoint protection—without incurring the significant upfront investments typical of traditional, on-premises models. At the same time, SECaaS solutions seamlessly integrate with existing IT environments, support hybrid and multi-cloud strategies, and use evolving technologies such as AI, blockchain, and zero trust.

At the same time, adoption is not without challenges. Beyond technical integration, SECaaS introduces ethical and trust considerations, including data sovereignty, provider accountability, and transparency in managing sensitive information. Comparative analyses show differing adoption patterns between SMEs and large enterprises, where issues such as cost–benefit trade-offs and vendor lock-in require careful strategic planning. Regulatory compliance further complicates adoption, as organizations must navigate different legal regimes such as GDPR, PDPA, HIPAA, ISO 27001, NIST, and CCPA, while also recognizing the enforcement gaps and resource disparities evident in real-world cases.

From a technological standpoint, machine learning has enhanced intrusion detection and prevention systems within SECaaS, but trade-offs remain between accuracy, computational cost, and susceptibility to adversarial threats. Scalability across multi-cloud environments and real-time deployment limitations remain pressing research challenges. Just as critically, organizational and human factors shape the success of SECaaS adoption. Resistance to change, the need for retraining IT staff, and cultural transitions from an on-premises mindset to outsourced security demand slow change management strategies and effective stakeholder communication.

Looking ahead, continuous innovation in AI-driven analytics, automated orchestration, and predictive intelligence will strengthen SECaaS capabilities, while governance frameworks, ethical trust models, and cross-border compliance mechanisms will determine its credibility and sustainability. As businesses expand their reliance on cloud and edge infrastructures, SECaaS must evolve to address emerging needs such as securing IoT ecosystems, supporting regulatory harmonization, and managing sociotechnical change. With robust integration, vigilant governance, and a balanced focus on technology, ethics, and people, SECaaS stands poised to become a cornerstone of cloud security in the digital era..

REFERENCES

Achankeng, S. (2025). Analysis of Prevention Techniques against DDoS and SQL Injection Attack in Network and Cloud Environment. *Journal of Cloud Computing (Heidelberg, Germany)*.

Ahn, S., Gim, G., Jang, S., & Hwang, J. (2024). *A Study on the Integration of End-point Security Service Operations Management*. Focusing on Cloud Services., DOI: 10.1007/978-3-031-53385-3_3

Aljuaid, W. H., & Alshamrani, S. S. (2024). A Deep Learning Approach for Intrusion Detection Systems in Cloud Computing Environments. *Applied Sciences (Basel, Switzerland)*, *14*(13), 5381. DOI: 10.3390/app14135381

Asghari, A., & Sohrabi, M. K. (2024). Server placement in mobile cloud computing: A comprehensive survey for edge computing, fog computing and cloudlet. *Computer Science Review*, *51*, 100616. DOI: 10.1016/j.cosrev.2023.100616

Ashraf, M. A., Jamal, H., Khan, S. A., Ahmed, Z., & Baig, M. I. (2016). A Heterogeneous Service-Oriented Deep Packet Inspection and Analysis Framework for Traffic-Aware Network Management and Security Systems. *IEEE Access : Practical Innovations, Open Solutions*, *4*, 5918–5936. DOI: 10.1109/ACCESS.2016.2609398

Awotunde, J. B., Ayo, F. E., Panigrahi, R., Garg, A., Bhoi, A. K., & Barsocchi, P. (2023). A Multi-level Random Forest Model-Based Intrusion Detection Using Fuzzy Inference System for Internet of Things Networks. *International Journal of Computational Intelligence Systems*, *16*(1), 31. DOI: 10.1007/s44196-023-00205-w

Casola, V., De Benedictis, A., Rak, M., & Villano, U. (2018). Monitoring Data Security in the Cloud: A Security SLA-Based Approach. In *Security and Resilience in Intelligent Data-Centric Systems and Communication Networks* (pp. 235–259). Elsevier. https://doi.org/DOI: 10.1016/B978-0-12-811373-8.00011-2

Chaisiri, S., Ko, R. K. L., & Niyato, D. (2015). A Joint Optimization Approach to Security-as-a-Service Allocation and Cyber Insurance Management. *2015 IEEE Trustcom/BigDataSE/ISPA*, 426–433. https://doi.org/DOI: 10.1109/Trustcom.2015.403

Conrad, E., Misenar, S., & Feldman, J. (2023). Domain 4: Communication and Network Security. In *CISSP® Study Guide* (pp. 225–293). Elsevier. https://doi.org/DOI: 10.1016/B978-0-443-18734-6.00003-9

Elsayed, M., & Zulkernine, M. (2019). Offering security diagnosis as a service for cloud SaaS applications. *Journal of Information Security and Applications*, *44*, 32–48. DOI: 10.1016/j.jisa.2018.11.006

Farnaaz, N., & Jabbar, M. A. (2016). Random Forest Modeling for Network Intrusion Detection System. *Procedia Computer Science*, *89*, 213–217. DOI: 10.1016/j.procs.2016.06.047

Fedele, G., D'Alfonso, L., & Chen, B. (2025). A matching problem between two decoupled multi-agent systems with reference tracking capabilities. *Automatica*, *173*, 112047. DOI: 10.1016/j.automatica.2024.112047

Fehis, S., Nouali, O., & Kechadi, T. (2021). Secure encryption key management as a SecaaS based on Chinese wall security policy. *Journal of Information Security and Applications*, *63*, 102975. DOI: 10.1016/j.jisa.2021.102975

García-Teodoro, P., Camacho, J., Maciá-Fernández, G., Gómez-Hernández, J. A., & López-Marín, V. J. (2022). A novel zero-trust network access control scheme based on the security profile of devices and users. *Computer Networks*, *212*, 109068. DOI: 10.1016/j.comnet.2022.109068

Genge, B., Graur, F., & Enăchescu, C. (2015). Non-intrusive Techniques for Vulnerability Assessment of Services in Distributed Systems. *Procedia Technology*, *19*, 12–19. DOI: 10.1016/j.protcy.2015.02.003

Greenleaf, G. (2012). *Singapore's New Data Protection Authority: Strong Enforcement Powers and Business Risks* .

Gupta, P., Sehgal, N. K., & Acken, J. M. (2025). *Trust and Security in a Cloud Environment*., DOI: 10.1007/978-3-031-59170-9_6

Hashizume, K., Rosado, D. G., Fernández-Medina, E., & Fernandez, E. B. (2013). An analysis of security issues for cloud computing. *Journal of Internet Services and Applications*, *4*(1), 5. DOI: 10.1186/1869-0238-4-5

Hnamte, V., & Hussain, J. (2023). DCNNBiLSTM: An Efficient Hybrid Deep Learning-Based Intrusion Detection System. *Telematics and Informatics Reports*, *10*, 100053. DOI: 10.1016/j.teler.2023.100053

Huang, M.-L. (2025). Digital Privacy in the Age of Surveillance: A Comparative Study of GDPR and CCPA. *OTS Canadian Journal*, *4*(7), 65–74. DOI: 10.58840/1t99rb13

Jafari, N., Alsadoon, A., Withana, C. P., Beg, A., & Elchouemi, A. (2016). Designing a Comprehensive Security Framework for Smartphones and Mobile Devices. *American Journal of Engineering and Applied Sciences*, *9*(3), 724–734. DOI: 10.3844/ajeassp.2016.724.734

Jayshree, J., & Leena, R. (2013). Intrusion Detection System using Support Vector Machine. [IJAIS]. *International Journal of Applied Information Systems*.

Jurgała, P., Kurek, T., & Niemiec, M. (2022). Preserving Privacy of Security Services in the SecaaS Model. *Information & Security: An International Journal, 53*, 47–64. DOI: 10.11610/isij.5304

Kaluvuri, S. P., Egner, A. I., den Hartog, J., & Zannone, N. (2015). SAFAX â€“ An Extensible Authorization Service for Cloud Environments. *Frontiers in ICT (Lausanne, Switzerland), 2*. Advance online publication. DOI: 10.3389/fict.2015.00009

Khan, A. R., Kashif, M., Jhaveri, R. H., Raut, R., Saba, T., & Bahaj, S. A. (2022). Deep Learning for Intrusion Detection and Security of Internet of Things (IoT): Current Analysis, Challenges, and Possible Solutions. *Security and Communication Networks*, *2022*, 1–13. DOI: 10.1155/2022/4016073

Kotilainen, P., Mäkitalo, N., Systä, K., Mehraj, A., Waseem, M., Mikkonen, T., & Murillo, J. M. (2025). Allocating distributed AI/ML applications to cloud-edge continuum based on privacy, regulatory, and ethical constraints. *Journal of Systems and Software*, *112333*. Advance online publication. DOI: 10.1016/j.jss.2025.112333

Lakshminarayana, S. K., & Basarkod, P. I. (2023). Unification of K-Nearest Neighbor (KNN) with Distance Aware Algorithm for Intrusion Detection in Evolving Networks Like IoT. *Wireless Personal Communications*, *132*(3), 2255–2281. DOI: 10.1007/s11277-023-10722-8

Mostafa, A. M., Rushdy, E., Medhat, R., & Hanafy, A. (2023). An identity management scheme for cloud computing: Review, challenges, and future directions. *Journal of Intelligent & Fuzzy Systems*, *45*(6), 11295–11317. DOI: 10.3233/JIFS-231911

Mukherjee, S., & Sharma, N. (2012). Intrusion Detection using Naive Bayes Classifier with Feature Reduction. *Procedia Technology*, *4*, 119–128. DOI: 10.1016/j.protcy.2012.05.017

Muneer, S., Farooq, U., Athar, A., Ahsan Raza, M., Ghazal, T. M., & Sakib, S. (2024). A Critical Review of Artificial Intelligence Based Approaches in Intrusion Detection: A Comprehensive Analysis. *Journal of Engineering, 2024*(1). https://doi.org/DOI: 10.1155/2024/3909173

Nikhitha, M., & Jabbar, Dr. M. A. (2019). K Nearest Neighbor Based Model for Intrusion Detection System. [IJRTE]. *International Journal of Recent Technology and Engineering*, *8*(2), 2258–2262. DOI: 10.35940/ijrte.B2458.078219

Pampus, J., & Heisel, M. (2025). A Delimitation of Data Sovereignty From Privacy. In *Empowering Digital Sovereignty* (pp. 1–24). IGI Global Scientific Publishing., DOI: 10.4018/979-8-3693-9137-2.ch001

Pawlicki, M., Pawlicka, A., Kozik, R., & Choraś, M. (2023). The survey and meta-analysis of the attacks, transgressions, countermeasures and security aspects common to the Cloud, Edge and IoT. *Neurocomputing*, *551*, 126533. DOI: 10.1016/j.neucom.2023.126533

Ranaweera, P., Imrith, V. N., Liyanag, M., & Jurcut, A. D. (2020). Security as a Service Platform Leveraging Multi-Access Edge Computing Infrastructure Provisions. *ICC 2020 - 2020 IEEE International Conference on Communications (ICC)*, 1–6. https://doi.org/DOI: 10.1109/ICC40277.2020.9148660

Rullo, A., Midi, D., Mudjerikar, A., & Bertino, E. (2024). Kalis2.0—A SECaaS-Based Context-Aware Self-Adaptive Intrusion Detection System for IoT. *IEEE Internet of Things Journal*, *11*(7), 12579–12601. DOI: 10.1109/JIOT.2023.3333948

Ruohonen, J., & Hjerppe, K. (2022). The GDPR enforcement fines at glance. *Information Systems*, *106*, 101876. DOI: 10.1016/j.is.2021.101876

Sarveshwaran, V., Pandiaraj, S., Bindu, G., Ganesan, V., & Swamidason, I. T. J. (2024). Binarized Spiking Neural Network with blockchain based intrusion detection framework for enhancing privacy and security in cloud computing environment. *Applied Soft Computing*, *154*, 111218. DOI: 10.1016/j.asoc.2023.111218

Settanni, F., Regano, L., Basile, C., & Lioy, A. (2023). A Model for Automated Cybersecurity Threat Remediation and Sharing. *2023 IEEE 9th International Conference on Network Softwarization (NetSoft)*, 492–497. https://doi.org/DOI: 10.1109/NetSoft57336.2023.10175486

Sharma, D. H., Dhote, C. A., & Potey, M. M. (2016). Implementing Intrusion Management as Security-as-a-service from cloud. *2016 International Conference on Computation System and Information Technology for Sustainable Solutions (CSITSS)*, 363–366. https://doi.org/DOI: 10.1109/CSITSS.2016.7779387

Shen, Y., Li, Y., Wu, L., Liu, S., & Wen, Q. (2013). *Security Information and Event Management Implementation Guidance*., DOI: 10.4018/978-1-4666-4801-2.ch005

Shirley, C. P., Thanga Helina, S., Thusita, S., & Okesh, A. (2025). Machine Learning for Cloud Security: A Systematic Review. *Journal of Information Systems Engineering & Management*, *10*(37), 517–529.

Srinadh, V., Swaminathan, B., & Vidyadhari, Ch. (2023). Blockchain-Integrated Advanced Persistent Threat Detection Using Optimized Deep Learning-Enabled Feature Fusion. *Journal of Uncertain Systems*, *16*(03). Advance online publication. DOI: 10.1142/S1752890922500179

Su, L., Bai, W., Zhu, Z., & He, X. (2021). Research on Application of Support Vector Machine in Intrusion Detection. *Journal of Physics: Conference Series, 2037*(1), 012074. DOI: 10.1088/1742-6596/2037/1/012074

Tahri, R., Lasbahani, A., Jarrar, A., & Balouki, Y. (2024). Intelligent Intrusion Detection Using Decision Trees and the NSL-KDD Dataset: An All-Inclusive Method for Cyber Attack Detection. *Journal of Southwest Jiaotong University, 59*(5). Advance online publication. DOI: 10.35741/issn.0258-2724.59.5.13

Talib, A. M., Atan, R., Abdullah, R., & Murad, M. A. A. (2012). Security Facilitation in Collaborative Cloud Data Storage Implementation Environment Based on Multi Agent System Architecture. *Journal of Software Engineering, 6*(3), 49–64. DOI: 10.3923/jse.2012.49.64

Mushtaque Temrekar, Ms. M. (2025). A Comparative Analysis of Global Data Privacy Regulations and Their Implementation by Major Cloud Service Providers. *INTERNATIONAL JOURNAL OF SCIENTIFIC RESEARCH IN ENGINEERING AND MANAGEMENT, 09*(05), 1–9. https://doi.org/DOI: 10.55041/IJSREM46907

Wang, Y., & Shen, J. (2013). CloudProxy: A NAPT Proxy for Vulnerability Scanners based on Cloud Computing. *Journal of Networks, 8*(3). Advance online publication. DOI: 10.4304/jnw.8.3.607-615

Yang, L., Moubayed, A., Hamieh, I., & Shami, A. (2019). Tree-Based Intelligent Intrusion Detection System in Internet of Vehicles. *2019 IEEE Global Communications Conference (GLOBECOM)*, 1–6. https://doi.org/DOI: 10.1109/GLOBECOM38437.2019.9013892

Yuan, H., Xia, Y., Zhang, J., Yang, H., & Mahmoud, M. S. (2020). Stackelberg-Game-Based Defense Analysis Against Advanced Persistent Threats on Cloud Control System. *IEEE Transactions on Industrial Informatics, 16*(3), 1571–1580. DOI: 10.1109/TII.2019.2925035

Zhao, J., Wang, L., Tao, J., Chen, J., Sun, W., Ranjan, R., Kołodziej, J., Streit, A., & Georgakopoulos, D. (2014). A security framework in G-Hadoop for big data computing across distributed Cloud data centres. *Journal of Computer and System Sciences, 80*(5), 994–1007. DOI: 10.1016/j.jcss.2014.02.006

Chapter 10
Solar and Wind Energy in Urban Transformation: Opportunities, Challenges, and Cybersecurity

Tamara Phillips Fudge
https://orcid.org/0000-0002-8682-9711
Purdue University Global, USA

Susan Shepherd Ferebee
https://orcid.org/0000-0002-3616-634X
Purdue University Global, USA

ABSTRACT

Green initiatives regarding energy generation is not just a social topic for debate; it is a necessity for ensuring our planet's future well-being. Both solar and wind energies are renewable sources that are gaining in popularity as replacements for fossil fuels. Along with the opportunities they bring to smart cities lie some issues that will need mitigation, and planning carefully will be crucial. It is useful to understand some history and the basics of current solar and wind technologies, as well as the cybersecurity concerns that can occur with smart grids. Citizen engagement, ethical and legal concerns, and industry standards, plus other options are explored, and a list of recommendations is offered for those who seek to plan a safe, green future for their cities.

DOI: 10.4018/979-8-3373-4455-3.ch010

INTRODUCTION

The limitations and environmental hazards caused by fossil fuels is well known, as is the fact there are alternatives in the form of renewable systems. Exploration of these technologies is prudent as cities realize the dangers of climate change and slowly convert into "smart cities." The need to invest in cybersecurity measures comes with goals for cost savings and other positives. The two most often espoused renewable sources are solar and wind energy; how and where these are constructed, the challenges of implementation, data privacy and other cybersecurity issues, and concerns are presented, as well as brief comparisons to marine and hydropower, geothermal energy, and bioenergy alternatives. Policy writing and other recommendations provide city administrators with a framework to begin the journey towards safe changes.

LITERATURE REVIEW: THE NEED FOR RENEWABLE ENERGY

The environmental benefits of energies that do not pollute air, water, or land are obvious. Fossil fuels and nuclear energy are limited and harm the planet's health (Majumder et al., 2025). Communities that Make use of renewable energy contribute positively to mitigating the effects of climate change (Nidhi et al., 2024). Mahesha et al. (2022) add that countries and communities often rely on imported energies and high, variable expenses, yet still have unstable grids, providing additional reasons for renewable and local energy sources. Smart city goals include the desire for management of natural resources, leading to clean air and a reduced carbon footprint (Mahesha et al, 2022).

There are also social issues to consider. Over a decade ago, Zahnd and Jennings (2012) noted inadequate sanitation in large parts of the world, resulting in billions afflicted by water-related illnesses; providing renewable energy sources can significantly improve health and hygiene and lead to positive community outcomes. Nidhi et al. (2024) use the phrase "energy poverty" to describe urgent needs in developing countries, with implications in completing simple tasks such as cooking, but also in education, healthcare, and even gender equality. Efficient, clean energies are also supportive of lower-income populations and promote economic growth (Mahesha et al., 2022). Renewable energy sources can provide positive changes for whole communities.

The burning of fossil fuels accounts for 66% of the world's electricity and 80% of the total energy production (IEEE Standards, 2024). Mishra et al. (2025) specify 75% of the world's energy resources are used in cities, while those areas are also being most responsible for greenhouse gases and the depletion of already-limited fossil fuels. This necessitates the concept of the "smart city," wherein a combination of technologies and strategies are crafted to provide affordability as well as better environmental quality (Mishra et al., 2025).

The Paris Agreement came about in 2015 as a treaty between 196 nations with the intent to curtail global warming. Nationally Determined Contributions (NDCs) are developed by each country to seek short-term and long-term solutions, share resources and financial assistance, and work towards zero-carbon solutions (United Nations, 2023). The effects of global warming are expected to include a rise in sea level and flooding, loss of most of the world's coral reefs, and other risks that can affect the well-being of living creatures (Stallard & Poynting, 2025). The United States is a leader in planet-warming emissions yet under Donald Trump withdrew from the Agreement in 2021; Joe Biden rejoined in 2021 (Stallard & Poynting, 2025). To worldwide consternation, Trump again withdrew the United States in early 2025; comments from other countries' officials and the scientific community included this is "contrary to scientific evidence" and there are "serious consequences for humanity" (Volcovici et al., 2025, para. 10). Current rules mean the U.S. will not be considered officially out for one year, and notably, the only other countries not included in this agreement are Iran, Libya, and Yemen (Stallard & Poynting, 2025).

Abu-Rayash and Dincer (2021) claim it is technically possible for all of Europe to switch to renewable sources by 2050, but the costs may be 10-15% higher than "business as usual" (p. 1). Majumder et al. (2025) claim 65-85% worldwide use of renewable energies is possible by that time, with solar energy being the leading technology, followed by wind energy. That being said, security issues must be in the forefront before attempting such major changes.

SOLAR ENERGY

A Short History

Making use of the sun for energy is far from a new idea. As early as the 7th century B.C., glass was used to magnify the sun's rays to create fire. For many centuries, various cultures have used south-facing windows or dwellings to capture the best heat; by the late 18th and early 19th centuries, solar cookers aided in food preparation (U.S. Department of Energy, 2004). These can be said to be direct use of sunlight rather than harnessing its potential, however.

In 1839, Edmond Becquerel of France discovered electricity could be generated when light was exposed to electrolytic cells. This phenomenon is known as the "photovoltaic effect." By 1865, Augutin Mouchot's "solar engine," which gathered the heat of the sun in a silver-plated cone-like apparatus with a copper "boiler" in the center, hand-cranked frequently to follow the sun's path, and ultimately resulting in a 140 liters-per-minute flow of steam (Woerlen, n.d.). Mouchot, a French mathematics professor, had expressed his concern that Europe would need alternatives to coal due to its finite availability (Collins, 2002).

John Ericsson, a Swedish-born American inventor, had worked with steam engines and other machinery, most notably designing the majority of the U.S.S. Monitor warship (Collins, 2002). After the Civil War, he devoted his time to inventing solar energy. His "Sun Motor" was invented somewhere around 1868 or thereafter, and was composed of:

> *a cylindrical heater, and a frame supporting a series of reflecting mirrors composed of narrow strips of window-glass coated with silver on the underside. The frame [was] provided with transverse ribs ... accurately bent to a parabolic curvature whose focus coincides with the axis of the cylindrical heater. ... [A] cylindrical heater, as stated, may be attached for generating steam or expanding the gases intended to actuate the piston of the motive engine (Ericsson, 1888, pp. 319-320).*

In the 1870s, selenium was found to be of value in the search for heat and electrical current (U.S. Department of Energy, 2004); this discovery predated its important use in today's solar energy collection.

There were other experiments, inventions, and papers written about solar energy. Notably, Albert Einstein published work and, by 1921, received the Nobel Prize for his work on the photoelectric effect (U.S. Department of Energy, 2004).

The Technology

Energy from the sun can be used for many purposes, including water irrigation pumps, heating and cooling systems, water treatment desalination, LED lighting, and other electrical needs (Majumder et al., 2025). Solar panels are commonly used to collect energy, and are composed of frames with glass covering encapsulated photovoltaic cells and connected to a junction box, which then creates the electrical direct current, sending the energy to an inverter box to transfer into alternating current (Majumder et al., 2025). Marsh (2024) states "A typical residential solar panel with 60 cells combined might produce anywhere from 220 to over 400 watts of power" (para. 8).

Photons are light energy (electromagnetic radiation) emitted by the sun. These massless particles move at the speed of light, and when they hit a semiconductor such as silicon, the activity breaks electrons away from the semiconductor material. This occurs because the side of the silicon facing the barrage of sunlight photons is "doped" with phosphorus, an element with an extra electron in comparison to the silicon and willing to discharge the extraneous electron; the other side is doped with boron, which has one less electron and thus provides a balance. The resulting electrical flow works much like a traditional battery with positive and negative poles; the electrons move towards the negative end, thus creating a flow of electricity that can be harnessed ("How does a photovoltaic cell," 2024). An anti-reflective coating prevents photons from bouncing off the cell (Marsh, 2024). There are additional photovoltaic cell creation methods, but Marsh (2024) indicates silicon is the most common. Cells might be monocrystalline (made from one crystal) or polycrystalline, which is made from melting multiple pieces of silicon. The former is considered higher quality but more expensive (Marsh, 2024). Figure 1 below shows panels are easily carried by installers, although great care must be taken to ensure there is no damage during installation.

Figure 1. Solar panel held by a worker

("A person," 2021)

Panels can be attached to roofs, walls, signposts, open park coverings, or fields. They can be slanted at an angle that, according to Majumder et al. (2025), should match the site's latitude for the best sun pathways.

During roof construction or reroofing, a building's air venting system can make a difference in the placement of solar panels. Ridge vents are placed at the peaks of sloping roofs to allow air to flow fully upward before being expelled; this allows most of the roof to be free for attaching solar panels. Box vents, also called turtle vents or louvres, are square or round, a few inches thick, and placed towards the top of a sloping roof but not at the apex (Johnson, 2023; Ragan, 2025). Since multiple box vents are needed to allow for sufficient attic cooling, this can limit the space needed for solar panel placement. There are additional types of vents such as turbine vents (sometimes called whirlybirds) which are shaped like a chef's hat and make use of wind to remove excessive heat, soffit vents that allow for lower intake of air, and options that use solar or other power to pull heat from under the roof. These are less often employed or may be used in combination with other methods (Johnson, 2023; Ragan, 2025). In Figure 2, both box and ridge vents are present on a rooftop; note placement of the solar panels is partially determined by the open roof space.

Figure 2. Rooftop solar panel installation

(Wilde, 2018)

Additional implementations of solar energy panels are shown in the next several figures. Stand-alone panels can be used to power street lights, radar speed signs, and flashing warning lights around stop signs that might otherwise be ignored by drivers. Large installations in car parks make active use of real estate while also keeping vehicles cooler and protected somewhat from the elements.

Figure 3. Stand-alone solar panel to power public lighting – and Solar-powered radar speed warning sign

(Недвига, 2017 and Dwernertl, 2007)

Figure 4. 1365 solar panels covering a second-floor parking area, KONE building in Moline, IL

(Fudge, 2025a)

Figure 5. Closeup of solar panels above parking area, KONE building

(Fudge, 2025b)

Rectangular panels are not the only design available. The Smartflower is made up of "petals" (like pie-shaped pieces); it fans open during morning hours and then repositions throughout the day to follow the sun, closing the petals again at sunset (Mack & Blok, 2023). Both residential and commercial consumers can use this system; while considered more costly than other installations and warranties are limited, Mack and Blok (2023) claim it generates "up to 40% more energy than typical fixed solar panels" (para. 5).

In spring of 2025, the University of California at Merced launched its Project Nexus: solar panels were placed over irrigation canals at Turlock in a bid to generate electricity also using already-developed land; scientists estimate 2 million homes might be powered in this way if most of the 4000 miles of irrigation canals in California were similarly managed (Guerra, 2025). In addition to the electrical benefits, Guerra (2025) notes that covering theses canals is expected to reduce algae and weed growth and keep the water at a cool temperature, thus helping to conserve precious water resources.

Solar energy can be harnessed for rail travel as well. Australia's Byron Bay Railroad placed panels on top of its refurbished vintage train and its barn; this provides about 1/4 of the energy needed to run the train, with the rest supplied by a "green energy provider" ("Sustainability," 2025, para. 2).

A distinctly different method of collecting sunlight energy is the solar pond, a shallow water basin in which salt is added. Kumar and Pal (2025) explain the concentration of salt works in layers, with the heaviest settling at the bottom. As the water is warmed by sunlight, the heat collects in the top layer and, via conduction, transfers heat to the bottom layer, known as the storage zone. Steam turbines and heat pumps can be used to extract the energy (Kumar & Pal, 2025). Drawbacks include the need for fresh water and a substantial amount of salt needing replenishing on a constant basis, but a benefit is that copper, iron, and other metals can be extracted along with the brine (Janusz-Szymańska et al., 2025).

There is also a method called Concentrated Solar Power (CSP), in which mirrors are used in towers, troughs, or dishes to maximize the heat caused by sunlight. At this point, the heat is converted into steam and usable energy (Majumder et al., 2025). Point-focused receptors include towers and dishes and use dual-axis tracking and refocus them into a single point, whereas linear-focused receptors such as parabolic troughs or Fresnel reflectors use single-axis tracking (Magalhães et al., 2025). Depending on the receptor, the sunlight may be directed to heating a synthetic oil or may more directly generate steam; Magalhães et al. (2025) indicate the robustness of the energy gathering finds use in industrial application.

Benefits and Drawbacks

Over recent years, solar energy storage has significantly improved. It has proven to be easily scaled, requires less infrastructure, and panels can be installed nearly anywhere (Majumder et al., 2025) as illustrated by the figures above.

One drawback of photovoltaic solar energy is the visual aspect of the panels; they might be said to distract from the aesthetics of the locale. Geospatial planning for where each type of energy is to be installed is important to meet the varied demands within a city (Ihsan et al., 2021). Another issue is that panels can degrade over time, necessitating replacement, and disposing of replaced panels can be environmentally unfriendly (Majumder et al., 2025). CSP systems do not operate as well on cloudy days and need substantial space; this is also more expensive than photovoltaic collection (Majumder et al., 2025). In developing countries, it may also be difficult to find skilled technologists who understand proper implementation (Nidhi et al., 2024).

Perhaps one of the most concerning drawbacks, however, is initial financing. Modernizing outdated energy infrastructures and ensuring grid stability are costly but crucial steps. A half century ago, McGarity (1977) explained a high initial cost can be balanced by low lifetime operating costs; a "life-cycle cost analysis" should figure costs over time, but is difficult because both fuel and maintenance costs tend to rise each year (p. 11). It should be noted Abu-Rayash and Dincer (2021) claim operational costs and maintenance in today's energy systems may be decreasing; this does not, however, reduce the need for analysis, the results of which may allay the reluctance of communities to espouse renewable energies.

Additional cost-related challenges for individual businesses and homeowners include the following:

- Professional installation is important; self-installation by the homeowner may nullify warranties;
- Some tax incentive programs only apply to new installations; buying a home that already has solar panels may not qualify;
- When a roof's shingles must be replaced, the panels must be removed first and then reinstalled;
- In locations where rainfall is insufficient to keep solar panels clean, an installer will need to be engaged (McMillin, 2022).

Smart cities must effectively use connectivity to manage lighting adjustments and other consumption, which can then minimize costs (Nidhi et al., 2024). Load sharing also can reduce costs (Abu-Rayash & Dincer, 2021) but must be configured well.

While this technology only gathers energy when the sun shines, combining solar with other technologies and well-designed storage systems still makes it worthwhile (Abu-Rayash & Dincer, 2021). Majumder et al. (2025) agree diversification of energy supplies is recommended, as this aids in stability.

WIND ENERGY

A Short History

Civilizations have used wind energy for thousands of years. The earliest known wind-powered machines date back to around 200 BC, when vertical-axis windmills were used in Persia to power water pumps and grain grinders. These early devices featured sails mounted on a vertical shaft and were primarily used in agricultural settings (Manwell et al., 2009).

By the 12th century, horizontal-axis windmills were common in Europe, quite notably in the Netherlands. These mills were more efficient and allowed for improved mechanical applications, such as draining wetlands and grinding grain. The Dutch refined windmill technology by introducing innovations such as adjustable sails and rotatable caps, which allowed the mills to face the wind (Gipe, 2004).

The late 19th and early 20th centuries witnessed the application of wind energy to electricity generation. In 1887, Scottish academic James Blyth built one of the first wind turbines to generate electricity for his home. Around the same time, Charles F. Brush in the United States constructed a large windmill to power his mansion in Cleveland, Ohio (Shahan, 2014). The image below shows an unusual design on top of a horse barn on a northwestern Illinois farm in 1910; the power generated by the windmill was used to grind corn on George R. Smith's farm.

Figure 6. Unusual Windmill, 1910, Geneseo IL

(Geneseo Public Library, 2025)

During the oil crisis in the 1970s, the modern era of wind energy began with governments and researchers investing in renewable energy. Denmark became a pioneer in wind energy, developing the first grid-connected turbines and initiating large-scale commercial production. By the early 2000s, wind energy had become a significant contributor to national energy portfolios in countries such as Germany, Spain, and the United States (Timmons et al., 2024).

Today, both onshore and offshore installations are expanding rapidly due to technological advancements, cost reductions, and climate policies. Wind power is now a cornerstone of the global transition to renewable energy.

The Technology

Wind turbine blades are key factors in converting the wind's kinetic energy into electricity. Turbine blades are affected by four pressures: lift, gravitational, drag, and centrifugal. Drag force is due to air molecules that come in contact with the blade facing the wind, and the size of the force varies based on the size of the blade and wind speed. Lift force occurs when wind passes over the blade, causing pressure differences between the back and front sides of the blade—the extent of the lift force changes with the size and shape of the blade and wind speed. Lift and drag pressures are perpendicular to one another. Each particle inside a blade changes direction and velocity as the rotor turns, causing the particle to accelerate toward the axis around which the blade is spinning. This is the centrifugal force in a radial direction which means it extends out from a central point. The fourth force is gravitational and this relies on the blades' size, shape, and density. The gravitational force is always toward the Earth's center so it varies continuously as the blade spins (Duval, 2024).

Figure 7. Wind Turbines Blade Forces

(Wind Turbine Professor, 2022)

While the horizontal-axis turbine is the most commonly in use, there are other designs as well, including vertical-axis machines which look like a kitchen eggbeater (U.S. Energy Information Administration, 2023b). There are also bladeless turbines that make use of vortex-induced vibration (VIV) technology with a horizontal cylindrical shape, however, exact positioning to take advantage of natural frequencies, drag, and centrifugal forces is needed for best performance (Mohammed et al., 2025).

The rapid evolution of wind energy technologies since 2021 has resulted in four categories of technology development: 1) novel turbine and blade designs, 2) advanced turbine materials, 3) wind energy storage development, and 4) the integration of wind energy with smart grid systems.

Novel blade designs have significantly advanced wind energy capability. Innovations in aerodynamic optimization, morphing mechanisms, alternative rotor configurations, and advances in blade profiles, active flow control, and adaptive blades with embedded sensors have enhanced efficiency, reduced loads, and improved noise attributes (Firoozi et al., 2024). Deformable blades that change their shape or size in response to external forces contribute to alleviating loads and improving power (Jauregui-Correa & Duran-Carillo, 2022). Two-bladed, dual-rotor, and vertical-axis turbines are being examined for their contribution to aerodynamic and performance trade-offs (Chen et al., 2025). Bio-inspired modifications, including nature-derived blade features such as tubercles and serrated trailing edges, contribute to improved performance and reduced noise (Omidvarnia & Sarhadi, 2024).

The transition from traditional composites toward advanced, non-enhanced, and sustainable materials, such as the adoption of carbon and glass fiber reinforced polymers, nanomaterials, and recyclable thermoplastics in turbine blades to improve mechanical performance, durability, recyclability, and life-cycle environmental impact, are significant advances for implementing wind energy systems and wind farms (Firoozi et al., 2024). Smart materials for real-time structural health monitoring and predictive maintenance are also emerging turbine material technologies (Tolasa & Furi, 2025).

The integration of wind energy with advanced storage solutions is crucial to advancing wind energy. Dhar and Chakraborty (2021) describe hybrid storage systems that combine technologies such as pumped storage hydroelectricity and vanadium redox flow batteries, co-located with wind turbines, to provide voltage stabilization and uninterrupted output in microgrid scenarios. Yu et al. (2022) found pumped hydro storage of wind energy is the most promising. This method is effected during times of low demand, and pumps water from a lower-level reservoir to one on higher elevation, then releasing it back down to the lower reservoir through turbines to generate electricity when the demand is high, essentially acting as a water battery, storing energy in the potential energy of the water at a higher elevation. Pumped storage hydropower is the world's largest battery technology, accounting for over 94% of the world's long-duration energy storage capacity (International Hydropower Association, 2022). A vanadium redox flow battery (VRB)uses vanadium ions, which act as both positive and negative electrodes, as the charge carrier (Knight, 2014).

In integrating wind energy with smart grids, digital twins —a virtual representation of a physical object, system, or process that updates in real-time —enable real-time monitoring, predictive analytics, and automated operational adjustments based on sensor data (Siddiqui et al., 2023). Machine learning enhances hub-height wind forecasting, which is crucial for routine operation and black start contexts (Hugeback et al., 2023). IoT-enabled controls, AI-driven diagnostics, and secure data communication are important to integrating wind turbines with smart grids (Madeswaran et al., 2024).

Turbines might be single for small projects but in "farms" for larger areas, including smart cities. Figures 8 and 9 illustrate two implementations; while they are not in urban areas, they can still be used to deliver energy to cities.

Figure 8. Wind farm in a wheat field

(Sjödin, 2018)

Figure 9. Offshore wind farm

(Enrique, 2022)

A recent and resourceful installation of small wind turbines at Dallas Love Field airport takes advantage of the powerful wind generated by airplanes as they depart from the tarmac (Romeo, 2025).

Benefits and Drawbacks

As global electricity systems decarbonize, onshore wind energy has become a central pillar of sustainable power supply, offering rapid deployment, modular scalability, and near-zero marginal emissions. However, its expansion at both small and large scales provokes ongoing debate around its ecological footprint, contributions to energy security, and the technical challenges of integration with power grids across diverse contexts (Uktamova, 2024).

As with solar energy, wind energy is also abundant, freely available, and does not produce dangerous pollutants. The land used for wind turbines can simultaneously be used for agriculture or other offshore activities. Wind turbine electricity is alternating current (AC), so it can easily be connected to existing AC grids. Wind generators can be placed closer to consumers to minimize power transmission loss (Nartowska & Rozenvalde, 2023). However, with all of the benefits of wind energy, there are also downsides.

Wind energy, again like solar energy, has storage limitations. Additionally, accurate wind forecasts are necessary to ensure continuous, reliable energy production, but forecast accuracy is imperfect. The up-front cost of initiating wind energy implementation and research is high, as are maintenance costs for the wind energy systems. Wind farms are detrimental to wildlife, particularly birds, and both noise and the flickering effect of the spinning wind turbine blades negatively impact individuals near the systems (Nartowska & Rozenvalde, 2023). Energy storage limitations are one of the most significant drawbacks of wind energy.

CONCERNS

Cybersecurity Issues

Ekechukwu and Simpa (2024) state “despite the existence of standards and protocols aimed at safeguarding these systems, the rapid evolution of cyber threats and the fragmented nature of existing standards pose significant challenge” (p. 1266). Indeed, renewable energies require a different infrastructure than traditional energy sources, as the “smart grid” relies on interconnectedness. The use of smart technology thus makes these grids prone to cyberattacks, which can affect energy supply and distribution, data security, and physical components (Ekechukwu & Simpa, 2024). While solar panels themselves are passive, solar power plant inverters, monitoring/recording devices, battery storage systems, and communication channels are especially prone to attack (Ledmaoui et al., 2025). The recent use of Artificial Intelligence for monitoring and control makes the chance of a threat much greater (Călin et al., 2024). Much of the problem is the use of wireless and cloud connections and the quick growth of the industry. Farrell and Dullea (2025) claim a 70% increase during 2024 for solar energy cyberattacks.

Reasons for energy hacking incidents vary, as they do with any cyberattack. Ukraine experienced an attack wherein administrative privileges were accessed; “cascading system-wide failures” ensued (Ledmaoui et al., 2025). Malware was injected into Ukraine's electrical grid, and the hackers were able to control circuit breakers to effect widespread power outages – plus they used a Denial of Service attack to prevent communication with customers (Rekeraho et al., 2025). In April 2024, a solar plant attack was perpetrated by Russia; this attack may have been unexpected, as the previous targets had typically been hydroelectric and thermal plants. A wind turbine was destroyed earlier that year by drones rather than cyberattack (Sanderson, 2024); however, this demonstrates additional vulnerabilities plus the fact a combination of methods was generating power.

In 2019, hackers were able to bypass a firewall and instigate a denial-of-service (DoS) attack on a solar energy station that affected several areas in the United States (Farrell & Dullea, 2025). Insertion of false measurements can affect data integrity and performance, and electrical surges could thwart the system physically (Călin et al., 2024). Brute force and man-in-the-middle attacks, delays in providing energy, and other issues can be caused by backdoor access, cross-site scripting, and other hacking means (Călin et al., 2024). Replay attacks in which real data is either delayed or repeated are possible; another concern is hardware being physically stricken (Rekeraho et al., 2024).

Firewalls, wireless connections, and poor configurations are not the only problems for solar energy cybersecurity. A recent report indicates inverters made in China were said to have nearly four dozen vulnerabilities that would allow hackers to inject malicious code or at least access equipment and Personal Identifiable Information (PII) data (Geller, 2025). Johnson et al. (2023) also mention the potential loss of financial data, damage to equipment, and loss of consumer trust.

Forescout Research – Vedere Labs (2025) report that nearly 35 thousand solar power devices worldwide have been exposed to hackers, and of these, 76% are found in Europe, 17% in Asia, and much smaller percentages in other continents. This might reflect the market share of manufacturers, who share responsibilities for cybersecurity. According to SMA Sunny WebBox devices were discontinued a decade ago but are still in use in many places; they "have always been among the most often exposed solar devices," (Forescout Research – Vedere Labs, para. 19).

In the past ten years, cyberattacks have impacted wind energy organizations in at least seven countries: the United States, Germany, Azerbaijan, Denmark, India, China, and Ukraine. Wind energy systems are increasingly vulnerable to cyberattacks because of the reliance on networked digital devices and remote monitoring and control. In addition, legacy technologies are often part of the networked systems. Proactive threat detection, robust security policies, and industry collaboration are necessary for improved cybersecurity (U.S. Department of Energy, 2024). A recent article points to recent discovery of covert communication devices being found in inverters manufactured in China (Pan, 2025). Pan (2025) explains these devices could potentially modify settings or cause shutdowns, thus enabling damage and interruption of power grids; however, a Chinese spokesperson denied any malicious intent and the U.S. Department of Energy acknowledges "challenges with … documenting functionalities of emerging technologies" (para. 6).

Virtual replication of energy systems (digital twin technology or DT) allows for monitoring in real time, predicting maintenance provisions, and analysis of security needs (Ba et al., 2025). DTs are composed of the physical system, a virtual counterpart, a communication system, and shared data; the virtual counterpart can be used for what-if scenarios, imitate machine and system behavior, and are synchronized with the system's actual physical assets. Ba et al. (2025) assert energy savings could be as much as 30% by use of this technology.

Ledmaoui et al. (2025) remind that cybersecurity measures also contribute to power plant financial stability. Monitoring in real time allows for efficiency and lessens the chance for threats (Ekechukwu & Simpa, 2024).

Smart Grid Cybersecurity

As urban environments continue evolving into highly connected ecosystems, the smart grid stands at the core of modern energy infrastructure. Designed to deliver solar and wind-generated electricity more efficiently, these advanced grids depend on digital communications, automation, and interconnected devices. While the benefits are substantial, this digital transformation introduces a complex web of cybersecurity challenges.

The Expanding Attack Surface

Smart grids, in contrast to traditional power grids, use distributed generation systems, real-time data exchange, and bi-directional communication. This means thousands of smart meters, SCADA (Supervisory Control and Data Acquisition) systems, intelligent electronic devices (IEDs), and IoT-based components now participate in energy distribution, monitoring, and feedback loops (Sridhar et al., 2012). Each endpoint increases the system's vulnerability, creating multiple vectors for cyber intrusion.

Smart meters report usage in real-time, and can be manipulated to falsify billing, overload transformers, or even serve as botnet access points. The use of insecure wireless communication protocols or outdated firmware further amplifies risk. Attackers targeting smart grids may aim to manipulate data, disrupt services, or even cause physical damage, particularly when they gain remote access to substations or power generation controls.

Common Threats in Smart Grid Systems

Smart grids face an array of cyber threats that target both data integrity and physical infrastructure. Some common threats include those in table 1 below.

Table 1. Typical Cyber Attacks

Name of attack	Definition
Denial of Service (DoS) Attacks	Overwhelming the target with excessive traffic, the system crashes or becomes slow and unresponsive. This can disrupt the flow of critical data needed to manage power distribution (CISA, 2021).
Man-in-the-Middle (MitM) Attacks	Unauthorized parties may intercept data transmissions, allowing them to alter commands or harvest sensitive information (Lindemulder & Kosinski, 2024).
Insertion of Rogue Devices	In some reported cases, compromised or counterfeit hardware has been used to bypass regular security checks and introduce malicious code into the grid (Pan, 2025).

Additionally, social engineering attacks and ransomware attacks against utility organizations and personnel continue to be an underestimated threat vector, especially in environments where cybersecurity training is inconsistent (Beeman, 2025).

Defense Strategies: A Layered Approach

An effective approach to smart grid cybersecurity emphasizes multiple layers of protection rather than relying on a single solution. Common strategies include those explained in table 2.

Table 2. Common Cyber Strategies

Strategy	Definition
Segmenting networks	Separating critical operational systems from general IT networks can prevent attackers from moving freely once inside.
Encryption and strong authentication	Securing communication channels and requiring multiple forms of identity verification helps ensure only authorized users gain access.
Device hardening	This involves configuring all equipment to minimize vulnerabilities, keeping firmware up to date, and disabling unnecessary features.
Intrusion Detection Systems (IDS)	These tools monitor network activity for suspicious behavior and can alert operators to potential breaches.
Automated security policies	Using policy-as-code techniques allows organizations to consistently apply rules across all devices and systems, reducing the chance of misconfiguration
Advanced threat detection	Applying machine learning to create robust AI threat-detection models is encouraged

Ideas from ("Smart grid," 2025)

The real-world implementation of these techniques is often hindered by budgetary constraints, a lack of technical expertise, and fragmented vendor ecosystems. Therefore, ongoing cross-sector collaboration is crucial to ensure interoperability, effective sharing of threat intelligence, and seamless coordination of responses (Fourrage, 2024).

Smart Grid Use Cases

Barcelona, Spain. Barcelona integrates its smart energy initiatives with urban mobility, water systems, and waste management through its "Urban Platform" infrastructure. The city employs a municipal data network to monitor energy consumption patterns in real time, adjusting lighting, HVAC, and water usage based on demand. Security is enhanced through a centralized monitoring center that oversees all smart infrastructure, incorporating anomaly detection tools and strict data encryption protocols (Aragón et al., 2017).

Singapore. Singapore has developed one of the most advanced smart grid initiatives in Asia. The city-state's Intelligent Energy System (IES) pilot incorporates advanced metering infrastructure, AI-driven demand forecasting, and predictive maintenance for grid assets. Cybersecurity is woven into the foundation through compliance with the Cybersecurity Code of Practice for Critical Information Infrastructure, alongside continuous stress testing and cyber drills ("Smart nation," 2023).

Copenhagen, Denmark. Copenhagen has made substantial strides in aligning renewable energy with smart grid development. The city uses integrated wind and solar generation, real-time grid monitoring, and electric vehicle (EV) charging networks. Security policies are enforced through Denmark's national cyber strategy, which mandates cybersecurity audits, supply chain assessments, and multi-sectoral coordination (Petrea & Ursache, 2023).

These examples illustrate how cities with varying geographies and governance structures are approaching the dual challenge of energy optimization and cyber resilience. They underscore the need for adaptive solutions tailored to local context, while reinforcing the global importance of cybersecurity in the smart grid era. Smart grids represent the future of energy, but with greater efficiency comes greater responsibility. By adopting a proactive, layered approach to cybersecurity, cities can better protect their critical infrastructure and maintain public trust.

Citizen Engagement and Digital Trust

Effective smart city initiatives depend not only on technological innovation but also on cultivating public trust and ensuring genuine citizen participation. As urban ecosystems collect and manage vast amounts of personal and community-generated data, engaging citizens meaningfully becomes a cornerstone of sustainable and ethical governance.

Cities like Barcelona have pioneered platforms which allow citizens to drive key decisions and control their data. Through Decidim, residents can propose, debate, and vote on municipal policies—70% of proposals come directly from citizens, with over 40,000 participants (Aragón et al., 2017). Additionally, Barcelona's DECODE project enables residents to manage IoT data (e.g., air quality sensors) through privacy-respecting tools, giving them control over what is shared and with whom. Transparent data practices are essential. Reports emphasize smart city deployments must embed security and privacy from the outset, rather than leaving them as afterthoughts (Calleja-López, 2019). Technologies like Barcelona's Sentilo, enhanced with AI, help surface meaningful, localized insights for citizens, reinforcing trust through visible, interactive dashboards.

Artificial Intelligence can scale citizen interactions. In Singapore's Smart Nation initiative, AI-driven chatbots and analytics offer real-time feedback on policies and services, making civic engagement more responsive and inclusive. However, the system also includes governance measures, such as digital identity frameworks and strict data sharing regulations, to limit surveillance risks ("Smart nation," 2023).

Research highlights that if trust and usability are not prioritized, smart city tools may fail to engage all residents equally. Adoption can vary significantly across neighborhoods due to disparities in digital literacy and concerns about privacy. Inclusive design strategies, such as multilingual interfaces, low-data mobile access, and offline engagement options, are essential to ensure equity and broad acceptance (van Zoonen, 2016).

Ethical and Legal Issues – and Standards

In addition to cyber problems, there are humanitarian concerns related to solar energy. For example, 95% of solar modules use polysilicon, and the Uyghur Region of China supplies nearly half of it; forced labor is said to be employed (Webb, 2022). Current employment in traditional energy sourcing could well mean loss of job, and costs of setting up renewables can be prohibitive in some communities, thus creating a social disparity (Tabibi, 2024). Solar energy fields in an agricultural area can cause land use disputes, and wildlife could be displaced (Tabibi, 2024).

Key ethical issues relating to wind energy include killing birds and bats, disrupting the peaceful and aesthetic use of the environment due to noise, flickering blades, and disrupting views. However, it can be argued these impacts are far less than the impacts of climate change and continued use of fossil fuels (Brown, 2012). Citizens in Idaho became concerned about the red lights on wind turbines creating light pollution at night; the lights are meant to help aircraft see potential obstructions but annoy residents. A law has been passed to instead use technology such as an Aircraft Detection Lighting System (ADLS) which only lights up when aircraft are within a designated zone (Hart, 2025).

Wind turbines can interfere with nearby military radar systems due to the inability of radar to filter out blade movement when surveilling for incoming missiles or enemy aircraft. In June 2025, wind farms being developed in the Irish Sea are causing this interference with Warton Aerodrome systems and mitigations are still in development (Sanderson, 2025).

There are three legal factors to consider in wind energy development: property rights, permissions, and taxes (property tax, generation tax, and sales tax). In terms of property rights, for example, mineral rights prevail over wind energy rights. An additional property right is eminent domain, the right to seize land for a public use such as electricity, water, and other power (Iowa State University, 2011). It must also be said that wind energy, like many commodities worldwide, is subject to the challenges of tariffs, which have been greatly increased in the current year (Bath, 2025).

IEEE Standards (2024) notes power grids are beginning a trend of decentralizing; instead of all energy coming from major power plants, there are also microgrids and other such structures. These require intense management so that power can be stored and distributed as needed. This means aggregation software is necessary for management, and circuit breakers and switches are needed to control the flow. Redundancy, which is the ability of one microgrid to be able to take over for another in an emergency, is an excellent feature of smart grids. The complexity of these systems do mean security is a primary concern, however (IEEE Standards, 2024). A search of the IEEE website reveals many standards that apply to solar, wind, and other smart energy systems, their digital twins, and more.

As of mid-2024, eighteen U.S. states and the District of Columbia adopted a Renewable Portfolio Standard requiring renewable energies comprise a certain percentage of the electricity used in those locations; eight states have a Clean Energy Standard which requires low-carbon emissions, and three states (Colorado, North Carolina, and Oregon) have set deadlines for "carbon neutrality" (Center for Climate and Energy Solutions, 2024).

The International Organization for Standardization (ISO) also published their standard 37120 in which requirements, recommendations, permissions, possibilities, and methodologies are outlined (International Organization for Standardization, 2018). The standard includes far more than just energy needs, but specifies items relating to climate change, energy consumption per capita, renewable energies, service interruptions, etc. (International Organization for Standardization, 2018).

Threats are real; according to Beetroot software company, "90% of the world's largest energy companies suffered a cybersecurity breach" in 2023, and this would include solar and wind companies ("Securing renewable data," 2025, para. 2). The main challenges for green technology options according to Beetroot help to summarize the importance of a multi-faceted approach:

- Infrastructure and attack surface: the energy collection devices for solar and wind energy are typically spread over large areas. They require many devices and sensors, all at risk.
- Systems architecture: the cloud and other internet connections provide risk.
- Standards and regulation: Inconsistencies in current standards, and small installations might not be following security protocols.
- Operational complexity: Coordination of remote controls, a wide variety of stakeholders, and other connections are complicated.
- Threat profile: hacking, ransomware, and threats from state actors must be considered.

(“Securing renewable data,” 2025)

POLICY WRITING AND RECOMMENDATIONS

Writing policies for clean energy solutions involves the need for accurate information to be used in basing decisions about the causal effects of changes, which may affect not just emissions, but public health, employment, and other consequences (Aldy, 2022). Aldy (2022) explains evaluative plans must be put in place at the very beginning of this venture; trust begins at the design stage, and most notably, “iterative improvements in policy over time” need to be included (p. 4).

Resources, time, initial funding, tax credits/expectations, economic changes anticipated over time, and meeting regulatory requirements must all be considered (Aldy, 2022). In understanding the latter, Omri and Boubaker (2024) claim “governments with higher control of corruption are more effective at enacting and executing laws and regulations dealing with environmental challenges which help achieve desirable environmental outcomes” (Abstract). The so-called Paris Agreement was an outgrowth of a United Nations conference in 1992; this led to Agenda 21 and the Kyoto Protocol, the latter of which was rejected by the United States so by 2009, a conference in Copenhagen was still working through details. Finally the 2015 conference in Paris found a commitment to measures against global warming (Omri & Boubaker, 2024).

Nidhi et al. (2024) mention “inconsistent regulations, bureaucratic barriers, and a lack of clear incentives” are major obstacles (p. 2). Gautam et al. (2024) include the idea of tax credits as an incentive.

A cybersecurity policy is not a simple task. Johnson et al. (2023) from the North American Electric Reliability Corporation recommend formal documentation of every step with solar energy implementation, including quality assurance during manufacturing, inspection, encryption, monitoring, physical security, and all other steps in planning, set-up, and use of hardware, software, and services. It is also recommended personnel be assigned to specific tasks, suitable training be developed and conducted, threat profiles be determined, and all processes be reviewed regularly (Johnson et al., 2023).

Recommendations include:

- Develop and maintain complete documentation of all aspects of the project from the onset, along with ongoing updates (Johnson et al., 2023).
- Ensure firewalls, network segmentation, and other cybersecure actions are made as expected for computer networks such as insisting on unique credentialling of all allowed persons (Johnson et al., 2023).
- Generate and enforce encryption of all data (Johnson et al., 2023).
- Employ a Digital Twin for real-time monitoring as well as issue monitoring (Ba et al., 2025).
- Identify physical security issues and develop rules (Johnson et al., 2023).
- Inspect all hardware as it arrives from vendors (Johnson et al., 2023). It would also be prudent to ensure at that time all purchases of hardware, software, and services meet industry standards.
- Appraise cloud services, sensors, nodes, and gateways as vulnerabilities (Rekeraho et al., 2025).
- Focus threat and risk modeling for Internet of Things systems (Rekeraho et al., 2025) and include predictive performance and maintenance solutions (Ledmaoui et al., 2025).
- Consider use of Machine Learning and Artificial Intelligence for detecting threats (Ekechukwu & Simpa, 2024) but balance with the knowledge of the limitations of such algorithms (Călin et al., 2024).
- Employ a battery of tools such as vulnerability assessment, behavior analysis, anomaly detection, and other detection and management tools (Rekeraho et al., 2024).
- Create and update "golden images" as a baseline to compare against any suspected alterations (Johnson et al., 2023).
- Establish a Security Operations Center, along with designating personnel who are tasked with security; include backup designees (Johnson et al., 2023).
- Devise robust training (Zahnd & Jennings, 2012; Johnson et al., 2023).
- Write policies to share with the public (Johnson et al., 2023).

ADDITIONAL RENEWABLE ALTERNATIVES

Over a decade ago, a hybrid photovoltaic turbine was developed in the United Kingdom, but the issues seem to outweigh any advantages: light emanating from the moving solar panels could potentially affect pilots in the area and it was worried the intense heat could cause fires on the ground. This might be mitigated by use of tinting on the glass enveloping the solar panels (Singh, 2013), but it appears the hybrid is not in common use today.

Solar and wind energy can be implemented almost anywhere, but alternatives must be mentioned, as each option could be used in conjunction with other energy supplies. Rogers et al. (2016) warn the market for energies can be volatile and quite competitive, which further indicates the need to explore various possibilities. Ember Energy in the U.S. announced 17% of the country's electricity in 2024 was generated by solar and wind systems, surpassing coal which dropped to 15% (Jones et al., 2025). Natural gas is still the top producer. Nuclear power has been consistent but should soon be overtaken by solar and wind if trends continue. Hydro and other generation methods generate the least amount of energy but have been mostly consistent in the last two decades (Jones et al., 2025).

The volatility of nuclear power plants makes them less attractive as alternatives. In addition to the well-publicized errors at Three Mile Island in Pennsylvania in 1979, other plants have had similar issues. A series of human errors, for example, occurred in 2023 at the Cordova, IL plant, where coolant needed to keep fuel rods at a safe temperature drained too quickly during maintenance, causing workers to be "soaked in radioactive coolant" and then they were not "appropriately decontaminated" (Christensen, 2025, para. 7). While a major disaster was averted, the Nuclear Regulatory Commission has been investigating a cover-up of the incident (Christensen, 2025). In May of 2025, an electrical power loss triggered coolant draining again; the reactor unit was shut down quickly and an outdoor battery was blamed, which three days later started a fire. In this case, employees were said to handle the situation per protocol (Franz, 2025). These situations point to various vulnerabilities of nuclear power generation, which include human error as well as physical threats and sabotage. While cyberattacks on these facilities are possible, the World Nuclear Association (2025) states that fortunately at this time, "no cyber-attack on a nuclear reactor's information and control system has compromised safety" (para. 2).

Hydropower or marine power uses the force of ocean or river waves to generate usable energy. This hydrokinetic energy can be captured by buoys placed in large bodies of water or turbines (U.S. Energy Information Administration, 2023a). In hydroelectric plants, energy is harnessed as water falls from an elevated location, such as a dam, then flows through a penstock to cause a turbine to rotate (Kumar & Pal, 2025). This kind of energy is consistent, and access to oceans and other bodies of water is a worldwide asset; more than half of the population of the United States, for example, lives 50 miles or less from a coast (U.S. Energy Information Administration, 2023a). Hoover Dam is a prime example of an hydroelectric power plant; constructed in 1931-36, it provides power to parts of Nevada and Arizona, provides water for irrigation of 2 million acres of land as well as communities far away (including Los Angeles), assists with previous issues of flooding (National Park Service, 2018). Mai et al. (2025) indicate that "phasor measurement units and area control error channels" are especially vulnerable to cyberattack, and Denial of Service and other attacks are not uncommon (p. 1).

Geothermal power is where energy is collected from heat trapped below the Earth's surface thanks to the "slow decay of radioactive particles in the earth's core" (U.S. Energy Information Administration, 2022, para. 2). Deep loops are dug into the ground for pumps to pull heat; warm and cool water are then sent from the energy station through pipes to end-users (U.S. Department of Energy, n.d.b.). This kind of energy sourcing can often be directed to the intended use without conversion. Since this involves drilling deep into the earth to extract hot water or steam, there can be environmental impacts such as groundwater contamination. Despite the shortcomings, the operating costs of geothermal power plants tend to be low (Kumar & Pal, 2025). Cybersecurity issues might include many of the same problems encountered by other energies: data breaches due to hacking, unauthorized access to the system, the need for constant threat monitoring and compliance checks, and plans for response and recovery ("Geothermal energy cyber security," 2024).

Bioenergy converts organic resources, known as biomass, from plants such as corn and algae-based materials into a liquid form, such as ethanol and biodiesel, that can replace or supplement fossil-based fuels. In addition to the conversion into liquid form, biomass can be converted to energy through burning or bacterial decay; this industry can also create new plastics and other chemical products (U.S. Department of Energy, n.d.a.). The supply of biomass needs to be of high quality and may include vegetable and other oils, wood waste, and both forestry and agricultural residues; in addition to transportation fuels, the output can include wood pellets and heating oils (Rogers et al., 2016). Notably, it is said that developing countries may have better access to biomass due to climate and labor costs; this indicates international trade possibilities (Zahnd & Jennings, 2012). Menghwani et al. (2024) note that inconsistencies in cross-jurisdictional policies can be a problem.

There are many possibilities afforded by these options, including the Organic Rankine Cycle, a method for converting low thermal energy from solar, biomass, geothermal, and other sources (Matuszewska, 2024). This captures heat and transfers it into a liquid which Matuszewska (2024) explains can be one of several "organic chemical fluids with high molecular weights" with a preference for isentropic fluids (pp. 5-6); the liquid is then expanded, condensed, and finally the energy can be pumped. Temperatures typically are 150 degrees C or less, and this method can be applied to "waste heat" such as exhaust, burners, dryers, etc. (Jiménez-García et al. (2023). Cybersecurity vulnerabilities for biomass power plants mirror the vulnerabilities in any power plant where typically up to date Information Technology (IT) is combined with legacy operational technologies (OT). It is increasingly difficult to segment the IT and OT networks. Biomass power plants are different than renewable energy sources, as the plant is running off of an exhaustible energy source. The cybersecurity landscape must be managed as would be a traditional power plant (Thompson, 2022).

CONCLUSION

The benefits of solar and wind energies are clear, with improvements to the environment and the ability to make use of sources that will not vanish like fossil fuels. Livestock and crops, irrigation ditches, parking areas for vehicles, and other projects can share space with these accoutrements. While the availability of adequate wind and sunlight may be somewhat irregular for gathering energy, Ghadami et al. (2021) remind that tourist influxes, water availability, and other factors—some of which may be seasonal—must also be considered, and "motivational citizenship programs" may be helpful (p. 14). Public awareness of the advantages is crucial in working towards practicable policies and programs. Smart cities and small communities alike relying on solar and/or wind energy must allow for robust storage, be diligent in watching for and mitigating cybersecurity and maintenance issues, and develop long-term strategic plans to ensure the viability of these resources, as the consequences will benefit generations to come.

REFERENCES

Abu-Rayash, A., & Dincer, I. (2021, August). Development and analysis of an integrated solar energy system for smart cities. *Sustainable Energy Technologies and Assessments*, *46*, 101170. DOI: 10.1016/j.seta.2021.101170

Aldy, J. (2022, August). Learning how to build back better through clean energy policy evaluation. *HKS Faculty Research Working Paper Series RWP22-010*. https://nrs.harvard.edu/URN-3:HUL.INSTREPOS:37373014

Aragón, P., Kaltenbrunner, A., Calleja-López, A., Pereira, A., Monterde, A., Barandiaran, X. E., & Gómez, V. (2017, September). Deliberative platform design: The case study of the online discussions in Decidim Barcelona. In G. Ciampaglia, A. Mashhadi, & T. Yasseri, T. (Eds.), *Social Informatics, Lecture Notes in Computer Science, 10540*, 277-287. https://doi.org/DOI: 10.1007/978-3-319-67256-4_22

Ba, L., Tangour, F., El Abbassi, I., & Absi, R. (2025, April 15). Analysis of Digital Twin applications in energy efficiency: A systematic review. *Sustainability*, *17*(8), 3560. DOI: 10.3390/su17083560

Bath, A. (2025, April 23). *Wind industry installs record capacity in 2024 despite policy instability*. Global Wind Energy Council. https://www.gwec.net/gwec-news/wind-industry-installs-record-capacity-in-2024-despite-policy-instability

Beeman, G. (2025, April 1). *The top cyber threats to energy & utilities in 2025 – and how to stay ahead.* Mattermost. https://mattermost.com/blog/top-cyber-threats-to-energy-utilities-in-2025

Brown, D. (2012, August 27). *Wind power ethics*. Ethics and Climate. https://ethicsandclimate.org/2012/08/27/wind-power-ethics

Călin, A.-M., Cotfas, D. T., & Cotfas, P. A. (2024, September). A review of smart photovoltaic systems which are using remote-control, AI, and cybersecurity approaches. *Applied Sciences (Basel, Switzerland)*, *14*(17), 7838. DOI: 10.3390/app14177838

Calleja-López, A. (2019, May 17). *Building alternatives: The digital democracy and data commons pilot*. Decode. https://decodeproject.eu/blog/building-alternatives-digital-democracy-and-data-commons-pilot.html

Center for Climate and Energy Solutions. (2024, August). *U.S. state electricity portfolio standards*. https://www.c2es.org/document/renewable-and-alternate-energy-portfolio-standards

Chen, S., Wang, K., Zhao, M., & Gao, Z. (2025, April 2). A review of the recent development of innovative wind turbines: Concepts and aerodynamic analyses. *Physics of Fluids, 37*(041302). Advance online publication. DOI: 10.1063/5.0256502

Christensen, M. (2025, June 5). Coverup in Cordova: How regulators caught nuclear operators lying about a 'near miss.' *KWQC News*. https://www.kwqc.com/2025/06/05/coverup-cordova-how-regulators-caught-nuclear-operators-lying-about-near-miss

CISA. (2021, February 1). *Understanding denial-of-service attacks.* https://www.cisa.gov/news-events/news/understanding-denial-service-attacks

Collins, P. (2002, Spring). The beautiful possibility: Here comes the sun. *Cabinet Magazine, 6.* https://www.cabinetmagazine.org/issues/6/collins.php

Dhar, P., & Chakraborty, N. (2021, October). A dual mode wind turbine operation with hybrid energy storage system for electricity generation at constant voltage in an islanded microgrid. *International Journal of Energy Research, 45*(13), 18885. DOI: 10.1002/er.6994

Duval, G. (2024, April 8). *How do wind turbines work?* Today's Homeowner. https://todayshomeowner.com/eco-friendly/guides/how-do-wind-turbines-work

Dwernertl. (2007, August 8). *Solar radar speed sign*. [Image]. Wikimedia Commons. https://commons.wikimedia.org/wiki/File:Solar_radar_speed_sign.jpg. Used per Creative Commons License (https://creativecommons.org/licenses/by-sa/3.0/deed.en), without alterations.

Ekechukwu, D. E., & Simpa, P. (2024, June). The future of cybersecurity in renewable energy systems: A review, identifying challenges and proposing strategic solutions. *Computer Science & IT Research Journal, 5*(6), 1265–1299. DOI: 10.51594/csitrj.v5i6.1197

Enrique. (2022, January 27). *Sea wind turbines.* [Image]. Pixabay. https://pixabay.com/photos/sea-wind-turbines-wind-farm-6972214

Ericsson, J. (1888, August 2). The Sun Motor. *Nature, 38,* 319-321. https://doi.org/ DOI: 10.1038/038319b0

Farrell, S., & Dullea, E. (2025, February 11). *Cybersecurity and solar power vulnerability.* Husch Blackwell. https://www.climatesolutionslaw.com/2025/02/cybersecurity-and-solar-power-vulnerability

Firoozi, A. A., Hejazi, F., & Firoozi, A. A. (2024, June 13). Advancing wind energy efficiency: A systematic review of aerodynamic optimization in wind turbine design. *Energies, 17*(12), 2919. DOI: 10.3390/en17122919

Forescout Research - Vedere Labs. (2025, June 3). *The security risks of internet-exposed solar power systems.* (2025, June 3). https://www.forescout.com/blog/the-security-risks-of-internet-exposed-solar-power-systems

Fourrage, L. (2024, April 9). *What are the challenges in implementing cybersecurity tools?* Nucamp. https://www.nucamp.co/blog/coding-bootcamp-cybersecurity-what-are-the-challenges-in-implementing-cybersecurity-tools

Franz, M. (2025, June 5). The NRC is conducting a special inspection at the Quad Cities nuclear plant. Here's why. *WQAD News*. https://www.wqad.com/article/news/local/nrc-investigation-quad-cities-nuclear-plant-why/526-1c61f08b-f817-42da-af6f-028d36f406f0

Fudge, J. (2025a, May 29). *Close-up of panels on the roof of the 2nd-floor garage.* [Image]. Fudgelink. https://fudgelink.com/solarpanels. Used by kind permission.

Fudge, J. (2025b, May 29). *View of the building from the south.* [Image]. Fudgelink. https://fudgelink.com/solarpanels. Used by kind permission.

Gautam, C. K., Da, N., Kumar, R., & Kulhar, K. S. (2024, January). Short review of solar energy markets and policies for smart cities development. *E3S Web of Conferences, 540*, 04002. https://doi.org/DOI: 10.1051/e3sconf/202454004002

Geller, E. (2025, March 28). *Solar power gear vulnerable to remote sabotage.* Cybersecurity Dive. https://www.cybersecuritydive.com/news/solar-power-gear-vulnerable-remote-sabotage/743806

Geneseo Public Library District. (2025, May 22). *First picture: Horse barn on the George R Smith farm with a unique windmill that provided power to grind corn.* [Image attached] [Status update]. Facebook. https://www.facebook.com/permalink.php?story_fbid=pfbid02xoTu2MWuA6is751aegoRjC8YEfRkf1h37D4foafDLVrv79CT5ipVGDV9Sab4qDngl&id=100079953789167. Used by kind permission.

Geothermal energy cyber security. (2024, November 4). Cyber Energia. https://cyberenergia.com/geothermal-energy-cyber-security

Ghadami, N., Gheibi, M., Kian, Z., Faramarz, M. G., Naghedi, R., Eftekhari, M., Fathollahi-Fard, A. M., Dulebenets, M. A., & Tian, G. (2021, July). Presentation of solar energy in smart cities using an integration of artificial neural network, photovoltaic system and classical Delphi methods. *Sustainable Cities and Society, 74*, 103149. DOI: 10.1016/j.scs.2021.103149

Gipe, P. (2004). *Wind power: Renewable energy for home, farm, and business.* Chelsea Green Publishing.

Guerra, P. (2025, March 27). *New multicampus consortium looks to expand solar-over-canal projects statewide.* University of California. https://www.universityofcalifornia.edu/news/new-multicampus-consortium-looks-expand-solar-over-canal-projects-statewide

Hart, K. (2025, June 2). New Idaho bill forces wind farms to get rid of 'Red Light District.' *East Idaho News.* https://www.eastidahonews.com/2025/06/new-idaho-bill-forces-wind-farms-to-get-rid-of-red-light-district

Недвига, A. (2017, August 6). *Solar clean battery energy.* [Image]. Pixabay. https://pixabay.com/photos/solar-battery-clean-energy-pillar-2602980

How does a photovoltaic cell work? (2024, May 23). Planete Energies. www.planete-energies.com/en/media/article/how-does-photovoltaic-cell-work

Hugeback, K. K., Gallus, W. A.Jr, & Pico, H. N. V. (2023, September). Machine learning-adjusted WRF forecasts to support wind energy needs in black start. *Weather and Forecasting*, *38*(9), 1553–1561. DOI: 10.1175/WAF-D-23-0023.1

IEEE Standards Association. (2024, March 22). *Evolving IEEE standards foster a more sustainable power grid.* Institute of Electrical and Electronics Engineers. https://standards.ieee.org/beyond-standards/ieee-2030-standards

Ihsan, K. T. N., Sakti, A. D., & Wikantika, K. (2021, March 29). Geospatial assessment for planning a smart energy city using rooftop solar photovoltaic in Bandung City, Indonesia. *International Archives of the Photogrammetry, Remote Sensing & Spatial Information Sciences, XLIV–. M*, *3*, 83–87. DOI: 10.5194/isprs-archives-XLIV-M-3-2021-83-2021

International Hydropower Association. (2022). *Pumped storage hydropower.* https://www.hydropower.org/factsheets/pumped-storage

International Organization for Standardization. (2018). *Sustainable cities and communities - Indicators for city services and quality of life.* (ISO Standard No. 37120:2018). https://www.iso.org/obp/ui/en/#iso:std:iso:37120

Iowa State University. (2011, June 20). *Wind energy production: Legal issues and related liability concerns for landowners.* Center for Agricultural Law and Taxation. https://www.calt.iastate.edu/system/files/CALT%20Legal%20Brief%20-%20Wind%20Energy%20Production.pdf

Janusz-Szymańska, K., Wiciak, G., Remiorz, L., & Hulak, D. (2025, February). Heat storage using solar pond technology and post-mining brine: Preliminary analysis. *Heat Transfer Engineering*, *46*(3), 310–320. DOI: 10.1080/01457632.2024.2308353

Jauregui-Correa, J. C., & Duran-Carillo, A. (2022, October 28). Optimum control scheme for deformable blades applied to horizontal wind turbine. *Proceedings of the ASME Turbo Expo 2022: Turbomachinery Technical Conference and Exposition, 11: Wind Energy*. Rotterdam Netherlands, June 13-17, 2022. https://doi.org/DOI: 10.1115/GT2022-81169

Jiménez-García, J. C., Ruiz, A., Pacheco-Reyes, A., & Rivera, W. (2023, June 30). A comprehensive review of Organic Rankine Cycles. *Processes (Basel, Switzerland), 11*(7), 1982. DOI: 10.3390/pr11071982

Johnson, J., Hurtado, J., Krishnappa, B., Collier, L., & Goodlett, D. (2023, June 1). *Recommendations for solar energy cybersecurity.* North American Electric Reliability Corporation. https://www.nerc.com/pa/Documents/Recommendations-for-Solar-Energy-Cybersecurity.pdf

Johnson, S. (2023, December 17). *11 best types of roof vents + understanding attic ventilation.* My Roof Hub. https://myroofhub.com/materials/roof-vents-attic-ventilation

Jones, D., Rangelova, K., Walter, D., & Worthington, B. (2025, March 12). *US electricity 2025 special report.* Ember Energy. https://ember-energy.org/app/uploads/2025/03/US-Electricity-2025-Special-Report.pdf

Knight, L. (2014, June 14). Vanadium: The metal that may soon be powering your neighbourhood. *BBC News*. https://www.bbc.com/news/magazine-27829874

Kumar, A., & Pal, D. B. (2025). Renewable energy development sources and technology: Overview. In S. Kumar & V. K. Singh (Eds.), *Renewable energy development: Technology, material and sustainability* (pp. 111-131). Clean Energy Production Technologies. Springer. https://doi.org/DOI: 10.1007/978-981-97-9626-7_6

Ledmaoui, Y., El Maghraoui, A., El Aroussi, M., & Saadane, R. (2025, January). Review of recent advances in predictive maintenance and cybersecurity for solar plants. *Sensors (Basel), 25*(1), 206. DOI: 10.3390/s25010206 PMID: 39796997

Lindemulder, G., & Kosinski, M. (2024, June 11). *What is a man-in-the-middle (MITM) attack?* IBM. https://www.ibm.com/think/topics/man-in-the-middle

Mack, E., & Blok, A. (2023, December 22). Smartflower solar review: Beautiful solar for up to $65,000. *CNet.* https://www.cnet.com/home/solar/smartflower-solar-review-beautiful-solar-sculpture

Madeswaran, A., Bisht, D., Yuvaraj, S., Reedy, M. U., Al-Attabi, K., & Dhablia, A. (2024). AI-controlled wind turbine systems: Integrating IoT and machine learning for smart grids. *E3S Web of Conferences, 540,* 03008. https://doi.org/DOI: 10.1051/e3sconf/202454003008

Magalhães, M. F., Mselle, B. D., & Galindo, F. (2025, March 31). Decision-making and selection framework for potential implementation of Concentrated Solar Power technologies: Case study. *Energies*, *18*(7), 1753. DOI: 10.3390/en18071753

Mahesha, C. R., Ramalingam, M., Sujith, S., Kalyanasundaram, P., Soni, N. B., Nalinashini, G., Suresh Kumar, S., Sathyamurthy, R., & Mohanavel, V. (2022, February). Sustainable cooling and heating in smart cities using solar energy system planning, from the International Conference on Energy Storage Technology and Power Systems. *Energy Reports*, *8*, 826–835. DOI: 10.1016/j.egyr.2022.09.208

Mai, V. T., Mohammadzadeh, A., Alattas, K. A., Taghavifar, H., & Ghaderpour, E. (2025, April). Cybersecurity in maritime power systems: A comprehensive review of cyber threats and mitigation techniques. *Electric Power Systems Research*, *247*, 111797. DOI: 10.1016/j.epsr.2025.111797

Majumder, S., Thakur, P., & Thakur, A. (2025, January 25). Solar energy and environmental application. In S. Kumar & V. K. Singh (Eds.), *Renewable energy development: Technology, material and sustainability* (pp. 43-66). Clean Energy Production Technologies. Springer. https://doi.org/DOI: 10.1007/978-981-97-9626-7_6

Manwell, J. F., McGowan, J. G., & Rogers, A. L. (2009). *Wind energy explained: Theory, design and application*. Wiley.

Marsh, J. (2024, July 25). *How do solar cells work? Photovoltaic cells explained.* Energy Sage. https://www.energysage.com/solar/solar-photovoltaic-cells

Matuszewska, D. (2024, October). Solar Organic Rankine Cycle (ORC) systems: A review of technologies, parameters, and applications. *Energies*, *17*(20), 5106. DOI: 10.3390/en17205106

McGarity, A. E. (1977). *Solar heating and cooling: An economic assessment*. National Science Foundation. https://files.eric.ed.gov/fulltext/ED145586.pdf

McMillin, D. (2022, September 2). *What to know about buying a house with solar panels.* Bankrate. https://www.bankrate.com/real-estate/buying-house-with-solar-panels

Menghwani, V., Wheat, R., Balicki, B., Poelzer, G., Noble, B., & Mansuy, N. (2024). Bioenergy for community energy security in Canada: Challenges in the business ecosystem. *Energies*, *16*(4), 1560. DOI: 10.3390/en16041560

Mishra, A., Alam, M. I., Pal, D. B., & Awasthi, S. (2025, January 25). Solar energy and its utilization in smart cities. In S. Kumar & V. K. Singh (Eds.), *Renewable energy development: Technology, material and sustainability* (pp. 111-131). Clean Energy Production Technologies. Springer. https://doi.org/DOI: 10.1007/978-981-97-9626-7_6

Mohamed, Z., Soliman, M., Feteha, M., & Saber, E. (2025, January 8). A novel optimal design approach for bladeless wind turbines considering mechanical properties of composite materials used. *Scientific Reports*, *15*, 1355. DOI: 10.1038/s41598-024-82385-9

Nartowska, E., & Rozenvalde, A. (2023). Renewable energy sources: Benefits and drawbacks from the perspective of the experiences of China, Brazil, Canada and the United States. *Civil and Environmental Engineering Reports*, *33*(1), 39–52. DOI: 10.59440/ceer-2023-0003

National Park Service. (2018, November 7). *Nevada and Arizona: Hoover Dam.* Discover our shared heritage travel itinerary series. https://www.nps.gov/articles/nevada-and-arizona-hoover-dam.htm

Nidhi, S., Megha, P., Kant, P. R. & Kulha, K. S. (2024, January). Solar energy in developing countries: Challenges and opportunities for smart cities. *E3S Web of Conferences, 540*, 04003. https://doi.org/DOI: 10.1051/e3sconf/202454004003

Omidvarnia, F., & Sarhadi, A. (2024, February 1). Nature-inspired designs in wind energy: A review. *Biomimetics*, *9*(2), 90. DOI: 10.3390/biomimetics9020090 PMID: 38392136

Omri, A., & Boubaker, S. (2024, March). When do climate change legislation and clean energy policies matter for net-zero emissions? *Journal of Environmental Management*, *354*, 120275. DOI: 10.1016/j.jenvman.2024.120275 PMID: 38364534

Pan, J. (2025, May 23). *US experts warn 'rogue' devices found in Chinese solar power inverters could trigger widespread blackouts, report says — effectively a 'built-in way' to destroy the grid. Are you prepared?* Money Wise. https://moneywise.com/news/top-stories/rogue-devices-reportedly-found-in-chinese-solar-power-inverters-batteries

A person in black shirt holding a solar panel. (2021, October 20). Kindel Media. [Image]. Pexels. https://www.pexels.com/photo/a-person-in-black-shirt-holding-a-solar-panel-while-standing-on-the-roof-9875441

Petrea, M. I. I., & Ursache, I.-M. (2023, October). Inside the world's most sustainable smart city: Lessons from Copenhagen. *International Conference on Sustainable Development of European Smart Cities,* Ia i, Romania, June 2023, 225-238. http://smarteu.uaic.ro/PublishingImages/Pages/Start/Smart%20EU%20volume_Conference%20Proceedings_2023.pdf

Ragan, B. (2025, February 28). *What are the types of attic ventilation systems?* Bill Ragan Roofing. https://www.billraganroofing.com/blog/types-attic-ventilation-systems

Rekeraho, A., Cotfas, D. T., Balan, T. C., Cotfas, P. A., Acheampong, R., & Tuyishime, E. (2025, March). Cybersecurity threat modeling for IoT-integrated smart solar energy systems: Strengthening resilience for global energy sustainability. *Sustainability, 17*(6), 2386. DOI: 10.3390/su17062386

Rekeraho, A., Cotfas, D. T., Cotfas, P. A., Bălan, T. C., Tuyishime, E., & Acheampong, R. (2024, February). Cybersecurity challenges in IoT-based smart renewable energy. *International Journal of Information Security, 23*, 101–117. DOI: 10.1007/s10207-023-00732-9

Rogers, J. N., Stokes, B., Dunn, J., Cai, H., Wu, M., Haq, Z., & Baumes, H. (2016, November 21). An assessment of the potential products and economic and environmental impacts resulting from a billion ton bioeconomy. *Biofuels, Bioproducts & Biorefining, 11*(1), 110–128. DOI: 10.1002/bbb.1728

Romeo, J. (2025, April 10). *Dallas Love Field turns jet blasts into renewable power.* Electrical Contractor. https://www.ecmag.com/magazine/articles/article-detail/dallas-love-field-turns-jet-blasts-into-renewable-power

Sanderson, C. (2024, April 25). *Russia launches 'first targeted strike' on a Ukrainian solar power facility.* Recharge News. https://www.rechargenews.com/energy-transition/russia-launches-first-targeted-strike-on-a-ukrainian-solar-power-facility/2-1-1622019

Sanderson, C. (2025, June 3). *'Unacceptable': BP bristles at BAE Systems wind farm radar shutdown demand.* Recharge News. https://www.rechargenews.com/wind/unacceptable-bp-bristles-at-bae-systems-wind-farm-radar-shutdown-demand/2-1-1827749

Securing renewable data: Green energy sector cybersecurity challenges. (2025, May 3). Beetroot. https://beetroot.co/business/securing-renewable-data-green-energy-sector-cybersecurity-challenges

Shahan, Z. (2014, November 21). *History of wind turbines*. Factor This. https://www.renewableenergyworld.com/wind-power/turbines-equipment/history-of-wind-turbines

Siddiqui, M. S., Keprate, A., Yang, L., & Malmedal, T. (2023, December). Towards an integrative framework for digital twins in wind power. *2023 IEEE International Conference on Industrial Engineering and Engineering Management (IEEM)*, Singapore. https://doi.org/DOI: 10.1109/IEEM58616.2023.10406340

Singh, T. (2013, April 1). *Scientists develop solar-powered wind turbine for ultimate energy generation.* Inhabit. https://inhabitat.com/scientists-develop-solar-powered-wind-turbine

Sjödin, M. (2018, March 13). *Turbine electricity.* [Image]. Pixabay. https://pixabay.com/photos/turbine-electricity-generator-3224747

Smart grid security: Attacks and defence techniques. (2025). Infosys. https://www.infosysbpm.com/blogs/business-transformation/smart-grid-security-attacks-and-defence-techniques.html

Smart nation and the digital government office partner with Google Cloud to launch an AI government cloud cluster. (2023, June 6). CIO. https://ciosea.economictimes.indiatimes.com/news/cloud-computing/smart-nation-and-digital-government-office-partners-with-google-cloud-to-launch-ai-government-cloud-cluster/100780836

Sridhar, S., Hahn, A., & Govindarasu, M. (2012). Cyber–physical system security for the electric power grid. *Proceedings of the IEEE, 100*(1), 210–224. DOI: 10.1109/JPROC.2011.2165269

Stallard, E., & Poynting, M. (2025, January 21). What is the Paris climate agreement and why has Trump withdrawn? *BBC News.* https://www.bbc.com/news/science-environment-35073297

Sustainability. (2025). Byron Solar Train. https://byronbaytrain.com.au/sustainability

Tabibi, A. (2024, January 30). *The ethics of solar energy: Balancing progress and responsibility*. Green.org. https://green.org/2024/01/30/the-ethics-of-solar-energy-balancing-progress-and-responsibility

Thompson, K. (2022). *How do power plants and renewables differ in cybersecurity requirements.* Integriti. https://itegriti.com/2022/compliance/how-do-power-plants-and-renewables-differ-in-cybersecurity-requirements/

Timmons, D., Harris, J. M., & Roach, B. (2024). *The economics of renewable energy*. Boston University Global Development Policy Center. https://www.bu.edu/eci/files/2024/03/renewable-energy-econ-module-final.pdf

Tolasa, D. G., & Furi, A. T. (2025, January 30). The role of advanced materials in the optimization of wind energy systems: A physics based approach. *Acceleron Aerospace Journal*, *4*(1), 847–857. DOI: 10.61359/11.2106-2504

Uktamova, D. (2024). Evaluating the onshore wind farms based on multi-criteria decision-making model under Neutrosophic Set. *Journal of Sustainable Development and Green Technology*, *4*(2), 22–33. DOI: 10.54216/JSDGT.040203

United Nations Climate Change. (2023, September). *The Paris Agreement*. https://unfccc.int/process-and-meetings/the-paris-agreement

U.S. Department of Energy. (2004, March 8). *The history of solar.* Energy Efficiency and Renewable Energy Office. https://www1.eere.energy.gov/solar/pdfs/solar_timeline.pdf

U.S. Department of Energy. (2024, May 21). *Protecting wind energy systems from cyberattacks*. Wind Energy Technologies Office. https://www.energy.gov/eere/wind/articles/protecting-wind-energy-systems-cyberattacks

U.S. Department of Energy. (n.d.a,). *Bioenergy basics.* Bioenergy Technology Office. https://www.energy.gov/eere/bioenergy/bioenergy-basics

U.S. Department of Energy. (n.d.b.). *Geothermal heating and cooling*. Geothermal Technologies Office. https://www.energy.gov/eere/geothermal/geothermal-heating-cooling

U.S. Energy Information Administration. (2022, December 27). *Geothermal explained.* https://www.eia.gov/energyexplained/geothermal

U.S. Energy Information Administration. (2023a, April 20). *Hydropower explained.* https://www.energy.gov/eere/water/marine-energy-basics

U.S. Energy Information Administration. (2023b, December 27). Wind explained: Types of wind turbines. https://www.eia.gov/energyexplained/wind/types-of-wind-turbines.php

van Zoonen, L. (2016, July). Privacy concerns in smart cities. *Government Information Quarterly*, *33*(3), 472–480. DOI: 10.1016/j.giq.2016.06.004

Volcovici, V., Abnett, K., Stanway, D., Farge, E., & Pineau, E. (2025, January 21). World reacts to Trump withdrawing US from Paris climate pact. *Reuters*. https://www.reuters.com/business/environment/world-reacts-trumps-plan-withdraw-us-paris-climate-pact-2025-01-20

Webb, S. (2022, February 24). Are solar panels in China made using slave labour? *Independent*. https://www.independent.co.uk/climate-change/are-solar-panels-in-china-made-using-slave-labour-b2022336.html

Wilde, C. (2018, May 6). *Architecture solar.* [Image]. Pixabay. https://pixabay.com/photos/architecture-solar-solar-panels-3379146

Wind Turbine Professor. (2022, October 17). *Forces acting on wind turbine blades.* [Image]. Wikimedia Commons. https://commons.m.wikimedia.org/wiki/File:Wind_Turbine_forces.png. Used per Creative Commons License (https://creativecommons.org/licenses/by-sa/4.0/deed.en), without alterations.

Woerlen, I. (n.d.). *Mouchot's sun engine.* Hot Air Engines. http://hotairengines.org/solar-engine/mouchot-1865

World Nuclear Association. (2025, February 12). *Security of nuclear facilities and material.* https://world-nuclear.org/information-library/safety-and-security/security/security-of-nuclear-facilities-and-material

Yu, H., Yang, X., Chen, H., Lou, S., & Lin, Y. (2022, November 6). Energy storage capacity planning method for improving offshore wind power consumption. *Sustainability, 14*(21), 14589. DOI: 10.3390/su142114589

Zahnd, A., & Jennings, O. (2012). The role of renewable energy technology in holistic community development. In M. D. Tiwari & A. Vaish, A. (Eds.), *Green Energy* (pp. 75-142). River Publishers.

KEY TERMS AND DEFINITIONS

Digital Twin: a digital representation of a system used for emulating issues and mitigations; useful in the development phase as well as after a system has been deployed.

Encryption: the transformation of data into computer code that must be decoded before it can be read.

Fossil fuels: energy-enabling substances, often carbon-based, such as oil, gas, and coal; these are finite resources.

Geospatial planning: land use planning for the use of something such as photovoltaic panels or wind turbines; can include social and economic factors, use of waterways, etc.

Internet of Things (IoT): interconnectivity of devices via the internet.

Kinetic energy: energy from motion.

Photovoltaic cell: a device that converts solar heat into energy; typically uses silicon as a major component.

Renewable energies: naturally-sourced energies that can be replenished faster than they are used.

Standards: industry criteria set by organizations such as ISO and IEEE with the purpose of ensuring stability, interoperability, and ethical development and use.

Turbine: a machine with moving, revolving parts that works via wind, water, steam, or other means.

Chapter 11

The Convergence of Artificial Intelligence and the Internet of Things for Next-Generation Smart Systems

G. Swetha
https://orcid.org/0000-0001-8620-7149
RR Institute of Technology, Bangalore, India

M. S. Veena
https://orcid.org/0000-0002-9960-4263
RR Institute of Technology, Bangalore, India

Tejaswini Krishnamurthy
RR Institute of Technology, Bangalore, India

S. Druva Kumar
https://orcid.org/0000-0001-5157-6294
Dayananda Sagar College of Engineering, India

M. Shruthi
Dayananda Sagar College of Engineering, India

S. Vishwanatha
https://orcid.org/0000-0002-0485-6194
Jain University, India

N. Raghu
https://orcid.org/0000-0002-2091-8922
Jain University, India

V. N. Trupti
https://orcid.org/0000-0002-3414-100X
Jain University, India

ABSTRACT

The convergence of Artificial Intelligence and the Internet of Things has paved the way for the development of smart environments that are efficient, adaptive and

DOI: 10.4018/979-8-3373-4455-3.ch011

sustainable. While IoT enables vast networks of interconnected sensors, device and actuators to capture real-time data, AI provides the intelligence needed to process, analyze and act upon this information. Together, they transform reactive systems into proactive, context-aware ecosystems capable of decision-making and automation. This chapter presents a comprehensive framework for integrating AI with IoT, highlighting its architecture, component and applicability across domains such as smart cities, healthcare, agriculture, transportation and industrial automation. The framework emphasizes enabling technologies including edge, fog, and cloud computing, communication protocols and open platforms like FIWARE, which collectively support scalability, interoperability and real-time analytics.

INTRODUCTION

The technological progress of Internet of Things (IoT) and Artificial Intelligence (AI) has created a total revolution in contemporary technological advancement. The first IoT idea required linking physical devices to internet protocols which allowed them to transfer and receive information. The first applications operated at a basic level to track and control operations. The growth of IoT networks brought forth three main technological solutions which included smart homes and connected health systems and industrial automation systems. AI experienced a transformation from basic rule-based systems and expert programs into complex machine learning and deep learning models which recognized patterns and made predictions and autonomous decisions. AI provided the intelligence to process real-time data that IoT delivered in vast quantities. AI and IoT joined forces to establish modern adaptable systems which will remain relevant in the future. These technologies enable both connected systems and environments which adapt while learning from their operations. The integration between AI and IoT enables cities to operate efficiently and produces wearable devices that track health data instantly thus reshaping modern living. AI-powered IoT stands at the innovation forefront to lead the world toward a more intelligent and sustainable future.

The Internet of Things and Machine learning have fundamentally altered our interactions with the environment and data utilization. The Internet of Things (IoT) is a network including interconnected devices, sensors, and actuators that gather data. Artificial intelligence (AI) refers to a collection of advancement that allows machines to replicate the abilities of humans. Technologies such as computer vision and machine learning, natural language processing exemplify this category. Nonetheless, the endeavor of deriving substantive insights from this enormous volume of data is far more arduous (Nagaraj, 2023). Help from AI in such a scenario with AI algorithms and techniques, which are derived from the data generated by Internet of Things new insights are gained that enable efficient decision-making processes and can also be used for automation. IoT + AI — The Two Are Inseparable Creating smart environments requires these two technologies combination of the Internet of Things (IoT) and Machine learning, gives rise to numerous opportunities for smarter, more energy-efficient, sustainable settings aware of human requirements.

The sensing capability of the Internet of Things gagdets along with the cognitive capabilities of artificial intelligence systems together can reinvent entire cities, healthcare, transportation, and agriculture. The Internet of Things combined with Machine learning, for example, can enable smart cities to deploy intelligent transportation systems that increase public safety and ease traffic congestion by better controlling the flow of cars. Internet of Things (IoT) gadgets used to screen patients remotely combined with artificial intelligence analytics which can identify patterns, forecast maladies and personalize treatments may help the healthcare business. One of the ways in which the transportation sector can simplify this daunting task and enhance efficiency at machines is through implementation connected automobiles as well as AI-driven traffic management.This research study's primary goal is to provide a comprehensive framework for combining machine learning with the internet of things to build intelligent settings. The framework will include the key technology, components, and design needed to successfully integrate artificial intelligence with the Internet of Things. The purpose of this essay is to analyze the issues, prospects, and possible applications of this all-encompassing framework in a number of industries.

The agricultural field is using Internet of Things sensors to keep track of the growing conditions of the crops. In addition, irrigation systems and crop management structures can be improved further by the use of approaches based on artificial intelligence. This research paper, therefore, is aimed at describing a comprehensive framework employing artificial intelligence with the internet of things. This framework will also cover design, components and appropriate technologies necessary for successful integration of internet of things with artificial intelligence. Furthermore, this article aims to examine the challenges, opportunities or possible domains of relevance of this hybrid framework in practice.

The figure 1 presents a succinct summary of the FIWARE Internet of Things architectural components. FIWARE, as an open-source platform, facilitates compatibility across the world of technology of Things, huge amounts of data, cloud computing, and the future Internet. It offers throughout a large number of the business sectors a full range of standards and technology which may be applied for the creation of modern and scalable applications and services. The following is an illustration of how FIWARE can easily fit in with these technologies: Assume that a network of several sorts of IoT devices is deployed in different areas of the city, collecting information in real time. Some of these devices might have sensors that track Air quality, traffic patterns, trash management, and energy consumption.

Figure 1. FIWARE framework for an integrated future of Internet of Things

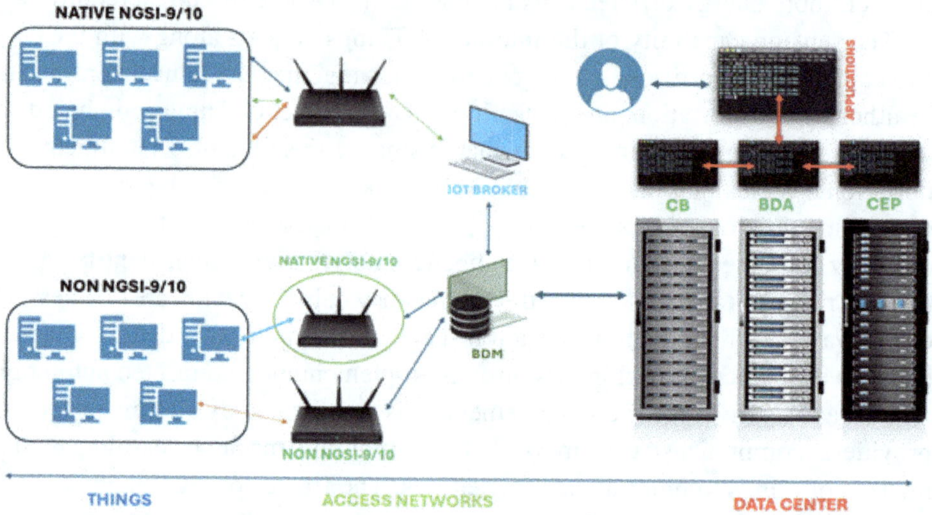

The explosion of IoT devices has created a massive flow of data every second. This information can be scattered and difficult to use. A FIWARE-based platform changes that by serving as a central hub where data is collected, stored, and analyzed. The support of big data technologies, it can detect patterns, identify trends, and spot unusual events turning raw numbers into insights that help guide better decisions. One of FIWARE's biggest strengths is its cloud-native design. As more devices connect and data volumes grow, the platform automatically scales to handle demand while staying reliable. Thanks to open APIs and standardized data models, developers can tap into this data with ease, reusing it to build useful applications. In smart mobility, for instance, real-time traffic updates can be transformed into accurate directions and optimized routes, cutting travel time and reducing congestion.

The impact goes far beyond traffic management. In waste collection, FIWARE can help cities create efficient schedules, reducing unnecessary trips and saving resources. Its open ecosystem of developers, service providers, and innovators ensures that raw IoT data is turned into practical tools that improve everyday services and urban living. The FIWARE stand out is the way it brings together IoT, cloud computing, and big data analytics in one platform. From gathering information to analyzing it and building applications, the platform supports the full journey through open standards. While often associated with smart cities, FIWARE is also driving progress in healthcare, agriculture, transportation, and industrial automation.

The merging IoT with Artificial Intelligence also raises challenges. Protecting data privacy, ensuring security, addressing ethical concerns, managing costs, and developing the right skills are all critical. Yet these challenges also bring opportunities. By finding solutions, platforms like FIWARE can unlock intelligent, adaptive environments that are not only smarter but also more sustainable. FIWARE is more than just infrastructure, it is a bridge between raw data and meaningful action, enabling the creation of digital ecosystems that make communities more connected, efficient, and responsive to real-world needs.

LITERATURE SURVEY

The Authors state that the dynamic junction of three cutting-edge technologies, namely Artificial Intelligence (AI), Internet of Things (IoT), and Cloud Computing, as well as the tremendous impact that these technologies have had on a variety of different fields. After providing an overview of artificial intelligence and the issues it faces, it then goes into Internet of Things applications in several industries, including transportation, industry 4.0, healthcare, and agriculture. Artificial intelligence (AI) on the cloud is investigated, with topics including finance, e-commerce, smart cities, healthcare, and robotics being covered. This section examines several applications, such as intelligent meters, smart buildings, intelligent farming, smart hospitals, and smart industry, focusing on the combination of artificial intelligence and cloud-based Internet of Things technologies (Nagaraj, 2023). Challenges such as security and confidentiality of information are examined, along with the prospective future trajectories of technologies like quantum computer technology and fog computing. A collection of use cases that illustrate the practical implementations of these transformational technologies across a variety of industries is presented in the final section of the book. In addition, a list of scholarly references is included at the end of each chapter which is intended for more advanced readers.

The authors illustrate that the Internet of Things (IoT) has established a globally interconnected environment, driven by wired and wireless sensors that generate heterogeneous data across various industries and applications. Advanced artificial intelligent (AI) technology, particularly deep learning (DL), has enhanced data analysis, prediction, and decision-making by extracting comprehensive information from data (Chang et al., 2021). The merging of AI with IoT has expedited the advancement of AI-of-Things (AIoT) technologies that intelligently evaluate and react to environmental stimuli autonomously. The amount, speed, and validity of data, along with catastrophic transmission delay, impair networking infrastructures, rendering cloud data processing challenging or unfeasible. Edge computing can address these significant challenges. This essay thoroughly examines an end-edge-cloud coordinated architecture for flexible AIoT systems. Fundamental concepts such as IoT, AI, and computing at the edge are presented. These principles direct its examination of the comprehensive AIoT architecture, a practical AIoT instance to illustrate AI's applications in real life, and prospective AIoT applications. The subsequent review focuses on the advancement of AI model interpretation and training techniques at the network edge. The remaining challenges and potential trajectories of this promising sector are examined.

The Authors have claimed that Internet of Things (IoT), billions of gadgets and sensors gather data from their surroundings, process it, send it to data centers in the cloud, and then receive feedback through the Internet to assist with perception and connection. However, it is challenging to communicate large quantities of diverse data, to perceive complicated situations from this data, and to make timely smart decisions. Deep learning and other forms of artificial intelligence (AI) have recently achieved notable success in a number of domains, such as computer vision, voice recognition, and NLP. When AI is integrated into the IoT, it signals the beginning of the AI of things (AIoT) era (Zhang, 2020). This article provides an extensive overview of AIoT to demonstrate how AI may enhance the IoT by making it more efficient, intelligent, environmentally friendly, and secure. In particular, we provide a high-level overview of the AIoT architecture within the framework of cloud, fog, and edge computing. Then, we cover the state of AI research for the Internet of Things (IoT) from four angles: 1) perception, 2) learning, 3) reasoning, and 4) behavior. We will now go on to a brief overview of several exciting AIoT uses that have the potential to change our world in a significant way. Lastly, we discuss the difficulties of AIoT and point out several areas where future study could be fruitful.

The authors states that the IoT is a network that allows physical objects to communicate with one another and share data through the use of applications, sensors, and actuators (Kankanhalli, 2019). Artificial intelligence (AI) might help governments build apps and learn from big data sets collected from individuals, sensors, and networks. Services in the areas of energy, transportation, medical care, schooling, and public safety can be developed with the use of the Internet of Things (IoT) and artificial intelligence (AI). The Internet of Things (IoT) and artificial intelligence (AI) are set to revolutionize smart government. In this special edition guest editorial, the authors address the obstacles that have so far prevented their widespread adoption and implementation in the public sector, and they present a thorough research methodology to address these issues. Following a brief editorial introduction, this special issue contains six papers. Using the suggested framework and existing literature gaps, the articles included in this special issue advocate for further study of the Internet of Things (IoT) and artificial intelligence (AI) in the context of smart government. On the agenda are studies that are specialized to certain domains, studies that go above adoption studies to look at how these technologies are put into practice and evaluated, studies that zero in on particular problems and successes quickly, and studies that broaden the scope of research methodologies and theoretical underpinnings.

The Authors have reported that Internet of Things (IoT) is industrializing in numerous real-world applications such as smart transportation, smart city to improve human life trustworthy (Singh, 2020). Industrial IoT sensors are producing too much sensing data as industrialization increases. AI is a powerful analytic tool for big data processing, providing scalable and accurate results in real time. However, centralized architecture, security, privacy, resource limits, and a lack of training data make AI-based big data analysis tool design and development difficult. Blockchain, a new technology, fosters decentralization. It encourages secure data and resource sharing between IoT network nodes to reduce centralized control and solve AI problems. The research aims to create a blockchain-AI IoT infrastructure for big data processing. To effectively integrate blockchain technology with AI for the Internet of Things, this article suggests a Blockchain-enabled Smart IoT Architecture that makes use of state-of-the-art methods and tools. As part of its quantitative and qualitative assessments, the suggested design defines "AI-driven Blockchain" and "Blockchain-driven AI" as they pertain to Internet of Things (IoT) systems. In order to compare studies on precision, delay, privacy and security, complexity of computation, and cost of energy in IoT applications, we objectively analyze the Block IoT Intelligent architecture. This evaluation covers gadget, fog, edge, and cloud intelligence. When compared to current Internet of Things (IoT) systems, the results show that the suggested architecture performs better and solves more problems.

The growth of intelligent services and apps driven by AI is expanding the reach of the Internet of Things (IoT) into a variety of people's everyday lives, as stated by the authors in (Baccour et al., 2021). Because of issues with data privacy and the scalability of IoT networks, traditional AI methods that rely on centralised data collection and processing may not function in practical application settings. The federated learning (FL) approach enables a plethora of intelligent IoT applications by facilitating AI training at dispersed IoT devices without requiring data transmission. From the inception of FL and the Internet of Things (IoT) to their integration, we cover every angle of FL's expanding use in IoT networks. Data sharing, unloading, caching, identifying attacks, location, mobile crowdsensing, privacy and security are some of the Internet of Things (IoT) services that we highlight as having the ability to be enabled by FL. Next, we take a close look at FL's applications in smart industries, smart cities, UAVs, smart transportation, and smart healthcare. The crucial lessons learned about FL-IoT services and applications are highlighted. At the end of this study, we will go over some of the present problems and future directions for research in this exciting new area (Rawat, 2023).

IoT and AI: Fundamentals and Principles

This class of gadgets can include the now commonplace product such as telephones, wearables, household apparatuses, automobiles, manufacturing tools, transport and structures. The architecture of the Internet of Things typically consists of four primary layers: Sensors, actuators, and embedded systems are the make-up of the perception layer; it is an extensive range. These are functional components which enable the organization to collect information from the external environment (Nguyen, 2021). These devices are equally able to monitor many aspects such as location, motion, temperature, and Humidity. Information that is collected by the devices can be transferred to the cloud or a central hub easier due to the network layer that facilitates. Some of the communication that it uses include cellular networks, Bluetooth, Zigbee, and Wi-Fi among others (Hao, 2021).

Data that is accumulated by gadgets can be communicated to the centralized system or cloud more easily thanks to the network layer, which is responsible for making this possible (Campolo et al., 2021). Technology like as cellular networks, Bluetooth, Zigbee, and Wi-Fi are among the communication tools and protocols that it employs.

The cloud and platform layer is responsible for storing, processing, and analyzing the massive amounts of data that are produced by Internet of Things devices (G. Muhammad, 2021). For the purposes of data management, analytics, and application development, cloud platforms provide scalable infrastructure as well as tools. Applications and services that utilize data make up the application layer from the Internet of Things for specific objectives such as the automation of smart homes, the monitoring of businesses, or the sensory analysis of the environment (W. Yu, 2022).

Figure 2. The overall order of conventional artificial intelligence.

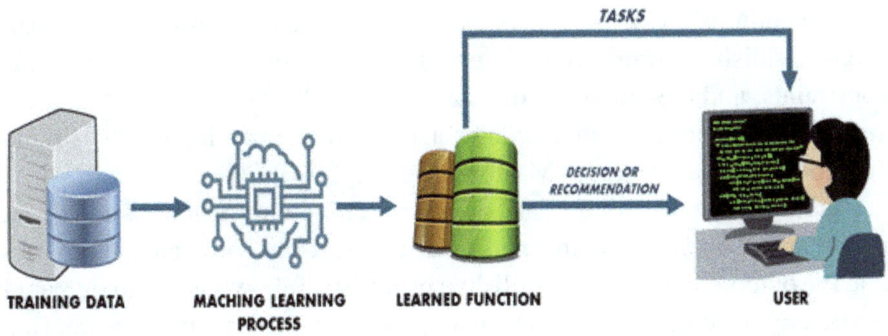

The phases involved in traditional artificial intelligence, also known as classical or symbolic AI, are depicted in Figure 2. These steps include general processing and problem-solving. An outline of the typical flow is shown in the following context:

Defining the problem that the artificial intelligence system is supposed to solve is the first step in the process. To accomplish this, it is necessary to have an understanding of the problem area, to determine the specific goal or objective, and to establish the criteria for success. Knowledge Acquisition: In traditional artificial intelligence, the process of acquiring knowledge involves collecting information about the topic matter from many sources, such as books, databases, experts, or other sources. In most cases, this information is communicated in the form of facts, rules, or claims that are logical. In the process of knowledge representation, the artificial intelligence system is able to process the information that it has learned after it has been organized and represented. In this context, formal languages may be utilized (Alberti et al., 2019). Some examples of these include logic-based representations, frames, semantic networks, and ontologies.

Inference and Reasoning

The artificial intelligence system use reasoning and inference in order to arrive at make or conclusions the judgments by utilizing the information that it has learnt and the problem that it has identified. The use of logical principles, deductive reasoning, or probabilistic reasoning is often required in order to arrive at conclusions that are logical or probabilistic. Planning and Problem-Solving: In certain applications of artificial intelligence, planning and problem-solving are essential initial steps. To accomplish this, one must devise a sequence of steps or actions that will allow one to finish a certain work while taking into account the resources available, the constraints, and the outcomes that are sought. AI system generates a plan or a solution, it can either put it into action by actually implementing it or by simulating the process to ensure accuracy (Mastorakis et al., 2020).

At this stage, physical systems, robotics, or the modeling of actions and their consequences are all on the table. In terms of assessment and comments, the AI system looks at the outcomes or the accomplished objectives following the implementation of the strategy or solution. Using feedback, we can examine performance, find out how efficient the method is, and perhaps enhance the approach for further iterations. The efficacy of the system can also be assessed through feedback. It is critical to realize that this general order is not exhaustive and may differ based on the specific issue domain, AI techniques, and methodologies applied. Because conventional AI can't handle complex and unpredictable real-world problems, new paradigms in AI like machine learning and deep machine learning have arisen. Among the most important topics related to the Internet of Things are features include interoperability, scalability, real-time analytics, and device management. Through the Internet of Things (IoT), it is possible to connect physical items into the digital world in a seamless manner, which ultimately results in a networked environment that can be utilized for a range of reasons (Shafique, 2020).

The Many AI Approaches, and Methods Computers that can mimic human intelligence are able to carry out a wide variety of jobs hitherto reserved for people, a phenomenon known as "artificial intelligence" (AI). It is possible for artificial intelligence systems to perceive, reason, learn, and make decisions on their own. Artificial intelligence can be divided into numerous categories, including the following:

- AI that is limited: Artificial intelligence systems that are too narrow, often called weak AI, are created to solve very specific issues or execute very specialized jobs. Such technologies include methods for image identification, voice assistants, and engines for recommendations, among others.
- AI in general: Across a wide range of activities and topics, the goal of general artificial intelligence is to display intellect that is comparable to that of humans. It has capacities that are comparable of humans in terms of comprehension, learning, and knowledge application. Achieving comprehensive general artificial intelligence remains a challenging task.
- The primary goal of machine learning, a subfield of artificial intelligence, is to automate the collection of data and the improvement of computer systems' performance through the application of specific algorithms and approaches.

All three types of learning supervised, reinforced, and unsupervised fall under one umbrella.

- "Deep learning" is shorthand for a branch of machine learning that uses multi-layered artificial neural networks to find hidden meaning in data. Artificial intelligence and the processing of natural languages are only two of the many fields that have benefited from its use.

IoT and AI Synergies and Complementarities

The combination of AI and the Internet of Things (IoT) produces a smart environment because of the complementary and synergistic effects of the two technologies: Through their connections to the IoT, everyday objects collect and generate vast amounts of data about their environments. This information can be analyzed and processed using machine intelligence and other AI approaches to provide useful predictions, discoveries, and patterns for the future (Alankar, 2021). It is now feasible to make decisions all at once with the aid of machine learning algorithms that can send information from the Internet of Things in real time. By evaluating data collected by Internet of Things sensors and making real-time adjustments to the timing of traffic lights, machine learning can be utilized to enhance traffic flow in a smart city environment. Internet of Things devices may automate operations and adapt to varying conditions simultaneously by employing intelligent automation (AI) (Yarlagadda, 2018). As an example, AI-driven systems in industrial automation can optimize machine performance by monitoring it using IoT sensors and then adjusting operations automatically. This means is that AI systems may use IoT data to essentially predict what the future holds. This capability is useful for such ideas as sales forecast or break-down prediction as artificial intelligence can use the sensor data expect issues in equipment and arrange for measures so as to be prepared for the maintenance. Adaptability and Personalization: The information provided by the internet of things AI algorithms can adjust interface to different user and make systems more perceptive about individual preferences (Balas et al., 2020). As an example, there are already AI-controlled smart home systems that can monitor IoT device use patterns and adjust settings like temperature and lighting accordingly. The combination of the IoT's data-creation powers with AI's decision-making and analysis capabilities can lead to new opportunity and effective advances in many different fields.

Integrated Framework for Smart Environments

The development of smart grids that maximize efficiency in power generation, distribution, and consumption is made feasible by the Internet of Things. This is referred to as smart energy management. Additionally, it enhances the management of inventory, enhances the efficiency of logistics and transportation, and reduces inefficiencies such as delays and losses. The effective monitoring of energy consumption, the implementation of demand response plans, and the incorporation of renewable energy sources are all made possible this way (Ma, Y, 2020). Monitoring of the Environment: Internet of Things sensors have the capability to monitor and collect data on a variety of environmental elements, such as the levels of noise, the quality of the water, and the qualities of the air (Haseeb, 2025).

The data analysis and analytics layers are responsible for processing and examining the collected data. Machine learning and deep learning are two methodologies within artificial intelligence utilized for deriving insights, recognizing patterns, and generating predictions. Big processing methods can be employed to manage the substantial volumes of data produced through Internet of Things gadgets (De Micco et al., 2025). Using the data that has been examined and the AI models, the decision-making and automation layer is responsible for making judgments and initiating certain automated activities (Alberti et al., 2019). While automation mechanisms are responsible for directing actuators and Internet of Things devices to carry out the operations that are required, real-time decision-making algorithms make it possible to respond quickly to changing situations (Alberti et al., 2018).

The layer of integration: The integration layer is responsible for ensuring that the integrated framework is able to operate in conjunction with and is connected to the infrastructure and systems that are already in place. Integration with business software, cloud platforms, legacy systems, and other data sources is required for this purpose in order to make more efficient use of the resources that are easily accessible.

Figure 3. Crucial Internet of Things

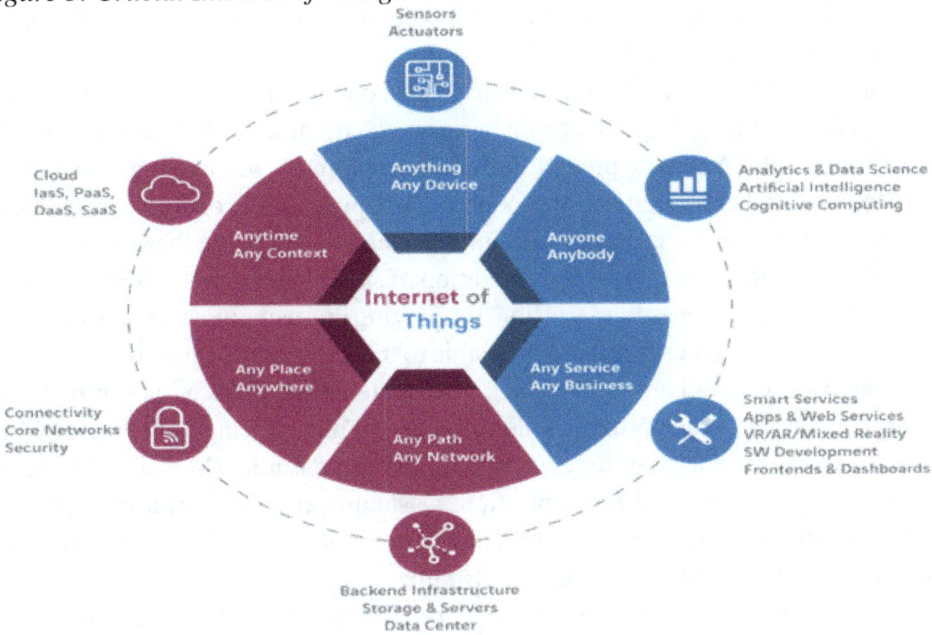

The Internet of Things (IoT) possesses extensive potential applications across various domains. Numerous significant Internet of Things applications are augmenting overall productivity and instigating transformations across various industries, as illustrated in Figure 3. The Internet of Things (IoT) now enables the automation and control of many home devices and systems. Homeowners can remotely control various domestic gadgets, such as lights, thermostats, and security systems, through linked devices or cellphones. The Industrial Network of Things is referred to as IIoT.

The IIoT links several pieces of industrial machinery, sensors, and other devices in order to gather and analyze data in real-time (E. F. Z. Santana, 2018). This makes it possible to perform predictive maintenance, which in turn optimizes operations and boosts productivity in industries such as manufacturing, energy, transportation, and agriculture. Applications of the Internet of Things in healthcare make it possible to collect health data in real time, to use intelligent medical devices, and to monitor patients remotely. Patient care is improved as a result of this technology since it enables medical practitioners to monitor vital signs, provide tailored treatment, and ensure rapid actions. The some of major IoT applications that are creating revolutions in various sectors and enhancing productivity in large are: It is now possible to automate and control most of the household equipments and systems with the help of Internet of Things or IoT. Homeowners are capable of working remote lighting, thermostats, security systems, appliances, and other home appliances with the use of linked devices or smartphone. IIoT is the acronym that denotes Industrial Internet of Things (O. B. Sezer, 2018).

Real-time data collection and analysis is the concept of the Industrial Internet of Things (IIoT) which connects machines, sensors, and other industrial equipment's. This makes it possible to do predictive maintenance and hence leading to efficiency in operations and enhancement of productivity in production, energy, transport and even agricultural sectors. Internet of things in healthcare enable the acquisitions of health information in real time, the utilization of smart health products and services, and the home-based patient supervision. Employing this technology enhances patient care because; the medical practitioner is able to track the signs, administer treatment from the data received and know what immediate action is necessary to be taken. Smart cities refer to the notions of the Internet of Things acting as the major factor for boosting the productivity and eco-friendliness of large cities (Veena, 2025). Smart grids, intelligent modes of transportation, waste and environmental management, and security-supporting apps are just a few of the innovations that emerge from the interconnected infrastructure (M. H. ur Rehman, 2020).

In precision agriculture, IoT sensors in conjunction with drones along with data collection and analytics are used for purposes of health condition of crops, irrigation, animal tracking, and conditions of the soil. Because of this, farmers are able to increase the yields in their farms by practicing modern farming techniques which do not require a lot of resources and end up wasting them while making sound decisions based on facts that are made available to them by technology. Due to IOT it has become feasible to trace and track product in real time starting from supply chain to consumption. Thanks to Internet of Things, it can be created smart grid systems in order to generate, transmit and use electricity more efficiently. This is referred to as smart energy management (Y. Liu, 2020). Further, it optimizes stocks, optimizes the processes of shipping and receiving, and minimizes such wastes as downtimes and damages. This way, it is possible to monitor the energy consumption, propose and manage demand response plans and integrate renewable energy sources. Monitoring of the Environment: Various Internet of Things sensors have the ability to detect as well as record. gather information on different elements of the environment including the levels of noise, quality of the water and even the quality of the air (Guo et al., 2018). The application of this information helps decision making on policies easier and ways and means on how to handle the risks that come with the environment. Wearable technology and individual fitness: Various gadgets for example fitness trackers and smart watches that are IoT enabled can also capture details of a person's health and fitness. They give data about such things as a pulse, sleep pattern, and exercises, which in turn assists people in tailoring their mode of living. Connected shelf and smart inventory are Internet of Things gadgets which are integrated into smart retail (Wang et al., 2021).

Deep Learning: Deep learning is highly effective for analyzing extensive quantities of complex data due to its utilization of neural network architectures (Chelloug & El-Zawawy, 2017). Consequently, deep learning is exceptionally efficacious. Unlike convolutional artificial neural networks (CNNs), which are primarily employed for the analysis of images, recurrent neural network networks (RNNs) are appropriate for processing time-series data.

Figure 4. The real-time decision-making and automation.

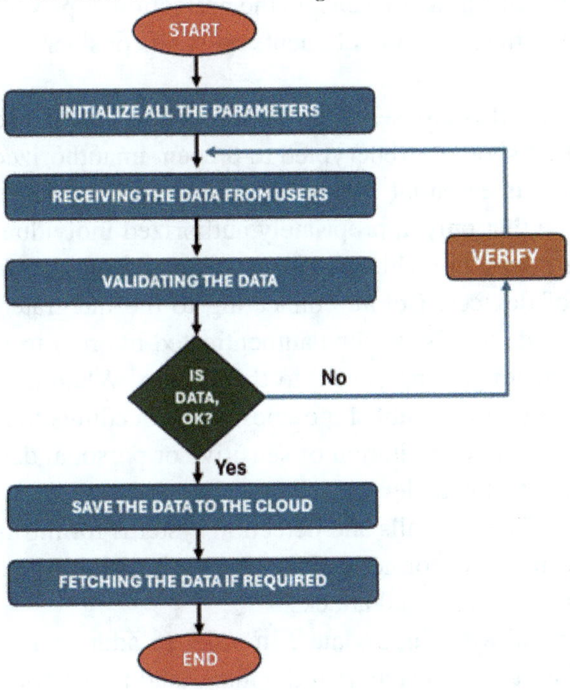

Decision-Making and Automation in Real-time Smart settings are able to respond rapidly to shifting situations as a result of real-time decision-making and automation as shown in figure 4. Using artificial intelligence algorithms and rule-based systems, judgments are formed based on the data that has been processed, and these decisions then begin automatic activities. There are numerous scenarios in which real-time decision-making and automation can be utilized (H. V Balachandra, 2025). One example of this is the implementation of traffic management systems that dynamically alter traffic lights based on information regarding the flow of traffic at the moment. equipment for industrial automation that can make adjustments to the parameters of machines in real time in order to improve production lines. regulating energy use in smart homes based on occupancy patterns and the time of day are systems that are included in smart homes.

Scalability, handling of information, and analytical capabilities are all made easier with the combination of cloud-based services with contemporary data processing and storage technologies. Through this integration, data created by the Internet of Things can be processed and stored using resources and services available in the cloud (Mohanty, 2016).

Important Things to Keep in Mind Regarding Security and Privacy: Concerns around security and privacy arise as a result of smart environments' use of machine learning and the Internet of Things. To ensure the protection of private data and the reliability of the system, the following elements must be considered:

- Encryption of Data: It is advised that data sent between IoT gadgets and the combined structure should be encrypted to prevent unauthorized access.
- Access Control: It is essential to provide robust access control methods in order to guarantee that only appropriately authorized individuals are able to interact with the Internet of Things devices and the integrated framework.
- Authentication of devices: Before connecting to the integrated framework, Internet of Things devices should be authenticated in order to prevent unauthorized devices from gaining access to the system. When it comes to data privacy, it is important to establish policies and procedures that regulate the collection, storage, and exploitation of sensitive or personal data that is produced by Internet of Things devices.
- Network Security: The firewalls and detection systems for intrusions are two types of security measures for networks that must be established to safeguard against unauthorized access and attacks.
- Security Patches and Regular Updates: In order to address any vulnerabilities that may exist, it is important that the integrated framework and Internet of Things devices receive regular updates and security patches. When these considerations are taken into account, the integrated framework is able to ensure that smart environments are operated in a secure and confidential manner, which in turn increases the level of user confidence in the system.

APPLICATIONS OF THE INTEGRATED FRAMEWORK

Smart cities utilize the Internet of Things and the artificial intelligence framework to improve several facets of urban life.

Integration with Existing Infrastructure and Infrastructure Systems: There is a need for IoT and Artificial Intelligence to be integrated and merged with the present environment so that it will be harmonious and compatible. Through such approaches as system integration of the existing infrastructure, applications and data sources, functionality and efficiency can be enhanced. The following are important factors that determine integration: Others have taken its meaning to mean "Application Programming Interface". Through application programming interface or API the connected framework and other current systems can communicate and share information. This is especially useful since both the coordination or integration of the operations of different platforms and the integration of information from a number of sources are enabled by this. Integration with Legacy Systems: The term Integration with Legacy Systems means enrichment involved in the current systems or addition of new systems to support the Internet of Things devices as well as the utilization of artificial intelligence. This may entail making modifications or adding new modules to allow the connection and exchange of information depending on the situation that prevails. The adoption of cloud platforms with the traditional storage and computing systems makes it possible to have scalability, data management and analysis at a given instance. We have seen that through integration, the data that is produced by the Internet of Things is processed and stored utilizing cloud services. Some Things to Think About Regarding Privacy and Safety: Smart space and Internet of Things with the help of AI and integration generates the issues of privacy and security.

The integrated framework contributes to the advancement of agriculture by maximizing the utilization of resources, crop management, and livestock monitoring. In order to facilitate precision farming, Internet of Things sensors are installed in the fields. These sensors collect data on the moisture content, nutrient content, and environmental aspects of the soil. AI algorithms are used to process this data in order to improve pest management, fertilization, and irrigation, which ultimately results in an increase in crop yield and a reduction in the amount of resources that are wasted.

Smart irrigation utilizes Internet of Things devices and artificial intelligence analyses to optimize watering schedules according to plant specifications, forecasts for the weather, and soil moisture levels. As a consequence of this, water is utilized more efficiently, there is less water that is wasted, and the health of the crop is enhanced. Through the use of Internet of Things devices such as GPS trackers and wearable sensors, it is feasible to do real-time monitoring of the health, behavior, and position of cattle. The data are then examined by artificial intelligence systems in order to identify anomalies, forecast disease outbreaks, and enhance strategies for livestock management.

The following considerations are essential for the aim of protecting private data and the system's integrity: Security of Data: Therefore, it is suggested that data transferred between the Internet of Things gadgets and integrated framework must be encrypted.

Access Control: To ensure that only the right people get to engage the IoT systems and the integrated architecture it is necessary to incorporate strong signal access control mechanism that shall only allow: Authentication of devices: In other words, every device to be connected to the integrated framework should go through an identification process to ensure only right devices access the system. Concerning data privacy, there exists a need to formulate measures on how the information generated and managed by the Internet of Things devices should be collected, stored, or exploited. Network Security: Security and access control mechanisms such as firewalls and IDS are two of the methods that should be put in place in a network to prevent web accesses and other forms of unlawful attacks. Security Patches and Regular Updates: To eliminate any possibilities of risk, it is invariably relevant that the integrated framework and the IoT devices should be updated frequently and should be guarded with updated security layers. When these factors are considered, the integrated framework is effective in making certain that smart environments are run in a secure and an optimal way of keeping the data a secret from other people hence enhancing the level of confidence in the system among the users.

Therefore, smart cities extend the use of IOT and AI in order to improve a number of affairs of urban life. Internet of Things (IoT) sensors and artificial intelligence algorithms can perform smart transportation activities which include constant traffic surveillance, estimation of traffic densities and optimal signal timing. It increases throughput and reduces congestion, enhances the environment for driving a car and optimizes public transport. Intelligent Energy Management: The IoT grows energy use reduction capabilities, pattern recognition, and the integration of renewable energy through AI analytics to energy management. This helps to mitigate inefficient use of energy and hence improve on the energy efficiency. Smart garbage can IoT sensors can view fill levels and improve waste collection routes so that the garbage cans are not full. This contributes to lowering of the number of avoidable trips and costs of operation. Besides, many AI systems can analyze data and recognize pattern for suggestion of the possible ways and means for minimizing the generation of wastes. Systems that involve the use of Internet of Things and artificial intelligence could improve public safety in different ways such as predictive policing, video surveillance and in optimizing disaster response. Thus, by applying real-time data analysis, there is a possibility to assess the possible security threats as well as to take appropriate and adequate measures in due time. Some of the uses of the integrated framework in the area of the healthcare business permit the practice of differential management of patients, deliver high-quality care to the patients, and improve the overall effectiveness of the operations in healthcare business.

ETHICS AND GOVERNANCE

As Artificial Intelligence (AI) and the Internet of Things (IoT) become more deeply embedded in everyday life, ethical concerns and governance have taken on increasing importance. These technologies can collect and process enormous amounts of information, which allows for powerful insights and automated decision-making but also introduces risks. Privacy, security, and accountability are central challenges. Without careful oversight, personal data can be misused, and decisions made by automated systems can unintentionally harm individuals or communities.

Addressing these challenges requires more than technical fixes. Ethical considerations must be integrated into every stage of design and development. Developers need to prioritize transparency, fairness, and inclusivity, ensuring that systems do not reinforce social biases or exclude certain groups. In the case of IoT, this means implementing strong protections for personal data and giving users clear control over how their information is used. For AI, it involves creating systems whose decisions can be traced and understood, so that they can be reviewed or corrected when necessary.

Governance frameworks complement these efforts by providing standards, regulations, and best practices. Governments, industry bodies, and international organizations play an important role in shaping policies that encourage innovation while protecting society. Public engagement and accountability mechanisms are equally essential, giving communities a voice in determining how these systems are used. Embedding ethical principles and strong governance into AI-powered IoT systems, it is possible to harness their potential safely. This approach ensures that future smart technologies are not only effective and intelligent but also responsible, trustworthy, and aligned with human values.

CHALLENGES AND OPPORTUNITIES

Problems with Scalability and Interoperability: Scaling Internet of Things installations and integrating a wide variety of devices, protocols, and platforms can be challenging because of the vast volume of data and devices involved. It is possible for interoperability issues to arise when equipment built by different manufacturers or utilizing different communication protocols are required to work together without any interruptions.

It is possible that scalability and interoperability can be improved by the standardization of frameworks and their protocols. The use of open standards and protocols makes it possible to integrate and communicate with devices, systems, and platforms without any interruptions. It is possible that attempts to achieve interoperability could be bolstered by collaboration between Standards organizations and industry stakeholders.

Challenges Related to Data Management and Processing: The Internet of Things (IoT) devices provide issues in storing, analyzing, and analysis due to the substantial volume, rapid generation, and diverse nature of the data they produce. Traditional data management solutions may be inadequate for managing the substantial volume and complexity of data created by the Internet of Things.

The application of big data, cloud computing technology, and edge computing to address data management challenges is a potential prospect. Cloud platforms provide scalable storage as well as processing capabilities, whereas edge computing minimizes latency and bandwidth requirements by relocating computation nearer to the data source. Enhancements can be implemented in AI algorithms to satisfy the processing demands of data generated by the Internet of Things (IoT). Security and privacy are important issues with IoT devices because of the cyber dangers they face, such as hacking, data leaks, and hostile attacks. Privacy issues are also brought up by the gathering and processing of personal or sensitive data.

Opportunity: The implementation of stringent security measures, including encryption, authentication techniques, and secure protocols, is essential to safeguard the data and devices linked to the Internet of Things (IoT). Technologies that enhance privacy, such as data anonymization and consent management, can be utilized to address concerns regarding security and confidentiality. An ongoing commitment to research and collaboration is essential in order to stay one step ahead of the ever-evolving cybersecurity threats.

Concerns Regarding Ethical Behavior and Responsible Artificial Intelligence the AI algorithms that are a part of the integrated framework ought to adhere to ethical standards of fairness and transparency. The potential for employment displacement, algorithmic bias, and accountability in decision-making are all challenges that need to be addressed.

Creating ethical paradigms, standards, and guidelines for the application of artificial intelligence in smart environments is an opportunity that must be taken advantage of Ethical AI principles such as explainability, justice, and human oversight should be incorporated into the process of developing and utilizing artificial intelligence technologies. It is absolutely necessary for politicians, industry, and academic institutions to work together in order to address these ethical concerns.

Deficiencies in Skills and Training Requirements within the Workforce: Confrontation: Successful integration of the Internet of Things with artificial intelligence necessitates a workforce proficient in developing, implementing, and maintaining these intricate systems. There can be a dearth of experts in fields related to artificial intelligence (AI), the Internet of Things (IoT), and their overlaps. Possibility: Learning programs, training initiatives, and interdisciplinary collaboration can effectively bridge skill gaps, allowing us to address this issue. Learners can acquire the information and skills needed to interact with IoT and AI technologies through educational programs offered by universities, corporate collaborations, and online learning platforms.

Business Models and Their Economic Implications: Degree of difficulty: The integration of the Internet of Things and machine learning may necessitate significant expenditures in gadgets, platforms, and infrastructure. Assessing the viability of business models, return on investments, and income streams in emerging applications and industries can be tough.

It is possible to discover new economic opportunities by conducting research on innovative business models. Some examples of these models are data monetization, service-oriented approaches, and value-added services. It is possible for stakeholders, such as technology companies, business leaders, and legislators, to contribute to the promotion of sustainable economic growth through collaborative efforts.

In order to completely realize the possibilities of smart circumstances, it is vital to overcome these challenges and exploit the opportunities given by the interconnected Internet of Things and intelligent machines framework. The only way to make smart surroundings deliver on their potential. Integration of the Internet of Things (IoT) and machine learning (AI) will need ongoing research, new ideas, and cooperation across many fields and stakeholders if it is to overcome these obstacles and make the most of AI's benefits.

FUTURE DIRECTIONS AND RESEARCH AGENDA

Explainable AI, 5G connectivity, learning federation, the Internet of Medical Things (IoMT), and edge computing are a few examples of the new developments in AI and the Internet of Things. Research can investigate and make use of these technologies. In order to stimulate further growth, it is necessary to investigate the possibilities offered by these technologies and to appreciate the implications that they have for intelligent settings.

Creating and implementing standardized protocols, frameworks, and architectures for the integration of artificial intelligence with the internet of things can be facilitated by research. Both regulatory frameworks and efforts to standardize are being made. Collaborative efforts with standardization bodies, industry participants, and legislators can assure the preservation of compatibility, confidentiality of data, and security in smart environments. Studying enables a comprehensive understanding of the rules and regulations governing the legal and responsible implementation of machine learning in Internet of Things platforms. When thinking about the challenges and limitations of integrating AI with the IoT, many issues must be considered. These include issues of scaling, connectivity, organizing data, security, and privacy. Smart environments can run smoothly and safely with the help of newly researched methods, tools, and algorithms that solve these problems. To maximize the integrated framework's potential, researchers can also look into state-of-the-art processing of data, resource utilization, and system reliability technologies.

Research has the ability to highlight the need of designing smart settings with users in mind, with a focus on usability, accessibility, and user experience, as well as human-centered approaches. Research on user habits, views, and opinions has the potential to pave the way for more personalized services, adaptable systems, and interfaces that are easy to use. The advancement of people-centric methodologies in intelligent surroundings may also be shaped by investigations into the social, cultural, and ethical implications of integrating IoT with AI.

Collaborative research across several fields: Interdisciplinary studies involving the integration of AI and the internet of things can be facilitated by the development of collaboration among investigators, practitioners, and industry experts from other domains. Smart environment innovation can be enhanced by interdisciplinary collaboration in engineering, computer science, social science, healthcare, and design. This can also provide you a full picture of what the integrated framework can do. Research that incorporates different fields of study can tackle intricate problems and provide all-encompassing solutions.

The integration of the Internet of Things (IoT) and machine learning (AI) for smart settings can continue to advance if researchers follow these future paths and prioritize these areas of study. Application efficiency, environmental impact, and user experience will all see significant improvements as a result. Ongoing research and collaboration are crucial for managing the ever-changing demands and obstacles of smart environments and making full use of the combined structure of the Internet of Things and machine learning.

RESULTS AND DISCUSSION

This research presents an integrated framework leveraging IoT and AI to create smart environments, significantly enhancing efficiency, productivity, and quality of life in smart cities, healthcare, transportation, and agriculture. Key findings include a comprehensive understanding of IoT and AI, detailed framework architecture, and practical applications across sectors. The study addresses critical challenges like scalability, interoperability, data management, security, privacy, ethics, and economic implications, proposing solutions and emphasizing standardization and interdisciplinary collaboration.

Implications:

- Efficiency: Intelligent automation and resource optimization boost productivity.
- Quality of Life: Enhanced public services and urban living.
- Sustainability: Improved energy use, waste reduction, and resource management.
- Personalization: AI-driven customization enhances user experiences.
- Economic Growth: Data-driven innovations and new business models foster development.

CONCLUSION

Intelligent machines (AI) and the Internet of Things (IoT) collaborate in the comprehensive smart environment framework to create responsive, efficient, and smart spaces. All of this is made possible by the framework's design and components. It connects to existing infrastructure, automates operations, makes choices in real time, processes data, and does analytics. It is talked about that worries about privacy, security, scaling, and interoperability are all taken care of. Intelligent cities, health care, agriculture, transportation, and industry automation are just some of the fields that can use the framework.

Important Findings and Contributions from the Research: This research paper offers a thorough analysis of the topic by combining the Internet of Things (IoT) with artificial intelligence (AI). The following are examples of important findings and contributions: Familiarity with the terminology, classifications, and processes of artificial intelligence and the Internet of Things has been achieved, by analyzing the similarities and differences between the two technologies demonstrates the combination of IoT and AI can improve automation, judgment, and efficiency. The practical applications in various industries will be investigated in this chapter, with a focus on smart cities, medical care, agriculture, transportation, and industrial automation.

REFERENCES

Alankar, B., Kaur, H., & Chauhan, R. (Eds.). (2021). *Transforming the Internet of Things for Next-generation Smart Systems*. IGI Global.

Alberti, M.. (2019). Platforms for Smart Environments and Future Internet Design: A Survey. *IEEE Access : Practical Innovations, Open Solutions*, *7*, 165748–165778. DOI: 10.1109/ACCESS.2019.2950656

Baccour, E., Mhaisen, N., Abdellatif, A., Erbad, A., Mohamed, A., Hamdi, M., & Guizani, M. (2021). Pervasive AI for IoT Applications: A Survey on Resource-Efficient Distributed Artificial Intelligence. *IEEE Communications Surveys and Tutorials*, *24*, 2366–2418. DOI: 10.1109/COMST.2022.3200740

Balas, V. E., Kumar, R., & Srivastava, R. (Eds.). (2020). *Recent trends and advances in artificial intelligence and internet of things*. Springer International Publishing.

Campolo, C., Genovese, G., Iera, A., & Molinaro, A. (2021). Virtualizing AI at the Distributed Edge towards Intelligent IoT Applications. *J. Sens. Actuator Networks*, *10*, 13. DOI: 10.3390/JSAN10010013

Chang, Z., Liu, S., Xiong, X., Cai, Z., & Tu, G. (2021). A Survey of Recent Advances in Edge-Computing-Powered Artificial Intelligence of Things. *IEEE Internet of Things Journal*, *8*, 13849–13875. DOI: 10.1109/JIOT.2021.3088875

Chelloug, S. A., & El-Zawawy, M. A. (2017). Middleware for internet of things: Survey and challenges. *Intelligent Automation & Soft Computing*, **•••**, 1–9. DOI: 10.1080/10798587.2017.1290328

De Micco, F., Di Palma, G., Ferorelli, D., De Benedictis, A., Tomassini, L., Tambone, V., & Scendoni, R. (2025). Artificial intelligence in healthcare: Transforming patient safety with intelligent systems—A systematic review. *Frontiers in Medicine*, *11*, 1522554. PMID: 39845830

Guo, H., Ren, J., Zhang, D., Zhang, Y., & Hu, J. (2018, August). A scalable and manageable IoT architecture based on transparent computing. *Journal of Parallel and Distributed Computing*, *118*, 5–13.

H. V Balachandra Achar and R. N. "The Impact and Future of Artificial Intelligence in Learning," *2025 3rd International Conference on Integrated Circuits and Communication Systems (ICICACS)*, Raichur, India, 2025, pp. 1-6, doi: DOI: 10.1109/ICICACS65178.2025.10967881

Hao, Q., Nazir, S., Li, M., Khan, H., Wang, L., & Ahmad, S. (2021). AI-Enabled Sensing and Decision-Making for IoT Systems. Complex., 2021, 6616279:1-6616279:9. https://doi.org/DOI: 10.1155/2021/6616279

Haseeb, K., Saba, T., Rehman, A., Abbas, N., & Kim, P. W. (2025). AI-driven IoT-fog analytics interactive smart system with data protection. *Expert Systems: International Journal of Knowledge Engineering and Neural Networks*, *42*(1), e13573.

Kankanhalli, A., Charalabidis, Y., & Mellouli, S. (2019). IoT and AI for Smart Government: A Research Agenda. *Government Information Quarterly*, *36*, 304–309. DOI: 10.1016/j.giq.2019.02.003

Liu, Y., Yuan, X., Xiong, Z., Kang, J., Wang, X., & Niyato, D. (2020, September). Federated learning for 6G communications: Challenges, methods, and future directions. *China Communications*, *17*(9), 105–118.

M. H. ur Rehman, K. Salah, E. Damiani, and D. Svetinovic, “Towards blockchain-based reputation- aware federated learning,” in Proc. IEEE INFOCOM Conf. Comput. Commun. Workshops (INFOCOM WKSHPS), 2020, pp. 183–188

Ma, Y., Ping, K., Wu, C., Chen, L., Shi, H., & Chong, D. (2020). Artificial Intelligence powered Internet of Things and smart public service. *Library Hi Tech*, *38*(1), 165–179.

Mastorakis, G., Mavromoustakis, C. X., Batalla, J. M., & Pallis, E. (Eds.). (2020). *Convergence of artificial intelligence and the Internet of Things*. Springer International Publishing.

Mohanty, S. P., Choppali, U., & Kougianos, E. (2016). Everything you wanted to know about smart cities: The Internet of things is the backbone. *IEEE Consumer Electronics Magazine*, *5*(3), 60–70. DOI: 10.1109/MCE.2016.2556879

Muhammad, G., & Alhussein, M. (2021). Convergence of Artificial Intelligence and Internet of Things in Smart Healthcare: A Case Study of Voice Pathology Detection. *IEEE Access : Practical Innovations, Open Solutions*, *9*, 89198–89209. DOI: 10.1109/ACCESS.2021.3090317

Nagaraj, A. (2023). *The Role of AI in Enhancing IoT-Cloud Applications*. Bentham Science Publishers., DOI: 10.2174/97898151657081230101

Nguyen, D., Ding, M., Pathirana, P., Seneviratne, A., Li, J., & Poor, F. (2021). Federated Learning for Internet of Things: A Comprehensive Survey. *IEEE Communications Surveys and Tutorials*, *23*, 1622–1658. DOI: 10.1109/COMST.2021.3075439

Rawat, R. (2023). Harnessing the Power of IoT and AI for Human Evolution. *International Journal of Research In Science & Engineering*, *33*(33), 58–68. DOI: 10.55529/ijrise.33.58.68

E. F. Z. Santana, A. P. Chaves, M. A. Gerosa, F. Kon and D. S. Milojicic, "Software platforms for smart cities: Concepts requirements challenges and a unified reference architecture", ACM Comput. Surv., vol. 50, no. 6, pp. 78:1-78:37, Nov. 2018.

Sezer, O. B., Dogdu, E., & Ozbayoglu, A. M. (2018, February). Context-aware computing learning and big data in Internet of Things: A survey. *IEEE Internet of Things Journal*, *5*(1), 1–27.

Shafique, K., Khawaja, B. A., Sabir, F., Qazi, S., & Mustaqim, M. (2020). Internet of things (IoT) for next-generation smart systems: A review of current challenges, future trends and prospects for emerging 5G-IoT scenarios. *IEEE Access : Practical Innovations, Open Solutions*, *8*, 23022–23040.

Singh, S., Rathore, S., & Park, J. (2020). BlockIoTIntelligence: A Blockchain-enabled Intelligent IoT Architecture with Artificial Intelligence. *Future Generation Computer Systems*, *110*, 721–743. DOI: 10.1016/j.future.2019.09.002

Veena, V., Manjunath, R., Asha, V., Gangaraju, V., Swetha, G., & Raghu, N. (2025). Smart Homes with IoT Technology Provide Safety and Security for Elderly Individuals. In Mallik, S., Mathivanan, S., Sangeetha, S., & Soufiene, B. (Eds.), *Real-World Applications of AI Innovation* (pp. 425–450). IGI Global Scientific Publishing., DOI: 10.4018/979-8-3693-4252-7.ch020

W. Yu, Y. Liu, T. Dillon, W. Rahayu and F. Mostafa, "An Integrated Framework for Health State Monitoring in a Smart Factory Employing IoT and Big Data Techniques," in IEEE Internet of Things Journal, vol. 9, no. 3, pp. 2443-2454, 1 Feb.1, 2022, https://doi.org/.DOI: 10.1109/JIOT.2021.3096637

Wang, Z., Qiu, J., Zhou, Y., Shi, Y., Fu, L., Chen, W., & Letaief, K. B. (2021). Federated learning via intelligent reflecting surface. *IEEE Transactions on Wireless Communications*, *21*(2), 808–822.

Yarlagadda, R. T. (2018). Internet of things & artificial intelligence in modern society. *International journal of creative research thoughts (IJCRT), ISSN*, 2320-2882.

Zhang, J., & Tao, D. (2020). Empowering Things With Intelligence: A Survey of the Progress, Challenges, and Opportunities in Artificial Intelligence of Things. *IEEE Internet of Things Journal*, *8*, 7789–7817. DOI: 10.1109/JIOT.2020.3039359

Chapter 12 The Ethics of Data Collection and Usage in Smart City Infrastructure

Zokir Mamadiyarov
Termez University of Economics and Service, Uzbekistan

Barno Matchanova
Urgench State Pedagogical Institute, Uzbekistan

Shokhjakhon Akhmedov
Urgench State University, Uzbekistan

Munir Ahmad
https://orcid.org/0000-0003-4836-6151
Survey of Pakistan, Pakistan

ABSTRACT

The rapid integration of data-driven technologies in urban environments offers significant opportunities for efficiency, sustainability, and citizen well-being, yet it introduces complex ethical challenges. This chapter examines privacy, consent, equity, and algorithmic bias concerns in smart city infrastructures. It highlights the importance of human-centered governance, transparency, accountability, and participatory decision-making. Comparative analysis of global frameworks reveals operational gaps, prompting actionable recommendations including ethics-by-design, stakeholder engagement, technological safeguards, and adaptive governance. By embedding ethics into urban data management, cities can achieve socially equitable, trustworthy, and sustainable smart city development.

DOI: 10.4018/979-8-3373-4455-3.ch012

INTRODUCTION

The use of the more advanced digital technologies, such as the Internet of Things (IoT) devices, networked sensors, real-time data solutions, and artificial intelligence systems, is becoming one of the defining features of smart cities. With these infrastructures, urban centres can maximize the circulation of traffic, energy, waste, security, and other required services, boosting the efficiency in the process and raising the quality of life among the citizens (Amy, 2024; Go Green, 2024; Stu, 2025). The smart city data ecosystem is humongous and ever-growing, which includes structured data of municipal records as well as unstructured social media and environmental sensors, and behavioral data of connected devices. It is an intricate network of information that provides unparalleled possibilities of innovation, evidence-based urban planning, but it also creates a variety of ethical issues that should be resolved to guarantee responsible governance (Adepoju et al., 2025; Bibri et al., 2023a).

The contemporary concern that drives the interest in analyzing the ethics of smart cities' data collection and usage can be related to the possible risks of pervasive surveillance (Masha, 2023), data leakage (Bibri et al., 2023b), illegal profiling (Sustainability Directory, 2025), and structural bias (Juvenile Ehwi et al., 2022). The lack of awareness or control of how personal information of individuals is recorded and disseminated, as well as the way it is analyzed, tends to raise concerns about privacy, consent, and ownership of data among citizens (Kim et al., 2025). In addition to personal rights, social aspects are involved: an unfair way to access the services, discriminating algorithms, and posing further emphasis on the preexisting societal disparities (Cowls & Floridi, 2018; Eubanks, 2018). Ethics is not a side issue; therefore, in the design and implementation of technologies in smart cities (Sharon, 2021). These problems can be addressed in advance so that they do not harm people, resulting in the establishment of firm relationships between them and building more socially accepted, inclusive urban spaces (Bayat & Kawalek, 2023; Cardullo & Kitchin, 2019).

The purpose of the chapter is to present a detailed analysis of ethical issues in the practice of smart cities with data and to discuss the guidelines of responsible data governance. It shall look at both positive and negative case studies, assess current regulatory strategies, and note what has been learned over global practice. In such a way, the chapter presents policy-relevant research findings by outlining feasible suggestions to policymakers, urban planners, and technologists with an emphasis on recommendations to produce transparent, accountable, and fair policies in data-driven urban projects. The outcome can be to encourage the development of smart cities, humanistic, and to make the technological innovation act in consonance with the values and the ethical aspects of society.

ETHICAL CHALLENGES IN SMART CITY DEPLOYMENTS

The sudden growth of smart city technologies has opened the door to never-before-seen potential in terms of improving the efficiency, sustainability, and quality of cities. Sophisticated digital infrastructure, including IoT-optimized streetlights and traffic monitors; AI-powered citizen services platforms, can enable cities to track, forecast, and act on sophisticated city dynamics in real-time. Nevertheless, besides these advantages, the gathering, archiving, and processing of large quantities of data present a set of ethical issues, which are not only intertwined but also complex. For example, 311 reporting in cities like Kansas City reveals that low-income and minority neighborhoods are less likely to report infrastructure issues despite having greater needs, leading to skewed data-driven decisions and unequal service delivery (Kontokosta & Hong, 2021). The challenges must be addressed so that technological innovation is streamlined according to the values of society and the rights of human beings. To better illustrate the multifaceted ethical concerns that accompany smart city data ecosystems, Table 1 summarizes the key challenges, their causes, and their potential societal impacts.

Table 1. Ethical Challenges in Smart City Data

Ethical Challenge	Key Causes/Drivers	Potential Impacts on Society
Privacy & Surveillance	Ubiquitous sensors, CCTV, drones, centralized databases	Loss of privacy, chilling effect, cyber vulnerabilities
Consent & Autonomy	Implicit consent, opaque data practices, passive collection	Reduced agency, lack of transparency, mistrust
Data Ownership & Equity	Proprietary control, restricted citizen access	Power imbalance, social disparities, reduced accountability
Bias & Discrimination	Incomplete or skewed datasets, algorithmic opacity	Inequitable services, social exclusion, and reinforced inequalities

Privacy and Surveillance

One of the major issues of developing smart cities is the privacy of the citizens in the face of an ever-growing surveillance infrastructure. Smart cities take advantage of the widespread CCTV camera systems, drones, GPS-enabled mass transport networks, cellular connectivity data, and the Internet of Things deployed into the infrastructure of places of business and commercial, and even personal locations. The result of these technologies is large-scale high-resolution data that monitors the movement, behaviors, and interactions of people at scale, many in real time, opening up new possibilities in optimizing transport systems, energy performance, safety, and urban planning (Fabrègue & Bogoni, 2023).

But such benefits bring with them deep privacy dangers, the risk of which is a product of the same systems that make such benefits possible. The same monitoring can create a so-called chilling effect when people can change their behavior because they are aware that they are constantly watched and thus interfere with the freedom of expression, association, and involvement in the civic sphere. Besides, the aggregation and central storage of sensitive data provide opportunities to be vulnerable to cyberattack, unauthorized access, and misuse of data, either by municipality officials, other third-party contractors, or commercial entities. In addition to technical risks, there is also the ethical question of informed consent, data ownership, and the discrimination that could ensue through discriminating profiling or social sorting (Sustainability Directory, 2025; Ziosi et al., 2024). Breached personal data can be exploited for identity theft, phishing, or ransomware targeting. Attackers often exploit insecure IoT endpoints or weak encryption protocols to infiltrate municipal systems, turning individual privacy violations into systemic cybersecurity crises. Figure 1 visualizes how surveillance technologies in smart cities create a chain of risks, beginning with pervasive data collection and culminating in societal implications such as reduced freedom and trust erosion.

Figure 1. Smart City Ethical Risk Flow

The answer to these challenges is strong privacy-preserving measures, such as decentralized data storage, end-to-end encryption, differential privacy approaches, and transparent governance policies. Also essential are control measures, checks by citizen authority, and ethical standards that harmonize the efficiency and innovation in data collection and usage in smart cities and constitutional rights. For example, Amsterdam canceled its smart traffic light initiative due to privacy and cybersecurity concerns related to data collection via mobile apps (The Times, 2025). Determining a balance between the two important tasks of developing a technological society and creating a network that can provide privacy to individuals remains crucial in the attainment of trust, legitimacy, and social cohesion in subsequent urban ecosystems.

Consent and Citizen Autonomy

Intimately relevant to many of those concerns of privacy is the all-important issue of informed consent, which is core to citizen autonomy in smart city ecosystems. Most smart city technologies are based on passive data collection or assumptions of implicit consent and provide little information about data capture, processing, storage, or sharing of personal data. Examples are tracking of locations using mobile apps, smart-meter data on usage, and behavioral data on IoT-enabled public services, and frequently tracked and monitored without the express awareness of individuals (Sustainability Directory, 2025; Trigen, 2025). Unauthorized or opaque data collection increases the risk of illicit data resale or unlawful access to sensitive records. Such opacity can mask vulnerabilities, allowing attackers to insert malware or spyware through compromised data pipelines, highlighting that ethical lapses in consent mechanisms can directly create security weaknesses.

Lack of meaningful consent kills the domain of citizen autonomy, because in this case, the objects remain disenfranchised in matters of making sound decisions with regard to disclosure and making use of their personal information. In addition to strictly being within the confines of the law, effectiveness in ethical governance of smart cities necessitates active systems, which give precedence to openness and individual choice. This involves clear communication of data collection practices, opt-in consent models, granular permission settings, and intensive processes that enable citizens to withdraw or change consent at any time. This kind of measure ensures the fact that the citizens can be brought into the fold of smart city schemes voluntarily, in an informed manner, without infringing on individual rights, promoting trust, responsibility, and citizenship. To highlight the role of informed consent and personal agency, Figure 2 presents a layered model of citizen autonomy in smart cities.

Figure 2. Layers of Citizen Autonomy in Smart Cities

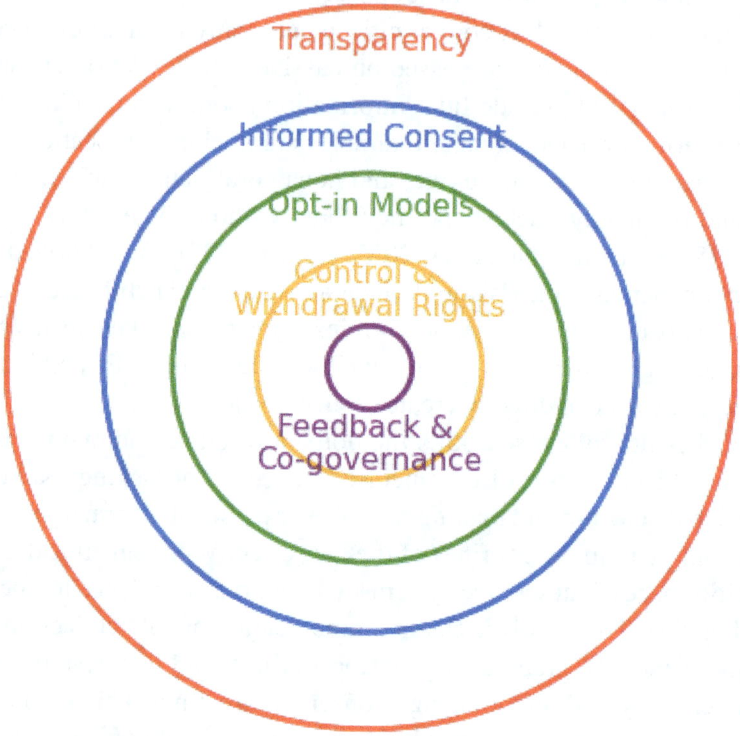

Further, the promotion of citizen autonomy can be done by enabling both residents to have access to instruments that allow them to observe and manage their data footprints, and incorporating feedback systems where the concerns of the masses come into play as both part and parcel of real-time policy and operations. Specifically, by integrating the model of consent as an evolving and active practice instead of a fixed legal procedure, smart cities can approach technological change and its ethics in line with each other, generating smart and inclusive cities.

Data Ownership, Access, and Equity

One of the overarching ethical issues in the smart city ecosystem is whether one should own the data or there should be fair access to it. The ownership over key datasets that impact urban life is, in most urban settings, held exclusively or majority by third-party technological companies, platform operators, or individual departments within a city, rather than by the people who contribute the data. This asymmetry gives rise to Sherman and Hugo Rouzer's power disparities that can be used by data controllers to gain business advantages, enter autonomously into the policy directing process, or act in their interests in optimizing operation without necessarily having the interests of the people in mind (Sustainability Directory, 2025; Trigen, 2025). Table 2 contrasts different data ownership and access scenarios, clarifying the implications for equity and governance.

Table 2. Data Ownership and Access Models in Smart Cities

Model	Controller of Data	Citizen Access	Social Implications
Proprietary (Private)	Tech companies	Minimal	Power concentration, commercial exploitation
Municipal Centralized	City authorities	Limited	Efficiency gains, risk of bureaucratic opacity
Open Data Framework	Shared between gov. & public	High	Transparency, shared innovation, civic trust

The lack of citizen access to their data would decrease the level of transparency and accountability since people usually do not understand how the insights, based on their data, are utilized and who gains the benefits. Data-driven advantages are also likely to increase social inequality: less privileged neighborhoods could have less of the benefits related to technology or online services, against the many technically and technologically advanced services that could be implemented in more fortunate spots.

These ethical and social issues need to be solved with governance systems that extend beyond legal ownership, imbuing values of justice, diversity, and joint value creation. This contains the means to provide citizens with useful access to data, the transparency of data use, and avoiding the monopoly of actions by business organizations. Policies that can stimulate equitable data access, community-based analytics, and open-data efforts can further contribute to democratizing the advantages of smart city technologies, and to social justice and the strength of public confidence in its management (Fabrègue & Bogoni, 2023).

Bias, Discrimination, and Social Exclusion

Algorithms and machine learning models are becoming an important part of smart ecosystems in cities since these systems analyze the data, optimize services, and help in decision-making. Though these technologies are efficient and predictive, they are by their very nature subject to bias when based on an incomplete or otherwise unrepresentative dataset or when based on historical inequalities. Prejudiced data may be presented in such a way as to uphold institutionalized interpersonal inequality, without significant thought to help the marginalized or underrepresented groups (Fabrègue & Bogoni, 2023; Trigen, 2025).

An example would be predictive policing systems that are trained based on the crime records that are biased to particular neighborhoods, thereby leading to over-policing of minority groups, a behavior that further promotes the patterns of discrimination. In the same manner, AI-enabled resource distribution, public service delivery systems, or traffic control systems might neglect low-income or minority neighbourhoods when these are underrepresented in the data. In addition to unequal service provision, unfair algorithms have been a source of lack of trust in the city by citizens, worsened social exclusion, and the advantages of pre-existing inequality in urban governance. Figure 3 depicts how biased data and algorithms can create feedback loops that reinforce systemic inequities within smart cities.

Figure 3. Algorithmic Bias Feedback Loop

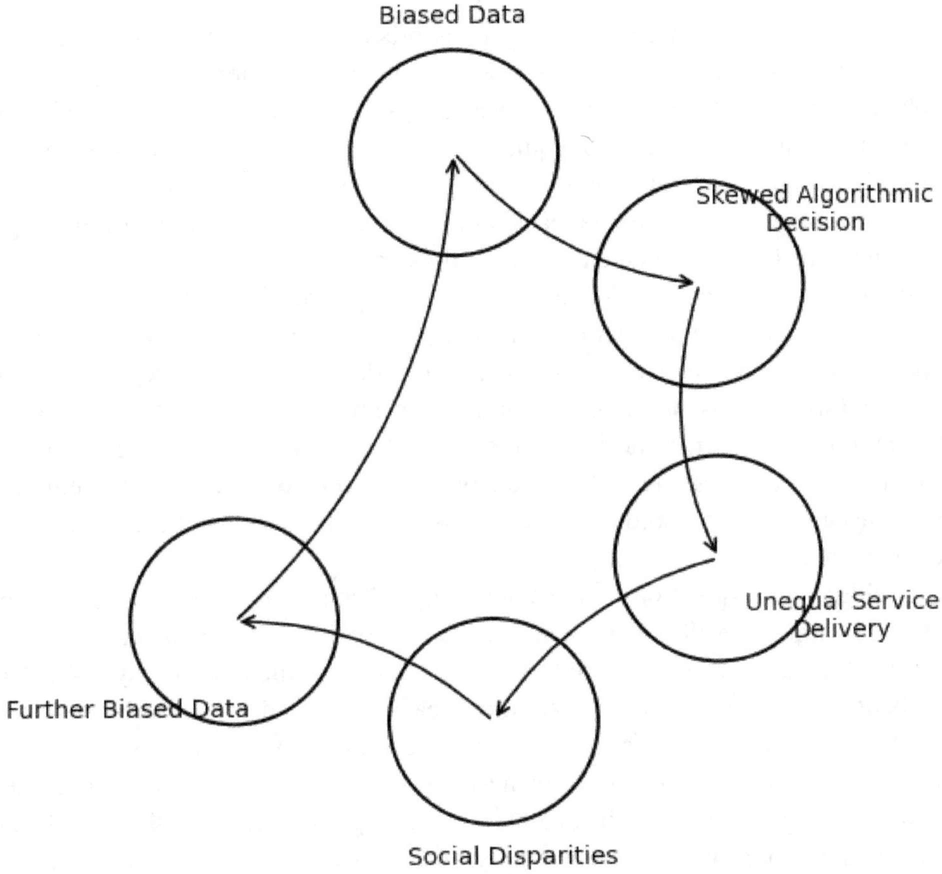

Fighting against these risks is a challenge that should be handled multilaterally. High-quality audit of datasets, bias detection processes, and methodological transparency of algorithmic assessment are the key requirements to be fair. Purposive engagement of different groups and communities through inclusive design processes can assist in determining blind spots and localized nuances. Frequent checking and cyclic reshaping of models should be done to identify new emerging biases and rectify them promptly. Incorporating the concept of ethical principles into the life journey of smart city technologies allows one to prevent discriminatory results and foster inclusive digital cities where all citizens are able to enjoy the outcomes of technical growth with benefits equally.

Interconnected Ethical Dimensions

Ethical issues in smart city ecosystems relate on many levels and create an overlapping network of interdependencies, with one problem throwing another problem into sharper relief. Privacy invasions, say, may directly interfere with the autonomy of the citizenry, and inequitable data access can further support bias due to the algorithms. On the same note, discriminatory algorithms can serve to reinforce social inequities, resulting in feedback loops that can rectify systemic disadvantage. Working to resolve an isolated concern is thus not adequate.

Ethical governance should be based on taking into consideration a complex view that involves the aspects of technical protection, legal aspects, and societal aspects. This encompasses the introduction of effective privacy safeguards, facilitating informed consent and citizen agency, establishing equity of accessing the data, auditing the algorithmic discrimination, and integrating inclusive participatory structures. The cornerstones of this strategy are the values of fairness, accountability, and transparency that would not only sit at the core of the rights of individuals and social equality.

Besides, the acquisition and sustainability of smart city initiatives cannot be achieved without developing trust among the population. When people, as citizens, feel that the data used deals with them responsibly, has their autonomy respected, and benefits are shared well, they are more ready to use and support urban technologies. With a careful consideration of the interdependence of ethical aspects, smart cities could be natural carriers of technological creativity and respect humanistic values, making the urban environments smart, integrated, and socially fair. The interdependence of privacy, consent, equity, and fairness can be illustrated through an interconnected framework (Figure 4), showing how challenges amplify each other.

Figure 4. Interconnected Ethical Dimensions in Smart Cities

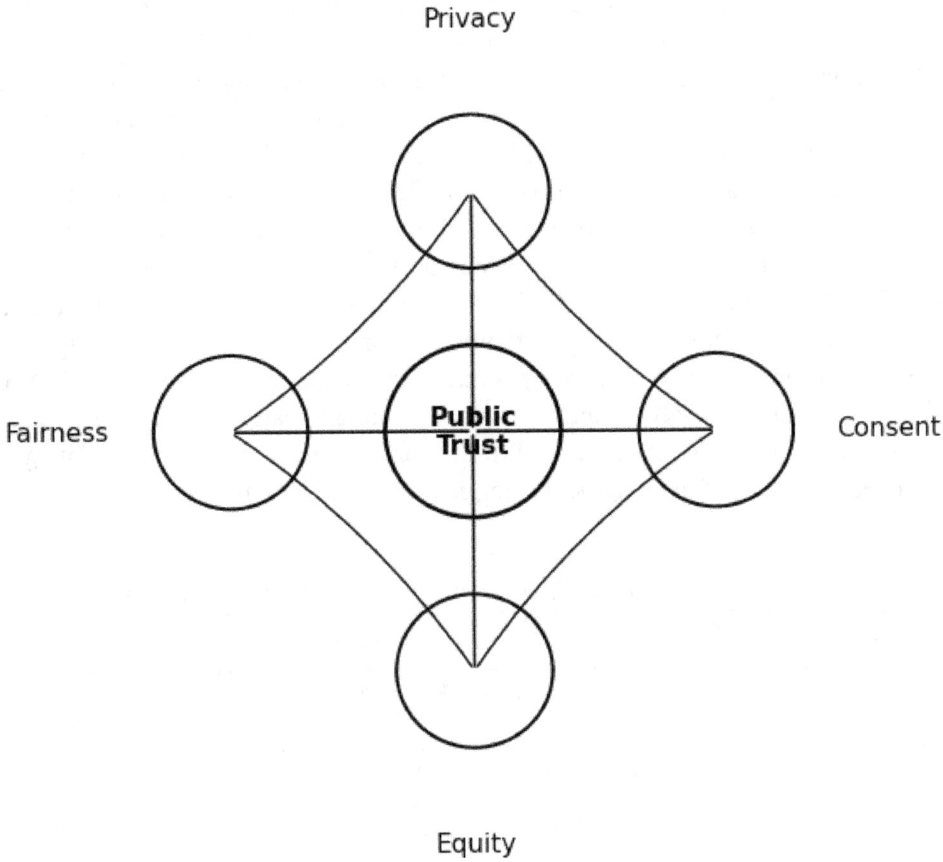

ETHICAL FRAMEWORKS AND REGULATORY APPROACHES

Smart city data governance is becoming more informed by international ethical principles and rule sets that seek to safeguard privacy, support citizen free motivation, and promote social fairness, whilst at the same time supporting ethical use of technological progress (Jørgensen & Ma, 2025). The General Data Protection Regulation (GDPR) of the European Union is one of the most influential legal tools that imposes rigorous requirements on personal data protection, transparency, and privacy of consent. GDPR aims at respecting the rights of individuals to access, correct, and erase personal information, and also explicitly and factually consent to data processing operations. In addition to compliance, in GDPR, there is a strong focus on accountability and the need to incorporate privacy by design principles, requiring data protection to be incorporated into cyber systems at the design stage and not retroactively (Danezis et al., 2015).

Inaugurating such legal frameworks, non-governmental international organizations like UNESCO have come up with principles of using ethical data in urban environments. These guidelines emphasize the priority of human rights, inclusivity, transparency, and accountability in the development and implementation of smart city technologies, with technological innovation needing to be subjected to the values held in society and the well-being of all inhabitants (UNESCO, 2021). Such industry initiatives as the IEEE Global Initiative on Ethics of Autonomous and Intelligent Systems have practical guidance on how to instill ethical principles into AI, IoT, and other intelligent systems, emphasizing ethical considerations of fairness, non-discrimination, and the human-centered design (IEEE, 2023). Table 3 summarizes the major international frameworks influencing smart city data governance, highlighting their scope, principles, and practical mechanisms.

Table 3. Key Global Ethical and Regulatory Frameworks for Smart Cities

Framework	Scope	Key Principles	Mechanisms	Relevance to Smart Cities
GDPR (EU)	Legal	Privacy, consent, transparency, accountability	Data protection officers, citizen rights to access/erase data, privacy-by-design	Strong legal safeguards, binding across EU
UNESCO Guidelines	Ethical	Human rights, inclusivity, transparency, accountability	Voluntary guidelines, capacity building	Normative guidance for cities globally
IEEE Global Initiative	Industry-led	Fairness, non-discrimination, human-centered AI/IoT design	Standards, best-practice protocols	Technical/ethical design support

Collectively, these regulatory and ethical frameworks put in place a layered method of managing the data of smart cities. The combination of legal requirements, international treaties, industry standards, and ideas should allow cities to develop an environment where the potential of technology can be equated with the preservation of personal values, social fairness, and confidence of the population. These holistic governance guarantees a kind of data-driven urban innovation that is both effective and improves efficiencies and the living standards, but in a way that is responsible and ethically appealing; in other words, these urban innovations should be inclusive.

Comparative Analysis of Regulatory Landscapes

The variance in city implementation of ethical principles in governance of smart city data is significant, with a comparative analysis of regulatory environments in countries around the world bringing out this fact. In Europe, cities are usually governed by strong national and regional data protection frameworks, and the General Data Protection Regulation (GDPR) underpins the law-making activities of the EU. This system has led to the creation of independent data protection bodies, institutionalized redress mechanisms for citizens, and strict control procedures, which provide adequate protection against the ill-use of urban data and increase citizen confidence in online governance.

Asian smart cities have different ways of approaching that are informed by the local legal cultures, expectations of society, and the prevailing priorities on technology. As one example, Singapore has built extensive systems combining data governance and privacy policies and proactive citizen consultation, whereas Seoul focuses on transparency and user involvement in data-driven urban programs. In the meantime, other cities in the area can rely mostly upon the policies of the private technology providers, whose interests in most cases lie in operational efficiency or commercial goals rather than in a citizen-centered approach, which constitutes the ethical weak spots (Calzada, 2018).

Such variations across the globe highlight the role that legal traditions, social norms, the role of government, and the degree of technological maturity have on managing smart city data. Global knowledge comparisons have shown that, although such critical elements as regulatory rigor and citizen empowerment are paramount in the context of ethical, equitable, and accountable smart city ecosystems, the adaptation to its local context should take place to recalibrate governance models to local realities and expected societal values.

Gaps and Limitations

Irrespective of rigorous regulatory and ethical codes, the majority of guidelines in existence deal mainly with the rights of the individual, namely privacy, consent, and data protection. These are necessary, but they do not offer too many guidelines on systemic or structural issues, such as algorithmic bias and equity, or social justice (Danezis et al., 2015; Jørgensen & Ma, 2025). The GDPR lays down stringent rules on consent and data protection, but nowhere does it specify how the use of predictive algorithms in the provision of a service policy, like the police, health benefits, or in traffic, would lead to unintended social inequality. This discrepancy indicates the necessity of frameworks that go beyond person-centered protection to introduce the steps that contribute to the fairness and equity of society.

Weak and Inconsistent Enforcement Mechanisms

The application of ethical and regulatory standards is not always consistent, fragmented, or weak, especially in multi-stakeholder ecosystems where various parties are involved: municipal agencies, business suppliers of technologies, and national regulatory authorities. Redundancy or shared authority may result in a lack of accountability, where a citizen has no adequate powers in case of misuse of data or ethical breach. These difficulties are further compounded by the effects of depending on voluntary compliance or corporate self-regulation, which suggests that effective enforcement mechanisms play a key role in the transformation of ethical principles into effective safeguards.

Lack of Operational Clarity

Ethical broad strokes are often too generalized to be practical to the city planner, systems designers, and technologists tasked with bringing them to life on the ground. Abstract norm does not in many cases give direction of real-life design, procedures to be taken by those making the decision, or auditing practices to make, and as such, decision-makers are reported to be in a dilemma on how to encompass the ethics in their system design and implementation (Daoudagh et al., 2021). In the absence of straightforward, executable implementation pathways, even the best-intended frameworks run a risk of becoming aspirational and do not have as much capacity to generate any practical change in the governance of smart cities.

Rapid Technological Evolution

The swiftness with which technologies in smart cities evolve, fueled by the rapid development of edge computing, AI-based surveillance, and ubiquitous real-world time sensor strings, usually exceeds the ability of regulatory systems to evolve. This brings on the legal gray areas and unexpected ethical aspects, which cannot be projected to an equal extent using statutory rules. Anticipatory, dynamic governance is thus needed where iterative policy design, cross-sector interactions, and continuous input by citizens are needed to make sure that ethical principles keep up with technological possibilities, but that rights of citizens are not severely harmed and that responsible urban innovation can be achieved. Table 4 outlines systemic limitations in existing frameworks, underscoring the need for more adaptive, enforceable, and operationally specific approaches.

Table 4. Gaps and Limitations in Current Ethical and Regulatory Frameworks

Gap	Example	Consequences
Narrow focus on individual rights	GDPR regulates consent & privacy but not algorithmic fairness	Risk of systemic inequities
Weak/inconsistent enforcement	Voluntary corporate compliance in North America	Accountability gaps
Lack of operational clarity	Ethical principles remain abstract	Uncertainty for technologists and policymakers
Pace of innovation outstrips regulation	AI-powered surveillance	Legal gray zones

Integrated and Adaptive Governance Models

Adaptive and integrated models of governance seek to balance legal, technical, and societal dimensions concerning smart city operations, which the traditional models tend to lack. These models unite straightforward legal rules and strong technological protection along with societal measures to attack an ethical governance issue in a comprehensive manner. This guarantees that policies, system designs, and work practices all guarantee respect of the citizen rights, take precautionary measures, and facilitate accountable urban innovation (Calzada, 2018).

Transparent Decision-Making

Through integrated models, good governance auctions are appreciated through transparency and accountability. Transparency through public information about data policies, transparent decision-making processes, and constant ethical auditing of algorithms, AI systems, and other automated technologies contributes to compliance control and prevents abuse. Accountability mechanisms, which are designed, clear, and delegated, would ensure responsibility in case of errors, harms, or violations, which turn the ethical oversight into reality in the context of smart city initiatives and not some kind of wishful thinking.

Contextualizing International Standards

Laws are necessary to govern the country, but the application of global ethical standards and best practices should be adapted to suit the local societies culturally and legally. Municipality can incorporate ethical values into the formulation of technology design and implementation in a manner that is reflective of local norms and values, and societal priorities. Such contextualization enables cities to harmonize innovation, efficiencies of operations, and rights of citizens as governance frameworks are both contemporaneous and commanding.

Operationalizing Ethical Principles

Such frameworks as participatory design workshops and the equity impact assessment, as well as the algorithmic fairness audits and privacy-preserving analytics, translate abstract ethical principles into action practices. Systemic approaches to these operations can guarantee the incorporation of human values like fairness, equity, and transparency in the day-to-day running of a smart city. In such a way, the city can be able to defend both the individual and community interests and present that ethical governance is the factor that does not and cannot hamper the sustainable and innovative city development, but, on the contrary, promotes it. Figure 5 presents a conceptual model of integrated governance, emphasizing the interplay of legal, technical, and societal safeguards in creating ethically robust smart city ecosystems.

Figure 5. Integrated and Adaptive Governance Model

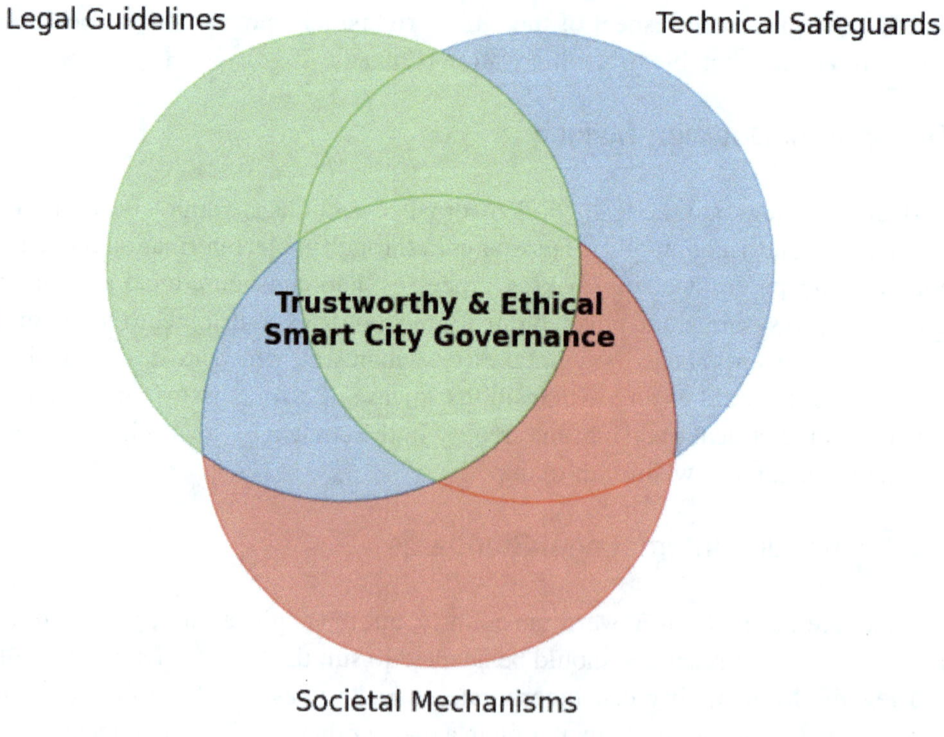

RESPONSIBLE SMART CITY DATA GOVERNANCE

With smart cities becoming more dependent on digital technologies connected to each other, it is essential to develop effective governance strategies to make sure that collecting and using data is ethical, the rights of citizens are preserved, and social equity is facilitated. A conscientious approach to data governance of a smart city is comprehensive and includes not only humanistic concerns, but also a transparent and responsible policy, sensible technological and organizational means. This type of governance not only helps address ethical risks but also helps create trust and social legitimacy among the population, which are a prerequisite to the long-term success of urban digital initiatives.

Principles for Human-Centered Data Collection

The fundamental idea of the responsible smart city governance is to have the humanities at the center of the governance approach that will not aim at furthering the operations or the technological convenience but can be based on the rights, needs, and well-being of the citizens. Other key sources in the approach are some guiding principles.

Privacy-by-Design

Privacy-by-design would be an active model where privacy protections become an ingredient in the architecture and processes of the technology at the ideation phase of technology development. That is to expect possible dangers to individual data, reduce the exposure of data to the limits, and ensure it is secure at each stage. Within the context of smart cities, privacy-by-design can include encrypting streams of data on IoT sensors, anonymizing data before retained, and inserting access controls on systems themselves. This incorporation of privacy as a core design requirement, instead of a retrofitted one, can minimize vulnerabilities and uphold the trust of the population of a city to the end (Cavoukian, 2012, 2020).

Data Minimization

Data minimization presupposes that only the absolute minimum amount of data that is required to provide a certain service is to be stored and gathered. Such a notion not only helps to decrease the possibility of the breakage of the data, but also the risk of its inappropriate use (Ganesh et al., 2025; Goldsteen et al., 2022). As an example, a smart parking system may lead to gathering data on vehicle location only at the stage of active parking and destroying such data as soon as it stops being utilized. When municipalities refrain from collecting data in excess or collecting unnecessary data, they can reduce the storage cost, enhance the privacy regulation compliance, and make the technology correspond to the specified scope.

Equity

Most importantly, equity in smart city governance means that there is a fair distribution of the uterine effects of the technologies to every social group, with special care to the marginalized, underserved, or vulnerable groups (Kempin Reuter, 2019). This implies that services and data-based optimizations cannot favor the wealthy neighborhoods at the cost of poor people. As an illustration of the initiatives to be implemented when analyzing data on energy consumption to quantify efficiency concerns, the interventions ought to be focused on well-linked areas and communities with ageing infrastructures. Equity is also concerned with mitigating digital losses in accessibility, literacy, and affordability so that smart city initiatives do more to curb rather than contribute to social inequity.

Informed Consent

Informed consent offers a stronger human aspect as it gives the citizens a chance to know precisely what data is going to be captured, how it can be handled, the reason behind its usage, and its intended recipients (Pickering, 2021). This needs to be in jargon-free, readable, and understandable language as opposed to the judicial documents. In an intelligent city scenario, it may involve giving informed consent by having interactive dashboards or notifications in different languages on the advantages and disadvantages of involving themselves in data initiatives. The informed consent actively and consciously permits people to make decisions regarding their interaction with urban technologies and strengthens both the principle of autonomy and trust.

Avoiding Exploitative Use of Data

Human-centered perspective requires that data collected should not be utilized in discriminatory, manipulative, and exploitative ways against individuals or groups (Ozmen Garibay et al., 2023; Rouse, 2024). This implies resisting the commodification of urban data to serve only commercial interests when such purposes are detrimental to the welfare of people at large or their privacy. Such as, location data collected by public transportation systems might not be sold to advertisers unless the citizens have been given clear consent to do it, and predictive analytics might not be used in a manner that stigmatizes certain neighborhoods. Since cities rely on data to address public interest issues in other areas like safety, sustainability, and social inclusion, they make sure technological advancements build a stronger civic society, not destroy it.

Operationalizing Human-Centered Governance

To achieve these principles, it is necessary to incorporate them in policies, in the design process, and in monitoring tools. Policies are transparent to allow commitments to be seen, participatory design processes allow the residents to be a part of the technology design process, and accountability structures work to ensure promises become a quantifiable reality. Such principles can be actionable tools such as equity impact assessments, algorithmic fairness audits, and public data dashboards. With the constant use, these kinds of measures can aid cities in reaching a sustainable balance between innovation and ethics, achieving long-term trust and legitimacy.

Technological and Organizational Measures

Smart cities require an ethical government that can be delivered by the integration of technological applications and organizational forms that instantiate human-centered values.

Technical Solutions

Technology is considered the initial security measure against the violation of the rights of citizens in smart cities to maintain fairness and privacy of the data. In certain cases, encryption is used to safeguard sensitive data, which may include personal identifiers, health data, or location history: this makes it impossible to access and use such data by unauthorized actors. Techniques to anonymize a dataset include deleting or obscuring personally identifiable information in databases so that they can be analyzed without compromising the privacy of individuals. Privacy-preserving analytics, such as approaches used in federated learning and differential privacy, allow insight into large amounts of data without the risk of re-identification. Not just privacy, a certain degree of fairness would need automated decision-making using algorithms, which would feature algorithmic auditing, systematic assessment of systems to find unintended biases, accuracy gaps, or discriminatory effects. Integrating these tools within the design and deployment phases would help the cities to make sure that technological systems are in alignment with the norms of ethical standards, legal necessities, and social equity goals.

Organizational Solutions

Although technology offers necessary protection, it is imperative to be institutionalized to allow accountability and ensure that the community feels safe enough to place trust. The formation of specialized ethics boards can make sure that the viewpoints of different bodies of knowledge are being expressed when making decisions, including legal, technical, and social viewpoints. Such boards can examine the policies, invest in high-risk projects, and provide advice on conflicted dilemmas. Intimately related to the preceding is capacity-building, which consists of educational opportunities to train municipal employees, technology developers, and data scientists on how to identify ethical risks, the compliance requirements, and how to implement ethical decision-making models practically. Moreover, periodic review and dynamic feedback mechanisms enable systems of governance to gracefully adapt to changing technology and changes in societal expectations to maintain relevance and performance over a longer period.

Examples of smart cities like Singapore and Toronto can offer strong examples of how smart cities can operationalize ethical governance through integration of both the technological and organizational patterns in action. The holistic approach can be seen in the Singapore Smart Nation plan, which incorporates systems to defend against potential cybersecurity threats to sensitive citizens' data, protocols to ensure such information is anonymized to protect privacy, and practices of algorithmic auditing to mitigate any unfairness or bias of automated decisions. These technological protection mechanisms are underpinned by robust institutional controls such as the Personal Data Protection Commission (PDPC), which carries out the enforcement of the data protection laws, and ethics review panels that review high-risk projects to determine their impact on society and their compatibility with human-centric values.

Technical safeguards and organizing considerations are integrated in both instances, but this fact highlights the point that ethical governance is not only illusory; it is also very doable, and it is not supposed to be optional. Integrating privacy, fairness, accountability, and citizen participation into the operations of smart city projects, Singapore and Toronto present models of how to create sustainability, inclusiveness, and trustworthy urban ecosystems capable of responding and evolving to new changes in the technological and social landscapes in responsible ways.

EMERGING TRENDS AND FUTURE DIRECTIONS

With urban settings becoming more digital, governing systems, service delivery, and citizen engagement are all being transformed immensely by emerging technologies. Smart cities now incorporate AI-based analytics, IoT edge computing, and intelligent mobility systems into the infrastructure to allow real-time observation, anticipative decision-making, and dynamic resource optimization, radically changing the way city services can be planned, delivered, and assessed. Such technologies yield the prospect of higher efficiency, lower operational expenditures, and higher life quality, yet complex ethical, social, and regulatory issues in the field that require being solved proactively.

AI and Predictive Analytics

The city can use huge amounts of collected data to make decisions through AI-based programs in the transportation sector, energy, safety, and service distribution. Indicatively, the platforms would allow the live monitoring of the flow of traffic, use real-time adjustments of sign light timings, and rerouting of vehicles to enhance flow, congestion reduction, minimize emissions, and provide a better experience by commuters because of the use of AI-driven traffic management technology. Predictive energy systems can take account of real-time consumption to optimize electricity distribution across neighborhoods to reduce carbon emissions, energy costs, and aid sustainable urban planning. Nonetheless, the ethics of AI applications has serious issues, such as bias in judgment, a lack of algorithmic transparency, and unfair results in cases where minority groups are underrepresented during the training. Efforts aimed at seeking egalitarian strategies, including algorithmic auditing and fairness-aware model design, and corrections based on ethics by design, are necessary to see that egalitarian principles of equity, transparency, and accountability are observed through AI-based solutions.

IoT and Edge Computing

Smart meters, environmental sensors, and connected transport infrastructure (IoT devices) make it possible to monitor and optimize operations in real-time. Edge computing improves these functions by enabling data to be processed near the source, which serves to lower latency, increase responsiveness, and enable essential systems such as emergency responders and smart grid systems to operate more smoothly. Nevertheless, decentralizing the processing of the data also presents the danger of losing privacy and cybersecurity, and data mismanagement in terms of some sensitive information being more vulnerable to leakage or misuse. Data security can only be achieved through the use of privacy-attributing analytics, heavy encryption, anonymization, and data ownership policies by law, as well as through organizational practices as staff training, standard operating procedures, and a committee that oversees and reviews ethical practices towards data.

Blockchain

Blockchain also promotes transparency, accountability, and traceability in urban management by allowing for transparent ledgers of unchangeable records of transactions, property, and public spending. Its decentralized architecture lowers corruption and trust between the citizens and institutions. Yet, the energy intensity of Blockchain, privacy implications, and governance fragmentation all cause ethical and environmental concerns. Policy and governance implications: Urban authorities should lay out green blockchain standards that prioritize energy-efficient consensus mechanisms (e.g. Proof of Stake), establish clear data protection and anonymization protocols, and work towards developing interoperability standards across municipal and national platforms to avoid fragmentation and to ensure sustainable scalability.

Digital Twins

Digital twins - high-fidelity virtual replicas of urban systems - allow simulation, scenario testing, and proactive planning in transportation, infrastructure and environmental management. By connecting the sensor data to predictive models, they enable evidence-based decision-making and resilience planning. However, digital twins are dependent on huge and continuous data flows, which have raised questions regarding privacy, consent and algorithmic bias. Policy and governance implications: Governments should adopt ethical data-sharing frameworks and implement AI transparency and accountability standards in model design. The development of public digital twin registries could guarantee the audibility, inclusiveness and representativeness of datasets being used for urban modeling. Additionally, integrating protocols for privacy-by-design and bias-mitigation into digital twin architectures would help to protect against misuse and inequitable outcomes.

Next Generation Networks

5G and next-generation 6G networks are the source of the ultra-fast and low-latency connectivity required to enable smart cities, including the IoT, autonomous systems, and real-time analytics. While these networks allow for the possibility of ubiquitous data exchange and automation, they also increase cybersecurity weakness, digital divides, and data sovereignty issues. Policy and governance implications: Policymakers should advocate for secure-by-design standards in network infrastructure, data localization and encryption policies, and universal access programs to avoid digital exclusion. Furthermore, there is a need for cross-sector Cybersecurity governance frameworks to manage the risks across connected systems and preserve public trust in data-driven urban services.

Autonomous Mobility and Robotics

Self-driving mass transit, delivery drones, self-driving garbage collection vehicles, self-driving robot cleaners, and the promise of an autonomous system can lead to increased efficiency, increased accessibility, and environmental sustainability. But they bring complex ethical and regulatory issues. The questions of liability, safety, fair distribution of services, and social acceptability should be resolved in advance. Thus, the routing algorithms should be elaborated so that the underserved neighborhoods are not left behind, and the safety plans should consider technological malfunctions, human contact, and contingency plans. Governance practices like adaptive regulation, ongoing surveilling practices, participatory testing, and impact assessments make sure that autonomous systems are safely, fairly, and all-inclusively in operation.

Integrating Ethical Considerations

The ethical issues relevant across AI, IoT, and autonomous technologies are immense. In order to achieve defensible security, cities need to consider fairness, transparency, privacy, accountability, and social inclusion throughout the entire course of deployment, including design of systems and protocols of operation, policy frameworks, and consultation with citizens. Incorporation of these guidelines can ensure that digital transformation is not only effective in making the city efficient and sustainable but also does not undermine the rights of citizens and instead implements equality and public trust. We can ensure that the cities realize the absolute power of new technologies, as well as reduce the risks and strengthen legitimacy by using a combination of technological safeguards and effective organization and participatory governance. As cities adopt AI, IoT, and autonomous systems, understanding the interplay between technological potential, associated risks, and governance strategies becomes critical. Table 5 summarizes key urban technologies, their primary benefits, challenges, and recommended governance or ethical considerations.

Table 5. Emerging Urban Technologies – Benefits, Challenges, and Governance Considerations

Technology / Application	Potential Benefits	Key Challenges & Risks	Governance & Ethical Considerations
AI-Driven Analytics (e.g., traffic management, predictive energy systems)	- Real-time decision-making - Reduced congestion & emissions - Optimized resource allocation	- Algorithmic bias - Lack of transparency in decision-making - Data dependency on quality & completeness	- Establish explainable AI protocols - Independent audits for fairness - Data quality and governance standards
IoT Edge Computing (e.g., smart grid, emergency response systems)	- Low latency & faster response - Improved operational efficiency - Decentralized processing reduces network load	- Increased attack surface for cyber threats - Data fragmentation risks - Higher complexity in system management	- Cybersecurity-by-design policies - Encryption & privacy-preserving processing - Interoperability standards
Autonomous Mobility Systems (e.g., self-driving transit, delivery drones, robotic waste collection)	- Improved accessibility - Operational cost reduction - Reduced environmental footprint	- Liability in accidents - Public safety concerns - Unequal service distribution	- Clear liability frameworks - Equity-focused service algorithms - Public engagement & acceptance strategies
Predictive Energy Systems (e.g., neighborhood-level demand optimization)	- Reduced energy waste - Lower operational costs - Support for renewable integration	- Over-reliance on automated control - Potential exclusion in underserved areas - Data privacy from consumption patterns	- Demand-side equity monitoring - Transparent usage of consumption data - Community inclusion in energy planning

With the implementation of such emerging urban technologies, there is an acute need to have a culture of constructing governance frameworks that are sensitive to contexts, dynamic, and ethically sound. To date, cities are using AI-based analytics, IoT infrastructures, autonomous mobility systems, and predictive energy platforms to operate equipment in the city, and governance needs to balance the aspects of promoting technological innovation and upholding ethical, legal, and social norms. Unless they are properly maintained, these technologies pose the danger of strengthening disparities, inciting the loss of privacy, or eroding customer confidence.

Such governance can be well-founded on global standards. As an example, the European General Data Protection Regulation (GDPR) imparts binding guidelines related to data protection and consent and transparency; the UNESCO Recommendation on the Ethics of Artificial Intelligence emphasizes upholding human dignity, fairness, accountability, and social responsibility; and the IEEE Ethically Aligned design guidelines provide recommendations applicable to actually introducing ethics in technological systems, such as connecting with stakeholders, reducing bias, and the evaluation of burdens or impact. The two frameworks intersect in domain-focused values, which are important assets in ethical digital urbanization.

Equity also needs to be adjusted to localities in demographics and socioeconomic realities. Urban development patterns, income inequality, and availability of digital infrastructure all affect those who gain access to technology interventions. The AI-augmented recommendations on accessible transportation services or energy-saving algorithms need to incorporate the more deprived areas to make sure that the software and app-based trend does not increase the current social disparity. The convergence of global best practices and locally based policies ensures that cities are able to develop models of governance that are influenced by what is going on globally and are also socially relevant. These strategies facilitate the ethical use of emerging technologies to harness innovation to maximize efficiency, sustainability, and enhance urban quality of life without abrogating citizen rights, facilitating inclusivity, and achieving the long-term goal of building public confidence in smart city projects.

Simultaneously, research and innovation priorities are critical to evidence-based governance and empowering smart cities initiatives in an ethical way. The breakthroughs in these spheres can help to achieve the balance between the technological implementation and human-oriented values to make the urban digitalization efficient and socially responsible. The research on participatory governance aims at creating the distinctive guidelines and procedures of real participation of its citizens in designing, monitoring, planning, and auditing of smart city technologies. Incorporating the view of the people in decision-making enables cities to achieve accountability, transparency, and trust. These may include co-design workshops, citizen advisory boards, and online platforms through which a citizen can provide feedback on the services and policies of a municipality in real time.

The research on algorithmic fairness tackles the issue created by prejudice in predictive models, automatic decision-making systems, and allocation algorithms. Techniques derived with the help of this domain can lead to the identification, alleviation, and avoidance of discriminatory consequences to ensure that each of the societal and socioeconomic categories can receive fair treatment. Its applications would run the gamut from fair distribution of traffic and energy, equal allocation of public services, and policing. The need to test privacy-preserving technologies is yet another avenue of interest, as the solutions promise a methodologically balanced approach between the strength of urban-scale analysis and the respect of individual rights. Techniques like differential privacy, federated learning, and secure multi-party computation enable leveraging the data to make optimization, forecasting, and research decisions without compromising sensitive personal data. These strategies limit any loss of privacy without having to compromise the innovation and efficiency of smart city systems.

Moving forward, smart cities of the future are hinged on how the city handles itself proactively, in the future, and how it can make seamless integrations of the technological innovations with ethical governance and citizen-centered practices. In order to do so, ethical assessment at all levels of system development, including the initial planning, data gathering, algorithm design, implementation, and maintenance processes, can be necessary so that newly emerging technologies can act as human beings with the same value system and human rights. The governance models should be dynamic and relevant to the social, cultural, and legal realities of the area, at the same time being guided by international guidelines and best practices. At the same time, constant research and evidence-based knowledge should inform decision-making processes, determine new threats, and work on solutions that underpin fairness, inclusivity, and privacy. Accountability, trust, and ensured legitimacy by the citizens are further tightened through the participatory mechanisms that incorporate citizens in the co-design, monitoring, and evaluation processes.

When innovation is accompanied by high standards of ethical oversight, cities can have a sustainable, inclusive, and resilient urban ecosystem that can provide substantial social and environmental goods. The interaction of cutting-edge innovation, like AI, IoT, and edge computing, with flexible governance can decide whether the Smart-Cities of the future can turn out to become the role model of responsible city transformation or a techno-geekism nightmare where the technological development can no longer keep pace with social and ethical restraints. After all, the key to successful smart cities can be their ability to take into account innovation, inclusivity, transparency, and accountability that can truly become those serving the greater good and promoting better lives amongst all inhabitants of the respective societies.

CONCLUSION AND POLICY RECOMMENDATIONS

Faster pace of data-driven technologies adoption in urban conditions provides cities with a transformational chance of optimizing their operational efficiency, resource distribution, green environmental issues, and better civic wellbeing. Today, smart city infrastructures powered with IoT sensors, real-time analytics, and AI-based decision-making help municipal authorities to deal with more complex issues in the city, like traffic jams, energy consumption, waste reduction, and public safety in a more efficient way than ever before. These developments are, however, associated with a lot of ethical and social challenges. As discussed in the chapter, extensive data collection can interfere with privacy, circumvent informed consent, establish unfairness in service delivery, and instill biases in their algorithmic decision-making.

These risks can undermine the trust people have and can cement inequalities in society, as well as decrease the legitimacy of smart city efforts without direct governance.

Human-empowerment style of governance is necessary in order to ensure that innovation promotes societal values. The solution to this would be a transparent, accountable, and inclusive method of deploying the technology in urban spaces and the ethical use of data throughout the entire process of urban technology deployment. Analysis of frameworks abroad shows that although the international guidance is comprehensive, there are still gaps in operation that need bridging in global frameworks such as the European GDPR, UNESCO ethical guidelines, and IEEE guidelines. Most cities are challenged to convert general philosophical inquiries regarding ethics into practical policies, guarantee fair access and distribution of benefits, and ensure that various stakeholders, such as urban agencies, private tech companies, and civic groups, may adhere to policies. On the basis of these reflections, a number of practical suggestions can be made that are listed below.

Institutionalizing Ethics-by-Design

Ethical concerns ought to be integrated in every phase of smart city initiatives, starting with planning, up to the implementation of systems and their ongoing management. That involves fixing privacy-by-design, data minimization, and equity-driven ones of approaches into the very architectures of systems. Overall, it is reasonable to say that in determining the technology, municipalities need to view ethics as a core as well as an add-on feature of technological applications to ensure that all systems of technological devices have their foundations rooted within their inherent ability to respect the rights of the citizen, promote fairness, and avoid causing harm. Another benefit of ethics-by-design is the possibility of ensuring conformance with legal frameworks and the further improvement of the trust of the public in the digital initiatives implemented in urban spaces.

Enhancing Citizen Participation and Transparency

Responsible and responsible governance requires some formal means of citizen participation. Public consultations, citizen advisory boards, participatory data workshops, and open data dashboards are all tools that can allow residents to have a say in policy-making and tracking the urban data collection, analysis, and use. Open processes not only build trust but also enable communities to have input into decision-making so that the technologies being adopted are smart city technologies that meet the local needs, cultural drivers, and equity.

Empowering Accountability Structures

Effective governance requires a clear division of responsibilities among all the stakeholders. The appointment of permanent ethics committees, algorithmic auditing systems, and internal reporting mechanisms can serve to perform a timely identification, treatment, and prevention of ethical violations. It cannot be solely the municipal agencies that are responsible, since governments, private technology providers, and contractors must also be accountable when they participate in the design, deployment, and operation of smart cities.

Investing in Technological and Organizational Structures

Such technical defenses as encryption, data anonymization, privacy-protecting analytics, and bias detectors are needed to safeguard sensitive data and avoid discriminatory effects in the automated systems. The combination of these technologies with the training of staff, as well as standard operating procedures and internal governance procedures, can make the principles of ethics actively work throughout all the layers of organizational structure. This combined action ascertains security and fairness in smart city programs.

Adopting Adaptive Governance Models

Considering the fast development of urban technologies, the governance structures have to remain elastic and adaptive. Constant monitoring, reviewing, and adaptation of policies are some of the measures that cities ought to take to respond to the new ethical, social, and technological dangers as they occur. Adaptive governance can enable municipalities to be ahead of the curve when it comes to legal gaps, operational challenges, and societal concerns so that smart city ecosystems can be considered ethically sound, resilient, and future-proof.

Eventually, the ethical development of smart cities demands and needs the context-sensitive, multidisciplinary planning strategies that re-align the global best practices with the local requirements in culture, social, and law. The deployment of emerging technologies (including AI-based predictive analytics, edge computing of the IoT, and autonomous mobility systems) must be made in conjunction with substantial social impact analysis, equity-related findings, and public opinion polls. Hedged-gambling betting games can be used to a great extent by expanded research into participatory governance, algorithmic fairness, and privacy-preserving technologies to give evidence-based policy design. Being based on ethics, transparency, and inclusivity, cities can be able to develop sustainable human-centric urban ecosystems that can exploit digital innovation to trigger sustainable development without undermining democratic principles or losing the trust of their residents.

REFERENCES

Adepoju, P. A., Ige, A. B., Akinade, A. O., & Afolabi, A. I. (2025). Smart Cities and Internet of Things (IoT): A Review of Emerging Technologies and Challenges. *International Journal of Research and Innovation in Social Science, IX*(I), 1536–1549. DOI: 10.47772/IJRISS.2025.9010127

Amy, N. (2024). *How AI is arming cities in the battle for climate resilience | Reuters*. https://www.reuters.com/sustainability/climate-energy/how-ai-is-arming-cities-battle-climate-resilience-2024-05-23/

Bayat, A., & Kawalek, P. (2023). Digitization and urban governance: The city as a reflection of its data infrastructure. *International Review of Administrative Sciences, 89*(1). Advance online publication. DOI: 10.1177/00208523211033205

Bibri, S. E., Alexandre, A., Sharifi, A., & Krogstie, J. (2023a). Environmentally sustainable smart cities and their converging AI, IoT, and big data technologies and solutions: an integrated approach to an extensive literature review. *Energy Informatics 2023 6:1, 6*(1), 1–39. https://doi.org/DOI: 10.1186/S42162-023-00259-2

Calzada, I. (2018). (Smart) Citizens from Data Providers to Decision-Makers? The Case Study of Barcelona. *Sustainability 2018, Vol. 10, Page 3252, 10*(9), 3252. https://doi.org/DOI: 10.3390/SU10093252

Cardullo, P., & Kitchin, R. (2019). Being a 'citizen' in the smart city: Up and down the scaffold of smart citizen participation in Dublin, Ireland. *GeoJournal, 84*(1). Advance online publication. DOI: 10.1007/s10708-018-9845-8

Cavoukian, A. (2012). Operationalizing Privacy by Design : A Guide to Implementing Strong Privacy Practices. *Information and Privacy Commissioner, Ontario, Canada, December*.

Cavoukian, A. (2020). Understanding How to Implement Privacy by Design, One Step at a Time. *IEEE Consumer Electronics Magazine, 9*(2). Advance online publication. DOI: 10.1109/MCE.2019.2953739

Cowls, J., & Floridi, L. (2018). Prolegomena to a White Paper on an Ethical Framework for a Good AI Society. *SSRN Electronic Journal*. https://doi.org/DOI: 10.2139/ssrn.3198732

Danezis, G., Domingo-Ferrer, J., Hansen, M., Hoepman, J.-H., Metayer, D. Le, Tirtea, R., & Schiffner, S. (2015). *Privacy and Data Protection by Design - from policy to engineering*. https://doi.org/DOI: 10.2824/38623

Daoudagh, S., Marchetti, E., Savarino, V., Bernabe, J. B., García-Rodríguez, J., Moreno, R. T., Martinez, J. A., & Skarmeta, A. F. (2021). Data Protection by Design in the Context of Smart Cities: A Consent and Access Control Proposal. *Sensors 2021, Vol. 21, Page 7154, 21*(21), 7154. https://doi.org/DOI: 10.3390/S21217154

Eubanks, V. (2018). *Automating inequality: How high-tech tools profile, police, and punish the poor*. St. Martin's Press.

Fabrègue, B. F. G., & Bogoni, A. (2023). Privacy and Security Concerns in the Smart City. *Smart Cities*, *6*(1), 586–613. DOI: 10.3390/smartcities6010027

Ganesh, P., Tran, C., Shokri, R., & Fioretto, F. (2025). The data minimization principle in machine learning. *Proceedings of the 2025 ACM Conference on Fairness, Accountability, and Transparency*, 3075–3093.

Goldsteen, A., Ezov, G., Shmelkin, R., Moffie, M., & Farkash, A. (2022). Data minimization for GDPR compliance in machine learning models. *AI and Ethics*, *2*(3). Advance online publication. DOI: 10.1007/s43681-021-00095-8

Green, Go. (2024). *SMART CITIES: AI & IOT SOLUTIONS FOR SUSTAINABILITY*. https://gogreengosmart.com/smart-cities-ai-iot-solutions-for-sustainability/

IEEE. (2023). *AI Ethics in Smart Cities: Starting Points for Discussion in Society*. https://smartcities.ieee.org/newsletter/may-2023/ai-ethics-in-smart-cities-starting-points-for-discussion-in-society?

Jørgensen, B. N., & Ma, Z. G. (2025). Impact of EU Regulations on AI Adoption in Smart City Solutions: A Review of Regulatory Barriers, Technological Challenges, and Societal Benefits. *Information 2025, Vol. 16, Page 568, 16*(7), 568. https://doi.org/DOI: 10.3390/INFO16070568

Juvenile Ehwi, R., Holmes, H., Maslova, S., & Burgess, G. (2022). The ethical underpinnings of Smart City governance: Decision-making in the Smart Cambridge programme, UK. *Urban Studies (Edinburgh, Scotland)*, *59*(14), 2968–2984. DOI: 10.1177/00420980211064983

Kempin Reuter, T. (2019). Human rights and the city: Including marginalized communities in urban development and smart cities. *Journal of Human Rights*, *18*(4). Advance online publication. DOI: 10.1080/14754835.2019.1629887

Kim, Y., Ahn, M., Park, J., Jung, C., Siano, P., Almulhim, A. I., & Yigitcanlar, T. (2025). Understanding Smart Governance of Sustainable Cities: A Review and Multidimensional Framework. *Smart Cities 2025, Vol. 8, Page 113, 8*(4), 113. https://doi.org/DOI: 10.3390/SMARTCITIES8040113

Kontokosta, C. E., & Hong, B. (2021). Bias in smart city governance: How socio-spatial disparities in 311 complaint behavior impact the fairness of data-driven decisions. *Sustainable Cities and Society, 64*, 102503. DOI: 10.1016/J.SCS.2020.102503

Masha, B. (2023). *Inside Safe City, Moscow's AI Surveillance Dystopia | WIRED*. https://www.wired.com/story/moscow-safe-city-ntechlab/

Ozmen Garibay, O., Winslow, B., Andolina, S., Antona, M., Bodenschatz, A., Coursaris, C., Falco, G., Fiore, S. M., Garibay, I., Grieman, K., Havens, J. C., Jirotka, M., Kacorri, H., Karwowski, W., Kider, J., Konstan, J., Koon, S., Lopez-Gonzalez, M., Maifeld-Carucci, I., & Xu, W. (2023). Six Human-Centered Artificial Intelligence Grand Challenges. *International Journal of Human-Computer Interaction, 39*(3). Advance online publication. DOI: 10.1080/10447318.2022.2153320

Pickering, B. (2021). Trust, but verify: Informed consent, AI technologies, and public health emergencies. *Future Internet, 13*(5). Advance online publication. DOI: 10.3390/fi13050132

Rouse, W. B. (2024). *From Human-Centered Design to Human-Centered Society: Creatively Balancing Business Innovation and Societal Exploitation*. Productivity Press.

Sharon, T. (2021). Blind-sided by privacy? Digital contact tracing, the Apple/Google API, and big tech's newfound role as global health policy makers. *Ethics and Information Technology, 23*. Advance online publication. DOI: 10.1007/s10676-020-09547-x PMID: 32837287

Stu, S. (2025). *How to build AI-powered cities intelligently | The Australian*. https://www.theaustralian.com.au/business/cfo-journal/how-to-build-aipowered-cities-intelligently/news-story/cac9476c0c284925d70b3abde2dcc785

Sustainability Directory. (2025). *What Ethical Frameworks Should Guide the Development and Deployment of Smart City Technologies?* https://sustainability-directory.com/question/what-ethical-frameworks-should-guide-the-development-and-deployment-of-smart-city-technologies/

The Times. (2025). *Amsterdam abandons smart traffic lights amid privacy fears*. https://www.thetimes.com/world/europe/article/amsterdam-abandons-smart-traffic-lights-amid-privacy-fears-l97g6rmtc?

Trigen. (2025). *Legal & Ethical Considerations for Smart Cities and IoT*. https://www.trigyn.com/insights/legal-and-ethical-considerations-smart-cities-and-iot

UNESCO. (2021). *Recommendation on the Ethics of Artificial Intelligence - Legal Affairs*. https://www.unesco.org/en/legal-affairs/recommendation-ethics-artificial-intelligence?

Ziosi, M., Hewitt, B., Juneja, P., Taddeo, M., & Floridi, L. (2024). Smart cities: Reviewing the debate about their ethical implications. *AI & Society*, *39*(3), 1185–1200. DOI: 10.1007/S00146-022-01558-0/METRICS PMID: 36212227

Chapter 13
The Threat Landscape of Smart Urban Ecosystems:
A Survey

Mohammad Albadareen
https://orcid.org/0009-0008-3034-7693
Hashemite University, Jordan

Abdullah Al-Husseaney
https://orcid.org/0009-0002-6061-4875
Hashemite University, Jordan

Mahmoud Aljawarneh
https://orcid.org/0000-0003-2003-6310
Applied Science Private University, Jordan

Qais Al-Na'amneh
Applied Science Private University, Jordan

Fadi Batah
https://orcid.org/0009-0001-8080-9429
Applied Science Private University, Jordan

Ahmad saleh Alhazaimeh
King Abdaulaziz University, Saudi Arabia

Rahaf Hazaymih
Jordan University of Science and Technology, Jordan

ABSTRACT

The digital transformation of cities into smart urban ecosystems creates a vast and complex cybersecurity attack surface. This paper provides a foundational survey of this threat landscape, systematically deconstructing the smart city's anatomy from a security perspective. We analyze inherent vulnerabilities within key technologies like IoT, 5G/6G, AI, and cloud/edge computing. The survey presents a multi-dimensional taxonomy of threats, classifying them by attacker intent, target asset, and vector, while examining domain-specific vulnerabilities in transportation, energy, and healthcare. A forward-looking analysis of emerging threats is also provided. The

DOI: 10.4018/979-8-3373-4455-3.ch013

objective is to establish a comprehensive, structured understanding of the threats themselves, offering an essential baseline for researchers, practitioners, and policymakers dedicated to securing the cities of tomorrow.

1 INTRODUCTION

The 21st century is defined by an inexorable shift towards urbanization, a trend that places immense pressure on city infrastructure, resources, and governance models. In response, municipalities worldwide are embracing the paradigm of the smart urban ecosystem, leveraging information and communication technologies (ICT) to fundamentally reimagine city operations and enhance the quality of urban life (Hollands, 2020). This transformation is driven by pressing socio-economic needs: the demand for sustainable energy consumption, the necessity of efficient and multimodal transportation, the call for more responsive public services, and the imperative to ensure public safety in increasingly dense population centers. The smart city, therefore, is not merely a technological pursuit but a strategic response to the core challenges of modern urban living.

These ecosystems are built upon a sophisticated, layered architecture of sensors, networks, data platforms, and applications, all powered by a convergence of powerful technologies. The Internet of Things (IoT) forms the nervous system, with billions of sensors collecting real-time data on everything from traffic flow to air quality. High-speed communication networks, particularly 5G and the forthcoming 6G, provide the ubiquitous connectivity essential for processing this data deluge. Artificial Intelligence (AI) and Machine Learning (ML) act as the brain, analyzing patterns to optimize services, predict failures, and automate decisions (Meijer & Bolívar, 2016). While this digital evolution offers immense benefits, it intrinsically introduces a complex and expanding array of cybersecurity risks. The very technologies that enable urban intelligence also serve as potential entry points for malicious actors, creating a dual-use dilemma.

Each connected device and automated service enlarges the digital attack surface, making cities vulnerable to a wide spectrum of malicious activities (Rejeb, Suhaiza, Rejeb, Seuring, & Treiblmaier, 2022). The consequences of security failures in these cyber-physical environments transcend typical IT incidents. A compromised power grid, a manipulated traffic control system, or a breached public health database can have immediate and severe physical-world consequences, disrupting critical infrastructure, compromising public safety, and eroding the fundamental trust between citizens and their governance (Cavoukian et al., 2009). Therefore, a granular understanding of the threat landscape is not merely a technical exercise but a prerequisite for building resilient and trustworthy smart cities. This paper addresses this need by providing a foundational survey focused exclusively on the threats themselves. Our primary objective is to deconstruct, categorize, and analyze the full spectrum of cybersecurity threats, vulnerabilities, threat actors, and attack vectors pertinent to smart urban ecosystems.

This survey serves as a systematic map of the problem space, structured to guide the reader from the technological underpinnings of vulnerabilities to the sophisticated tactics of adversaries. Section 2 examines the anatomy of smart cities from a security viewpoint, identifying vulnerabilities in the enabling technologies as summarized in Table 1. Section 3 presents a multi-dimensional taxonomy of threats, classifying them by origin, target, and method, with concepts illustrated in Figure 3 and Table 2. Section 4 delves into the specific vulnerability landscapes of core urban domains, highlighting crossdomain risks as shown in Figure 2. Section 5 provides a forward look at emerging and sophisticated threats that will define future security challenges, visualized in part by Figure 5. The paper concludes by synthesizing this foundational view of the threat landscape, providing a critical reference for all stakeholders involved in smart city development and security.

2 THE ANATOMY OF EVOLVING SMART URBAN ECOSYSTEMS: A SECURITY PERSPECTIVE

Evolving smart urban ecosystems are complex socio-technical assemblages, characterized by a deep integration of digital technologies into the physical fabric and operational processes of cities. Understanding their anatomy from a security perspective necessitates a survey of the key enabling technologies, the interdependencies they foster, the resultant expansion of the attack surface, and the persistent challenges posed by legacy system integration. As illustrated in Figure 1, these vulnerabilities permeate every layer of the smart city architecture.

A foundational survey of key enabling technologies, summarized in Table 1, reveals a diverse yet vulnerable portfolio. The Internet of Things (IoT) is the most pervasive layer, deploying vast networks of sensors and actuators (Alavi, Jiao, Buttlar, & Lajnef, 2018). Their vulnerability stems from inherent resource constraints; low-cost microcontrollers often preclude the implementation of robust cryptographic algorithms, secure boot processes, or comprehensive logging capabilities. Furthermore,

Figure 1. Layered Architecture of a Smart Urban Ecosystem Highlighting Key Vulnerability Concepts.

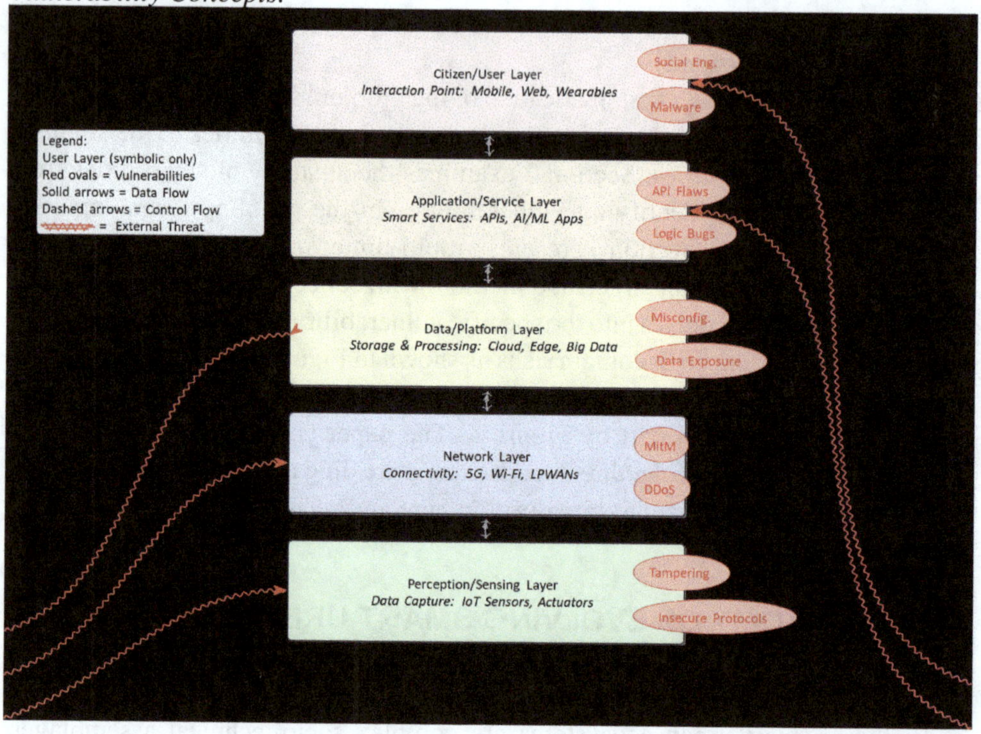

patching vast fleets of physically dispersed devices presents a logistical nightmare, leaving many devices permanently vulnerable to known exploits and susceptible to large-scale botnet conscription (Neshenko, Bou-Harb, Crichigno, Kaddoum, & Ghani, 2019; Bakhshi, Ghita, & Kuzminykh, 2024; Coston, Plotnizky, & Nojoumian, 2025; Al-Na'amneh, Dhifallah, et al., 2025).

Fifth-generation (5G) and future wireless communication technologies are critical enablers, but their software-defined nature introduces new risks. Unlike legacy hardware-based networks, 5G architectures rely heavily on virtualization (NFV) and Software-Defined Networking (SDN). This exposes new attack surfaces at the orchestration and management layers. An attacker who compromises the SDN controller could potentially reroute, monitor, or drop traffic across large segments of the city network. Similarly, vulnerabilities in virtualized network functions or network slicing mechanisms could allow an attacker to break out of their designated slice and impact other critical services sharing the same physical infrastructure (Scalise et al., 2024; Park et al., 2021).

Artificial Intelligence (AI) and Machine Learning (ML) act as the "brain" of many smart services, but this brain can be deceived. Adversarial attacks demonstrate that subtle, often human-imperceptible modifications to input data can cause models to misclassify information with high confidence (Nobles, 2024; Humayun et al., 2024). In a smart city, this could mean tricking a traffic camera into ignoring a stop sign or fooling a security system into not recognizing a threat. Data poisoning, where attackers subtly corrupt training data over time, can install hidden backdoors or biases into models, making them unreliable or unfair in their decision-making (Benouachane, 2025).

Cloud and Edge Computing provide the necessary data processing power. However, the complexity of cloud environments often leads to security misconfigurations (e.g., public storage buckets, overly permissive IAM roles), which are a leading cause of data breaches. Edge computing pushes processing closer to the source, reducing latency but also creating a more distributed and harder-to-defend perimeter. These numerous edge nodes may lack the physical security of a centralized data center and become prime targets for compromise (Albshaier, Almarri, & Albuali, 2025; Ometov, Molua, Komarov, & Nurmi, 2022). Digital Twins, while powerful for simulation, introduce a new risk: the fidelity of the virtual model. An attack that corrupts the link between the physical asset and its digital twin can lead to disastrous decisions based on flawed virtual data (Lv et al., 2022).

The profound interdependencies across urban systems create the potential for cascading failures, as visualized in Figure 2. Smart cities are not collections of independent systems but tightly coupled networks where a failure in one domain can trigger a catastrophic chain reaction in others (Brunner, Peer, Zorn, Paulik, & Logan, 2024; Salehpour, Al-Anbagi, Yow, & Cheng, 2022). For instance, a cyberattack on a regional power grid (energy domain) could initiate a widespread blackout. This immediately impacts the transportation domain (traffic signals fail, public transit stops), the healthcare domain (hospitals switch to limited backup power), the governance domain (emergency services communication is strained), and the economic domain (financial transactions halt). This interconnectedness means attackers can target a less secure system as a pivot point to reach a more critical one, making holistic, cross-domain risk assessment essential yet incredibly difficult to perform (Rehak, Senovsky, Hromada, Lovecek, & Novotny, 2018; Hayat, Adnan, & Iqbal, 2024).

Consequently, the digital attack surface in smart cities is vast, dynamic, and porous. Every connected device is a potential ingress point (Choo, 2021). This necessitates a shift from traditional perimeter security to adaptive, zero-trust architectures that assume no implicit trust and continually verify every user and device (Stafford, 2020).

Finally, legacy systems integration presents a persistent vulnerability source. Many cities have operational technology (OT) like industrial control systems (ICS) that predate modern cybersecurity (Stouffer, Falco, Scarfone, et al., 2011; Nankya, Chataut, & Akl, 2023). Integrating these systems, which may lack basic authentication or use insecure protocols, into modern IP networks creates weak links that attackers can easily exploit to pivot from IT networks into critical OT environments (Byres & Lowe, 2004; Harkat, Camarinha-Matos, Goes, & Ahmed, 2024). Addressing this requires careful segmentation and compensating controls like specialized intrusion detection systems (Ali et al., 2025).

Table 1. Key Enabling Technologies in Smart Urban Ecosystems: Functions, Vulnerabilities, and Example Threats.

Technology	Primary Function(s)	Key Vulnerabilities	Example Scenario
Internet of Things (IoT)	Real-time data collection (sensors), automation (actuators) across various domains.	Resource constraints (power, memory), insecure default credentials, unpatched firmware, weak communication protocols.	Compromised IoT sensors feeding false data to traffic management, leading to gridlock or accidents.
5G/6G Networks	Ultra-high bandwidth, low latency, massive connectivity for advanced applications (autonomous vehicles, AR).	Network slicing vulnerabilities, insecure virtualization (NFV/SDN), complex management interfaces, increased attack surface.	Exploitation of a 5G core network vulnerability to disrupt communication for emergency services city-wide.
Artificial Intelligence / Machine Learning (AI/ML)	Optimization (traffic, energy), prediction (maintenance, crime), anomaly detection, decision support.	Adversarial attacks (evasion, poisoning), model theft/extraction, biased algorithms, lack of explainability, data privacy concerns.	AI-powered traffic system fooled by adversarial inputs on vehicle cameras, causing misclassification and dangerous maneuvers.
Cloud Computing	Scalable data storage, processing power, application hosting for city services.	Misconfigurations (e.g., public buckets), insecure APIs, multi-tenancy risks, data breaches, vendor lock-in, data sovereignty issues.	Misconfigured cloud storage exposing sensitive citizen PII collected by various smart city applications.
Edge Computing	Local data processing near IoT devices, reduced latency for real-time applications.	Physical security of edge nodes, distributed security management, limited resources on edge devices, insecure edge-to-cloud communication.	Compromise of an edge server controlling local utility infrastructure, leading to localized service disruption.
Digital Twins	Virtual replicas of physical assets/ systems for simulation, monitoring, and planning.	Data synchronization vulnerabilities, compromise of the twin leading to flawed physical control, inaccurate simulations, exposure of sensitive operational models.	Manipulation of a digital twin for a critical bridge, hiding structural weaknesses from maintenance systems.

3 SYSTEMATIC CATEGORIZATION OF CYBERSECURITY THREATS

A systematic understanding of cybersecurity threats within smart urban ecosystems necessitates a multidimensional categorization, reflecting the diverse motivations of attackers, the variety of assets targeted, the manifold vectors of attack, and the common forms these threats take. Figure 3 provides a high-level mapping of threat actors to their primary targets.

Classification by attacker intent reveals a spectrum of adversaries. Cybercrime syndicates, motivated purely by profit, have adapted their models for municipal targets, offering

Figure 2. Interconnected Smart City Domains Highlighting Critical Dependencies and Cascading Threat Scenarios.

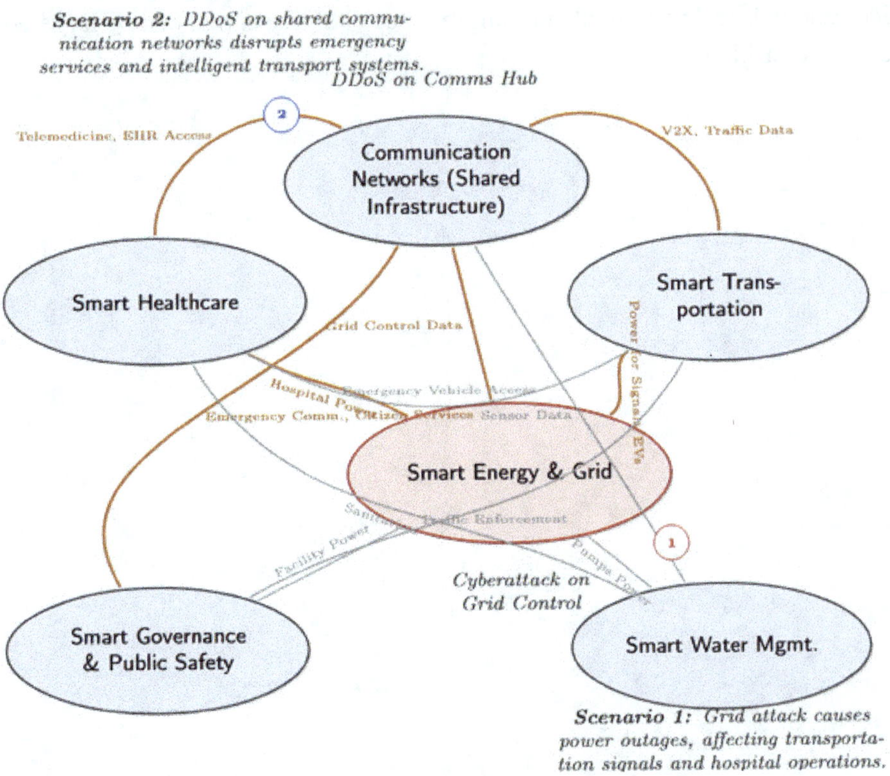

Ransomware-as-a-Service (RaaS) that lowers the bar for attacking under-funded city governments (Europol, 2020). Nation-state actors represent the most sophisticated threat, conducting long-term espionage campaigns to steal intellectual property or pre-positioning disruptive payloads in critical infrastructure, to be activated during geopolitical conflict (Adeniran, Adeniran, Familusi, & Adedayo, 2024). Hacktivists leverage cyber disruption as a form of protest, defacing city websites or leaking documents to draw attention to political causes (Gönç, 2022). Insider threats remain particularly dangerous, as a trusted employee or contractor can bypass perimeter defenses to cause sabotage or exfiltrate data with intimate knowledge of internal systems (Cappelli, Moore, & Trzeciak, 2012; Al-Na'amneh, Aljawarneh, & Hazaymih, 2025).

Classification by target asset shows what is at stake. Critical Infrastructure remains a high-value target because its disruption has immediate physical consequences (Salehpour et al., 2022). Data is the "new oil" of the smart city, and its theft or manipulation can undermine city operations and citizen privacy (ENISA (European Union Agency for Cybersecurity), 2019). The integrity of municipal Services and public Trust are also intangible but vital assets that can be targeted to erode civic confidence.

Figure 3. Taxonomy of Threat Actors in Smart Urban Ecosystems and Their Primary Target Assets.

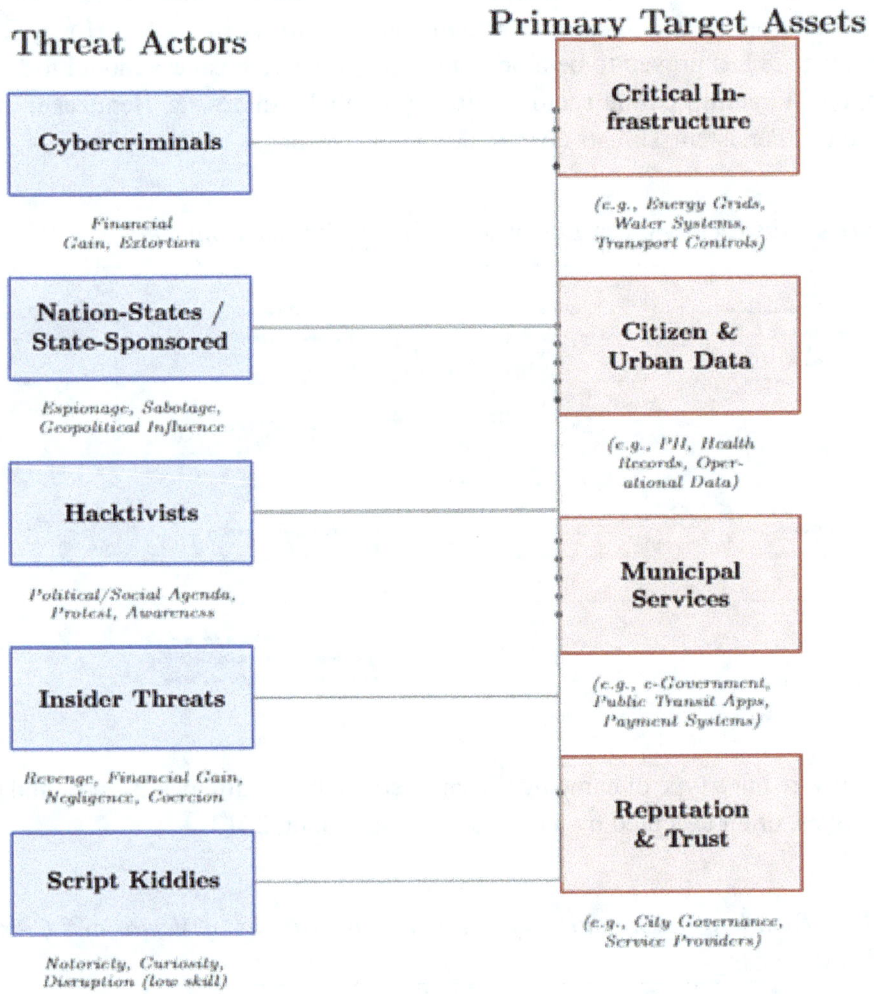

Classification by attack vector, detailed in Table 2, describes the "how" of an attack. These vectors are often combined in a multi-stage attack lifecycle, as depicted in Figure 4. Network-based attacks like DDoS can paralyze services (Ahmed, 2020), while software-basedattacks exploit vulnerabilities in the vast and complex codebases of smart city applications (McGraw, 2012). The physical accessibility of many IoT devices opens them up to tampering, while social engineering continues to be a highly effective vector for bypassing technical controls by exploiting human psychology (Ch, 2014). The supply chain vector is particularly insidious, as it allows threats to be embedded in trusted products before they are even deployed (Hassija, Chamola, Gupta, Jain, & Guizani, 2020).

Common threat types are the specific manifestations of these vectors. Malware is a general-purpose tool for various malicious activities (Sikorski & Honig, 2012). Ransomware has proven to be a devastatingly effective business model for cybercriminals targeting public sector entities (Greubel, Andres, & Hennecke, 2023). Advanced Persistent Threats (APTs) are not a type of

Figure 4. Abstracted Attack Lifecycle for Smart City Environments.

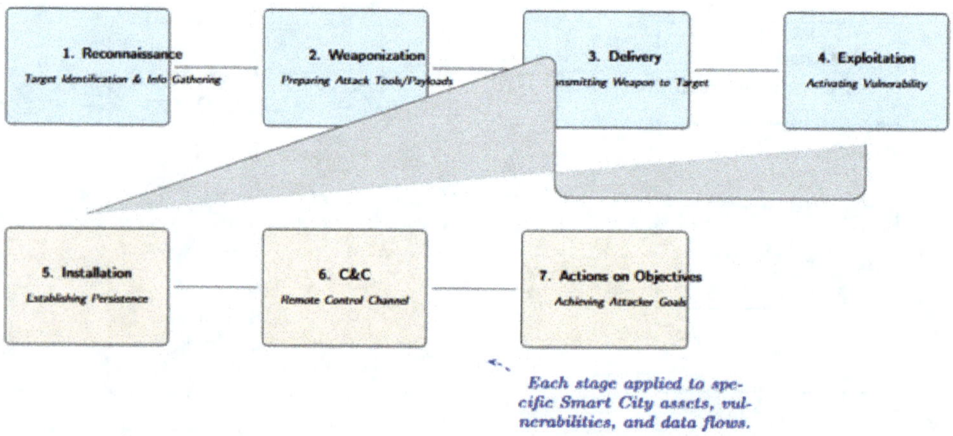

malware but a type of campaign, characterized by stealth, persistence, and clear objectives, often executed by nation-states (Mandiant, 2013).

Table 2. Detailed Classification of Cybersecurity Threats by Vector and Common Manifestations.

Attack Vector	Description	Common Techniques	Example Impact
Network based	Exploiting vulnerabilities in network protocols, configurations, or devices to intercept, disrupt, or gain unauthorized access.	DDoS, Man-in-the-Middle (MitM), IP/MAC Spoofing, DNS Poisoning, Session Hijacking, Network Sniffing, Rogue Access Points.	DDoS attack renders city's e-government portal or emergency alert system unavailable.

continued on following page

Table 2. Continued

Attack Vector	Description	Common Techniques	Example Impact
Software based	Leveraging flaws in operating systems, applications (web, mobile, embedded), firmware, or APIs.	Malware (Ransomware, Spyware), Zero-day Exploits, SQL Injection, Cross-Site Scripting (XSS), Insecure Deserialization, API abuse.	Ransomware encrypts patient data in a smart hospital system, halting operations. SQL injection on a smart parking app steals user payment details.
Physical Access	Gaining unauthorized physical proximity or access to devices, systems, or infrastructure components.	Device Tampering, Theft of Hardware, Installation of Rogue Devices (e.g., malicious USBs), Bypassing Physical Security Controls.	Unauthorized physical access to a traffic control cabinet allows manipulation of signals, causing deliberate congestion.
Social Engineering	Manipulating human psychology to trick individuals into divulging confidential information or performing actions that compromise security.	Phishing, Spear-Phishing, Vishing (Voice Phishing), Smishing (SMS Phishing), Baiting, Pretexting.	City employee tricked by a spear-phishing email into revealing credentials, giving attackers access to internal municipal networks.
Supply Chain	Targeting less secure elements in the lifecycle (design, development, manufacturing, distribution, update) of components.	Embedding Malware/Backdoors in firmware/software, Using Counterfeit/Compromised Hardware, Hijacking Update Mechanisms.	Compromised IoT sensors with pre-installed malware are deployed across the city, forming a large-scale botnet for future attacks.
Human Error / Misconfiguration	Unintentional actions or incorrect setup of systems or security controls by legitimate users or administrators.	Weak/Default Passwords, Unpatched Systems, Misconfigured Firewalls or Cloud Services, Accidental Data Exposure.	Public cloud storage bucket for smart city data misconfigured to allow public read access, exposing sensitive citizen information.

4 VULNERABILITY LANDSCAPE SURVEY ACROSS CORE URBAN DOMAINS

While foundational technologies introduce risks, these vulnerabilities manifest in unique ways within specific urban domains. A domain-centric survey, summarized in Table 3, is essential for targeted risk management.

In Smart Transportation Systems (STS), the attack surface spans from the vehicle to the cloud. The in-vehicle network (e.g., CAN bus) was historically isolated but is now connected via telematics units, creating pathways for remote attacks. Vulnerabilities in V2X communication protocols could enable an attacker to spoof messages, creating "ghost vehicles" to cause chaos or triggering mass braking events (Lippi et al., 2025). Furthermore, the centralized traffic management systems that ingest data and control signals are high-value targets; compromising one could paralyze a city's transport network (Ghena, Beyer, Hillaker, Pevarnek, & Halderman, 2014).

The Smart Energy & Grid domain is a primary target due to its critical nature. The convergence of traditional Operational Technology (OT) with modern Information Technology (IT) is a major source of risk. An attacker breaching the utility's corporate IT network could potentially pivot into the OT network that controls SCADA systems and physical grid components (Nambundo, de Souza Martins Gomes, de Souza, & Machado, 2025). Smart meters, while enabling efficiency, create millions of new endpoints on the grid edge, each a potential target for energy theft or as an entry point for larger-scale attacks (Sheng, Yao, Fu, & Yang, 2021). The Stuxnet malware remains the canonical example of a sophisticated cyberphysical attack designed to cause physical destruction in an industrial setting (Langner, 2011; Rai & Nain, 2024).

Smart Healthcare faces a dual threat: data privacy and patient safety. The Internet of Medical Things (IoMT) includes devices like infusion pumps and pacemakers where a software vulnerability could have lethal consequences (Yaqoob, Abbas, & Atiquzzaman, 2019). Hospitals are frequently targeted by ransomware because the urgency of restoring access to patient records creates immense pressure to pay the ransom, making them a lucrative target for cybercriminals (Coventry & Branley, 2018).

In Smart Buildings and Homes, vulnerabilities in Building Management Systems (BMS) for commercial properties can be exploited to control HVAC, lighting, and physical access systems, posing risks of sabotage or enabling corporate espionage. In the residential space, the proliferation of insecure consumer IoT devices creates significant privacy risks, turning homes into sources of surveillance data or nodes in a botnet (Shah, Aljawarneh, & Akbar, 2025; Angrishi, 2017).

Finally, Smart Governance and Public Safety systems are targets for both disruption and influence. Compromising emergency alert systems can incite public panic, while hacking public surveillance networks enables illicit monitoring or the creation of deepfakes for disinformation campaigns (Moore, 2023). These attacks aim not just at technical systems but at the fabric of social order and trust.

Table 3. Vulnerability Hotspots and Threat Examples Across Key Smart City Domains.

Domain Critical Components		Specific Vulnerabilities	Plausible Threat Example
Smart Transportation	Connected Vehicles (V2X), Traffic Light Controllers, Public Transit Systems, EV Charging Stations.	Insecure V2X communication, default credentials in controllers, unpatched firmware, CAN bus vulnerabilities.	Remote hijacking of connected vehicle functions; manipulation of traffic signals to cause gridlock or facilitate other crimes.
Smart Energy & Grid	Smart Meters, SCADA/ICS Systems, Distributed Energy Resources (DERs), Substation Automation.	Weak authentication in meters, insecure legacy SCADA protocols (Modbus, DNP3), lack of IT/OT segmentation.	Attackers compromise smart meters to commit energy theft or disrupt grid stability; Stuxnet-like attack on a power generation facility.
Smart Healthcare	Connected Medical Devices (pumps, pacemakers), EHR systems, Hospital Networks, Telemedicine Platforms.	Unpatched medical device firmware, insecure PHI transmission, weak EHR access controls, ransomware susceptibility.	Ransomware attack locks access to critical patient EHRs, forcing hospitals to divert patients; remote manipulation of a connected infusion pump.
Smart Buildings & Homes	BMS/BAS, Smart Locks, IP Cameras, Voice Assistants, HVAC controllers.	Insecure BMS protocols (e.g., BACnet exposed), default IoT credentials, firmware vulnerabilities, data privacy leaks.	Attacker gains unauthorized access to a commercial building via a vulnerable BMS to disable security systems or conduct corporate espionage.
Smart Governance	E-Government Portals, Public Surveillance (CCTV) Networks, Emergency Alert Systems, Citizen Databases.	Web app vulnerabilities (SQLi, XSS), insecure CCTV feeds, lack of encryption in emergency comms, poor data anonymization.	Defacement of city website; compromised CCTV network used for unauthorized surveillance or to create deepfakes for disinformation.
Smart Water & Waste	Water Quality Sensors, SCADA for Water Treatment, Smart Bins, Automated Collection Systems.	Sensor spoofing/tampering, vulnerabilities in ICS for water purification, insecure data transmission from smart bins.	Attackers provide false sensor readings to a water treatment plant, leading to incorrect chemical dosing and potential public health risks.

5 EMERGING THREAT VECTORS: A FORWARD LOOK

The cybersecurity threat landscape is not static; it continually evolves as attackers devise new methods and exploit advancements in technology. For smart urban ecosystems, a survey of emerging and sophisticated threat vectors, as summarized in Table 4, is crucial for anticipating future challenges.

AI-Powered Attacks and Adversarial Machine Learning represent a paradigm shift. Attackers are no longer just targeting systems; they are targeting the logic of the AI models themselves. Adversarial ML is particularly concerning because it can undermine the reliability of AI-driven systems in subtle ways that are difficult for traditional signature-based or anomaly detection systems to identify (Rubin, 2022; Khazane, Ridouani, Salahdine, & Kaabouch, 2024). A successful poisoning attack on a city's predictive policing model, for instance, could introduce biases that lead to discriminatory outcomes, eroding public trust without ever triggering a typical security alert.

The threat from Quantum Computing is strategic and long-term. The most immediate concern is the "harvest now, decrypt later" scenario, where adversaries are already intercepting and storing

Figure 5. Conceptual Flow of an Advanced Persistent Threat (APT) Targeting a Smart City Environment.

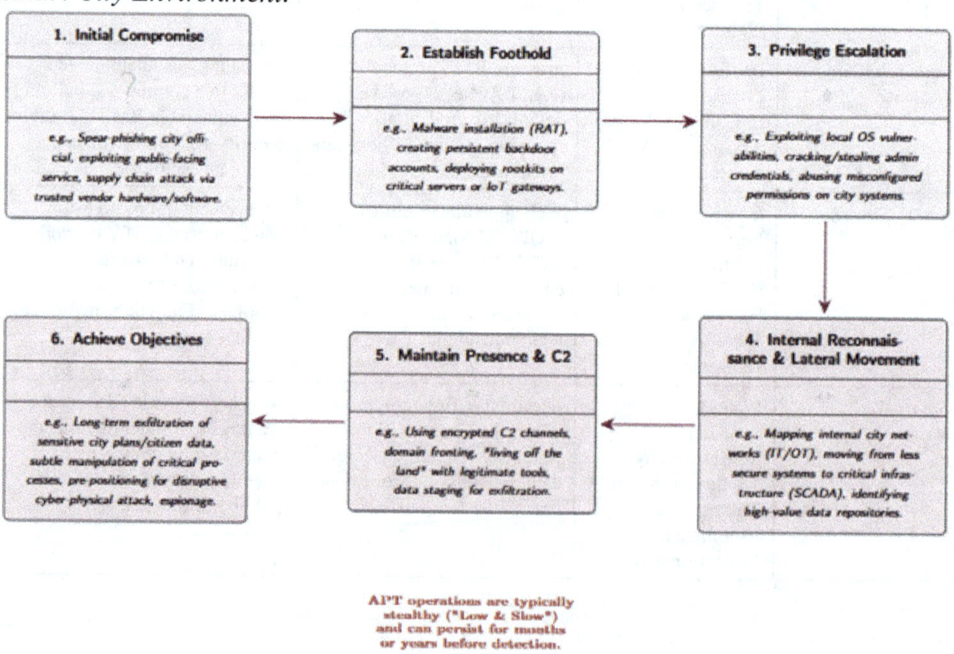

encrypted data from government, infrastructure, and commercial communications. While this data is secure today, the expectation is that it can be decrypted retroactively once a fault-tolerant quantum computer is built (Bernstein & Lange, 2017). This creates an existential risk for any data with a long secrecy lifetime, forcing a slow and costly migration to Post-Quantum Cryptography (PQC) standards, a process that will take over a decade to complete for complex urban systems (Alagic et al., 2022).

Advanced Persistent Threats (APTs), visualized in Figure 5, are becoming more focused on OT environments. Instead of simple disruption, adversaries may seek to cause subtle, long-term degradation of physical equipment by manipulating control processes just within operational tolerances, causing premature wear and tear that is difficult to attribute to a cyberattack (Chen, Desmet, & Huygens, 2014).

Sophisticated Supply Chain Attacks are moving beyond simple software compromises. Hardware-level threats, such as malicious modifications to microchips (hardware Trojans) or compromised firmware, are incredibly difficult to detect post-deployment. The increasing reliance on a globalized, opaque supply chain for the millions of devices required by a smart city makes it a prime vector for high-impact, widespread attacks initiated by well-resourced nation-state actors (Hassija et al., 2020; Nguyen, Durlauf, & Tikalsky, 2023).

Finally, Data Integrity Attacks are emerging as a more insidious threat than simple data theft. An attacker who can subtly alter environmental sensor data, financial transaction records, or traffic flow information can undermine the entire value proposition of a data-driven smart city, leading to flawed decisions, economic chaos, and a complete loss of trust in the city's digital infrastructure (Garagad, Iyer, & Wali, 2020).

Table 4. Analysis of Emerging and Sophisticated Threat Vectors in Smart Urban Ecosystems.

Emerging Threat	Description & Modus Operandi	Risks to Critical Functions	Detection & Mitigation Challenges
AI-Powered Attacks & Adversarial ML	Attackers use AI for enhanced reconnaissance, adaptive malware, and sophisticated social engineering. Adversarial ML targets AI models via evasion, poisoning, or extraction.	Manipulation of AI-driven traffic control, compromised facial recognition, biased AI in public service allocation, automated discovery of zero-days.	Detecting subtle adversarial inputs, securing AI training data, lack of robust defenses for AI models, attributing AI-generated attacks.

continued on following page

Table 4. Continued

Emerging Threat	Description & Modus Operandi	Risks to Critical Functions	Detection & Mitigation Challenges
Quantum Computing Threats	Future quantum computers could break current public-key cryptography (RSA, ECC) used for secure communication and data protection.	Widespread compromise of encrypted city data, invalidated digital signatures, breakdown of secure V2X or smart grid communications.	"Harvest now, decrypt later" risk, long transition time to PQC, cost and complexity of upgrading legacy systems.
Advanced IoT Botnets	Large-scale networks of compromised IoT devices capable of sophisticated, coordinated attacks beyond simple DDoS.	Coordinated sensor data manipulation, synchronized attacks on infrastructure control points, large-scale privacy violations.	Securing vast numbers of heterogeneous IoT devices, identifying sophisticated botnet C&C, mitigating physical-layer impacts.
Supply Chain Attacks	Compromise of hardware/ software components during design, manufacturing, or distribution, embedding backdoors before deployment.	Pre-compromised critical infrastructure components (SCADA controllers, routers), widespread deployment of vulnerable IoT devices.	Lack of transparency in global supply chains, difficulty verifying hardware/software integrity, detecting deeply embedded malicious code.
Data Integrity Attacks	Subtle manipulation of data inputs or stored data to undermine decision-making; advanced attacks on data availability.	Flawed urban planning from corrupted datasets, compromised AI models due to data poisoning, manipulation of financial systems.	Detecting subtle data manipulations, ensuring end-to-end data provenance, robust backup and recovery against advanced wipers.
CPS Convergence Threats	Exploitation of the tight coupling between cyber and physical components to cause intended physical damage or disruption.	Sabotage of industrial processes in water/energy sectors, intentional accidents in autonomous transport, manipulating building automation for physical harm.	Complex cyber-physical interactions, lack of safety-engineered cybersecurity, difficulty modeling physical consequences of cyber attacks.

6 CONCLUSION

This survey has systematically deconstructed the multifaceted cybersecurity threat landscape confronting modern smart urban ecosystems. Our analysis establishes that the digital transformation of cities, while offering profound benefits, is fundamentally intertwined with the introduction of complex and pervasive security risks. The very technologies that enable urban innovation—from the ubiquitous sensors of the Internet of Things and the intelligent algorithms of AI to the high-speed connectivity of 5G and the scalable infrastructure of cloud platforms—each contribute to a complex matrix of inherent vulnerabilities. As detailed in our examination of the smart city's anatomy, this technological convergence creates a vastly expanded and dynamic attack surface, where deep-seated interdependencies between critical domains like energy, transport, and healthcare present the constant threat of cascading failures with profound societal impact.

Our systematic taxonomy of threats reveals a diverse and motivated adversarial ecosystem. Smart cities are not merely facing opportunistic hackers; they are strategic targets for a spectrum of actors, from profit-driven cybercriminals leveraging ransomware to sophisticated nation-states conducting espionage and preparing for future disruption. These adversaries employ a multifaceted arsenal of attack vectors, exploiting weaknesses across every layer of the urban architecture, from the physical security of a sensor to the application logic of a city service platform. By cataloging specific vulnerabilities within core urban domains and providing a forward look at emerging threats like adversarial AI, quantum computing risks, and insidious supply chain compromises, this paper provides a comprehensive and foundational map of the problem space.

Ultimately, this detailed understanding of the threat landscape is the essential, non-negotiable first step for any stakeholder involved in urban development. Without a granular appreciation of the vulnerabilities, the adversaries, and their methods, any attempt to build a secure city will be superficial and reactive at best. The findings presented herein serve as a critical baseline for the subsequent development of robust defensive strategies, resilient architectures, and effective governance policies. Securing the city of the future begins with a clear-eyed assessment of the dangers it faces today. This survey provides that assessment, offering a vital resource for building the robust, resilient, and trustworthy smart cities of tomorrow.

REFERENCES

Adeniran, A. A., Adeniran, A. O., Familusi, O. B., & Adedayo, O. (2024). The outlook of cyber security in african businesses: Issues and way-out. *Management analytics and social insights, 1*(2), 260–271.

Ahmed, S. (2020). Security and privacy in smart cities: Challenges and opportunities. *International Journal of Engineering Trends and Technology, 68*(2), 1–8.

Al-Na'amneh, Q., Aljawarneh, M., & Hazaymih, R. (2025). A framework for insider threat detection using role-based profile assessment and threshold. In *Utilizing ai in network and mobile security for threat detection and prevention* (pp. 97–114). IGI Global Scientific Publishing.

Al-Na'amneh, Q., Dhifallah, W., Hazaymih, R., Almaiah, M. A., Alsheyab, A., Alshinwan, M., & Qadoumi, B. (2025). Dis flooding attack impact in rpl-based 6lowpan network. In *Machine intelligence applications in cyber-risk management* (pp. 69–84). IGI Global Scientific Publishing.

Alagic, G., Alagic, G., Apon, D., Cooper, D., Dang, Q., Dang, T., ... others (2022). Status report on the third round of the nist post-quantum cryptography standardization process.

Alavi, A. H., Jiao, P., Buttlar, W. G., & Lajnef, N. (2018). Internet of things-enabled smart cities: State-of-the-art and future trends. *Measurement, 129*, 589–606.

Albshaier, L., Almarri, S., & Albuali, A. (2025). Federated learning for cloud and edge security: A systematic review of challenges and ai opportunities. *Electronics (Basel), 14*(5), 1019.

Ali, S., Alshinwan, M., Khashan, O. A., Hijjawi, M., Altawil, A., Al-Na'amneh, Q., ... others (2025). Intrusion detection for wireless sensor networks using parrot algorithm. In *Machine intelligence applications in cyber-risk management* (pp. 345–366). IGI Global Scientific Publishing.

Angrishi, K. (2017). Turning internet of things (iot) into internet of vulnerabilities (iov): Iot botnets. *arXiv preprint arXiv:1702.03681*.

Bakhshi, T., Ghita, B., & Kuzminykh, I. (2024). A review of iot firmware vulnerabilities and auditing techniques. *Sensors (Basel), 24*(2), 708. PMID: 38276399

Benouachane, H. (2025). Cyber security challenges in the era of artificial intelligence and autonomous weapons. In *Cyber security in the age of artificial intelligence and autonomous weapons* (pp. 24–42). CRC Press.

Bernstein, D. J., & Lange, T. (2017). Post-quantum cryptography. *Nature*, *549*(7671), 188–194. PMID: 28905891

Brunner, L. G., Peer, R., Zorn, C., Paulik, R., & Logan, T. (2024). Understanding cascading risks through real-world interdependent urban infrastructure. *Reliability Engineering & System Safety*, *241*, 109653.

Byres, E., & Lowe, J. (2004). The myths and facts behind cyber security risks for industrial control systems. In *Proceedings of the vde kongress* (Vol. 116, pp. 213–218).

Cappelli, D. M., Moore, A. P., & Trzeciak, R. F. (2012). *The cert guide to insider threats: How to prevent, detect, and respond to information technology crimes (theft/sabotage/fraud)*. AddisonWesley Professional.

Cavoukian, A., ... (2009). Privacy by design: The 7 foundational principles. *Information and privacy commissioner of Ontario, Canada, 5*(2009), 12.

Ch, H. (2014). *Social engineering: The science of human hacking*. Wiley.

Chen, P., Desmet, L., & Huygens, C. (2014). A study on advanced persistent threats. In *Ifip international conference on communications and multimedia security (cms 2014)* (Vol. 8557, pp. 63–72). Springer.

Choo, K.-K. R. (2021). Internet of things (iot) security and forensics: Challenges and opportunities. In *Proceedings of the 2th workshop on cps&iot security and privacy* (pp. 27–28).

Coston, I., Plotnizky, E., & Nojoumian, M. (2025). Comprehensive study of iot vulnerabilities and countermeasures. *Applied Sciences (Basel, Switzerland)*, *15*(6), 3036.

Coventry, L., & Branley, D. (2018). Cybersecurity in healthcare: A narrative review of trends, threats and ways forward. *Maturitas*, *113*, 48–52. PMID: 29903648

ENISA (European Union Agency for Cybersecurity). (2019). *Good practices for iot and smart infrastructures security* (Tech. Rep.). Heraklion, Greece: ENISA.

Europol. (2020). *Internet organised crime threat assessment (iocta) 2020* (Tech. Rep.). The Hague: Europol Public Information.

Garagad, V. G., Iyer, N. C., & Wali, H. G. (2020). *Data integrity: a security threat for internet of things and cyber-physical systems. In 2020 international conference on computational performance evaluation (compe).*

Ghena, B., Beyer, W., Hillaker, A., Pevarnek, J., & Halderman, J. A. (2014). Green lights forever: Analyzing the security of traffic infrastructure. In *8th usenix workshop on offensive technologies (woot 14).*

Gönç, D. (2022). An evaluation of cyber threat taxonomies in the framework of cyber activism. *Bilgi ve Iletis¸im Teknolojileri Dergisi˙*, *4*(2), 171–196.

Greubel, A., Andres, D., & Hennecke, M. (2023). Analyzing reporting on ransomware incidents: A case study. *Social Sciences*, *12*(5), 265.

Harkat, H., Camarinha-Matos, L. M., Goes, J., & Ahmed, H. F. (2024). Cyber-physical systems security: A systematic review. *Computers & Industrial Engineering*, *188*, 109891.

Hassija, V., Chamola, V., Gupta, V., Jain, S., & Guizani, N. (2020). A survey on supply chain security: Application areas, security threats, and solution architectures. *IEEE Internet of Things Journal*, *8*(8), 6222–6246.

Hayat, F., Adnan, M., & Iqbal, S. (2024). Expert and intelligent systems for assessment and mitigation of cascading failures in smart grids: Research challenges and survey.

Hollands, R. G. (2020). Will the real smart city please stand up?: Intelligent, progressive or entrepreneurial? In *The routledge companion to smart cities* (pp. 179–199). Routledge.

Humayun, M., Tariq, N., Alfayad, M., Zakwan, M., Alwakid, G., & Assiri, M. (2024). Securing the internet of things in artificial intelligence era: A comprehensive survey. *IEEE Access : Practical Innovations, Open Solutions*, *12*, 25469–25490.

Khazane, H., Ridouani, M., Salahdine, F., & Kaabouch, N. (2024). A holistic review of machine learning adversarial attacks in iot networks. *Future Internet*, *16*(1), 32.

Langner, R. (2011). Stuxnet: Dissecting a cyberwarfare weapon. *IEEE Security and Privacy*, *9*(3), 49–51.

Lippi, G., Aljawarneh, M., Al-Na'amneh, Q., Hazaymih, R., & Dhomeja, L. D.. (2025). Security and privacy challenges and solutions in autonomous driving systems: A comprehensive review. *Journal of Cyber Security and Risk Auditing*, *2025*(3), 23–41.

Lv, Z., Chen, D., Feng, H., Singh, A. K., Wei, W., & Lv, H. (2022). Computational intelligence in security of digital twins big graphic data in cyber-physical systems of smart cities. [TMIS]. *ACM Transactions on Management Information Systems*, *13*(4), 1–17.

Mandiant. (2013). *Apt1: Exposing one of china's cyber espionage units* (Tech. Rep.). Alexandria, VA: Mandiant.

McGraw, G. (2012). Software security: Building security in. *Datenschutz und Datensicherheit-DuD*, *36*(9), 662–665.

Meijer, A., & Bolívar, M. P. R. (2016). Governing the smart city: A review of the literature on smart urban governance. *International Review of Administrative Sciences, 82*(2), 392–408.

Moore, A. D. (2023). Privacy, security, and surveillance. In *Technology ethics* (pp. 160–168).

Nambundo, J. M., de Souza Martins Gomes, O., de Souza, A. D., & Machado, R. C. S. (2025). Cybersecurity and major cyber threats of smart meters: A systematic mapping review. *Energies, 18*(6), 1445.

Nankya, M., Chataut, R., & Akl, R. (2023). Securing industrial control systems: Components, cyber threats, and machine learning-driven defense strategies. *Sensors (Basel), 23*(21), 8840. PMID: 37960539

Neshenko, N., Bou-Harb, E., Crichigno, J., Kaddoum, G., & Ghani, N. (2019). Demystifying iot security: An exhaustive survey of iot vulnerabilities and a first empirical look at internet-scale iot exploitations. *IEEE Communications Surveys and Tutorials, 21*(3), 2702–2733.

Nguyen, P., Durlauf, S., & Tikalsky, M. (2023). *Software bill of materials: A catalyst to a more secure software supply chain* (Unpublished doctoral dissertation). Acquisition Research Program.

Nobles, C. (2024). The weaponization of artificial intelligence in cybersecurity: A systematic review. *Procedia Computer Science, 239*, 547–555.

Ometov, A., Molua, O. L., Komarov, M., & Nurmi, J. (2022). A survey of security in cloud, edge, and fog computing. *Sensors (Basel), 22*(3), 927. PMID: 35161675

Park, J. H., Rathore, S., Singh, S. K., Salim, M. M., Azzaoui, A., Kim, T. W., & Park, J. H. (2021). A comprehensive survey on core technologies and services for 5g security: Taxonomies, issues, and solutions. *Hum.-. Centric Comput. Inf. Sci, 11*(3), 1–22.

Rai, P., & Nain, V. (2024). Stuxnet unveiled: The blueprint for modern cyber conflict. In *2024 3rd edition of ieee delhi section flagship conference (delcon)* (pp. 1–4).

Rehak, D., Senovsky, P., Hromada, M., Lovecek, T., & Novotny, P. (2018). Cascading impact assessment in a critical infrastructure system. *International Journal of Critical Infrastructure Protection, 22*, 125–138.

Rejeb, A., Suhaiza, Z., Rejeb, K., Seuring, S., & Treiblmaier, H. (2022). The internet of things and the circular economy: A systematic literature review and research agenda. *Journal of Cleaner Production, 350*, 131439.

Rubin, V. L. (2022). *Misinformation and disinformation: Detecting fakes with the eye and ai*. Springer Nature.

Salehpour, A., Al-Anbagi, I., Yow, K.-C., & Cheng, X. (2022). Modeling cascading failures in coupled smart grid networks. *IEEE Access : Practical Innovations, Open Solutions, 10*, 81054–81070.

Scalise, P., Boeding, M., Hempel, M., Sharif, H., Delloiacovo, J., & Reed, J. (2024). A systematic survey on 5g and 6g security considerations, challenges, trends, and research areas. *Future Internet, 16*(3), 67.

Shah, S. M., Aljawarneh, M. M., & Akbar, S. (2025). Assistive living in iot-based smart home systems for aging in place: A review. *VFAST Transactions on Software Engineering, 13*(2), 83–98.

Sheng, C., Yao, Y., Fu, Q., & Yang, W. (2021). A cyber-physical model for scada system and its intrusion detection. *Computer Networks, 185*, 107677.

Sikorski, M., & Honig, A. (2012). *Practical malware analysis: the hands-on guide to dissecting malicious software*. No Starch Press.

Stafford, V. (2020). Zero trust architecture. *NIST special publication, 800*(207), 800–207.

Stouffer, K., Falco, J., Scarfone, K., et al. (2011). Guide to industrial control systems (ics) security. *NIST special publication, 800*(82), 16–16.

Yaqoob, T., Abbas, H., & Atiquzzaman, M. (2019). Security vulnerabilities, attacks, countermeasures, and regulations of networked medical devices—A review. *IEEE Communications Surveys and Tutorials, 21*(4), 3723–3768.

Chapter 14
Trust Through Transparency:
Blockchain-Enabled Supply Chain Traceability for Smart Urban Ecosystems

Yahaya Saidu
https://orcid.org/0009-0000-8909-8806
Universiti Teknologi PETRONAS, Malaysia & Taraba State University, Jalingo, Nigeria

Suwaiba Siuto Adamu
https://orcid.org/0009-0005-9522-2777
Taraba State University, Jalingo, Nigeria

Shuhaida Mohamed Shuhidan
Universiti Teknologi PETRONAS, Malaysia

Jameel Shehu Yalli
https://orcid.org/0009-0006-2602-4862
Universiti Teknologi PETRONAS, Malaysia

Dahiru Adamu Aliyu
https://orcid.org/0009-0009-9803-3604
Universiti Teknologi PETRONAS, Malaysia

Hussaini Mamman
https://orcid.org/0009-0005-0404-3125
Universiti Teknologi PETRONAS, Malaysia

ABSTRACT

As urban ecosystems evolve into data-intensive infrastructures, the transparency of supply chains has become pivotal to cybersecurity, governance, and trust. This chapter explores how blockchain, initially developed for decentralized finance, is now foundational for traceability in smart urban logistics. It examines its convergence with IoT and governance systems to enable tamper-resistant, auditable, and privacy-aware data flows. The chapter outlines blockchain's core features, immutability, decentralization, smart contracts, and permissioned architectures, and maps

DOI: 10.4018/979-8-3373-4455-3.ch014

these to urban sectors like food safety, pharmaceuticals, procurement, and waste. Real-world deployments across Asia, Europe, and North America demonstrate its role in enhancing collaboration, preventing fraud, and supporting compliance with regulations such as the GDPR. The chapter also identifies adoption challenges and offers ethical governance models and a strategic roadmap to position blockchain as a socio-technical foundation for trust, sovereignty, and equity in the smart city era.

1. INTRODUCTION: URBAN SUPPLY CHAINS IN THE AGE OF SMART CITIES

Modern urban life relies on the continuous circulation of goods and information. Supply chains (SC), which link production, distribution, and consumption, serve as critical infrastructures for food security, public health, transportation, and emergency response (Sarkheyli & Sarkheyli, 2019). As cities become increasingly interdependent and data-driven, ensuring the integrity and traceability of these chains is no longer a purely operational task but a strategic imperative for resilience, public trust, and equitable service delivery.

Urban supply chains(USC) sustain the ecosystemic metabolism of cities. Whether transporting perishable food, delivering vaccines, or maintaining energy systems, they enable cities to function effectively and adapt to crises. Yet, they often remain invisible until disruptions expose their fragility (Ding et al., 2023). The COVID-19 pandemic underscored this vulnerability: shortages of medical equipment and essential goods emerged not from absolute scarcity but from fragmented coordination, hoarding, and the absence of real-time data (Agarwal et al., 2022). These failures reveal deeper structural problems rooted in limited visibility and reliance on centralized, siloed infrastructures.

Traditional logistics models perpetuate trust asymmetries and data fragmentation. Legacy systems often depend on intermediaries, proprietary databases, and batch-based recordkeeping, creating vulnerabilities to fraud, counterfeiting, and manipulation. Centralized authorities also introduce single points of failure; a compromised database or ERP platform can paralyze an entire urban supply chain (Jinor & Bridgelall, 2024; Theodorou & Sklavos, 2019). In complex metropolitan environments, where municipal agencies, private vendors, and community stakeholders must coordinate, fragmented data stewardship undermines both cybersecurity and systemic resilience.

The lack of transparency also limits accountability to consumers and regulators. Citizens rarely have reliable means to verify the origin, quality, or ethical sourcing of goods, while city managers often lack audit trails necessary to enforce environmental and social compliance. From contaminated food in Europe to counterfeit vaccines in Southeast Asia, recent scandals demonstrate the costs of opacity for both human well-being and institutional legitimacy (Sarkheyli & Sarkheyli, 2019; Shchekhovska, 2025).

To address these weaknesses, cities are increasingly turning to the convergence of logistics, the Internet of Things (IoT), and blockchain. IoT devices such as sensors, RFID tags, and GPS trackers now generate real-time data throughout SC. When anchored immutably on blockchain ledgers, these data streams enable tamper-resistant provenance tracking and auditable records of environmental conditions and handover events (Saidu et al., 2025). Blockchain's strength lies not only in data immutability but also in distributed validation and programmable automation. Smart contracts can, for instance, trigger payment holds or regulatory alerts if temperature thresholds are breached during vaccine distribution (Baranidharan et al., 2025; Thakur, 2025).

Urban governance is beginning to adapt to these innovations. Cities such as Dubai and Amsterdam are integrating blockchain-enabled provenance into food and waste management systems, embedding verifiability and privacy-by-design into urban platforms (Bai et al., 2022; Shen & Pena-Mora, 2018; Zhu et al., 2024). Yet, this shift also raises new challenges. Immutable ledgers may conflict with data protection principles such as the "right to be forgotten" under GDPR, and without inclusive design, traceability systems risk excluding small vendors, informal workers, and digitally marginalized communities. Blockchain promises to decentralize trust, but without robust governance, consumer protection, and equity safeguards, it may reproduce or even exacerbate digital inequalities (Singh et al., 2021).

As cities digitize further, their ability to secure and verify SC will shape resilience to future disruptions, from pandemics to climate shocks. Blockchain-enabled traceability must therefore be viewed not only as a technical innovation but as a socio-technical infrastructure for accountability, ethical sourcing, and democratic oversight. Realizing its promise requires more than technology adoption: it demands governance frameworks, consumer protection policies, and strategies that support equity for diverse suppliers, including small and medium enterprises (SMEs) in developing economies. As illustrated in Figure, by situating blockchain within both technological and policy contexts, this chapter frames traceability as a shared civic infrastructure that balances efficiency with inclusivity, laying foundations for trustworthy and equitable urban governance.

The remainder of this chapter will explore the cybersecurity and privacy risks inherent in traditional SC, identify the unique capabilities blockchain offers to address these concerns, and evaluate real-world architectures and policy frameworks that can guide the implementation of blockchain-based traceability systems in smart urban contexts

Figure 1. Convergence of USC, Smart City Infrastructure, and Blockchain Traceability.

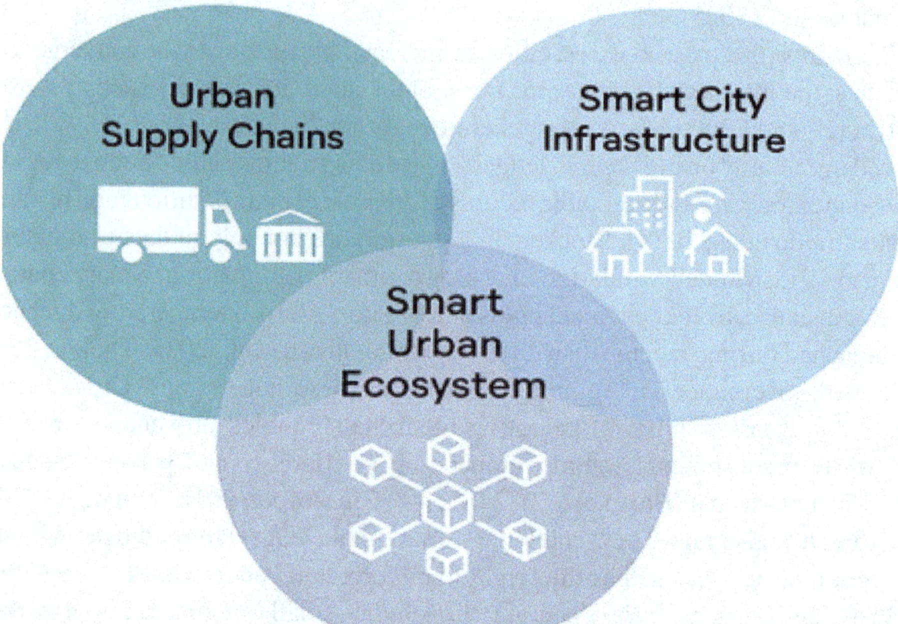

2. CYBERSECURITY AND PRIVACY RISKS IN TRADITIONAL SUPPLY CHAINS

Traditional SC have historically ensured the movement of goods and services across regions, but their design is increasingly misaligned with the demands of digital and interconnected urban ecosystems. These infrastructures, often reliant on centralized databases and siloed information flows, lack the agility, transparency, and security required in smart city contexts. The consequences of such structural rigidity are not only operational delays but also heightened exposure to cyberattacks, data breaches, and regulatory non-compliance. Figure 2 illustrates the common vulnerabilities that characterize conventional USC, including fragmented data silos, single points of failure, and insufficient safeguards for data privacy and integrity.

2.1 Data Silos and Access Control Failures

A prominent vulnerability in legacy SC is the persistence of data silos, where manufacturers, distributors, and retailers maintain isolated databases with limited interoperability. This fragmented architecture hampers visibility and complicates authentication across networks, obstructing real-time verification of provenance or compliance (Mazumdar, 2023). The lack of unified access controls amplifies the risks: a study by Agnes et al. (2024) found that 62% of logistics breaches were linked to misconfigurations or inadequate role-based permissions (Agnes et al., 2024). During the distribution of pandemic-related medical equipment in 2020, outdated access logs and overlapping procurement roles led to unauthorized approvals and misallocations across multiple cities (Tan et al., 2025). These examples highlight how governance weaknesses, particularly inadequate oversight of data stewardship, compound cybersecurity risks in urban supply ecosystems.

Figure 2. Common vulnerabilities in traditional USC

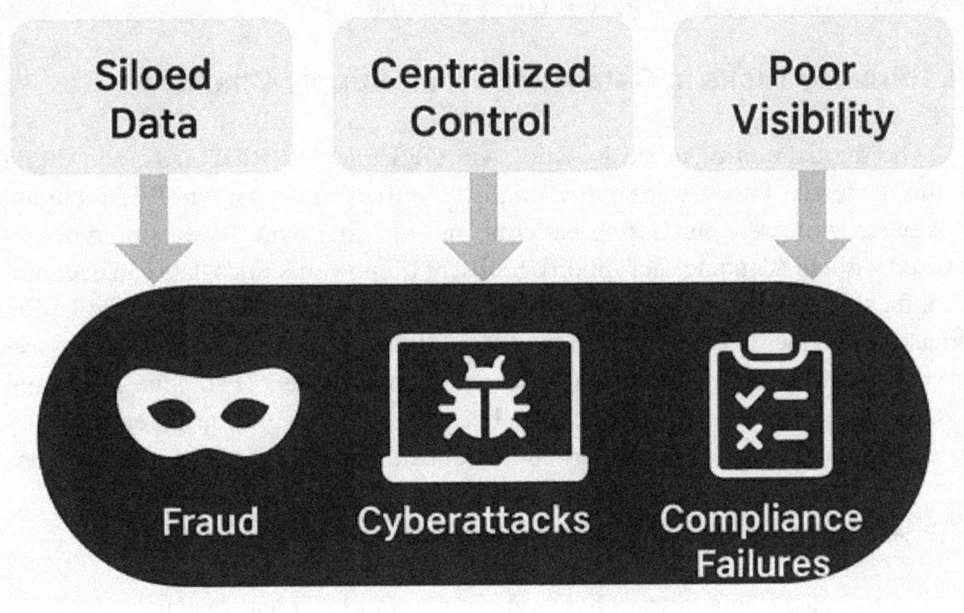

2.2 Centralization and Systemic Vulnerabilities

Reliance on centralized Enterprise Resource Planning (ERP) systems and databases creates systemic fragility in USC. A single attack or technical failure can disrupt the operations of hospitals, transport hubs, or energy distribution networks. The 2021 ransomware attack on JBS Foods, which paralyzed meat SC in North America and Australia, demonstrated how cybercriminals exploit central points of control to cause cascading urban disruptions (Agarwal et al., 2022). Such incidents underscore the urgency of rethinking governance models and adopting resilience-focused approaches that minimize single points of failure.

2.3 Fraud, Counterfeiting, and Provenance Gaps

Weak verification mechanisms in traditional systems create opportunities for fraud and counterfeit goods to enter SC. This is particularly damaging in pharmaceuticals, food safety, and high-value goods, where substandard or falsified products threaten public health and consumer confidence (Hastig & Sodhi, 2020). For instance, the World Health Organization (2022) reported a surge of counterfeit COVID-19 vaccines and test kits in 2022, largely facilitated by unauthorized intermediaries manipulating paper-based and spreadsheet-based records. Such cases reveal that beyond technical flaws, governance lapses and inadequate cross-border oversight exacerbate risks to safety and consumer protection.

2.4 Privacy Risks in Data-Rich Urban Supply Chains

The digitization of urban logistics, via GPS trackers, RFID tags, and digital twins, generates vast streams of personally identifiable information (PII), including customer addresses, purchasing patterns, and mobility data. When stored or processed without adequate encryption or consent frameworks, such data can become a tool for surveillance and profiling. A 2023 breach at a Southeast Asian ride-hailing logistics provider led to the exposure of 20 million delivery records containing user coordinates and timestamps, later sold on darknet markets (Fabrègue & Bogoni, 2023). These incidents reveal a tension between the drive for transparency and the need to uphold privacy rights, particularly considering data protection regulations.

2.5 Case Examples: Failures in Urban Supply Chains

Several cases demonstrate how cyber vulnerabilities and opaque governance undermine USC:

- **Food Contamination in China (2021):** Falsified safety certificates and altered delivery logs allowed tainted dairy products to reach multiple cities, exposing the lack of integrated traceability and regulatory enforcement (Z. Wang, 2023).

- **Counterfeit Electronics in Africa (2020):** Nearly 35% of imported consumer electronics in Nairobi and Lagos were counterfeit, facilitated by falsified customs records during intermodal transfers. The absence of shared audit mechanisms delayed detection until consumer complaints surged (Maima, 2024).
- **Medical Cold Chain Failures in Argentina (2021):** Temperature excursions during vaccine distribution in Buenos Aires were concealed through manual overwriting of logs, a vulnerability revealed only after a neighboring city's blockchain pilot exposed discrepancies (Fazekas et al., 2021).

These cases show how fragmented oversight, cost-cutting practices, and weak auditing frameworks can translate into systemic risks for urban populations.

2.6 Regulatory and Compliance Implications

The vulnerabilities above intersect directly with emerging regulatory, and governance demands. Global frameworks such as the EU's GDPR, California Consumer Privacy Act (CCPA), and India's data localization mandates require robust data protection, consent management, and auditability. Newer directives, such as the EU's Corporate Sustainability Due Diligence Directive (CSDDD), compel firms to demonstrate transparent monitoring of environmental and human rights impacts across supply networks (Mokale, 2021). Traditional supply chain infrastructures, built on siloed and unverified data flows, are ill-equipped to meet these requirements (Danyluk, 2021).

Equally critical are socio-economic and ethical considerations. SMEs, especially in the Global South, often lack the financial and technical resources to comply with blockchain-based traceability mandates. These risks creating a two-tier system in which large corporations meet compliance expectations while smaller actors face exclusion, further entrenching inequalities in access to urban markets. Moreover, without consumer protection frameworks, blockchain-enabled transparency could inadvertently shift liability onto smaller suppliers while shielding larger actors.

Addressing these challenges requires more than technological fixes. Hybrid governance models that combine blockchain's auditability with flexible oversight, capacity-building initiatives, and inclusive policymaking are essential. Cities and regulators must ensure that traceability systems reinforce accountability and privacy without undermining equity, thereby aligning cybersecurity and transparency goals with the broader objectives of sustainable and inclusive smart urban governance.

3. BLOCKCHAIN AS AN ENABLER OF TRUST AND TRACEABILITY

As cities evolve into data-driven, cyber-physical systems, the integrity of SC has become a cornerstone of urban resilience. SC are no longer discrete commercial processes but digital arteries linking food, pharmaceuticals, construction materials, and utilities across urban environments logistics (Saidu et al., 2024). However, legacy infrastructures characterized by centralization and fragmented data cannot provide the verifiable trust demanded by smart cities. Blockchain, originally designed to support cryptocurrencies, has emerged as a foundational infrastructure for traceability, offering distributed validation, automated compliance, and tamper-resistant records (Saidu, Shuhidan, Aliyu, et al., 2025).

3.1 Key Features and Their Strategic Role

At its foundation, blockchain functions as a distributed ledger, recording transactions across a peer-to-peer network in a verifiable and permanent manner (Ghaffari et al., 2023). Its core attributes, immutability, decentralization, consensus mechanisms, and smart contracts, are not ends in themselves but enablers of higher-order outcomes. Together, they provide tamper-proof provenance records, ensure that no single authority can unilaterally alter data, and support automated enforcement of contractual rules (Yakubu et al., 2024). These features are summarized analytically in Figure 3, which illustrates how blockchain's technical properties underpin traceability capabilities and ultimately foster trust: The diagram illustrates three tiers: Blockchain Features (immutability, decentralization, consensus, smart contracts) feeding into Traceability Capabilities (secure provenance, real-time compliance, collaborative auditability), which ultimately enhance Trust Outcomes (consumer confidence, regulatory oversight, stakeholder equity). This highlights how blockchain's value stems not from isolated technical novelty but from its capacity to reshape socio-technical trust relationships across USC.

Figure 3. Conceptual Model Linking Blockchain Features to Trust Outcomes in USC

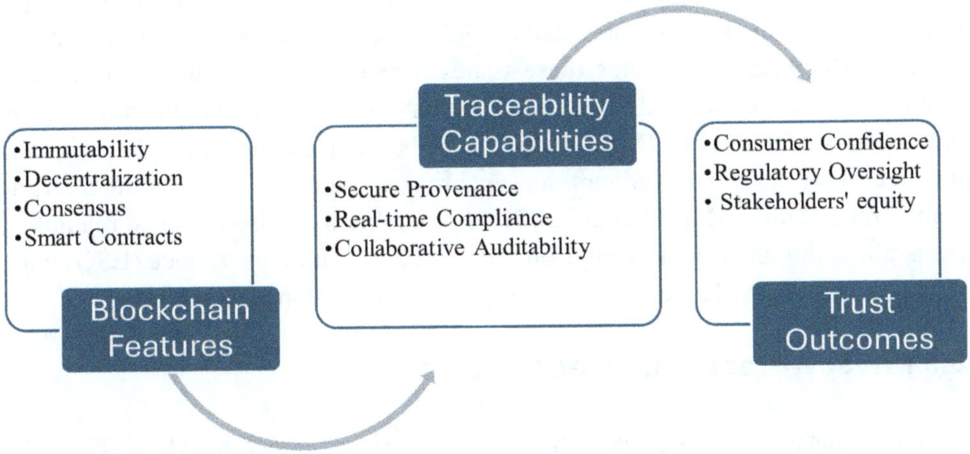

3.2 Smart Contracts and Automated Compliance

Smart contracts, self-executing scripts embedded on blockchain, extend these capabilities by automating governance processes. They can release payments only after delivery is confirmed, flag deviations in cold chain temperature data, or suspend transactions when compliance breaches occur (Chang et al., 2019) (Zhang et al., 2024). Such mechanisms reduce reliance on manual oversight and accelerate enforcement in time-sensitive urban contexts, particularly in public health logistics. By embedding rules into digital protocols, smart contracts act as automated compliance agents, reducing administrative overhead while strengthening accountability.

3.3 Product Provenance and Authenticity

Growing consumer demand for ethical sourcing and sustainability has intensified calls for end-to-end visibility. Blockchain enables continuous provenance tracking from raw material extraction to point of sale, creating a transparent and verifiable chain of custody. The IBM Food Trust reduced produce recall times from 6.5 days to 2.2 seconds (IBM, 2021), while MediLedger has improved pharmaceutical authentication and reduced counterfeit infiltration (Uddin et al., 2021). These measurable outcomes demonstrate how blockchain directly supports consumer protection and regulatory compliance by making authenticity auditable in real time.

3.4 Multi-Stakeholder Collaboration and Auditability

USC require coordination among diverse actors with varying priorities and information systems. This often leads to information asymmetry and governance disputes. Blockchain mitigates these issues through permissioned visibility and role-based access control, allowing participants to share relevant data without compromising confidentiality. Dubai's blockchain-based licensing and logistics system illustrates how distributed ledgers can synchronize operations across municipal and commercial actors (Majeed et al., 2021). Immutable logs also enhance regulatory oversight in domains such as Environmental, Social, and Governance (ESG) compliance, enabling evidence-based auditing rather than reliance on self-reported data.

3.5 Privacy-Preserving Mechanisms

While transparency is a strength, it can raise privacy concerns when SC involve sensitive contracts or personally identifiable information. Emerging techniques such as selective disclosure and zero-knowledge proofs (ZKPs) allow participants to prove compliance without exposing underlying data (Aljabhan & Obaidat, 2023; Karaduman & Gülhas, 2025). In Amsterdam's smart waste pilot, ZKPs were used to confirm waste origins while protecting household identities. These methods illustrate how blockchain can reconcile verifiability with privacy, aligning with legal frameworks such as GDPR and supporting citizen trust in data-intensive urban systems.

3.6 Permissioned vs. Permissionless Models

USC operate within regulated environments where accountability and performance are essential. Permissionless blockchains like Bitcoin or Ethereum offer openness but face scalability and governance challenges. In contrast, permissioned platforms such as Hyperledger Fabric or Quorum provide controlled participation, high throughput, and tailored privacy policies suited for municipal oversight (Z. Wang, 2023). Consortium-based models allow city agencies, logistics partners, and regulators to share data under agreed governance rules, balancing decentralization with institutional accountability.

3.7 Comparative Advantages Over Traditional Systems

Compared with traditional ERP-based systems, blockchain offers a more resilient and interoperable foundation for SC. While conventional systems suffer from centralized vulnerabilities and opaque audit trails, blockchain enables real-time verification, automated compliance, and cross-stakeholder accountability. As summarized in Table 1, these capabilities address persistent risks of fraud, counterfeiting, and regulatory blind spots, positioning blockchain as a civic infrastructure that supports trasparency and resilience in smart urban ecosystems.

Table 1. Comparison of Traditional and Blockchain-Based Supply Chain Systems

Feature	Traditional Systems	Blockchain-Based Systems
Data Integrity	Centrally editable	Cryptographically immutable
Interoperability	Vendor-dependent	Open, API-driven interoperability
Auditability	Manual, non-uniform	Automated, verifiable logs
Transparency	Opaque to outsiders	Configurable visibility by design
Trust Requirements	Third-party verification	Trustless, consensus-based validation

The technology addresses key vulnerabilities in traditional systems, such as fraud, opacity, and slow response, while enabling real-time, automated, and privacy-aware compliance. As we will explore in the next section, deploying blockchain in practice requires architectural planning, IoT integration, and system-level optimization to manage scalability and privacy. Nonetheless, blockchain lays the groundwork for traceability as a civic asset, rather than a proprietary feature, in the age of urban digital transformation.

4. ARCHITECTURE OF A BLOCKCHAIN-ENABLED URBAN SUPPLY CHAIN

Deploying blockchain in the context of smart USC is not merely a matter of technology adoption, it requires a coherent, layered architectural framework that aligns real-world logistics with digital traceability goals. Such architecture must support secure data ingestion from physical assets, enforce integrity through consensus, and present usable, role-specific insights to diverse urban stakeholders, including regulators, operators, and end-users. It must also be built with scalability, privacy preservation, and urban data governance in mind, particularly as cities face increasing demands for interoperability, transparency, and real-time responsiveness (Radmanesh et al., 2023). As illustrated in Figure 4, a robust blockchain-enabled urban supply chain architecture typically consists of four core layers, the Data Acquisition Layer, the Network Layer, the Blockchain Layer, and the Application Layer, complemented by privacy-preserving mechanisms and performance optimization strategies. Each layer contributes to a unified system that captures, validates, and distributes trusted logistics information across smart city environments (Agrawal et al., 2023).

4.1 Data Acquisition Layer

The first and most foundational layer involves the capture of real-world logistics data using a variety of embedded sensing and identification technologies. Devices across the supply chain, whether installed in warehouses, transport vehicles, shipping containers, or retail shelves continuously monitor and log key environmental and logistical metrics. These include IoT sensors for temperature, humidity, and vibration; RFID tags and QR codes for tracking individual items; GPS modules for geolocation; and video surveillance systems for visual verification. In a cold chain scenario, for instance, temperature sensors embedded in refrigerated trucks constantly monitor and record conditions throughout transit. Each data point is timestamped and structured as a potential blockchain transaction. However, ensuring the integrity of this raw data at the edge, before it enters the blockchain, is critical. This is where edge computing and secure device provisioning come into play. By authenticating device firmware and filtering invalid data streams at the source, this layer minimizes the risk of data spoofing or injection, which could compromise the trustworthiness of the entire system (Nagarajan et al., 2022; Tripathi et al., 2023).

Figure 4. Layered architecture of a blockchain-integrated supply chain for smart urban ecosystems.

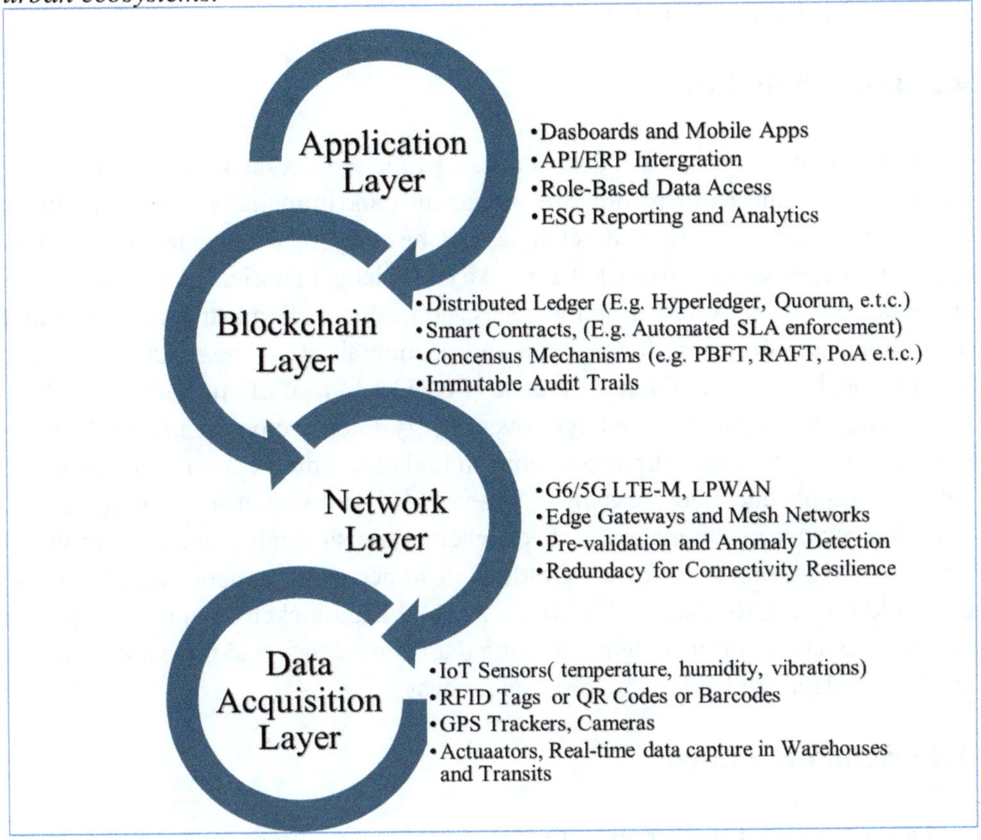

4.2 Network Layer

The second layer focuses on transmitting the acquired data from physical devices to blockchain nodes. In urban settings where infrastructure is dense and operational environments are varied; the network layer must support diverse connectivity protocols. High-speed communication methods like 5G and LTE-M are ideal for mobile logistics assets in busy city routes, while Wi-Fi and LPWAN technologies such as LoRa or NB-IoT are better suited for localized smart warehouses or long-range low-power applications. To ensure that only clean, structured data reaches the blockchain, smart gateways perform pre-validation, local aggregation, and even lightweight anomaly detection. These gateways act as both traffic controllers and quality filters, reducing network congestion and shielding the system from faulty or malicious data. Given the potential for urban disruptions, ranging from traffic congestion to power outages, the network layer also incorporates redundancy strategies and mesh networking topologies to maintain uptime and data continuity in the face of instability (Yau et al., 2024)

4.3 Blockchain Layer

At the system's core, the blockchain layer functions as the trust infrastructure, where verified transaction records are permanently and immutably stored. It includes consensus protocols, smart contract logic, and the distributed ledger itself. For urban applications, permissioned blockchains, like Hyperledger Fabric, Quorum, or Corda, are preferred, as they allow granular access control and align better with legal and institutional requirements for privacy and accountability. Consensus algorithms like Practical Byzantine Fault Tolerance (PBFT) or Proof of Authority (PoA), or RAFT offer performance advantages over energy-intensive public protocols, making them suitable for real-time operations in logistics. Smart contracts, meanwhile, automate supply chain business logic. For example, in a vaccine distribution chain, a smart contract can automatically check whether transit conditions adhere to WHO standards, triggering alerts or withholding clearance if a shipment exceeds an 8°C threshold for over 30 minutes (Tan et al., 2025). Each blockchain node maintains a synchronized copy of the ledger, ensuring data consistency and traceability across all stakeholders involved in the logistics process.

4.4 Application Layer

The application layer serves as the interface between users and the blockchain-based system, presenting validated logistics data through intuitive, role-based dashboards, APIs, and analytics tools. It must accommodate a wide spectrum of users, from frontline workers managing shipments to regulators auditing ESG compliance to consumers verifying product provenance. Real-time monitoring dashboards and mobile apps provide operational visibility, while APIs facilitate integration with existing ERP, SCM, or municipal logistics systems. Regulatory agencies may use built-in analytics engines to generate compliance reports or track emissions data. Equally important is the need for role-based data access: a public health official might require granular logs for cold chain audits, while a consumer-facing interface might only expose high-level traceability summaries. This differentiation protects sensitive information while maintaining user relevance and usability (Nagarajan et al., 2022).

4.5 Privacy-Preserving Techniques

In USC, data often includes sensitive commercial contracts, proprietary formulations, or personally identifiable information. As a result, the architecture must embed privacy-by-design principles into its core. Techniques like Zero-Knowledge Proofs (ZKPs) allow actors to demonstrate compliance with specific rules, such as temperature control or ethical sourcing, without revealing the underlying operational data. Additionally, off-chain storage is used for large or sensitive payloads, with only cryptographic proofs (e.g., hashes or Merkle roots) anchored on-chain. This reduces on-chain bloat while preserving verifiability. Private channels or sub-ledgers are also implemented in permissioned blockchains to allow confidential interactions between specific participants, such as city procurement officials and private vendors. Real-world projects like VeChain and MediLedger demonstrate the viability of this approach. These platforms offer public traceability for batches and logistics events, while concealing business-critical or legally sensitive data such as pharmaceutical recipes or price contracts (Bernal Bernabe et al., 2019; Padma & Ramaiah, 2024).

4.6 Urban Scalability and Performance Considerations

Urban environments present unique challenges in terms of scale, heterogeneity, and system legacy integration. A viable blockchain architecture must be engineered for high throughput, resilience, and extensibility. Techniques such as block size optimization, transaction batching, and sharding help handle peak data loads across congested logistics hubs. To accommodate intermittent connectivity, a common issue in urban terrain, edge synchronization protocols and local caching mechanisms ensure that data is not lost and is committed once a stable connection is reestablished. Furthermore, the architecture must support seamless integration with legacy infrastructure, often achieved through middleware that wraps existing ERP or logistics software into blockchain-compatible formats. The Dubai Blockchain Strategy exemplifies this approach. It integrates blockchain incrementally across sectors such as shipping, health, and food safety, using modular frameworks that allow for gradual, low-risk deployment (Majeed et al., 2021). This flexibility is crucial for cities that need to balance innovation with operational continuity.

In summary, a blockchain-enabled urban supply chain is best conceived as a layered, modular architecture, not a one-size-fits-all solution. Its strength lies in harmonizing data acquisition, network reliability, distributed validation, and user-facing applications within a privacy-preserving and scalable framework. By integrating IoT sensing, edge computing, smart contracts, and role-based access, this architecture delivers trustworthy, real-time traceability tailored to the nuanced realities of smart city logistics. As we move to the next section, we turn from theory to practice, exploring real-world implementations that demonstrate how this architecture performs under regulatory pressure, resource constraints, and operational complexity in diverse urban settings.

5. REAL-WORLD USE CASES AND IMPLEMENTATION EXAMPLES

Moving from conceptual design to lived application, this section examines real-world deployments of blockchain in diverse urban sectors. It analyzes how blockchain has been implemented across food safety, pharmaceuticals, fashion, automotive SC, waste management, and agriculture, the discussion illustrates how "trust through transparency" is operationalized in practice.

5.1 Methodological Approach

Blockchain's potential for supply chain transparency is most evident through real-world deployments rather than theoretical promise trust (Baharmand et al., 2021; Rijanto, 2021). To ensure relevance and analytical depth, case studies in this chapter were selected using a three-layer methodology illustrated in Figure 5. Layer 1 ensured *sectoral diversity*, covering food, pharmaceuticals, fashion, automotive, waste management, and agriculture. Layer 2 required *documented implementation outcomes*, prioritizing cases with measurable results such as efficiency gains or compliance improvements. Layer 3 applied *urban relevance*, focusing on SC and citizen-facing services in smart city contexts. Only cases meeting all three criteria were included as the final case studies for analysis. This systematic approach ensures that the examples highlight not just technical feasibility but also governance and societal relevance, reinforcing the central theme of "trust through transparency."

Figure 5. Case Study Selection Funnel Methodology

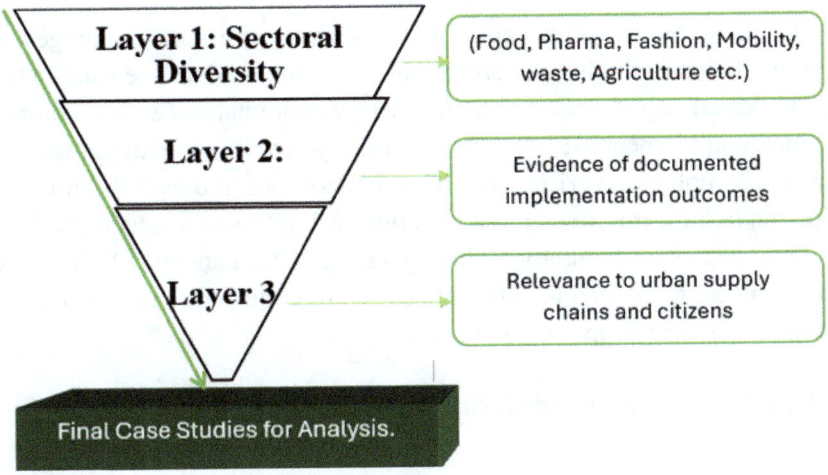

5.1 Case Studies

The following case studies illustrate how blockchain has been applied across diverse urban supply chain contexts. Each example is structured around three dimensions: context, intervention, and outcomes, to provide clarity and comparability. By presenting both sector-specific challenges and measurable results, the cases demonstrate how blockchain operationalizes the principle of "trust through transparency" in practice (Shahid et al., 2020; Subramanian et al., 2020).

5.2.1 Food Safety and Contamination Control: IBM Food Trust

Urban food networks remain highly vulnerable to contamination events, where even minor lapses in monitoring can lead to widespread public health risks. A notable example comes from Walmart's collaboration with IBM through the Food Trust blockchain platform. This initiative enabled end-to-end tracing of produce provenance, allowing retailers to pinpoint the exact source of contaminated mangoes in just 2.2 seconds, compared to the 6.5 days required under traditional tracking systems (IBM, 2021). By drastically accelerating recall processes and ensuring the authenticity of safety data, the project strengthened consumer confidence and illustrated blockchain's role in safeguarding urban food supplies.

5.2.2 Pharmaceutical Integrity: MediLedger Network

Pharmaceutical SC in urban environments face persistent challenges from counterfeit medicines, which threaten patient safety and undermine trust in health systems. The MediLedger consortium, involving major pharmaceutical companies and distributors, implemented a blockchain-based system to record drug provenance and automate compliance verification. This intervention reduced the infiltration of falsified medicines, improved authentication of legitimate products, and shortened reporting cycles for regulators (Ghadge et al., 2023; Pandey, 2025). The case demonstrates blockchain's potential to embed accountability and enhance regulatory oversight in life-critical supply networks.

5.2.3 Ethical Sourcing in Fashion: Aura Consortium

In the fashion industry, urban consumers are increasingly concerned about sustainability, ethical labor practices, and authenticity of branded products. To respond, leading luxury brands established the Aura Blockchain Consortium, a shared ledger system designed to record and verify product sourcing and production histories (Bullón Pérez et al., 2020; Guo et al., 2023). By enabling consumers to trace garments back to their origin, the initiative reduced sourcing misrepresentation and strengthened brand credibility. Early evaluations suggest that the availability of verifiable records contributes positively to consumer trust indices (Aura, 2023), showing how blockchain can reinforce ethical consumption in urban markets.

5.2.4 Automotive Supply Chains and Sustainable Mobility

The rapid adoption of electric vehicles (EVs) in urban centers has heightened scrutiny of SC for critical minerals such as cobalt, often associated with environmental degradation and labor exploitation. Companies like Volvo and Mercedes have piloted blockchain-based "battery passports" that capture detailed records of mineral provenance and carbon emissions across the supply chain. Independent audits confirmed that blockchain improved the transparency of cobalt sourcing and provided verifiable data on CO_2 emissions, thereby enhancing compliance with stringent European sustainability regulations (Jain et al., 2021; Raj Kumar Reddy et al., 2021). This example highlights blockchain's ability to link ethical sourcing with urban sustainability agendas.

5.2.5 Waste Management and the Circular Economy: Amsterdam Pilot

Urban waste management systems often suffer from illegal dumping, fragmented oversight, and weak accountability mechanisms. To address these issues, the City of Amsterdam piloted a blockchain-based system for recording waste collection, transfer, and recycling activities. By creating an immutable audit trail of waste handling events, the platform exposed discrepancies in contractor reporting and reduced unauthorized waste flows (França et al., 2020; Jiang et al., 2023). The pilot demonstrated how blockchain can support municipal authorities in building transparent, accountable, and sustainable waste management systems within smart cities.

5.2.6 Agricultural Supply Chains: AgriDigital and VeChain

Agricultural SC play a vital role in urban food security but are often hindered by disputes over payment delays and concerns about product authenticity. In Australia, AgriDigital introduced a blockchain-based platform that digitizes contracts and automates settlement between farmers and buyers, reducing payment delays from several weeks to just a few days. Similarly, in Asia, VeChain has applied blockchain for crop provenance, enabling exporters and urban retailers to verify compliance with food safety standards (Mohammed et al., 2025). These cases highlight how blockchain can empower producers, particularly SMEs, by fostering timely transactions and providing transparent access to international markets.

Table 2. Blockchain Case Studies in Urban SC

Sector	Problem / Context	Intervention	Outcomes / Metrics
Food Safety	Contamination, slow recalls	IBM Food Trust (Walmart)	Traceback ↓ 6.5 days → 2.2 sec; ↑ consumer trust
Pharmaceuticals	Counterfeit drugs	MediLedger	Improved authentication; faster compliance reporting
Fashion	Ethical sourcing misrepresentation	Aura Consortium	↑ Brand credibility; ↑ consumer trust indices
Automotive	Ethical minerals, carbon tracking	Volvo & Mercedes battery passports	Verified sourcing; transparent CO_2 reporting
Waste	Illegal dumping, opacity	Amsterdam blockchain pilot	Reduced unauthorized waste flows; improved oversight
Agriculture	Payment delays, provenance issues	AgriDigital, VeChain	Settlements reduced weeks → days; verified compliance

5.4 Synthesis and Implications

Table 2 consolidates the case studies, showing how blockchain addresses sectoral problems through interventions that improve provenance verification, reduce fraud, accelerate recalls, and strengthen compliance. From Walmart's rapid food recalls to Volvo's battery sourcing and Amsterdam's waste tracking, the cases demonstrate blockchain's versatility in operationalizing "trust through transparency." However, adoption is dominated by large corporations, with SMEs facing cost and technical barriers (Shahid et al., 2020). Achieving equitable impact requires supportive governance, inclusive onboarding, and hybrid oversight, setting the stage for the next section on adoption challenges (Singh et al., 2020).

6. CHALLENGES AND LIMITATIONS OF BLOCKCHAIN ADOPTION IN USC

Blockchain offers significant opportunities for enhancing supply chain transparency, but its deployment in urban ecosystems is constrained by multiple factors (Kouhizadeh et al., 2021). These challenges span technical, financial, organizational, and social dimensions, and they must be critically addressed to achieve equitable and sustainable adoption. This section explores the multifaceted challenges that must be addressed to ensure blockchain's successful integration into smart urban logistics systems. Figure 6 visualizes the summary of these barrier categories.

6.1 Technical Challenges

USC demand high throughput, real-time traceability, and interoperability across diverse systems. Current blockchain platforms face infrastructure limitations, integration complexity, and scalability constraints. Latency issues further hinder performance, especially in cold chain logistics or just-in-time delivery contexts where delays can compromise safety and service quality.

6.2 Organizational Barriers

Adoption Adoption requires cultural as well as technical shifts. Stakeholders often show resistance to change, particularly when transparency exposes inefficiencies. A lack of awareness about blockchain's potential and a shortage of technical expertise within municipal agencies and SMEs further impede integration.

6.3 Economic Constraints

Akella et al. (2023) emphazised that high infrastructure and onboarding costs create barriers to widespread adoption. Implementation costs for blockchain platforms, IoT sensors, and system maintenance can be prohibitive, particularly for SMEs. Broader resource constraints in cities of the Global South exacerbate this challenge, risking uneven participation in blockchain-enabled ecosystems (W. Wang et al., 2025).

6.4 Environmental Impacts

Although more efficient than early proof-of-work systems, blockchain still carries sustainability concerns. Energy consumption, carbon emissions, and e-waste generation from hardware upgrades can conflict with urban climate neutrality goals (Hong & Xiao, 2024).. Aligning blockchain adoption with green energy strategies is essential to avoid undermining sustainability commitments.

6.5 Legal and regulatory Issues

Uncertainty persists regarding the legal recognition of blockchain records, cross-border data governance, and liability in case of disputes. Regulatory uncertainty and compliance complexity make firms reluctant to commit to large-scale deployment, particularly in international SC that traverse multiple jurisdictions (Kouhizadeh et al., 2021).

6.6 Privacy and Data Protection

Immutable ledgers create tensions with privacy regulations such as GDPR. Challenges include data privacy concerns, conflicts with GDPR principles, and the contradiction between immutability and the right to be forgotten. Although cryptographic tools such as zero-knowledge proofs offer solutions, their complexity limits practical adoption at scale (Karaduman & Gülhas, 2025).

6.7 Governance Challenges

Permissioned systems, often favored in urban contexts, risk over-centralization if dominated by large corporations or government entities. Without incentives for broad participation, adoption may stall. Unequal power dynamics can emerge, leading to uneven distribution of decision-making authority and undermining the democratic potential of blockchain (Najati, 2025).

Figure 6. Multidimensional Barriers to Blockchain Adoption in USC

6.8 Equity and Inclusion

A critical challenge is ensuring that blockchain adoption does not reinforce digital inequalities. SME exclusion, capacity barriers in the Global South, and the digital divide limit participation of smaller or resource-constrained actors. This risks creating a two-tier supply chain where larger firms reap the benefits while vulnerable suppliers are marginalized. Inclusive design, subsidized onboarding, and capacity-building measures are needed to close these gaps (Karaduman & Gülhas, 2025).

The challenges to blockchain adoption extend beyond technical performance to include economic, organizational, regulatory, governance, and equity dimensions. As shown in Figure 6, these multi-faceted barriers call for hybrid approaches that balance innovation with inclusivity and compliance. Addressing them is essential to creating traceability frameworks that are technologically robust, socially equitable, and politically feasible.

Blockchain's promise in urban SC lies in its ability to deliver tamper-proof transparency, automated trust, and resilience. Yet realizing this potential requires overcoming technical limits, high costs, regulatory uncertainty, and organizational resistance. These constraints do not diminish blockchain's value; rather, they highlight the need for thoughtful, context-aware implementation embedded within supportive policy and governance frameworks. Regulatory clarity, stakeholder coordination, ethical oversight, and public–private collaboration are vital to ensure blockchain adoption advances equity, protects privacy, and supports urban resilience and sustainability sustainability (Uddin et al., 2023). The next section explores these governance dimensions and outlines strategies for integrating blockchain traceability into urban policy and infrastructure.

7. POLICY AND GOVERNANCE CONSIDERATIONS FOR BLOCKCHAIN IN URBAN SUPPLY CHAINS

As blockchain technologies transition from experimental pilots to mission-critical infrastructure within smart USC, the importance of robust policy and governance frameworks cannot be overstated. While the technical aspects of blockchain adoption are often emphasized, long-term success depends equally on navigating legal ambiguity, data ethics, and institutional capacity. Governance in this context must be understood not just as top-down regulation, but as a multi-layered, participatory process that involves legal institutions, technical standard bodies, city governments, private enterprises, and civil society actors (Bae et al., 2025). This section examines the evolving landscape of blockchain governance and identifies key considerations shaping its trajectory in urban logistics ecosystems.

7.1 Regulatory Landscape and Legal Frameworks

The regulatory environment surrounding blockchain remains fluid and highly fragmented across jurisdictions. Governments worldwide are working to balance innovation with risk management, aiming to create legal certainty for decentralized technologies while protecting public interest. In the European Union, the introduction of the Markets in Crypto-Assets (MiCA) regulation represents a significant step toward establishing a unified legal framework for digital assets, with implications for traceability and transactional integrity in blockchain-enabled SC. In the United States, the Executive Order on Ensuring Responsible Development of Digital Assets has called for cross-agency coordination to assess the risks and opportunities posed by blockchain and cryptocurrencies. Meanwhile, countries like Singapore, Japan, and South Korea have adopted proactive, innovation-friendly stances, providing regulatory sandboxes, clear licensing regimes, and data protection rules that facilitate responsible experimentation. These efforts collectively signal a trend toward formalizing the legal status of blockchain-based data, smart contracts, and decentralized identifiers (DIDs) in commercial and public-sector applications (Ghadge et al., 2023).

7.2 Data Governance, Privacy and Consumer protection

A defining tension in blockchain-enabled traceability is the conflict between immutability and modern data protection rights, such as the GDPR's "right to be forgotten." Recording personal or commercially sensitive data on an immutable ledger may expose citizens to surveillance and limit their ability to control personal information. Hybrid storage models, where sensitive data is retained off-chain and only cryptographic proofs are anchored on-chain, offer one solution. Emerging tools such as zero-knowledge proofs (ZKPs) and selective disclosure mechanisms provide further privacy-preserving capabilities (Akanfe et al., 2024). At the policy level, consumer protection must be explicitly integrated, ensuring that traceability frameworks not only secure supply chain data but also safeguard individual rights, prevent misuse, and comply with privacy regulations.

7.3 Interoperability and Standardization

The lack of interoperability across blockchain platforms poses a major governance and operational challenge. USC often span multiple sectors, agencies, and private actors, all of whom may deploy different systems with incompatible data formats or consensus mechanisms. This fragmentation inhibits system-wide coordination and undermines the benefits of traceability. Global standardization efforts are currently underway to address these gaps. The International Organization for Standardization (ISO), for instance, has established working groups to define blockchain standards for terminology, architecture, privacy, and interoperability. Other initiatives, such as those by the World Economic Forum (WEF) and ITU-T, are promoting cross-sector dialogue to accelerate the development of shared technical and governance frameworks. Establishing interoperable protocols is crucial not only for seamless data exchange, but also for ensuring accountability, scalability, and cross-border cooperation in globalized urban logistics networks (Saidu, Shuhidan, Aziz, et al., 2025; G. Wang et al., 2023).

7.4 Economic Constraints and Resource Demands

Blockchain adoption often requires significant upfront investment in digital infrastructure, IoT integration, and specialized workforce training. For large multinational firms, these costs can be justified by efficiency and compliance benefits. However, for SMEs, particularly in developing economies, the financial and technical barriers are substantial. Without mechanisms such as public–private financing schemes, cooperative platforms, and shared digital infrastructure, the burden of compliance may exclude smaller actors from urban SC, creating asymmetries in access and participation.

7.5 Environmental and Sustainability Concerns

Although permissioned blockchains mitigate the energy intensity of proof-of-work systems, sustainability concerns persist. Energy consumption, carbon emissions, and electronic waste from hardware upgrades remain challenges for cities pursuing climate neutrality. Governance frameworks must integrate blockchain adoption with broader environmental policies, promoting energy-efficient consensus mechanisms and coupling blockchain with green energy and circular economy initiatives. Only then can blockchain-enabled traceability align with urban sustainability goals (Gloerich et al., 2020).

7.6 Governance and Institutional Barriers

Beyond regulation, governance involves how decisions are distributed among stakeholders. Urban SC require collaborative and hybrid governance models that balance state authority with private-sector innovation and community oversight. Over-centralization within permissioned blockchains risks replicating the same power imbalances that blockchain seeks to overcome. Additionally, organizational resistance to transparency and a lack of digital capacity within municipal agencies and SMEs remain critical obstacles. Incentive structures that reward participation, combined with regulatory oversight, can help ensure balanced decision-making and institutional trust (Tafuro et al., 2023).

7.6 Future Directions and Policy Recommendations

Looking forward, policymakers must adopt adaptive, forward-compatible governance models that can evolve alongside technological advancements. Rather than static regulation, this requires continuous dialogue between technologists, regulators, researchers, and community representatives. Regulatory sandboxes, living policy frameworks, and open consultation platforms can enable real-time feedback and iterative improvement. Investing in education and capacity-building is equally critical. Municipal leaders, logistics managers, and community advocates need not become blockchain engineers, but they must understand its governance implications. Curricula, training workshops, and cross-sector fellowships can equip these stakeholders to navigate blockchain's opportunities and limitations, fostering a governance ecosystem that is both informed and inclusive.

Governing blockchain in USC is not merely a matter of protocol selection or legal compliance, it is a multi-dimensional process that spans law, ethics, civic engagement, and institutional innovation. As cities integrate blockchain into their core logistics and traceability systems, governance must become a guiding architecture, ensuring that decentralized systems are deployed with transparency, inclusivity, and adaptability. Yet even the most sophisticated governance frameworks cannot guarantee success in isolation. For blockchain to deliver on its transformative promise, it must be part of a strategic and systemic redesign of supply chain infrastructures, one that reflects not only technical best practices but also policy priorities and human development goals (Kouhizadeh et al., 2021). The final section of this chapter turns toward that future, outlining a strategic roadmap for scaling blockchain-enabled traceability in ways that are sustainable, equitable, and aligned with the evolving needs of smart urban ecosystems.

8. STRATEGIC ROADMAP AND POLICY RECOMMENDATIONS

As blockchain technology matures from conceptual promise to practical deployment, the successful integration of blockchain into USC requires more than technical blueprints; it demands strategic foresight, policy alignment, institutional capacity, and social inclusiveness. This final section distills the key insights presented throughout the chapter into a coherent roadmap for action, offering policymakers, city planners, technologists, and industry leaders concrete pathways to move from isolated pilots to scalable, sustainable solutions. Figure 7 depicts this strategic roadmap, where each recommendation addresses a critical facet of blockchain implementation and governance, grounded in the understanding that technology alone cannot deliver transformation, intentional strategy must drive its application.

8.1 Establishing Clear Regulatory Frameworks

A foundational step for blockchain integration lies in the formulation of robust and forward-compatible regulatory frameworks. Ambiguities around data sovereignty, digital identity, smart contracts, and cross-border transactions continue to hinder adoption. Governments must engage with industry stakeholders, standards bodies, and academic researchers to develop comprehensive legal frameworks that address privacy, cybersecurity, interoperability, and liability. For example, the European Union's Markets in Crypto-Assets (MiCA) regulation, though primarily targeting digital assets, provides a governance model that can be adapted for supply chain traceability. Local governments and urban authorities should adopt a similar approach, crafting sector-specific rules that provide regulatory clarity without stifling innovation, thereby fostering confidence among potential adopters.

8.2 Promoting Public–Private Partnerships

Blockchain implementation in USC is inherently cross-sectoral, requiring collaboration between city governments, logistics firms, platform developers, and civil society organizations. Public–private partnerships (PPPs) provide a mechanism for pooling resources, aligning goals, and leveraging complementary strengths. Cities such as Dubai and Seoul have demonstrated how PPPs can accelerate innovation, enabling governments to frame regulatory sandboxes while private actors deliver technical capabilities. These partnerships should not be transactional but strategic in nature, involving co-design processes, shared risk frameworks, and joint ownership of outcomes. Effective PPPs also create pathways for integrating startups and SMEs into larger digital infrastructure projects, promoting both scalability and local innovation ecosystems.

8.3 Investing in Infrastructure and Capacity Building

No blockchain deployment can succeed without the underlying infrastructure to support it. Reliable internet connectivity, edge computing capabilities, secure storage, and robust cybersecurity systems are prerequisites, particularly in urban logistics environments where real-time data capture and verification are essential. In parallel, there is an urgent need for capacity building at multiple levels. Decision-makers must understand the policy implications of blockchain, while operational staff require hands-on training in system usage, data entry, and smart contract interpretation. Universities, vocational institutions, and city innovation labs should develop curricula and professional certification programs focused on blockchain for supply chain traceability, enabling a digitally fluent urban workforce.

8.4 Encouraging Interoperability and Standardization

USC span diverse actors and technologies. Without common standards, the risk of fragmentation, inefficiency, and vendor lock-in becomes significant. To avoid this, stakeholders must prioritize interoperability and open standards in blockchain system design. International standardization bodies such as the ISO (e.g., ISO/TC 307) and regional consortia like the Asia Blockchain Alliance are already developing guidelines for terminology, security, interoperability, and governance. Cities should adopt and contribute to these efforts, ensuring that local implementations can interconnect across jurisdictions, sectors, and platforms. Open APIs, modular design principles, and blockchain-agnostic middleware can further reinforce this goal.

8.5 Ensuring Ethical and Inclusive Implementation

Technology that improves efficiency while reinforcing exclusion or surveillance is not a win for cities. Ethical design and implementation must be a non-negotiable priority. Blockchain solutions should be built with inclusivity in mind, accessible to people across socio-economic strata, literacy levels, and digital proficiencies. Engaging underrepresented communities in design workshops, using human-centered design, and conducting equity impact assessments are practical ways to ensure inclusive implementation. Furthermore, ethical concerns such as algorithmic bias in smart contracts, potential misuse of immutable data, and disproportionate surveillance risk must be proactively addressed through governance safeguards, transparency mechanisms, and public oversight bodies.

8.6 Fostering Innovation through Pilot Projects

Before scaling city-wide or regionally, pilot projects provide critical testbeds for assessing blockchain's performance, usability, and institutional fit. These pilots should be real-world in scope, covering logistics operations, waste management, food traceability, or pharmaceutical delivery chains, domains with tangible pain points and data flows. Importantly, these pilots should not be treated as public relations exercises. They must be scientifically evaluated, documented, and peer reviewed. Iterative feedback from users, regulators, and communities should inform system redesigns. Governments can support this process by providing funding, regulatory waivers, and access to public data, creating learning ecosystems that catalyze responsible innovation.

Figure 7. Strategic Roadmap for Blockchain Integration in USC

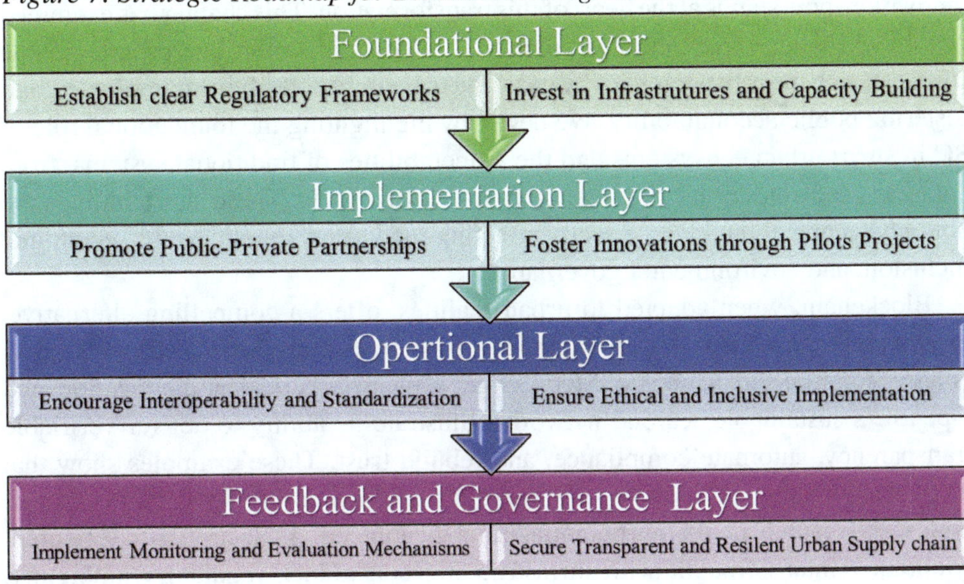

8.7 Implementing Monitoring and Evaluation Mechanisms

Sustainable blockchain adoption requires continuous evaluation using metrics such as throughput, traceability coverage, compliance accuracy, and user satisfaction. Robust frameworks combining quantitative KPIs with qualitative feedback, supported by dashboards, audits, and participatory reviews, can ensure transparency, equity, and accountability. Blockchain-enabled SC are an evolving transformation spanning infrastructure, governance, and innovation. Viewed not as an endpoint but as a foundation, they offer pathways to build resilient, transparent, and citizen-centric urban ecosystems. The final section synthesizes key lessons, identifies future research needs, and situates blockchain traceability within the broader trajectory of digital urban governance.

9. CONCLUSION

As cities navigate the intertwined demands of digitization, climate resilience, and equitable development, the integrity and transparency of USC have become pivotal concerns. Blockchain technology, once confined to the fringes of financial innovation, now stands at the heart of this transformation. This chapter has examined how blockchain's core features, immutability, decentralization, and programmable trust, can reshape urban logistics by ensuring traceability, verifying compliance, and fostering public accountability. We began by highlighting the foundational role of SC in smart urban ecosystems and the vulnerabilities of traditional systems, from data silos and counterfeit risks to compliance blind spots. These shortcomings are not only technical but civic, directly affecting food safety, public health, economic inclusion, and environmental governance.

Blockchain, when adapted to urban realities, offers a compelling alternative. Real-world case studies, from Walmart's food traceability and VeChain's provenance solutions in China to MediLedger's pharmaceutical authentication and OpenSC's sustainable seafood networks, illustrate its ability to deliver verifiable transparency, automate compliance, and rebuild trust. These examples show that blockchain's value extends beyond operational efficiency to advancing fairness, ethics, and resilience. Yet this potential is not guaranteed. As Section 6 underscored, adoption remains fraught with infrastructural constraints, regulatory ambiguity, privacy tensions, and organizational inertia. Addressing these requires governance innovation, public–private collaboration, standardization efforts, and policies that promote inclusivity, particularly for SMEs and actors in the Global South who risk exclusion without targeted support.

The analysis suggests that blockchain traceability is not merely a technical upgrade but a form of digital public infrastructure. When embedded within supportive governance and policy frameworks, it enables cities to restore confidence in institutions, extend protections to vulnerable populations, and create systems that balance innovation with accountability. Looking forward, continued research should evaluate blockchain's long-term impacts on labor equity, sustainability goals, and algorithmic governance in smart cities. Inclusive pilot programs, interdisciplinary assessments, and community-driven design processes will be critical to ensure that benefits reach not only corporations and regulators but also citizens themselves.

The future of urban SC lies not simply in digitization, but in the cultivation of trustworthy, transparent, and participatory infrastructures. If guided by vision and responsibility, blockchain can support the transition from reactive logistical networks to proactive ecosystems of digital trust, resilient in crisis, equitable by design, and governed in the public interest.

REFERENCES

Agarwal, U., Rishiwal, V., Tanwar, S., Chaudhary, R., Sharma, G., Bokoro, P. N., & Sharma, R. (2022). Blockchain Technology for Secure Supply Chain Management: A Comprehensive Review. *IEEE Access : Practical Innovations, Open Solutions, 10*(July), 85493–85517. DOI: 10.1109/ACCESS.2022.3194319

Agnes, C. O., Sodrudeen, A. A., & Emmanuel, A. A. (2024). Securing the digital supply chain: Cybersecurity best practices for logistics and shipping companies. *World Journal of Advanced Science and Technology, 5*(1), 026–030. https://doi.org/ DOI: 10.53346/wjast.2024.5.1.0030

Agrawal, T. K., Angelis, J., Khilji, W. A., Kalaiarasan, R., & Wiktorsson, M. (2023). Demonstration of a blockchain-based framework using smart contracts for supply chain collaboration. *International Journal of Production Research, 61*(5), 1497–1516. DOI: 10.1080/00207543.2022.2039413

Akanfe, O., Lawong, D., & Rao, H. R. (2024). Blockchain technology and privacy regulation: Reviewing frictions and synthesizing opportunities. *International Journal of Information Management, 76*, 102753. DOI: 10.1016/j.ijinfomgt.2024.102753

Akella, G. K., Wibowo, S., Grandhi, S., & Mubarak, S. (2023). A Systematic Review of Blockchain Technology Adoption Barriers and Enablers for Smart and Sustainable Agriculture. *Big Data and Cognitive Computing, 7*(2), 86. DOI: 10.3390/bdcc7020086

Aljabhan, B., & Obaidat, M. A. (2023). Privacy-Preserving Blockchain Framework for Supply Chain Management: Perceptive Craving Game Search Optimization (PCGSO). *Sustainability, 15*(8), 6905. DOI: 10.3390/su15086905

Bae, S. H., Saberi, S., Kouhizadeh, M., & Sarkis, J. (2025). Examining blockchain's role in supply chain finance structure and governance. *International Review of Financial Analysis, 99*, 103955. DOI: 10.1016/j.irfa.2025.103955

Baharmand, H., Maghsoudi, A., & Coppi, G. (2021). Exploring the application of blockchain to humanitarian supply chains: Insights from Humanitarian Supply Blockchain pilot project. *International Journal of Operations & Production Management, 41*(9), 1522–1543. DOI: 10.1108/IJOPM-12-2020-0884

Bai, Y., Hu, Q., Seo, S.-H., Kang, K., & Lee, J. J. (2022). Public Participation Consortium Blockchain for Smart City Governance. *IEEE Internet of Things Journal, 9*(3), 2094–2108. DOI: 10.1109/JIOT.2021.3091151

Baranidharan, K., Mahalakshmi, R., & Anagha, S. (2025). Blockchain Technology for Enhancing Supply Chain Transparency: Opportunities and Challenges. *International Journal of Advanced Research in Science. Tongxin Jishu*, •••, 345–353. DOI: 10.48175/IJARSCT-23039

Bernal Bernabe, J., Canovas, J. L., Hernandez-Ramos, J. L., Torres Moreno, R., & Skarmeta, A. (2019). Privacy-Preserving Solutions for Blockchain: Review and Challenges. *IEEE Access : Practical Innovations, Open Solutions*, *7*, 164908–164940. DOI: 10.1109/ACCESS.2019.2950872

Bullón Pérez, J. J., Queiruga-Dios, A., Gayoso Martínez, V., & Martín del Rey, Á. (2020). Traceability of Ready-to-Wear Clothing through Blockchain Technology. *Sustainability*, *12*(18), 7491. DOI: 10.3390/su12187491

Chang, S. E., Chen, Y. C., & Lu, M. F. (2019). Supply chain re-engineering using blockchain technology: A case of smart contract based tracking process. *Technological Forecasting and Social Change*, *144*(March), 1–11. DOI: 10.1016/j.techfore.2019.03.015

Danyluk, M. (2021). Supply-Chain Urbanism: Constructing and Contesting the Logistics City. *Annals of the Association of American Geographers*, •••, 1–16. DOI: 10.1080/24694452.2021.1889352

Ding, T., Chen, J., Fang, L., Ji, J., & Fang, Z. (2023). Urban ecosystem services supply-demand assessment from the perspective of the water-energy-food nexus. *Sustainable Cities and Society*, *90*, 104401. DOI: 10.1016/j.scs.2023.104401

Fabrègue, B. F. G., & Bogoni, A. (2023). Privacy and Security Concerns in the Smart City. *Smart Cities*, *6*(1), 586–613. DOI: 10.3390/smartcities6010027

Fazekas, M., Borges de Oliveira, A., & Regos, N. (2021). *Lowering Prices of Pharmaceuticals, Medical Supplies, and Equipment : Insights from Big Data for Better Procurement Strategies in Latin America*. World Bank., DOI: 10.1596/1813-9450-9689

França, A. S. L., Amato Neto, J., Gonçalves, R. F., & Almeida, C. M. V. B. (2020). Proposing the use of blockchain to improve the solid waste management in small municipalities. *Journal of Cleaner Production*, *244*, 118529. DOI: 10.1016/j.jclepro.2019.118529

Ghadge, A., Bourlakis, M., Kamble, S., & Seuring, S. (2023). Blockchain implementation in pharmaceutical supply chains: A review and conceptual framework. *International Journal of Production Research*, *61*(19), 6633–6651. DOI: 10.1080/00207543.2022.2125595

Ghaffari, F., Bertin, E., Crespi, N., & Hatin, J. (2023). Distributed ledger technologies for authentication and access control in networking applications: A comprehensive survey. *Computer Science Review, 50*. Advance online publication. DOI: 10.1016/j.cosrev.2023.100590

Gloerich, I., De Waal, M., Ferri, G., Cila, N., & Karpinski, T. (2020). The City as a License. Implications of Blockchain and Distributed Ledgers for Urban Governance. *Frontiers in Sustainable Cities, 2*. Advance online publication. DOI: 10.3389/frsc.2020.534942

Guo, S., Sun, X., & Lam, H. K. S. (2023). Applications of Blockchain Technology in Sustainable Fashion Supply Chains: Operational Transparency and Environmental Efforts. *IEEE Transactions on Engineering Management, 70*(4), 1312–1328. DOI: 10.1109/TEM.2020.3034216

Hastig, G. M., & Sodhi, M. S. (2020). Blockchain for Supply Chain Traceability: Business Requirements and Critical Success Factors. *Production and Operations Management, 29*(4), 935–954. DOI: 10.1111/poms.13147

Hong, Z., & Xiao, K. (2024). Digital economy structuring for sustainable development: The role of blockchain and artificial intelligence in improving supply chain and reducing negative environmental impacts. *Scientific Reports, 14*(1), 3912. DOI: 10.1038/s41598-024-53760-3 PMID: 38365912

Jain, S., Ahuja, N. J., Srikanth, P., Bhadane, K. V., Nagaiah, B., Kumar, A., & Konstantinou, C. (2021). Blockchain and Autonomous Vehicles: Recent Advances and Future Directions. *IEEE Access : Practical Innovations, Open Solutions, 9*, 130264–130328. DOI: 10.1109/ACCESS.2021.3113649

Jiang, P., Zhang, L., You, S., Van Fan, Y., Tan, R. R., Klemeš, J. J., & You, F. (2023). Blockchain technology applications in waste management: Overview, challenges and opportunities. *Journal of Cleaner Production, 421*, 138466. DOI: 10.1016/j.jclepro.2023.138466

Jinor, E., & Bridgelall, R. (2024). Bibliometric Insights into Balancing Efficiency and Security in Urban Supply Chains. *Urban Science (Basel, Switzerland), 8*(3), 100. DOI: 10.3390/urbansci8030100

Karaduman, Ö., & Gülhas, G. (2025). Blockchain-Enabled Supply Chain Management: A Review of Security, Traceability, and Data Integrity Amid the Evolving Systemic Demand. *Applied Sciences (Basel, Switzerland), 15*(9), 5168. DOI: 10.3390/app15095168

Kouhizadeh, M., Saberi, S., & Sarkis, J. (2021). Blockchain technology and the sustainable supply chain: Theoretically exploring adoption barriers. *International Journal of Production Economics*, *231*, 107831. DOI: 10.1016/j.ijpe.2020.107831

Maima, A. J. (2024). Evaluation of Counterfeit Antimalarial Drug Awareness and Knowledge Among Pharmacy Attendants in Nairobi County, Kenya. *African Journal of Pharmacy and Alternative Medicine*, *2*(1), 21–31. DOI: 10.58460/ajpam.v2i1.84

Majeed, U., Khan, L. U., Yaqoob, I., Kazmi, S. M. A., Salah, K., & Hong, C. S. (2021). Blockchain for IoT-based smart cities: Recent advances, requirements, and future challenges. *Journal of Network and Computer Applications*, *181*, 103007. DOI: 10.1016/j.jnca.2021.103007

Mazumdar, S. (2023). *How to Reduce Information Silos While Blockchain-ifying Recycling Focused Supply Chain Solutions?* https://doi.org/DOI: 10.24251/HICSS.2023.057

Mohammed, S., Singh, A., & Kumar, G. R. (2025). Transforming Agricultural Supply Chains: The Power of Blockchain Technology. *2025 International Conference on Intelligent and Innovative Technologies in Computing, Electrical and Electronics (IITCEE)*, 1–8. https://doi.org/DOI: 10.1109/IITCEE64140.2025.10915510

Mokale, M. (2021). Navigating Global Data Privacy Regulations: A Guide for Telecom Operators. *International Journal For Multidisciplinary Research*, *3*(4). Advance online publication. DOI: 10.36948/ijfmr.2021.v03i04.39051

Nagarajan, S. M., Deverajan, G. G., Chatterjee, P., Alnumay, W., & Muthukumaran, V. (2022). Integration of IoT based routing process for food supply chain management in sustainable smart cities. *Sustainable Cities and Society*, *76*, 103448. DOI: 10.1016/j.scs.2021.103448

Najati, I. (2025). Exploring the failure factors of blockchain adopting projects: A case study of tradelens through the lens of commons theory. *Frontiers in Blockchain*, *8*. Advance online publication. DOI: 10.3389/fbloc.2025.1503595

Padma, A., & Ramaiah, M. (2024). Blockchain Based an Efficient and Secure Privacy Preserved Framework for Smart Cities. *IEEE Access : Practical Innovations, Open Solutions*, *12*(February), 21985–22002. DOI: 10.1109/ACCESS.2024.3364078

Pandey, A. (2025). Blockchain for Pharmaceutical Industry: Present, Past and Future. *INTERANTIONAL JOURNAL OF SCIENTIFIC RESEARCH IN ENGINEERING AND MANAGEMENT*, *09*(03), 1–9. DOI: 10.55041/IJSREM42252

Radmanesh, S.-A., Haji, A., & Fatahi Valilai, O. (2023). Blockchain-Based Architecture for a Sustainable Supply Chain in Cloud Architecture. *Sustainability, 15*(11), 9072. DOI: 10.3390/su15119072

Raj Kumar Reddy, K., Gunasekaran, A., Kalpana, P., Raja Sreedharan, V., & Arvind Kumar, S. (2021). Developing a blockchain framework for the automotive supply chain: A systematic review. *Computers & Industrial Engineering, 157*, 107334. DOI: 10.1016/j.cie.2021.107334

Rijanto, A. (2021). Blockchain Technology Adoption in Supply Chain Finance. *Journal of Theoretical and Applied Electronic Commerce Research, 16*(7), 3078–3098. DOI: 10.3390/jtaer16070168

Saidu, Y., Shuhaida, M. S., Dahiru, A. A., Yau, S., Muhammad, M. Y., & Babando, A. A. (2024). Charting the Course : A Bibliometric Exploration of Blockchain Traceability Systems. *International Conference on Technological Solutions for Smart Economy*, 1–8. https://library.ncs.org.ng/download/charting-the-course-a-bibliometric-exploration-of-blockchain-traceability-systems/

Saidu, Y., Shuhidan, S. M., Aliyu, D. A., Aziz, I. A., & Adamu, S. (2025). Convergence of Blockchain, IoT, and AI for Enhanced Traceability Systems: A Comprehensive Review. *IEEE Access : Practical Innovations, Open Solutions, 13*, 16838–16865. DOI: 10.1109/ACCESS.2025.3528035

Saidu, Y., Shuhidan, S. M., Aziz, I. A., Adamu, D. A., Yau, S., & Adamu, S. (2025). A Bibliometric Analysis on Blockchain Consensus Algorithms: Unveiling Trends, Contributors, and Intellectual Structures. In M. Hisham, H. Mohd Hilmi, A. Said Jadid, & S. Nasir (Eds.), *Proceedings of the International Conference on Smart Cities* - Volume 2 *ICSC 2024, September 10-11, Kota Kinabalu, Malaysia* (pp. 579–593). Springer Singapore. https://doi.org/DOI: 10.1007/978-981-96-5848-0_47

Sarkheyli, A., & Sarkheyli, E. (2019). Smart Megaprojects in Smart Cities, Dimensions, and Challenges. In *Smart Cities Cybersecurity and Privacy* (pp. 269–277). Elsevier., DOI: 10.1016/B978-0-12-815032-0.00019-6

Shahid, A., Almogren, A., Javaid, N., Al-Zahrani, F. A., Zuair, M., & Alam, M. (2020). Blockchain-Based Agri-Food Supply Chain: A Complete Solution. *IEEE Access : Practical Innovations, Open Solutions, 8*, 69230–69243. DOI: 10.1109/ACCESS.2020.2986257

Shchekhovska, L. (2025). Transparency and sustainability: a new paradigm for supply chain management. *Electronic Scientific Journal Intellectualization of Logistics and Supply Chain Management #1 2020, 30*, 47–53. https://doi.org/DOI: 10.46783/smart-scm/2025-30-4

Shen, C., & Pena-Mora, F. (2018). Blockchain for Cities—A Systematic Literature Review. *IEEE Access : Practical Innovations, Open Solutions*, *6*, 76787–76819. DOI: 10.1109/ACCESS.2018.2880744

Singh, S., Hosen, A. S. M. S., & Yoon, B. (2021). Blockchain Security Attacks, Challenges, and Solutions for the Future Distributed IoT Network. *IEEE Access : Practical Innovations, Open Solutions*, *9*, 13938–13959. DOI: 10.1109/ACCESS.2021.3051602

Singh, S., Sharma, P. K., Yoon, B., Shojafar, M., Cho, G. H., & Ra, I.-H. (2020). Convergence of blockchain and artificial intelligence in IoT network for the sustainable smart city. *Sustainable Cities and Society*, *63*, 102364. DOI: 10.1016/j.scs.2020.102364

Subramanian, N., Chaudhuri, A., & Kayikci, Y. (2020). Blockchain Applications in Food Supply Chain. In *Blockchain and Supply Chain Logistics* (pp. 21–29). Springer International Publishing., DOI: 10.1007/978-3-030-47531-4_3

Tafuro, A., Dammacco, G., & Costa, A. (2023). A Conceptual Study on the Role of Blockchain in Sustainable Development of Public–Private Partnership. *Administrative Sciences*, *13*(8), 175. DOI: 10.3390/admsci13080175

Tan, Z., Parambath, S. P., Anagnostopoulos, C., Singer, J., & Marnerides, A. K. (2025). Advanced Persistent Threats Based on Supply Chain Vulnerabilities: Challenges, Solutions, and Future Directions. *IEEE Internet of Things Journal*, *12*(6), 6371–6395. DOI: 10.1109/JIOT.2025.3528744

Thakur, C. K. (2025). Blockchain in Enhancing Supply Chain Transparency. *International Journal for Research in Applied Science and Engineering Technology*, *13*(1), 2093–2095. DOI: 10.22214/ijraset.2025.66746

Theodorou, S., & Sklavos, N. (2019). Blockchain-Based Security and Privacy in Smart Cities. In *Smart Cities Cybersecurity and Privacy* (pp. 21–37). Elsevier., DOI: 10.1016/B978-0-12-815032-0.00003-2

Tripathi, A. K., Akul Krishnan, K., & Pandey, A. C. (2023). A Novel Blockchain and Internet of Things-Based Food Traceability System for Smart Cities. *Wireless Personal Communications*, *129*(3), 2157–2180. DOI: 10.1007/s11277-023-10230-9 PMID: 36987505

Uddin, M., Salah, K., Jayaraman, R., Pesic, S., & Ellahham, S. (2021). Blockchain for drug traceability: Architectures and open challenges. *Health Informatics Journal*, *27*(2). Advance online publication. DOI: 10.1177/14604582211011228 PMID: 33899576

Uddin, M., Selvarajan, S., Obaidat, M., Arfeen, S. U., Khadidos, A. O., Khadidos, A. O., & Abdelhaq, M. (2023). From Hype to Reality: Unveiling the Promises, Challenges and Opportunities of Blockchain in Supply Chain Systems. *Sustainability*, *15*(16), 12193. DOI: 10.3390/su151612193

Wang, G., Wang, Q., & Chen, S. (2023). Exploring Blockchains Interoperability: A Systematic Survey. *ACM Computing Surveys*, *55*(13s), 1–38. DOI: 10.1145/3582882

Wang, W., Chen, Y., Wang, Y., Deveci, M., Al-Hinai, A., & Kadry, S. (2025). Analyzing the barriers to blockchain adoption in supply chain finance using an integrated interval-valued Fermatean fuzzy RAFSI model. *Financial Innovation*, *11*(1), 9. DOI: 10.1186/s40854-024-00670-y

Wang, Z. (2023). *Blockchain Technology—A New Traceability System in Prevention of Fraud-Ridden Food Safety Issues* (pp. 1062–1073). https://doi.org/DOI: 10.2991/978-94-6463-010-7_108

Yakubu, M. M., Hassan, M. F. B., Danyaro, K. U., Junejo, A. Z., Siraj, M., Yahaya, S., Adamu, S., & Abdulsalam, K. (2024). A Systematic Literature Review on Blockchain Consensus Mechanisms' Security: Applications and Open Challenges. *Computer Systems Science and Engineering*, *48*(6), 1437–1481. DOI: 10.32604/csse.2024.054556

Yau, S., Aliyu, A., Saidu, Y., Ibrahim, A., & Aliyu, F. M. (2024). Prospect of Smart Agriculture Using IoT and Data Analytics: A Perspective of Kebbi State, Northwestern Nigeria. *International Journal of Advanced Networking and Applications*, *15*(06), 6194–6203. DOI: 10.35444/ijana.2024.15606

Zhang, Y., Tang, Y., Li, C., Dong, M., Huang, M., Zhang, H., & Ota, K. (2024). Privacy-Preserving for Blockchain-Enabled Cold-Chain Logistics System With IoV and Linkable Ring Signature. *IEEE Transactions on Vehicular Technology*, *73*(9), 12585–12596. DOI: 10.1109/TVT.2024.3391419

Zhu, X., Chen, Z., Cheng, T., Yang, C., Wu, D., Wu, Y., & Wang, H. (2024). Blockchain for urban governance: Enhancing trust in smart city systems with advanced techniques. *Sustainable Cities and Society*, *108*, 105438. DOI: 10.1016/j.scs.2024.105438

Conclusion

Navigating Cybersecurity and Privacy in the Evolution of Smart Urban Ecosystems makes a profound contribution to the interdisciplinary fields of cybersecurity, urban technology, and smart city development. In an era marked by rapid digital transformation, this book serves as a critical link where technical accuracy meets ethical reflection and governance innovation, all of which are critical for achieving sustainable and resilient urban transformation. By bridging these domains, the volume addresses not only the immediate practical challenges but also the long-term implications of integrating advanced technologies into complex urban environments.

At the heart of this work sits a multidisciplinary approach that trains readers with a well understanding as necessary to anticipate and respond to the evolving cyber threat faced by smart cities today. It goes beyond conventional technical analyses, incorporating considerations from data ethics, privacy law, and governance frameworks to ensure the knowledge imparted is both deep and broad. This synthesis empowers cybersecurity professionals, urban planners, and scholars to deploy innovative defensive strategies that are sensitive to the privacy and justice needs of diverse urban developments.

The book's comprehensive discussion of a wide range of technologies — including artificial intelligence, blockchain, the Internet of Things, industrial automation, and edge computing — reflects the varied and integrated nature of smart urban ecosystems. It sheds light on the vulnerabilities inherent to each component and explores cutting-edge defense mechanisms that collectively strengthen cities' security. Equally important, it explains the ethical dilemmas and governance challenges emerging from such technological convergence, reminding readers that the future of urban intelligence is inseparable from questions of transparency, fairness, and inclusiveness.

Moreover, this book's coherent structure, which systematically addresses digital threats alongside governance and ethical pathways, provides a foundational script for the smart city concept. It fills a critical gap by integrating technical sophistication with social responsibility, thus setting a benchmark for how academic work and practical guidance can blend to shape the next generation of urban infrastructures and services.

As cities worldwide become more interconnected and complex, they also become more susceptible to multifaceted cyber risks, ranging from data breaches to attacks on critical infrastructure. This book offers the intellectual tools necessary to understand these interconnected risks. It advances strength not just through technology but through adaptive governance and collaborative community engagement. The integration of concepts such as cyber resilience, privacy innovation, and ethical AI highlights the multifaceted strategies required to build urban systems that are not only functionally advanced but also just and trusted by citizens.

The impact of this book extends beyond theory into actionable insights. It serves as a practical guide for implementing security frameworks and privacy safeguards for the unique characteristics of smart urban ecosystems. From innovative sensor deployment algorithms and cloud security models to ethical data management and green cybersecurity practices, the work equips practitioners with the capabilities to implement real-world solutions that are sensitive to ecological, social, and technological factors.

Furthermore, by emphasizing transparency and equitable access, the book addresses one of the most pressing challenges in smart city development: ensuring that technological progress benefits all citizens without exacerbating existing inequalities. It calls for a future where the digital development of cities is handled carefully and thoughtfully, always considering its effects on society.

In academic terms, this publication provides a rich foundation for further research by mapping emerging trends and identifying critical knowledge gaps in smart city security and privacy. It encourages interdisciplinary collaboration among engineers, social scientists, legal experts, and urban planners, advancing a universal research culture that reflects the complexity of smart ecosystems.

Navigating Cybersecurity and Privacy in the Evolution of Smart Urban Ecosystems stands as an essential contribution to the global effort to build smarter, safer, and more ethical cities. It illustrates a roadmap for understanding and managing the predictable tensions between innovation and risk, efficiency and privacy, automation and human values. Readers of this book will be well-prepared to lead in the design, implementation, and governance of urban environments that are not only intelligent and efficient but also fundamentally secure, equitable, and resilient —accurate models for the cities of tomorrow.

Compilation of References

(2014). World Development Indicators. (2014). *World Development Indicators*, •••. Advance online publication. DOI: 10.1596/978-1-4648-0163-1

. Malik, S., & Sun, W. (2020, February 1). Analysis and Simulation of Cyber Attacks Against Connected and Autonomous Vehicles. IEEE Xplore. https://doi.org/DOI: 10.1109/MetroCAD48866.2020.00018

. Manas. (2023). Role of Privacy Metrics in Next Generation Smart Cities. *Tuijin Jishu/Journal of Propulsion Technology, 44*(4), 3151–3159. https://doi.org/DOI: 10.52783/tjjpt.v44.i4.1407

A person in black shirt holding a solar panel. (2021, October 20). Kindel Media. [Image]. Pexels. https://www.pexels.com/photo/a-person-in-black-shirt-holding-a-solar-panel-while-standing-on-the-roof-9875441

Abbas, K., Tawalbeh, L A A., & Rafiq, A. (2021). Convergence of Blockchain and IoT for Secure Transportation Systems in Smart Cities. *Security and Privacy in Smart Cities, 15*(3), 567–589. DOI: 10.1000/wiley.blockchainiottransportation2021

Abkenar, F. S., Ramezani, P., Iranmanesh, S., Murali, S., Chulerttiyawong, D., Wan, X., & Raad, R. (2022). A survey on mobility of edge computing networks in iot: State-of-the-art, architectures, and challenges. *IEEE Communications Surveys and Tutorials, 24*(4), 2329–2365.

Abu-Dabaseh, F., Alghizzawi, M., Alkhlaifat, B. I., Ezmigna, A. A. R., Alzghoul, A., AlSokkar, A. A., & Al-Gasawneh, J. (2024). Enhancing privacy and security in decentralized social systems: blockchain-based approach. In *2024 2nd international conference on cyber resilience (iccr)* (pp. 1–6).

Abu-Dabaseh, F., & Alghizzawi, M. (2024). "Enhancing Privacy and Security in Decentralized Social Systems: Blockchain-Based Approach." *Proceedings of the International Conference on Cybersecurity*, Vol. 15(3), pp. 567–589. DOI: DOI: 10.1000/ieeexplore.blockchainprivacysecurity2024

Abu-Rayash, A., & Dincer, I. (2021, August). Development and analysis of an integrated solar energy system for smart cities. *Sustainable Energy Technologies and Assessments*, *46*, 101170. DOI: 10.1016/j.seta.2021.101170

Abu-Salma, R. (2020). Designing user-centered privacy-enhancing technologies (Doctoral dissertation, UCL (University College London)).

Achaal, B., Adda, M., Berger, M., Ibrahim, H., & Awde, A. (2024). Study of smart grid cyber-security, examining architectures, communication networks, cyber-attacks, countermeasure techniques, and challenges. *Cybersecurity*, *7*(1), 10. PMID: 38707764

Achankeng, S. (2025). Analysis of Prevention Techniques against DDoS and SQL Injection Attack in Network and Cloud Environment. *Journal of Cloud Computing (Heidelberg, Germany).*

Acquisti, A., Brandimarte, L., & Loewenstein, G. (2015). Privacy and human behavior in the age of information. *Science*, *347*(6221), 509–514. DOI: 10.1126/science.aaa1465 PMID: 25635091

Adeniran, A. A., Adeniran, A. O., Familusi, O. B., & Adedayo, O. (2024). The outlook of cyber security in african businesses: Issues and way-out. *Management analytics and social insights, 1*(2), 260–271.

Adepoju, P. A., Ige, A. B., Akinade, A. O., & Afolabi, A. I. (2025). Smart Cities and Internet of Things (IoT): A Review of Emerging Technologies and Challenges. *International Journal of Research and Innovation in Social Science*, *IX*(I), 1536–1549. DOI: 10.47772/IJRISS.2025.9010127

Adil, M., Khan, M. K., Kumar, N., Attique, M., Farouk, A., Guizani, M., & Jin, Z. (2024). Healthcare internet of things: Security threats, challenges, and future research directions. *IEEE Internet of Things Journal, 11*(11), 19046–19069.

Adjorlolo, G., Tang, Z., Wauk, G., Adu Sarfo, P., Braimah, A. B., & Blankson Safo, R., & N-yanyi, B. (2025). Evaluating Corruption-Prone Public Procurement Stages for Blockchain Integration Using AHP Approach. *Systems*, *13*(4), 267. DOI: 10.3390/systems13040267

Agarwal, U., Rishiwal, V., Tanwar, S., Chaudhary, R., Sharma, G., Bokoro, P. N., & Sharma, R. (2022). Blockchain Technology for Secure Supply Chain Management: A Comprehensive Review. *IEEE Access : Practical Innovations, Open Solutions*, *10*(July), 85493–85517. DOI: 10.1109/ACCESS.2022.3194319

Agnes, C. O., Sodrudeen, A. A., & Emmanuel, A. A. (2024). Securing the digital supply chain: Cybersecurity best practices for logistics and shipping companies. *World Journal of Advanced Science and Technology, 5*(1), 026–030. https://doi.org/ DOI: 10.53346/wjast.2024.5.1.0030

Agrawal, N., Binns, R., Van Kleek, M., Laine, K., & Shadbolt, N. (2021, May). Exploring design and governance challenges in the development of privacy-preserving computation. In *Proceedings of the 2021 CHI Conference on Human Factors in Computing Systems* (pp. 1-13).

Agrawal, T. K., Angelis, J., Khilji, W. A., Kalaiarasan, R., & Wiktorsson, M. (2023). Demonstration of a blockchain-based framework using smart contracts for supply chain collaboration. *International Journal of Production Research, 61*(5), 1497–1516. DOI: 10.1080/00207543.2022.2039413

Ahmad Jan, M., Adil, M., Brik, B., Harous, S., & Abbas, S. (2025). Making Sense of Big Data in Intelligent Transportation Systems: Current Trends, Challenges and Future Directions. *ACM Computing Surveys, 57*(8), 1–43.

Ahmad, K., Maabreh, M., Ghaly, M., Khan, K., & Qadir, J. (2022). Developing Future Human-Centered Smart Cities: Critical Analysis of Smart City Security, Data Management, and Ethical Challenges. *Computer Science & AI Systems, 39*(2), 101–120. DOI: 10.1000/elsevier.smartcitysecurity2022

Ahmad, K., Maabreh, M., Ghaly, M., Khan, K., Qadir, J., & Al-Fuqaha, A. (2022). Developing future human-centered smart cities: Critical analysis of smart city security, Data management, and Ethical challenges. *Computer Science Review, 43*, 100452. DOI: 10.1016/j.cosrev.2021.100452

Ahmed, E., Yaqoob, I., Hashem, I. A. T., Khan, I., Ahmed, A. I. A., Imran, M., & Vasilakos, A. V. (2017). The role of big data analytics in Internet of Things. *Computer Networks, 129*, 459–471.

Ahmed, M. R., Islam, A. K. M. M., Shatabda, S., & Islam, S. (2022). Blockchain-Based Identity Management System and Self-Sovereign Identity Ecosystem: A Comprehensive Survey. *IEEE Access : Practical Innovations, Open Solutions, 10*, 567–589. DOI: 10.1000/ieeexplore.blockchainidentity2022

Ahmed, R. A., Hemdan, E. E. D., & El-Shafai, W. (2022). Climate-Smart Agriculture Using Intelligent Techniques, Blockchain and Internet of Things: Concepts, Challenges, and Opportunities. *Transactions on Emerging Telecommunications Technologies, 33*(4), e4607. DOI: 10.1002/ett.4607

Ahmed, S. (2020). Security and privacy in smart cities: Challenges and opportunities. *International Journal of Engineering Trends and Technology*, *68*(2), 1–8.

Ahmed, S., Hossain, M. F., Kaiser, M. S., Noor, M. B. T., Mahmud, M., & Chakraborty, C. (2021). Artificial intelligence and machine learning for ensuring security in smart cities. In *Data-driven mining, learning and analytics for secured smart cities: Trends and advances* (pp. 23–47). Springer International Publishing.

Ahn, S., Gim, G., Jang, S., & Hwang, J. (2024). *A Study on the Integration of Endpoint Security Service Operations Management*. Focusing on Cloud Services., DOI: 10.1007/978-3-031-53385-3_3

Akanfe, O., Lawong, D., & Rao, H. R. (2024). Blockchain technology and privacy regulation: Reviewing frictions and synthesizing opportunities. *International Journal of Information Management*, *76*, 102753. DOI: 10.1016/j.ijinfomgt.2024.102753

Akella, G. K., Wibowo, S., Grandhi, S., & Mubarak, S. (2023). A Systematic Review of Blockchain Technology Adoption Barriers and Enablers for Smart and Sustainable Agriculture. *Big Data and Cognitive Computing*, *7*(2), 86. DOI: 10.3390/bdcc7020086

Akhter, R., & Sofi, S. A. (2022). Precision agriculture using IoT data analytics and machine learning. In Journal of King Saud University – Computer and Information Sciences (Vols. 34–34, pp. 5602–5618). https://doi.org/10.1016/j.jksuci.2021.05.013

Alagic, G., Alagic, G., Apon, D., Cooper, D., Dang, Q., Dang, T., ... others (2022). Status report on the third round of the nist post-quantum cryptography standardization process.

Alajlan, R., Alhumam, N., & Frikha, M. (2023). Cybersecurity for Blockchain-Based IoT Systems: A Review. *Applied Sciences (Basel, Switzerland)*, *12*(6), 765–788. DOI: 10.1000/mdpi.blockchainiotsecurity2023

Alam, K. M., Ashfiqur Rahman, J. M., Tasnim, A., & Akther, A. (2022). A Blockchain-based Land Title Management System for Bangladesh. *Journal of King Saud University. Computer and Information Sciences*, *34*(6), 3096–3110. DOI: 10.1016/j.jksuci.2020.10.011

Alam, S., Shuaib, M., Khan, W. Z., Garg, S., & Kaddoum, G. (2021). Blockchain-Based Initiatives: Current State and Challenges. *Computer Networks*, *15*(3), 567–589. DOI: 10.1000/elsevier.blockchaininitiatives2021

Alankar, B., Kaur, H., & Chauhan, R. (Eds.). (2021). *Transforming the Internet of Things for Next-generation Smart Systems*. IGI Global.

Alavi, A. H., Jiao, P., Buttlar, W. G., & Lajnef, N. (2018). Internet of things-enabled smart cities: State-of-the-art and future trends. *Measurement, 129*, 589–606.

Alberti, M.. (2019). Platforms for Smart Environments and Future Internet Design: A Survey. *IEEE Access : Practical Innovations, Open Solutions*, *7*, 165748–165778. DOI: 10.1109/ACCESS.2019.2950656

Albino, V., Berardi, U., & Dangelico, R. M. (2015). Smart Cities: Definitions, dimensions, performance, and initiatives. *Journal of Urban Technology*, *22*(1), 3–21. DOI: 10.1080/10630732.2014.942092

Albshaier, L., Almarri, S., & Albuali, A. (2025). Federated learning for cloud and edge security: A systematic review of challenges and ai opportunities. *Electronics (Basel)*, *14*(5), 1019.

Aldy, J. (2022, August). Learning how to build back better through clean energy policy evaluation. *HKS Faculty Research Working Paper Series RWP22-010*. https://nrs.harvard.edu/URN-3:HUL.INSTREPOS:37373014

Al-Farsi, S., Rathore, M. M., & Bakiras, S. (2021). Security of Blockchain-Based Supply Chain Management Systems: Challenges and Opportunities. *Applied Sciences (Basel, Switzerland)*, *15*(3), 567–589. DOI: 10.1000/mdpi.blockchainsupplychain-security2021

Alfiani, F. R. N., & Sara, R. (2024). The Improvement of Digital Literacy to Secure Data and Privacy in the Digital Age. *INJURITY: Journal of Interdisciplinary Studies*, *3*(12), 832–839.

Al-Huthaifi, R., Li, T., Huang, W., Gu, J., & Li, C. (2023). Federated learning in smart cities: Privacy and security survey. *Information Sciences*, *632*, 833–857.

Ali, S., Alshinwan, M., Khashan, O. A., Hijjawi, M., Altawil, A., Al-Na'amneh, Q., ... others (2025). Intrusion detection for wireless sensor networks using parrot algorithm. In *Machine intelligence applications in cyber-risk management* (pp. 345–366). IGI Global Scientific Publishing.

Ali, S., Wang, J., & Leung, V. C. M. (2025). AI-driven fusion with cybersecurity: Exploring current trends, advanced techniques, future directions, and policy implications for evolving paradigms– A comprehensive review. *Information Fusion*, *118*, 102922. DOI: 10.1016/j.inffus.2024.102922

Aljabhan, B., & Obaidat, M. A. (2023). Privacy-Preserving Blockchain Framework for Supply Chain Management: Perceptive Craving Game Search Optimization (PCGSO). *Sustainability*, *15*(8), 6905. DOI: 10.3390/su15086905

Aljaidi, M., Alsarhan, A., Al-Fraihat, D., Al-Arjan, A., Igried, B., El-Salhi, S. M., . . . Al-Na'amneh, Q. (2023). Cybersecurity threats in the era of ai: Detection of phishing domains through classification rules. In *2023 2nd international engineering conference on electrical, energy, and artificial intelligence (eiceeai)* (pp. 1–6).

Aljuaid, W. H., & Alshamrani, S. S. (2024). A Deep Learning Approach for Intrusion Detection Systems in Cloud Computing Environments. *Applied Sciences (Basel, Switzerland), 14*(13), 5381. DOI: 10.3390/app14135381

Al-Makkawi, T., Alsarhan, A., Al-Na'amneh, Q., Aljaidi, M., Almaiah, M. A., Al-Jamal, M., & Aljawarneh, M. (2025). Open-source forensics tools for recovery of deleted data in unconventional ways. In *Cryptography, biometrics, and anonymity in cybersecurity management* (pp. 41–60). IGI Global Scientific Publishing.

Almeida, F. (2023). Prospects of cybersecurity in smart cities. *Future Internet, 15*(9), 285.

Al-Na'amneh, Q. (2025). Secure cloud-marketplaces: A trust framework for evaluating. *Utilizing AI in Network and Mobile Security for Threat Detection and Prevention*, 255.

Al-Na'amneh, Q., Aljaidi, M., Nasayreh, A., Gharaibeh, H., Mamlook, A., Emhamed, R., ... Samara, G. (2024). Journal of intelligent systems: Enhancing iot device security: Cnn-svm hybrid approach for real-time detection of dos and ddos attacks.

Al-Na'amneh, Q., Almomani, A., Nasayreh, A., Nahar, K. M., Gharaibeh, H., Al Mamlook, R. E., & Alauthman, M. (2024). Next generation image watermarking via combined dwt-svd technique. In *2024 2nd international conference on cyber resilience (iccr)* (pp. 1–10).

Al-Na'amneh, Q., Aljawarneh, M., & Hazaymih, R. (2025). A framework for insider threat detection using role-based profile assessment and threshold. In *Utilizing ai in network and mobile security for threat detection and prevention* (pp. 97–114). IGI Global Scientific Publishing.

Al-Na'amneh, Q., Dhifallah, W., Hazaymih, R., Almaiah, M. A., Alsheyab, A., Alshinwan, M., & Qadoumi, B. (2025). Dis flooding attack impact in rpl-based 6lowpan network. In *Machine intelligence applications in cyber-risk management* (pp. 69–84). IGI Global Scientific Publishing.

Alnahari, M. S., & Ariaratnam, S. T. (2022). The Application of Blockchain Technology to Smart City Infrastructure. *Smart Cities, 5*(3), 979–993. DOI: 10.3390/smartcities5030049

Al-Raeei, M. (2024). The smart future for sustainable development: Artificial intelligence solutions for sustainable urbanization. *Sustainable Development*. Advance online publication. DOI: 10.1002/sd.3131

Al-Sada, B., Sadighian, A., & Oligeri, G. (2024). Mitre att&ck: State of the art and way forward. *ACM Computing Surveys*, *57*(1), 1–37.

Alshmrany, S. (2025). Securing smart cities: Privacy-preserving IoT with optimized gated lounge attention dropout mechanism. *Neural Computing & Applications*, 1–26.

Al-Shurbaji, T., Anbar, M., Manickam, S., Hasbullah, I. H., Alfriehat, N., Alabsi, B. A., Alzighaibi, A. R., & Hashim, H. (2025). Deep learning-based intrusion detection system for detecting IoT botnet attacks: A review. *IEEE Access : Practical Innovations, Open Solutions*, *13*, 11792–11822. DOI: 10.1109/ACCESS.2025.3526711

Al-Taleb, N., & Saqib, N. A. (2022). Towards a hybrid machine learning model for intelligent cyber threat identification in smart city environments. *Applied Sciences (Basel, Switzerland)*, *12*(4), 1863.

Al-Turjman, F., Zahmatkesh, H., & Shahroze, R. (2022). An overview of security and privacy in smart cities' IoT communications. *Transactions on Emerging Telecommunications Technologies*, *33*(3), e3677.

Alturki, N., Alharthi, R., Umer, M., Saidani, O., Alshardan, A., Alhebshi, R. M., Alsubai, S., & Bashir, A. K. (2024). Efficient and Secure IoT Based Smart Home Automation Using Multi-Model Learning and Blockchain Technology. *Computer Modeling in Engineering & Sciences*, *139*(3), 3387–3415. DOI: 10.32604/cmes.2023.044700

Amy, N. (2024). *How AI is arming cities in the battle for climate resilience | Reuters*. https://www.reuters.com/sustainability/climate-energy/how-ai-is-arming-cities-battle-climate-resilience-2024-05-23/

Anagnostopoulos, T., Kostakos, P., Zaslavsky, A., Kantzavelou, I., Tsotsolas, N., Salmon, I., & Harle, R. (2021). Challenges and solutions of surveillance systems in IoT-enabled smart campus: A survey. *IEEE Access : Practical Innovations, Open Solutions*, *9*, 131926–131954.

Anakhov, P., Zhebka, V., & Popereshnyak, S. (2023). Protecting Objects of Critical Information Infrastructure from Wartime Cyber Attacks by Decentralizing the Telecommunications Network. *Cybersecurity Providing in Information and Telecommunication Systems*, *3550*, 240–245. DOI: 10.1000/elibrary.wartimecybersecurity2023

Andrade, R. O., Yoo, S. G., Tello-Oquendo, L., & Ortiz-Garcés, I. (2020). A comprehensive study of the IoT cybersecurity in smart cities. *IEEE Access : Practical Innovations, Open Solutions, 8*, 228922–228941.

Andrade, R., Ortiz-Garcés, I., Tintin, X., & Llumiquinga, G. (2022). Factors of risk analysis for IoT systems. *Risks, 10*(8), 162.

Angrishi, K. (2017). Turning internet of things (iot) into internet of vulnerabilities (iov): Iot botnets. *arXiv preprint arXiv:1702.03681.*

Anisetti, M., Ardagna, C., Cremonini, M., Damiani, E., Sessa, J., & Costa, L. (2020). Security threat landscape. *White Paper Security Threats.*

Aragón, P., Kaltenbrunner, A., Calleja-López, A., Pereira, A., Monterde, A., Barandiaran, X. E., & Gómez, V. (2017, September). Deliberative platform design: The case study of the online discussions in Decidim Barcelona. In G. Ciampaglia, A. Mashhadi, & T. Yasseri, T. (Eds.), *Social Informatics, Lecture Notes in Computer Science, 10540*, 277-287. https://doi.org/DOI: 10.1007/978-3-319-67256-4_22

Arslan, S., Ozkaya, M., & Kardas, G. (2023). Modeling languages for internet of things (IoT) applications: A comparative analysis study. *Mathematics, 11*(5), 1263.

Artuso, M. (2014). UN Habitat, State of the World's Cities 2012/13 – prosperity of cities, London, Earthscan, 2013, 184 pp., ISBN 13: 978-0-415-83888-7. Tab. Graph. Images. Urban Research & Practice, 7(3), 359–360. https://doi.org/10.1080/17535069.2014.968363

ARTYUSHINA. A. (2023). DATA GOVERNANCE IN SMART CITIES: PERSONAL DATA AS PRIVATE ASSET, COMMONS, AND/OR PUBLIC GOOD? (Doctoral dissertation, YORK UNIVERSITY TORONTO).

Asghari, A., & Sohrabi, M. K. (2024). Server placement in mobile cloud computing: A comprehensive survey for edge computing, fog computing and cloudlet. *Computer Science Review, 51*, 100616. DOI: 10.1016/j.cosrev.2023.100616

Ashraf, M. A., Jamal, H., Khan, S. A., Ahmed, Z., & Baig, M. I. (2016). A Heterogeneous Service-Oriented Deep Packet Inspection and Analysis Framework for Traffic-Aware Network Management and Security Systems. *IEEE Access : Practical Innovations, Open Solutions, 4*, 5918–5936. DOI: 10.1109/ACCESS.2016.2609398

Asio, J. M. R., & Suero, A. N. (2025). Global Synergy: Cross-Border Collaborations in AI-Enabled Smart City Development. In *AI and Emerging Technologies for Emergency Response and Smart Cities* (pp. 259-286). IGI Global Scientific Publishing. DOI: 10.4018/979-8-3693-9770-1.ch012

Aslam, M., Khan Abbasi, M. A., Khalid, T., Shan, R. U., Ullah, S., Ahmad, T., & Ahmad, R. (2022). Getting smarter about smart cities: Improving data security and privacy through compliance. *Sensors (Basel)*, *22*(23), 9338. PMID: 36502039

Athanere, S., & Thakur, R. (2022). Blockchain-Based Hierarchical Semi-Decentralized Approach Using IPFS for Secure and Efficient Data Sharing. *Journal of King Saud University. Computer and Information Sciences*, *34*(3), 211–230. DOI: 10.1000/elsevier.blockchainipfs2022

Atzori, L., Iera, A., & Morabito, G. (2010). The internet of things: A survey. *Computer Networks*, *54*(15), 2787–2805.

Awotunde, J. B., Ayo, F. E., Panigrahi, R., Garg, A., Bhoi, A. K., & Barsocchi, P. (2023). A Multi-level Random Forest Model-Based Intrusion Detection Using Fuzzy Inference System for Internet of Things Networks. *International Journal of Computational Intelligence Systems*, *16*(1), 31. DOI: 10.1007/s44196-023-00205-w

Ayalon, O., & Toch, E. (2021). User-centered privacy-by-design: Evaluating the appropriateness of design prototypes. *International Journal of Human-Computer Studies*, *154*, 102641.

Babel, K., Daian, P., & Kelkar, M. (2023). "Clockwork Finance: Automated Analysis of Economic Security in Smart Contracts." *Proceedings of the IEEE Security and Privacy Symposium*, Vol. 15(3), pp. 567–589. DOI: DOI: 10.1000/ieeexplore.clockworkfinance2023

Bacco, M., Delmastro, F., Ferro, E., & Gotta, A. (2017). Environmental monitoring for smart cities. *IEEE Sensors Journal*, *17*(23), 7767–7774. DOI: 10.1109/jsen.2017.2722819

Baccour, E., Mhaisen, N., Abdellatif, A., Erbad, A., Mohamed, A., Hamdi, M., & Guizani, M. (2021). Pervasive AI for IoT Applications: A Survey on Resource-Efficient Distributed Artificial Intelligence. *IEEE Communications Surveys and Tutorials*, *24*, 2366–2418. DOI: 10.1109/COMST.2022.3200740

Bada, A. O., Damianou, A., Angelopoulos, C. M., & Katos, V. (2021). Towards a green blockchain: A review of consensus mechanisms and their energy consumption. In *2021 17th International Conference on Distributed Computing in Sensor Systems (DCOSS)* (pp. 503–511). IEEE. https://doi.org/DOI: 10.1109/DCOSS52077.2021.00083

Bae, S. H., Saberi, S., Kouhizadeh, M., & Sarkis, J. (2025). Examining blockchain's role in supply chain finance structure and governance. *International Review of Financial Analysis*, *99*, 103955. DOI: 10.1016/j.irfa.2025.103955

Baharmand, H., Maghsoudi, A., & Coppi, G. (2021). Exploring the application of blockchain to humanitarian supply chains: Insights from Humanitarian Supply Blockchain pilot project. *International Journal of Operations & Production Management, 41*(9), 1522–1543. DOI: 10.1108/IJOPM-12-2020-0884

Bai, Y., Hu, Q., Seo, S.-H., Kang, K., & Lee, J. J. (2022). Public Participation Consortium Blockchain for Smart City Governance. *IEEE Internet of Things Journal, 9*(3), 2094–2108. DOI: 10.1109/JIOT.2021.3091151

Bakhshi, T., Ghita, B., & Kuzminykh, I. (2024). A review of iot firmware vulnerabilities and auditing techniques. *Sensors (Basel), 24*(2), 708. PMID: 38276399

Ba, L., Tangour, F., El Abbassi, I., & Absi, R. (2025, April 15). Analysis of Digital Twin applications in energy efficiency: A systematic review. *Sustainability, 17*(8), 3560. DOI: 10.3390/su17083560

Balas, V. E., Kumar, R., & Srivastava, R. (Eds.). (2020). *Recent trends and advances in artificial intelligence and internet of things*. Springer International Publishing.

Balcerzak, A. P., Nica, E., Rogalska, E., Poliak, M., Klieštik, T., & Sabie, O.-M. M. (2022). Blockchain Technology and Smart Contracts in Decentralized Governance Systems. *Administrative Sciences, 12*(3), 96. DOI: 10.3390/admsci12030096

Bannerman, S., & Orasch, A. (2020). Privacy and smart cities. *Canadian Journal of Urban Research, 29*(1), 17–38.

Baranidharan, K., Mahalakshmi, R., & Anagha, S. (2025). Blockchain Technology for Enhancing Supply Chain Transparency: Opportunities and Challenges. *International Journal of Advanced Research in Science. Tongxin Jishu*, •••, 345–353. DOI: 10.48175/IJARSCT-23039

Baskar, K., Muthuraj, S., Sangeetha, S., Vengatesan, K., Aishwarya, D., & Yuvaraj, P. (2022). *Framework for implementation of smart driver assistance system using augmented reality.* Paper presented at the International Conference on Big data and Cloud Computing.

Bath, A. (2025, April 23). *Wind industry installs record capacity in 2024 despite policy instability.* Global Wind Energy Council. https://www.gwec.net/gwec-news/wind-industry-installs-record-capacity-in-2024-despite-policy-instability

Bayat, A., & Kawalek, P. (2023). Digitization and urban governance: The city as a reflection of its data infrastructure. *International Review of Administrative Sciences, 89*(1). Advance online publication. DOI: 10.1177/00208523211033205

Beeman, G. (2025, April 1). *The top cyber threats to energy & utilities in 2025 – and how to stay ahead.* Mattermost. https://mattermost.com/blog/top-cyber-threats-to-energy-utilities-in-2025

Beerman, J., Berent, D., Falter, Z., & Bhunia, S. (2023, May). A review of colonial pipeline ransomware attack. In 2023 IEEE/ACM 23rd International Symposium on Cluster, Cloud and Internet Computing Workshops (CCGridW) (pp. 8-15). IEEE.

Belli, L., Cilfone, A., Davoli, L., Ferrari, G., Adorni, P., Di Nocera, F., & Bertolotti, E. (2020). IoT-enabled smart sustainable cities: Challenges and approaches. *Smart Cities*, *3*(3), 1039–1071.

Bellini, P., Nesi, P., & Pantaleo, G. (2022). IoT-enabled smart cities: A review of concepts, frameworks and key technologies. *Applied Sciences (Basel, Switzerland)*, *12*(3), 1607.

Benouachane, H. (2025). Cyber security challenges in the era of artificial intelligence and autonomous weapons. In *Cyber security in the age of artificial intelligence and autonomous weapons* (pp. 24–42). CRC Press.

Bera, S., Misra, S., & Rodrigues, J. J. (2014). Cloud Computing Applications for smart Grid: A survey. *IEEE Transactions on Parallel and Distributed Systems*, *26*(5), 1477–1494. DOI: 10.1109/tpds.2014.2321378

Bernal Bernabe, J., Canovas, J. L., Hernandez-Ramos, J. L., Torres Moreno, R., & Skarmeta, A. (2019). Privacy-Preserving Solutions for Blockchain: Review and Challenges. *IEEE Access: Practical Innovations, Open Solutions*, *7*, 164908–164940. DOI: 10.1109/ACCESS.2019.2950872

Bernstein, D. J., & Lange, T. (2017). Post-quantum cryptography. *Nature*, *549*(7671), 188–194. PMID: 28905891

Bhaduri, M. (2025). AI and IoT Solutions for Efficient Public Service Delivery in Smart Cities. *Soft Computing Fusion with Applications*, *2*(1), 153–163. DOI: 10.22105/scfa.v2i1.41

Bhardwaj, A., Kaushik, K., Bharany, S., Rehman, A. U., Hu, Y.-C., Eldin, E. T., & Ghamry, N. A. (2022). IIoT: Traffic data flow analysis and modeling experiment for smart IoT devices. *Sustainability*, *14*(21), 14645.

Bhardwaj, T., Kamat, V. A., & Dwivedi, G. (2022). Blockchain-Based Solutions for Cybersecurity: Architecture, Applications, and Review. *Security and Privacy in Cyberspace*, *15*(3), 567–589. DOI: 10.1000/springer.blockchainsecurity2022

Bibri, S. E., Alexandre, A., Sharifi, A., & Krogstie, J. (2023a). Environmentally sustainable smart cities and their converging AI, IoT, and big data technologies and solutions: an integrated approach to an extensive literature review. *Energy Informatics 2023 6:1, 6*(1), 1–39. https://doi.org/DOI: 10.1186/S42162-023-00259-2

Bouacida, N., & Mohapatra, P. (2021). Vulnerabilities in federated learning. *IEEE Access : Practical Innovations, Open Solutions, 9*, 63229–63249.

Breuer, J., & Pierson, J. (2021). The right to the city and data protection for developing citizen-centric digital cities. *Information Communication and Society, 24*(6), 797–812.

Brown, D. (2012, August 27). *Wind power ethics*. Ethics and Climate. https://ethicsandclimate.org/2012/08/27/wind-power-ethics

Brunner, L. G., Peer, R., Zorn, C., Paulik, R., & Logan, T. (2024). Understanding cascading risks through real-world interdependent urban infrastructure. *Reliability Engineering & System Safety, 241*, 109653.

Buczak, A. L., & Guven, E. (2015). A survey of data mining and machine learning methods for cyber security intrusion detection. *IEEE Communications Surveys and Tutorials, 18*(2), 1153–1176.

Buettner, T. (2015). Urban Estimates and Projections at the United Nations: The strengths, weaknesses, and underpinnings of the world Urbanization Prospects. *Spatial Demography, 3*(2), 91–108. DOI: 10.1007/s40980-015-0004-2

Bullón Pérez, J. J., Queiruga-Dios, A., Gayoso Martínez, V., & Martín del Rey, Á. (2020). Traceability of Ready-to-Wear Clothing through Blockchain Technology. *Sustainability, 12*(18), 7491. DOI: 10.3390/su12187491

Byres, E., & Lowe, J. (2004). The myths and facts behind cyber security risks for industrial control systems. In *Proceedings of the vde kongress* (Vol. 116, pp. 213–218).

Călin, A.-M., Cotfas, D. T., & Cotfas, P. A. (2024, September). A review of smart photovoltaic systems which are using remote-control, AI, and cybersecurity approaches. *Applied Sciences (Basel, Switzerland), 14*(17), 7838. DOI: 10.3390/app14177838

Calleja-López, A. (2019, May 17). *Building alternatives: The digital democracy and data commons pilot*. Decode. https://decodeproject.eu/blog/building-alternatives-digital-democracy-and-data-commons-pilot.html

Calzada, I. (2018). (Smart) Citizens from Data Providers to Decision-Makers? The Case Study of Barcelona. *Sustainability 2018, Vol. 10, Page 3252, 10*(9), 3252. https://doi.org/DOI: 10.3390/SU10093252

Calzada, I., & Almirall, E. (2020). Data ecosystems for protecting European citizens' digital rights. Transforming government: People, process and policy, 14(2), 133-147.

Campolo, C., Genovese, G., Iera, A., & Molinaro, A. (2021). Virtualizing AI at the Distributed Edge towards Intelligent IoT Applications. *J. Sens. Actuator Networks, 10*, 13. DOI: 10.3390/JSAN10010013

Capdevila, I., & Zarlenga, M. I. (2015). Smart city or smart citizens? The Barcelona case. *Journal of Strategy and Management, 8*(3), 266–282. DOI: 10.1108/jsma-03-2015-0030

Cappa, F., Franco, S., & Rosso, F. (2022). Citizens and cities: Leveraging citizen science and big data for sustainable urban development. *Business Strategy and the Environment, 31*(2), 648–667.

Cappelli, D. M., Moore, A. P., & Trzeciak, R. F. (2012). *The cert guide to insider threats: How to prevent, detect, and respond to information technology crimes (theft/sabotage/fraud)*. AddisonWesley Professional.

Cardullo, P., & Kitchin, R. (2019). Being a 'citizen' in the smart city: Up and down the scaffold of smart citizen participation in Dublin, Ireland. *GeoJournal, 84*(1). Advance online publication. DOI: 10.1007/s10708-018-9845-8

Casola, V., De Benedictis, A., Rak, M., & Villano, U. (2018). Monitoring Data Security in the Cloud: A Security SLA-Based Approach. In *Security and Resilience in Intelligent Data-Centric Systems and Communication Networks* (pp. 235–259). Elsevier. https://doi.org/DOI: 10.1016/B978-0-12-811373-8.00011-2

Cavoukian, A. (2012). Operationalizing Privacy by Design : A Guide to Implementing Strong Privacy Practices. *Information and Privacy Commissioner, Ontario, Canada, December.*

Cavoukian, A., ... (2009). Privacy by design: The 7 foundational principles. *Information and privacy commissioner of Ontario, Canada, 5*(2009), 12.

Cavoukian, A. (2020). Understanding How to Implement Privacy by Design, One Step at a Time. *IEEE Consumer Electronics Magazine, 9*(2). Advance online publication. DOI: 10.1109/MCE.2019.2953739

Cecco, L. (2020, May 7). *Google affiliate Sidewalk Labs abruptly abandons Toronto smart city project.* The Guardian; The Guardian. https://www.theguardian.com/technology/2020/may/07/google-sidewalk-labs-toronto-smart-city-abandoned?

Center for Climate and Energy Solutions. (2024, August). *U.S. state electricity portfolio standards*. https://www.c2es.org/document/renewable-and-alternate-energy-portfolio-standards

Chaisiri, S., Ko, R. K. L., & Niyato, D. (2015). A Joint Optimization Approach to Security-as-a-Service Allocation and Cyber Insurance Management. *2015 IEEE Trustcom/BigDataSE/ISPA*, 426–433. https://doi.org/DOI: 10.1109/Trustcom.2015.403

Cha, J., Singh, S. K., Kim, T. W., & Park, J. H. (2021). Blockchain-Empowered Cloud Architecture Based on Secret Sharing for Smart City. *Journal of Information Security and Applications*, *58*, 102791. DOI: 10.1016/j.jisa.2021.102791

Chang, S. E., Chen, Y. C., & Lu, M. F. (2019). Supply chain re-engineering using blockchain technology: A case of smart contract based tracking process. *Technological Forecasting and Social Change*, *144*(March), 1–11. DOI: 10.1016/j.techfore.2019.03.015

Chang, Z., Liu, S., Xiong, X., Cai, Z., & Tu, G. (2021). A Survey of Recent Advances in Edge-Computing-Powered Artificial Intelligence of Things. *IEEE Internet of Things Journal*, *8*, 13849–13875. DOI: 10.1109/JIOT.2021.3088875

Chaudhuri, A., & Bozkus Kahyaoglu, S. (2023). Cybersecurity assurance in smart cities: A risk management perspective. *Edpacs*, *67*(4), 1–22.

Chelloug, S. A., & El-Zawawy, M. A. (2017). Middleware for internet of things: Survey and challenges. *Intelligent Automation & Soft Computing*, •••, 1–9. DOI: 10.1080/10798587.2017.1290328

Chen, Y., Meng, L., Zhou, H., & Xue, G. (2021). A Blockchain-Based Medical Data Sharing Mechanism with Attribute-Based Access Control and Privacy Protection. *Wireless Communications and Mobile Computing, 2021*(1). https://doi.org/DOI: 10.1155/2021/6685762

Chen, D., Wawrzynski, P., & Lv, Z. (2021). Cyber security in smart cities: A review of deep learning-based applications and case studies. *Sustainable Cities and Society*, *66*, 102655.

Chen, J., Chen, S., Liu, Q., & Shen, M. I. (2021). Applying Blockchain Technology to Reshape the Service Models of Supply Chain Finance for SMES in China. *The Singapore Economic Review*. Advance online publication. DOI: 10.1142/S0217590821480015

Chen, P., Desmet, L., & Huygens, C. (2014). A study on advanced persistent threats. In *Ifip international conference on communications and multimedia security (cms 2014)* (Vol. 8557, pp. 63–72). Springer.

Chen, S., Wang, K., Zhao, M., & Gao, Z. (2025, April 2). A review of the recent development of innovative wind turbines: Concepts and aerodynamic analyses. *Physics of Fluids, 37*(041302). Advance online publication. DOI: 10.1063/5.0256502

Ch, H. (2014). *Social engineering: The science of human hacking*. Wiley.

Chian, Y. X. (2023). Sustainable, inclusive city-making through smart, playable environments: developing and testing the CO2rdinates pervasive mobile game. *26th International Academic Mindtrek Conference*, 321–328. https://doi.org/DOI: 10.1145/3616961.3617803

Chin, G. H. Y., & Chow, K. K. N. (2023). Technology-Enabled Interventions for Sustaining Behaviour Change in Adolescents: A Scoping Review for Research Gaps. *Proceedings of the ACM on Human-Computer Interaction, 7*(CSCW2), 1–30. https://doi.org/DOI: 10.1145/3610211

Choo, K.-K. R. (2021). Internet of things (iot) security and forensics: Challenges and opportunities. In *Proceedings of the 2th workshop on cps&iot security and privacy* (pp. 27–28).

Christensen, M. (2025, June 5). Coverup in Cordova: How regulators caught nuclear operators lying about a 'near miss.' *KWQC News*. https://www.kwqc.com/2025/06/05/coverup-cordova-how-regulators-caught-nuclear-operators-lying-about-near-miss

Christine, D., & Thinyane, M. (2020). Cyber resilience in asia-pacific: a review of national cybersecurity strategies.

Christofi, A., Wauters, E., & Valcke, P. (2021). Smart Cities, Data Protection and the Public Interest Conundrum: What Legal Basis for Smart City Processing? *European Journal of Law and Technology, 12*(1), 1–36.

CISA. (2021, February 1). *Understanding denial-of-service attacks*. https://www.cisa.gov/news-events/news/understanding-denial-service-attacks

Cities of the Future. (2025, May 3). NIS2 directive casts a wider net over smart city infrastructure. Cities of the Future. https://citiesofthefuture.eu/nis2-directive-casts-a-wider-net-over-smart-city-infrastructure/

Colding, J., Nilsson, C., & Sjöberg, S. (2024). Smart Cities for All? Bridging digital divides for socially sustainable and inclusive cities. *Smart Cities, 7*(3), 1044–1059. DOI: 10.3390/smartcities7030044

Collins, P. (2002, Spring). The beautiful possibility: Here comes the sun. *Cabinet Magazine, 6*. https://www.cabinetmagazine.org/issues/6/collins.php

Conrad, E., Misenar, S., & Feldman, J. (2023). Domain 4: Communication and Network Security. In *CISSP® Study Guide* (pp. 225–293). Elsevier. https://doi.org/DOI: 10.1016/B978-0-443-18734-6.00003-9

Coston, I., Plotnizky, E., & Nojoumian, M. (2025). Comprehensive study of iot vulnerabilities and countermeasures. *Applied Sciences (Basel, Switzerland)*, *15*(6), 3036.

Coventry, L., & Branley, D. (2018). Cybersecurity in healthcare: A narrative review of trends, threats and ways forward. *Maturitas*, *113*, 48–52. PMID: 29903648

Cowls, J., & Floridi, L. (2018). Prolegomena to a White Paper on an Ethical Framework for a Good AI Society. *SSRN Electronic Journal*. https://doi.org/DOI: 10.2139/ssrn.3198732

Cremonezi, B., Vieira, A. B., Nacif, J., Silva, E. F., & Nogueira, M. (2024). Identity management for internet of things: Concepts, challenges and opportunities. *Computer Communications*.

Cukier, V. M.-S. (2018). *Big Data: A Revolution that Will Transform how We Live, Work, and Think* (Revised Ed). Eamon Dolan/Houghton Mifflin Harcourt.

Cvitić, I., & Vujić, M. (2015). CLASSIFICATION OF SECURITY RISKS IN THE IOT ENVIRONMENT. *Annals of DAAAM & Proceedings*, *26*(1).

Cybersecurity & Infrastructure Security Agency. (2021, February 12). *Compromise of U.S. water treatment facility*. https://www.cisa.gov/news-events/cybersecurity-advisories/aa21-042a

Danezis, G., Domingo-Ferrer, J., Hansen, M., Hoepman, J.-H., Metayer, D. Le, Tirtea, R., & Schiffner, S. (2015). *Privacy and Data Protection by Design - from policy to engineering*. https://doi.org/DOI: 10.2824/38623

Danyluk, M. (2021). Supply-Chain Urbanism: Constructing and Contesting the Logistics City. *Annals of the Association of American Geographers*, •••, 1–16. DOI: 10.1080/24694452.2021.1889352

Daoudagh, S., Marchetti, E., Savarino, V., Bernabe, J. B., García-Rodríguez, J., Moreno, R. T., Martinez, J. A., & Skarmeta, A. F. (2021). Data Protection by Design in the Context of Smart Cities: A Consent and Access Control Proposal. *Sensors 2021, Vol. 21, Page 7154*, *21*(21), 7154. https://doi.org/DOI: 10.3390/S21217154

Das, D. K. (2024). Exploring the Symbiotic Relationship between Digital Transformation, Infrastructure, Service Delivery, and Governance for Smart Sustainable Cities. *Smart Cities*, *7*(2), 806–835. DOI: 10.3390/smartcities7020034

De Micco, F., Di Palma, G., Ferorelli, D., De Benedictis, A., Tomassini, L., Tambone, V., & Scendoni, R. (2025). Artificial intelligence in healthcare: Transforming patient safety with intelligent systems—A systematic review. *Frontiers in Medicine*, *11*, 1522554. PMID: 39845830

Decidim Barcelona | Barcelona Digital City | Barcelona City Council. (n.d.). Ajuntament.barcelona.cat. https://ajuntament.barcelona.cat/digital/en/technology-accessible-everyone/accessible-and-participatory/accessible-and-participatory-5

Decidim. (n.d.). Free Open-Source participatory democracy for cities and organizations | Decidim. Decidim.org. https://decidim.org/

Dehouche, N. (2025). Blockchain as urban governance infrastructure in private cities: An exploratory review. *Frontiers in Sustainable Cities*, *7*, 1–12. DOI: 10.3389/frsc.2025.1594711

Delgado, I., Sancristobal, E., Martin, S., & Robles-Gómez, A. (2023). Exploring IoT Vulnerabilities in a Comprehensive Remote Cybersecurity Laboratory. *Sensors (Basel)*, *23*(22), 9279. DOI: 10.3390/s23229279 PMID: 38005664

Demertzi, V., Demertzis, S., & Demertzis, K. (2023). An overview of cyber threats, attacks and countermeasures on the primary domains of smart cities. *Applied Sciences (Basel, Switzerland)*, *13*(2), 790.

Dhar, P., & Chakraborty, N. (2021, October). A dual mode wind turbine operation with hybrid energy storage system for electricity generation at constant voltage in an islanded microgrid. *International Journal of Energy Research*, *45*(13), 18885. DOI: 10.1002/er.6994

Ding, T., Chen, J., Fang, L., Ji, J., & Fang, Z. (2023). Urban ecosystem services supply-demand assessment from the perspective of the water-energy-food nexus. *Sustainable Cities and Society*, *90*, 104401. DOI: 10.1016/j.scs.2023.104401

Diwan, T. D., Kittusamy, L., Narasimhan, L., Ghige, O., William, P., & Badholia, A. (2024, November 25). AI Analysis of Edge- Cloud Computing on IOT-based Large Data Storage Systems with Deep Learning. In *2024 International Conference on Intelligent & Innovative Practices in Engineering & Management (IIPEM)*. DOI: 10.1109/iipem62726.2024.10925648

Dragonetti, W., & Garcia, R. (2025, May 3). Cities discuss regulation of AI and its many challenges. Eurocities. https://eurocities.eu/latest/cities-discuss-regulation-of-ai-and-its-many-challenges/

Dragos Inc. (2017). *CrashOverride: Analysis of the threat to electric grid operations* [Technical report]. Dragos Inc. https://www.dragos.com/wp-content/uploads/CrashOverride-01.pdf

Dubber, M. D., Pasquale, F., & Das, S. (Eds.). (2020). *The Oxford handbook of ethics of AI*. Oxford University Press.

Dutta, S. (2025). AI and IoT-Based Smart Healthcare Solutions in Urban Area. *Trends in Health Informatics*, *2*(1), 18–26. DOI: 10.22105/thi.v2i1.27

Duval, G. (2024, April 8). *How do wind turbines work?* Today's Homeowner. https://todayshomeowner.com/eco-friendly/guides/how-do-wind-turbines-work

Dwernertl. (2007, August 8). *Solar radar speed sign*. [Image]. Wikimedia Commons. https://commons.wikimedia.org/wiki/File:Solar_radar_speed_sign.jpg. Used per Creative Commons License (https://creativecommons.org/licenses/by-sa/3.0/deed.en), without alterations.

Dwivedi, R., Dave, D., Naik, H., Singhal, S., Omer, R., Patel, P., Qian, B., Wen, Z., Shah, T., Morgan, G., & Ranjan, R. (2023). Explainable AI (XAI): Core ideas, techniques, and solutions. *ACM Computing Surveys*, *55*(9), 1–33. DOI: 10.1145/3561048

Dziundziuk, B., & Dziundziuk, V. (2025). Methodology for integrating blockchain into digital governance systems: analysis of challenges, benefits, and opportunities for society. *Science and Public Policy, scaf022*, 1–23. https://doi.org/DOI: 10.1093/scipol/scaf022

E. F. Z. Santana, A. P. Chaves, M. A. Gerosa, F. Kon and D. S. Milojicic, "Software platforms for smart cities: Concepts requirements challenges and a unified reference architecture", ACM Comput. Surv., vol. 50, no. 6, pp. 78:1-78:37, Nov. 2018.

Ekechukwu, D. E., & Simpa, P. (2024, June). The future of cybersecurity in renewable energy systems: A review, identifying challenges and proposing strategic solutions. *Computer Science & IT Research Journal*, *5*(6), 1265–1299. DOI: 10.51594/csitrj.v5i6.1197

Elassy, M., Al-Hattab, M., Takruri, M., & Badawi, S. (2024). Intelligent transportation systems for sustainable smart cities. *Transportation Engineering*, *16*, 100252. DOI: 10.1016/j.treng.2024.100252

Elsayed, M., & Zulkernine, M. (2019). Offering security diagnosis as a service for cloud SaaS applications. *Journal of Information Security and Applications*, *44*, 32–48. DOI: 10.1016/j.jisa.2018.11.006

ENISA (European Union Agency for Cybersecurity). (2019). *Good practices for iot and smart infrastructures security* (Tech. Rep.). Heraklion, Greece: ENISA.

Enrique. (2022, January 27). *Sea wind turbines.* [Image]. Pixabay. https://pixabay.com/photos/sea-wind-turbines-wind-farm-6972214

Ericsson, J. (1888, August 2). The Sun Motor. *Nature, 38,* 319-321. https://doi.org/ DOI: 10.1038/038319b0

Eubanks, V. (2018). *Automating inequality: How high-tech tools profile, police, and punish the poor*. St. Martin's Press.

Europol. (2020). *Internet organised crime threat assessment (iocta) 2020* (Tech. Rep.). The Hague: Europol Public Information.

Fabrègue, B. F., & Bogoni, A. (2023). Privacy and security concerns in the smart city. *Smart Cities*, *6*(1), 586–613. DOI: 10.3390/smartcities6010027

Far A Z, Far M Z, Gharibzadeh S, Naeini H K, (2024). "Artificial Intelligence for Secured Information Systems in Smart Cities: Collaborative IoT Computing with Deep Reinforcement Learning and Blockchain." arXiv Preprint, Vol. 15(3), pp. 567–589. DOI: DOI: 10.1000/arxiv.aiiotsecurity2024

Farnaaz, N., & Jabbar, M. A. (2016). Random Forest Modeling for Network Intrusion Detection System. *Procedia Computer Science*, *89*, 213–217. DOI: 10.1016/j.procs.2016.06.047

Farrell, S., & Dullea, E. (2025, February 11). *Cybersecurity and solar power vulnerability*. Husch Blackwell. https://www.climatesolutionslaw.com/2025/02/cybersecurity-and-solar-power-vulnerability

Fazekas, M., Borges de Oliveira, A., & Regos, N. (2021). *Lowering Prices of Pharmaceuticals, Medical Supplies, and Equipment : Insights from Big Data for Better Procurement Strategies in Latin America*. World Bank., DOI: 10.1596/1813-9450-9689

Fazeldehkordi, E., & Grønli, T.-M. (2022). A survey of security architectures for edge computing-based iot. *IoT*, *3*(3), 332–365.

Fedele, G., D'Alfonso, L., & Chen, B. (2025). A matching problem between two decoupled multi-agent systems with reference tracking capabilities. *Automatica*, *173*, 112047. DOI: 10.1016/j.automatica.2024.112047

Fehis, S., Nouali, O., & Kechadi, T. (2021). Secure encryption key management as a SecaaS based on Chinese wall security policy. *Journal of Information Security and Applications*, *63*, 102975. DOI: 10.1016/j.jisa.2021.102975

Feng, L., Yang, Z., Guo, S., Qiu, X., Li, W., & Yu, P. (2022). Two-Layered Blockchain Architecture for Federated Learning Over the Mobile Edge Network. *IEEE Network, 36*(1), 45–51. DOI: 10.1109/MNET.011.2000339

Feng, Q., He, D., Zeadally, S., Khan, M. K., & Kumar, N. (2019). A survey on privacy protection in blockchain system. *Journal of Network and Computer Applications, 126*, 45–58. DOI: 10.1016/j.jnca.2018.10.020

Fernandez-Monge, F., Barns, S., Kattel, R., & Bria, F. (2024). Reclaiming data for improved city governance: Barcelona's New Data Deal. *Urban Studies (Edinburgh, Scotland), 61*(7), 1291–1307. DOI: 10.1177/00420980231204835

Ferrer, A. J., Marquès, J. M., & Jorba, J. (2019). Towards the decentralised cloud: Survey on approaches and challenges for mobile, ad hoc, and edge computing. *ACM Computing Surveys, 51*(6), 1–36.

Firoozi, A. A., Hejazi, F., & Firoozi, A. A. (2024, June 13). Advancing wind energy efficiency: A systematic review of aerodynamic optimization in wind turbine design. *Energies, 17*(12), 2919. DOI: 10.3390/en17122919

Forescout Research - Vedere Labs. (2025, June 3). *The security risks of internet-exposed solar power systems*. (2025, June 3). https://www.forescout.com/blog/the-security-risks-of-internet-exposed-solar-power-systems

Fourrage, L. (2024, April 9). *What are the challenges in implementing cybersecurity tools?* Nucamp. https://www.nucamp.co/blog/coding-bootcamp-cybersecurity-what-are-the-challenges-in-implementing-cybersecurity-tools

França, A. S. L., Amato Neto, J., Gonçalves, R. F., & Almeida, C. M. V. B. (2020). Proposing the use of blockchain to improve the solid waste management in small municipalities. *Journal of Cleaner Production, 244*, 118529. DOI: 10.1016/j.jclepro.2019.118529

Franz, M. (2025, June 5). The NRC is conducting a special inspection at the Quad Cities nuclear plant. Here's why. *WQAD News*. https://www.wqad.com/article/news/local/nrc-investigation-quad-cities-nuclear-plant-why/526-1c61f08b-f817-42da-af6f-028d36f406f0

Fudge, J. (2025a, May 29). *Close-up of panels on the roof of the 2nd-floor garage*. [Image]. Fudgelink. https://fudgelink.com/solarpanels. Used by kind permission.

Fudge, J. (2025b, May 29). *View of the building from the south.* [Image]. Fudgelink. https://fudgelink.com/solarpanels. Used by kind permission.

Fugini, M., Finocchi, J., & Locatelli, P. (2021). A big data analytics architecture for smart cities and smart companies. *Big Data Research, 24*, 100192.

Fu, Y., & Zhu, J. (2021). Trusted Data Infrastructure for Smart Cities: A Blockchain Perspective. *Building Research and Information, 49*(5), 567–589. DOI: 10.1000/taylorfrancis.blockchainsmartcities2021

Gade, D. S., & Aithal, P. S. (2022). ICT and Digital Technology based Solutions for Smart City Challenges and Opportunities. International Journal of Applied Engineering and Management Letters, 1–21. DOI: 10.47992/ijaeml.2581.7000.0116

Ganesh, P., Tran, C., Shokri, R., & Fioretto, F. (2025). The data minimization principle in machine learning. *Proceedings of the 2025 ACM Conference on Fairness, Accountability, and Transparency*, 3075–3093.

Gao, S., Su, Q., Zhang, R., Zhu, J., & Sui, Z. (2021). A Privacy-Preserving Identity Authentication Scheme Based on the Blockchain. *Security and Privacy in Cyberspace, 15*(3), 567–589. DOI: 10.1000/wiley.blockchainprivacyauthentication2021

Garagad, V. G., Iyer, N. C., & Wali, H. G. (2020). *Data integrity: a security threat for internet of things and cyber-physical systems. In 2020 international conference on computational performance evaluation (compe).*

García-Teodoro, P., Camacho, J., Maciá-Fernández, G., Gómez-Hernández, J. A., & López-Marín, V. J. (2022). A novel zero-trust network access control scheme based on the security profile of devices and users. *Computer Networks, 212*, 109068. DOI: 10.1016/j.comnet.2022.109068

Gautam, C. K., Da, N., Kumar, R., & Kulhar, K. S. (2024, January). Short review of solar energy markets and policies for smart cities development. *E3S Web of Conferences, 540*, 04002. https://doi.org/DOI: 10.1051/e3sconf/202454004002

Geller, E. (2025, March 28). *Solar power gear vulnerable to remote sabotage.* Cybersecurity Dive. https://www.cybersecuritydive.com/news/solar-power-gear-vulnerable-remote-sabotage/743806

Geneseo Public Library District. (2025, May 22). *First picture: Horse barn on the George R Smith farm with a unique windmill that provided power to grind corn.* [Image attached] [Status update]. Facebook. https://www.facebook.com/permalink.php?story_fbid=pfbid02xoTu2MWuA6is751aegoRjC8YEfRkf1h37D4foafDLVrv79CT5ipVGDV9Sab4qDngl&id=100079953789167. Used by kind permission.

Genge, B., Graur, F., & Enăchescu, C. (2015). Non-intrusive Techniques for Vulnerability Assessment of Services in Distributed Systems. *Procedia Technology, 19*, 12–19. DOI: 10.1016/j.protcy.2015.02.003

Geothermal energy cyber security. (2024, November 4). Cyber Energia. https://cyberenergia.com/geothermal-energy-cyber-security

Ghadami, N., Gheibi, M., Kian, Z., Faramarz, M. G., Naghedi, R., Eftekhari, M., Fathollahi-Fard, A. M., Dulebenets, M. A., & Tian, G. (2021, July). Presentation of solar energy in smart cities using an integration of artificial neural network, photovoltaic system and classical Delphi methods. *Sustainable Cities and Society*, *74*, 103149. DOI: 10.1016/j.scs.2021.103149

Ghadge, A., Bourlakis, M., Kamble, S., & Seuring, S. (2023). Blockchain implementation in pharmaceutical supply chains: A review and conceptual framework. *International Journal of Production Research*, *61*(19), 6633–6651. DOI: 10.1080/00207543.2022.2125595

Ghaffari, F., Bertin, E., Crespi, N., & Hatin, J. (2023). Distributed ledger technologies for authentication and access control in networking applications: A comprehensive survey. *Computer Science Review*, *50*. Advance online publication. DOI: 10.1016/j.cosrev.2023.100590

Gheisari, M., Najafabadi, H. E., Alzubi, J. A., Gao, J., Wang, G., Abbasi, A. A., & Castiglione, A. (2021). OBPP: An ontology-based framework for privacy-preserving in IoT-based smart city. *Future Generation Computer Systems*, *123*, 1–13.

Gheisari, M., Shojaeian, E., Javadpour, A., Jalili, A., Esmaeili-Najafabadi, H., Bigham, B. S., & Rezaei, M. (2023). An agile privacy-preservation solution for IoT-based smart city using different distributions. *IEEE Open Journal of Vehicular Technology*, *4*, 356–362.

Ghena, B., Beyer, W., Hillaker, A., Pevarnek, J., & Halderman, J. A. (2014). Green lights forever: Analyzing the security of traffic infrastructure. In *8th usenix workshop on offensive technologies (woot 14).*

Gimenez-Aguilar, M., & De Fuentes, J. M. (2021). Achieving Cybersecurity in Blockchain-Based Systems: A Survey. *Future Generation Computer Systems*, *29*(5), 620–640. DOI: 10.1000/elsevier.cybersecurityblockchain2021

Gipe, P. (2004). *Wind power: Renewable energy for home, farm, and business*. Chelsea Green Publishing.

Gloerich, I., De Waal, M., Ferri, G., Cila, N., & Karpinski, T. (2020). The City as a License. Implications of Blockchain and Distributed Ledgers for Urban Governance. *Frontiers in Sustainable Cities*, *2*. Advance online publication. DOI: 10.3389/frsc.2020.534942

Goldsteen, A., Ezov, G., Shmelkin, R., Moffie, M., & Farkash, A. (2022). Data minimization for GDPR compliance in machine learning models. *AI and Ethics*, *2*(3). Advance online publication. DOI: 10.1007/s43681-021-00095-8

Gomes, J., Khan, S., & Svetinovic, D. (2023). Fortifying the Blockchain: A Systematic Review and Classification of Post-Quantum Consensus Solutions for Enhanced Security and Resilience. *IEEE Access : Practical Innovations, Open Solutions*, *11*, 74088–74100. DOI: 10.1109/ACCESS.2023.3296559

Gönç, D. (2022). An evaluation of cyber threat taxonomies in the framework of cyber activism. *Bilgi ve Iletis¸im Teknolojileri Dergisi˙*, *4*(2), 171–196.

Goswami, S. S., Mondal, S., & Licensee System Analytics. (2024). The Role of 5G in Enhancing IoT Connectivity: A Systematic review on applications, challenges, and future prospects [Original Article]. Big Data and Computing Visions, 4–4, 314–326. DOI: 10.22105/bdcv.2024.486159.1215

Green, Go. (2024). *SMART CITIES: AI & IOT SOLUTIONS FOR SUSTAINABILITY*. https://gogreengosmart.com/smart-cities-ai-iot-solutions-for-sustainability/

Greenleaf, G. (2012). *Singapore's New Data Protection Authority: Strong Enforcement Powers and Business Risks* .

Greubel, A., Andres, D., & Hennecke, M. (2023). Analyzing reporting on ransomware incidents: A case study. *Social Sciences*, *12*(5), 265.

Grimm, D. (2019). The Dark Data Quandary. *The American University Law Review*, *68*(3), 761–821. PMID: 30919611

Guerra, P. (2025, March 27). *New multicampus consortium looks to expand solar-over-canal projects statewide*. University of California. https://www.universityofcalifornia.edu/news/new-multicampus-consortium-looks-expand-solar-over-canal-projects-statewide

Gu, H., Zhang, X., Li, J., Wei, H., Li, B., & Huang, X. (2024). Federated learning vulnerabilities: Privacy attacks with denoising diffusion probabilistic models. In *Proceedings of the acm web conference 2024* (pp. 1149–1157).

Guha Roy, D., & Srirama, S. N. (2021). A Blockchain-Based Cyber Attack Detection Scheme for Decentralized Internet of Things Using Software-Defined Network. *Software, Practice & Experience*, *51*(7), 1540–1556. DOI: 10.1002/spe.2956

Guo, H., Ren, J., Zhang, D., Zhang, Y., & Hu, J. (2018, August). A scalable and manageable IoT architecture based on transparent computing. *Journal of Parallel and Distributed Computing*, *118*, 5–13.

Guo, S., Sun, X., & Lam, H. K. S. (2023). Applications of Blockchain Technology in Sustainable Fashion Supply Chains: Operational Transparency and Environmental Efforts. *IEEE Transactions on Engineering Management*, *70*(4), 1312–1328. DOI: 10.1109/TEM.2020.3034216

Guo, X., & Guo, X. (2023). A Research on Blockchain Technology: Urban Intelligent Transportation Systems in Developing Countries. *IEEE Access : Practical Innovations, Open Solutions*, *11*, 40724–40740. DOI: 10.1109/ACCESS.2023.3270100

Gupta, P., Sehgal, N. K., & Acken, J. M. (2025). *Trust and Security in a Cloud Environment.*, DOI: 10.1007/978-3-031-59170-9_6

H. V Balachandra Achar and R. N. "The Impact and Future of Artificial Intelligence in Learning," *2025 3rd International Conference on Integrated Circuits and Communication Systems (ICICACS)*, Raichur, India, 2025, pp. 1-6, doi: DOI: 10.1109/ICICACS65178.2025.10967881

Hajny, J., Ricci, S., Piesarskas, E., Levillain, O., Galletta, L., & De Nicola, R. (2021). Framework, Tools and Good Practices for Cybersecurity Curricula. *IEEE Access : Practical Innovations, Open Solutions*, *9*, 94723–94747. DOI: 10.1109/ACCESS.2021.3093952

Hamledari, H., & Fischer, M. (2021). Role of Blockchain-Enabled Smart Contracts in Automating Construction Progress Payments. *Journal of Legal Affairs and Dispute Resolution in Engineering and Construction*, *13*(4), 04521034. DOI: 10.1061/(ASCE)LA.1943-4170.0000483

Han, M. J. N., & Kim, M. J. (2024). A systematic review of smart city research from an urban context perspective. *Cities (London, England)*, *150*, 105027.

Hao, Q., Nazir, S., Li, M., Khan, H., Wang, L., & Ahmad, S. (2021). AI-Enabled Sensing and Decision-Making for IoT Systems. Complex., 2021, 6616279:1-6616279:9. https://doi.org/DOI: 10.1155/2021/6616279

Hao, J., & Tao, Y. (2022). Adversarial attacks on deep learning models in smart grids. *Energy Reports*, *8*, 123–129. DOI: 10.1016/j.egyr.2021.11.026

Harkat, H., Camarinha-Matos, L. M., Goes, J., & Ahmed, H. F. (2024). Cyber-physical systems security: A systematic review. *Computers & Industrial Engineering*, *188*, 109891.

Hart, K. (2025, June 2). New Idaho bill forces wind farms to get rid of 'Red Light District.' *East Idaho News*. https://www.eastidahonews.com/2025/06/new-idaho-bill-forces-wind-farms-to-get-rid-of-red-light-district

Hasan, H. R., Salah, K., Jayaraman, R., Omar, M., Yaqoob, I., Pesic, S., Taylor, T., & Boscovic, D. (2020). A Blockchain-Based Approach for the Creation of Digital Twins. *IEEE Access : Practical Innovations, Open Solutions*, *8*, 34113–34126. DOI: 10.1109/ACCESS.2020.2974810

Haseeb, K., Saba, T., Rehman, A., Abbas, N., & Kim, P. W. (2025). AI-driven IoT-fog analytics interactive smart system with data protection. *Expert Systems: International Journal of Knowledge Engineering and Neural Networks*, *42*(1), e13573.

Hashizume, K., Rosado, D. G., Fernández-Medina, E., & Fernandez, E. B. (2013). An analysis of security issues for cloud computing. *Journal of Internet Services and Applications*, *4*(1), 5. DOI: 10.1186/1869-0238-4-5

Hassija, V., Chamola, V., Gupta, V., Jain, S., & Guizani, N. (2020). A survey on supply chain security: Application areas, security threats, and solution architectures. *IEEE Internet of Things Journal*, *8*(8), 6222–6246.

Hastig, G. M., & Sodhi, M. S. (2020). Blockchain for Supply Chain Traceability: Business Requirements and Critical Success Factors. *Production and Operations Management*, *29*(4), 935–954. DOI: 10.1111/poms.13147

Hausken, K. (2020). Cyber resilience in firms, organizations and societies. *Internet of Things : Engineering Cyber Physical Human Systems*, *11*, 100204. DOI: 10.1016/j.iot.2020.100204

Hayat, F., Adnan, M., & Iqbal, S. (2024). Expert and intelligent systems for assessment and mitigation of cascading failures in smart grids: Research challenges and survey.

He, G., Li, C., Shu, Y., & Luo, Y. (2024). Fine-grained access control policy in blockchain-enabled edge computing. *Journal of Network and Computer Applications*, *221*, 103706.

He, K., Kim, D. D., & Asghar, M. R. (2023). Adversarial machine learning for network intrusion detection systems: A comprehensive survey. *IEEE Communications Surveys and Tutorials*, *25*(1), 538–566.

Helmi, R. A. A., Baskaran, N. A.-L., Jamal, A., & Mohammed, M. N. (2022). Dark Net Forum Analyzer Using Meta Data Search Bots. *2022 IEEE 10th Conference on Systems, Process & Control (ICSPC)*, 73–76. https://doi.org/DOI: 10.1109/ICSPC55597.2022.10001746

He, M., Wang, H., Sun, Y., Bie, R., Lan, T., Song, Q., Zeng, X., Pustisěk, M., & Qiu, Z. (2024). T^{2}L: A traceable and trustable consortium blockchain for logistics. *Digital Communications and Networks*. Advance online publication. DOI: 10.1016/j.dcan.2022.06.015

Hevner, A. R., March, S. T., Park, J., & Ram, S. (2004). Design science in information systems research. *Management Information Systems Quarterly*, ●●●, 75–105.

Недвига, A. (2017, August 6). *Solar clean battery energy*. [Image]. Pixabay. https://pixabay.com/photos/solar-battery-clean-energy-pillar-2602980

Hnamte, V., & Hussain, J. (2023). DCNNBiLSTM: An Efficient Hybrid Deep Learning-Based Intrusion Detection System. *Telematics and Informatics Reports*, *10*, 100053. DOI: 10.1016/j.teler.2023.100053

Hollands, R. G. (2020). Will the real smart city please stand up?: Intelligent, progressive or entrepreneurial? In *The routledge companion to smart cities* (pp. 179–199). Routledge.

Hong, Y., & Furnell, S. (2021). Understanding cybersecurity behavioral habits: Insights from situational support. *Journal of Information Security and Applications*, *57*, 102710. DOI: 10.1016/j.jisa.2020.102710

Hong, Z., & Xiao, K. (2024). Digital economy structuring for sustainable development: The role of blockchain and artificial intelligence in improving supply chain and reducing negative environmental impacts. *Scientific Reports*, *14*(1), 3912. DOI: 10.1038/s41598-024-53760-3 PMID: 38365912

Hossain, S. T., Yigitcanlar, T., Nguyen, K., & Xu, Y. (2024). Local government cybersecurity landscape: A systematic review and conceptual framework. *Applied Sciences (Basel, Switzerland)*, *14*(13), 5501.

How does a photovoltaic cell work? (2024, May 23). Planete Energies. www.planete-energies.com/en/media/article/how-does-photovoltaic-cell-work

Hsu, A. J., Pruckner, S., Satterthwaite, E. V., Weatherdon, L. V., Hadley, K., & Nguyen, E. T. T. (2021). Challenges and Recommendations for Equitable Use of Aerial Tools for Mangrove Research. *Frontiers in Marine Science*, *8*. Advance online publication. DOI: 10.3389/fmars.2021.643784

Huang, M.-L. (2025). Digital Privacy in the Age of Surveillance: A Comparative Study of GDPR and CCPA. *OTS Canadian Journal*, *4*(7), 65–74. DOI: 10.58840/1t99rb13

Hugeback, K. K., Gallus, W. A.Jr, & Pico, H. N. V. (2023, September). Machine learning-adjusted WRF forecasts to support wind energy needs in black start. *Weather and Forecasting*, *38*(9), 1553–1561. DOI: 10.1175/WAF-D-23-0023.1

Hu, M., Behar, E., & Ottenheimer, D. (2023). National Security and Federalizing Data Privacy Infrastructure for AI Governance. *Fordham Law Review*, *92*, 1829.

Humayun, M., Tariq, N., Alfayad, M., Zakwan, M., Alwakid, G., & Assiri, M. (2024). Securing the internet of things in artificial intelligence era: A comprehensive survey. *IEEE Access : Practical Innovations, Open Solutions, 12*, 25469–25490.

IBM Report: Escalating Data Breach Disruption Pushes Costs to New Highs. (2024). IBM Newsroom. https://newsroom.ibm.com/2024-07-30-ibm-report-escalating-data-breach-disruption-pushes-costs-to-new-highs?

Ibrahim, T. M., Abdulhamid, S. M., Alarood, A. A., Chiroma, H., Al-garadi, M. A., Rana, N., Muhammad, A. N., Abubakar, A., Haruna, K., & Gabralla, L. A. (2019). Recent advances in mobile touch screen security authentication methods: A systematic literature review. *Computers & Security, 85*, 1–24. DOI: 10.1016/j.cose.2019.04.008

IEEE Standards Association. (2024, March 22). *Evolving IEEE standards foster a more sustainable power grid.* Institute of Electrical and Electronics Engineers. https://standards.ieee.org/beyond-standards/ieee-2030-standards

IEEE. (2023). *AI Ethics in Smart Cities: Starting Points for Discussion in Society.* https://smartcities.ieee.org/newsletter/may-2023/ai-ethics-in-smart-cities-starting-points-for-discussion-in-society?

Ietto, B., Rabe, J., Muth, R., & Pascucci, F. (2023). Blockchain for citizens' participation in urban planning: The case of the city of Berlin. A value sensitive design approach. *Cities (London, England), 140*, 104382. DOI: 10.1016/j.cities.2023.104382

Ihsan, K. T. N., Sakti, A. D., & Wikantika, K. (2021, March 29). Geospatial assessment for planning a smart energy city using rooftop solar photovoltaic in Bandung City, Indonesia. *International Archives of the Photogrammetry, Remote Sensing & Spatial Information Sciences, XLIV–. M, 3*, 83–87. DOI: 10.5194/isprs-archives-XLIV-M-3-2021-83-2021

International Hydropower Association. (2022). *Pumped storage hydropower.* https://www.hydropower.org/factsheets/pumped-storage

International Organization for Standardization. (2018). *Sustainable cities and communities - Indicators for city services and quality of life.* (ISO Standard No. 37120:2018). https://www.iso.org/obp/ui/en/#iso:std:iso:37120

Iowa State University. (2011, June 20). *Wind energy production: Legal issues and related liability concerns for landowners.* Center for Agricultural Law and Taxation. https://www.calt.iastate.edu/system/files/CALT%20Legal%20Brief%20-%20Wind%20Energy%20Production.pdf

Ismagilova, E., Hughes, L., Rana, N. P., & Dwivedi, Y. K. (2022). Security, privacy and risks within smart cities: Literature review and development of a smart city interaction framework. *Information Systems Frontiers*, ●●●, 1–22.

Jafari, N., Alsadoon, A., Withana, C. P., Beg, A., & Elchouemi, A. (2016). Designing a Comprehensive Security Framework for Smartphones and Mobile Devices. *American Journal of Engineering and Applied Sciences*, *9*(3), 724–734. DOI: 10.3844/ajeassp.2016.724.734

Jain, S., Ahuja, N. J., Srikanth, P., Bhadane, K. V., Nagaiah, B., Kumar, A., & Konstantinou, C. (2021). Blockchain and Autonomous Vehicles: Recent Advances and Future Directions. *IEEE Access : Practical Innovations, Open Solutions*, *9*, 130264–130328. DOI: 10.1109/ACCESS.2021.3113649

Janusz-Szymańska, K., Wiciak, G., Remiorz, L., & Hulak, D. (2025, February). Heat storage using solar pond technology and post-mining brine: Preliminary analysis. *Heat Transfer Engineering*, *46*(3), 310–320. DOI: 10.1080/01457632.2024.2308353

Jaradat, A. S., Nasayreh, A., Al-Na'amneh, Q., Gharaibeh, H., & Al Mamlook, R. E. (2023). *Genetic optimization techniques for enhancing web attacks classification in machine learning. In 2023 ieee intl conf on dependable, autonomic and secure computing, intl conf on pervasive intelligence and computing, intl conf on cloud and big data computing, intl conf on cyber science and technology congress (dasc/picom/cbdcom/cyberscitech) (pp. 0130–0136).*

Jauregui-Correa, J. C., & Duran-Carillo, A. (2022, October 28). Optimum control scheme for deformable blades applied to horizontal wind turbine. *Proceedings of the ASME Turbo Expo 2022: Turbomachinery Technical Conference and Exposition, 11: Wind Energy*. Rotterdam Netherlands, June 13-17, 2022. https://doi.org/DOI: 10.1115/GT2022-81169

Jayakumari, B., Sheeba, S. L., Eapen, M., Anbarasi, J., Ravi, V., Suganya, A., & Jawahar, M. (2024). E-voting system using cloud-based hybrid blockchain technology. *Journal of Safety Science and Resilience = An Quan Ke Xue Yu Ren Xing (Ying Wen)*, *5*(1), 102–109. DOI: 10.1016/j.jnlssr.2024.01.002

Jayshree, J., & Leena, R. (2013). Intrusion Detection System using Support Vector Machine. [IJAIS]. *International Journal of Applied Information Systems*.

Jha, A., & Jha, A. (2024). Securing tomorrow's urban frontiers: A holistic approach to cybersecurity in smart cities. Information System and Smart City, 3(1).

Jha, S., Shakya, S. R., Ahmad, S., & Zhou, Z. (2024). *Quality assessment and security in industrial internet of things*. CRC Press.

Jiang, P., Zhang, L., You, S., Van Fan, Y., Tan, R. R., Klemeš, J. J., & You, F. (2023). Blockchain technology applications in waste management: Overview, challenges and opportunities. *Journal of Cleaner Production*, *421*, 138466. DOI: 10.1016/j.jclepro.2023.138466

Jiménez-García, J. C., Ruiz, A., Pacheco-Reyes, A., & Rivera, W. (2023, June 30). A comprehensive review of Organic Rankine Cycles. *Processes (Basel, Switzerland)*, *11*(7), 1982. DOI: 10.3390/pr11071982

Jimmy, F. (2024). Enhancing Data Security in Financial Institutions With Blockchain Technology. [JAIGS]. *Journal of Artificial Intelligence General Science*, *15*(3), 567–589. DOI: 10.1000/newjaigs.blockchainfinancialsecurity2024

Jinor, E., & Bridgelall, R. (2024). Bibliometric Insights into Balancing Efficiency and Security in Urban Supply Chains. *Urban Science (Basel, Switzerland)*, *8*(3), 100. DOI: 10.3390/urbansci8030100

Jithish, J., Alangot, B., Mahalingam, N., & Yeo, K. S. (2023). Distributed anomaly detection in smart grids: A federated learning-based approach. *IEEE Access : Practical Innovations, Open Solutions*, *11*, 7157–7179. DOI: 10.1109/ACCESS.2023.3237554

Johnson, J., Hurtado, J., Krishnappa, B., Collier, L., & Goodlett, D. (2023, June 1). *Recommendations for solar energy cybersecurity.* North American Electric Reliability Corporation. https://www.nerc.com/pa/Documents/Recommendations-for-Solar-Energy-Cybersecurity.pdf

Johnson, S. (2023, December 17). *11 best types of roof vents + understanding attic ventilation.* My Roof Hub. https://myroofhub.com/materials/roof-vents-attic-ventilation

Jones, D., Rangelova, K., Walter, D., & Worthington, B. (2025, March 12). *US electricity 2025 special report.* Ember Energy. https://ember-energy.org/app/uploads/2025/03/US-Electricity-2025-Special-Report.pdf

Jørgensen, B. N., & Ma, Z. G. (2025). Impact of EU Regulations on AI Adoption in Smart City Solutions: A Review of Regulatory Barriers, Technological Challenges, and Societal Benefits. *Information 2025, Vol. 16, Page 568*, *16*(7), 568. https://doi.org/DOI: 10.3390/INFO16070568

Jøsang, A. (2024). Secure by design. In *Cybersecurity: Technology and governance* (pp. 243–270). Springer.

Jumani, A. K., Siddique, W. A., Siddiqui, M. F., & Kanwal. (2024). Blockchain security for fog computing and internet of things. *Fog Computing for Intelligent Cloud IoT Systems*, 379–403.

Jurgała, P., Kurek, T., & Niemiec, M. (2022). Preserving Privacy of Security Services in the SecaaS Model. *Information & Security: An International Journal, 53*, 47–64. DOI: 10.11610/isij.5304

Juvenile Ehwi, R., Holmes, H., Maslova, S., & Burgess, G. (2022). The ethical underpinnings of Smart City governance: Decision-making in the Smart Cambridge programme, UK. *Urban Studies (Edinburgh, Scotland), 59*(14), 2968–2984. DOI: 10.1177/00420980211064983

Kalinaki, K., Fahadi, M., Alli, A. A., Shafik, W., Yasin, M., & Mutwalibi, N. (2023). Artificial intelligence of internet of medical things (aiomt) in smart cities: a review of cybersecurity for smart healthcare. *Handbook of security and privacy of ai-enabled healthcare systems and internet of medical things*, 271–292.

Kaluarachchi, Y. (2022). Implementing Data-Driven Smart City Applications for future cities. *Smart Cities, 5*(2), 455–474. https://doi.org/10.3390/smartcities5020025

Kaluvuri, S. P., Egner, A. I., den Hartog, J., & Zannone, N. (2015). SAFAX â€" An Extensible Authorization Service for Cloud Environments. *Frontiers in ICT (Lausanne, Switzerland), 2*. Advance online publication. DOI: 10.3389/fict.2015.00009

Kanellopoulos, D., Sharma, V. K., Panagiotakopoulos, T., & Kameas, A. (2023). Networking architectures and protocols for IoT applications in smart cities: Recent developments and perspectives. *Electronics (Basel), 12*(11), 2490.

Kankanhalli, A., Charalabidis, Y., & Mellouli, S. (2019). IoT and AI for Smart Government: A Research Agenda. *Government Information Quarterly, 36*, 304–309. DOI: 10.1016/j.giq.2019.02.003

Karaduman, Ö., & Gülhas, G. (2025). Blockchain-Enabled Supply Chain Management: A Review of Security, Traceability, and Data Integrity Amid the Evolving Systemic Demand. *Applied Sciences (Basel, Switzerland), 15*(9), 5168. DOI: 10.3390/app15095168

Kassen, M. (2025). Blockchain and digital governance: Decentralization of decision making policy. *The Review of Policy Research, 42*(1), 95–121. DOI: 10.1111/ropr.12585

Kaushal, R. K., Kumar, N., & Panda, S. N. (2021). Blockchain Technology, Its Applications and Open Research Challenges. In A. null, K. A., M. R.K., D. V., & K. B. (Eds.), *Journal of Physics: Conference Series* (Vol. 1950, Issue 1). IOP Publishing Ltd. https://doi.org/DOI: 10.1088/1742-6596/1950/1/012030

Keerthana, N., Sakthivel, D., Balasubramaniyan, D., Gunasekaran, K., & Marimuthu, M. (2020). Enhanced Privacy Based Authenticity for Smart e-Health Cares using Light Weight ECC. *GEDRAG & ORGANISATIE Учредители: UITGEVERIJ LEMMA BV, 33*(2), 644–653.

Kempin Reuter, T. (2019). Human rights and the city: Including marginalized communities in urban development and smart cities. *Journal of Human Rights, 18*(4). Advance online publication. DOI: 10.1080/14754835.2019.1629887

Kezron, I. E. (2025). AI and the future of cybersecurity in smart cities: A framework for secure and resilient urban environments. *Iconic Research and Engineering Journals, 8*(7).

Khalifeh, A., Darabkh, K. A., Khasawneh, A. M., Alqaisieh, I., Salameh, M., AlAbdala, A., & Al-Wardat, R. (2021). Wireless sensor networks for smart cities: Network design, implementation and performance evaluation. *Electronics (Basel), 10*(2), 218.

Khaliji, M. A., & Jafarpour Ghalehteimouri, K. (2024). Urban Security Challenges in Major Cities, with a Specific Emphasis on Privacy Management in the Metropolises. *Discover Environment, 4*(1), 78–94. DOI: 10.1000/springer.urbanprivacy-security2024

Khan, A. R., Kashif, M., Jhaveri, R. H., Raut, R., Saba, T., & Bahaj, S. A. (2022). Deep Learning for Intrusion Detection and Security of Internet of Things (IoT): Current Analysis, Challenges, and Possible Solutions. *Security and Communication Networks, 2022*, 1–13. DOI: 10.1155/2022/4016073

Khan, A., Jhanjhi, N. Z., & Humayun, M. (2022). The role of cybersecurity in smart cities. In *Cyber Security Applications for Industry 4.0* (pp. 195–208). Chapman and Hall/CRC.

Khan, M. I., Arif, A., & Khan, A. R. A. (2024). The most recent advances and uses of ai in cybersecurity. *BULLET: Jurnal Multidisiplin Ilmu, 3*(4), 566–578.

Khanna, A., Sah, A., Bolshev, V., Jasinski, M., Vinogradov, A., Leonowicz, Z., & Jasiński, M. (2021). Blockchain: Future of e-governance in smart cities. *Sustainability (Switzerland), 13*(21), 11840. DOI: 10.3390/su132111840

Khan, S., Shael, M., Majdalawieh, M., Nizamuddin, N., & Nicho, M. (2022). Blockchain for Governments: The Case of the Dubai Government. *Sustainability (Switzerland), 14*(11), 6576. DOI: 10.3390/su14116576

Khazane, H., Ridouani, M., Salahdine, F., & Kaabouch, N. (2024). A holistic review of machine learning adversarial attacks in iot networks. *Future Internet, 16*(1), 32.

Kibria, M. G., Nguyen, K., Villardi, G. P., Zhao, O., Ishizu, K., & Kojima, F. (2018). Big data analytics, machine learning, and artificial intelligence in Next-Generation wireless networks. IEEE Access, 6, 32328–32338. 6–97. https://doi.org/10.1007/s11524-007-9171-9DOI: 10.1109/access.2018.2837692

Kim, Y., Ahn, M., Park, J., Jung, C., Siano, P., Almulhim, A. I., & Yigitcanlar, T. (2025). Understanding Smart Governance of Sustainable Cities: A Review and Multidimensional Framework. *Smart Cities 2025, Vol. 8, Page 113, 8*(4), 113. https://doi.org/DOI: 10.3390/SMARTCITIES8040113

Kim, B. G., Cho, Y.-S., Kim, S.-H., Kim, H., & Woo, S. S. (2021). A security analysis of blockchainbased did services. *IEEE Access : Practical Innovations, Open Solutions*, *9*, 22894–22913.

Kim, K., Alshenaifi, I. M., Ramachandran, S., Kim, J., Zia, T., & Almorjan, A. (2023). Cybersecurity and Cyber Forensics for Smart Cities: A Comprehensive Literature Review and Survey. *Sensors (Basel)*, *23*(7), 1–25. DOI: 10.3390/s23073681 PMID: 37050740

Kitchin, R. (2021). Black Data Matter. In *Data Lives* (pp. 197–204). Bristol University Press., DOI: 10.2307/j.ctv1c9hmnq.29

Kitchin, R., & Moore-Cherry, N. (2021). Fragmented governance, the urban data ecosystem and smart city-regions: The case of Metropolitan Boston. *Regional Studies*, *55*(12), 1913–1923.

Kjellstrom, T., Friel, S., Dixon, J., Corvalan, C., Rehfuess, E., Campbell-Lendrum, D., Gore, F., & Bartram, J. (2007). Urban Environmental Health Hazards and health equity. *Journal of Urban Health*, *84*(S1), 8.

Knight, L. (2014, June 14). Vanadium: The metal that may soon be powering your neighbourhood. *BBC News*. https://www.bbc.com/news/magazine-27829874

Kong, L., Liu, Z., & Wu, J. (2020). A systematic review of big data-based urban sustainability research: State-of-the-science and future directions. *Journal of Cleaner Production*, *273*, 123142. DOI: 10.1016/j.jclepro.2020.123142

Kontokosta, C. E., & Hong, B. (2021). Bias in smart city governance: How socio-spatial disparities in 311 complaint behavior impact the fairness of data-driven decisions. *Sustainable Cities and Society*, *64*, 102503. DOI: 10.1016/J.SCS.2020.102503

Kotilainen, P., Mäkitalo, N., Systä, K., Mehraj, A., Waseem, M., Mikkonen, T., & Murillo, J. M. (2025). Allocating distributed AI/ML applications to cloud-edge continuum based on privacy, regulatory, and ethical constraints. *Journal of Systems and Software*, *112333*. Advance online publication. DOI: 10.1016/j.jss.2025.112333

Kouhizadeh, M., Saberi, S., & Sarkis, J. (2021). Blockchain technology and the sustainable supply chain: Theoretically exploring adoption barriers. *International Journal of Production Economics*, *231*, 107831. DOI: 10.1016/j.ijpe.2020.107831

Kshetri, N. (2017). Blockchain's roles in strengthening cybersecurity and protecting privacy. *Telecommunications Policy*, *41*(10), 1027–1038.

Kumar, A., & Pal, D. B. (2025). Renewable energy development sources and technology: Overview. In S. Kumar & V. K. Singh (Eds.), *Renewable energy development: Technology, material and sustainability* (pp. 111-131). Clean Energy Production Technologies. Springer. https://doi.org/DOI: 10.1007/978-981-97-9626-7_6

Kundu, D. (2019). Blockchain and Trust in a Smart City. *Environment & Urbanization Asia*, *10*(1), 31–43. DOI: 10.1177/0975425319832392

Kuzior, A., Pakhnenko, O., Tiutiunyk, I., & Lyeonov, S. (2023). E-governance in smart cities: Global trends and key enablers. *Smart Cities*, *6*(4), 1663–1689.

Laguerre, M. S. (2006). The digital city: The American metropolis and information technology. *Choice Reviews Online*, *44*(04), 44–2421. DOI: 10.5860/choice.44-2421

Lakhouit, A. (2025). Revolutionizing Urban Solid Waste Management with AI and IoT: A review of smart solutions for waste collection, sorting, and recycling. *Results in Engineering*, *25*, 104018. DOI: 10.1016/j.rineng.2025.104018

Lakshminarayana, S. K., & Basarkod, P. I. (2023). Unification of K-Nearest Neighbor (KNN) with Distance Aware Algorithm for Intrusion Detection in Evolving Networks Like IoT. *Wireless Personal Communications*, *132*(3), 2255–2281. DOI: 10.1007/s11277-023-10722-8

Langner, R. (2011). Stuxnet: Dissecting a cyberwarfare weapon. *IEEE Security and Privacy*, *9*(3), 49–51.

Ledmaoui, Y., El Maghraoui, A., El Aroussi, M., & Saadane, R. (2025, January). Review of recent advances in predictive maintenance and cybersecurity for solar plants. *Sensors (Basel)*, *25*(1), 206. DOI: 10.3390/s25010206 PMID: 39796997

Lee, I. (2020). Internet of Things (IoT) cybersecurity: Literature review and IoT cyber risk management. *Future Internet*, *12*(9), 157.

Liang, X., Konstantinou, C., Shetty, S., & Bandara, E. (2023). Decentralizing Cyber Physical Systems for Resilience: An Innovative Case Study from a Cybersecurity Perspective. *Computers & Security*, *14*(8), 342–363. DOI: 10.1000/elsevier.cyber-physicalsecurity2023

Lindemulder, G., & Kosinski, M. (2024, June 11). *What is a man-in-the-middle (MITM) attack?* IBM. https://www.ibm.com/think/topics/man-in-the-middle

Lin, I. C., Kuo, Y. H., Chang, C. C., Liu, J. C., & Chang, C. C. (2024). Symmetry in Blockchain-Powered Secure Decentralized Data Storage: Mitigating Risks and Ensuring Confidentiality. *Symmetry, 15*(3), 567–589. DOI: 10.1000/mdpi.blockchainconfidentiality2024

Lippi, G., Aljawarneh, M., Al-Na'amneh, Q., Hazaymih, R., & Dhomeja, L. D.. (2025). Security and privacy challenges and solutions in autonomous driving systems: A comprehensive review. *Journal of Cyber Security and Risk Auditing, 2025*(3), 23–41.

Liu, Y., He, D., Obaidat, M. S., Kumar, N., Khan, M. K., & Choo, K.-K. R. (2020). Blockchain-based identity management systems: A review. *Journal of Network and Computer Applications, 166*, 102731.

Liu, Y., Yuan, X., Xiong, Z., Kang, J., Wang, X., & Niyato, D. (2020, September). Federated learning for 6G communications: Challenges, methods, and future directions. *China Communications, 17*(9), 105–118.

Li, Y., & Huang, Y. (2025). Social security, digital literacy, and relative poverty in China. *Finance Research Letters, 71*, 106446.

Lv, Z., Chen, D., Feng, H., Singh, A. K., Wei, W., & Lv, H. (2022). Computational intelligence in security of digital twins big graphic data in cyber-physical systems of smart cities. [TMIS]. *ACM Transactions on Management Information Systems, 13*(4), 1–17.

Lv, Z., Qiao, L., Kumar Singh, A., & Wang, Q. (2021). AI-empowered IoT security for smart cities. *ACM Transactions on Internet Technology, 21*(4), 1–21.

Lyon, D. (2018). No TitleThe Culture of Surveillance: Watching as a Way of Life. *Polity*.

Lyu, Q., Liu, S., & Shang, Z. (2024). Securing Urban Landscape: Cybersecurity Mechanisms for Resilient Smart Cities. *IEEE Access : Practical Innovations, Open Solutions*.

M. H. ur Rehman, K. Salah, E. Damiani, and D. Svetinovic, "Towards blockchain-based reputation- aware federated learning," in Proc. IEEE INFOCOM Conf. Comput. Commun. Workshops (INFOCOM WKSHPS), 2020, pp. 183–188

Ma, C. (2021). Smart city and cyber-security; technologies used, leading challenges and future recommendations. *Energy Reports, 7*, 7999–8012.

Mack, E., & Blok, A. (2023, December 22). Smartflower solar review: Beautiful solar for up to $65,000. *CNet.* https://www.cnet.com/home/solar/smartflower-solar-review-beautiful-solar-sculpture

Madeswaran, A., Bisht, D., Yuvaraj, S., Reedy, M. U., Al-Attabi, K., & Dhablia, A. (2024). AI-controlled wind turbine systems: Integrating IoT and machine learning for smart grids. *E3S Web of Conferences, 540,* 03008. https://doi.org/DOI: 10.1051/e3sconf/202454003008

Magalhães, M. F., Mselle, B. D., & Galindo, F. (2025, March 31). Decision-making and selection framework for potential implementation of Concentrated Solar Power technologies: Case study. *Energies*, *18*(7), 1753. DOI: 10.3390/en18071753

Mahadev Madgule, N. (2023). Vinayaka, Yeshwant M. Sonkhaskar, Dhiren Ramanbhai Patel R. Karthikeyan P. Selvakumar, (2023). Mechanical properties and microstructure of activated TIG welded similar joints of Inconel alloys by desirability approaches. *Materials Today: Proceedings*, *77*, 528–533.

Mahesha, C. R., Ramalingam, M., Sujith, S., Kalyanasundaram, P., Soni, N. B., Nalinashini, G., Suresh Kumar, S., Sathyamurthy, R., & Mohanavel, V. (2022, February). Sustainable cooling and heating in smart cities using solar energy system planning, from the International Conference on Energy Storage Technology and Power Systems. *Energy Reports*, *8*, 826–835. DOI: 10.1016/j.egyr.2022.09.208

Maima, A. J. (2024). Evaluation of Counterfeit Antimalarial Drug Awareness and Knowledge Among Pharmacy Attendants in Nairobi County, Kenya. *African Journal of Pharmacy and Alternative Medicine*, *2*(1), 21–31. DOI: 10.58460/ajpam.v2i1.84

Mai, V. T., Mohammadzadeh, A., Alattas, K. A., Taghavifar, H., & Ghaderpour, E. (2025, April). Cybersecurity in maritime power systems: A comprehensive review of cyber threats and mitigation techniques. *Electric Power Systems Research*, *247*, 111797. DOI: 10.1016/j.epsr.2025.111797

Majeed, U., Khan, L. U., Yaqoob, I., Kazmi, S. M. A., Salah, K., & Hong, C. S. (2021). Blockchain for IoT-based smart cities: Recent advances, requirements, and future challenges. *Journal of Network and Computer Applications*, *181*, 103007. DOI: 10.1016/j.jnca.2021.103007

Makani, S., Pittala, R., Alsayed, E., Aloqaily, M., & Jararweh, Y. (2022). A survey of blockchain applications in sustainable and smart cities. *Cluster Computing*, *25*(6), 3915–3936. DOI: 10.1007/s10586-022-03625-z

Mandiant. (2013). *Apt1: Exposing one of china's cyber espionage units* (Tech. Rep.). Alexandria, VA: Mandiant.

Manwell, J. F., McGowan, J. G., & Rogers, A. L. (2009). *Wind energy explained: Theory, design and application*. Wiley.

Marsh, J. (2024, July 25). *How do solar cells work? Photovoltaic cells explained.* Energy Sage. https://www.energysage.com/solar/solar-photovoltaic-cells

Masha, B. (2023). *Inside Safe City, Moscow's AI Surveillance Dystopia | WIRED*. https://www.wired.com/story/moscow-safe-city-ntechlab/

Masoumi, Z., & van Genderen, J. (2024). Artificial intelligence for sustainable development of smart cities and urban land-use management. *Geo-Spatial Information Science*, *27*(4), 1212–1236.

Mastorakis, G., Mavromoustakis, C. X., Batalla, J. M., & Pallis, E. (Eds.). (2020). *Convergence of artificial intelligence and the Internet of Things*. Springer International Publishing.

Matuszewska, D. (2024, October). Solar Organic Rankine Cycle (ORC) systems: A review of technologies, parameters, and applications. *Energies*, *17*(20), 5106. DOI: 10.3390/en17205106

Ma, Y., Goyal, S. B., Rajawat, A. S., Bedi, P., & Yasmeen, S. (2024). Blockchain-based Human Intelligent Systems for Smart City Safety. *Transactions on Emerging Telecommunications Technologies*, *35*(2). Advance online publication. DOI: 10.1002/ett.4939

Ma, Y., Ping, K., Wu, C., Chen, L., Shi, H., & Chong, D. (2020). Artificial Intelligence powered Internet of Things and smart public service. *Library Hi Tech*, *38*(1), 165–179.

Mazumdar, S. (2023). *How to Reduce Information Silos While Blockchain-ifying Recycling Focused Supply Chain Solutions?* https://doi.org/DOI: 10.24251/HICSS.2023.057

McGarity, A. E. (1977). *Solar heating and cooling: An economic assessment*. National Science Foundation. https://files.eric.ed.gov/fulltext/ED145586.pdf

McGraw, G. (2012). Software security: Building security in. *Datenschutz und Datensicherheit-DuD*, *36*(9), 662–665.

McMillin, D. (2022, September 2). *What to know about buying a house with solar panels.* Bankrate. https://www.bankrate.com/real-estate/buying-house-with-solar-panels

Md Ajis, A. F., & Hajar Baharin, S. (2019). Dark Data Management as frontier of Information Governance. *2019 IEEE 9th Symposium on Computer Applications & Industrial Electronics (ISCAIE)*, 34–37. https://doi.org/DOI: 10.1109/ISCAIE.2019.8743915

Meijer, A., & Bolívar, M. P. R. (2016). Governing the smart city: A review of the literature on smart urban governance. *International Review of Administrative Sciences*, *82*(2), 392–408.

Menghwani, V., Wheat, R., Balicki, B., Poelzer, G., Noble, B., & Mansuy, N. (2024). Bioenergy for community energy security in Canada: Challenges in the business ecosystem. *Energies*, *16*(4), 1560. DOI: 10.3390/en16041560

Midani, M. T. (2023). AI-Based Smart Access Systems and Applications for Smart Cities and Living Spaces. In *Role of 6G Wireless Networks in AI and Blockchain-Based Applications* (pp. 80–111). IGI Global., DOI: 10.4018/978-1-6684-5376-6.ch004

Mircea, M., Stoica, M., & Ghilic-Micu, B. (2022). Analysis of the Impact of Blockchain and Internet of Things (BIoT) on Public Procurement. *IEEE Access : Practical Innovations, Open Solutions*, *10*, 63353–63374. DOI: 10.1109/ACCESS.2022.3182656

Mishra, R., & Mishra, A. (2025). Current research on internet of things (iot) security protocols: A survey. *Computers & Security*, •••, 104310.

Moch, N., & Wereda, W. (2024). Management of Urban Security and New Technologies. *European Research Studies Journal*, *27*(1), 145–159. DOI: 10.1000/ersj.urbansecurity2024

Mohamed, N., Al-Jaroodi, J., & Jawhar, I. (2020, July). Opportunities and challenges of data-driven cybersecurity for smart cities. In 2020 IEEE systems security symposium (SSS) (pp. 1-7). IEEE.

Mohamed, Z., Soliman, M., Feteha, M., & Saber, E. (2025, January 8). A novel optimal design approach for bladeless wind turbines considering mechanical properties of composite materials used. *Scientific Reports*, *15*, 1355. DOI: 10.1038/s41598-024-82385-9

Mohammadi, F. (2021). Emerging challenges in smart grid cybersecurity enhancement: A review. *Energies*, *14*(5), 1380.

Mohammed, S., Singh, A., & Kumar, G. R. (2025). Transforming Agricultural Supply Chains: The Power of Blockchain Technology. *2025 International Conference on Intelligent and Innovative Technologies in Computing, Electrical and Electronics (IITCEE)*, 1–8. https://doi.org/DOI: 10.1109/IITCEE64140.2025.10915510

Mohanty, S. P., Choppali, U., & Kougianos, E. (2016). Everything you wanted to know about smart cities: The Internet of things is the backbone. *IEEE Consumer Electronics Magazine*, *5*(3), 60–70. DOI: 10.1109/MCE.2016.2556879

Mokale, M. (2021). Navigating Global Data Privacy Regulations: A Guide for Telecom Operators. *International Journal For Multidisciplinary Research*, *3*(4). Advance online publication. DOI: 10.36948/ijfmr.2021.v03i04.39051

Moore, A. D. (2023). Privacy, security, and surveillance. In *Technology ethics* (pp. 160–168).

Morley, J., Elhalal, A., Garcia, F., Kinsey, L., Mökander, J., & Floridi, L. (2021). Ethics as a Service: A Pragmatic Operationalisation of AI Ethics. *Minds and Machines*, *31*(2), 239–256. DOI: 10.1007/s11023-021-09563-w PMID: 34720418

Mostafa, A. M., Rushdy, E., Medhat, R., & Hanafy, A. (2023). An identity management scheme for cloud computing: Review, challenges, and future directions. *Journal of Intelligent & Fuzzy Systems*, *45*(6), 11295–11317. DOI: 10.3233/JIFS-231911

MOVEit data breach: 45,000 NYC students among victims. (2023, June 23). Chalkbeat. https://www.chalkbeat.org/newyork/2023/6/23/23772027/nyc-student-data-breach-security-moveit-department-education-hack/

Mrabet, M., & Sliti, M. (2024). Integrating machine learning for the sustainable development of smart cities. *Frontiers in Sustainable Cities*, *6*. Advance online publication. DOI: 10.3389/frsc.2024.1449404

Muhammad, G., & Alhussein, M. (2021). Convergence of Artificial Intelligence and Internet of Things in Smart Healthcare: A Case Study of Voice Pathology Detection. *IEEE Access : Practical Innovations, Open Solutions*, *9*, 89198–89209. DOI: 10.1109/ACCESS.2021.3090317

Mukherjee, S., & Sharma, N. (2012). Intrusion Detection using Naive Bayes Classifier with Feature Reduction. *Procedia Technology*, *4*, 119–128. DOI: 10.1016/j.protcy.2012.05.017

Muneer, S., Farooq, U., Athar, A., Ahsan Raza, M., Ghazal, T. M., & Sakib, S. (2024). A Critical Review of Artificial Intelligence Based Approaches in Intrusion Detection: A Comprehensive Analysis. *Journal of Engineering*, *2024*(1). https://doi.org/DOI: 10.1155/2024/3909173

Muniz, R., Nied, A., Da Costa Júnior, C., González, G., & Buratto, W. (2023). The Sustainability Concept: A Review Focusing on Energy. Sustainability. *Sustainability*. https://doi.org/https://doi.org/10.3390/su151914049

Musa, S. I., Hashim, M., & Reba, M. N. M. (2017). A review of geospatial-based urban growth models and modelling initiatives. *Geocarto International*, *32*(8), 813–833.

Mushtaque Temrekar, Ms. M. (2025). A Comparative Analysis of Global Data Privacy Regulations and Their Implementation by Major Cloud Service Providers. *INTERNATIONAL JOURNAL OF SCIENTIFIC RESEARCH IN ENGINEERING AND MANAGEMENT, 09*(05), 1–9. https://doi.org/DOI: 10.55041/IJSREM46907

Mustafa, G., Rafiq, W., Jhamat, N., Arshad, Z., & Rana, F. A. (2025). Blockchain-based governance models in e-government: A comprehensive framework for legal, technical, ethical and security considerations. *International Journal of Law and Management*, *67*(1), 37–55. DOI: 10.1108/IJLMA-08-2023-0172

Nagaraj, A. (2023). *The Role of AI in Enhancing IoT-Cloud Applications*. Bentham Science Publishers., DOI: 10.2174/97898151657081230101

Nagarajan, S. M., Deverajan, G. G., Chatterjee, P., Alnumay, W., & Muthukumaran, V. (2022). Integration of IoT based routing process for food supply chain management in sustainable smart cities. *Sustainable Cities and Society*, *76*, 103448. DOI: 10.1016/j.scs.2021.103448

Najati, I. (2025). Exploring the failure factors of blockchain adopting projects: A case study of tradelens through the lens of commons theory. *Frontiers in Blockchain*, *8*. Advance online publication. DOI: 10.3389/fbloc.2025.1503595

Nambundo, J. M., de Souza Martins Gomes, O., de Souza, A. D., & Machado, R. C. S. (2025). Cybersecurity and major cyber threats of smart meters: A systematic mapping review. *Energies*, *18*(6), 1445.

Nankya, M., Chataut, R., & Akl, R. (2023). Securing industrial control systems: Components, cyber threats, and machine learning-driven defense strategies. *Sensors (Basel)*, *23*(21), 8840. PMID: 37960539

Nartowska, E., & Rozenvalde, A. (2023). Renewable energy sources: Benefits and drawbacks from the perspective of the experiences of China, Brazil, Canada and the United States. *Civil and Environmental Engineering Reports*, *33*(1), 39–52. DOI: 10.59440/ceer-2023-0003

Nasir, M. H., Arshad, J., Khan, M. M., Fatima, M., Salah, K., & Jayaraman, R. (2022). Scalable blockchains — A systematic review. *Future Generation Computer Systems*, *126*, 136–162. DOI: 10.1016/j.future.2021.07.035

National Park Service. (2018, November 7). *Nevada and Arizona: Hoover Dam.* Discover our shared heritage travel itinerary series. https://www.nps.gov/articles/nevada-and-arizona-hoover-dam.htm

Nations, U. (2015). *Transforming our world: The 2030 Agenda for Sustainable Development.* https://sdgs.un.org/2030agenda

Neshenko, N., Bou-Harb, E., Crichigno, J., Kaddoum, G., & Ghani, N. (2019). Demystifying iot security: An exhaustive survey of iot vulnerabilities and a first empirical look at internet-scale iot exploitations. *IEEE Communications Surveys and Tutorials, 21*(3), 2702–2733.

Neshenko, N., Bou-Harb, E., Crichigno, J., Kaddoum, G., & Ghani, N. (2019). Demystifying iot security: An exhaustive survey on iot vulnerabilities and a first empirical look on internet-scale iot exploitations. *IEEE Communications Surveys and Tutorials, 21*(3), 2702–2733.

Nguyen, P., Durlauf, S., & Tikalsky, M. (2023). *Software bill of materials: A catalyst to a more secure software supply chain* (Unpublished doctoral dissertation). Acquisition Research Program.

Nguyen, D., Ding, M., Pathirana, P., Seneviratne, A., Li, J., & Poor, F. (2021). Federated Learning for Internet of Things: A Comprehensive Survey. *IEEE Communications Surveys and Tutorials, 23*, 1622–1658. DOI: 10.1109/COMST.2021.3075439

Nicholson, B., Nielsen, P., Sahay, S., & Sæbø, J. I. (2022). Digital public goods platforms for development: The challenge of scaling. *The Information Society, 38*(5), 364–376. DOI: 10.1080/01972243.2022.2105999

Nidhi, S., Megha, P., Kant, P. R. & Kulha, K. S. (2024, January). Solar energy in developing countries: Challenges and opportunities for smart cities. *E3S Web of Conferences, 540*, 04003. https://doi.org/DOI: 10.1051/e3sconf/202454004003

Nikhitha, M., & Jabbar, Dr. M. A. (2019). K Nearest Neighbor Based Model for Intrusion Detection System. [IJRTE]. *International Journal of Recent Technology and Engineering, 8*(2), 2258–2262. DOI: 10.35940/ijrte.B2458.078219

Nobles, C. (2022). Stress, burnout, and security fatigue in cybersecurity: A human factors problem. *Holistica Journal of Business and Public Administration, 13*(1), 49–72.

Nobles, C. (2024). The weaponization of artificial intelligence in cybersecurity: A systematic review. *Procedia Computer Science, 239*, 547–555.

Obaidat, M. A., Obeidat, S., Holst, J., Al Hayajneh, A., & Brown, J. (2020). A comprehensive and systematic survey on the internet of things: Security and privacy challenges, security frameworks, enabling technologies, threats, vulnerabilities and countermeasures. *Computers, 9*(2), 44.

Okorie, I. J. (2024, June 24). *Suspected Chinese hackers targeted Kenya government agencies*. Techpoint Africa. https://techpoint.africa/news/chinese-hackers-kenya-government-agencies/.

Oliha, J. S., Biu, P. W., & Obi, O. C. (2024). Securing the smart city: A review of cybersecurity challenges and strategies. *Open Access Research Journal of Multidisciplinary Studies*, *7*(1), 94–101.

Ometov, A., Molua, O. L., Komarov, M., & Nurmi, J. (2022). A survey of security in cloud, edge, and fog computing. *Sensors (Basel)*, *22*(3), 927. PMID: 35161675

Omidvarnia, F., & Sarhadi, A. (2024, February 1). Nature-inspired designs in wind energy: A review. *Biomimetics*, *9*(2), 90. DOI: 10.3390/biomimetics9020090 PMID: 38392136

Omri, A., & Boubaker, S. (2024, March). When do climate change legislation and clean energy policies matter for net-zero emissions? *Journal of Environmental Management*, *354*, 120275. DOI: 10.1016/j.jenvman.2024.120275 PMID: 38364534

Ouaddah, A., Abou Elkalam, A., & Ait Ouahman, A. (2016). Fairaccess: A new blockchain-based access control framework for the internet of things. *Security and Communication Networks*, *9*(18), 5943–5964.

Ozmen Garibay, O., Winslow, B., Andolina, S., Antona, M., Bodenschatz, A., Coursaris, C., Falco, G., Fiore, S. M., Garibay, I., Grieman, K., Havens, J. C., Jirotka, M., Kacorri, H., Karwowski, W., Kider, J., Konstan, J., Koon, S., Lopez-Gonzalez, M., Maifeld-Carucci, I., & Xu, W. (2023). Six Human-Centered Artificial Intelligence Grand Challenges. *International Journal of Human-Computer Interaction*, *39*(3). Advance online publication. DOI: 10.1080/10447318.2022.2153320

Padma, A., & Ramaiah, M. (2024). Blockchain Based an Efficient and Secure Privacy Preserved Framework for Smart Cities. *IEEE Access : Practical Innovations, Open Solutions*, *12*(February), 21985–22002. DOI: 10.1109/ACCESS.2024.3364078

Paiva, S., Ahad, M. A., Tripathi, G., Feroz, N., & Casalino, G. (2021). Enabling Technologies for Urban Smart Mobility: Recent Trends, Opportunities, and Challenges. *Sensors (Basel)*, *19*(4), 432–455. DOI: 10.1000/mdpi.smartmobility2021 PMID: 33803903

Pajooh, H. H., Rashid, M., Alam, F., & Demidenko, S. (2021). Multi-layer blockchain-based security architecture for internet of things. *Sensors (Switzerland)*, *21*(3), 1–26. DOI: 10.3390/s21030772

Pampus, J., & Heisel, M. (2025). A Delimitation of Data Sovereignty From Privacy. In *Empowering Digital Sovereignty* (pp. 1–24). IGI Global Scientific Publishing., DOI: 10.4018/979-8-3693-9137-2.ch001

Pan, J. (2025, May 23). *US experts warn 'rogue' devices found in Chinese solar power inverters could trigger widespread blackouts, report says — effectively a 'built-in way' to destroy the grid. Are you prepared?* Money Wise. https://moneywise.com/news/top-stories/rogue-devices-reportedly-found-in-chinese-solar-power-inverters-batteries

Pandey, A. (2025). Blockchain for Pharmaceutical Industry: Present, Past and Future. *INTERANTIONAL JOURNAL OF SCIENTIFIC RESEARCH IN ENGINEERING AND MANAGEMENT*, *09*(03), 1–9. DOI: 10.55041/IJSREM42252

Park, J. H., Rathore, S., Singh, S. K., Salim, M. M., Azzaoui, A., Kim, T. W., & Park, J. H. (2021). A comprehensive survey on core technologies and services for 5g security: Taxonomies, issues, and solutions. *Hum.-. Centric Comput. Inf. Sci*, *11*(3), 1–22.

Pawlicki, M., Pawlicka, A., Kozik, R., & Choraś, M. (2023). The survey and meta-analysis of the attacks, transgressions, countermeasures and security aspects common to the Cloud, Edge and IoT. *Neurocomputing*, *551*, 126533. DOI: 10.1016/j.neucom.2023.126533

Pelluru, K. (2021). Cryptographic Assurance: Utilizing Blockchain for Secure Data Storage and Transactions. *Journal of Innovative Technologies*, *15*(3), 567–589. DOI: 10.1000/acadexpinnara.blockchainsecurity2021

Pemmasani, P. K., & Osaka, M. (2021). The future of smart cities: Cybersecurity challenges in public infrastructure management. *International Journal of Modern Computing*, *4*(1), 72–85. https://yuktabpublisher.com/index.php/IJMC/article/view/249

Perera, C., Zaslavsky, A., Christen, P., & Georgakopoulos, D. (2014). Context Aware Computing for The Internet of Things: A Survey. *IEEE Communications Surveys and Tutorials*, *16*(1), 414–454. DOI: 10.1109/SURV.2013.042313.00197

Perez, A. J., & Zeadally, S. (2022). Secure and Privacy-Preserving Crowdsensing Using Smart Contracts: Issues and Solutions. *Computer Science Review*, *44*, 100456. DOI: 10.1016/j.cosrev.2022.100456

Petrea, M. I. I., & Ursache, I.-M. (2023, October). Inside the world's most sustainable smart city: Lessons from Copenhagen. *International Conference on Sustainable Development of European Smart Cities,* Ia i, Romania, June 2023, 225-238. http://smarteu.uaic.ro/PublishingImages/Pages/Start/Smart%20EU%20volume_Conference%20Proceedings_2023.pdf

Pickering, B. (2021). Trust, but verify: Informed consent, AI technologies, and public health emergencies. *Future Internet, 13*(5). Advance online publication. DOI: 10.3390/fi13050132

Pise, R., & Patil, S. (2021). "Enhancing Security of Data in Cloud Storage Using Decentralized Blockchain." *Proceedings of the Third International Conference on Blockchain Security*, Vol. 15(3), pp. 567–589. DOI: DOI: 10.1000/ieeexplore.cloudblockchainsecurity2021

Poláková, M., Suleimanová, J. H., Madzík, P., Copuš, L., Molnárová, I., & Polednová, J. (2023). Soft skills and their importance in the labour market under the conditions of Industry 5.0. *Heliyon, 9*(8), e18670. DOI: 10.1016/j.heliyon.2023.e18670 PMID: 37593611

Pollard, M. (2024) "A Case Study of Russian Cyber-Attacks on the Ukrainian Power Grid: Implicationsand Best Practices for the United States,"Pepperdine Policy Review: Vol. 16, Article 1.Available at:https://digitalcommons.pepperdine.edu/ppr/vol16/iss1/1

Prasad, K. R., Karanam, S. R., Ganesh, D., Liyakat, K. K. S., Talasila, V., & Purushotham, P. (2024). AI in public-private partnership for IT infrastructure development. *The Journal of High Technology Management Research, 35*(1), 100496.

Priyadarshini, I., Alkhayyat, A., Gehlot, A., & Kumar, R. (2022). Time series analysis and anomaly detection for trustworthy smart homes. *Computers & Electrical Engineering, 102*, 108193. DOI: 10.1016/j.compeleceng.2022.108193

Przeybilovicz, E., Cunha, M. A., Geertman, S., Leleux, C., Michels, A., Tomor, Z., Webster, C. W. R., & Meijer, A. (2020). Citizen participation in the smart city: Findings from an international comparative study. *Local Government Studies, 48*(1), 23–47. DOI: 10.1080/03003930.2020.1851204

Radmanesh, S.-A., Haji, A., & Fatahi Valilai, O. (2023). Blockchain-Based Architecture for a Sustainable Supply Chain in Cloud Architecture. *Sustainability, 15*(11), 9072. DOI: 10.3390/su15119072

Radu, L.-D. (2017). Green Cloud Computing: A Literature Survey. *Symmetry, 9*(12), 295. DOI: 10.3390/sym9120295

Ragan, B. (2025, February 28). *What are the types of attic ventilation systems?* Bill Ragan Roofing. https://www.billraganroofing.com/blog/types-attic-ventilation-systems

Ragothaman, K., Wang, Y., Rimal, B., & Lawrence, M. (2023). Access control for IoT: A survey of existing research, dynamic policies and future directions. *Sensors (Basel)*, *23*(4), 1805. PMID: 36850403

Rahouti, M. (2019). Board 129: Facilitation of Cybersecurity Learning Through Real-world Hands-on Labs. *2019 ASEE Annual Conference & Exposition Proceedings*. https://doi.org/DOI: 10.18260/1-2--32228

Rai, P., & Nain, V. (2024). Stuxnet unveiled: The blueprint for modern cyber conflict. In *2024 3rd edition of ieee delhi section flagship conference (delcon)* (pp. 1–4).

Raj Kumar Reddy, K., Gunasekaran, A., Kalpana, P., Raja Sreedharan, V., & Arvind Kumar, S. (2021). Developing a blockchain framework for the automotive supply chain: A systematic review. *Computers & Industrial Engineering*, *157*, 107334. DOI: 10.1016/j.cie.2021.107334

Rameder, H., Di Angelo, M., & Salzer, G. (2022). Review of Automated Vulnerability Analysis of Smart Contracts on Ethereum. *Frontiers in Blockchain*, *5*, 814977. DOI: 10.3389/fbloc.2022.814977

Rana, M. U., Shah, M. A., Al-Naeem, M. A., & Maple, C. (2024). Ransomware attacks in cyber-physical systems: Countermeasure of attack vectors through automated web defenses. *IEEE Access : Practical Innovations, Open Solutions*, *12*, 149722–149739. DOI: 10.1109/ACCESS.2024.3477631

Ranaweera, P., Imrith, V. N., Liyanag, M., & Jurcut, A. D. (2020). Security as a Service Platform Leveraging Multi-Access Edge Computing Infrastructure Provisions. *ICC 2020 - 2020 IEEE International Conference on Communications (ICC)*, 1–6. https://doi.org/DOI: 10.1109/ICC40277.2020.9148660

Ranjitha, P. K., Selvakumar, P., Anute, N., Manjunath, T., Sureshkrishna, G., & Pougajendy, S. (2025). Transportation Challenges In Islands Tourism. In Hassan, V. (Ed.), *Navigating Mass Tourism to Island Destinations: Preservation and Cultural Heritage Challenges* (pp. 287–312). IGI Global Scientific Publishing., DOI: 10.4018/979-8-3693-9107-5.ch011

Rashid, M. M., Kamruzzaman, J., Hassan, M. M., Imam, T., & Gordon, S. (2020). Cyberattacks detection in iot-based smart city applications using machine learning techniques. *International Journal of Environmental Research and Public Health*, *17*(24), 9347.

Rathore, M. M., Attique Shah, S., Awad, A., Shukla, D., Vimal, S., & Paul, A. (2021). A cyber-physical system and graph-based approach for transportation management in smart cities. *Sustainability*, *13*(14), 7606.

Rathore, R., Kaushik, P., Sikarwar, S. S., Joshi, H., Mishra, A. K., & Hudda, Y. (2024, March 14). Intelligent Transportation Systems Make Use of Fog and Edge Computing for Navigation. In In *2024 IEEE International Conference on Interdisciplinary Approaches in Technology and Management for Social Innovation (IATMSI)* (Vol. 2, Pp. 1-6). IEEE. https://doi.org/10.1109/iatmsi60426.2024.10502525

Rawat, R. (2023). Harnessing the Power of IoT and AI for Human Evolution. *International Journal of Research In Science & Engineering*, *33*(33), 58–68. DOI: 10.55529/ijrise.33.58.68

Razaque, A., Al Ajlan, A., Melaoune, N., & Alotaibi, M. (2021). Avoidance of Cybersecurity Threats with the Deployment of a Web-Based Blockchain-Enabled Cybersecurity Awareness System. *Applied Sciences (Basel, Switzerland)*, *25*(4), 375–398. DOI: 10.1000/mdpi.blockchaincybersecurityawareness2021

Razmjoo, A., Østergaard, P. A., Denaï, M., Nezhad, M. M., & Mirjalili, S. (2021). Effective policies to overcome barriers in the development of smart cities. *Energy Research & Social Science*, *79*, 102175. DOI: 10.1016/j.erss.2021.102175

Rehak, D., Senovsky, P., Hromada, M., Lovecek, T., & Novotny, P. (2018). Cascading impact assessment in a critical infrastructure system. *International Journal of Critical Infrastructure Protection*, *22*, 125–138.

Rejeb, A., Suhaiza, Z., Rejeb, K., Seuring, S., & Treiblmaier, H. (2022). The internet of things and the circular economy: A systematic literature review and research agenda. *Journal of Cleaner Production*, *350*, 131439.

Rekeraho, A., Cotfas, D. T., Balan, T. C., Cotfas, P. A., Acheampong, R., & Tuyishime, E. (2025, March). Cybersecurity threat modeling for IoT-integrated smart solar energy systems: Strengthening resilience for global energy sustainability. *Sustainability*, *17*(6), 2386. DOI: 10.3390/su17062386

Rekeraho, A., Cotfas, D. T., Cotfas, P. A., Bălan, T. C., Tuyishime, E., & Acheampong, R. (2024, February). Cybersecurity challenges in IoT-based smart renewable energy. *International Journal of Information Security*, *23*, 101–117. DOI: 10.1007/s10207-023-00732-9

Rifat Hossain, M., Nirob, F. A., Islam, A., Rakin, T. M., & Al-Amin, M. (2024). A Comprehensive Analysis of Blockchain Technology and Consensus Protocols Across Multilayered Framework. *IEEE Access : Practical Innovations, Open Solutions, 12*, 63087–63129. DOI: 10.1109/ACCESS.2024.3395536

Rijanto, A. (2021). Blockchain Technology Adoption in Supply Chain Finance. *Journal of Theoretical and Applied Electronic Commerce Research, 16*(7), 3078–3098. DOI: 10.3390/jtaer16070168

Rizi, M. H. P., & Seno, S. A. H. (2022). A systematic review of technologies and solutions to improve security and privacy protection of citizens in the smart city. *Internet of Things : Engineering Cyber Physical Human Systems, 20*, 100584.

Rogers, J. N., Stokes, B., Dunn, J., Cai, H., Wu, M., Haq, Z., & Baumes, H. (2016, November 21). An assessment of the potential products and economic and environmental impacts resulting from a billion ton bioeconomy. *Biofuels, Bioproducts & Biorefining, 11*(1), 110–128. DOI: 10.1002/bbb.1728

Romeo, J. (2025, April 10). *Dallas Love Field turns jet blasts into renewable power*. Electrical Contractor. https://www.ecmag.com/magazine/articles/article-detail/dallas-love-field-turns-jet-blasts-into-renewable-power

Rouse, W. B. (2024). *From Human-Centered Design to Human-Centered Society: Creatively Balancing Business Innovation and Societal Exploitation*. Productivity Press.

Roy, A., Dhar, A., & Tinny, S. S. (2024). Strengthening iot cybersecurity with zero trust architecture: A comprehensive review. *Journal of Computer Science and Information Technology, 1*(1), 25–50.

Rubin, V. L. (2022). *Misinformation and disinformation: Detecting fakes with the eye and ai*. Springer Nature.

Rullo, A., Midi, D., Mudjerikar, A., & Bertino, E. (2024). Kalis2.0—A SECaaS-Based Context-Aware Self-Adaptive Intrusion Detection System for IoT. *IEEE Internet of Things Journal, 11*(7), 12579–12601. DOI: 10.1109/JIOT.2023.3333948

Ruohonen, J., & Hjerppe, K. (2022). The GDPR enforcement fines at glance. *Information Systems, 106*, 101876. DOI: 10.1016/j.is.2021.101876

Saha, A., Mattei, J., Blasco, J., Cavallaro, L., Votipka, D., & Lindorfer, M. (2025). Expert insights into advanced persistent threats: Analysis, attribution, and challenges. In *Proceedings of the 34th usenix security symposium (usenix sec)*.

Saidu, Y., Shuhaida, M. S., Dahiru, A. A., Yau, S., Muhammad, M. Y., & Babando, A. A. (2024). Charting the Course : A Bibliometric Exploration of Blockchain Traceability Systems. *International Conference on Technological Solutions for Smart Economy*, 1–8. https://library.ncs.org.ng/download/charting-the-course-a-bibliometric-exploration-of-blockchain-traceability-systems/

Saidu, Y., Shuhidan, S. M., Aziz, I. A., Adamu, D. A., Yau, S., & Adamu, S. (2025). A Bibliometric Analysis on Blockchain Consensus Algorithms: Unveiling Trends, Contributors, and Intellectual Structures. In M. Hisham, H. Mohd Hilmi, A. Said Jadid, & S. Nasir (Eds.), *Proceedings of the International Conference on Smart Cities* - Volume 2 *ICSC 2024, September 10-11, Kota Kinabalu, Malaysia* (pp. 579–593). Springer Singapore. https://doi.org/DOI: 10.1007/978-981-96-5848-0_47

Saidu, Y., Shuhidan, S. M., Aliyu, D. A., Aziz, I. A., & Adamu, S. (2025). Convergence of Blockchain, IoT, and AI for Enhanced Traceability Systems: A Comprehensive Review. *IEEE Access : Practical Innovations, Open Solutions, 13*, 16838–16865. DOI: 10.1109/ACCESS.2025.3528035

Saidu, Y., Shuhidan, S. M., Aziz, I. A., Alam, M. M., Aliyu, D. A., Yakubu, M. M., & Adamu, S. (2025). Exploring Blockchain–IoT Convergence for Logistics Traceability: A Systematic Review and Future Outlook. *IEEE Access : Practical Innovations, Open Solutions, 13*, 112390–112416. DOI: 10.1109/ACCESS.2025.3583927

Saleem, M. U., Usman, M. R., Usman, M. A., & Politis, C. (2022). Design, deployment and performance evaluation of an IoT based smart energy Management system for demand side management in smart Grid. *IEEE Access : Practical Innovations, Open Solutions, 10*, 15261–15278. DOI: 10.1109/access.2022.3147484

Saleh, A. M. S. (2024). “Blockchain for Secure and Decentralized Artificial Intelligence in Cybersecurity: A Comprehensive Review.” Blockchain. *Research and Applications, 6*(1), 55–72. DOI: 10.1000/elsevier.blockchaincybersecurity2024

Salehpour, A., Al-Anbagi, I., Yow, K.-C., & Cheng, X. (2022). Modeling cascading failures in coupled smart grid networks. *IEEE Access : Practical Innovations, Open Solutions, 10*, 81054–81070.

Sallam, K., Mohamed, M., & Mohamed, A. W. (2023). Internet of things (iot) in supply chain management: challenges, opportunities, and best practices. *Sustainable machine intelligence journal, 2*, 3–1.

Sameer Babu, M., Karunakaran, N. B., Selvakumar, P., Sethumadhavan, R., & Chandel, P. S. (2025). The Role of Chatbots in Educational Leadership. In Musundire, A. (Ed.), *Chatbots in Educational Leadership and Management* (pp. 321–346). IGI Global Scientific Publishing., DOI: 10.4018/979-8-3693-8734-4.ch013

Sanchez, T. W., Brenman, M., & Ye, X. (2024). The ethical Concerns of artificial intelligence in urban planning. *Journal of the American Planning Association*, •••, 1–14. DOI: 10.1080/01944363.2024.2355305

Sanderson, C. (2024, April 25). *Russia launches 'first targeted strike' on a Ukrainian solar power facility.* Recharge News. https://www.rechargenews.com/energy-transition/russia-launches-first-targeted-strike-on-a-ukrainian-solar-power-facility/2-1-1622019

Sanderson, C. (2025, June 3*). 'Unacceptable': BP bristles at BAE Systems wind farm radar shutdown demand.* Recharge News. https://www.rechargenews.com/wind/unacceptable-bp-bristles-at-bae-systems-wind-farm-radar-shutdown-demand/2-1-1827749

Sarkheyli, A., & Sarkheyli, E. (2019). Smart Megaprojects in Smart Cities, Dimensions, and Challenges. In *Smart Cities Cybersecurity and Privacy* (pp. 269–277). Elsevier., DOI: 10.1016/B978-0-12-815032-0.00019-6

Sarveshwaran, V., Pandiaraj, S., Bindu, G., Ganesan, V., & Swamidason, I. T. J. (2024). Binarized Spiking Neural Network with blockchain based intrusion detection framework for enhancing privacy and security in cloud computing environment. *Applied Soft Computing*, *154*, 111218. DOI: 10.1016/j.asoc.2023.111218

Satyanarayanan, M. (2017). The emergence of edge computing. *Computer*, *50*(1), 30–39. DOI: 10.1109/ MC.2017.17

Scalise, P., Boeding, M., Hempel, M., Sharif, H., Delloiacovo, J., & Reed, J. (2024). A systematic survey on 5g and 6g security considerations, challenges, trends, and research areas. *Future Internet*, *16*(3), 67.

Schembera, B., & Durán, J. M. (2020). Dark Data as the New Challenge for Big Data Science and the Introduction of the Scientific Data Officer. *Philosophy & Technology*, *33*(1), 93–115. DOI: 10.1007/s13347-019-00346-x

Securing renewable data: Green energy sector cybersecurity challenges. (2025, May 3). Beetroot. https://beetroot.co/business/securing-renewable-data-green-energy-sector-cybersecurity-challenges

Settanni, F., Regano, L., Basile, C., & Lioy, A. (2023). A Model for Automated Cybersecurity Threat Remediation and Sharing. *2023 IEEE 9th International Conference on Network Softwarization (NetSoft)*, 492–497. https://doi.org/DOI: 10.1109/NetSoft57336.2023.10175486

Seyam, H., & Habbal, A. (2023). "A Systematic Review of Blockchain-Based Identity Management Solutions." *Proceedings of the International Conference on Recent Academic Research*, Vol. 15(3), pp. 567–589. DOI: DOI: 10.1000/academia.blockchainidentityreview2023

Sezer, O. B., Dogdu, E., & Ozbayoglu, A. M. (2018, February). Context-aware computing learning and big data in Internet of Things: A survey. *IEEE Internet of Things Journal*, *5*(1), 1–27.

Shafique, K., Khawaja, B. A., Sabir, F., Qazi, S., & Mustaqim, M. (2020). Internet of things (IoT) for next-generation smart systems: A review of current challenges, future trends and prospects for emerging 5G-IoT scenarios. *IEEE Access : Practical Innovations, Open Solutions*, *8*, 23022–23040.

Shahan, Z. (2014, November 21). *History of wind turbines*. Factor This. https://www.renewableenergyworld.com/wind-power/turbines-equipment/history-of-wind-turbines

Shahid, A., Almogren, A., Javaid, N., Al-Zahrani, F. A., Zuair, M., & Alam, M. (2020). Blockchain-Based Agri-Food Supply Chain: A Complete Solution. *IEEE Access : Practical Innovations, Open Solutions*, *8*, 69230–69243. DOI: 10.1109/ACCESS.2020.2986257

Shah, S. M., Aljawarneh, M. M., & Akbar, S. (2025). Assistive living in iot-based smart home systems for aging in place: A review. *VFAST Transactions on Software Engineering*, *13*(2), 83–98.

Shahzad, A., Chen, W., & Zhang, Y. (2025). Zero-Trust Medical Image Sharing: A Secure and Decentralized Approach Using Blockchain and the IPFS. *Symmetry*, *17*(2), 112–132. DOI: 10.1000/ebscohost.medicalblockchain2025

Shankar, G., Singh, P., & Dewangan, N. K. (2024). DEMRISEC: Security Enhancement of Patient Data in Decentralized Medical Records with IPFS. *Multimedia Tools and Applications*, *15*(3), 567–589. DOI: 10.1000/springer.blockchainmedicalsecurity2024

Sharma, D. H., Dhote, C. A., & Potey, M. M. (2016). Implementing Intrusion Management as Security-as-a-service from cloud. *2016 International Conference on Computation System and Information Technology for Sustainable Solutions (CSITSS)*, 363–366. https://doi.org/DOI: 10.1109/CSITSS.2016.7779387

Sharmin, N. S., & Chowdhury, N. R. H. (2025). Digital Transformation in Governance: The Impact of e-governance on Public Administration and Transparency. *Journal of Computer Science and Technology Studies*, *7*(1), 362–379. DOI: 10.32996/jcsts.2025.7.1.27

Sharon, T. (2021). Blind-sided by privacy? Digital contact tracing, the Apple/Google API, and big tech's newfound role as global health policy makers. *Ethics and Information Technology*, *23*. Advance online publication. DOI: 10.1007/s10676-020-09547-x PMID: 32837287

Shayea, G. G., Zabil, M. H. M., Habeeb, M. A., Khaleel, Y. L., & Albahri, A. (2025). Strategies for protection against adversarial attacks in ai models: An in-depth review. *Journal of Intelligent Systems*, *34*(1), 20240277.

Shchekhovska, L. (2025). Transparency and sustainability: a new paradigm for supply chain management. *Electronic Scientific Journal Intellectualization of Logistics and Supply Chain Management #1 2020*, *30*, 47–53. https://doi.org/DOI: 10.46783/smart-scm/2025-30-4

Shen, C., & Pena-Mora, F. (2018). Blockchain for Cities—A Systematic Literature Review. *IEEE Access : Practical Innovations, Open Solutions*, *6*, 76787–76819. DOI: 10.1109/ACCESS.2018.2880744

Shende, A. D., Tekade, S. A., Deshmukh, A. A., Tembhurkar, S. P., & Selvakumar, P. (2025). Water Quality Monitoring and Control With AI. In Ruiz-Vanoye, J., & Díaz-Parra, O. (Eds.), *Smart Water Technology for Sustainable Management in Modern Cities* (pp. 51–80). IGI Global Scientific Publishing., DOI: 10.4018/979-8-3693-8074-1.ch003

Sheng, C., Yao, Y., Fu, Q., & Yang, W. (2021). A cyber-physical model for scada system and its intrusion detection. *Computer Networks*, *185*, 107677.

Shen, Y., Li, Y., Wu, L., Liu, S., & Wen, Q. (2013). *Security Information and Event Management Implementation Guidance*., DOI: 10.4018/978-1-4666-4801-2.ch005

Sheoran, S., & Vij, S. (2022). A Review of E-Government Assessment Frameworks: E-Readiness, Adoption, Citizen Engagement and Quality: E-Readiness, Adoption, Citizen Engagement and Quality. JeDEM-eJournal of eDemocracy and Open Government, 14(2), 197-213.

Shin, S., Kim, D., & Chun, S. A. (2021). Digital divide in advanced smart city innovations. *Sustainability*, *13*(7), 4076. DOI: 10.3390/su13074076

Shirley, C. P., Thanga Helina, S., Thusita, S., & Okesh, A. (2025). Machine Learning for Cloud Security: A Systematic Review. *Journal of Information Systems Engineering & Management, 10*(37), 517–529.

Short, J. R. (2004). Black Holes and Loose Connections in a Global Urban Network. *The Professional Geographer, 56*(2), 295–302. DOI: 10.1111/j.0033-0124.2004.05602012.x

Shostack, A. (2014). *Threat modeling: Designing for security*. Wiley.

Shuaib, M., Hassan, N. H., & Usman, S. (2022). Self-Sovereign Identity Solution for Blockchain-Based Land Registry System: A Comparison. *Mobile Information Systems, 2022*, 567–589. DOI: 10.1000/wiley.blockchainlandregistry2022

Siddiqui, M. S., Keprate, A., Yang, L., & Malmedal, T. (2023, December). Towards an integrative framework for digital twins in wind power. *2023 IEEE International Conference on Industrial Engineering and Engineering Management (IEEM)*, Singapore. https://doi.org/DOI: 10.1109/IEEM58616.2023.10406340

Sikorski, M., & Honig, A. (2012). *Practical malware analysis: the hands-on guide to dissecting malicious software*. No Starch Press.

Singh, T. (2013, April 1). *Scientists develop solar-powered wind turbine for ultimate energy generation.* Inhabit. https://inhabitat.com/scientists-develop-solar-powered-wind-turbine

Singh, J., Sajid, M., & Gupta, S. K. (2022). Artificial Intelligence and Blockchain Technologies for Smart City. *Sustainable Smart Cities, 15*(3), 567–589. DOI: 10.1000/wiley.blockchainai2022

Singh, S. K., Azzaoui, A. E., Choo, K. K. R., & Yang, L. T. (2023). A Comprehensive Survey on Blockchain for Secure IoT-Enabled Smart City Beyond 5G: Approaches, Processes, Challenges, and Opportunities. *Human-Centric Computing and Information Sciences, 15*(3), 567–589. DOI: 10.1000/hcisj.blockchainsmartcity2023

Singh, S., Hosen, A. S. M. S., & Yoon, B. (2021). Blockchain Security Attacks, Challenges, and Solutions for the Future Distributed IoT Network. *IEEE Access : Practical Innovations, Open Solutions, 9*, 13938–13959. DOI: 10.1109/ACCESS.2021.3051602

Singh, S., Rathore, S., & Park, J. (2020). BlockIoTIntelligence: A Blockchain-enabled Intelligent IoT Architecture with Artificial Intelligence. *Future Generation Computer Systems, 110*, 721–743. DOI: 10.1016/j.future.2019.09.002

Singh, S., Sharma, P. K., Yoon, B., Shojafar, M., Cho, G. H., & Ra, I.-H. (2020). Convergence of blockchain and artificial intelligence in IoT network for the sustainable smart city. *Sustainable Cities and Society, 63*, 102364. DOI: 10.1016/j.scs.2020.102364

Sjödin, M. (2018, March 13). *Turbine electricity.* [Image]. Pixabay. https://pixabay.com/photos/turbine-electricity-generator-3224747

Smart grid security: Attacks and defence techniques. (2025). Infosys. https://www.infosysbpm.com/blogs/business-transformation/smart-grid-security-attacks-and-defence-techniques.html

Smart nation and the digital government office partner with Google Cloud to launch an AI government cloud cluster. (2023, June 6). CIO. https://ciosea.economictimes.indiatimes.com/news/cloud-computing/smart-nation-and-digital-government-office-partners-with-google-cloud-to-launch-ai-government-cloud-cluster/100780836

Sridhar, S., Hahn, A., & Govindarasu, M. (2012). Cyber–physical system security for the electric power grid. *Proceedings of the IEEE, 100*(1), 210–224. DOI: 10.1109/JPROC.2011.2165269

Srinadh, V., Swaminathan, B., & Vidyadhari, Ch. (2023). Blockchain-Integrated Advanced Persistent Threat Detection Using Optimized Deep Learning-Enabled Feature Fusion. *Journal of Uncertain Systems, 16*(03). Advance online publication. DOI: 10.1142/S1752890922500179

Stafford, V. (2020). Zero trust architecture. *NIST special publication, 800*(207), 800–207.

Stallard, E., & Poynting, M. (2025, January 21). What is the Paris climate agreement and why has Trump withdrawn? *BBC News.* https://www.bbc.com/news/science-environment-35073297

Stouffer, K., Falco, J., Scarfone, K., et al. (2011). Guide to industrial control systems (ics) security. *NIST special publication, 800*(82), 16–16.

Stu, S. (2025). *How to build AI-powered cities intelligently | The Australian.* https://www.theaustralian.com.au/business/cfo-journal/how-to-build-aipowered-cities-intelligently/news-story/cac9476c0c284925d70b3abde2dcc785

Subashini, B., & Hemavathi, D. (2023). Scalable Blockchain Technology for Tracking the Provenance of the Agri-Food. *Computers, Materials & Continua, 75*(2), 3339–3358. DOI: 10.32604/cmc.2023.035074

Subramanian, M., Portia, R., Mishra, B. R., & Selvakumar, P. P. V., R., & T. C., M. (2025). Assessment and Evaluation in Personalized STEAM Education. In N. Son (Ed.), *Integrating Personalized Learning Methods Into STEAM Education* (pp. 103-122). IGI Global Scientific Publishing. https://doi.org/DOI: 10.4018/979-8-3693-7718-5.ch005

Subramanian, N., Chaudhuri, A., & Kayikci, Y. (2020). Blockchain Applications in Food Supply Chain. In *Blockchain and Supply Chain Logistics* (pp. 21–29). Springer International Publishing., DOI: 10.1007/978-3-030-47531-4_3

Sugumaran K M D, Pandiyarajan V Y B S, Selvakumar P. and M. S, (2024). "Analysis of Electromyography Signals for Control of Mechanical Prosthesis using Machine Learning Techniques," 2024 2nd International Conference on Intelligent Data Communication Technologies and Internet of Things (IDCIoT), Bengaluru, India, 2024, pp. 1059-1067, doi: .DOI: 10.1109/IDCIoT59759.2024.10467707

Su, L., Bai, W., Zhu, Z., & He, X. (2021). Research on Application of Support Vector Machine in Intrusion Detection. *Journal of Physics: Conference Series*, *2037*(1), 012074. DOI: 10.1088/1742-6596/2037/1/012074

Sustainability Directory. (2025). *What Ethical Frameworks Should Guide the Development and Deployment of Smart City Technologies?* https://sustainability-directory.com/question/what-ethical-frameworks-should-guide-the-development-and-deployment-of-smart-city-technologies/

Sustainability. (2025). Byron Solar Train. https://byronbaytrain.com.au/sustainability

Sutheekshan, B., Basheer, S., Thangavel, G., & Sharma, O. P. (2024). *Evolution of malware targeting iot devices and botnet formation. In 2024 ieee international conference on computing, power and communication technologies (ic2pct)* (Vol. 5).

Syed, N. F., Shah, S. W., Shaghaghi, A., Anwar, A., Baig, Z., & Doss, R. (2022). Zero trust architecture (zta): A comprehensive survey. *IEEE Access : Practical Innovations, Open Solutions*, *10*, 57143–57179.

Szabo, J., Bernard, C., & Philip, L. (2024). Legal Implications and Challenges of Blockchain Technology and Smart Contracts. *Computer Life*, *12*(2), 6–10. DOI: 10.54097/ztn2w848

Tabibi, A. (2024, January 30). *The ethics of solar energy: Balancing progress and responsibility*. Green.org. https://green.org/2024/01/30/the-ethics-of-solar-energy-balancing-progress-and-responsibility

Tafuro, A., Dammacco, G., & Costa, A. (2023). A Conceptual Study on the Role of Blockchain in Sustainable Development of Public–Private Partnership. *Administrative Sciences, 13*(8), 175. DOI: 10.3390/admsci13080175

Tahri, R., Lasbahani, A., Jarrar, A., & Balouki, Y. (2024). Intelligent Intrusion Detection Using Decision Trees and the NSL-KDD Dataset: An All-Inclusive Method for Cyber Attack Detection. *Journal of Southwest Jiaotong University, 59*(5). Advance online publication. DOI: 10.35741/issn.0258-2724.59.5.13

Talib, A. M., Atan, R., Abdullah, R., & Murad, M. A. A. (2012). Security Facilitation in Collaborative Cloud Data Storage Implementation Environment Based on Multi Agent System Architecture. *Journal of Software Engineering, 6*(3), 49–64. DOI: 10.3923/jse.2012.49.64

Tan, E., Lerouge, E., Du Caju, J., & Du Seuil, D. (2023). Verification of Education Credentials on European Blockchain Services Infrastructure (EBSI): Action Research in a Cross-Border Use Case between Belgium and Italy. *Big Data and Cognitive Computing, 7*(2), 79. DOI: 10.3390/bdcc7020079

Tan, E., Mahula, S., & Crompvoets, J. (2022). Blockchain governance in the public sector: A conceptual framework for public management. *Government Information Quarterly, 39*(1), 101625. DOI: 10.1016/j.giq.2021.101625

Tanim, A. H., McRae, C. B., Tavakol-Davani, H., & Goharian, E. (2022). Flood detection in urban areas using satellite imagery and machine learning. *Water (Basel), 14*(7), 1140.

Tan, Z., Parambath, S. P., Anagnostopoulos, C., Singer, J., & Marnerides, A. K. (2025). Advanced Persistent Threats Based on Supply Chain Vulnerabilities: Challenges, Solutions, and Future Directions. *IEEE Internet of Things Journal, 12*(6), 6371–6395. DOI: 10.1109/JIOT.2025.3528744

Tekinerdogan, B., Köksal, Ö., & Çelik, T. (2023). System architecture design of IoT-based smart cities. *Applied Sciences (Basel, Switzerland), 13*(7), 4173.

Thakur, C. K. (2025). Blockchain in Enhancing Supply Chain Transparency. *International Journal for Research in Applied Science and Engineering Technology, 13*(1), 2093–2095. DOI: 10.22214/ijraset.2025.66746

The Times. (2025). *Amsterdam abandons smart traffic lights amid privacy fears.* https://www.thetimes.com/world/europe/article/amsterdam-abandons-smart-traffic-lights-amid-privacy-fears-l97g6rmtc?

Theisen, C., Munaiah, N., Al-Zyoud, M., Carver, J. C., Meneely, A., & Williams, L. (2018). Attack surface definitions: A systematic literature review. *Information and Software Technology*, *104*, 94–103.

Thompson, K. (2022). *How do power plants and renewables differ in cybersecurity requirements.* Integriti. https://itegriti.com/2022/compliance/how-do-power-plants-and-renewables-differ-in-cybersecurity-requirements/

Timmons, D., Harris, J. M., & Roach, B. (2024). *The economics of renewable energy*. Boston University Global Development Policy Center. https://www.bu.edu/eci/files/2024/03/renewable-energy-econ-module-final.pdf

Tolasa, D. G., & Furi, A. T. (2025, January 30). The role of advanced materials in the optimization of wind energy systems: A physics based approach. *Acceleron Aerospace Journal*, *4*(1), 847–857. DOI: 10.61359/11.2106-2504

Treude, M. (2021). Sustainable Smart City—Opening a Black Box. *Sustainability*, *13*(2), 769. DOI: 10.3390/su13020769

Trevisan, A. H., Lobo, A., Guzzo, D., Gomes, L. A. de V., & Mascarenhas, J. (2023). Barriers to employing digital technologies for a circular economy: A multi-level perspective. *Journal of Environmental Management*, *332*, 117437. DOI: 10.1016/j.jenvman.2023.117437 PMID: 36801533

Trigen. (2025). *Legal & Ethical Considerations for Smart Cities and IoT.* https://www.trigyn.com/insights/legal-and-ethical-considerations-smart-cities-and-iot

Tripathi, A. K., Akul Krishnan, K., & Pandey, A. C. (2023). A Novel Blockchain and Internet of Things-Based Food Traceability System for Smart Cities. *Wireless Personal Communications*, *129*(3), 2157–2180. DOI: 10.1007/s11277-023-10230-9 PMID: 36987505

Truong, N. B., Sun, K., Lee, G. M., & Guo, Y. (2020). GDPR-Compliant Personal Data Management: A Blockchain-Based Solution. *IEEE Transactions on Information Forensics and Security*, *15*, 1746–1761. DOI: 10.1109/TIFS.2019.2948287

Tyagi, A. K., Kumari, S., & Surve, T. (2024). Integration of Digital Twin and Blockchain for Smart Cities. In *Digital Twin and Blockchain for Smart Cities* (pp. 81–100). Wiley., DOI: 10.1002/9781394303564.ch5

U.S. Department of Energy. (2004, March 8). *The history of solar.* Energy Efficiency and Renewable Energy Office. https://www1.eere.energy.gov/solar/pdfs/solar_timeline.pdf

U.S. Department of Energy. (2024, May 21). *Protecting wind energy systems from cyberattacks.* Wind Energy Technologies Office. https://www.energy.gov/eere/wind/articles/protecting-wind-energy-systems-cyberattacks

U.S. Department of Energy. (n.d.a,). *Bioenergy basics.* Bioenergy Technology Office. https://www.energy.gov/eere/bioenergy/bioenergy-basics

U.S. Department of Energy. (n.d.b.). *Geothermal heating and cooling.* Geothermal Technologies Office. https://www.energy.gov/eere/geothermal/geothermal-heating-cooling

U.S. Energy Information Administration. (2022, December 27). *Geothermal explained.* https://www.eia.gov/energyexplained/geothermal

U.S. Energy Information Administration. (2023a, April 20). *Hydropower explained.* https://www.energy.gov/eere/water/marine-energy-basics

U.S. Energy Information Administration. (2023b, December 27). Wind explained: Types of wind turbines. https://www.eia.gov/energyexplained/wind/types-of-wind-turbines.php

Uddin, M., Salah, K., Jayaraman, R., Pesic, S., & Ellahham, S. (2021). Blockchain for drug traceability: Architectures and open challenges. *Health Informatics Journal, 27*(2). Advance online publication. DOI: 10.1177/14604582211011228 PMID: 33899576

Uddin, M., Selvarajan, S., Obaidat, M., Arfeen, S. U., Khadidos, A. O., Khadidos, A. O., & Abdelhaq, M. (2023). From Hype to Reality: Unveiling the Promises, Challenges and Opportunities of Blockchain in Supply Chain Systems. *Sustainability, 15*(16), 12193. DOI: 10.3390/su151612193

Uktamova, D. (2024). Evaluating the onshore wind farms based on multi-criteria decision-making model under Neutrosophic Set. *Journal of Sustainable Development and Green Technology, 4*(2), 22–33. DOI: 10.54216/JSDGT.040203

Ullah, A., Anwar, S. M., Li, J., Nadeem, L., Mahmood, T., Rehman, A., & Saba, T. (2023). Smart cities: The role of Internet of Things and machine learning in realizing a data-centric smart environment. *Complex & Intelligent Systems, 10*(1), 1607–1637. https://doi.org/10.1007/s40747-023-01175-4

UNESCO. (2021). *Recommendation on the Ethics of Artificial Intelligence - Legal Affairs.* https://www.unesco.org/en/legal-affairs/recommendation-ethics-artificial-intelligence?

United Nations Climate Change. (2023, September). *The Paris Agreement*. https://unfccc.int/process-and-meetings/the-paris-agreement

van Twist, A., Ruijer, E., & Meijer, A. (2023). Smart cities & citizen discontent: A systematic review of the literature. *Government Information Quarterly, 101799*. Advance online publication. DOI: 10.1016/j.giq.2022.101799

van Zoonen, L. (2016, July). Privacy concerns in smart cities. *Government Information Quarterly*, *33*(3), 472–480. DOI: 10.1016/j.giq.2016.06.004

Veena, V., Manjunath, R., Asha, V., Gangaraju, V., Swetha, G., & Raghu, N. (2025). Smart Homes with IoT Technology Provide Safety and Security for Elderly Individuals. In Mallik, S., Mathivanan, S., Sangeetha, S., & Soufiene, B. (Eds.), *Real-World Applications of AI Innovation* (pp. 425–450). IGI Global Scientific Publishing., DOI: 10.4018/979-8-3693-4252-7.ch020

Veeramachaneni, V. (2025). Edge computing: Architecture, applications, and future challenges in a decentralized era. *Recent Trends in Computer Graphics and Multimedia Technology*, *7*(1), 8–23.

Vijayakumar, G. (2024). Muniyandi Rajkumar, Rajiv Chandar N, Selvakumar P and Ramesh Duraisamy, (2024). Environmentally friendly TDS removal from waste water by electrochemical ion exchange batch-type recirculation (EIR) technique. *Environmental Science. Water Research & Technology*, *10*, 826–835. DOI: 10.1039/D3EW00793F

Viljoen, S. (2021). A relational theory of data governance. *The Yale Law Journal*, •••, 573–654.

Vishwarupe, V., Zahoor, S., Akhter, R., Bhatkar, V. P., Bedekar, M., Pande, M., Joshi, P. M., Patil, A., & Pawar, V. (2023, December 26). Designing a human-centered AI-based cognitive learning model for industry 4.0 applications. Bentham Science Publishers. https://www.benthamdirect.com/content/books/9789815179187.chapter-5

Volcovici, V., Abnett, K., Stanway, D., Farge, E., & Pineau, E. (2025, January 21). World reacts to Trump withdrawing US from Paris climate pact. *Reuters*. https://www.reuters.com/business/environment/world-reacts-trumps-plan-withdraw-us-paris-climate-pact-2025-01-20

W. Yu, Y. Liu, T. Dillon, W. Rahayu and F. Mostafa, "An Integrated Framework for Health State Monitoring in a Smart Factory Employing IoT and Big Data Techniques," in IEEE Internet of Things Journal, vol. 9, no. 3, pp. 2443-2454, 1 Feb.1, 2022, https://doi.org/.DOI: 10.1109/JIOT.2021.3096637

Wang, Z. (2023). *Blockchain Technology—A New Traceability System in Prevention of Fraud-Ridden Food Safety Issues* (pp. 1062–1073). https://doi.org/DOI: 10.2991/978-94-6463-010-7_108

Wang, G., Wang, Q., & Chen, S. (2023). Exploring Blockchains Interoperability: A Systematic Survey. *ACM Computing Surveys*, *55*(13s), 1–38. DOI: 10.1145/3582882

Wang, S., Ouyang, L., Yuan, Y., Ni, X., Han, X., & Wang, F. Y. (2019). Blockchain-Enabled Smart Contracts: Architecture, Applications, and Future Trends. *IEEE Transactions on Systems, Man, and Cybernetics. Systems*, *49*(11), 2266–2277. DOI: 10.1109/TSMC.2019.2895123

Wang, W., Capitaneanu, S. L., Marinca, D., & Lohan, E.-S. (2019). Comparative analysis of channel models for industrial IoT wireless communication. *IEEE Access : Practical Innovations, Open Solutions*, *7*, 91627–91640.

Wang, W., Chen, Y., Wang, Y., Deveci, M., Al-Hinai, A., & Kadry, S. (2025). Analyzing the barriers to blockchain adoption in supply chain finance using an integrated interval-valued Fermatean fuzzy RAFSI model. *Financial Innovation*, *11*(1), 9. DOI: 10.1186/s40854-024-00670-y

Wang, Y., & Shen, J. (2013). CloudProxy: A NAPT Proxy for Vulnerability Scanners based on Cloud Computing. *Journal of Networks*, *8*(3). Advance online publication. DOI: 10.4304/jnw.8.3.607-615

Wang, Z., Qiu, J., Zhou, Y., Shi, Y., Fu, L., Chen, W., & Letaief, K. B. (2021). Federated learning via intelligent reflecting surface. *IEEE Transactions on Wireless Communications*, *21*(2), 808–822.

Wani, S., Imthiyas, M., Almohamedh, H., & Alhamed, K. M. (2021). Distributed Denial of Service (DDoS) Mitigation Using Blockchain—A Comprehensive Insight. *Symmetry*, *13*(2), 227. DOI: 10.3390/sym13020227

Wasif, N. (2022). Securing Smart Cities: AI-Based Cybersecurity Strategies for Urban Digital Infrastructure.

Webb, S. (2022, February 24). Are solar panels in China made using slave labour? *Independent*. https://www.independent.co.uk/climate-change/are-solar-panels-in-china-made-using-slave-labour-b2022336.html

Weder, F. (2023). Cultivation of sustainability in a discourse of change. *Journal of Language and Politics*, *22*(5), 577–600. DOI: 10.1075/jlp.22122.wed

Westraadt, L., & Calitz, A. (2020). A modelling framework for integrated smart city planning and management. *Sustainable Cities and Society*, *63*, 102444. DOI: 10.1016/j.scs.2020.102444

Wilde, C. (2018, May 6). *Architecture solar.* [Image]. Pixabay. https://pixabay.com/photos/architecture-solar-solar-panels-3379146

Wind Turbine Professor. (2022, October 17). *Forces acting on wind turbine blades.* [Image]. Wikimedia Commons. https://commons.m.wikimedia.org/wiki/File:Wind_Turbine_forces.png. Used per Creative Commons License (https://creativecommons.org/licenses/by-sa/4.0/deed.en), without alterations.

Woerlen, I. (n.d.). *Mouchot's sun engine.* Hot Air Engines. http://hotairengines.org/solar-engine/mouchot-1865

World Economic Forum. (2021, January). *The global risks report 2021* (16th ed.). Geneva, Switzerland. Retrieved from https://www3.weforum.org/docs/WEF_The_Global_Risks_Report_2021.pdf (In partnership with Marsh McLennan, SK Group and Zurich Insurance Group)

World Nuclear Association. (2025, February 12). *Security of nuclear facilities and material.* https://world-nuclear.org/information-library/safety-and-security/security/security-of-nuclear-facilities-and-material

Wu, Y., Ru, Y., Lin, Z., Liu, C., & Xue, T. (2022). Research on Cyber Attacks and Defensive Measures of Power Communication Network. *IEEE Internet of Things Journal*, *9*(6), 3181698. DOI: 10.1109/JIOT.2022.3181698

Xia, G., Chen, J., Yu, C., & Ma, J. (2023). Poisoning attacks in federated learning: A survey. *IEEE Access : Practical Innovations, Open Solutions*, *11*, 10708–10722. DOI: 10.1109/ACCESS.2023.3238823

Xia, M., Xie, Z., Lin, H., & He, X. (2022). Synergistic Mechanism of the High-Quality Development of the Urban Digital Economy from Blockchain Adoption Perspective—A Configuration Approach. *Journal of Theoretical and Applied Electronic Commerce Research*, *17*(2), 704–721. DOI: 10.3390/jtaer17020037

Xu, Y., Chong, H. Y., & Chi, M. (2021). A Review of Smart Contracts Applications in Various Industries: A Procurement Perspective. *Advances in Civil Engineering*, *2021*(1). https://doi.org/DOI: 10.1155/2021/5530755

Yakubu, M. M., Hassan, M. F. B., Danyaro, K. U., Junejo, A. Z., Siraj, M., Yahaya, S., Adamu, S., & Abdulsalam, K. (2024). A Systematic Literature Review on Blockchain Consensus Mechanisms' Security: Applications and Open Challenges. *Computer Systems Science and Engineering*, *48*(6), 1437–1481. DOI: 10.32604/csse.2024.054556

Yamin, M., Alsaawy, Y., & Alkhodre, B., A., & Abi Sen, A. A. (2019). An innovative method for preserving privacy in Internet of Things. *Sensors (Basel)*, *19*(15), 3355. PMID: 31370150

Yang, C. (2020). Remapping Songdo: A genealogy of a smart city in South Korea. https://www.ideals.illinois.edu/handle/2142/107879

Yang, L., He, W., Qiang, X., Zheng, J., & Huang, F. (2024). Research on remote sensing image storage management and a fast visualization system based on cloud computing technology. *Multimedia Tools and Applications*, *83*(21), 59861–59886. DOI: 10.1007/s11042-023-17858-6

Yang, L., Moubayed, A., Hamieh, I., & Shami, A. (2019). Tree-Based Intelligent Intrusion Detection System in Internet of Vehicles. *2019 IEEE Global Communications Conference (GLOBECOM)*, 1–6. https://doi.org/DOI: 10.1109/GLOBECOM38437.2019.9013892

Yang, X., Luo, Z., Huang, Z., Zhao, Y., Xue, Z., Wang, Y., Liu, W., Liu, S., Zhang, H., Xu, K., Dou, S., Xu, J., Hu, W., & Deng, Y. (2020). Development Status and Prospects of Artificial Intelligence in the Field of Energy Conversion Materials. *Frontiers in Energy Research*, *8*. Advance online publication. DOI: 10.3389/fenrg.2020.00167

Yang, Z., Alfauri, H., Farkiani, B., Jain, R., Di Pietro, R., & Erbad, A. (2024). A Survey and Comparison of Post-Quantum and Quantum Blockchains. *IEEE Communications Surveys and Tutorials*, *26*(2), 967–1002. DOI: 10.1109/COMST.2023.3325761

Yan, Z., Zhao, X., & Liu, Y. (Alison), & Luo, X. (Robert). (2024). Blockchain-driven decentralized identity management: An interdisciplinary review and research agenda. *Information & Management*, *61*(7), 104026. DOI: 10.1016/j.im.2024.104026

Yaqoob, T., Abbas, H., & Atiquzzaman, M. (2019). Security vulnerabilities, attacks, countermeasures, and regulations of networked medical devices—A review. *IEEE Communications Surveys and Tutorials*, *21*(4), 3723–3768.

Yarlagadda, R. T. (2018). Internet of things & artificial intelligence in modern society. *International journal of creative research thoughts (IJCRT), ISSN*, 2320-2882.

Yau, S., Aliyu, A., Saidu, Y., Ibrahim, A., & Aliyu, F. M. (2024). Prospect of Smart Agriculture Using IoT and Data Analytics: A Perspective of Kebbi State, North-western Nigeria. *International Journal of Advanced Networking and Applications*, *15*(06), 6194–6203. DOI: 10.35444/ijana.2024.15606

Yigit, Y., Duran, K., Moradpoor, N., Maglaras, L., Van Huynh, N., & Canberk, B. (2024). Machine learning for smart healthcare management using IoT. In Studies in computational intelligence (pp. 135–166). DOI: 10.1007/978-981-97-5624-7_4

Yousefpoor, M. S., Yousefpoor, E., Barati, H., Barati, A., Movaghar, A., & Hosseinzadeh, M. (2021). Secure data aggregation methods and countermeasures against various attacks in wireless sensor networks: A comprehensive review. *Journal of Network and Computer Applications*, *190*, 103118.

Yuan, H., Xia, Y., Zhang, J., Yang, H., & Mahmoud, M. S. (2020). Stackelberg-Game-Based Defense Analysis Against Advanced Persistent Threats on Cloud Control System. *IEEE Transactions on Industrial Informatics*, *16*(3), 1571–1580. DOI: 10.1109/TII.2019.2925035

Yu, H., Yang, X., Chen, H., Lou, S., & Lin, Y. (2022, November 6). Energy storage capacity planning method for improving offshore wind power consumption. *Sustainability*, *14*(21), 14589. DOI: 10.3390/su142114589

Zahnd, A., & Jennings, O. (2012). The role of renewable energy technology in holistic community development. In M. D. Tiwari & A. Vaish, A. (Eds.), *Green Energy* (pp. 75-142). River Publishers.

Zahoor, S., Akhter, R., Vishwarupe, V., Bedekar, M., Pande, M., Bhatkar, V. P., Joshi, P. M., Pawar, V., Mandora, N., & Kuklani, P. (2023, December 26). A Comprehensive Study of State-of-the-Art App- lications and Challenges in IoT, and Blockchain Technologies for Industry 4.0. Bentham Science Publishers. https://www.benthamdirect.com/content/books/9789815179187.chapter-1

Zanella, A., Bui, N., Castellani, A., Vangelista, L., & Zorzi, M. (2014). Internet of things for smart cities. *IEEE Internet of Things Journal*, *1*(1), 22–32.

Zeadally, S., Adi, E., Baig, Z., & Khan, I. A. (2020). Harnessing Artificial Intelligence Capabilities to Improve Cybersecurity. *IEEE Access : Practical Innovations, Open Solutions*, *8*, 23817–23837. DOI: 10.1109/ACCESS.2020.2968045

Zeng, J., & Glaister, K. W. (2018). Value creation from big data: Looking inside the black box. *Strategic Organization*, *16*(2), 105–140. DOI: 10.1177/1476127017697510

Zhang, J., & Tao, D. (2020). Empowering Things With Intelligence: A Survey of the Progress, Challenges, and Opportunities in Artificial Intelligence of Things. *IEEE Internet of Things Journal*, *8*, 7789–7817. DOI: 10.1109/JIOT.2020.3039359

Zhang, N., Chen, H., Chen, X., & Chen, J. (2016). Semantic framework of internet of things for smart cities: Case studies. *Sensors (Basel)*, *16*(9), 1501. PMID: 27649185

Zhang, Y., Tang, Y., Li, C., Dong, M., Huang, M., Zhang, H., & Ota, K. (2024). Privacy-Preserving for Blockchain-Enabled Cold-Chain Logistics System With IoV and Linkable Ring Signature. *IEEE Transactions on Vehicular Technology*, *73*(9), 12585–12596. DOI: 10.1109/TVT.2024.3391419

Zhao, J., Wang, L., Tao, J., Chen, J., Sun, W., Ranjan, R., Kołodziej, J., Streit, A., & Georgakopoulos, D. (2014). A security framework in G-Hadoop for big data computing across distributed Cloud data centres. *Journal of Computer and System Sciences*, *80*(5), 994–1007. DOI: 10.1016/j.jcss.2014.02.006

Zhao, W., Aldyaflah, I. M., Gangwani, P., Joshi, S., Upadhyay, H., & Lagos, L. (2023). A Blockchain-Facilitated Secure Sensing Data Processing and Logging System. *IEEE Access : Practical Innovations, Open Solutions*, *11*, 21712–21728. DOI: 10.1109/ACCESS.2023.3252030

Zhu, X., Chen, Z., Cheng, T., Yang, C., Wu, D., Wu, Y., & Wang, H. (2024). Blockchain for urban governance: Enhancing trust in smart city systems with advanced techniques. *Sustainable Cities and Society*, *108*, 105438. DOI: 10.1016/j.scs.2024.105438

Ziegeldorf, J. H., Morchon, O. G., & Wehrle, K. (2014). Privacy in the internet of things: Threats and challenges. *Security and Communication Networks*, *7*(12), 2728–2742.

Ziosi, M., Hewitt, B., Juneja, P., Taddeo, M., & Floridi, L. (2024). Smart cities: Reviewing the debate about their ethical implications. *AI & Society*, *39*(3), 1185–1200. DOI: 10.1007/S00146-022-01558-0/METRICS PMID: 36212227

Zwilling, M., Klien, G., Lesjak, D., Wiechetek, Ł., Cetin, F., & Basim, H. N. (2022). Cyber security awareness, knowledge and behavior: A comparative study. *Journal of Computer Information Systems*, *62*(1), 82–97.

About the Contributors

Asma'a Alhakimi obtained her Diploma in Computer Programming in 2006 from the University of Science and Technology in Sanaa, Yemen. She earned her bachelor's degree in computer studies in 2008 from Northumbria University in Newcastle, UK, followed by a master's degree in software engineering in 2011 from Staffordshire University, UK. She completed her Ph.D. in Software Engineering at Universiti Putra Malaysia. Dr. Asma'a has extensive experience in the networking field and served as a lecturer at Asia Pacific University (APU) in Malaysia for five years. She is recognized for her expertise in conducting industrial cybersecurity training. Her research interests encompass Cybersecurity, Reverse Engineering, Software Engineering, and Artificial Intelligence. In addition to her teaching and research responsibilities, Dr. Asma'a is an Editorial Board Member of the American Journal of Electrical and Computer Engineering (AJECE) and is affiliated with the Association for Computing Machinery (ACM) and IEEE Access. Currently, she is a senior lecturer and researcher at MSU University, where she leads a research group focused on cybersecurity and forensics. Dr. Asma'a is dedicated to her work and is known for her innovative contributions across various domains. She has a strong publication record in cybersecurity and smart cities and has participated in an international exhibition showcasing a cybersecurity project that received significant recognition. Her numerous publications highlight advancements in smart cities and cybersecurity.

Safaa Najah Saud Al-Humairi is an Associate Professor at Management and Science University, serving as the Deputy Dean of Research, International, and Industry. He is at the forefront of technological innovation with over 15 years of research experience in robotics, drone technologies, and nanotechnology. His work focuses on integrating nanomaterials and nanoelectronics into drones and robots, leading to advancements in miniaturization, energy efficiency, and the development of highly sensitive sensors and communication devices. His research also explores advanced communication technologies to enhance the security and efficiency of robotic systems, which is vital for applications in military operations and emergency response. Dr. Safaa's interdisciplinary approach addresses contemporary challenges by deeply understanding robotic systems and advanced materials. In addition to his academic and research roles, Dr. Safaa is a registered professional engineer and has authored over 150 research articles in prestigious journals. His work has earned him numerous awards, including special, gold, silver, and bronze medals at national and international engineering exhibitions. He also serves as an editor and reviewer for several leading journals, contributing significantly to his field.

Saddaf Rubab is Assistant Professor at the Department of Computer Engineering, College of Computing and Informatics, University of Sharjah, UAE. She is also affiliated with the National University of Sciences and Technology, Pakistan. She completed her doctoral studies at Universiti Teknologi PETRONAS, Malaysia in 2018. She received her MSc in Computer Software Computer Engineering from NUST College of Electrical & Mechanical Engineering (CEME), in 2012 and worked on different academic positions from 2009 to 2013. She has worked on forecasts and implementing AI techniques in various interdisciplinary areas. Her research interests include distributed computing, security, and prediction systems.

I Wayan Budi Sentana is a senior lecturer in the Department of Information Technology at Politeknik Negeri Bali, where he specializes in cybersecurity and blockchain technology. In 2019, he was awarded the prestigious LPDP scholarship to pursue his PhD at Macquarie University, Australia. His research focuses on enhancing the security of internet routing protocols (BGP) and mobile applications. In addition to his academic contributions, Dr. Sentana serves as an expert consultant at DUCO Inc. in California and is an active member of IEEE. He holds industry-recognized certifications, including Cisco DevOps and EC-Council CHFI, further solidifying his expertise in cybersecurity. Dr. Sentana's accomplishments include being a recipient of the 2018 Research Bridging Program in Taiwan and a finalist in the 2022 Cyber Thesis Competition at UNSW Sydney.

***

Suwaiba Adamu Siuto holds a B.Sc. in Computer Science from Taraba State University, Jalingo, Nigeria. Her academic and professional interests include blockchain applications in smart cities and web development. She is passionate about emerging technologies and their role in shaping secure and sustainable urban systems.

Munir Ahmad is a seasoned professional in the realm of Spatial Data Infrastructure (SDI), Geo-Information Productions, Information Systems, and Information Governance, boasting over 25 years of dedicated experience in the field. With a PhD in Computer Science, Dr. Ahmad's expertise spans Spatial Data Production, Management, Processing, Analysis, Visualization, and Quality Control. Throughout his career, Dr. Ahmad has been deeply involved in the development and deployment of SDI systems specially in the context of Pakistan, leveraging his proficiency in Spatial Database Design, Web, Mobile & Desktop GIS, and Geo Web Services Architecture. His contributions to Volunteered Geographic Information (VGI) and Open Source Geoportal & Metadata Portal have significantly enriched the geospatial community. As a trainer and researcher, Dr. Ahmad has authored over 50 publications, advancing the industry's knowledge base and fostering innovation in Geo-Tech, Data Governance, and Information Infrastructure, and Emerging Technologies. His commitment to Research and Development (R&D) is evident in his role as a dedicated educator and mentor in the field.

Rabiya Akhter holds a strong academic background in Electronics and Communication Engineering (ECE). She completed her B.Tech in ECE from the Islamic University of Science and Technology (IUST) in 2020, where she built a foundation in core electronics and communication technologies. She then pursued her M.Tech in ECE from the University of Kashmir, graduating in 2024 with advanced knowledge and research exposure in the field. Her research interests include wireless sensor networks (WSN), Internet of Things (IoT), machine learning (ML), deep learning (DL), data analytics, and modern communication technologies. Her academic journey reflects dedication to technical growth and continuous learning in emerging areas of engineering.

Ravesa Akhter is a Ph.D. scholar in the Department of Information Technology at the National Institute of Technology Srinagar, Hazratbal, Jammu and Kashmir, India. She obtained her M.Tech in Information Technology from the Central University of Kashmir, Tulmulla Ganderbal, in 2018, with her research focusing on load balancing in cloud computing. She completed her B.Tech in Information Technology from NIT Srinagar in 2016. Her research interests include the Internet of Things (IoT), Cloud Computing, Wireless Sensor Networks, Fog Computing, and Machine Learning. She is actively engaged in exploring innovative solutions at the intersection of these domains to address real-world challenges.

Mohammad Albadareen is an accomplished software engineer with a Master's degree, recognized for his strong passion for technological advancements and creative problem-solving. With a solid foundation in software development,

Mohammad has made significant strides in the field of cybersecurity. His career is defined by innovative research, especially at the intersection of cybersecurity and artificial intelligence (AI), where he continues to explore and push the boundaries of what's possible.

Balqees Alhaddad Master's student in Education Instructional Technology at Universiti Geomatika Malaysia, with a Bachelor's degree in Kindergarten from King Faisal University, Saudi Arabia (4.5/5 GPA). Experienced educational leader with a background in kindergarten management, curriculum development, and school administration. Passionate about integrating technology into education, with growing interests in cybersecurity, information security, and smart city innovations. Aspiring to bridge the gap between education management and advanced digital solutions to enhance learning environments and community development.

Abdullah Al-Hussenaey holds a Master's degree in Software Engineering and has published research in the fields of artificial intelligence, cybersecurity, and blockchain-based IoT systems. His academic interests include intrusion detection systems, machine learning applications in security, and decentralized technologies. He actively contributes to scholarly publications and collaborative research in the domain of emerging technologies.

Syed Muqthadar Ali received B.Tech degree in CSE from Anwarul Uloom College of Engineering & Technology, Vikarabad, affiliated to Jawaharlal Nehru Technological University, Hyderabad, A.P. in 2003. He received his M.Tech Degree in CSE from CVR College of Engineering, Rangareddy, affiliated to Jawaharlal Nehru Technological University Hyderabad, Hyderabad, Telangana in 2013. He is currently working as a Senior Assistant Professor, Department of Computer Science & Engineering, CVR College of Engineering, Rangareddy, Telangana, India.

Dahiru Adamu Aliyu received a B.Tech. in Information Management Technology with First Class Honors from Modibbo Adama University of Technology (MAUTECH), Nigeria, and is currently pursuing an MSc in Information Systems at Universiti Teknologi PETRONAS (UTP), Malaysia. He has worked as a software developer and has taught courses in data analytics and business intelligence. His research interests include deep learning, machine learning, reinforcement learning, and medical information systems. He has authored publications in journals and conferences

Mohammad Aljawarneh. Received the B.S., M.S. and PhD degree in Information Technology from University of Sindh, Jamshoro, Pakistan, in 2011, 2014, and 2019 respectively. From 2012 to 2014 and 2016 to 2018, he was a Research

Assistant with the Institute of Information and Communication Technology, University of Sindh, Jamshoro, Pakistan. And From January 2020 to March 2022: he was an Assistant Professor, Computer Science Department, Szabist University, Hyd Campus, Pakistan. And From October 2022 to Current: he is working as an Assistant Professor, Faculty of Information Technology, Applied Sciences Private University, Amman, Jordan. His research interest includes, Cybersecurity, Pervasive Computing, Context-awareness, Internet of Things (IoT), Machine Learning (ML).

Ayoub Alsarhan received the Ph.D. degree in computer engineering in the field of cyber security and wireless networks from Concordia University, Canada. He is currently a Full Professor with the Information Technology Department, The Hashemite University, Zarqa, Jordan. He contributed to several journal and conference papers. His research interests include cybersecurity, network security, wireless networks, and cloud computing.

Zainab Attar Bashi is an assistant professor at Department of Computer Science, Kulliyyah of Information and Communication Information at International Islamic University Malaysia (IIUM). She received her PhD, MSc and BEng in Computer and Information Engineering from IIUM. Her research areas are computer networking, information & network security, Blockchain, IoT, and cloud computing.

F. Shabina Fred Rishma is a dedicated faculty member in the Department of Computer Science and Engineering (CSE) at Vel Tech Rangarajan Dr. Sagunthala R & D Institute of Science and Technology, located in Chennai, Tamil Nadu (600062). She completed her Bachelor of Engineering (BE) from Anna University and her Master of Engineering (ME) from Sathyabama University, Chennai. Additionally, she holds a Bachelor of Library Science (B.Lib.Sc.) from Alagappa University. With over three years of experience in the teaching profession, Shabina has developed a deep expertise in areas such as Machine Learning and Artificial Intelligence. Her passion for these cutting-edge fields drives her commitment to delivering high-quality education and contributing to the academic development of her students. Through her work, she aims to inspire and shape the future of technology enthusiasts.

Susan Ferebee earned her Ph.D. in Information Systems at Nova Southeastern University in Ft. Lauderdale, Florida. She also has an Executive Juris Doctorate from Concord Law School, and has a Masters in Educational Psychology from Purdue University Global.. She is a faculty member in the School for Business and Information Technology at Purdue University Global and has also served as a consultant with more than 25 years of experience working directly with organizations and higher education institutions. Susan has published many peer-reviewed articles. Her current research in progress includes studies on machine learning in environment forecasting, metaverse ethics, and Society 5.0 business models, Susan also served as a guest editor for a special issue of International Journal of Conceptual Structures and Smart Applications. Susan serves as an Editorial Review Board member for International Journal of Cognitive Informatics and Natural Intelligence. She is an active presenter at international and national conferences. Susan has received numerous teaching and outstanding contributor awards and has been awarded several research grants.

Tamara Phillips Fudge is a full-time professor in the graduate technology programs at Purdue University Global. She has won fellowships and awards for innovation and teaching, and has taught a wide variety of topics, including web development, human-computer interaction, systems analysis and design, and those featuring documentation, diagramming, problem-solving, and presentation. Her career started with music degrees from Indiana University and Florida State University. She sang opera, oratorio, and in recital; her compositions have been heard on Public Radio, at various universities, and a state choral convention. She taught vocal and choral music, piano, pedagogy, foreign language diction, opera production, music theory, composition, and related courses in the traditional college classroom for 20-odd years. For 7 years, she was a weekend correspondent for the Quad-City Times (Davenport, IA). Following a brief stint as an agent/registered representative selling life and health insurance and variable products, she returned to school with a keen interest in technology and has since distinguished herself in online teaching, coordination of large projects, and curriculum development.

Aliyu Garba received both his B.Sc. and M.Sc. degrees in Computer Science from Ahmadu Bello University (ABU), Zaria, Nigeria. He is currently a Lecturer at the Department of Computer Science, ABU, and a Graduate Research Assistant pursuing a Ph.D. in Information Technology at Universiti Teknologi PETRONAS, Malaysia. His research interests include machine learning, grid computing, and software engineering. He has authored several articles in peer-reviewed journals and international conference proceedings.

Syed Hassan Imam Gardezi serves as the Executive Director and Board Member at Union Investments LLC, based in Ras Al Khaimah, United Arab Emirates. With a strategic leadership role in the organization, Dr. Gardezi brings extensive experience in corporate governance, investment planning, and executive management. His contributions to Union Investments LLC reflect a strong commitment to driving business growth, fostering innovation, and ensuring sustainable development. Through his role on the board, he plays a key part in shaping the company's strategic direction and long-term vision.

Aisha Hassan Abdalla Hashim received her Ph.D in Computer Engineering (2007), M.Sc. in Computer Science (1996) and B.Sc. in Electronics Engineering (1990). She won the Best Graduating Ph.D Student Award during the IIUM Convocation ceremony in 2007. She joined IIUM in 1997 and is currently a Professor at the Department of Electrical and Computer Engineering. Professor Aisha has taught several courses related to Communication and Computer Engineering and is actively involved in curriculum development and programme accreditation. She has been a member of the Department Board of Studies for several years. She received the Best Teacher Award during IIUM Quality Day in 2007. Prof. Aisha has been appointed as external examiner/visiting professor/adjunct professor at different universities. Professor Aisha who is actively involved in research and postgraduate programmes, has published more than 200 journal/conference papers, and supervised/ co-supervised more than 40 Ph.D/Master's students. She received the Promising Researcher Award in 2009 during IIUM Quality Day. She has also received many medals/awards in different national/international research exhibitions. One of her research exhibitions won the Promising Commercial Value Award (Second Runner Up) in IRIIE 2014. As a researcher, she has secured research grants from IIUM, Ministry of Higher Education (MOHE) and Ministry of Science, Technology and Innovation (MOSTI). She has actively contributed as a reviewer /technical committee member in many journals/conferences. Professor Aisha has established several teaching/ research networks between IIUM and overseas universities. She has been appointed as IIUMÂ Internationalisation Ambassador to Sudan (October 2014) and has participated in initiating several MoUs as well as encouraging the PhD Student Mobility programme between IIUM and Sudanese Universities. Professor Aisha also participates in community services. She was appointed as a Board of Studies member at the International Islamic School, Malaysia. She also served as Parent/ Teacher Committee member at the school for more than 10 years.

Syeda Nida Hassan holds a Master's degree in Cybersecurity from Ravensbourne University London and a Bachelor's degree in Software Engineering. She has engaged in international research collaborations on federated learning security and is a member of IEEE and the IEEE Women in Engineering Society.

Bashar Khassawneh is a faculty member in the Department of Computer Science, Faculty of Information Technology at Amman Arab University, Amman, Jordan. My academic and research interests focus on computer science, cybersecurity, artificial intelligence, machine learning, deep learning, and the Internet of Things (IoT).

Zokir Mamadiyarov is working in the Department of Finance and Tourism at Termez University of Economics and Service, Termez, Uzbekistan.

Hussaini Mamman is a Ph.D. candidate in Information Technology at Universiti Teknologi PETRONAS, Malaysia. His research focuses on fairness testing in machine learning systems, with the aim of developing frameworks that enhance transparency, mitigate algorithmic bias, and uphold ethical standards in AI technologies. He holds a B.Tech. in Information Technology (2010) and an M.Sc. in Management Information Technology (2018) from Abubakar Tafawa Balewa University, Nigeria. With a background in software engineering and a strong interest in responsible AI, his work contributes to advancing inclusive, fair, and accountable intelligent systems

T.C. Manjunath was born on 6th February 1967. He did his B.E. from RV College of Engg. in 1989 (B'lore Univ), M.E. in Robotics & Automation from Govt.'s LD College of Engg., (Gujarat Univ., Ahmedabad) in 1992 with FCD-First Rank & PhD in Systems & Control Engg. from IIT Bombay in the year 2007, got best research scholar award for the entire IITB. He is currently working as the Dean Research (R & D) and as Professor in Dept. of Computer Science & Engg. with specialization in IoT, Cyber Security, Blockchain Technology in Rajarajeswari College of Engineering, Bengaluru, Karnataka. He has got a teaching (academic), research & administrative experience of more than 35+ years (10 years as Principal & 8 years as HoD, 1 year as Dean Research & rest as faculty) and has published more than 1500+ research papers in various national & international journals & conferences, with 175+ patents, 100+ book-chapters, 25 awards, 100s of Keynote talks and also published 25 text books in various field of science, engineering & technology, completed projects worth Rs. 9 Crores till date & guided 10 PhD scholars in VTU. He is a member of 30 Professional Society Chapters and is a fellow of IE, IETE, AMIEE, Sr. Member of IEEE and a chartered engineer.

Nur-Adib is currently working as an assistant professor at department of computer science at International Islamic University Malaysia. She did her Ph.D. under Disaster Prevention and Preparedness Center at Malaysian - Japan International Institute of Technology (MJIIT). Her research area is applying Machine Learning in flood prediction.

Barno Matchanova is working at Department of National Idea and Philosophy, Urgench State Pedagogical Institute, Uzbekistan

Swaroop Mohanty is an esteemed Associate Professor at the Amity University Kolkata, within the Department of ACCFK (Accounting, Finance, and Commerce).

With a robust academic background and a keen interest in the fields of finance and commerce, Dr. Mohanty has established himself as a respected educator and researcher. His teaching style emphasizes both theoretical understanding and practical application, preparing students for the dynamic challenges of the business world. At Amity University, Kolkata, he contributes not only to the academic development of his students but also to the broader research initiatives of the institution. His expertise and commitment to higher education have earned him recognition as a valuable member of the university community.

Azana Hafizah Mohd Aman received her PhD, MSc and BEng in Computer and Information Engineering from International Islamic University Malaysia. She is currently working as senior lecturer at Research Center for Cyber Security, Faculty of Information Science and Technology (FTSM), The National University of Malaysia (UKM), Malaysia. Her research areas are computer system & networking, information & network security, IoT, cloud computing, and big data.

Raghu N has Ten years of experience in Academic and Research. He received the Ph.D. (2020) in Electronics Engineering from Jain University, and B.E. in Electronics and Telecommunications Engineering from VTU University, Karnataka. His research interests were in RF Communication and Image Processing. He has published his research findings in various Scopus indexed Journals and International conferences. He is a member of various professional bodies.

Keerthana N V is an Assistant Professor with 8 Years of experience in teaching and 1-year experience in research (IUCAA LIGO Data Centre, Pune). Her area of interest is Network Security, Blockchain Security, and Machine Learning Algorithms. She is pursuing PhD at Anna University in Security in Blockchain. She has a working experience in High-Performance Computing (HTCondor) in LIGO INDIA Project. She has written many research articles in Network Security and assisted Scientists in analyzing Datasets in HTCondor.

Daniel Oyefidein is currently a Ph.D. student in Information Technology at Universiti Teknologi PETRONAS, Malaysia. He holds an M.Sc. in Information and Telecommunication Engineering from the University of Port Harcourt and a B.Sc. in Electrical Engineering from Rivers State University, Nigeria. With over six years of teaching experience, he also serves as a Teaching Assistant at UTP and a Cambridge AS & A Level examiner. His research interests include immersive learning, generative AI, blockchain, and AR/VR in support of SDG 4 (Quality Education). He has presented at the Teaching and Learning Innovation Festival (CADeX) and holds multiple professional certifications.

P. Selvakumar is currently an Associate Professor in the Department of Science and Humanities at Nehru Institute of Technology, Coimbatore, Tamil Nadu, India. Prior to joining Nehru Institute of Technology, he held positions as an Assistant Professor in the Department of Science and Humanities various engineering colleges in Coimbatore, Tamil Nadu, India, spanning from 2011 to 2023. Dr.P. Selvakumar's academic and research interests lie primarily in the field of phytochemistry. He has made significant contributions to his field, with an impressive record that includes 30 journal publications, 12 patents, and 20 conference papers. Additionally, he has organized 5 seminars and conferences, further demonstrating his commitment to academic and scientific exchange. Throughout his career, Dr. P.Selvakumar has been recognized for his dedication and excellence in teaching, having been honored with several awards, including the Best Teacher Awards. He holds a prominent position in the academic community, contributing actively to research.

Vishwanatha S, currently working as an Assistant Professor at JAIN (Deemed-to-Be University), obtained his Master's degree from Bangalore University, Bengaluru. He is pursuing a Ph.D. at Visvesvaraya Technological University (VTU), Belgaum. With over 13 years of experience in teaching and imparting knowledge in Mathematics. He has made significant contributions to the field through the publication of numerous research papers in various international journals. Additionally, he holds several patents, showcasing his innovative thinking and commitment to advancing knowledge. His research interests primarily focus on Fluid Mechanics and Magneto Hydrodynamics. He has presented at various national and international conferences. He is a member of the Indian Mathematical Society (IMS) and the International Association of Engineering (IAENG).

Yahaya Saidu (Graduate Student Member, IEEE) is a PhD candidate in Information Technology at Universiti Teknologi PETRONAS (UTP), Malaysia, and a lecturer in the Department of Computer Science, Taraba State University, Nigeria. He holds BSc and MSc degrees in computer science from Taraba State University and Bayero University, respectively. His research interests include blockchain, cloud computing, machine learning, and deep learning. He has published in peer-reviewed journals and presented at international conferences.

Salem Sati has a PhD in computer science from HHU University in Dusseldorf, Germany (2017), and an MSc degree in computer engineering from Higher Industrial Institute in Misurata, Libya (2008). Also he completed his BSc in computer engineering in Higher Industrial Institute in 1997. Dr. Sati has contributed to several local conferences in Libya, Also International IEEE conferences in North America. Asia and Europe in the fields of computer networks. He has many publications in

IEEE conferences. He is currently a Doctor at the faculty of Information Technology in Misurata University.

Insha Shafi completed her BCA from Women's College M.A. Road, Srinagar in 2013, after which she earned her MCA from the University of Kashmir in 2017. She further enhanced her academic profile by completing a B.Ed from the University of Kashmir in 2022. Her research interests lie in modern and evolving areas of computer science, including machine learning, Internet of Things (IoT), and data analytics. She is passionate about applying computational techniques to solve real-world problems and continues to develop her knowledge in emerging digital technologies.

Shuhaida Mohamed Shuhidan is a senior lecturer and head of the Centre for Research in Data Science (CeRDaS) at Universiti Teknologi PETRONAS (UTP), Malaysia. She holds a PhD in Computer Science from RMIT University, Australia, an MSc in Information Technology from Universiti Teknologi MARA, and a BSc in Information Technology from UTP. Her expertise includes data analytics, polygraph technology, and digital innovation. She has authored over 60 publications and led more than 20 funded research projects, contributing to 35 innovations.

Shabir Ahmad Sofi is an Assistant Professor and Head of the Department of Information Technology at the National Institute of Technology (NIT) Srinagar, with around 17 years of academic and research experience. He completed his Bachelor of Engineering in Electronics and Communication from the former Regional Engineering College Srinagar, followed by a Master of Technology in Communication and Information Technology, and later earned his Ph.D. in Computer Science and Engineering, all from NIT Srinagar. As an author and research contributor, Sofi has published numerous works in emerging areas such as Wireless Sensor Networks, the Internet of Things, Artificial Intelligence, Big-Data applications, Data Analytics, Precision Agriculture, and Blockchain Technologies. His academic output includes research publications in journals, conference papers, multiple book chapters, books, patents, and review articles, through which he has contributed to research to a large extent. He has actively participated in faculty development programs, delivered technical sessions, and contributed to the advancement of engineering education through his teaching, research activities, publications, and involvement in academic development initiatives.

Ahgalya Subbiah lecturer and researcher at Management and Science University. Her research focuses on Smart City, Transportation, Service System Value, Healthcare Informatics, HCI, e-Government, Public Policy, Health Informatics, Gerontology and IoT. Her research in the last decade has revolved around the following theme: Service Innovation & Co-Creation of Value between the computational complexity of various computational problems, particularly lattice problems. and has a background in the education industry, including her role as Head of School at Cosmopoint International College of Technology. 10 years of experience in education industry with many levels of degree, attained recognition as higher management level for student centered teaching and learning. Trained as Duke of Edinburgh Award trainer to encourage students to dream big. Conducted various research on co creation of service value between students and society.

Bharathi V is a dedicated faculty member in the Department of Computer Science and Engineering at Vel Tech Rangarajan Dr. Sagunthala R&D Institute of Science and Technology, Chennai, Tamil Nadu. She is committed to delivering high-quality education and fostering technical excellence among students. With a strong foundation in computer science, Ms. Bharathi focuses on both theoretical and practical aspects of the discipline, ensuring that students are industry-ready and academically strong. She actively contributes to departmental initiatives, engages in continuous learning, and encourages innovation and research among her students, playing a key role in the academic growth of the institution.

Jameel Shehu Yalli received his BSc. in Computer Science, MSc. in Computer and Information Engineering. He is currently pursuing a PhD in Information Technology at Universiti Teknologi PETRONAS, Malaysia. He has gained industry experience and currently a Teaching Assistant and Researcher at Universiti Teknologi PETRONAS. His research interests include Internet of Things (IoT), cybersecurity, authentication models, wireless networks, the intersection of cybercrime/cybersecurity and Islamic ethics.

Shuaibu Yau received a B.Sc. in Computer Science from Kano University of Science and Technology, and an M.Sc. in Computer Science from Bayero University Kano, Nigeria. He is currently pursuing a Ph.D. in Computer Science at Chiang Mai University, Thailand, and serves as a Lecturer at the Department of Computer Science, Federal University Birnin Kebbi, Nigeria. His research focuses on cloud and edge computing, optimization techniques, machine learning, multimedia streaming, and intelligent systems. He has published several peer-reviewed journal and conference articles.

Index

A

B

C

D

E

F

G

H

I

M

P

R

S

T

U

W

Z

www.ingramcontent.com/pod-product-compliance
Lightning Source LLC
LaVergne TN
LVHW061528290926
849162LV00004B/711